Building the National Parks

To the designers of national parks, presenting nature meant bringing visitors to the parks. Roads and trails were located and designed to show nature's wonders from the best point of view while leaving scenic vistas and natural features unimpaired. A memorandum of agreement with the Bureau of Public Roads enabled the National Park Service to build roads according to the highest technical standards and ensure that designs were in harmony with nature. *(Photograph by George A. Grant, courtesy National Park Service Historic Photography Collection)*

BUILDING
THE
NATIONAL
PARKS

Historic
Landscape
Design and Construction

Linda Flint McClelland

The Johns Hopkins University Press
Baltimore & London

This book has been brought to publication with the generous assistance of the Laurence Hall Fowler Fund.

Published in cooperation with the Center for American Places, Harrisonburg, Virginia.

Building the National Parks: Historic Landscape Design and Construction was published in paperback as *Presenting Nature: The Historic Landscape Design of the National Park Service, 1916 to 1942* in 1993 by the U.S. Government Printing Office. All new material in this updated and expanded edition © 1998 The Johns Hopkins University Press
9 8 7 6 5 4 3 2 1

The Johns Hopkins University Press
2715 North Charles Street
Baltimore, Maryland 21218–4319
The Johns Hopkins Press Ltd., London

Library of Congress Cataloging-in-Publication Data will be found at the end of this book.
A catalog record for this book is available from the British Library.

Frontispiece: Tunnel on Going-to-the-Sun Highway, Glacier National Park, 1933

ISBN 0–8018–5582–9
ISBN 0–8018–5583–7 (pbk.)

*To keep the natural beauty of mountain, forest, lake and waterfall
unspoiled and yet within easy access of such a multitude of visitors
is an interesting though often difficult problem. Quoting the landscape
architects, upon whom devolves the responsibility for this phase of
park activities, . . . roads, trails, and buildings all should provide a
maximum of scenic view, at the same time being as inconspicuous as
possible themselves. . . . The landscape process begins with selecting
locations which do not tear up the landscape or obtrude into
important views. This is followed by a study of the design, which
endeavors to use native materials and other architectural features that
will harmonize the structure with its surroundings. The last phase of
the problem is the placing of any plant materials necessary to cure
unavoidable damage that may have resulted from the construction.*

—National Park Service, *The National Parks and Emergency Conservation Work*, 1936

Contents

The Employment Stabilization Act of 1931
Plans as a Tool for Landscape Preservation
The Planning Process in Action: The Story of Yakima Park

Part IV *Park and Recreation Progress since 1933*

Illustrations

Foreword

J ust over fifty years ago, the Civilian Conservation Corps (CCC) ended, and
with it concluded a grand era of park building marked by naturalistic principles, craftsmanship, and native materials. Rooted in the American park
movement of the nineteenth century, naturalistic park design flourished under
the stewardship of the National Park Service in the early twentieth century. Park
designers — landscape architects, architects, and engineers — forged a rich legacy
of roads and trails that blended with the natural scenery, picturesque park villages, campgrounds and picnic areas, scenic overlooks, and majestic views. Many
of these places have fulfilled the National Park Service's dual mission to conserve
the natural scenery and to provide for public use, enjoyment, and appreciation.
They have continued to serve visitors for several generations. Park managers,
public officials, and preservationists are now being called upon to recognize
these places, appreciate their historical significance, and protect them as cultural
resources.

This study was developed by the National Register of Historic Places, a program of the National Park Service in the U.S. Department of the Interior, which
maintains the official federal list of districts, buildings, sites, structures, and objects significant in American history, architecture, archeology, engineering, and
culture. The primary purpose of the study is to encourage the nomination of
historic park landscapes in national and state parks to the National Register of
Historic Places. The idea stemmed from the growing interest in landscape preservation and the concern that, although significant park buildings and structures
were being recognized, the larger landscapes of which they were an integral part
were being overlooked. The study provides a national context for identifying,
evaluating, and registering the vast number of historic park landscapes influenced by the design ethic developed and practiced by the National Park Service.
The largest group of these are areas of national, state, and local parks developed
by the CCC under the direction of landscape architects, architects, and engineers of the National Park Service in the 1930s. The initial funding for this study
came from a grant from the Horace Albright (now Albright-Wirth) Employee
Development Fund of the National Park Foundation, a nonprofit organization
devoted to supporting National Park Service employees and initiatives.

The study is written from the perspective of landscape architecture, the profession having primary responsibility for the physical development of the parks from 1916 to 1942. Just after the turn of the century, prominent landscape architects proclaimed their stewardship of significant natural areas, set forth naturalistic theories for park development, and advocated the founding of the National Park Service. Part I traces the roots of a naturalistic ethic of park design from landscape gardener Andrew Jackson Downing and park builder Frederick Law Olmsted Sr. to twentieth-century practitioners such as Henry Hubbard and Frank Waugh.

As called upon in a 1918 statement of policy, National Park Service officials looked to landscape engineers and landscape architects to locate and design facilities in ways that harmonized with the natural setting and ensured that natural features and scenery remained unimpaired. Part II describes the contributions of the park service's first landscape engineers to the creation of a design ethic for national parks. Part III tells the story of the founding and growth of the Landscape Division of the Western Field Office, which was modeled after a professional design office and guided the development of national parks through a process of master planning and advances in the naturalistic design of roads, trails, overlook, bridges, and buildings. It also closely examines the planning process through which areas of each park were designated for various types of development or set aside as wilderness to remain undeveloped.

Landscape concerns continued to dominate the development of national parks during the New Deal. Part IV includes chapters on the period from 1933 to 1942, when the park system greatly expanded and planning and construction proceeded on an unprecedented scale through programs such as the CCC and Public Works Administration. It also examines the role of the National Park Service in the development of state and local parks during the 1930s and the origins of a state and federal partnership for outdoor recreation.

An understanding of the landscape design of the National Park Service provides a basis for evaluating the historical significance of park landscapes in national, state, and, in some cases, local parks. These areas are cultural and natural landscapes containing roads, trails, overlooks, bridges, buildings, parking areas, vistas, plantings, and small elements such as signs and water fountains. Because these places reflect the manifold contributions of several generations of creative national park designers who were committed to the use and preservation of parks, many of these areas meet criteria for the National Register of Historic Places. For this reason, the results of this study have also been incorporated into a multiple property documentation form entitled "Historic Park Landscapes in National and State Parks." This documentation form can be used by park agencies at various levels of government, state preservation offices, local governments, and others to facilitate the National Register listing of parks and park landscapes associated with the context. Our intention is to eliminate the duplicative efforts that result when each park agency and state historic preservation office sets out to evaluate and register properties sharing the same historic context and characteristics.

By defining and describing the characteristics of park landscapes, the study is also intended as a guide to identifying the component resources that were part of the legacy of the National Park Service designers from 1917 to 1942. As a result, the study should be useful to those surveying the cultural resources of national, state, and local parks; those compiling the List of Classified Structures (LCS) and Cultural Landscape Inventory (CLI); and those preparing National Register forms. Furthermore, the documentation and references given in the study on features, such as stonemasonry specifications for guardrails, bridges, and culverts, should be useful to those planning rehabilitation or restoration projects.

We hope that this study will encourage further scholarship on the landscape design of national, state, and local parks. The research methods used herein can be applied to studies of individual parks. The text, notes, and bibliography are intended to help researchers find and interpret primary sources, such as master plans, development outlines, historic photographs, plans and drawings, narrative reports of CCC camp superintendents, and reports of the resident landscape architects. These historical documents, which can be found in the National Archives and park archives, provide a wealth of detailed, interesting, and relevant information. The study also draws attention to some of the valuable finding aids available to the researcher. Foremost among these are the computerized index and microfilmed files of historic drawings and plans maintained by the Technical Information Center of the Denver Service Center.

This study is also intended as a model statement of historic context for a theme that can be meaningfully examined from a national perspective and applied to a large number of cultural landscapes. It has been developed according to the Secretary of the Interior's Standards and Guidelines for Archeology and Historic Preservation and guidelines developed by the National Register of Historic Places for documenting and registering multiple property groups. It is hoped that this national context will assist national, state, and local park agencies in developing historic contexts for their jurisdictions relating to conservation, park development, recreation, landscape architecture, architecture, and engineering. Our intent is to consolidate the information relating to the national context and thereby eliminate the need to reestablish the chronology of events, the physical and associative characteristics, and the historical importance of this group of cultural resources in subsequent, separate reports. As a result this information will streamline the documentation of historic contexts for National Register nominations, historic resource studies, and cultural landscape reports of the National Park Service in keeping with the National Park Service's *Cultural Resource Management Guideline* (NPS-28).

The history of the landscape design of the National Park Service in the early twentieth century is diverse and complex, and the National Park Service is actively involved in further contextual research in this field. Currently under way is a National Historic Landmark Theme Study on the landscape architecture designed by the National Park Service between 1917 and 1941. The study will provide a comparative analysis of national, state, and local parks developed with the technical assistance of the park service for the purposes of visitor use, interpretation, and administration and identify those of exceptional value to the nation. This study will be the first to nominate a series of properties for National Historic Landmark designation under the theme of American landscape architecture.

Stewardship remains a challenge today, even more than it was for the National Park Service's founders in 1916. Our knowledge of the causes and effects of human use on the natural landscape has grown considerably in recent decades. The concerns of park design and development have become increasingly complex, as we are faced with issues of highway safety, pollution, and species extinction. Park managers are being asked to achieve an ecological balance and to manage cultural and natural resources effectively. At such a time, it is worthwhile to look backward and trace our progress in presenting and preserving nature's wonders. In so doing, we can appreciate and perhaps recapture the spirit, commitment, and principles that guided park managers and designers earlier in this century. We can better understand and plan for the parks as both natural and cultural places. Above all, we will be better equipped to make decisions that will succeed in leaving the parks and the wonders they hold unimpaired for the enjoyment of future generations.

John J. Reynolds, FASLA
Former Deputy Director
National Park Service

Acknowledgments

Many individuals contributed to this study, and I am indebted to them all for their interest, support, and comments. First of all, I wish to thank those who have supported this project from the beginning. I extend my appreciation to the National Park Foundation and the members of the selection committee of the Horace Albright Employee Development Fund, which provided the sponsorship and initial funding for this study. I wish to recognize my supervisor, Carol D. Shull, chief of registration and keeper of the National Register of Historic Places, and Lawrence E. Aten, former chief, Interagency Resources Division, for supporting my continuing research and making this publication possible. For their inspiration, I thank my parents, George and Pauline Flint. To my husband, Lindsay R. McClelland, and my daughter, Karen, I extend thanks for their patience, understanding, and encouragement.

Several individuals have generously shared their own research and ideas. To Hugh Miller, formerly the chief historical architect, National Park Service, whose pioneering groundwork in landscape preservation has led to the preservation of many cultural landscapes, I credit the idea for this study. I offer special thanks to James W. Steely of the Texas Historical Commission for sharing his master's thesis and continuing research on the history of Texas state parks. To Barry Mackintosh, bureau historian for the National Park Service History Program, I extend my thanks for his review and comments on an early draft. To William C. Tweed of Sequoia National Park and Laura E. Soullière of Arkansas Post National Memorial I am indebted for their fine research on rustic park architecture. I wish to thank Richard W. Sellars of the Southwest Support Office for sharing his research on the history of natural resource policy in the National Park Service. I extend my appreciation to Dorothy Waugh, Edward Ballard, and Charles Peterson for their thoughtful correspondence and recollections. For sharing their research and documents in their care, I wish to thank Stephanie S. Toothman of the Columbia Cascade Support Office and Clifford I. Tobias of the Chesapeake/Allegheny Support Office.

In addition, I wish to acknowledge the contributions of others to this field of research: Mary Shivers Culpin, National Park Service; Cathy Gilbert and

Gretchen A. Luxenberg of the Columbia Cascade Support Office; John C. Paige of the Denver Service Center; Claudette Stager of the Tennessee Historical Commission; Rolf Anderson, consultant for the Minnesota Historical Society; Carol Ahlgren of the Nebraska State Historical Society; James Denny of the Missouri Division of Parks, Recreation, and Historic Preservation; Ian Firth of the University of Georgia; Lee Maddex of the Institute for the History of Technology and Industrial Archaeology, West Virginia University; and Joyce McKay, consultant for the State Historical Society of Iowa.

My thanks are extended to a number of people who assisted me in my research of historical documents: Jodi Morrison and Edna Ramey of the National Park Service's Technical Information Center, Denver Service Center; Margaret Yates, former park ranger and librarian at Mount Rainier National Park; Jim Rush and Raymond Cotton, archivists of the National Archives; Tom DuRant of the National Park Service Historic Photography Collection; Rolf Diamant, superintendent, and Joyce Connally, registrar, of the Frederick Law Olmsted National Historic Site; Jackie Holt of the Blue Ridge Parkway; Harriet Rusin and Donald Chase of the Natural Resources Library, U.S. Department of the Interior.

Appreciation is also extended to those who shared their parks with me: James Carrico, former superintendent, and Tom Alex, cultural resource manager, Big Bend National Park; John Debo Jr., superintendent, and David Humphrey, landscape architect, Cuyahoga Valley National Recreation Area; Felix Hernandez, former chief ranger, Carlsbad Caverns National Park; Barbara Stewart, ranger, and Dale Hoak, former assistant chief of maintenance, Shenandoah National Park; Angela Cartwright, assistant manager, Indian Lodge, Davis Mountains State Park in Texas; and Jessie Aronow, planner, Blue Hills Reservation in Massachusetts.

I wish to thank several of my colleagues in the National Register of Historic Places, National Park Service, for their assistance in making this publication a reality: Patty Sackett Chrisman, Rama Ramakrishna Badamo, Jennifer Meisner, and Antoinette J. Lee. I also extend my appreciation to Jill Nicholl of the National Park Foundation for her assistance in making this publication available to a wide audience.

Many other individuals associated with the National Park Service shared information, offered comments, and supported this project in various ways. I wish to thank Victoria Clarke and Albert Werking, Employee Development Division; Linda Eade, Don Fox, and James Snyder of Yosemite National Park; Denis P. Galvin, deputy director; the late William Penn Mott, former director of the National Park Service; Randall Biallas, chief historical architect; Edwin C. Bearss, former chief historian; Eric DeLony, Historic American Engineering Record; John Byrne and Beth Savage, National Register of Historic Places; Lindsay R. McClelland, Geologic Resources Division; Karl Esser, formerly of the National Park Service's Management Services Division; Warren Brown, Park

Planning; Ethan Carr and Robert Page, Park Historic Structures and Cultural Landscapes Programs; and Pat Sacks and Carey Feierabend, Denver Service Center.

And finally, for their interest and comments, I wish to thank Terry Wood, executive director, Employees and Alumni Association of the National Park Service; Shary Page Berg, former president of the Alliance for Historic Landscape Preservation; and Noel Dorsey Vernon of the American Society of Landscape Architects and California Polytechnical Institute.

For their helpful comments on the draft of this study, I extend my thanks to Harvey Kaiser, Syracuse University; Robert E. Grese, University of Michigan; Ian Firth, University of Georgia; James W. Steely, Texas Historical Commission; Craig Shafer, National Natural Landmarks Program; Steve Elkinton, National Trails and Greenways; Ben Levy, former chief of the National Historic Landmarks Program; Randall Biallas, Park Historic Architecture Division; Linda W. Greene, Jere L. Krakow, and Harlan D. Unrau of the Denver Service Center; William C. Tweed of Sequoia National Park; Lucy Lawless and Lenard E. Brown, Southeast Support Office; and Lynn R. Wightman, Morristown National Historical Park.

Building the National Parks

Introduction

The future of the national parks depends on the action of thoughtful men all over the country, who will help to bring the American people to realize what national parks really are, and how they ought to be developed as great pleasure grounds, as great scenic reserves, and as holding inviolate the notabilities of nature. . . . I shall hope that this sort of education . . . will lead to the establishment of a national park service, with its skilled and permanent force, with its civil and not military guards and rangers, with its engineers and advisers, so that these parks cannot be made . . . the victims of an incidental political change.

—J. Horace McFarland to the American Society of Landscape Architects, 1916

The 1916 act creating the National Park Service charged the new bureau with promoting and regulating the use of national parks in ways that would "conserve the scenery and the natural and historic objects and the wild life therein and . . . provide for the enjoyment of the same in such manner and by such means as will leave them unimpaired for the enjoyment of future generations."[1]

During the formative years of the National Park Service, from 1916 to 1942, landscape architects, architects, and engineers forged a cohesive style of landscape design which fulfilled the demands for park development while preserving the outstanding natural qualities for which each park had been designated. This style subordinated all built features to the natural, and often cultural, influences of the environment in which they were placed. Through time it achieved in each park a cohesive unity that in many cases became inseparable from the park's natural identity.

Park roads followed nature's contours, affording scenic vistas and achieving remarkable engineering feats. Crushed stone surfaces and rugged boulder walls along graded roads provided safe and convenient access for the increasing numbers of visitors carried to the parks by automobile. Networks of trails in every park not only aided the service in patrolling and protecting the natural landscape but also gave visitors, on horseback or foot, access to the park's hidden wonders. Facilities for lodging, camping, comfort, picnicking, and purchasing supplies and gasoline were needed for visitors, and ranger stations, residences, workshops, and garages were needed to manage the park and accommodate staff. Even providing the necessary utility systems — electricity, water, sewerage, and telephone — presented challenges in remote and rugged places.

Development affected the landscape, threatened its natural integrity, and demanded a consistent, responsible policy for management and planning. This policy emerged as the National Park Service made decisions about where to locate development and what form such development was to take. The park service introduced the concept of identifying "wilderness" areas to be left untouched and accessible only by foot or horseback at the same time that it was drafting solutions for developments that could serve increasing numbers of visitors in wholesome and educational ways without sacrificing natural values. A concept of park planning evolved, calling for the creation of park development outlines and general development plans. A system of review and approval ensured adherence to fundamental principles and design solutions that harmonized with nature and upheld the service's twofold responsibility for stewardship and visitor use.

In the National Park Service's first fifteen years, from park to park and through one project after another, service officials, superintendents, landscape architects, engineers, and architects proceeded to define a servicewide policy. Development was carefully situated and then constructed to blend unobtrusively into the natural setting. Existing development was reviewed, improved, and, in some cases, removed. Roads and trails were laid gently upon the land, and construction techniques were developed to create the illusion that the natural landscape had never been disturbed. Wood, stone, and clay were fashioned with native or pioneer building techniques to create facilities for the comfort and convenience of visitors and for the efficient administration of the park. These included entrance or checking stations, inns and lodges, museums, administration buildings, gas stations, maintenance shops, and even small elements such as signs, guardrails, water fountains, fireplaces, bridges, and culverts. Vegetation was selectively thinned, transplanted, cleared, or reintroduced to open up scenic vistas, screen facilities, prevent fire hazards, or blend construction with the natural setting of the park.

Development responded to the expanding park service's programs of natural history interpretation, forestry, engineering, and recreation while conforming to a design ethic based on landscape preservation and harmonization. Principles of naturalistic or informal landscape design were adopted as the chief means for blending construction with the natural setting. These principles included the preservation of existing natural features and vegetation, the selection and enframement of vistas, the screening of obtrusive elements, the planting of native species, the use of local native materials and traditional or pioneer methods of construction, and the avoidance of straight lines and right angles in all aspects of design.

The design of natural parks and rustic park structures was rooted in the nineteenth-century English gardening tradition, popularized in the United States by the writings of Andrew Jackson Downing and by the urban parks designed by Frederick Law Olmsted and others. Principles of naturalistic gardening were carried into the twentieth century in the designs for park and parkway systems and cemeteries in U.S. metropolitan areas, scenic parks and reservations developed at various levels of government, and many private estates and residential subdivisions.

By the end of the nineteenth century, several advances had been made in landscape theory and gardening design which would profoundly influence the design of national and state parks. First was a growing body of literature on the development of wild gardens and naturalistic effects using rockwork and native vegetation, principally in the works of William Robinson, a British master gardener, and Samuel Parsons, an American landscape gardener who for many years was the superintendent of Central Park. The work of Charles Eliot in the reservations of metropolitan Boston demonstrated the value of comprehensive park planning and introduced a philosophy and techniques for the management of vegetation in natural areas. His techniques included vista clearing, vegetation studies, and general landscape forestry, allowing the park designer to manipulate the character of vegetation to attain a healthy and scenic landscape.

In the early twentieth century, naturalistic gardening practices merged with an increasing interest in the native vegetation of the United States. This new blend of ideas became recognized as the principal style of American landscape architecture by Wilhelm Miller in *What England Can Teach Us about Gardening* (1911), Henry Hubbard and Theodora Kimball in *An Introduction to the Study of Landscape Design* (1917), and Frank Waugh in *The Natural Style in Landscape Gardening* (1917). It had important regional expressions such as the Prairie style of the Midwest and the arid and semiarid forms of California gardening. The increasing interest in the vegetation and forms of the American landscape as a source for conscious landscape design coincided with the founding of the National Park Service. The landscape profession, through the American Civic Association and the American Society of Landscape Architects, avidly supported the establishment of the National Park Service and influenced its organization.

In the 1880s Olmsted and Henry Hobson Richardson collaborated in forging a sturdy, rustic style of architecture for park buildings and structures. This new style drew from the rugged proportions, naturalistic siting, and use of native stone and timbers characteristic of the Shingle style and the rusticated stonework and bold arches of Richardsonian Romanesque. This style, with variations, was widely adopted in the design of shelters, bridges, and other structures for urban parks and parkways and the earliest state parks in the late nineteenth century. In the twentieth century, it would influence the design of suburban and rural bungalows and be embraced by the Arts and Crafts movement. This movement, promoted by Gustav Stickley, combined a variety of "naturalistic" influences, including Japanese architectural and landscape design, the Western Bungalow and Prairie styles of architecture, and the naturalistic gardening techniques promoted by Downing, Robinson, and Parsons. In several editions of the *Introduction to the Study of Landscape Design,* Henry Hubbard and Theodora Kimball upheld the appropriateness of the style for constructions in natural or country parks.

These influences, coupled with Downing's direct role in the frame-and-timber construction and romantic Swiss and Scandinavian style architecture of the camps and lodges of the Adirondacks, led to the design of the great inns and hotels in Glacier National Park, the El Tovar at Grand Canyon National Park, Old Faithful Inn in Yellowstone National Park, and the Bear Mountain Inn in New York's Interstate Palisades Park.

After the National Park Service assumed administrative control of the national parks in 1917, policies and practices for the design of park improvements emerged. A statement issued by Secretary of the Interior Franklin Lane in 1918 established a policy for landscape preservation and harmonization to guide all park development and use. The hiring of a "landscape engineer" in 1918 to advise on all decisions affecting the landscape character of each park and the eventual expansion of the Landscape Division in 1927 were critical steps in aligning the needs for development and the role of stewardship.

Roads were a primary necessity. Beginning in 1924, Congress granted appropriations annually for the development of roads and trails in national parks. In 1926, the service signed a cooperative agreement with the Bureau of Public Roads under which park roads attained the most up-to-date engineering and standards of road design. This agreement resulted in a long-term relationship whereby park designers set aesthetic standards of workmanship, location, and design of roads while bureau engineers provided the latest technology. The close interaction between the park service's civil engineers and landscape architects led to clear distinctions in standpoint and in role. Concerned with landscape preservation and harmonization, the landscape designers called for practices of clearing, blasting, cutting and filling, rounding and flattening slopes, bank blending, and planting which harmonized with the natural environment; they called for methods of construction which located roads and overlooks to present scenery at its best and to blend them naturalistically with the surrounding landscape. They designed bridges and culverts to fit their site and setting. Specifications for the masonry rockwork of bridges, guardrails, and culverts emerged which blended construction inconspicuously into the natural setting.

Many park trails received similar attention by both civil engineers and landscape architects. Standards for trail construction were issued by the engineers in 1934. The landscape architects had continuing responsibility for the location of trails and the treatment of trail surfaces and embankments to achieve harmony with local conditions.

Designs for new kinds of park structures emerged to fill the need for entrance stations, administration buildings, comfort stations, community buildings, lookouts, and museums. Principles of informality and naturalism were applied to park structures. Prototypes of indigenous workmanship and design using native materials were studied and adapted to form simple and functional park buildings. The park shelter, a feature of interest and great use in landscape architecture, was central to the design of many park structures, and the prototypes provided by Downing, Hubbard, and others were adopted and improved upon. While efficient design solutions were developed for floor plans and the functional layout of structures, exterior standards of design called for durability and above all harmony with the specific characteristics of each location.

Principles of landscape preservation and harmonization rather than prototypes were followed in the external design of these structures. Structures took on unique character as construction followed and blended with the natural landform and character of each site and as native materials and pioneering techniques of a region were employed. Naturalistic effects — including the roughened, irregular character of stonemasonry walls, the battering of boulder foundations to give them the appearance of having sprung naturally from the ground, and the overscaling of architectural features in mountainous areas — evolved from general landscape principles. By 1928, many of these practices were formulated and began to appear in the specifications for contracts; on plans and drawings for bridges, guardrails, and buildings; and in the lessons of experienced park designers such as chief landscape architect Thomas Vint and museum designer Herbert Maier to the service's growing corps of landscape architects. Such adherence to model principles and practices, rather than prototypical, standard designs, distinguished the design of National Park Service structures and led to the originality of ideas and diversity of expression.

Concern for the harmonization of construction and nature led park designers to adapt principles of natural landscape design for restoring building sites to a natural condition after construction. In 1930 the recognition of landscape naturalization as an ordinary and advantageous consequence of park development coincided with a policy prohibiting the introduction of exotic plants in national parks. Native ferns were planted along foundation walls, climbing vines were planted in the interstices of earth cuts along roadways, and trees were planted to screen buildings and to frame vistas. Plantings erased the lines between the earth and constructed features, returned construction sites to their natural condition, and overall enhanced the natural beauty of the parks. Landscape naturalization included the beautification of park entrances

I.1. In the Western Field Office from 1928 to 1933, chief landscape architect Thomas Vint (*middle left*) created a central design office of landscape architects and architects whose clients were the superintendents of the national parks. This office met the growing demand for master plans, specifications for park roads, and drawings of guardrails, culverts, bridges, overlooks, and buildings. By 1934 when this photograph was taken, Vint's staff had grown dramatically in response to the make-work programs of President Franklin Roosevelt's New Deal. The master plan for Lassen Volcanic National Park lies on the table. (*Photograph by George A. Grant, courtesy National Park Service Historic Photography Collection*)

and villages, vista clearing, the development of overlooks, the rehabilitation of springs and streams, and "cleanup" projects to remove fallen timber and snags or to restore areas damaged by flood, fire, or blight. By combining the planting and transplanting of native materials with naturalistic road or trail improvements — curbing, sidewalks, paths, parking, curvilinear stone steps, and planted islands — park designers were able to erase the scars of construction and control pedestrian and automobile traffic in heavily visited areas. The overall intent of the program was to allow access while at the same time protecting surrounding vegetation and natural features and harmonizing the built improvements with the natural setting. This program "beautified" the grounds of administration buildings, entrance stations, park residences, museums, concession buildings, and other buildings in developed areas. It also created the illusion in the minds of visitors that the landscape had never been disturbed.

A program for general planning began in the mid-1920s to enable park superintendents to schedule the construction and improvement of park roads and trails and other facilities over a five-year period. By 1932, this process had evolved into a program of master planning which programmed all park improvements for six-year periods. By 1939, it encompassed the many emerging programs of the National Park Service, from engineering and forest protection to interpretation and recreation.

In the 1930s, through emergency conservation and public works projects, the naturalistic landscape design of the national parks matured and flourished. Master plans became reality as, project by project, work was carried out under the direction of the park's resident landscape architect.

The beginnings of the Civilian Conservation Corps and Emergency Conservation Work coincided with the U.S. Forest Service's introduction of a new approach to campground design, called the "Meinecke plan." This approach, published in E. P. Meinecke's *Camp Ground Policy* (1932) and further developed in his *Camp Planning and Camp Reconstruction* (ca. 1934), was immediately adopted by the National Park Service. It became the basis for many innovative site plans and facilities for camping and picnicking in national and state parks in following years.

The design principles, process, and practices of the National Park Service were institutionalized nationwide in the development of state parks in the 1930s. This was accomplished through the park service's supervision of state park Emergency Conservation Work, the acquisition and development of recreational demonstration areas, and the publication of manuals and portfolios. Through a program of technical assistance, the National Park Service reviewed and approved project plans for the work of the Civilian Conservation Corps (CCC) and the Works Progress Administration (WPA) in state parks and hired inspectors, architects, landscape architects, and engineers to design and supervise CCC and WPA projects. Several publications—The National Park Service's *Portfolio of Comfort Stations and Privies* (1934) and *Portfolio of Park Structures* (1934) and Albert Good's *Park Structures and Facilities* (1935) and three-volume *Park and Recreation Structures* (1938)—provided models and principles for designing park structures. Frank Waugh's *Landscape Conservation* (1935) gave instructions on blending the edges of plantations, lakes, and artificial ponds through a process of studying and re-creating naturalistic zones of native vegetation based on soil, moisture, climate, and natural associations.

The work of the National Park Service in state park development went beyond the design of parks to the broader concern for park and parkway planning, recreational development, and the creation of statewide systems of parks and recreation. The reclamation of submarginal lands for park development implemented the landscape naturalization program on a monumental scale as large areas were reforested and streams dammed to provide pleasing scenery and recreational facilities for hiking, swimming, boating, fishing, skiing, and skating. Major advances were made in the design and development of campgrounds for automobiles and trailers and in the design of day-use areas and picnic grounds and waysides that were integrated with recreational areas and scenic parkways. The concept of organization camps took the material form of clusters of cabins, eating halls, and comfort stations scenically sited in secluded wooded areas or alongside open meadows or lakeshores and connected to scenic and recreational areas by paths and trails. Today these recreational facilities are the physical manifestation of the broad social philosophy of the New Deal. They are also the tangible results of a state and federal partnership that began when National Park Service director Stephen Mather convened the first state park conference in Des Moines, Iowa, in 1921, and gained tremendous impetus through the leadership of the park service during the 1930s.

Stewardship for a National Park Service

The wording of the National Park Service Act of 1916 has been attributed to Frederick Law Olmsted Jr., a preeminent landscape architect and the son of the Olmsted who had written an important report on Yosemite half a century earlier. The involvement of the Olmsteds in park conservation is indicative of the advocacy of the landscape architecture profession for the preservation of natural areas of national importance. In the early decades of the twentieth century, as concern over the uses and management of national parks increased, landscape architects called for the organization of a government agency to establish a policy and process for park development.[2]

Beginning in the early twentieth century, the American Civic Association (ACA) and the American Society of Landscape Architects (ASLA) were influential advocates for national parks. In a letter to the ASLA, J. Horace McFarland, president of the ACA and the leader of the movement to establish a bureau to administer the national parks, called upon the profession of landscape architects to educate the public. Professional standards, not politics, in McFarland's opinion, should determine the future of the parks.

In February 1916, the ASLA held a conference devoted to the subject of national parks and the bills pending before Congress to create a national park service. The ACA, with the cooperation of members of the ASLA, had drawn up the bill (H.R. 8668) introduced in the House of Representatives by William Kent of California on January 11, 1916. At its February conference, the ASLA resolved to support the bill and pledged to cooperate with the new agency in any way possible, consistent with the recognized ethics of the profession. This conference promoted the stewardship of the landscape architecture profession for national parks and the preeminence of a landscape preservation ethic in the development of natural areas of outstanding value.[3]

The society recommended the formation of an advisory board composed of landscape architects and an engineer, whose services could be called for whenever landscape questions in existing parks or proposals for new parks were considered. Although this measure was dropped from the bill, conference speaker Richard Watrous predicted that the profession would have a continuing role: "I have no doubt they will call on you frequently for such advice. Planning for the proper treatment of the parks is no small undertaking. In respect to its scenic beauty, each park is an entity in itself, and for such treatment as may be necessary each park presents its own special problems" (104).

Landscape architects were fully aware of the dilemma posed by the park service's twofold mission, to protect the resources of the national parks and at the same time make them accessible. James Sturgis Pray, president of the ASLA, warned against the overexploitation of the national parks. Recalling John Muir's advocacy of the preservation of unimpaired examples of primeval landscape, Pray called upon members of the profession to educate Americans about the sacredness of these areas. Pray outlined the vital role of the landscape architecture profession:

> Let me now go on record as believing that the surpassing beauty of our National Parks is neither safe, nor will be made enjoyable, for the maximum number of people with the minimum of injury to that landscape beauty, unless the administration of the National Park areas employs the best counsel it can secure in the profession of Landscape Architecture, and that this is needed for four principal purposes: First, a careful determination of proper boundaries of the National Parks . . . in consonance with the topography and landscape unity; second, the development of comprehensive general plans for every National Park and Monument, showing roads, bridges, trails, buildings, etc., so far as these may be needed, and at the same time can be built without injury to the landscape, and the adoption of a definite policy of development; third, the approval of designs for buildings or other special structures; fourth, prescribing a system of intelligent and scrupulous maintenance having particular regard to the protection of the beauty of the landscape.[4]

Henry Vincent Hubbard, a professor of landscape architecture at Harvard University and partner in Olmsted Brothers, upheld the profession's stewardship role the following year in *An Introduction to the Study of Landscape Design,* which he coauthored with Theodora Kimball, Harvard's librarian for landscape architecture. Having visited Yosemite shortly before, Hubbard called upon members of his profession to work toward preserving the primeval and characteristic scenery of what he called America's "wild landscape."

> A possession of inestimable value to mankind, which once was so common that it went unheeded, is now becoming in our country so rare that we are beginning to appreciate its preciousness; and the responsibility rests upon us, especially upon our landscape architects, as it has never rested upon any generation of men before, to see to it that the scattered remnants of natural character and natural beauty, which we still have left to us, are preserved for the recreation and inspiration of the generations to come.[5]

Removing natural scenery from economic use and preserving it for public enjoyment as state and national parks was a civic and professional obligation. Hubbard called for the nationwide planning of areas to be preserved as landscape parks and reservations at all levels, town and city, state and nation. He urged members of his profession to take responsibility for identifying areas of outstanding scenic beauty and for educating the public about their value (323).

Similarly, in 1917, Frank Albert Waugh, a professor of landscape architecture at Massachusetts Agricultural College, recognized the development of national parklands as the domain of the landscape architect:

> We have, therefore, in hand several millions of acres of national park lands (including the national forests and the national monuments), with other millions fairly in sight, and we are just organizing a national park service to develop these unimagined resources in the public interest. . . . And this magnificent enterprise will soon be in the hands of the landscape gardeners; for who can deal with it except the men best trained in the love of the landscape and in the technical methods by which it alone can be conserved, restored, improved, clarified, made available and spiritually effective in the hearts of men and women?[6]

Outstanding scenic character distinguished national parks from national forests, which were set apart for economic purposes with the by-product of recreation. According to Frederick Law Olmsted Jr.,

> The National Parks are set apart primarily in order to preserve to the people for all time the opportunity of a peculiar kind of enjoyment and recreation, not measurable in economic terms and to be obtained only from the remarkable scenery which they contain — scenery of those primeval types which are in most parts of the world rapidly vanishing for all eternity before the increased thoroughness of the economic use of land. In the National Parks direct economic returns, if any, are properly the by-products; and even rapidity and efficiency in making them accessible to the people, although of great importance, are wholly secondary to the

one dominant purpose of preserving essential esthetic qualities of their scenery unimpaired as a heritage to the infinite numbers of the generations to come.[7]

The vision and wisdom of this generation of landscape designers, which included Pray, Hubbard, Olmsted Jr., Warren H. Manning, and others, provided the philosophical underpinnings of the new bureau. From 1916 to 1942, the landscape profession, in practice and in theory, would have a leading role in the development of parklands for public use and enjoyment. The ASLA followed the events and legislation concerning national parks, supporting bills that would limit and prohibit economic uses of the parks, and established a committee to follow national park issues.

Beginning in 1918, the National Park Service hired landscape architects to plan and design park villages, campgrounds, roads and trails, and facilities and to provide advice on issues affecting the scenery of the parks. The first of these so-called landscape engineers—Charles P. Punchard, Daniel R. Hull, and Thomas C. Vint—integrated the principles and practices of their profession with the fundamental conservationist philosophy of park service directors Stephen T. Mather and Horace M. Albright. These landscape engineers and architects relied heavily upon their educational training and the principles published by Andrew Jackson Downing, Henry Hubbard, Samuel Parsons Jr., Frank Waugh, and others. Some of the national park designers, including Punchard, Hull, Merel S. Sager, and Conrad L. Wirth, had studied under Hubbard at Harvard or Waugh at Massachusetts Agricultural College. Others received their training in some of the leading landscape design programs in the nation, including those at the University of California, Berkeley; Cornell University; the University of Illinois; and Iowa State College.

In numerous instances, formally and informally, the service called upon national experts and private practitioners to help solve some of its most pressing problems. Frederick Law Olmsted Jr. had a strong presence in the parks and remained a steadfast supporter of landscape preservation. In 1920 and 1921, he visited the national parks and forests of the West, accompanying Director Mather on some occasions. Experiencing the sense of freedom and independence stimulated by the vast untouched tracts of these reservations, Olmsted became more than ever convinced of the need to preserve these areas "substantially unimpaired by the intrusion of other functions" and to set aside wilderness areas in national parks and forests.[8]

Olmsted served on Yosemite's expert advisory committee from 1928 to 1956 and wrote numerous comprehensive reports for the committee. In the park, he helped the superintendent and the Landscape Division work out problems regarding traffic and circulation in Yosemite Valley, access to Glacier Point from the valley, and the landscape preservation of the park's meadows. He also offered advice on the location of facilities and the design of roads at Crater Lake

National Park and participated in the earliest planning of Acadia National Park and later in the design of a shoreline motor road. Olmsted's influence went far beyond the projects on which he commented. Yosemite's problems were some of the service's most vexing, and Olmsted's continuing involvement provided in-depth analyses of special problems and carefully worked out solutions that affected how similar problems in other parks were treated. His private practice, including the design of the grounds of the Ahwahnee Hotel in Yosemite Valley and the development of a plan for California's state parks, provided models for the development and management of natural areas.

Henry Hubbard also remained involved in the affairs of the National Park Service. He was a delegate and committee member of the National Conference on Outdoor Recreation in the 1920s. He served on the National Capital Park and Planning Commission from 1932 until his death in 1947. As a professor of landscape architecture at Harvard from 1906 to 1941 and as coauthor of the field's primary textbook, first published in 1917 and revised in 1929, Hubbard exerted widespread influence on the practice and character of park design in national and state parks.

Hubbard continued to write on park issues and, as editor of *Landscape Architecture,* circulated information about the national parks. At the request of the service, he wrote an article for the *1941 Yearbook: Park and Recreation Progress* entitled "The Designer in National Parks." Here he described the park designer's concerns and contrasted the landscape architect's approach with that of the architect.

> Now it is with the preservation of this natural character that the landscape designer has to deal in considering a national park, and usually in considering a "landscape park." He thus starts with an attitude of mind in one respect directly opposite from that of the architect. The landscape designer is just as much bound as is the architect by the requirements of stability and practicality. Like the architect, he also must put before the beholder compositions esthetically effective. But, unlike the architect, the good landscape designer must think in terms of natural beauty and natural expression. He is often an interpreter, a sympathetic showman, a loving conservator, rather than a self-expressing creator. He builds roads and bridges and houses, to be sure, and they are—and should normally look—manmade; but they are not there for their own sake, and usually the less they are noticed the better. They are merely necessary conveniences in presenting the pictures of nature. The national park designer cannot, of course, design the mountains. But, if he is from long and humble study an interpreter of natural beauty, he can present the mountains to the observer effectively.[9]

In 1939, Hubbard published "Landscape Development Based on Conservation, As Practiced in the National Park Service" in *Landscape Architecture.*

I.2. In November 1922, James Greenleaf (*far left*) of the federal Commission of Fine Arts visited Yosemite National Park and conferred with Daniel Hull (*middle left*) and Arno B. Cammerer (*far right*) on plans for the new village in Yosemite Valley. *(Photograph courtesy National Park Service Historic Photography Collection)*

In this comprehensive article, he summarized the master planning process behind the park service's program of landscape protection and harmonization: First came the location of the elements of park development—roads, trails, and buildings—and then the design of architectural features using native materials and harmonizing principles. And finally came the reestablishment of the natural setting through the planting of native materials.[10]

The National Park Service called upon members of the federal Commission of Fine Arts to review questionable issues and designs using its authority as a federal land-managing agency under Executive Order 1010 of January 19, 1909. Olmsted served as the commission member for landscape architecture from 1910 to 1918, including the years when the National Park Service was being promoted and organized. In 1919, Chairman Charles Moore visited Yosemite, and shortly thereafter the commission helped the park service retain the services of Myron Hunt, a Los Angeles landscape architect, to develop a new plan for Yosemite

Valley. As the commission member for landscape architecture from 1918 to 1927, James L. Greenleaf, whose private estate work included informal, naturalistic designs, visited Yosemite in 1922 to consult with landscape engineer Daniel Hull on plans for Yosemite Village. For several years, he advised Hull on the naturalistic design of masonry for guardrails and bridges. In 1928, Ferruccio Vitale, who succeeded Greenleaf as the commission's landscape architecture representative, traveled west to help chief landscape architect Thomas Vint locate several park museums and to study landscape problems at Mammoth Hot Springs in Yellowstone. On this trip, Vitale also reviewed problems in the Many Glacier area of Glacier National Park and later provided designs for the park's Swiftcurrent Bridge.

The nation's leading authority on parkways, Gilmore D. Clarke of New York's Westchester County Parks Commission, also developed close ties with the service. After Vitale's visit to Yellowstone's Mammoth Hot Springs headquarters, Vint had concluded that no more development should occur there until a general plan had been worked out; it was Clarke who created general development plans for the area in 1930. Vint and Clarke also ran a program in which they exchanged staff for periods of several months as a way of mutually enhancing their design programs. Clarke served on the Commission of Fine Arts from 1932 to 1950, during which time he helped develop parkways around the nation's capital. He also trained landscape architects such as Stanley W. Abbott, who later worked for the National Park Service and designed the Blue Ridge Parkway. Clarke and Charles W. Eliot II, planner for the National Capital Park and Planning Commission, visited Rocky Mountain National Park in 1930 to help the park service work out the final boundaries for the park and develop a plan for restoring the park's natural vegetation.

Other landscape designers advised on landscape matters, sometimes without compensation. Jens Jensen, for instance, supervised some planting at Hot Springs Reservation in 1919; Harold A. Caparn advised on boundary issues at Yellowstone in 1926; and Beatrix J. Farrand was hired by John D. Rockefeller to make recommendations for clearing vistas and adding plantings along the carriage roads at Acadia. Others experienced as educators or park designers, including P. H. Elwood Jr., Frank H. Culley, Saco R. de Boer, George L. Nason, and Harvey H. Cornell, carried the ethics of landscape preservation and rustic landscape design to state parks through the New Deal's Emergency Conservation Work program as National Park Service inspectors or, in the case of Waugh, as authors of technical manuals for conservation work.

PART I

*The Origins
of a Design Ethic
for Natural Parks*

Chapter 1

From Pleasure Grounds
to Public Parks

*Here commences a long walk, which is the favorite morning ramble of
guests. Deeply shaded, winding along the thickly wooded bank, with
the refreshing sound of the tide-waves gently dashing against the rocky
shores below, or expending themselves on the beach of gravel, it curves
along the bank for a great distance. Sometimes overhanging cliffs,
crested with pines, frown darkly over it; sometimes thick tufts of fern
and mossy-carpeted rocks border it, while at various points, vistas or
long reaches of the beautiful river scenery burst upon the eye. Half-
way along this morning ramble, a rustic seat, placed on a bold little
plateau, at the base of a large tree, eighty feet above the water, and
fenced about with a rustic barrier, invites you to linger and gaze at the
fascinating river landscape here presented. It embraces the distant
mountains, a sylvan foreground, and the broad river stretching away
for miles, sprinkled with white sails. The* coup-d'oeil *is heightened by
its being seen through a dark framework of thick leaves and branches,
which open here just sufficiently to show as much as the eye can enjoy
or revel in, without change of position.*

Andrew Jackson Downing, "A Visit to Montgomery Place," 1847

The historical development of national parks drew from the mainstream
principles and practices of the American landscape design profession. To
meet the challenge of subordinating development to natural character
and scenic values, park designers adopted naturalistic and informal practices of
landscape design with roots in nineteenth-century ideas about landscape preservation and harmonization of built features. These ideas were accompanied by
specific practices for accommodating development, whether roads or structures,

which caused minimal disruption of natural topography and which blended built structures with natural surroundings.

This ethic of design, commonly referred to as rustic, applied to the treatment of the natural features of the landscape as well as to the style of structures and buildings. It drew heavily on the nineteenth-century naturalistic tradition of landscape gardening in private pleasure grounds and urban parks which valued scenic views, variations in topography, and natural features such as vegetation, streams, and rock outcroppings. This design ethic spurred a growing appreciation for and use of native materials for construction and for naturalistic plantings. It also drew from architectural styles such as the Shingle style, the Adirondack style, the Prairie style, and the vernacular forms and methods of pioneer settlers and indigenous cultures, which all used native materials of log, wood, stone, clay, or thatch and situated constructed elements in harmony with the natural topography and surroundings. All of these influences were embraced at the turn of the century by the Arts and Crafts movement, which fostered an appreciation of handcrafted forms, pioneer and indigenous prototypes, natural settings, and naturalistic appearances.

As heirs to this rich legacy, national park designers not only adopted naturalistic principles and practices but also advanced them by forging a cohesive ethic of naturalism which simultaneously applied to the design of structures, the construction of roads and trails, and the successful blending of constructed and natural features of the park. Their work was aimed at presenting the scenic beauty of the parks and enhancing the visitors' experience while preserving the natural features. The principles and practices they advanced would in turn influence the design and development of state parks in the 1930s.

The Writings of Andrew Jackson Downing

The landscape design of national and state parks evolved from the eighteenth- and early-nineteenth-century English landscape gardening tradition of William Kent, Capability Brown, and Humphry Repton. This tradition came to America at the beginning of the nineteenth century and was first manifested in the pleasure grounds of the wealthy along the Hudson River in New York. Country estates such as Montgomery Place were celebrated in the writings of Andrew Jackson Downing in the periodical the *Horticulturalist.* Downing's *Treatise on the Theory and Practice of Landscape Gardening,* first published in 1841, was the standard American guide for landscape gardening in the nineteenth century and was revised by a number of authors as late as the 1920s. Downing, who had visited many English landscapes and was familiar with Repton's treatises, adapted the ideas and practices of the English designers to the American landscape and fos-

1.1. A. J. Downing cultivated in the American imagination an appreciation of wilderness and the wilderness experience. When Yellowstone National Park was created in 1872, it was envisioned as a "pleasuring-ground for the benefit and enjoyment of the people." Through the years, park roads and a system of paths and scenic overlooks brought park visitors on foot or horseback to the edge of one of the most spectacular scenes in America—the Grand Canyon of the Yellowstone. Concern for the encroachment of development led to the canyon's designation as a sacred area in the 1930s and the eventual removal of the hotel and campground still visible (*upper center*) in this 1936 view. (*Photograph by George A. Grant, courtesy National Park Service Historic Photography Collection*)

tered a strong awareness and appreciation of a native landscape that was inherently sublime and picturesque.

The Wilderness

Downing's writings provided a philosophical basis for preserving America's natural areas and translated the idea of "wilderness," as evocative of the sublime and picturesque, into design terms. His principles reflected the landscape interests of contemporary writers, such as Nathaniel Hawthorne, Washington Irving, William Cullen Bryant, and Henry David Thoreau, and artists of the Hudson River School, including Thomas Cole and Asher B. Durand.

Montgomery Place was an estate of about four hundred acres devoted to "pleasure grounds and ornamental purposes." Its "natural boundaries" consisted of an oak wood, a wooded valley with a broad stream containing many waterfalls, the post road, and, to the west, the Hudson River. Downing praised the natural specimens of hemlock, lime, ash, and fir and described the broad undulating lawn, margined with rich foliage and bordered by the river, which provided a view of the distant Catskills. He was elated by the panoply of colors seen at sunset from the terrace or the pavilion: "The eye is filled with wonder at the various dyes that bathe the receding hills—the most distant of which are twenty or thirty miles away."[1]

Downing cultivated in the American mind an aesthetic appreciation of wild places and stimulated images of the picturesque qualities of such places. He was intensely aware of the tremendous power that primeval nature, with its dramatically changing landform, variations of light and shadow, sounds of moving water, and enveloping vegetation, could exert on the human senses. Influenced by the popular writings of William Gilpin and Sir Uvedale Price, he described the "Wilderness" at Montgomery Place, a wooded area of the estate which retained the natural character of the Hudson River valley and evoked feelings of the sublime:

> Leaving the morning walk, we enter at once into "The Wilderness." This is a large and long wooded valley. It is broad, and much varied in surface, swelling into deep ravines, and spreading into wide hollows. In its lowest depths runs a large stream of water, that has, in portions, all the volume and swiftness of a mountain torrent. But the peculiarity of "The Wilderness," is in the depth and massiveness of its foliage. It is covered with the native growth of trees, thick, dark and shadowy, so that once plunged in its recesses, you can easily imagine yourself in the depths of an old forest, far away from the haunts of civilization. Here and there, rich thickets of the kalmia or native laurel clothe the surface of the ground, and form the richest underwood. (197)

Sparing no picturesque detail, Downing proceeded to describe the experience of moving through the wilderness. The sequence of changing vistas was central to Downing's vision. After crossing an "airy looking rustic bridge," one was plunged for a moment into the thicket and emerged again in full view of the first cataract. By "a flight of steps made in the precipitous banks of the stream," one entered another scene, which was "scarcely less-spirited and picturesque," and proceeded to the lake and after that another waterfall. The memory of what was past and the anticipation of what lay ahead heightened the individual's response (198–200).

The untamed ambiance of the place was relieved by paths, "ingeniously and naturally conducted" to reach the most interesting points. Constructed features—bridges, steps, seats, and shelters—along the way provided access, comfort, and shelter and were themselves picturesque details. A great variety of rustic seats "formed beneath the trees, in deep secluded thickets, by the side of the swift rushing stream, or on some inviting eminence" enabled one to enjoy fully the richly wooded valley (198).

Downing's description of Montgomery Place illustrated the meaning of scenery, vista, enframement, and sequence and stressed the role that rustic constructed features played in enhancing the individual's enjoyment and experience. Downing's romantic vision of the sylvan retreat—with its broad vistas, rustic seats, rock steps, thatch-roofed shelters, dense thickets of native wood, and expansive terraces and porches from which distant views across open lawns could be enjoyed—captured the imagination of the designers of parks and suburban homes alike in the nineteenth century. Downing's principles would continue to attract followers well into the twentieth century, even after other styles gained popularity.

Downing's *Treatise on the Theory and Practice of Landscape Gardening* established the key components of the pleasure ground. Apart from a fashionable manor house and formal gardens, pleasure grounds contained serpentine drives, open meadows, winding paths, picturesque rockwork, rustic bridges, and wooded glades. Rustic summerhouses and pavilions of unpeeled logs and branches provided shade and seating for rest and contemplation. Natural elements—groves of hemlocks and pines, bubbling streams, rock outcrops, waterfalls, and scenic river views—defined the wild and untamed areas of these places.

Rustic Seats, Shelters, and Bridges

Downing identified the "embellishments" that pleasure grounds should possess. Many were functional, adding to the comfort of visitors while enhancing the beauty of the natural setting. The shelter, with its seat and view, was an essential furnishing. Such structures provided shade, seating, comfort, and rest. As overlooks or windows for contemplating the natural scenery, shelters served as the objective of walks through the woods. Downing urged his readers to locate seats at points providing "agreeable prospects or extensive views of the surrounding country," so they could afford the double benefit of comfort and view. They could also be the object of visual interest from afar.[2]

There was no limit to the variety of forms and patterns in which rustic seats, arbors, summerhouses, and such structures could be constructed. In all cases, these structures were to be appropriate to their location and use and in

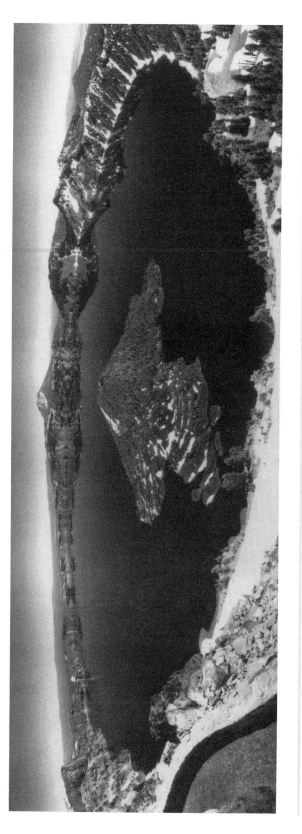

1.2. Downing's shelters and prospect towers would have corollaries in the lookouts, fire towers, picnic shelters, nature shrines, and observation towers of national parks. The Watchman, a combination fire lookout and observation tower built in 1931 through the collaboration of the Landscape and Forestry Divisions, provided the perfect vantage point for viewing Crater Lake, captured here in 1936 with a panoramic camera designed to register park locations for forest fire control. (*Photograph by Lester M. Moe, courtesy National Park Service Historic Photography Collection*)

harmony with the scene; thus, a classic temple pavilion could crown a prominent knoll, but a rustic seat demanded a secluded quiet place where "undisturbed meditation [could] be enjoyed." Downing's idea of harmonization was to blend the structure into its setting by using woodland materials and by imitating the natural form of nearby trees. He advocated rustic constructions made from the trunks and branches of trees in their natural, unpeeled, and often twisted forms. Thatching and climbing vines added attractive details to roofs and helped blend structures with surrounding vegetation. Not only did the materials of Downing's shelters echo the textures and colors of their surroundings, but also the slender sinuous elements repeated the vertical and arching forms of tree trunks and branches (411–12, 392–96).

Downing provided numerous illustrations of suitable rustic shelters that would serve as the prototypes for public and private pleasure grounds for decades to come. His "covered seat or rustic arbor" was a circular form with a thatched roof of straw supported by twelve posts and window openings framed by branches, each about three inches in diameter, fastened together to form an irregular lattice pattern. Bark and unpeeled logs were also suggested roofing materials. This type of naturalistic construction was carried to its extreme in the example of a shelter built around a living tree, with both roof and sides forming an open lattice of branches, and the whole "covered by a grape, bigonian or some other vine or creeper of luxuriant growth." Downing encouraged the construction of shelters in the form of "prospect towers" from which observers could gain a bird's-eye view of the surrounding country. Downing's rustic prospect tower was three stories in height with a double thatched roof. It had rustic pillars or columns joined by a fanciful lattice of rustic branches; a spiral staircase wound around the interior of the platform to the second and third stories, where visitors could enjoy the view in the shade of the thatched roof. Another example showed a circular thatch-covered seat surrounding a cabinet where collections of "minerals, shells, or any other curious objects for which an amateur might have a penchant" or the "geological or mineralogical specimens of the adjacent neighborhood" could be displayed (figs. 78, 79, 82; 394–98).

Downing's shelters would have corollaries in the lookouts, fire towers, picnic shelters, nature shrines, and observation towers of the national and state parks. Although his designs using twisted unpeeled branches would eventually be rejected in favor of sturdier structures built of large peeled logs or native stone, Downing established the link between a structure's material and its setting and set the precedent for the use of native materials in naturalistic forms as a technique for harmonizing built structures with a natural setting.

A similar concern for naturalism extended to the design of bridges. He recognized both the functional necessity and the decorative value of bridges. Readers were to consider the scale of the stream to be crossed, the character of the surroundings, and the appropriateness of materials to the site. Stately bridges of stone or timber were most suitable for large streams because they emitted a sense of permanence and solidity. Downing recommended a bridge when a stream was "only a winding rivulet or crystal brook, [meandering] along beneath the shadow of tufts of clustering foliage of the pleasure-ground or park" (399).

Downing's design for a rustic bridge of unpeeled logs set upon stone abutments provided the prototype for the footbridge of public parks. Although primitive in form, it would influence the evolution of sturdier bridges on national park foot and bridle trails and even park roads in the twentieth century. Downing described the bridge:

> The foundation is made by laying down a few large square stones beneath the surface on both sides of the stream to be spanned; upon these are stretched two round posts or sleepers with the bark on, about eight or ten inches in diameter. The rustic hand-rail is framed into these two sleepers. The floor of the bridge is made by laying down small posts of equal size, about four or six inches in diameter, crosswise upon the sleepers, and nailing them down securely. The bark is allowed to remain on in every piece of wood employed in the construction of this little bridge; and when the wood is cut at the proper season (durable kinds being chosen), such a bridge, well made will remain in excellent order for many years. (Fig. 83; 399)

Bridges of entwined unpeeled branches and tree trunks, inspired by Downing, appeared in urban parks in the late nineteenth century. The designs for rustic bridges in Henry Tyrrell's *Artistic Bridge Design* of 1912 included a double-span example used for foot traffic in a Minneapolis park; the bridge was described as "ordinary but satisfying because of its fitness" to its location over a ravine and surrounded by forest. Tyrrell's book also, in contrast, illustrated a sturdy timber type from Rock Creek Park in the District of Columbia.

Although constructions of unpeeled trunks remained popular as backyard garden furnishings, by 1917 landscape architects such as Frank Waugh were criticizing them as affectations and discouraging their use. Bridges made of sturdy, peeled members were more likely to withstand insect attack and rotting. The national park designers in the 1930s cautioned against such examples of "twig" architecture. In public parks, the twisted, narrow, peeled branches of Downing's bridge gave way to sturdier bridges made of larger peeled timbers with fewer irregularities. The logs for rails, stringers, braces, and trusses were selected for durability, scale with the surrounding forest, and general naturalistic character. Bridges closer in style to the Rock Creek bridge could be designed to carry varying loads and to serve foot, bridle, or automobile traffic. Among the grandest of these were Mount Rainier's Shaw Creek Bridge (1929) and Yellowstone's Lewis River Bridge (1936) and Fishing Bridge (1936). Exceptions to the bold new timber designs were several bridle trail bridges built of slender unpeeled branches

1.3. The rustic footbridge (1928) over Indian Creek in Yosemite Valley was one of the last bridges built in the national parks to follow A. J. Downing's prototype for a picturesque bridge fashioned from unpeeled branches and tree trunks. *(Photograph courtesy National Archives, Record Group 79)*

across Indian Creek in Yosemite Valley in 1926; by the mid-1930s, however, they were already in need of replacement.[3]

Rockwork

Rockwork was central to naturalistic landscape design. When it occurred in nature, it added greatly to the scenic interest of a woodland, ravine, or cliff. Downing drew attention to the inherent beauty of natural outcrops of rock, especially as they created waterfalls, inclines, and precipitous peaks affording scenic vistas. He saw rockwork of native stones as a compositional element that could be introduced and manipulated, fashioned into naturalistic groupings, or enhanced by plantings.

Rockwork could also be contrived artificially to imitate nature. Downing offered detailed instructions for developing rockwork which were used by generations of landscape architects and, in the twentieth century, by designers of national and state parks. Used as a construction material, rock could unite and harmonize built elements with a park's natural setting. Downing called for the use of moss- and lichen-covered rocks, gathered locally, set in artificial groupings such as a rocky bank. He encouraged the study of natural groupings and cautioned that great skill was necessary to achieve, in artificial rockwork, "a natural and harmonious expression." Downing urged the designer to begin his rockwork in a place where a rocky bank or knoll already partially existed or where an arrangement of rocks would be in keeping with the form of the ground and the character of the scene.

> But let us take the case of the large rugged rock, and commence our picturesque operations upon it. We will begin by collecting from some rocky hill or valley in the neighborhood of the estate, a sufficient quantity of rugged rocks, and, in size from a few pounds to half a ton or more, if necessary, preferring always such as already coated with mosses and lichens. These we will assemble around the base of a large rock, in an irregular somewhat pyramidal group, bedding them sometimes partially, sometimes almost entirely in soil heaped in irregular piles around the rock. The rocks must be arranged in a natural manner, avoiding all regularity and appearance of formal art, but placing them sometimes in groups of half a dozen together, overhanging each other, and sometimes half bedded in the soil, and a little distance apart.[4]

Rocks were to be embedded in the soil to one-half or three-fourths of their depth to create the appearance of a natural rocky ridge "just cropping out." Plants were to be arranged to increase the naturalism of the rockwork. Downing advised further,

> The rockwork once formed, choice trailing, creeping, and alpine plants, such as delight naturally in similar situations, may be planted in the soil which fills the interstices between the rocks; when these grow to fill their proper places, partly concealing and adorning the rocks with their neat green foliage and pretty blossoms, the effect of the whole, if properly done, will be like some exquisite portion of a rocky bank in wild scenery, and will be found to give an air at once striking and picturesque to the little scene where it is situated. (402)

Moist, secluded areas, such as woodland streams and ponds, and caves or rocky spots having a source of water, offered ideal sites for enhancing rockwork, either natural or naturalistic, with moisture-loving plants such as ferns, mosses, low shrubs, and climbing plants like wild clematis. Where a place was naturally picturesque with rocky banks, the best thing to do was to leave the scene alone

1.4. A. J. Downing's instructions for creating naturalistic rockwork and basins to catch water from naturally flowing springs inspired landscape designers for generations. The landscape architects of the Civilian Conservation Corps in national and state parks in the 1930s, who created picturesque springs such as this one at Backbone State Park, Iowa, were among his greatest followers. *(Photograph by Ralph H. Anderson, courtesy National Archives, Record Group 79)*

or, if necessary, enhance it by planting beautiful shrubs and climbers. Rockwork was inappropriate where rocks of any kind were unknown (402–4).

Recognizing the aesthetic possibilities of combining rocks, water, and vegetation, Downing offered instructions for creating a "rustic fountain." A conduit pipe was concealed among a group of rocks, and water flowing through it spilled out in the form of a cascade, a weeping fountain, or a perpendicular jet. The water could then fall into little basins among the rocks or at the foot of the rockwork. "The cool, moist atmosphere afforded by the trickling stream," in Downing's mind, offered "a most congenial site for aquatic plants, ferns, and mosses" (409–10).

Downing introduced Americans to the English gardener's aesthetic preference for rough stone surfaces covered with moss and lichens and worn by weather and time. This aesthetic would continue to appeal to park designers working in the rustic tradition and serve as the basis of naturalistic rock design both in landscape design and in the construction of walls, bridges, and buildings well into the twentieth century. The use of native stone, in boulder and split form, would be expanded in later treatises on landscape architecture by Samuel Parsons Jr. and Henry Hubbard. Native rock would have numerous applications in the design of national and state parks, from the embedding of rough boulders as guardrails along roads or barriers in campgrounds to the massive boulder foundations and chimneys of park buildings. It would appear in the construction of park structures of all sizes, from water fountains to refectories and administration buildings. Park designers during the New Deal also used Downing's ideas to create naturalistic lakes, channelize streams, create waterfalls, rehabilitate springs, and construct buildings that emerged naturalistically from the ground. Downing's advice on planting was followed to beautify springs, control erosion along streams, restore eroded or disturbed areas, plant foundations and bridge abutments, and naturalize road and trail cuts.

Roads and Walks

Emphasizing the importance of circulation within the pleasure ground, Downing specified several types of roads and paths. His ideas, many drawn from Repton, would be developed in the public parks and parkways of the late nineteenth century and would directly influence the location and design of roads in national and state parks in the twentieth century.

First was the approach road, which connected the estate or pleasure ground with the public highway and led to the house. Developed with artistic skill in easy curvilinear lines, it wound through the grounds until it arrived at the main house at an angle so that the facade and one of the side elevations could be viewed. The road was to be laid out in gradual, graceful curves that seemed to flow naturally up and down the contours of the land and in and around groups of trees. Downing noted, "The most natural method of forming a winding Approach where the ground is gently undulating, is to follow, in some degree, the depressions of the surface and to curve round the eminences." Groups of trees were to be planted inside the curves of the road so that when the trees were grown, it would appear that they had always stood there and that the road turned to avoid them. Views of the house were to be carefully planned and viewpoints sited on the ground. Right angles were to be avoided where the approach road left the highway and where roadways intersected (288–90).

Next was the drive, intended to lead visitors in carriages or on horseback to points of interest and to enhance their enjoyment of the grounds. Intersecting with the approach road, the drive proceeded in a similar curvilinear fashion through the grounds, revealing interesting spots and views or simply giving access to outlying areas of the estate. Finally came the walks, laid out for purposes similar to those of the drives but exclusively for travel by foot. Walks were to be laid out in easy flowing curves so that they opened up new scenes to the beholder and thereby led the traveler forth. What Downing called the "genius of a place" was to dictate the nature of a walk so that it corresponded to the scene through which it passed, being rugged where the scene was rough and picturesque, being smooth and easy where a scene was gentler and more refined. Walks were to be dry and firm. Downing described the varied character of such walks:

> Some may be open to the south, sheltered with evergreens, and made dry and hard for a warm promenade in winter; others formed of closely mown turf, and thickly shaded by a leafy canopy of verdure, for a cool retreat in the midst of summer. Others again may lead to some sequestered spot, and terminate in a secluded rustic seat, or conduct to some shaded dell or rugged eminence, where an extensive prospect can be enjoyed. Indeed, the genius of the place must suggest the direction, the length, and number of the walks to be laid out, as no fixed rules can be imposed in a subject so everchanging and different. (294)

Vegetation

Trees, in the form of plantations and small groups, had aesthetic as well as functional value. Natural groups were "full of openings and hollows, of trees advancing before or retiring behind each other; all productive of intricacy, of variety, of deep shadows and brilliant lights." Downing's writings on trees would influence the identification of natural areas to be set aside for parks, the selection of park boundaries, and the preservation or development of certain areas within a park (294).

Trees also had great value for enframing desirable vistas and screening undesirable ones: "*Wood,* in its many shapes, is then one of the greatest sources of interest and character in Landscapes. Variety, which we need scarcely allude to as a fertile source of beauty, is created in a wonderful degree by a natural arrangement of trees. To a pile of buildings, or even of ruins, to a group of rocks or animals, they communicate new life and spirit by their irregular outlines, which, by partially concealing some portions, and throwing others into stronger light, contribute greatly to produce intricacy and variety, and confer an expression, which, without these latter qualities, might in a great measure be wanting. By shutting out some parts, and inclosing others they divide the extent embraced by the eye into a hundred different landscapes, instead of one tame scene bounded by the horizon" (70–71).

Trees created unity between buildings and the land and could be used to enhance the appearance of buildings or other structures. Trees could also be used to conceal buildings, to beautify roads and paths, and to provide natural boundaries around a property and block out scenes beyond: "Buildings which are tame, insipid, or even mean in appearance, may be made interesting and often picturesque, by a proper disposition of trees. Edifices, or parts of them that are unsightly, or which it is desirable partly or wholly to conceal, can readily be hidden or improved by wood; and walks and roads, which otherwise would be but simple ways of approach from one point to another, are, by an elegant arrangement of trees on their margins, or adjacent to them, made the most interesting and pleasing portions of the residence" (71–72).

The image of the picturesque, visible in what Downing called "spiry-topped" trees, engendered the most imaginative design possibilities for natural areas. Although parks frequently had a combination of deciduous and evergreen trees, it was the evergreen, in the form of stately pines, hemlocks, balsams, firs, redwoods, and sequoias, which inspired the greatest awe in park visitors. Recalling the words of Sir Uvedale Price's *An Essay on the Picturesque, as Compared with the Sublime and the Beautiful* (1794), Downing described the effect of spiry-topped trees:

> "The situations where they have most effect is among rocks and in very irregular surfaces, and especially on the steep sides of high mountains, where their forms and the direction of their growth seem to harmonize with the pointed rocky summits." Fir and pine forests are extremely dull and monotonous in sandy plains and smooth surfaces (as in the pine barrens of the southern states); but among the broken rocks, craggy precipices, and otherwise endlessly varied surfaces (as in the Alps, abroad, and the various rocky heights in the Highlands of the Hudson and the Alleghanies [*sic*], at home) they are full of variety. . . . In all grounds where there are abruptly varied surfaces, steep banks, or rocky precipices, this class of trees lends its efficient aid to strengthen the prevailing beauty, and to complete the finish of the picture. (106–7)

In "On the Employment of Ornamental Trees and Shrubs in North America," first published in 1835 in *Hovey's Magazine of Horticulture,* Downing praised many American trees, saying that no country on the globe produced a greater variety of fine forest trees than North America. Downing was interested in the beauty of each tree as an individual specimen or as part of a grouping. He had little concern for native habitat or groupings based on natural ecological relationships. He treated North American species as he did those introduced from abroad, as part of a full and rich palette from which the designer could fashion an estate, park, or country home. Of the deciduous trees of North America, he praised the oak for its "broad ample limbs and aged form" that gave "a very impressive air of dignity" to a scene. He wrote of the "pendulous" branches of the American elm, the "light foliage" of the birch, the "cheerful vernal appearance" of some maples, the "delicate" leaf of the locust, and the "heavy masses of verdure" produced by the beech.[5]

While he praised the Kentucky coffee (*Gymnocladus canadensis*) and the deciduous cypress (*Taxodium rich*), he considered "the most splendid, most fragrant, and most celebrated ornamental production" of American woodlands to be the *Magnolia grandiflora* of the southern states. Among native evergreens, he prized the white pine (*Pinus strobus*), the spruces of the Middle Atlantic states (*Pinus alba, rubra,* and *fraseri*), the balsam fir (*Pinus balsamea*), and the arborvitae (*Thuja occidentalis*). In an article entitled "A Word in Favor of Evergreens," first published in the *Horticulturalist* in 1848, Downing praised the hemlock (*Abies canadensis*). "In its wild haunts, by the side of some steep mountain, or on the dark wooded banks of some deep valley, it is most often a grand and picturesque tree; when, as in some parts of the northern States, it covers countless acres of wild forest land, it becomes gloomy and monotonous."[6]

Noting the beauty of America's autumnal foliage, known throughout the world, Downing regretted the increasing loss of these "wide masses of rich coloring" to the axe of the woodsman. He urged the mass planting of colorful groupings that included the scarlet of the scarlet oak (*Quercus coccinea*), the deep crimson of the dogwood (*Cornus florida*), the yellow and deep orange of the tupelo and sour gum (*Nyssa villosa*) and different species of maple (*Acer* spp.), the reddish purple of the sweet gum (*Liquidambar styraciflua*), and the somber purple of the American ash (*Fraxinus americana*). He noted that the intermediate shades came from the numerous species of birches, sycamores, elms, chestnuts, and beeches and that the effect of the whole was "thrown into lively contrast by a rich intermingling of the deep green in the thick foliage of the pines, spruces, and hemlocks" (381–82).

Downing offered complete instructions for transplanting large trees in the *Horticulturalist* of January 1850. Relying heavily upon Henry Stuart's instructions published about fifteen years earlier in Great Britain, Downing offered a simple formula: "First, the greatest respect for the roots of a tree, and some knowledge of the functions of the roots and branches; second, a pair of large wheels, with a strong axle and pole; third, practical skill and patience in executing the work." He noted that elms and maples were well adapted for transplanting, whereas oaks or hickories were not because of their deep-growing taproots (350–51).

Although Downing is most often acclaimed for his descriptions of foreign specimens and cultivars, he did not overlook the value of many fine American cultivars. At Montgomery Place he praised the ash, hemlock, and fir, as well as the flowering laurels that provided a rich underwood in the "Wilderness." Frank Waugh, one of Downing's strongest twentieth-century followers, recognized in 1917 that Downing did much to stimulate an appreciation for America's native plants. In addition to the native trees of the United States, Downing praised and encouraged the planting of many native shrubs and ground covers, which he valued not only for the inherent beauty of their foliage and flowers but also for their ability to enhance the character of a natural scene.

In an article in the *Horticulturalist* entitled "Neglected American Plants" in 1851, Downing regretted the "apathy and indifference of Americans to the beautiful sylvan and floral products of their own country." Americans, he claimed, imported every new and rare exotic from abroad but remained unappreciative of native plants: "How many rich and beautiful shrubs, that might embellish our walks and add variety to our shrubberies, . . . are left to wave on the mountain crag, or overhang the steep side of some forest valley; how many rare and curious flowers . . . bloom unseen amid the depths of silent woods, or along the margin of wild water-courses."[7]

Downing believed that American woods and swamps were full of the most exquisite plants, many of which could embellish "even the smallest garden." He called the azaleas, laurels, rhododendrons, cypripediums, and magnolias the "loveliest flowers, shrubs, and trees of temperate climates." He praised the English fashion of planting masses of American mountain laurel, azaleas, and rhododendrons. Downing drew attention to two native broad-leaved evergreen shrubs abundant in the middle states—the holly (*Ilex opaca*) and laurel (*Kalmia latifolia*)—and urged Americans to plant them in their pleasure grounds:

> Let our readers who wish to decorate their grounds with something *new and beautiful,* undertake now, *in this month of May* (for these plants are best transplanted *after* they have commenced a new growth), to plant some laurels and hollies. If they would do this quite successfully, they must not stick them here and there among other shrubs in the common border—but prepare a bed or clump, in some cool, rather shaded aspect—a north slope is better than a southern one—where the subsoil is rather damp than dry. The soil should be sandy or gravelly, with a mixture of black earth well decomposed, . . . to retain moisture in a long drought. A bed of these fine evergreens, made in this way, will be a *feature* in the grounds, which after it has been well established for a few years, will convince you far better than any words of ours, of the neglected beauty of our American plants. (342)

In an essay entitled "Vines and Climbing Plants," Downing praised the Virginia creeper (*Ampelopsis hederacea*). Calling it the American ivy, he compared it to English ivy:

> The leaves are as large as the hand, deeply divided into five lobes, and the blossoms are succeeded by handsome dark blue berries. The Virginia Creeper is a most luxuriant grower, and we have seen it climbing to the extremities of trees 70 or 80 feet in height. Like the Ivy, it attaches itself to whatever it can lay hold of, by little

rootlets which spring out of the branches; and its foliage, when it clothes thickly a high wall, or folds itself in clustering wreaths around the trunk and branches of an open tree, is extremely handsome and showy. Although the leaves are not ever-green, like those of the Ivy, yet in autumn they far surpass those of that plant in the rich and gorgeous coloring which they then assume.[8]

Downing also praised the wild grape for its ability to create a verdant canopy and draperylike effects. He noted the value of other native climbing plants, including bittersweet, pipe vine or birthwort, clematis, trumpet creeper, wisteria, honeysuckle, and climbing roses, all of which had native forms in the United States. Downing encouraged the planting of climbing vines to relieve the bleak, sun-bleached elevations of country cottages (286).

National park designers would highly value the native vegetation of the parks. Although they studied natural patterns of vegetation, they frequently chose the more ornamental flowering shrubs, climbing vines, and ferns and the most picturesque trees of an area's natural community to use as the dominant materials for planting around park buildings, roads, and bridges. Aesthetics often determined the selection of materials to be preserved or transplanted from areas being cleared for construction or selectively thinned for campgrounds, roads, or forest protection. Although many of the native species of the western parks were unknown to Downing, they possessed qualities comparable to those he praised in the East.

Where species praised by Downing existed in nature, they readily became favored materials in the palette of the park designers. The qualities of many of these species helped serve the purposes for which the parks had been set aside. Laurels, rhododendrons, and azaleas were used for screening and decorative pur-poses along the scenic drives of the Blue Ridge in Virginia and North Carolina. Virginia creeper was planted in the interstices of freshly cut rocks along Shenan-doah's Skyline Drive, while laurels and azaleas were planted in masses on the drive's flattened slopes. Douglas firs, western hemlocks, and Alaskan cedar were used at Longmire to blend the village with the dense forests of Mount Rainier. Elsewhere, corollaries were found, such as the deciduous azalea (*Rhododendron occidentale*) and chinquapin (*Castanopsis sempervirens*) of Yosemite, the laurels (*Umbellularia californica*) of Sequoia, the salal (*Gualtheria shallon*) of Mount Rainier, the junipers (*Juniperus osteosperma*) of the Grand Canyon's South Rim, and the evergreen sumac (*Rhus lanceolata*) of Big Bend. This appreciation for native species carried over into state parks, where rhododendrons (*Rhododen-dron maximum*) were planted along trails and at overlooks in Tennessee, birch (*Betula alleghaniensis*) in Michigan, laurels (*Kalmia latifolia*) in Pennsylvania, and yaupon (*Ilex vomitoria*), a native holly, in central Texas.

Downing's principles established an ethic for landscape preservation and harmonization which would reach maturity in the work of the National Park

Service in the 1920s and 1930s. Downing fostered an appreciation of landscape character and the sequence of landscape effects. In this he established an aesthetic basis for the preservation of natural scenery and its use for pleasure and enjoyment. He introduced the fundamental concepts of selecting viewpoints, enframing vistas, and moving the visitor through a sequence of views and scenes along curvilinear paths and steps to ensure pleasure and comfort while fostering appreciation and sensibility. He stimulated an appreciation for vegetation and rockwork as objects to be preserved and as vital design elements in enhancing the beauty of a place or scene and in blending constructed features with a natural setting. The conceptual foundation provided by the private pleasure ground was consciously adapted in the setting aside of natural reserves for public use and enjoyment. Yellowstone National Park, when established by law in 1872, was envisioned as "a public park or pleasuring-ground for the benefit and enjoyment of the people."[9]

The various components of the nineteenth-century pleasure ground would find practical and utilitarian counterparts in national and state parks in the twentieth century. The gatehouse would become the entrance station. Summerhouses would become overlooks and picnic shelters. Rustic seats would become sturdy benches and picnic tables. Moss- and lichen-covered rocks would be incorporated into the foundations and walls of park structures, while natural outcrops and formations would be developed as points of interest and picturesque elements along trails and roads. Woodland paths would become rugged hiking and bridle trails through which visitors experienced the natural beauty of the parks. The circular drives would become the loop roads that facilitated the flow of traffic in campgrounds and picnic areas or encircled parks to provide access and scenic views from many points. The prospect tower on the crest of a hill, which allowed visibility in all directions, would be transformed into a functional fire lookout or observation tower. And even Downing's cabinet of local curios would find its successor in trailside museums and nature shrines. Plantations of native trees, evergreen wherever appropriate, would be preserved or planted to screen undesirable views or structures. Spiry-topped trees, flowering shrubs, ferns, and climbing vines from Virginia creeper to wild clematis would be planted and transplanted to naturalize areas disturbed by construction, to erase the lines between built structures and natural settings, and to integrate development into the natural surroundings of the park. The ideas of Downing and American practitioners of the English gardening style would evolve through several stages, however, before being transformed into the policy and practices of the National Park Service.

1.5. Capturing the "genius of the place" was A. J. Downing's primary concern for laying out pathways through the wilderness. With the advent of the automobile and the desire to open up the splendid scenery of the West, park designers faced the challenge of creating a transmountain road across the Continental Divide in Glacier National Park in the 1920s. The Going-to-the-Sun Highway, photographed here near the summit at Logan Pass in 1933, became one of the greatest achievements of park road design. It combined picturesque and naturalistic techniques drawn from landscape architecture with the state-of-the-art technology of highway engineering. *(Photograph by George A. Grant, courtesy National Park Service Historic Photography Collection)*

The American Park Movement

The transition from the pleasure ground to the public park occurred in the second half of the nineteenth century through the work of Frederick Law Olmsted Sr., Calvert Vaux, and others. These parks were urban and often created through earth moving and extensive planting. Natural features, such as meadows, streams, lakes, waterfalls, and wooded glens, were improved or artificially created to provide picturesque effects. Rustic features and picturesque areas such as the Ramble and Ravine in Central Park would provide miniaturized versions of Montgomery Place's Wilderness.

Downing's principles held that all improvements should be subordinate to and in keeping with natural beauty. The designer's work was to strengthen the inherent expression of beautiful or picturesque natural character. The urban parks of the late nineteenth century were developed with this principle in mind. In 1917 Henry Hubbard recognized the incorporation of the natural landscape, with its landform and vegetation, into naturalistic designs as one of the distinguishing aspects of American landscape design.[10]

Frederick Law Olmsted Sr.

Frederick Law Olmsted Sr. developed six principles guiding the landscape design of public parks. These principles pertained to scenery, suitability, sanitation, subordination, separation, and spaciousness. They called for designs that were in keeping with the natural scenery and topography and consisted of "passages of scenery" and scenic areas of plantings. The principle of sanitation called for designs that promoted physical and mental health and provided adequate drainage and facilities. All details, natural and artificial, were to be subordinated to the character of the overall design. Areas having different uses and character were to be separated from each other, and separate byways were to be developed for different kinds of traffic. Designs were to make an area appear larger than it was by creating bays and headlands of plantings and irregular visual boundaries.[11]

Olmsted's ideas were shaped not only by the writings of Repton, Downing, and others but also by the example of English parks, particularly Birkenhead Park in Liverpool, which he had visited. He was familiar with the writings and work of Prince H. L. H. von Pückler-Muskau of Germany, whose private park exhibited his own interpretation of the principles of English landscape gardening. Von Pückler-Muskau advocated an approach to park building in which all design was subordinate to a "controlling scheme" and was carried out with simplicity, outwardness, and respect for nature. He had a keen understanding of the relationship between indoor and outdoor space and developed shaded sitting areas at scenic points. Perhaps most significant was the prince's ecological appreciation for native vegetation and his insistence that pleasure grounds should represent nature—nature arranged for the use and comfort of people— and should be true to the character of the country and climate to which they belonged. For this reason, the prince permitted the planting only of trees and shrubs that were native or thoroughly acclimated to the area, avoiding foreign ornamental plants.[12]

By 1858, when Olmsted and Vaux, an architect, submitted their award-winning design for Central Park, Olmsted was also acquainted with the improvements for the Bois de Boulogne in Paris being carried out by Baron Haussmann and his chief engineer, J. C. Adolphe Alphand. These improvements further developed the English gardening idea for public use and enjoyment. Olmsted would meet with Alphand and visit the Parisian park in 1859.[13]

According to Olmsted, the main purpose of a park was to "exact the predominance of nature." Improvements of any type were to be subordinate to the natural character: "In all much frequented pleasure-grounds, constructions of various kinds are necessary to the convenience and comfort of those to be benefited; their number and extent being proportioned to the manner in which they are to be used, and to the number of expected users. If well adapted to their purpose, strongly and truly built, the artificial character of many of these must be more or less displayed. It is not, then, by the absence nor by the concealment of construction that the natural school is tested. . . . In natural gardening artificial elements are employed adjunctively to designs, the essential pleasure-giving character of which is natural."[14]

In 1864, the commissioners of Central Park established a policy for subordinating constructed elements to the natural character of the park landscape. This policy clearly established a precedent for park structures that were inconspicuous and harmonized with nature: "So far as is consistent with the convenient use of the grounds, vegetation should hold first place of distinction; it is the work of nature, invulnerable to criticism, accepted by all . . . and affords a limitless field for interesting observation and instruction. . . . Such as finds a place in the Park in answer to the demands of convenience and pleasure should therefore be subordinate to its recognized natural features and in harmony with them, not impertinently thrusting itself into conspicuous notice, but fitly fulfilling the purposes for which it is admitted."[15]

Buildings should be limited in number, small in scale, and concealed behind groves of trees. Olmsted's design for Central Park had few structures. The old arsenal was temporarily left in place for museum purposes. Olmsted put great effort into making the building less conspicuous by painting it a subdued color, reducing its height, and covering it with vines.

Most of the structures for Central Park were part of the circulation system. Olmsted had laid out a system of independent ways for carriages, horses, and pedestrians. To a substantial extent, the circulation network of curvilinear paths and drives unified the park and guided the visitor through a sequence of predetermined scenes. The system was designed so that one could pass through the park on foot without crossing the carriage roads. Olmsted achieved this by constructing an intricate network of bridges and tunnels, called "arches," which allowed paths and roads to cross over or under each other on separate levels. These passageways also became shelters and were designed to blend into the surrounding scenery, whether earthen banks or rock outcrops. Rocky banks were "worked up boldly against the masonry of the arches" and planted so that visitors were scarcely aware of the structures. The most rustic of these were Olm-

1.6. The 1880s plan for Franklin Park in Boston shows Frederick Law Olmsted's concept of a country park, with areas for passive and active recreation and systems of footpaths and carriage roads. Although stone walls and boulders were removed from former fields and pastures to create open playing fields and meadows, the park's designers left large areas in the northwest of the park as wilderness. A circuit drive relied upon bridges, curving alignment, and points of interest to immerse carriage traffic in an unraveling panorama of country beauty. Separate paths and stairways led pedestrians to scenic overlooks and picturesque features. (*Plan courtesy National Park Service, Frederick Law Olmsted National Historic Site*)

sted's random masonry arch at the Ramble which tightly hugged the natural bedrock and the Boulder Bridge, in which massive slabs of rock were arranged in a bold, exaggerated manner, as if piled up by some great cataclysmic force. These designs, particularly the bridge, used natural materials and blended with the natural setting. In the design of the bridge, Olmsted's naturalism took on exaggerated proportions as the effects of a wild place were not only assimilated but amplified to create highly romantic, picturesque results. These two structures were later illustrated in Samuel Parsons' *Art of Landscape Architecture* (1915) and, like the designs of other features in Central Park, inspired the work of park designers for decades to come. Calvert Vaux designed many of the lesser structures following Downing's suggestions for constructions of unpeeled tree trunks and twisted branches; these included boathouses, footbridges, shelters, and benches.[16]

By 1872, the Tweed administration had very different ideas for the park and planned the construction of large museums. Olmsted responded by offering the following criteria for park buildings: "To determine whether any structure on the Park is undesirable, it should be considered, first, what part of the necessary accommodation of the public on the Park is met by it, how this much of accommodation could be otherwise or elsewhere provided, and in what degree and whence the structure will be conspicuous after it shall have been toned by weather, and the plantations about and beyond it shall have taken a mature character."[17]

Of Olmsted's greatest parks, Franklin Park in Boston, designed in the 1880s, established the strongest precedent for the design of natural areas. It adapted Downing's ideas about a private pleasure ground to the demands of an urban location, heavy public use, and public management. Envisioned as a "country park" from the start, the park preserved natural wooded areas and picturesque outcrops of Roxbury pudding stone, a local conglomerate. Open meadows were carved out of what had been farms and fields; natural vegetation was retained and enhanced by new plantings, many of which were native to the region; a pond was excavated and planted; overlooks were developed at scenic points; and an expanded repertoire of sturdy park structures and outside furniture was installed to provide for comfort and pleasure. A circuit drive led carriages around the park, up and down natural hills, to stopping places where passengers could climb rustic stone stairways lined with coping boulders to scenic overlooks and picturesque shelters. Henry Hubbard thought highly of Franklin Park and drew extensively from its example in his *Introduction to the Study of Landscape Design* (1917) and thereby set it forth as a model for the development of natural areas in the twentieth century.

The roads in Franklin Park were designed to enable visitors to take in the fresh air and enjoy the kinetic experience of viewing the scenery at a relatively slow speed. Because of the limited speed of horse-drawn carriages, the roads could round many tight curves and ascend steep gradients in order to follow the natural topography. In his "Notes on the Plan of Franklin Park," Olmsted wrote, "The roads of the park have been designed less with a purpose of bringing visitors to points of view at which they will enjoy set scenes or landscapes, than to provide for a constant mild enjoyment of simply pleasing rural scenery while in easy movement, and thus by curves and grades avoiding unnecessary violence to nature."[18]

Rockwork was an important unifying feature in the design of Franklin Park. Local stone gathered as old walls were dismantled and former pastures cleared provided construction materials for the buildings, bridges, and other built structures in the park and elsewhere in the city's emerging system of parks and parkways. Large, rugged boulders of Roxbury pudding stone were incorporated into the design of many landscape and architectural features. On the open field called the "playstead," Olmsted erected a massive terrace of boulders six hundred feet long on which a large two-story Shingle style recreation building was built. The building provided changing rooms for athletes, rest rooms, and, upstairs, a dining room with a large fireplace. A smaller Shingle style shelter in the form of an open-air lookout was built on the summit of Schoolmaster's Hill. The walls of these buildings were constructed of boulders and weathered wooden shingles. The solidity and proportions of their forms conveyed a permanence and sturdiness that was lacking in Downing's constructions of twisted branches. Rockwork provided rustic accents in an overgrown curving stairway of ninety-nine steps and in the edging of overlooks, paths, and roads. A circuit road and system of meandering paths were installed, and grades for strolling and driving were separated by stone bridges and the vine-covered Ellicotdale Arch, a rustic foot tunnel that passed beneath the carriage road. Functional landscape features, such as benches, water fountains, and springs, were characterized by the use of rustic boulders embedded in the soil, laid in courses, or sometimes fashioned into round arches. Water fountains were built from large boulders or slabs of pudding stone, often informally juxtaposed with little or no mortar. Benches were constructed in segments consisting of rough pudding stone piers and horizontal wooden slats forming seats and backrests; segments were fit together to wrap around the curves of the paths they served.[19]

The rockwork at Franklin Park further developed the rustic boulder and split-stone constructions of Central Park. The romantic exaggeration of Central Park's Boulder Bridge gave way to more subdued and less conspicuous forms of rockwork more in keeping with the arch in the Ramble. Overall the features developed for the park in the 1880s and 1890s shared a stronger functionalism and greater architectural unity than those developed earlier at Central Park. For the first time, park furniture and conveniences, including benches, water fountains, springs, and shelters, assumed sturdy permanent forms of native rock material.

Franklin Park set a standard for the design of rustic park structures and ex-

1.7. One of many overlooks in Franklin Park in Boston illustrates Frederick Law Olmsted's use of stone steps and coping to create a viewing terrace and an objective for park visitors. *(Photograph courtesy National Park Service, Frederick Law Olmsted National Historic Site)*

plored new uses of rockwork and native vegetation. It provided a model for the arrangement of a country park in relation to existing natural features and transportation needs. The Olmsted firm's work at Franklin Park forged a design ethic for natural parks which would be carried into the twentieth century by landscape architects, be adopted and adapted by National Park Service designers, and flourish in the park conservation work of the 1930s in national, state, and metropolitan parks.

Several significant developments had occurred in Olmsted's career by the time Franklin Park was being laid out. The firm had been creating the Emerald Necklace, a system of parks and parkways, for the city of Boston and was embroiled in debates over the appropriate design of bridges at various sites. Nationwide, the idea of "wilderness" had taken on monumental dimensions through the exploration and geological surveys of the West. Olmsted had become concerned with the conservation of natural areas. He had been to the West, working for the Mariposa Mining Company and serving as a commissioner for the Yosemite Valley and Mariposa Big Tree Grove. Olmsted was also enmeshed in efforts to save Niagara Falls. His continuing involvement at Central Park also

1.8. Typical of the sturdy park structures at Franklin Park, this rustic water fountain was made from slabs of local pudding stone laid up in monolithic fashion to imitate the natural rock outcroppings that abounded throughout the park. *(Photograph courtesy National Park Service, Frederick Law Olmsted National Historic Site)*

enabled Olmsted to test the durability of the park structures over several years and to plan more appropriately for the needs and comforts of visitors to public parks. There is some indication that he found Vaux's unpeeled log pavilions and bridges, built in the spirit of Downing's rustic structures, unable to withstand the use and weathering and, by the end of the 1870s, realized that park structures needed to be sturdier and easier to maintain.

1.9. The benches at Franklin Park in Boston were made of wooden planks and massive piers of Roxbury pudding stone, a local conglomerate. They were designed to follow the flowing curves of the drive and to blend with the surrounding woodlands and rock out-croppings. *(Photograph courtesy National Park Service, Frederick Law Olmsted National Historic Site)*

Franklin Park reflected two strong aesthetic influences that had affected Olmsted's work in the 1870s and 1880s. First, he began to collaborate with the architect Henry Hobson Richardson, who was the preeminent practitioner of the Shingle style. Second, he began to work more with wild plants to achieve effects that were highly picturesque and naturalistic.

Olmsted began collaborating with Richardson in the 1870s. Their collaboration resulted in major works such as the Ames Memorial Hall in North Easton, the Niagara Monument in Buffalo, and the state capitol in Albany, as well as many small structures such as gatehouses in city parks and waiting stations on the Boston and Albany Railroad line. One joint project to have substantial influence on the design of park structures was the Boylston Street Bridge, the first major structure that the Olmsted firm designed for the Emerald Necklace. Olmsted desired a bridge that would have a "rustic quality" and be "picturesque" in material, as well as in outline and shadow. He preferred an arch of Roxbury pudding stone or a bridge of rough fieldstones with an arch of cut voussoirs. Richardson sketched a simple arch that fit into the riverbanks and was likely to be built with boulders of local fieldstone. Although much debate ensued among city leaders before the bridge, very different in character from Richardson's single boulder arch, was built, a working relationship had been established between the master park builder and the great architect. Richardson went on to execute designs for several simple gatehouses and water fountains for the Emerald Necklace.[20]

In the early 1880s, Olmsted also collaborated with Richardson on the estate of the Ames family, the town hall, and several other projects in North Easton, Massachusetts. These commissions called for Richardson's bold arches, rusticated stonemasonry, and Shingle style design as well as Olmsted's naturalistic blending of wild plants with existing rugged outcroppings. The gatehouse at the Ames estate, with its bold arch, was a hallmark of Richardsonian design.

The first structures in Franklin Park were three temporary shelters designed by Richardson in 1884, shortly after the park opened. No drawings or photographs of these remain, but circumstances indicate that, in Olmsted's opinion, Richardson was capable of designing structures, no matter how small or unpretentious, which were functional, inconspicuous, harmonious with nature, and appropriate to a natural setting. In 1886, Richardson died, ending the fortuitous collaboration. By then the Olmsted firm had absorbed his ideas, which left an enduring legacy to park designers for generations to come.[21]

The Playstead Shelter at Franklin Park was one of the largest park buildings designed by the Olmsted firm. It appears to be Olmsted's design and clearly reflects Richardson's influence. Designed in 1887, the building was completed in 1889. Olmsted planned a six-hundred-foot boulder terrace, intended as a natural platform for viewing sports, as an integral feature of the park; it was built up of innumerable stones and boulders taken from the stone walls of former farms and from the rock-strewn pastures left by the glaciers and cleared by the park engineers. The shelter's lower walls and foundation were made of boulders and were part of the terrace. The lower story provided dressing and shower facilities for players and could be entered from the field through an arch in the terrace. The main floor, with its central area open to the roof with exposed rafters and flanked by two massive fireplaces, consisted of a soda fountain and eating facilities. Because of its horizontal proportions, its native shingle and stone materials, and its connection to the ground through the boulder terrace, the building blended harmoniously into its site.[22]

Although much debate raged over the construction of the Boylston Street Bridge, Richardson's sketch and Olmsted's thinking certainly influenced the design of two masonry stone bridges at Franklin Park's Scarborough Pond by George F. Shepley, Charles H. Rutan, and Charles A. Coolidge, the successors to Richardson's firm. Here in the setting of a country park, the bridges were constructed of fieldstones carefully placed to appear random, with a simple single arch of voussoir stones cut to size but fit together so that the weathered surfaces were exposed to view. Stone arch bridges were promoted in Repton's writings and commonly found across the English countryside as well as in parks such as Emmonville in France. Olmsted's collaboration with Richardson, however, encouraged Olmsted to explore new possibilities in rustic stonework, the park bridge being one of its most important applications and the one that would be most used in the design of rock-faced concrete bridges for national and state parks in the twentieth century. The debate over whether walls should be of rounded boulders or of cut stone laid in a random fashion led to experiments in park design in the Boston parks and parkways. The Scarborough Pond bridges, the large one with a streamlined curving parapet and the other with a stepped parapet, represent pivotal steps away from the picturesque boulder compositions toward designs of rusticated stone cut and arranged randomly to suit a natural setting. These bridges, particularly the larger one, provided models for the designers of national parks and were featured as appropriate for natural areas by Hubbard in his *Introduction to the Study of Landscape Design.*

The collaboration between Richardson and Olmsted was cut short by Richardson's untimely death, but its integration of landscape and architectural concerns would continue to be reflected in the work of the Olmsted firm and in metropolitan park and parkway systems across the country. Above all, Richardson's techniques for using native rock in bold, rusticated arches and masonry walls would be carried on in the development of landscape features such as bridges, tunnels, and shelters. Although many of the structures at Franklin Park were designed by others, they clearly show the profound influence that Richardson had on the work of the Olmsted firm and the design of park structures in general.

The other development to affect profoundly Olmsted's work and ultimately the twentieth-century park designers was the creation of wild gardens, espoused by British master gardener William Robinson in *The Wild Garden or the Naturalization and Natural Grouping of Hardy Exotic Plants* of 1870. Robinson's ideas on introducing the wild species of many nations into the English garden in the form of wild borders, woodland settings, fern gardens, and water gardens in ponds or along streams met with great popularity in England. Small wild plants such as ground covers, ferns, climbing vines, and water plants could embellish the pleasure ground, adding to the already existing interest in trees and shrubs for their aesthetic character. Robinson's ideas would be further expanded into treatises on creating English cottage gardens and would find an avid following in the English Arts and Crafts movement and among practitioners such as Gertrude Jekyll and William Morris.[23]

By the 1880s, Robinson's ideas were practiced in America and reflected in the work of the Olmsted firm and others. In 1872, Olmsted encouraged a more naturalistic treatment of vegetation in Central Park to avoid a gardenlike appearance and to enhance the park's picturesque qualities. He recommended that shrubbery and trees be thinned, pruned, and blended to avoid uniformity and that vines, such as clematis and honeysuckle, be planted. He offered extensive advice on the wild planting of the Ramble and sent the gardener an annotated copy of Robinson's *Wild Garden,* noting that Robinson's ideas coincided with what he had all along intended for the Ramble. Olmsted viewed the Ramble as the place most suitable for a "perfect realization of the wild garden":

> The rocks in the upper part of the Ramble are to be made permanently visible from the terrace. Tall trees are to be retained and encouraged in the outer parts; dark evergreens on the nearer parts of the ridges, right and left, with a general gradation of light foliage upon and near Vista Rock. The recently made moss gardens are to be revised and the ground rendered natural by the removal of some of the boulders, making larger, plainer surfaces, and by the introduction of more varied and common materials. Evergreen shrubs, ferns, moss, ivy, periwinkle, rock plants and common bulbs (snowdrop, dog tooth violet, crocuses, etc.), are to be largely planted in the Ramble, and while carefully keeping to the landscape character required in the general view from the Terrace, and aiming at a much more natural wild character in the interior views than at present, much greater variety and more interest of detail is to be introduced.[24]

At Franklin Park, wild grapevines clung to the walls of arches, springs, and water fountains built from rustic boulders and split stone. Low-growing plants flanked the sides of curving stone steps and stairways. Climbing vines, wild ground covers, and perennial plants were planted in the interstices of the massive boulder wall beneath the Playstead Shelter. Vegetation draped the Ellicotdale Arch, the arbor on Schoolmaster's Hill, and the many springs and water fountains. The carriage road and footpaths were lined with mixed displays of shrubbery and low-growing plants. The abutments of the Scarborough Pond bridges were planted in a rich display of shrubbery.

Robinson's ideas were assimilated into American landscape gardening in the 1880s and 1890s. Articles on the embellishment of dwellings with wild vegetation appeared in *Garden and Forest.* These included "How to Mask the Foundations of A Country House" in 1889 and "Architecture and Vines" in 1894. The driving force behind an almost excessive use of vegetation to adorn and to hide architecture was, on the one hand, romantic nostalgia for overgrown ruins and, on the other hand, an aesthetic belief that structures, although necessary, distracted from the scenic beauty of a country or natural place and were to be concealed by natural means wherever possible.

The profuse and dense vegetation that resulted from Robinson's techniques in the nineteenth century became less fashionable in the twentieth century. His

1.10. The development of springs was an important aspect of designing natural parks. Echoing the bold rusticated arches of H. H. Richardson's architecture and the wild gardening of William Robinson, the housing for this spring in Franklin Park was made of weathered pudding stone and planted with climbing vines of native grape. The spring was transformed into a quiet and picturesque grotto that blended with the park's natural setting. *(Photograph courtesy National Park Service, Frederick Law Olmsted National Historic Site)*

ideas, however, continued to attract followers into the twentieth century, when they took the form of wild gardens filling remote and often naturally wooded ravines of estates during the "country place era" from the early 1890s through the 1920s. These gardens included work by Hubbard, James Greenleaf, the Olmsteds, Warren Manning, Ferruccio Vitale, and Beatrix Farrand, practitioners who were also involved with the design of national parks. The practice of using wild plants, shrubs, and trees to conceal construction scars, to blend built structures with natural vegetation, and to screen undesirable objects from view would continue into the twentieth century and serve the National Park Service's program of landscape naturalization decades later.

Another important development of the nineteenth-century park movement was the creation of regional park systems that included large reservations and scenic natural features. In 1872, park designer H. W. S. Cleveland called for a system of metropolitan parks for Minneapolis which would include the nearby river bluffs along the Mississippi and the land encompassing the nearby lakes, hills, and valleys as well as suitable park areas within the city limits.[25]

Charles Eliot

Charles Eliot, a Boston landscape architect who had worked in the Olmsted office, was a pioneer in developing a methodology for preserving regional character and outstanding natural features and for developing and managing scenic reservations. Eliot defended the preservation of a stand of virgin trees and presented a plan for conserving scenic areas in an article, "Waverly Oaks," printed in *Garden and Forest* in February 1890. His argument resulted in the formation of the Trustees of Public Reservations in Massachusetts in 1891 and state legislation in 1893 which established the Metropolitan Park System around Boston; the first such system in the country, it included parks of natural scenic character such as Blue Hills and Middlesex Fells.[26]

Highly prizing regional character and scenic values, Eliot was greatly concerned with the development of vistas within parks and series of parks connected by natural systems such as rivers and meadows. Eliot advocated clearing vegetation to reveal and maintain scenic vistas that expressed regional character and united disparate geographical features. Eliot's understanding of vista and regional character had considerable influence on the landscape design of national parks, which often covered many thousands of acres, great variations in landform, and unified systems of mountains and valleys.

Eliot was strongly influenced by Prince von Pückler-Muskau's theories and his naturalistic pleasure ground at Muskau, Germany, which Eliot had visited in the early 1890s. Von Pückler-Muskau summarized his philosophy: "Wherever Nature has herself glorified a country, and made a picture bounded only by the horizon . . . we should content ourselves with laying out good roads, to make the fine points more accessible, and here and there the cutting of a few trees, to open vistas which Nature has left closed." Eliot was also influenced by his own formative experience at Mount Desert Island in Maine, his affiliation with the Olmsted firm, and his other travels abroad. His career was cut short by an untimely death in 1897. His reports and letters to the commissioners of the Boston metropolitan reservations and his speeches and writings were published by his father in 1902.[27]

One of Eliot's most important contributions to park design was his insistence on planning before developing a natural park for public use. Vegetation management and the preservation of vistas were important aspects of planning in his opinion. Although planning was an accepted part of the design of public squares and buildings, its use for natural areas was generally considered unnecessary. In a letter to the commissioners of June 22, 1896, Eliot urged planning for the rural park just as for a public square or building. He recognized, however, essential differences:

Unlike the architect, the landscape architect starts in the new reservations, for example, with broad stretches of existing scenery. It will be his calling and duty to discover, and then to evolve and make available, the most characteristic, interesting, and effective scenery. Practically, his work will be confined to planning such control or modification of vegetation as may be necessary for the sake of scenery, and to devising the most advantageous courses for the roads and paths from which the scenery will be viewed. (655–56)

Eliot recognized that what made certain areas distinctive and significant was the beauty of their vegetation or the scenic views they provided. For these reasons, Eliot emphasized that planning should be "comprehensive and not fragmentary" and should include controlling and modifying vegetation to expose scenic vistas and removing poor trees and encouraging better ones to improve woodlands (658).

In an article in *Garden and Forest* of August 26, 1896, entitled "The Necessity of Planning," Eliot asserted that planning with attention to the environment was needed "to make the wildest place . . . accessible or enjoyable." He argued that public reservations of any sort would only be saved from "decorative and haphazard development by the early adoption of rational and comprehensive plans." Several years earlier Eliot advised the commissioners: "If consistent and fine results are to be attained, the engineer must be ever ready to subordinate his special works for the sake of the general effect or 'landscape,' and the forester must likewise be willing to work in the same spirit. Administered in these ways by sufficiently active men, the forest scenery may, in a few years, be restored to that fortunate state the beauty of which, barring fires and other accidents, is inevitably increased by the passage of time."[28]

Eliot pioneered in the field of landscape forestry. In a study entitled *Vegetation and Forest Scenery for the Reservations* for the Boston Metropolitan Park Commission in 1896, he set forth a plan through which reservations could be rehabilitated by following the ecology and natural systems of the region. Eliot had distinguished between the roles of landscape architects, landscape engineers, and landscape foresters. Work in the metropolitan reservations to date had consisted of removing dead wood, both standing and fallen, and constructing preliminary roads on the lines of the old woodpaths. Because the reservations had suffered from forest fires or been used as woodlots, fields, and pastures, the existing forests consisted mostly of sprout and seedling woods. He estimated that the "restoration" of the land to an interesting and beautiful condition would "require years of labor in accordance with a well-laid scheme of economical management."[29]

The use of the axe in public reservations was a much-debated issue at the time. Frederick Law Olmsted Sr. and J. B. Harrison had published a pamphlet entitled "Observations on the Treatment of Public Plantations," in which they defended the selective cutting of trees and other vegetation to improve the overall character and health of forest plantations. In a letter to the editor of *Garden and Forest* of January 27, 1897, Eliot further defended this point of view: "A good park plan is fundamentally a scheme for the creation of more and more pleasing scenery through modifications to be made in the preexisting vegetation, by clearings, thinnings, plantings, and the like, and only secondarily a scheme for making the resulting scenery agreeably accessible by roads and walks."[30]

Eliot noted that the axe could achieve good work in the reservations, including the removal of trees to encourage shrubby ground cover and to reveal distant prospects and fine crags concealed by existing vegetation. The selective removal of competing species encouraged the growth of desirable plants, such as white dogwood on southern slopes, winterberry in swamps, bearberry on rocky summits, and white pine on ridges. Eliot explained, "The axe, if it be guided wisely, may gradually effect the desired rescue and enhancement of that part of the beauty of the scenery of the reservations which depends upon the seedling woods and shrubberies" (711).

Eliot's plan for restoration entailed several steps. First, the present condition of vegetation, including types and variations, was to be recorded on topographical maps. This information was then to be used to define the principal landscape types. In the case of the metropolitan reservations, these types included summits, swamps, areas of sprout growth called coppices, fields and pastures, bushy pastures, and seedling forests. Each type was to be analyzed according to its character and the proportion to which it covered the overall parkland, and recommendations were to be made for the treatment of each type. Eliot's study concluded that, in the case of the metropolitan reservations, the vegetation resulted from repeated or continuous interference with the natural processes by humans, fire, and browsing animals. This finding helped justify a plan of vegetation control and management that, under the skillful guidance of a landscape professional, would slowly induce the "greatest possible variety, interest, and beauty of landscape." Eliot summarized the practices that would preserve, restore, and enhance the scenic beauty of natural areas:

> To preserve existing beauty, grass-lands must continue to be mowed or pastured annually, trees must be removed from shrubberies, competing trees must be kept away from veteran Oaks and Chestnuts. . . . To restore beauty in such woods as are now dull and crop-like, large areas must be gradually cleared of sprout-growth . . . [and] the stumps must be subsequently killed, and seedling trees encouraged to take possession. To prepare for increasing the interest and beauty of the scenery, work must be directed to removing screens of foliage, to opening vistas through "notches," to substituting low ground-cover for high-woods in many places, and other like operations. (732)

Eliot's work, immediately recognized as seminal by the profession, had major applications for both national and state park work. First of all, it established a methodology for selecting parks based upon their representative characteristics. It further established a process for planning and managing natural areas, whereby the protection of natural vegetation took preeminence over the development of roads and trails. His approach was particularly useful for park landscapes that had been damaged by previous land uses. Although the first national parks were in the West and were essentially primeval in character, many parks contained former homesteads or Native American camping grounds and thus had been altered by the intervention of humans as well as by natural flooding, fires, or blights. Eliot's report also provided a well-ordered process and philosophy for preserving scenery, and his advice on clearing vistas was followed by national park designers as early as 1919. From Eliot came a philosophical basis for much of the common landscape work in national and state parks, including clearing for vistas, meadow protection, roadside and lake cleanup, and selective thinning of trees.

As more and more areas affected by human intervention entered the national park system and as the National Park Service began to transform submarginal land into state parks and recreational areas in the 1930s, Eliot's ideas and the field of landscape forestry assumed greater importance. From meadow clearing to fire protection by selective thinning of wooded areas, Eliot's principle that cutting should be based on long-range goals of beauty and scenery enhancement would predominate for many decades. His lessons on managing viewpoints and vistas would have far-reaching applications in the development of park roads and scenic parkways.

The Development of State and National Parks

While the concept of urban parks expanded to take in parkways and outlying reservations, a movement was beginning to set aside outstanding natural features and scenic areas, such as Niagara Falls and Yosemite Valley, for public enjoyment. This movement began with an act of Congress of June 30, 1864, when the United States government granted Yosemite Valley and the Mariposa Grove of Big Trees to California for the purpose of public use and recreation. Shortly thereafter, a commission was appointed to make recommendations for opening up the land for public use. Although this was the first park set aside by Congress for scenic purposes, it remained under state control until 1906, when it was added to the Yosemite National Park established in 1890.

As a member of Yosemite's board of commissioners, Frederick Law Olmsted Sr. prepared a preliminary report on the development of Yosemite Valley and the Mariposa Grove. Although intended for presentation to the California legislature, the report never passed beyond the commission and was lost for many years. Olmsted's report set forth a philosophical and practical framework for the development of natural areas for the use and enjoyment of the public. In the early 1860s, only a forty-mile trail in poor condition led into the valley, and a twenty-mile trail led to the Mariposa Grove. Better roads and arrangements for guides and horses to transport visitors were needed, Olmsted argued, so that the strenuous three- or four-day journey into the valley could be reduced to a one-day trip that many people could afford and enjoy. The roads would also make it possible to transport timber, food, and other supplies necessary for accommodating visitors, thereby making the destruction of native groves or the cultivation of parkland unnecessary. Areas for camping and other provisions could be supplied in the valley.[31]

Olmsted envisioned a circular or loop road around the Mariposa Grove which would also serve as a protective barrier against the fires common in the surrounding country. For Yosemite Valley, he proposed a circuit drive leading off the approach road from the west, encircling the wide portions of the valley, crossing the meadows at certain points, and "reaching all the finer points of view." The drive would be a double trail, wide enough for one vehicle with resting places and turnouts for passing at frequent intervals. An arrangement whereby carriages would travel up one side and down the other side of the valley would reduce the need for artificial construction, "destroying as it must the natural conditions of the ground and presenting an unpleasant object to the eye in the midst of the scenery." Such a road could be laid out in the shade, take a more picturesque course, and be more economical to repair. Footpaths could lead off the road to scenic points of view, and small bridges could be built where needed (24).

Olmsted's report established a basis for protecting natural features and scenery while at the same time making them accessible for the enjoyment of the public. It extended his respect of natural character, which was apparent in his plan for Central Park, to areas of outstanding scenic value and extensive wilderness. It defined the concept of circulation systems for natural areas which included approach roads, circuit drives, resting places, turnouts, paths leading to points of interest and scenic views, and, where necessary, bridges. While these features would be incorporated in Olmsted's urban parks, it was clearly the relationship of these features to wild, unspoiled land and vistas of supreme beauty which made the Yosemite recommendations relevant to the development of natural areas.

Olmsted's recommendations were based on a firm belief that although roads and facilities were needed, they must be located and designed in such a way that scenic character and timber were preserved as much as possible. The report reflected ideas that Olmsted practiced on a smaller scale at Franklin Park and elsewhere: roads and trails were fundamental to park planning; they should be laid out to connect sequential points of scenic interest; and, by their de-

A Design Ethic for Natural Parks

sign, they should engage the traveler in a pleasurable experience. The report, furthermore, reflected the philosophy that development must serve the public and minimally affect natural scenery, which Olmsted would espouse in other conservation matters, including his efforts to save Niagara Falls.

Set aside in 1872 as a "pleasuring-ground for the benefit and enjoyment of the people," Yellowstone became the first national park. Others followed. Sequoia and General Grant were established in 1890, the same year as Yosemite, and Mount Rainier (1899) and Crater Lake (1902) roughly a decade later. Between 1902 and 1906, Wind Cave, Sully's Hill, Platt, and Mesa Verde were made parks. The Antiquities Act of 1906 enabled a number of national monuments to be added to the list; these included missions, ruins of prehistoric cultures, and unusual natural features such as Devil's Tower and Petrified Forest. Glacier was added to the list of parks in 1910, followed by Rocky Mountain in 1915, Hawaii and Lassen in 1916, and Grand Canyon, Acadia (originally called Lafayette), and Zion in 1919. By the time the National Park Service took charge in 1917, there were seventeen national parks and twenty-two national monuments covering an area greater than ninety-eight hundred square miles.[32]

Although the idea of setting aside scenic reservations for public enjoyment emerged in the mid-nineteenth century, it did not gain widespread momentum until the early twentieth century. Efforts to save Niagara Falls began in the 1860s, but it was not until 1885 that the reservation was finally established as New York's first state park. New York created the Adirondack Forest Preserve (eight hundred thousand acres) the same year and in 1894 designated a park encompassing much of the region's public and private land and having protective restrictions. In 1891, Minnesota founded Itasca State Park, setting aside the headwaters of the Mississippi River as the state's first scenic park. In 1897, New York prohibited the cutting of timber in the Adirondack Forest Preserve and two years later set aside a similar reserve in the Catskills. In 1895, the Palisades Interstate Park in New York and New Jersey was established in an effort to save the scenic palisades that extended many miles up the Hudson River from quarrying and other forms of destruction. A system of state parks took form in New York as parks such as Watkins Glen (1906) and Letchworth (1907) were created and separate regional commissions were established. Connecticut established its first park in 1887 and created a state park commission in 1912.

At the turn of the century, Minnesota and Wisconsin set aside parks on opposite shores of the Saint Croix River, and Massachusetts established the Mount Tom and Mount Greylock reservations. Shortly thereafter, Ohio began to set aside land around public reservoirs as public parks. Wisconsin established a state parks board in 1907 and soon after hired landscape architect John Nolen to conduct a state park survey with the purpose of founding new state parks. Idaho set aside its first park, Payette Lake, in 1909, and Illinois established its first natural park, Starved Rock, in 1911. In 1915, North Carolina set aside Mount

Mitchell as its first park, and in 1916 Indiana established its first parks, McCormick's Creek and Turkey Run. In 1918, Iowa established its first state park, Backbone. California established the ten-thousand-acre Redwoods State Park in 1918, and in 1920 the state's legislature created a state park system. The years 1919 and 1920 saw the establishment of South Dakota's first park, Custer State Park; the addition of Clifty Falls to Indiana's parks, Old Salem to Illinois's parks, and Enfield to New York's parks; and the creation of a state park system in Iowa.[33]

By 1920, the movement to create state parks and park systems had taken hold nationwide. The movement was spurred by a number of regional organizations founded to identify significant areas of scenic or historic interest and to urge state legislatures to preserve them. The first such organization was the American Scenic and Historic Preservation Society, founded in 1895 in New York. Others included the Save-the-Redwoods League, founded in California in 1918, and the Friends of Our Native Landscape, founded in Illinois in 1913. Landscape architects were among the conservation-minded individuals who founded and fostered these organizations.

The state park to gain the most attention for the development of recreational facilities was the Palisades Interstate Park, particularly the area surrounding Bear Mountain on the west shore of the Hudson forty miles north of New York City. Here development was concentrated at the base of the mountain near Fort Montgomery in an area that had been extensively quarried and was formerly intended as the site for a prison. This area was developed in the early twentieth century under the direction of Major William A. Welch, a civil engineer and the interstate park's general manager. It is an important link between the nineteenth-century urban parks, such as Franklin Park, and the scenic and recreational state parks of the twentieth century.

By the end of 1916, Bear Mountain was a center for year-round recreation and the gateway to extensive tracts of wilderness which lay to the west and contained heavily wooded and well-watered mountains abounding in deciduous forests, streams, and lakes. It attracted throngs of visitors, who arrived by boat, ferry, and rail. On the riverfront were several docks for the steamers that daily carried visitors from the city, a railroad station, a swimming beach with bathhouses, and trails and ramps leading to the highland. One hundred and sixty-five feet above the Hudson lay Hessian Lake, a forty-acre spring-fed lake at the center of a large recreational area or "playground." The lake provided pleasure boating and fishing. Playing fields, tennis courts, a track, a children's play area, and other areas for sports were developed nearby. On the shores of the lake were picnic groves, a boathouse, a dancing pavilion, and a large rustic inn. Camping took place at the far end of the lake. The wooded and mountainous land west of Bear Mountain was minimally developed with hiking trails and, as early as 1913, rustic camps for youth groups and other social organizations. In 1916, more than two million conifers had been planted in the region, adding greatly to its beauty and undisturbed character.[34]

Bear Mountain Inn could accommodate more than three thousand diners at one time. The first story was built of moss-covered boulders taken from the old stone fences on the property. The second story was built of huge chestnut logs from surrounding forests. The building, with its massive stone fireplaces and chimneys and broad sloping and overhanging roof supported on massive log brackets, echoed the Swiss-influenced lodges of the Adirondacks. Its size, bold use of moss-covered boulders, rusticated arched entrances, and gabled roof, however, clearly reflected the Playstead Shelter in Franklin Park. Although it lacked the grandeur of the great inns that were being built at the same time in the national parks, such as Old Faithful Inn at Yellowstone and the lodges and inns the Great Northern Railway was building at Glacier, it very much reflected the rustic tradition. For more than two decades, it remained the only rustic hotel in a state or national park in the eastern United States.

The state park movement experienced rapid growth during the 1920s, through the efforts of many individuals and organizations, including the director of the National Park Service, Stephen Mather. During the 1920s, many states, including Arkansas, Kansas, Maine, Missouri, Nebraska, Oregon, Texas, Utah, and Washington, acquired their first state parks. In 1923, Texas appointed a state park board, and by 1927, it had established twenty-four parks, most of which were waysides along state roads. Other states either had no state parks or had designated only historical areas as state parks but had an extensive system of national forests available for recreational use. One of these was Pennsylvania, which by 1928 had more than one million acres of land in state forests.[35]

Existing state park systems also expanded rapidly during the 1920s. By 1928, Iowa's park system included thirty-nine parks and 7,413 acres. In 1924, New York's regional commissions were consolidated in a centralized state agency, and by 1928, New York had fifty-six parks and more than 2 million acres of parkland. In 1927, the California legislature established a state park commission, created a bond issue of six million dollars for the acquisition of state parks, and hired Frederick Law Olmsted Jr. to conduct a survey for new parklands. Olmsted's survey, known as the California State Parks Survey, was completed in 1929 and identified seventy-nine areas for acquisition. It also set out criteria for the selection and management of state parks and is recognized as a pivotal document in the history of state parks in the United States.[36]

One major catalyst for the movement was the founding of the National Conference on State Parks. The organization was formed at a meeting organized by Iowa's governor and Stephen Mather and held in Des Moines in 1921. The organization's purpose was to urge governments—local, county, state, and national—to acquire additional land and water areas for the study of natural history and its scientific aspects, for the preservation of wildlife, and for recreation. Its goal was to put public parks, forests, and preserves within reach of all citizens. The national conference also aimed to educate the public about the values and uses of recreational areas and encouraged private individuals to acquire and maintain similar areas for public pleasure.

Although focused on state parks, the national conference was the meeting ground for officials and interested professionals from all levels of government and from forests as well as parks. Common concerns and solutions were shared; principles and practices of park development were exchanged. The organization met annually and charted the progress being made nationwide in state legislation for state parks and the organization of statewide park systems. Mather followed the conference's progress and included it in his annual reports. Conferences were held in various state and national parks. From 1922 to 1927, the conference met at the Palisades Interstate Park in New York, Turkey Run State Park in Indiana, Gettysburg National Military Park, the proposed Shenandoah National Park, and Hot Springs National Park. During this time, regional conferences also formed in the Ohio River valley and the Southwest.

Bear Mountain quickly became the model for state park development and Welch a leading spokesperson. In introducing Welch at the fourth national parks conference, Enos Mills recalled Robert B. Marshall's advice that the parks be developed for all people and that the buildings be attractive and fit harmoniously into the surroundings. Mills highly commended Welch's work at the Palisades Interstate Park and particularly at Bear Mountain as fitting these requirements. A civil engineer by training, Welch was successful in establishing the systems for roads, water, power, and other utilities that supported the park's operation. By the early 1920s, his engineering work gained attention nationwide when he carved the Storm King Highway into the precipitous cliffs above the Hudson several miles north of Bear Mountain. He maintained close ties with the National Park Service and, in 1921, made an extensive tour of national parks, visiting Rocky Mountain, Mesa Verde, Grand Canyon, Sequoia, Yosemite, Mount Rainier, Glacier, and Yellowstone. In each park he offered park superintendents suggestions for practical improvements, particularly related to road and camp problems and water supply. Welch spoke at the 1917 national parks conference, numerous meetings of the National Conference on State Parks, and the National Conference on Outdoor Recreation in 1925 and was a member of the Southern Appalachian National Park Commission in the 1920s. In 1924, Welch's designs for the Bear Mountain complex and the Storm King Highway were the only state park works featured in *American Landscape Architecture,* a portfolio of premier works of landscape design selected by a committee consisting of Olmsted Jr., Charles Lowrie, and Noel Chamberlin.[37]

The second annual meeting of the National Conference on State Parks, held in 1922 at Bear Mountain, enabled visiting officials to view firsthand a model recreational park and Welch's engineering achievement on Storm King. The conference also visited the Bronx River Parkway, the nation's first limited access parkway, being constructed nearby under the direction of Jay Downer and Gilmore Clarke. The seventh annual conference of 1927 was also held at Bear Mountain, where new development included additional facilities for winter sports and a naturalistic swimming pool that had been created by damming a stream and filling a rocky ravine.

Several aspects of the Palisades Interstate Park would strongly influence the development of other state parks and the National Park Service's policies on recreational development. First was the program of organized camping which began in 1913 when the state built a camp for the Boy Scouts of America in the heavily wooded and mountainous area west of Bear Mountain. This program grew quickly, and the park became known for introducing urban youth to the experience of the woods. Organizational camping would be institutionalized by the National Park Service and the Resettlement Administration in the development of recreational demonstration areas in the 1930s. Second were the park's educational programs, including nature centers within the organization camps, hiking trails, and later a centralized museum and nature trail. Third were its pioneering facilities for winter sports, including skiing, skating, and tobogganing, which gained popularity in national and state parks in the early 1930s. Bear Mountain and the Cook County Forest Preserve, outside Chicago, were leaders in the development of facilities for winter sports by the end of the 1920s.

In May 1925, President Calvin Coolidge convened the National Conference on Outdoor Recreation, which covered diverse aspects of public recreation and drew individuals from many national organizations. Committees were formed to examine seventeen topics ranging from educational programs to waterway pollution and drainage and including federal land policy and policies dealing with state and county parks and forests. Among the speakers were many longtime friends and advocates of the national parks, including the executive secretary of the National Parks Association, Robert Sterling Yard, and Henry Hubbard. Hubbard spoke on the national provision for the enjoyment of scenic resources. William Welch spoke on the place of state and interstate parks in a national recreational policy, and Barrington Moore of the Council on National Parks, Forests, and Wildlife outlined a national outdoor recreational policy based on the role of federal agencies. While this meeting embraced many groups and professions, it brought together for the first time those involved in the municipal playground movement and those involved in the preservation of scenic and natural areas. Furthermore, it laid the groundwork for a federal recreational policy that would take form in the 1930s.[38]

In 1926, the National Conference on State Parks published *State Parks and*

Recreational Uses of State Forests, a study requested by the conference on outdoor recreation the previous year. By this time, forty-three states possessed state parks, state forests, or similar areas for outdoor recreation, covering more than 6.5 million acres. It was the first of a series of publications to appear in the next five years charting the progress of the state parks movement. Beatrice Ward Nelson's *State Recreation: Parks, Forests, and Game Preserves* of 1928 analyzed the various approaches and methods state governments were using to acquire parks and administer them. It was a reference book that contained state-by-state essays and, in the form of a chart, provided a comprehensive list of the recreational areas in each state and information about their founding, location, size, special characteristics, and recreational facilities. Herbert Evison's *State Park Anthology* of 1930 was a compendium of papers given at the annual meetings, reports by members, and articles written by specialists.[39]

During these years, several state and local park officials gained prominence for their leadership, wise management, and noteworthy practices and designs. In addition to Major William Welch of the Palisades Interstate Park, these included Colonel Richard Lieber of Indiana; Charles G. Sauer, a designer of Indiana parks and later the superintendent for the Cook County Forest Preserve District; Albert M. Turner of Connecticut; and Herbert S. Wagner of the Akron metropolitan parks.

Several members of the landscape profession played a major role in the state park movement. Warren Manning and Henry Hubbard were the ASLA's official representatives to the 1925 National Conference on Outdoor Recreation; James Greenleaf and several others also attended, and John Nolen was appointed to the permanent executive council. Manning, Nolen, and Frederick Law Olmsted Jr. conducted surveys and developed master plans for several state parks and park systems. Harold Caparn in 1917 wrote "Some Reasons for a General System of State Parks" in *Landscape Architecture.* Evison's *State Park Anthology* of 1930 included articles by Harold Caparn, James Greenleaf, S. Herbert Hare, Emerson Knight, Frederick Law Olmsted Jr., and many park officials. The following year, the ASLA's journal, *Landscape Architecture,* devoted an entire issue to the subject of state park acquisition and development and carried articles drawn from papers given by Wagner, Hare, Laurie D. Cox, and P. H. Elwood at that year's national conference meeting in St. Louis.

In their stewardship role, landscape architects were concerned with selecting parks on the one hand and planning for their development on the other. It is likely through members of the landscape profession that the distinctions between recreational development and scenery preservation in state park design were raised and became a matter of serious consideration and policymaking. Speaking on the basic principles of state park selection and design at the 1931 meeting of the national conference, Laurie D. Cox called for a new type of park design which could reconcile the differences between the national park or the scenic reservation envisioned by Charles Eliot and the country park or city play-ground that was better suited for recreational use. Such a task was difficult but, he believed, achievable through the careful consideration of questions such as how much public use or human service is possible or desirable and what kinds of recreation should be provided.[40]

Chapter 2

An American Style
of Natural Gardening

By 1917, Frank Waugh, Henry Hubbard, and others recognized the emergence of a unique American style of landscape design based on indigenous plant materials and naturalistic principles of design. There were a number of reasons for the emergence of this new style. In part, it was one manifestation of the back-to-the-woods movement and a progressive philosophy of conservation. To a certain degree, it reflected the general nostalgia and sense of loss experienced by a nation that had reached its westernmost limits and which turned inward toward national parks to recapture the experience of wilderness. Nevertheless, the movement for an American style coincided with the growing role of stewardship within the landscape design profession.

In the 1840s, Downing urged American gardeners to heed the beauty and potential of American plants for landscape gardening. He advocated, however, preserving the natural landform while introducing plants from other locations for their aesthetic quality. William Robinson's idea of naturalization in 1870 was to introduce exotic wild plants from all over the world into wild gardens; he was especially impressed with the diversity and beauty of American plants and urged English gardeners to naturalize them in their wild borders, woodlands, and water gardens. It was not until the end of the nineteenth century that the creative possibilities of native plants for American landscape design gained widespread interest among American practitioners.

American landscape designers began to urge strongly the use of native species over exotics about 1890, with the development of mass plantings by Frederick Law Olmsted Sr. at Biltmore, the Vanderbilt estate outside Asheville, North Carolina. Mass planting, Waugh wrote, "represents a most substantial advance, since nature manifestly offers her plantings nearly always in large masses. The white pine, for instance, used to exist in solid unbroken forest masses hundreds of miles in extent. There used to be thousands of miles of prairies in this country covered with blue stem and bunch grass."[1]

In the early twentieth century, the idea of an indigenous style derived from the principles and practices of Downing and Robinson was promoted in the United States by several leading landscape architects and writers. The style was dominated by a concern for preserving and enhancing natural character and harmonizing constructed improvements with the natural setting and topography, using informal and naturalistic elements of design. The preservation of existing vegetation and rock formations, the creation of naturalistic rockwork, the development of vistas and viewpoints, the construction of rustic shelters, and the planting of native vegetation were central to the interests of the style's practitioners.

Wilhelm Miller and the Prairie Style

In 1911, Wilhelm Miller, a horticultural writer and editor, published *What England Can Teach Us about Gardening*, a series of writings that had previously appeared in *Garden Magazine* and *Country Life in America*. His ideas were based on his interest in America's native flora and a trip to England, where he visited Robinson's home and gardens at Gravetye. Miller advised his readers, "Let every country use chiefly its own native trees, shrubs, vines and other permanent material, and let the style of gardening grow naturally out of necessity, the soil and the new conditions." At the time, Americans had only a few books contributing to what Miller called an "American Style of Gardening." These included writings of Downing, Olmsted, and Eliot, as well as Liberty Hyde Bailey's *Cyclopedia* and Neltje Blanchan's *American Flower Garden*. A complete analysis of American wildflowers worth cultivating had appeared in *Country Life in America* in July 1906, and an article on the roadside gathering of plants appeared in *Garden Magazine* in July 1908.[2]

Miller promoted the creation of both formal and informal gardens, drawing on Robinson's work and writings. Most valuable, however, was his adaptation of Robinson's ideas for creating irregular borders around a home or estate with perennials that in time would spread and create meandering displays of great beauty and require a minimum of upkeep. He adopted Robinson's love of vines, ground covers, masses of perennial plants, ferns, roses, and water gardens. Although he encouraged Americans to adopt Robinson's techniques, Miller abandoned Robinson's call for the naturalization of exotic wild plants in favor of using only native species. Miller envisioned a style that synthesized nature and landscape design. He praised the beauty of American landforms and scenery and saw them as features worthy of enhancement by the planting of native materials. Seeing the potential for such art in a waterfall in Virginia, he wrote, "America has thousands of natural cascades, the beauty of which we can enhance by planting" (48–49).

In 1915, Miller wrote a circular for the University of Illinois's Agricultural Experiment Station called *The Prairie Spirit in Landscape Gardening*. Here, he recognized and promoted a style of landscape gardening which drew inspiration from the native landscape of the Midwest, its landforms, waterways, and vegetation. This "spirit" could be displayed in both formal and informal gardens. This emerging school of gardening was based on the principles of preserving, restoring, or repeating some aspect of the prairie: "The prairie style of gardening is an American mode of design based upon the practical needs of the middle-western people and characterized by preservation of the typical western scenery, by restoration of local color, and by repetition of the horizontal line of land and sky, which is the strongest feature of prairie scenery."[3]

Miller attributed the origins of the style to O. C. Simonds, who had worked at Graceland Cemetery in Chicago beginning in 1880 and had transplanted from the wild many of Illinois's common shrubs and trees. These included oak, maple, hornbeam, ash, pepperidge, thorn apple, witch hazel, dogwood, sheepberry, and elder. Simonds had similarly worked with native materials at Lincoln Park in Chicago and on the grounds of several homes along Chicago's North Shore (2).

To Jens Jensen, Miller credited the original idea for taking the prairie as a "leading motive" in landscape design. Jensen, inspired by the natural beauty of the Midwest, incorporated fields of wildflowers and used natural and naturalistic features such as waterfalls, brooks, streams, and lakes in his work. At Chicago's Humboldt and West Side Parks, Jensen elevated the imitation of nature to a fine art for the enhancement of public parks and recreation. Miller quoted "one member of the new middle-western school of artists," who, although unidentified, was obviously Jensen:

> Of course, the primary motive was to give recreation and pleasure to the people, but the secondary motive was to inspire them with the vanishing beauty of the prairie. Therefore, I used many symbols of the prairie, i.e., plants with strongly horizontal branches or flower clusters that repeat in obvious or subtle ways the horizontal line of the land and sky which is the most impressive phenomenon on the boundless plains. Also, I aimed to re-create the atmosphere of the prairie by restoring as high a proportion as possible of the trees, shrubs, and flowers native to Illinois.[4]

Jensen's work in the mass planting at the three-hundred-acre Ford estate in Dearborn, Michigan, illustrated what Miller called "restoration." Here eighty acres were planted to create the effect of a thirty-year-old forest after one year.[5]

Miller's circular promoted "The Illinois Way," a statewide program of beautification based on public and private gardening. The program's original goal was to see that 90 percent of all planting statewide be composed of trees and shrubs native to Illinois. The program was supported to a large degree by the state's agricultural extension program and applied to urban design, suburban neighborhoods, farmsteads, estates, public parks, and roadsides.

Miller, who had been teaching horticulture at the University of Illinois since 1912, recommended planting trees, shrubs, and wildflowers for shade and beauty beside streams, rivers, waterfalls, and naturally occurring rockwork to restore the "ancient" feeling of primordial Illinois. Urban dwellers and farmers alike were urged to plant around foundations, to screen unsightly outbuildings, and to plant hedges instead of building fences. Property owners were urged to plant trees to frame their houses or to conceal them under a cover of vines and to plant irregular borders around their property. Farmers were urged to plant vegetation along creeks and in woodlots and unused areas. Miller recommended roadside planting in the form of trees and shrubbery to enframe views of farms, to beautify the roadside, and to create a parklike setting (13).

Eight types of Illinois scenery, in Miller's opinion, had picturesque character and merited preservation and beautification. They were lake bluffs, ravines, riverbanks, ponds and lakes, rocks, dunes, woods, and roadsides. In describing how riverbanks can be restored, he drew attention to the Prairie River in Chicago's Humboldt Park, where Jens Jensen had created a quintessential Illinois river. Modeled after Rock River, it was 1,650 feet long, varied from 52 to 108 feet in width, and abounded with cascades and rockwork (14–15).

Miller noted the emergence of "a new type of rock gardening" suited to the region's scenery and climate (14). Rock outcroppings did not dominate the midwestern landscape as they did the hills and coastal areas of the Northeast. Dry, hot summers and the scarcity of rocks in the Midwest made the creation of rocky glens and fern gardens popular in the East impossible. Beds of native limestone, however, were visible in the bluffs along rivers and lakes and in road cuts. This new technique, exemplified by the stratified rockwork of the Prairie River in Humboldt Park, called for embedding quarried stone, called tufa, to create ledgelike formations that could be planted with rock-loving plants that grew locally. He also recommended the use of a Wisconsin limestone that had become popular in northern Illinois for steppingstones, ledges, springs, cascades, and other forms of naturalistic rockwork. Miller assured readers that removing vegetation to expose rugged and picturesque ledges was landscape "restoration" because it restored to the scenery a dramatic element otherwise hidden (14).

Miller's ideas on stratified rockwork were not unique. The Illinois Agricultural Experiment Station had published a circular on stratified rockwork several years before.[6] Not only had Jens Jensen creatively used this natural form of limestone in creating naturalistic rockwork for swimming pools, dams, waterfalls, and springs, but the architects working in the Prairie style were also exploring its use as a construction material for buildings. To a large degree, the stratified materials reinforced the horizontality of the beloved prairie as well as the natural formation of native bedrock.

Jensen was a pioneer in highway beautification and the roadside planting of native vegetation in the early 1920s, when he designed the "ideal section" of the coast-to-coast Lincoln Highway. Here, in a $1^1/_3$-mile stretch between Schererville and Dyer, Indiana, Jensen created a landscape that followed the area's natural character. He planted native grasses, flowers, and occasional clusters of hawthorn or crabapple where the road passed through the open prairie and groves of native bur oak where it passed through upland areas and crossed wooded ravines. Jensen viewed his work as a model not only for the Lincoln Highway but for other roads as well. Jensen urged the highway association to secure a wide right-of-way, 100 to 150 feet to each side of the roadway, especially in developed areas. Jensen's design for the highway included a forty-acre campground that provided parking areas, a council ring with a campfire, rest rooms, a gas station, and a store.[7]

Jensen's many contributions to the landscape design of public parks were both great and modest. He forged an appreciation of the physical landforms and the native vegetation of the Midwest. A conservationist, Jensen was the leading member of the Friends of Our Native Landscape, founded in 1913, to gather information about areas of historic and scenic interest and to promote legislation to preserve these areas. He studied nature firsthand, explored the use of native rock and vegetation, and emulated natural cascades, pools, and rivers in his designs. His swimming pools and outdoor theaters had naturalistic rather than geometric forms and therefore blended gracefully with the surrounding natural or naturalistic topography. Jensen, too, was interested in providing park visitors, especially the youth of Chicago, with a vivid out-of-doors experience and in fostering an appreciation of nature through assimilated versions of the wilderness. His belief in the educational and interpretive value of landscape design led him to select native vegetation that was not only visually interesting and lush but also attractive to birds and wildlife. Jensen's greatest contributions to park landscape design were his creative adaptation of basic principles to local conditions and his ability to bring together social ideals and design principles (76, 85).

The influence of Jensen's ideas extended to the national parks. Mather saw the Lincoln Highway as an important link in the park-to-park highway he envisioned for the nation, and it is likely that his own concern about approach roads to parks was influenced by Jensen's ideas. Jensen's rule of a two-hundred-foot right-of-way was later adopted by Illinois's highway department and used by the National Park Service in its development of parkways and approach roads. Although never constructed, his plan for the camping area with a loop road, crescent-shaped tier, and component features was probably the prototype for the waysides of national parks and parkways in the 1930s.

Landscape architects working in the Prairie landscape style shared the same appreciation and idealization of the midwestern landscape as the architects of the Prairie style of architecture, Frank Lloyd Wright, Walter Burley Griffin, Dwight H. Perkins, Marion Mahoney, and Robert Spencer. Jensen worked with these designers through his office at Steinway Hall in Chicago and through his membership in the Cliff Dwellers, a club of prominent Chicago men. Jensen and Wright collaborated on a number of projects in the early twentieth century, including the Avery Coonley House in Riverside, Illinois. In addition to echoing the horizontal planes of the prairie landscape in their work through low-lying and overhanging eaves, Prairie style architects respected the contours of the land and let their designs follow the natural topography. Wright and Griffin, who was trained as a landscape architect, also used terraces, pools, walls, and planting boxes to extend their work into the surrounding site. These characteristics were also adopted by practitioners of the Arts and Crafts movement. Through the work of various practitioners and publications such as the *Craftsman* and Simonds' *Landscape-Gardening* of 1920, the ideas of the Prairie style about the unity of architecture and landscape were diffused to other parts of the country. The architect Myron Hunt, for example, had shared offices with Jensen at Steinway Hall and in 1903 moved to southern California, where his practice flourished. Hunt had a great understanding of the relationship of landscape and architecture and an ability to integrate landscape elements in his work. In the early 1920s, he was called upon to help plan a new village for Yosemite and design the park's administration building.[8]

California Gardening

The Midwest was not the only region of the country to develop a characteristic style of native gardening. In California, a style emerged which used plants native to specific climatic zones within the state. This style was generally called California gardening after Eugene O. Murmann, who laid out designs for the yards of bungalow homeowners and popularized the style in 1914 through an illustrated book of plans and photographs entitled *California Gardening*. Murmann said of California gardening, "California gardens are classed among the most beautiful in the world. Many of the best gardens in Southern California and, in fact, the whole state are remarkably unusual, not simply because palms and semitropical plant life thrive in California, but because the general arrangement was taken into consideration and each tree and plant set in its proper place."[9]

Subtitled "How to Plan and Beautify the City Lot, Suburban Grounds and Country Estate, including 50 Garden Plans and 103 Illustrations of Actual Gardens from Photographs by the Author," Murmann's book was both a portfolio of California gardens and a mail-order catalog from which homeowners could order plans and planting lists according to their tastes and local conditions. The photographs, illustrating various views and details of gardens and grounds, appeared to be taken at homes, estates, and parks in southern California. Some were recognizable as city parks or estates designed by Pasadena architects Charles and Henry Greene. Murmann's plans covered a variety of garden types popular in the United States and abroad which, he claimed, could be adapted to California's local conditions by substituting plants. There were alpine gardens, bog gardens, Japanese gardens, natural gardens, rock and water gardens, perennial borders, Old English gardens, and semiformal gardens. The idea behind Murmann's book was that each home should have a garden of "surprising beauty and color harmony" (8–9).

Plans for "natural gardens" dominated Murmann's catalog. These drew heavily from the nineteenth-century English gardening tradition espoused by Downing and Robinson. They incorporated curving paths, rustic stone stairways, curvilinear expanses of lawn bordered by shrubbery and trees, rustic seats and shelters, and naturalistic rock walls. The grounds of California homes were often considered outdoor living spaces. One of Murmann's plans featured a backyard lawn enveloped by borders of shrubs laid out in an irregular line; a curvilinear path of steppingstones led to an octagonal rustic pavilion for outdoor dining and recreation. There were rockeries in front of the pavilion and near the path leading to the kitchen entrance. Flowers were scattered across the lawn in little colonies and allowed to grow "in a natural way." Although California gardens used many exotic plants, native species were commonly preferred because they were well suited to the local climate and soil conditions. They were also inexpensive and readily accessible (plan 3, p. 63).

Murmann drew on the landscape work of Greene and Greene, especially that inspired by Japanese landscape traditions. Several views appear to be details of the six-acre grounds of Greene and Greene's Robert R. Blacker house in Pasadena, where a meandering stone-edged pool and rock garden graced the foot of the sloping knoll where the house was situated. Curving paths led from the house to the garden. The Japanese landscape style, commonly practiced in California in the early twentieth century, featured miniaturized gardens with tightly curving walks, small ponds and streams edged with irregular borders of boulders and cobbles, miniature hills called "hillocks," steppingstones, and rockwork in the form of stairways, walls, and water fountains. Plants included lotuses, lilies, grasses, evergreens, and other plants that thrived in or near the water or on rocky slopes. Structural elements included pergolas, rustic bridges, templelike shelters, and lanterns.

A distinctive movement was also emerging in favor of arid and semiarid gardens using desert plants and local sand and stones. Murmann depicted scenes in what appeared to be urban parks, estate grounds, and yards in residential developments. Many of these displayed plants such as yucca, agave, and cactus set on the banks of curving rock-edged drives and paths. Drives were also lined with irregular meandering walls of boulders and rocks embedded gently into the dry soil. There were masses of junipers and other evergreens capable of growing in semiarid conditions. The desert gardens, too, had rustic pergolas and garden seats often constructed of juniper trunks. Dry-laid boulder walls and meandering paths studded with boulders and rustic stone stairways provided rich accents to displays of perennial, alpine, and even desert plants (38–41, 56–57).

Today Murmann's book is a revealing index of the common landscape designs intended for the yards of California homes. It shows how Downing's and Robinson's principles were adapted to different climatic conditions and how these principles were combined with the compatible influence of Japanese landscape gardening. Thomas Vint, Daniel Hull, Herbert Maier, and other National Park Service designers were familiar with this style, if not with Murmann's book. Murmann's designs also fulfilled the tenets of the Arts and Crafts movement, with their use of native materials and unity of structures and natural setting. California gardens, many of the earliest of which were at the arboretum at the University of California, Berkeley, provided ready models for grading and planting the grounds of park buildings and for developing interpretive wild gardens in national parks and monuments, particularly in the Southwest.

The Arts and Crafts Movement

The Arts and Crafts movement, which espoused the early-twentieth-century back-to-nature philosophy, claimed California gardening as one of several styles appropriate for homes that sought to blend dwelling and nature and to create a flowing sense of space that linked the interior with views and passageways to the out-of-doors. The porte-cochères and pergolas so popular in California gardening were intermediary structures that could be adorned with vines and hanging plants. They belonged both to the house and to the garden, to the work of the architect and to that of the landscape architect.

Through his writings in the *Craftsman, Craftsman Homes,* and *More Craftsman Homes,* Gustav Stickley was perhaps one of the strongest influences on the general acceptance of the natural style of gardening in the early twentieth century. Stickley advocated a philosophy of harmony between home and nature which called for the siting of buildings in harmony with nature. Homes were to be built so that they became a part of the natural surroundings and blended with the general contour of the site and the surrounding country. This was achieved by designing buildings to fit the existing terrain and by using local materials and natural colors.

The 1909 essay "The Natural Garden: Some Things That Can Be Done When Nature Is Followed instead of Thwarted" in *Craftsman Homes* advised gardeners, "It is best to let Nature alone just as far as possible, following her suggestions and helping her to carry out her plans by adjusting our own to them, rather than attempting to introduce a conventional element into the landscape." Nature could be followed in several ways. The designer could allow the paths "to take the directions that would naturally be given to footpaths across the meadows or through the woods,—paths which invariably follow the line of the least resistance and so adapt themselves perfectly to the contour of the ground." A curving flight of steps conforming to the contour of a hillside with rustic railings and steps of heavy rounded boards could be draped with vines and natural undergrowth to create an effect of "rare and compelling charm." Vines could be made to grow over the walls of the house and around foundations, "where they naturally belong," and fast-growing vines could give "a leafy shade" to the porch that served as an outdoor living room and was more a part of the garden than the house. Such drapery was necessary to bring cobblestone and rough cement walls into a closer relationship with their surroundings. Stickley also recommended thatch for the roofing of a summerhouse for a "picturesque" effect, reviving Downing's romantic practice.[10]

The advice of the *Craftsman* reflected the English landscape gardening practices espoused by William Robinson. Robinson's ideas on naturalizing the wild species of many nations into the English garden found an avid following in the English Arts and Crafts movement. This movement called for exuberant displays of wild grapevines and other foliage and the use of native trees and shrubbery, often in combination with rockwork or bodies of water. These landscape effects were well suited to the concept of harmony held by the Arts and Crafts movement in America and were strongly advocated by Stickley, Wilhelm Miller, and Frank Waugh. They added to the picturesque quality of the bungalow home and enabled designers to merge indoor and outdoor elements.

The influence of Japanese design was especially strong in the landscape architecture and residential landscaping on the West Coast in the first two decades of the twentieth century. Stickley drew attention to the West Coast work and popularized Japanese techniques and designs. An essay in *Craftsman Homes* entitled "What May Be Done with Water and Rocks in a Little Garden," illustrated with photographs from the *Craftsman* and Wilhelm Miller's *Country Life in America*, applied the principles and features of Japanese gardens to the American home. The essay described a small garden about one hundred feet in diameter with a small stream of water running over a pile of rocks as producing the effect of a "mountain glen [where] so perfect [were] the proportions and so harmonious the arrangement that there [was] no sense of incongruity in the fact that the whole thing [was] on such a small scale." Although the example was intended for the gardener of small residential grounds, the author enjoined the reader to imagine "what could be done with large and naturally irregular grounds, say on a hillside, or where a natural brook wound its way through the garden, giving every opportunity for the picturesque effects that could be created by very simple treatment of the banks, by a bridge or a pool here and there and by a little adjustment of the rocks lying around."[11]

An essential part of the Japanese tradition was the interplay of rocks, waterfalls, meandering streams, and curvilinear ponds. In the Japanese garden, rocks were placed in groups or singly to display the inherent beauty of their shape, texture, form, color, and contrast of light and shadow. Stickley attributed the popularity of cobblestone in western design to the influence of Japanese design. Rock-edged pools and streams, commonplace in Japanese gardens, were one of the major characteristics through which these gardens, often on a miniaturized scale, created an illusionary and symbolic representation of nature.

Many of the designs and ideas popularized by Stickley's publications in the early twentieth century were rediscovered and used as naturalistic prototypes by the landscape designers of state and national parks several decades later. The use of thatch would find application in warmer climates where it had been used indigenously. Its use on ramadas in Mexico and the Southwest, for example, inspired the use of thatching on shelters in Phoenix's South Mountain Park. Juniper bark thatching was used to cover the shelters along Bright Angel Trail in the Grand Canyon. Its most elaborate expression came in the use of fronds of local palmetto (*Sabal minor*) for the roof of the refectory at Palmetto State Park in Texas. The water fountain built in front of the Paradise community house at Mount Rainier in 1933 displayed a tall assemblage of boulders which strongly resembled a backyard rock fountain first published in 1904 in the *Craftsman*. Park designers consciously imitated the rockwork and the planting of streambeds of Japanese gardens in the swimming pool at the Grand Canyon's Phantom Ranch, in a series of rock-edged pools and ponds in Minnesota's Camden State Park, and in the cleanup of streams and springs at Palmetto State Park in Texas.[12]

Another much emulated characteristic of Japanese gardens was the picturesque wooden bridge. Henry Tyrrell, in his treatise and portfolio *Artistic Bridge Design,* recognized the rustic effect of bridges in the Japanese Tea Garden in San Francisco and illustrated designs for both drum and bow types of bridges found in Japanese gardens. Both types were single arched forms, the first based on a semicircular radial curve, the other on a chord. The rustic arched bridge fashioned of wood constructed in a number of state parks, including Parvin in New Jersey and Ludington in Michigan, shows this influence. At Ludington, a series of bridges along the meandering Lost Lake Trail reflected the Japanese tradition on a larger scale.[13]

The Writings of Henry Hubbard

In 1917, two publications on the theory of landscape gardening appeared strongly promulgating an American style of natural gardening based on indigenous ma-

2.1. The footbridge over the Big Sable River in Ludington State Park, Michigan, built in 1934 by Company 1666 of the Civilian Conservation Corps, resembled the bow-type bridges of Japanese gardens and was hand-hewn from a single log. *(Photograph courtesy National Archives, Record Group 79)*

terials. They would have far-reaching influence on the landscape architecture of national and state parks. These were *An Introduction to the Study of Landscape Design* by Henry Vincent Hubbard and Theodora Kimball, the major textbook in schools of landscape architecture until the 1950s, and the lesser-known *The Natural Style in Landscape Gardening* by Frank Albert Waugh. It is no coincidence that both of these advocated a study of nature as the basis for informal or naturalistic landscape gardening and upheld the stewardship of landscape architects for natural areas of various types, including country parks, county and state parks, national forests, and national parks.

Henry V. Hubbard, a professor in Harvard's School of Landscape Architecture, had an extensive role in perpetuating the principles and practices of naturalistic landscape design in the twentieth century. Primarily through his *Introduction,* which was published in 1917, revised in 1929, and printed in many editions, Hubbard influenced several generations of students of landscape architecture. His text was comprehensive in its treatment of composition and description of numerous design features. It included a comprehensive bibliography of both American and European writings on landscape design. Hubbard was an experienced and versatile practitioner of both informal and formal landscape styles.

Unlike architects, who tended to work in the prevailing style of the period, landscape architects had freedom of choice, a wide palette of materials, and a panoply of styles from which to fashion each landscape according to its purpose and the tastes of the client. It should be no surprise, then, that in an era when Beaux Arts and Italianate influences and formal geometric design dominated urban planning and estate design, a style of park design based on naturalistic principles and the inspiration of nature should also flourish. Landscape architects of renown were versatile in their art, employing both formal and informal styles in their designs of gardens, parks, and estate grounds. Even the axial symmetry of formal promenades in urban systems of parks and parkways was relieved by meandering sinuous parkways that followed natural stream valleys and landforms. Hubbard practiced the naturalistic style in the spirit of Downing and Robinson in his own work and illustrated in his text the spring—complete with ferns and rockwork—which he designed for the wild garden of an estate in Newport, Rhode Island. He also showed numerous views of the work of the Olmsted firm at Franklin Park and along Boston's Emerald Necklace.[14]

Although influenced by Downing's theory and principles, Hubbard was far removed from the romantic idealism of the mid-nineteenth century. Hubbard was enlightened by the Columbian Exposition of 1893 and City Beautiful movement with its Beaux Arts formality that would transform naturalistic landscapes, such as the National Mall, into formal axial designs regimented by formal balustrades, regularly spaced rows of trees and shrubs, and patriotic memorials with their monuments and statuary. He, however, recognized and perpetuated an informal style of landscape architecture, which he called the Modern American Landscape style.

Hubbard replaced nineteenth-century romanticism with principles of composition which often echoed the tradition of American landscape painting. He also provided pragmatic solutions for substantial, durable, and harmonious designs. Although harmonious composition was imperative, Hubbard advocated as a general rule that it was better for the work to be recognizable either as a structure or as an element of natural beauty. This principle distinguished twentieth-century park structures from the nineteenth-century romanticized examples such as Central Park's Boulder Bridge with its cataclysmic collection of rocks and ledges and ambiguity between natural and constructed forms. In this way, he distinguished the transitory romantic trends of a bygone era from universal principles and an empirical approach to naturalism, thereby setting the stage for the flowering of a naturalistic American style, the greatest practitioners of which would be the designers of national and state parks (206–7).

Hubbard and Kimball's book was a compilation illustrating the professional practice of landscape architecture as it had evolved in America from Downing, the Olmsted firm, and others, assimilating English gardening style, Italian influences, and other trends, European and Eastern. For Hubbard, the design elements of texture, color, line, balance, and form and the basic principles of composition could be applied to landscape design for artistic and functional purposes. He translated Downing's concepts into practical approaches and techniques that the twentieth-century designer could follow. He gave detailed instructions on creating landscapes in both formal and informal styles, focusing mostly on landscape composition and principles of design rather than horticultural advice. Hubbard frequently pointed out what was appropriate for informal or naturalistic situations. For this reason, his ideas easily found their way into the practices of national park designers. Theodora Kimball was the librarian of Harvard's growing collection of literature on landscape architecture; her contributions to the book lay in the many literary references and extensive bibliography.

Hubbard's techniques included the natural coloration of park structures, use of native stone in rustic steps and bridges, variation in the contours of parapets to avoid monotony, construction of cobblestone gutters for drainage, creation of park shelters that repeated the verticality and branching of surrounding trees of the forest, curving paths rising to scenic overlooks, and use of plantings to integrate buildings and ground. Hubbard explored the development of vistas through devices such as screening and enframement and the construction of terraces, paths, and roads.

The Modern American Landscape style was a unique American version of the English landscape gardening tradition. What made American parks and private estates different from their English antecedents was the greater appreciation and interest of American designers in preserving and interpreting natural character. Focused on assimilating natural features and using native vegetation, American designers forged an informal style suitable for natural settings, whether a private home, residential subdivision, or country park. Hubbard defined the style: "The choice of indigenous plant material, the study of the arrangement of this material in accordance with its own character and of that in the landscape in which it appeared, is therefore an important consideration in this American style. The . . . 'natural' landscape scenes, which this style usually seized upon to enhance and reproduce, are seldom the unhampered work of nature; more usually they are the scenes of pasture and woodlot, shrub-grown wall, and elm-dotted river bottom, which are partly the results of man's activity in the less intensively used farm lands" (58).

Hubbard linked the landscape architects' inspiration from nature with their civic obligation of stewardship. He sought to give credibility to informal and naturalistic landscape design as a high artistic form, which, although simple in appearance, was a complex and exacting endeavor. He explained the process:

The greater and more striking examples of Nature's handiwork will serve the designer as inspiration and as training in appreciation, and he may by his knowledge of their peculiar value to the race have the duty and the great opportunity of defending them from destruction. But the humbler and less striking characters will be those to which he will usually go for models and for materials in his designs, since these will be the forms most commonly lying near the homes of the city-bred people for whom he works. His work will be on a small scale relatively to the great free landscape; the character which he will endeavor to produce will be of a less striking sort, and it will therefore be doubly necessary for him to make the expression of this character as complete, as unified, and as distinct as possible. He must be sensitive to feel what character is latent in the more or less inchoate scene on which he is called to work; he must know what of the elements now present are masking this character, and should be removed; he must know what can be added to perfect it without confusing it. (70–71)

In Hubbard's opinion, the designer's challenge was to arrange natural materials in such a way that they not only expressed the natural character of the landscape but also produced harmony of form, color, texture, repetition, sequence, and balance. Designs were to be both interpretations of natural character and effective pictorial compositions.

The original source of this style, according to Hubbard, was the work of the Olmsted firm at Franklin Park. His text included five illustrations of the park, depicting the circuit drive, one of the bridges over Scarborough Pond, the tennis courts at Ellicotdale, steps in a "naturalistic setting," and the Playstead Shelter and overlook. With its spaces, vistas, circuit drive, shelters, and facilities, Franklin Park became fixed in the minds of students and practitioners of landscape architecture in the 1920s and 1930s. Through Hubbard and Kimball's book, the park, described as a large landscape, or "country park," became the prototype for the development of natural areas, and the Scarborough Bridges, the Playstead Shelter, boulder-lined roads and paths, and meandering paths with rustic steps leading to scenic overlooks became models for rustic park structures and landscape features. The lessons of Franklin Park were applied to state and national parks and forests, as well as country parks and metropolitan reservations through the 1930s (56–58, 296–99, plates 31–35).

Hubbard's text abounded with advice useful to the twentieth-century park designer. Some of his most important lessons related to the development of vistas and the use of vegetation for screening and enframement. Hubbard explained how these devices enabled designers to control their designs and even enhance natural beauty: "In naturalistic design it normally happens that in any given important view the designer does what he can to enhance the character of the pond or valley or other small naturalistic unit which forms the principal part of a particular scene. Sometimes, by judicious screening out of incongruous

2.2. Clover Creek Bridge on the Generals Highway, Sequoia National Park, photographed shortly after construction in 1933, illustrates the simple arch and irregular stone-faced masonry prototype derived from the Scarborough bridges at Franklin Park. The wall and arch rings of native rock were perfectly designed to increase the irregularity and random character of the surface so that the bridge blended into and harmonized with the natural setting, a deeply cut rock creek amidst a towering forest. *(Photograph by George A. Grant, courtesy National Park Service Historic Photography Collection)*

elements and careful concentration of attention on those elements which are of the character intended to be brought out, a special character may be given to a scene as beheld from a certain point of view" (121).

Hubbard described in pictorial terms the development of vistas, which he considered to be one of the most unified of all types of landscape compositions. Vistas were to have a single central focal point and to be enframed by trees or other masses that screened all other objects. This essentially created a window that could be manipulated by the designer, who could arrange one scene after another in a sequence. Enframement prevented the visual intrusion of undesirable objects, setting definite limits to the composition being considered and fixing its center. Trees planted at the edges of viewpoints enframed the composition along the sides while overhanging foliage framed the view from above as well. The shadows of the trees, a long shadow from an object at the side, or perhaps a low mass of shrubbery in the foreground would similarly enframe a view at the base (126–27).

Expanding on Downing's advice, Hubbard enjoined landscape designers to use native rock, vegetation, and functional structures as elements of harmonious design. He drew the reader's attention to the size, coloration, texture, and natural arrangement of rocks and the growth of lichens and mosses upon them:

> The landscape architect is not infrequently called upon to design a unit in a naturalistic landscape, or to treat a part of a natural landscape, in which rocks form the principal objects to be arranged. . . . If rockwork is to be esthetically good, it must be apparently organized. If . . . it is to simulate the work of nature, then it must be organized as groups of rocks in nature are,—the rocks must be related one to another as though they formed part of a sea beach, of a talus slope, of a water-eroded slope, of an outcropping ledge, or of whatever natural rock-made form the designer chooses, or the circumstances require. (143)

Designers were to study carefully the character of existing natural rock and heed a few elementary geological facts. Hubbard explained further,

> Rock appears also in the landscape as outcropping ledges of natural stone. Sometimes it has evidently been exposed by some of the forces which we have discussed; sometimes, lying at steep slopes or at high altitudes, in cliffs or mountain summits, it has apparently never been clothed by any softer covering, at least not in recent geologic times. Such rock ledges, subjected to the action of the weather and in a great part of the world to frost, will in time break up on their surface into separate rocks. If the slope is not too great, these rocks will still remain more or less in their original position, and by their related forms and the direction of their fissures and perhaps their stratification, show the character of their parent ledge. Groups of rocks so formed are likely to produce, in nature, particularly unified and interesting compositions. (145)

The color and texture of rocks were valuable qualities that normally gave strength and solidity to constructed rockwork without making it conspicuous. Hubbard urged designers to use weathered or moss- and lichen-covered rocks and ledges to give an appearance of age. He discouraged the use of light-colored rocks dug from the ground because they had not been exposed to the weather and appeared barren. Designers were told to place rocks in conditions of sunlight or shade and dampness similar to those of the location where they were collected, so that mosses and lichens could continue to grow. Noting their deep fissures often filled with moist loam suitable for rock-loving plants, Hubbard,

2.3. Henry Hubbard encouraged designers to use moss- and lichen-covered local stone in the construction of bridges, parapets, and steps for natural parks. In building a stone bridge in Mount Nebo State Park, Arkansas, the Civilian Conservation Corps followed Hubbard's advice that rockwork have a pleasing irregularity of form and color and be located under conditions that would encourage the accumulation of moss and lichens to blend the rockwork with nature. *(Photograph courtesy National Archives, Record Group 79)*

like Downing, saw natural outcroppings and rock formations as ideal places to encourage rock gardens. Artificial rockwork was to be planted in similar ways to create the textures and character of natural outcrops or groups of boulders. Pragmatic in his advice, Hubbard recognized the difficulty in achieving a "final consistent natural effect." He cautioned designers that although they could draw rockwork easily enough on a plan, "skillful, patient, practical superintendence" of the work itself was necessary to "give results worthy of consideration" (144–47; plates 27, 35).

Hubbard encouraged designers to use local stone in the construction of steps, parapets, terraces, shelters, and walks. Local material yielded harmonies of color, as well as texture, between the stonework and any natural ledges nearby. Recognizing that built structures were bound to be conspicuous, Hubbard challenged designers to incorporate them into harmonious compositions that blended with nature. He suggested that "such structures should have some pleasing irregularity of form and color in their surface and some possibility of accumulating moss and lichens, and growing old gracefully with the rest of the design" (195).

Hubbard illustrated the curvilinear flight of stone steps that led to the overlook on Schoolmaster's Hill in Franklin Park. Although function determined the basic design, the stone steps fit tightly into the steep grade of the hill and were enframed by large coping boulders and low-growing plants and shrubs. Hubbard also suggested that stairways be set under overarching trees or built along the side of a projecting ledge for naturalistic effect. The careful selection of stones for color and texture and good masonry technique were imperative to achieve harmony of form and setting. The Franklin Park steps were particularly fine: they were sturdy; the treads and risers were evenly sized; and the coping of large boulders was embedded firmly in the ground as if part of the natural hillside (203–4; plate 34).

Stone walls gained texture and interest and could even be concealed when covered with vines hanging from above or climbing from below. Hubbard, like others, suggested creating pockets among the stones which could be filled with loam, planted, and watered. The results could relieve the harshness of form, change the texture of the construction, and provide a panel of green—the effect being to conceal the architectural character beneath.

Shelters required special treatment to blend into a natural setting: "Where some actual or apparent use of the pleasure structure is the first consideration— shelter or shade, for instance—and where no considerable architectural effect is desired, as often in a naturalistic design, the shelter may be made very much a part of its wilder surroundings. The roof may be thatched, the supporting posts left rough, or even with the bark on; the whole structure may be covered and concealed with vines. A greater departure from architectural form is permissible in such shelters, because they have an unimportant and temporary look, and a lightness of imaginative touch is not out of place in their design" (198).

Hubbard illustrated a circular pavilion with a thatched roof not unlike Downing's in form and function. Hubbard, however, replaced Downing's lattice of intertwined and bark-covered trunks with evenly spaced sturdy timber posts that had a somewhat knotted and irregular appearance. Sturdier than Downing's and Stickley's designs, the posts branched to create braces for the roof in a naturalistic way that imitated the natural branching of a woodland tree. So effective was Hubbard's shelter, in its imitation of the natural branching of tree limbs, its thatched roofing, and its fulfillment of the functional needs of the design, that the design would become an identifiable prototype for the construction of park shelters and lookouts. Its influence is most obvious in the circular and octagonal picnic shelters in Iowa state parks illustrated in Good's *Park and Recreation Structures.* The basic materials, method of construction, and branchlike braces have been adapted in parks across the country (drawing 26).

2.4. The boathouse at Iowa's Gull Point State Park, built by the Civilian Conservation Corps in the mid-1930s, incorporated a prospect tower for viewing the lake. The design echoed Henry Hubbard's call for sturdy timber constructions using knotted and irregular logs and having bracketed posts that imitated the natural branching of trees. *(Photograph by Ralph H. Anderson, courtesy National Archives, Record Group 79)*

Hubbard paid little attention to smaller park structures, other than to suggest that it was possible to build seats and drinking fountains that were inconspicuous by fashioning them after natural boulders. Such rustic features had been fashioned by the Olmsted firm for Franklin Park. This practice was readily adopted by the designers of national and state parks by the end of the 1930s and resulted in many imaginative variations, from water fountains made from large single boulders to picnic tables made of mammoth flagstones supported on masonry piers of native stone (316).

As an ideal for larger park structures, Hubbard presented the large, multipurpose Playstead Shelter, which he called the Overlook Shelter, at Franklin Park. Although the shelter was built upon a massive six-hundred-foot boulder terrace overlooking the playing fields, the terrace was not visible from the circuit drive. From this point of view, the building appeared to spring out of the natural rock outcrop, its weathered materials of stone and shingle blending with the natural rock and trees. The pitch of the hipped roof was flattened and given an undulating surface; it had broad overhanging eaves and was interrupted by a wide intersecting front gable. The design of the hipped roof enabled designers to "tuck in" the ends of the roof and eliminate the right angles that marked artificial construction. The roof overhung the shingled walls and was pierced by a large chimney of local stone. The ribbon of windows characteristic of the Shingle style extended across the gable illuminating the upper-story interior (plate 35).

The Overlook Shelter illustrated Hubbard's advice: "We should bear in mind . . . in our endeavors to subordinate a building to a natural or naturalistic landscape, the fact that it is not essential for harmony that the shape of the buildings should resemble any natural form. . . . The building should be beautiful, convenient, efficient after its own kind. In fact, fitness to local conditions, and simple form obviously expressing a practical need in construction or in use, tend of themselves to make the building less expressive of man's will, more expressive of man's necessity, and so less incongruous with natural expression" (190).

Although Hubbard discouraged the construction of buildings in a park, he admitted they were often necessary. Small buildings, such as comfort stations, were best located where they could be easily concealed and where signs could direct visitors to them. Large buildings, however, such as the Overlook Shelter, were to be set and enframed so that they were inconspicuous and were to be built of materials that harmonized with the landscape. Hubbard suggested that such buildings take on an irregular shape or be fitted closely to the irregularities of the land. Buildings could be subordinated to the landscape through harmonization of texture and color. Stone from local quarries could be used to match the nearby outcrops. Thatch roofing or lichen-covered walls could echo the character of nearby trees or grasses. Hubbard, too, suggested using "mantling" vines and overhanging foliage to screen constructed walls. He felt it unnecessary to go to the extreme of actually imitating natural forms in the shape of rooflines or other features (189, 316).

Hubbard also suggested that designers create a transition between a building and its natural setting by constructing terraces, ramps, steps, and stairs. These features effectively could connect the two areas and be combined with intermediary trees, shrubs, and vines to unify the building and its setting. By the late nineteenth century, transitional features such as terraces were increasingly becoming a standard part of the vocabulary of both architects and landscape architects and would become a strong characteristic of the Prairie and Adirondack styles, the West Coast work of Greene and Greene and Bernard Maybeck, and those works generally categorized as Craftsman and Bungaloid. With its use of native wood and stone and its tendency to weather over time in a way that enhanced the building's ability to blend into natural surroundings, the Shingle style provided the ideal medium for park construction, particularly when enhanced by naturalistic landscape features constructed of the same native materials. In 1917, the Overlook Shelter was already thirty years old. Yet Hubbard's interest gave it a timeless quality, demonstrating that architectural fashion mattered little when nature was the dominant feature in a naturalistic landscape (191).

Published one year after Congress had established the National Park Service, Hubbard's textbook was probably the single most influential source that inspired national and state park designers in the 1920s and 1930s. Hubbard, one of the profession's strongest advocates for the creation of the National Park Service, had visited Yosemite and used his photographs, experiences, and observations of the park extensively in his text. He appreciated national park scenery as an object for the study of landscape character as well as conservation (plate 8; 67).

Many of Hubbard's ideas were translated directly into the National Park Service's principles for park design. Numerous techniques, from using cobblestones in drains and ditches alongside park roads to varying the line of a parapet by introducing crenellations to relieve monotony, were incorporated into the work of National Park Service designers in the 1920s and continued to be applied in new and creative ways in state and national parks in the 1930s. As a professor at Harvard, Hubbard had an even greater influence on park landscape architects such as Daniel Hull, Merel Sager, George Nason, and Frank Culley, who had all been his students in the early twentieth century.

The Writings of Frank Waugh

In *The Natural Style in Landscape Gardening* of 1917, Frank Albert Waugh, a professor of landscape gardening at Massachusetts Agricultural College, promoted a style of landscape design based on an imitation of natural forms and the use of native vegetation. Born and educated in the Midwest, Waugh had close ties with Wilhelm Miller, Jens Jensen, and other advocates of the Prairie style in landscape gardening. Although Waugh was strongly influenced by the ideas of Miller and Jensen, his own work and teaching followed a different course. Waugh became increasingly interested in the challenge of making parks and forests accessible to the public and advocated an approach in which the finest of natural features and scenic beauty were to be preserved, interpreted, shaped, and presented to enhance the visitor's enjoyment. At the same time he pursued developments in the emerging field of ecology.[15]

Waugh called his approach the "natural style" to distinguish it from Downing's and Repton's naturalistic style, which imitated nature's forms but not its vegetation. To Waugh, the natural style endeavored "to present its pictures in forms typical of the natural landscape and made vital by the landscape spirit."

By landscape spirit, Waugh meant the informal order and feeling of vegetation and landscape features found in nature. He advocated a close study of nature for practitioners and adherence to the principles of composition followed by nature. This meant studying four principal types of native landscape—sea, mountains, plains, and forest—and several minor types including great rivers, little brooks, rolling hills, and lakes. "The ideas, motives, and methods must come mainly from nature," he told readers. Designers were to bring to this work "a critical understanding of nature's landscape and a love of the native landscape at once ardent, sane, discriminating, and balanced."[16]

Waugh claimed that the natural style was a fundamental garden form informal in character, that is, "unsymmetrical, not obviously balanced, not apparently enclosed and not marked by visible boundaries." Like Hubbard, Waugh recognized the style as one that resulted from conscious choice and adherence to the principles of composition followed by nature (20).

Waugh admitted that in many cases the natural style was best described as "intelligently letting alone a natural landscape." When called upon to treat an attractive stretch of natural scenery, the landscape gardener needed to "first and foremost, endeavor to understand the spirit of his landscapes." The designer was then "to simplify and accentuate the characteristic natural forms (chiefly topography and flora), and to clarify and interpret the spirit of the place." Waugh believed that the classification and interpretation of spiritual values was the work of the true artist (24).

Waugh applauded the development of national parks and forests as a "magnificent enterprise . . . in the hands of the landscape gardeners" who were "best trained in the love of the landscape and in the technical methods by which it alone can be conserved, restored, improved, clarified, made available and spiritually effective in the hearts of men and women." The natural style of landscape gardening was most suitable for this work: "Yes, indeed, the natural style of landscape gardening has before it the greatest opportunities ever offered to any art at any time in the world's history. It is high time that this old, yet ever new, natural style received a more thoroughgoing study at the hands of all thoughtful persons, but especially by those who call themselves professional landscape architects" (144–45).

Waugh's unique contribution to American literature was his introduction of an ecological approach to landscape gardening—an approach that called for the planting of trees, shrubs, and ground covers according to the conditions of soil and moisture and associations with other plants that occurred in nature. This was especially true of mass plantings. Waugh credited the second edition (1909) of Willy Lange's German work, *Die Garten-Gestaltung der Neuzeit,* with the best explanation of this ecological principle. He also recognized the work done by Dr. Engler and Dr. Peters, the curator and planting foreman at the botanical garden in Berlin, who apparently were the first to plant large masses of trees and shrubs in strict reference to soil and drainage conditions (48–52).

Just gaining recognition as a science in the early twentieth century, ecology led to the general understanding that very few species of plants existed alone in nature. Waugh wrote, "Practically every one associates habitually with certain other species. Thus they form set clubs or societies. And these friendly associations, based upon similarity of tastes and complementary habits of growth, should not be broken up. If we as landscape gardeners desire to preserve the whole aspect of nature, with all its forms intact, we will keep all plants in their proper social groupings" (50–51).

To Waugh, vegetation was the most critical aspect of creating the form and spirit of the natural style: "Unquestionably the selection and management of the plant materials does play a major role in practical landscape gardening, and especially in the natural style. . . . We must be able to use plants as nature uses them, to found our selections and our groupings on the same fundamental laws which govern these matters in the wild and native landscape" (48–49).

Mass planting was a comparatively recent innovation in landscape gardening in 1917. Waugh believed it marked one of the greatest advances in the evolution of a genuinely naturalistic style. It included planting trees by the thousands for screens or backgrounds, the introduction of rhododendrons "by carloads" for underplanting, and the development of considerable forest tracts as elements of scenic beauty. Mass plantings were of two kinds: pure masses, which were composed of a single species or variety, and mixed masses, which contained several different ones. Mixed mass plantings were composed of social groups, which included trees, shrubs, and ground covers that grew naturally together under the same conditions of soil, moisture, and climate (98, 101, 103).

The art of grouping trees and shrubs was fundamental to the natural style. Waugh identified seven patterns: (1) the single specimen, which was "a rarity in nature"; (2) the group of two, which according to Waugh was to be avoided in common practice; (3) the group of three, arranged in an irregular row; (4) the larger group of five or more; (5) the row, which was never used in naturalistic planting; (6) the mass planting; and (7) the social group. Although the group of three was particularly favored by designers, Waugh preferred the group of five or more: "With anywhere from five to twelve, according to species, we have individuals enough to make a genuine and effective group. At this stage grouping comes to its real meaning; and it must be allowed that most plantings are more successful in groups of this size than in any other scale. . . . This unit gives the most advantageous effect." Waugh cited several simple rules for grouping five or more trees: The law of simplicity cautioned against using too many species; the law of dominance called for one species to dominate the group; the law of harmony said that species must harmonize in color, form, and habit of growth;

the law of ecology required that plants "be socially compatible"; and the law of adaptation meant that all plants were to be adapted to the local conditions such as soil, drainage, and light (93, 96–98).

Waugh, like Hubbard, recognized the value of vistas in developing natural areas for public use and enjoyment. Waugh advanced Downing's principles on vistas through his work on roads and recreational areas in national forests. Developing views required at least three things: "First, the line of the best view must be determined and kept open; second, this view must be framed by suitable plantings; third, inferior views must be blocked out or reduced to more promissory glimpses." Vistas were to be focused on a definite object of interest or beauty such as a hill, mountain, or lake (120–21).

Every scenic feature, whether a natural pond, cliff, outcrop of rock, glacier-placed boulder, or old plantation of pine or oak, was to be "seized upon and developed with skill and imagination." On the unlimited possibilities of brooks and streams, Waugh said,

> If there is only a trickle of water in it one can set back certain stretches so as to make reaches of flat water on which the shadows lie and on the margin of which all manner of aquatic plants will thrive. Then there will be alternating stretches of water singing over stones or flashing in the sun. Foot bridges or stepping stones at suitable places add to the picture. There may be seats in shady nooks from which one can watch the panorama of life upon the brook; while at other points there will be sunny, grassy glades opening back into neighboring meadows or looking out to adjoining lawns. (122–23)

The sequence of scenes and views was particularly important in Waugh's opinion. On the design of roads or trails, Waugh said that at each climax of view the byway should turn and proceed upward to the next climax. Waugh called these places "paragraphic" points and described the ways in which a series of scenes could unfold through the careful location of trails, roads, and overlooks. Designers were to draw attention to special views by placing "at the optimum point of observation" a seat, carriage turn, or rest house so that the stranger was "directed unmistakably to the main feature, the desirable vista or the glorious outlook" (82–84).

Waugh recognized the value of natural areas for recreational activities and felt that structures for golf, skating, bathing, boating, and fishing belonged in the informal landscape. On shelters compatible with the natural style, he wrote, "Instead of the pergola and the classical 'temple' or 'gazebo' or 'music house,' there may be an 'arbor,' the 'summerhouse,' the 'log cabin,' the boat house or the fishing lodge." He reiterated Downing's advice for developing scenic viewpoints: "Wherever there are shelters there will nearly always be places to sit, but there ought to be ample temptation to linger and rest at other points in the park. Especially at those stations where good views are to be enjoyed, should there be ample provision of seats." He disapproved (as would national park designers a decade later) of Downing's use of saplings in woven furniture and the lattice-work of pavilions: "The extreme rustic fad of the 'fifties—twisted and contorted tree stems grotesquely woven into settees or chairs—should be forgotten; but the plain rough-sawed or hewn planks of modern times, stained or weathered, are both appropriate in the picture and comfortable in the using" (136–38).

While Henry Hubbard gave the park designer the practical tools for identifying landscape characteristics and the design principles for achieving an informal or natural style of landscape, Waugh laid a philosophical and practical basis for landscape naturalization, particularly the creation of mass plantings along ponds, roads, and streams and at the edges of forests that followed the natural patterns of growth and plant associations. Both men continued to be involved in the issues of developing natural areas for public use and enjoyment during the next twenty-five years. Both would substantially influence the landscape practices of national and state park designers.

In 1917, Waugh began consulting on the recreational development of national forests and within two years produced several reports for the U.S. Forest Service, including *Recreation Uses on the National Forests* and *A Plan for Grand Canyon Village.* Waugh brought together the concerns for developing natural scenic areas through subsequent work in Bryce, Kings Canyon, and Mount Hood national forests. It was no surprise that Conrad Wirth, an assistant director of the National Park Service during the New Deal era and Waugh's former student, called upon Waugh to write a handbook, *Landscape Conservation,* for Emergency Conservation Work in state parks; the book was first published in 1935 and several years later in the Civilian Conservation Corps's Project Training series. Waugh applied his style of natural gardening to the work of recreational development in national forests and later state parks. He wrote extensively on a variety of subjects, including outdoor theaters, roadside ecology, and the recreational uses of national forest lands. In addition to Conrad Wirth, Frank H. Culley and Albert Taylor were among his students at Massachusetts Agricultural College whose careers would in some way affect national and state park design.

Other Writings

Two other books that appeared in the same period also provided practical advice that was reflected in the work of park designers. In 1915, Samuel Parsons Jr. published principles of naturalistic gardening, including descriptive details of designs from Central Park such as the arch and cave in the Ramble and the Boulder Bridge, in *The Art of Landscape Architecture*. In 1920, O. C. Simonds published *Landscape-Gardening* as part of a rural science series directed at farmers, civil engineers, and others outside the landscape profession.

Drawing on his strong horticultural knowledge, Samuel Parsons Jr. enlightened American readers with instructions and advice on creating effects with natural vegetation. Parsons very much reflected Robinson's appreciation of native plants and promoted the creation of vegetation features from pine plantations, called "pintums," to water gardens with ferns and other low-growing, moisture-seeking plants and stone walls covered with randomly climbing vines. His *Art of Landscape Architecture* was also strongly influenced by Central Park, where he had been superintendent for many years, and by the writings and work of Prince Pückler-Muskau. Parsons would, in fact, edit an English translation of the prince's 1834 treatise for American audiences in 1917.

Parsons expanded Downing's advice on rockwork to the creation of rock structures such as walls and gate piers that could be planted with ferns and vines. Parsons offered some of the most detailed instructions for rockwork published at the time. These instructions would be particularly useful for park designers in the twentieth century.

> No chisel should be allowed to touch the stones except to break off chunks. The stone or rock masses should be laid lengthwise in the wall, not with the narrow parts up and down, and naturally the larger pieces should rest on the ground. Where the stones rest on the ground, the point of junction of the stone and soil should be at least two or three inches above the actual rock base. There is a principle involved in the idea. Concealment serves to suggest that the rocks have not been brought to the spot, but have grown there, and the soil gradually gathered about them.[17]

Stones, whether for bridges or walls, were to be collected in nearby fields or taken from quarries where the rock had the same color, grain, and cleavage, or lamination, as that found in the area where it is was to be used. Parsons recommended the use of rough-grained stone that was likely to weather, such as limestone, granite, or sandstone. Any concrete necessary in the core of the wall was to remain out of sight, with the crevices left exposed and open to allow pockets of soil to form for planting. At the base of walls ferns, irises, saxifrage, and other medium-sized herbaceous plants were to be planted (172, 176).

O. C. Simonds' *Landscape-Gardening* conveyed his ideas on the use of native vegetation. Although this was a practical guide directed at an audience of farmers, highway engineers, and residents of rural areas nationwide, it reflected the ideas of the Prairie style of landscape design. He, too, urged readers to use the trees, shrubs, and native flowers that were "close at hand" to develop a restful retreat that could be called "an American garden" and increase one's interest in the vegetation that grew along roadsides, margins of woodland streams, and other out-of-the-way places. Simonds included native wildflowers, mosses, lichens, ferns, and climbing vines as well as trees and shrubs among the gardener's materials.[18]

Calling for the beautification of roadways and noting the progress being made in New York and Massachusetts, Simonds advocated the planting of country roads with naturally arranged groups of trees and shrubbery of several different species. This approach allowed designers freedom to leave open spaces between groups where views of the surrounding countryside were scenic and to plant trees closely together where views were not desirable. Native species were to be planted because they matched the landscape and were hardy and dependable. The sequence of scenic views along a river road could be enhanced by planting screens in certain places and by preserving openings in others (198).

On the construction of artificial lakes and ponds, Simonds urged his readers to follow nature and to locate buildings far back from the shoreline so they would be unobtrusive yet still allow delightful views over the water. He advised sloping and planting steep banks to prevent erosion and creating borders along streams with cattails, pickerelweed, and sedges. He cautioned against concrete edges for ponds and suggested that boulders be laid in a naturalistic fashion where reinforcement was needed. He suggested that the cement aprons of dams be concealed by inserting boulders while the cement was soft, by using cobblestones and gravel to roughen the appearance, and by planting bushes that would provide overhanging foliage. He also described the development of earthen dams (11, 106).

Simonds suggested a wide range of native plants, shrubs, and trees for planting the various slopes of a lake according to moisture and exposure to sun. Virginia creepers and other vines, violets, marsh marigolds, bluets, forget-me-nots, white clover, and ground ivy were suggested for the lower banks. Hemlocks and birches with a ground covering of yews and ferns were suitable for southern banks. For sunny northern slopes in the Northeast and upper Midwest, he recommended sugar maples. Elsewhere, he recommended trees noted for autumn colors: sassafras, white ash, sweet gum, tulip trees, dogwood, pepperidge, blue beech, pin cherries, and some oaks. Appropriate for lakes were mountain laurels, rhododendrons, azaleas, sweet pepper bushes, bayberries, andromeda, wild roses, and hollies. Among the spring-flowering woody plants, he included Juneberry, redbud, crabapples, thorn apples, and elderberries. He suggested herbaceous plants that could be planted in moist areas for sequence of bloom; these included marigolds, iris, marshmallows, lilies, ironweed, lobelias, gentians, asters, and grass of Parnassus. He recommended columbines, saxifrage, harebells, butterfly weeds, goldenrods, and asters for steep, gravelly banks and trilliums, hepaticas, wild ginger, adder's-tongues, bloodroots, squirrel corn, maidenhair ferns, mosses, and liverworts for steep but moist and shady banks (115–17).

Simonds' knowledge of planting practices was, of course, limited by his regional knowledge of the Midwest. He did, however, include a chapter on landscape gardening for arid and semiarid regions, where the usual gardening practices were impossible to carry out. He pointed out the beauty of mountain views and natural rock formations in the Southwest, which were indigenous elements of landscape design. For arid areas, he suggested cactus gardens in combination with rocks and urged the planting of herbaceous plants that bloomed at certain seasons and were attractive as ground covers even in dry periods. In keeping with his own practice, Simonds wrote, "The problem for a landscape gardener in any location is to make the most of available materials. It is wise always to work in harmony with what nature has done in the surrounding territory. In any locality, whether dry or moist, planting material should be used which is indigenous to the region or which grows in some other locality having similar soil and climate" (185, 189–90).

Several other publications appeared which indicated the growing interest in gardening with native materials and a revival of the English landscape gardening tradition. Downing's essays from the *Horticulturalist* were compiled and published as one volume in 1894. The first American edition of Humphry Repton's principles for landscape gardening was published with an introduction by John Nolen in 1907. In 1917, Parson's editing of an English translation of Prince Pückler-Muskau's 1834 treatise was issued. Waugh published a revised edition of Downing's *Theory and Practice* in 1921. In 1929, Edith Roberts and Elsa Rehmann published *American Plants for American Gardens,* which further applied the principles of ecology to gardening with native plants.

While the appreciation for native plants was growing within the horticultural and landscape-architectural circles, scientific theory on plant ecology was advancing in the United States. In 1899, Henry C. Cowles of the University of Chicago published his landmark study on the ecological succession of plant life in the Indiana dunes of Lake Michigan. Between 1904 and 1930, Frederic E. Clements of the University of Nebraska and later the Carnegie Institution in Washington, D.C., published several important studies on ecology as a dynamic process and advanced theories on plant succession, plant competition, and climax communities. Clements did extensive research from laboratories in the Rocky Mountains and southern California, and in the 1930s his scientific theories were applied to the national effort to promote soil conservation and stabilization. Willis Linn Jepson's *Manual of the Flowering Plants of California,* first published in 1925, and the faculty of the University of California, Berkeley, would directly influence the pioneering educational programs of the National Park Service, which got under way in Yosemite National Park in the 1920s. Cowles became one of the founding members of the Friends of our Native Landscape, and Clements later advised the National Park Service on controlling erosion along park roads in Yosemite National Park.[19]

A Design Ethic for Natural Parks

Also influential on park design was the publication in 1928 of a volume of the senior Olmsted's writings on Central Park. Editors Frederick Law Olmsted Jr. and Theodora Kimball Hubbard intended the volume, entitled *Forty Years of Landscape Architecture: Central Park,* to be a history and case study of an urban park over several decades. It made available to large audiences information about Olmsted's philosophy and practices of park design. Olmsted's letters and reports covered a large number of subjects relating to the design and management of a public park, some of which applied to reservations of natural landscape as well. Subjects included the choice and care of plantations, boundaries and entrances, public use and abuse, park buildings, and various encroachments.

Technical instructions and plans for the construction of many landscape features, including well-drained earthen paths, dry-laid walls and ha-has, swimming pools, and amphitheaters, which would influence the development of national and state parks appeared in the ASLA's journal, *Landscape Architecture,* in the 1920s and early 1930s. Many of these were written by Cleveland landscape architect Albert Taylor (a former student of Waugh's) and directly applied to design problems common to natural areas. Articles in *Landscape Architecture* by Stephen Hamblin and Frank Waugh drew attention to native plants and their use in the design of roadsides and gardens and on the shores of lakes and ponds.

The greatest practitioners of the American style of natural gardening were the designers of national and state parks in the 1920s and 1930s. These designers, commonly called landscape engineers or landscape architects, readily and confidently drew inspiration from a variety of sources, borrowing both principles and practices that were in keeping with their desire to harmonize and naturalize their construction work and preserve or enhance the inherent scenic beauty of each park. Their work was part of a continuing tradition that began in nineteenth-century urban parks and matured and flourished in the 1930s. Developments in the twentieth century which called for the planting of native plants and trees according to their natural associations and conditions for moisture and drainage opened up new opportunities for park designers. Results included the naturalistic planting of roadsides and the shores of artificial lakes and ponds, the channelization and beautification of streams, and the return of development sites to nature after construction. New demands for public recreation, an increasingly mobile society, and the challenges of managing public lands called for the application of these principles and practices to new uses and at greater scales than they had ever been intended. Designers of national and state parks responded with vigor and creative genius and, in the process, forged a coherent and advanced form of naturalistic landscape design.

Chapter 3

Sources of
Rustic Architectural Design

The late nineteenth century saw the evolution of a design ethic for sturdy rustic structures. In the United States, this ethic made use of Downing's naturalistic principles and prototypes for rural architecture. A variety of practitioners seeking harmony between structure and setting and solutions to building homes in rugged and scenic places developed expressions of rustic architecture in the Adirondacks, along the Atlantic coast, in the San Francisco Bay Area, and in the Sierras. As the idea of developing wilderness for personal pleasure extended to an increasing number of public parks—local, metropolitan, state, and national—the rustic style was adopted for a multitude of park structures. By the turn of the century, the various expressions were embraced by the American Arts and Crafts movement, where they fused with regional styles, indigenous forms, and Japanese influences in both architectural design and gardening styles based on native materials.

The Shingle Style and Henry Hobson Richardson

Emerging in the northeastern United States in the 1870s, the Shingle style of architecture would have enduring expression in the architecture of parks and resort areas well into the twentieth century. Certain characteristics of the style were well suited to buildings and smaller structures that were required to fit the often rugged topography of natural parks and to blend harmoniously with a natural setting. The style offered a flexible system for massing a building according to interior function and space and the physical and scenic aspects of the site. The addition of porches, porte-cochères, viewing bays, towers, and terraces further allowed the framing of views and vistas from several vantage points and integrated the interior space and exterior setting. Construction materials of weathered local stone and timber further joined the building with its site and setting. The style featured massive interior fireplaces and capped chimneys that often pierced flat, low-pitched, and overhanging roofs. Rich wood paneling and crafted details adorned interiors. These characteristics would suit the functional, recreational, and aesthetic purposes of resort architecture. The style was especially suited to homes by the sea, on lakes, and in wooded enclaves such as Llewelyn Park in New Jersey and Tuxedo Park in New York. Most influential was the work of Henry Hobson Richardson, particularly his work for the Ames family in North Easton, Massachusetts. The style reached its zenith in Kragsyde in Manchester-by-the-Sea, Massachusetts, by Robert S. Peabody and John G. Stearns. Other practitioners included William Ralph Emerson, John Calvin Stevens, Hugo Lamb and Charles A. Rich, Arthur Little, and Charles F. McKim, William R. Mead, and Stanford White.

Many features of the Shingle style were incorporated in park buildings beginning in the 1880s and formed the vocabulary for structures in national and state parks in the 1920s and 1930s. These include an irregular massing of interlocking units on various levels, towers, gable-ended projections, octagons, overhanging roofs, projecting gables, flowing interior space, use of shingles for siding and roofing, entrance porches, porte-cochères, high chimneys, horizontal window bands in the gables, open interior spaces, battered foundations of stone which often merged with great stone chimneys and battered porch piers, and broad, open verandas to serve as out-of-door rooms. In addition to the integration of varied levels to suit the existing topography, the most commonly borrowed feature was a rusticated and often battered stone wall that extended from the ground into the lower story, uniting the building and its natural site.[1]

The Shingle style, according to scholar Vincent Scully, was essentially an American development that "did not destroy but enhanced and grew upon vernacular building." With their native materials, rustic craftsmanship, and environmental adaptations, Shingle style dwellings could also incorporate features drawn from local vernacular forms such as the homes of pioneers, early settlers, and indigenous peoples and probably reached its epitome in the Adirondack style. The use of native materials allowed designers to match the textures and coloration of the surrounding natural site and to unify groups of buildings and structures built for different functions and at varying scales. This recognition and connection with vernacular traditions was adopted later by the American Arts and Crafts movement and appears in the use of indigenous and pioneering prototypes, materials, and craftsmanship in park buildings of the 1920s and 1930s (89).

The Ames Gate Lodge (1880–81), designed by Richardson during his period of collaboration with Olmsted, represents an important stage in Richardson's work which would have influence on the design of park structures. Scully has written that the lodge was "a demonstration and an object lesson" in rock-

3.1. The Ames Gate Lodge, located in North Easton, Massachusetts, was designed in 1880–81 by architect H. H. Richardson during his period of collaboration with landscape architect Frederick Law Olmsted. Constructed of massive, weathered boulders, the lodge contains a gently sloped and curving roof and is bisected by a rusticated arched entrance to the Ames family estate. Richardson's use of natural materials, the bold arch, and forms to harmonize with the surrounding landscape made the Ames Gate Lodge a model of rustic, Shingle-style architecture which would be adopted by park designers for several generations. *(Photography courtesy William H. Pierson)*

work and that the "cyclopean rubble . . . culminated this development and brought violently to the attention of American architects the expressive possibilities inherent in construction with rough stone, up to boulder size." Although the bold rusticated arch and rubble construction of the lodge would become hallmarks of the Richardsonian Romanesque style of architecture, their use in park structures would continue to be more characteristic of the Shingle style (91).

Rusticated arched entrances of large weathered boulders similar to those of Richardson's Ames Gate Lodge and McKim, Mead, and White's Casino at Narragansett, Rhode Island, appeared again and again in park bridges, culverts, fireplaces, and buildings. For naturalistic park design this stylistic development was particularly important, for it extended Downing's ideas about naturalistic rockwork to the construction of structures having a more permanent and sturdy character than those constructed of unpeeled poles and twisted branches.

Richardson and Olmsted collaborated and influenced each other's work from the late 1870s until Richardson's death in 1886. Richardson's work extended to bridges, memorials, and other park structures. In addition to several stone-masonry bridges for the Boston parks, he also designed a gatehouse and a fountain for the Muddy River improvements that Olmsted's office was working on in Boston at the time. In 1879, Richardson designed a memorial commemorating the roles of Oakes Ames and Oliver Ames II in building the first transcontinental railroad. The result was a stepped pyramid that emerged from an isolated peak in Wyoming. It was more than fifty feet high and constructed of rough local granite. Olmsted praised this monument for its successful union of structure and setting. Richardson apparently designed several of the earliest shelters for Franklin Park in 1884. Olmsted seized upon Richardson's ideas for designing structures with rough masonry walls and bold arches and adopted a similar approach for the shelters, springs, water fountains, and benches made of large boulders and slabs of Roxbury pudding stone at Franklin Park in the 1880s.[2]

The Shingle style influenced the designers of the national and state parks through several channels. The first was in the rustic stone and shingle structures of nineteenth-century parks. In his *Introduction to the Study of Landscape Design,* Henry Hubbard recognized the suitability of the Shingle style for structures in natural parks and popularized the Olmsted firm's work at Franklin Park, influenced by Richardson, as a model for park design decades after the style had fallen out of fashion elsewhere. The Shingle style also fulfilled the basic principles of naturalistic gardening—the use of native materials, a design that fit the topography and blended with natural aspects of the setting, and the use of vegetation to blend and harmonize construction.

By the turn of the century, architects in the Adirondacks, the Midwest, and the West had already incorporated many characteristics of the style in their work. By 1910, these ideas were acclaimed by practitioners and promoters of the Arts and Crafts movement in America and had been absorbed into mainstream residential design as part of the "bungalow" craze.

The Great Camps of the Adirondacks

The great camps of New York's Adirondack region provided one of the earliest and strongest expressions of Downing's ideas for a picturesque rustic style appropriate for a natural area or wilderness. Nestled at the edge of deep forests, the camps were frequently lakeside resorts consisting of several buildings separated by function. The camps were sited to fit the natural contours of the land, to take advantage of the scenic views of the surrounding lakes, mountains, and woodlands, and to offer outdoor activities such as fishing and boating. As it evolved in the late nineteenth century, the Adirondack style adopted features of the Shingle style, the local vernacular of pioneer log cabins, and the romantic European

3.2. The dining hall at Camp Uncas, the Adirondack camp built for financier J. P. Morgan between 1893 and 1895, illustrates characteristics typical of the Adirondack style. The hall was carefully sited above Mohegan Lake to afford views, to disturb as few trees as possible, and to blend with the natural setting. It features a stone rubble foundation, spruce log walls, and a gable roof with overhangs and exposed purlins. A massive native stone chimney projects through the roof. *(Photograph by John Haggard, courtesy New York State Office of Parks, Recreation, and Historic Preservation)*

styles of country homes, especially the chalet form of the Swiss Alps and the German farmhouse with jerkinhead gables. These European styles had been popularized in America by Downing in his *Architecture of Country Houses* of 1850 and by Calvert Vaux in his *Villas and Cottages* of 1857. The resulting fusion of pattern-book sources and pioneer traditions was compatible with Downing's principles for picturesque and rustic forms that used natural materials in naturalistic forms.

The Adirondack camps, with their cabins, boathouses, and lodges, drew heavily on Downing's suggestions for rustic and picturesque constructions of twisted, unpeeled trunks and branches. Their architectural forms and functional designs, however, were derived from the pioneer building traditions of a region with a severe climate and an abundant local supply of logs and boulders. The

Adirondack region had heavy snowfalls in winter and extended periods of rain in the spring and summer. Log structures were therefore set upon foundations of stone built up around the first story and battered to shed rain and snow. Oversized timbers were used to support roofs that could hold heavy loads of snow. Overhanging roofs prevented ice and snow from building up against the walls and foundations. Logs were tightly joined and chinked to keep out driving rain and cold wind. Builders raised all log and timber elements off the ground onto stones to reduce interior dampness and prevent the rotting of timbers by rising dampness. The notching of logs at the corners of buildings strengthened the walls, and roof trusses and beams were exposed. The most successful designs, according to the historian Harvey H. Kaiser, were those where the building materials repeated the qualities of the surrounding forest, such as natural color, the scale of local timber, and even the natural grain of wood used for decorative effects.[3]

Fear of fire led builders to construct tall chimneys that rose high above the roof ridge. Capping around the tops trapped sparks. Fireplaces were built of cyclopean rocks and capped by massive stone slabs for mantles. Fireplaces needed to be sturdy and safe and draw well. This type of fireplace, a signature of the Adirondack lodge, would be incorporated in the lodges of state and national park concessionaires, from the Bear Mountain and Shenandoah lodges of the East to the Old Faithful and Glacier hotels of the West (67).

Another feature of the Adirondack camps was the placement of separate functions in individual buildings informally arranged within the natural topography. The construction of many small buildings often attached by covered walkways was motivated by concern for fire. The idea of the sylvan village derived first from the building of tent platforms in the woods and was later carried over into permanent buildings. Sleeping accommodations were housed in small cabins or on the second stories of the lakeside boathouses. Eating and social gatherings often took place in separate buildings. Later they were located in the second-story rooms of the lodge, constructed as a central gathering place. Buildings were connected by covered boardwalks and enclosed passageways. This arrangement enabled the camps to increase in size through the year and become small villages. Staff housing and utilities were commonly built in separate "service complexes" located away from the central camp (65).

Published in 1889, *Log Cabins: How to Build and Furnish Them* by William S. Wicks was likely the first published guide to siting, constructing, and furnishing log cabins for recreational purposes in keeping with the Adirondack tradition. Wicks told his readers to select sites based on scenic views, accessibility, frontage on the water, and protection by trees. He was one of the first to promote the idea that structures should be an outgrowth of the site and harmonize with it.[4]

The Adirondack style expanded Downing's methods of construction for

3.3. The concern for harmonizing with nature extended to the design of the many small structures associated with the Adirondack camps. The pump house at Camp Uncas was constructed of exterior pole framing made of native cedar logs and sheathing of spruce bark. A cobblestone chimney projects through the shingled gable roof. *(Photograph by Richard Youngken, courtesy New York State Office of Parks, Recreation, and Historic Preservation)*

rural architecture into a major form of picturesque architectural ornamentation. Previously confined to park and garden use in gazebos, fences, outdoor furniture, gateways, and bridges, Downing's twisted branches and tree trunks found their way into elaborate rustic embellishments from peeled-bark sheathing for walls to elaborate porch railings and gable vergeboards made of sinuous branches and roots. Branches from the surrounding woodland and roots exposed along the lakeshore were gathered, entwined, and tied to create a wide variety of imaginative forms, such as the name of the camp or a decorative porch railing. These forms became an insignia of the Adirondack style and were copied elsewhere in rustic resorts and recreational architecture and appeared in signs, gateways, bridges, and cabins from the White Mountains to Camp Curry in Yosemite by the turn of the century. A whole style of decorative arts grew up around this type of rustic ornamentation and extended to handcrafted furniture and interior design as well as exterior features. As a major manifestation of the Arts and Crafts movement in America, variations appeared in the West which incorporated discarded antlers of elk and the leather and hides of domestic and wild animals. A number of the early hotels in national parks, such as those of Glacier National Park and Yellowstone National Park's Old Faithful Inn, were influenced by the architecture as well as the decorative arts characteristic of the Adirondack style. In fact, antlers were fashioned into a movable gate for the Entrance Arch for Yellowstone National Park in Gardiner, Montana, and they dressed the stone foundation of the park's Cook entrance station in the mid-1930s, a variation of the "naturalistic garden."

By 1917, however, such embellishment was seen as an impractical and undesirable affectation and rejected in favor of more sturdy, functional, and unadorned structures. The movement away from ornamented designs reflected the emergence of the "form follows function" principle of the twentieth century, urged by Louis Sullivan and Frank Lloyd Wright. Henry Hubbard suggested more simple lattice patterns constructed of small vertical, horizontal, and diagonal logs, while Frank Waugh decried the "twig-like" ornamentation. National Park Service spokesman Herbert Maier classified such ornamentation as "gingerbread" and, in 1935, cautioned state park designers against its use for park structures.

Although influenced by pioneer traditions, the Adirondack style adopted characteristics of European design, especially that of Switzerland and Scandinavia, which Downing had strongly recommended as appropriate for American homes in a rural setting. The influence of Swiss architecture dominated in the Adirondack camps, mainly because it was widely used by entrepreneur William West Durant in his four camps—Pine Knot, Uncas, Sagamore, and Kill Kare. Swiss-influenced characteristics included the chalet form of a compact two-story building with a gabled front, broad overhanging roofs, a projecting second-story balcony extending across the gable with railings of roughly sawn boards with simple cutout designs, and horizontal ribbons of small-paned windows. The Swiss style adopted by Durant suited the practical conditions and needs of the Adirondacks and capitalized on the romantic appeal of a remote northern retreat. So popular was the Swiss imagery that William S. B. Dana published *The Swiss Chalet Book* in 1913. In the first three decades of the twentieth century, the designers of national park lodges at Glacier, Bryce, Zion, Grand Canyon, and Yellowstone national parks continued to be influenced by the romantic mountain imagery of Swiss architecture. Swiss-inspired details remained a part of the park designer's vocabulary long after the recognizable chalet form itself was abandoned (75–77).

Influences on the Adirondack style came from other parts of the world as well. The arrangement of the camps in a "compound-plan tradition" was derived from the forest camps of Japan, Europe, and Russia. At Durant's Camp Pine Knot, buildings were scattered informally across the land, each being situated for views while maintaining proximity to one another. This type of arrangement would be imitated in many of the cabin clusters built during the 1930s in state and national parks and would become a model for the arrangement of the organization camps in recreational demonstration areas. This arrangement afforded privacy and fire protection and allowed the siting of individual buildings for view and accommodation to the terrain without destroying the sense of community and settlement (81).

The jerkinhead gable, used extensively at Sekon Lodge in the Adirondacks, had its origins in the country architecture of southern Germany. The use of the jerkinhead gable suggests shelter, brings buildings closer to the ground, and adds the same domestic scale to all buildings. It was sometimes supported on a cross brace formed by an unpeeled log. The jerkinhead gable was frequently used by Gilbert Stanley Underwood, who designed park lodges for the Utah Parks Company in the mid-1920s, and was promoted by Herbert Maier for use in state park structures (155).

The William A. Read Camp (1906) by the architectural firm of Davis, McGrath, and Shepard was one of the few camps designed by an architect. The lodge with living room and bedrooms was sited on a knoll projecting into the lake; the dining room, kitchen, and servants' quarters were situated two hundred feet away on a rocky point. The two were connected by a covered passage of ramps and stairs which provided scenic views and allowed for changes in grade. A square viewing pavilion was built midway between the lodge and dining room.

A 1907 article in *House and Garden* described the picturesque effect created at the lakeside retreat and the efforts that the builder and owner had taken to harmonize the construction with the natural setting. The article pointed out that no attempt had been made at landscape gardening but that the grounds had been left in a natural state and natural grades had been preserved. Logs, carefully selected for size, had been cut from the surrounding forest. Only a single tree was taken from any one place, so that its loss would not be noticed from the lake. Stone for foundations, fireplaces, and chimneys was quarried from nearby but out-of-sight mountainsides. The railings along the covered walkway and porches were made of peeled logs arranged in a rhythmic pattern of diagonal crosses alternating with parallel uprights. Drawings of the elevations of the Read Camp were published in 1906 in the *American Architect and Building News* showing the carefully cut and laid logs stepped out to meet the foundation and support the broad overhanging roof and upper-story balconies. The two-story lodge was built into the naturally rising grade on a foundation of stone. A porch was built along three sides, and a covered passageway supported on rustic columns connected the wings of the north elevation facing away from the lake. Chimneys pierced the overhanging roofs. The elevation rising from the stone foundation showed an alternating design of dark-stained logs and white plaster chinking made of portland cement over lath.[5]

The Read Camp established an aesthetic for rustic construction which surpassed both pioneer log cabins and the earlier fussy yet primitive camps. The ingenious integration of a hillside site and the rich display of rusticated details provided a perfect prototype for natural park design. Projecting gable ends, broad overhangs, corbeled logs, stepped corner logs at the foundations and roof supports, scrolled brackets, and porch and balcony railings made of vertical planks added a Swiss feeling to the building's decor. Although features such as the second-story balcony and gable ends drew from the Swiss chalet prototype, the sophisticated log construction and detailing, the overall massing, and the penetration of the massive stone chimneys through the overhanging roof were of American derivation. Solid hewn beams with chamfered edges were supported on corbeled brackets. Great importance was attached to the small-paned windows, which resembled those of frontier cabins and added to the quaintness of the building. The dining room was a large octagonal room with an exposed roofing system of heavy hand-hewn trusses and a huge stone fireplace measuring six and a half feet wide by five feet high (191).

These characteristics would find their way to national parks through popular appeal and contemporary journals and magazines, including *American Architect and Building News, House and Garden,* and the *Craftsman.* Designs and ideas were also published in many popular bungalow pattern books, such as William Comstock's *Bungalows, Camps, and Mountain Houses,* which appeared in the first two decades of the twentieth century.

In 1931, an illustrated manual on Adirondack architecture was published which included numerous plans, details, and photographs. Entitled *Camps in the Woods* and written by Augustus D. Shepard, an architect of the Read Camp and a number of other Adirondack buildings, it was a compendium of the lodges, boathouses, and camps the author had designed at the Adirondack League Club — a private reserve of one hundred thousand acres within the Adirondacks. Shepard's book reveals how the Adirondack style evolved in the twentieth century, accommodating new ideas arising from the Prairie style of architecture, the American Arts and Crafts movement, and other sources. No longer primitive rustic cabins of the 1880s, the twentieth-century camps were "summer homes in the woods." Built of the best materials, they were "permanent, liveable, comfortable" and provided every modern convenience. They could be constructed and equipped for year-round use by building a cellar with a heating plant and by installing weatherproofed water and sewage systems.[6]

Shepard considered the lakeside boathouse to be the most important feature of a camp in the woods. Located at the water's edge, the boathouse had docks and piers and often served as the main entrance to a camp. The ground level was designed to store boats and equipment, and the second story contained guest rooms. Shepard showed many rustic boathouses, some with porches adorned with entwined branchwork, others built of stone and log. One common feature was the balcony, generally located on the second story above the

3.4. The guest cabin, whimsically called the "Bishop's Palace," at Camp Wild Air in the Adirondack region of New York dates from 1908. Sited on the shore of Upper St. Regis Lake amidst towering fir trees, the cabin features a polygonal shape that affords panoramic views of the lake and surrounding wilderness. It is constructed of solid logs and features a massive stone chimney and pavilionlike hipped roof with overhanging eaves. A walkway of immense, irregularly shaped flagstones provides further harmony between the structure and the natural setting. *(Photograph by Richard Youngken, courtesy New York State Office of Parks, Recreation, and Historic Preservation)*

boat dock. This balcony, often large enough to be called a porch, provided a lake view and an outdoor sitting area. An enclosed living room could be reached through a door at the back of the balcony and was graced by a massive stone fireplace. One of the most interesting examples was at the Riker Camp, where massive irregularly shaped and sized blocks made up the masonry of the lower level. The upper story was fronted by an open, semioctagonal porch having log columns with branching brackets, sawn wood rails, and an overhanging roof with exposed purlins (3).

The octagon was an architectural feature widely adopted wherever a broad or panoramic view from several angles was desirable. Popularized by Orson S. Fowler in *A Home for All,* first published in 1848, it had been common in dwellings, schoolhouses, and lighthouses since the nineteenth century. Downing had shown shelters of octagonal form. The octagon was easy to construct and afforded the same advantages as the circular form, such as offering wide views and having no dominant elevation. Architects working in the Shingle style adopted the octagon in sections or as a whole for viewing rooms or bays that could be joined to the mass of interlocking units that made up the house. The octagon's uses and aesthetic advantages made it suitable for adaptation by designers in the Midwest, the San Francisco Bay Area, and the Adirondacks, who were all interested in capturing views and integrating their structures with the natural surroundings. Its popularity continued in resort and recreational architecture and resulted in many creative forms and uses in state and national parks in the 1930s.

In Shepard's opinion, camp buildings were to be located where they best conformed to the contour of the land and provided a southern exposure so that occupants could enjoy the morning sunrise and midday sun. The direction of prevailing winds and summer storms were other important considerations. Shepard pointed out the particular importance of views and recommended that the windows of the main living rooms face the lake to enframe the reflection of the woods and mountains on the still waters of the lake (7).

Protecting the native trees was of utmost importance. Shepard showed a contour plan of the camp for George W. Vanderhoef Jr. which indicated the location of important trees. It is interesting to note that shortly after the publication of Shepard's book, national park designers similarly began to plot important trees on the topographic maps from which they made plans and drawings. Shepard recognized the experience and knowledge that forestry contributed to the creation of the great camp. He urged architects to seek out professional advice in determining the trees to be removed without disturbing the scenery and consider the proper treatment for the trees and flora that were to remain (6–7).

Upholding the idea that camps should be designed in a style inspired by the woods, Shepard stated that buildings should be designed so that they "appeared to grow out of the ground" and could not be distinguished from the woods of which they were a part. This could be accomplished by using stone posts and walls, stone and earth terraces, and hand-hewn wood steps, as nineteenth-century park designers had done. Unlike his nineteenth-century predecessors, however, who fit their buildings somewhat awkwardly onto the existing terrain, Shepard fit his lodges more closely into their natural sites and settings. The cutting of natural slopes and backfilling made it possible to fit a building tightly into its natural site and to eliminate unsightly voids under porches or boardwalks. Terraces, walls, and curving stairways further integrated the buildings and sites and created viewpoints where scenery could be enjoyed. Shepard's lodges were improved by flagstone walks and steppingstones, foundation plantings of ferns, and native stone walls. Many of these features followed the advances made by Prairie style and West Coast architects in the first two decades of the twentieth century. Similar techniques were being used in the design of park buildings in the late 1920s (24).

Like Downing and practitioners in the Arts and Crafts movement, Shepard saw planting vegetation as a way to erase further the lines between natural setting and construction. He recommended, "By planting Virginia Creeper at the base of the stonework and placing luxurious ferns and other wild flora at appropriate locations, the relation between the building and its setting is made even more intimate" (25).

National park designers drew heavily on the Adirondack tradition, adopting the following characteristics: the use of native logs and rock in a rustic unfinished form, naturalistic siting of structures, incorporation of porches and viewing platforms, the climatic adaptation of using native stone for the foundation and lower story and native timber above, stone chimneys with massive fireplaces and mantles, open interiors with ceilings of exposed rafters and trusses, and a multitude of windows. These characteristics perfectly suited the need to attract visitors to the parks and to harmonize amenities with natural setting. The characteristics of the Adirondack style first found their way into the national parks through the hotels, lodges, and camps of public operators and concessionaires. Glacier, Grand Canyon, Yellowstone, and Yosemite national parks all boasted accommodations in the finest rustic style by 1920. Published sources and examples from the Adirondacks and those inspired by the Adirondack style continued to be valuable sources for national and state park designers through the 1930s.

There is no question that Shepard's book was known to the designers of national and state parks. Chief landscape architect Thomas Vint recommended it as a useful reference to at least one person writing him about the design of park structures. Shepard's book provided a source of designs and ideas, even though his theory was more indicative of how the building practices of the day were already being applied to the problem of rustic design in a natural setting. The book, however, strongly reinforced the interest of designers such as Vint and Herbert Maier in the architecture of the Adirondacks as prototypes for the architecture of natural areas. Appearing just two years before the beginning of the Civilian Conservation Corps and public works program, the book was filled with practical ideas and detailed drawings, diagrams, plans, and photographs of actual examples that were compatible with National Park Service principles. The park service chose a similar format when publishing its own pattern books, *Park Structures and Facilities* of 1935 and the three-volume *Park and Recreation Structures* of 1938. The park service books, edited by Albert Good, an architect from Akron, Ohio, echoed many of the principles presented in Shepard's book, and Herbert Maier incorporated many of Shepard's ideas in his inspector's guide for state park Emergency Conservation Work.

The Prairie Style of Architecture

At the beginning of the twentieth century emerged the Prairie style of architecture, which made radical advances in the construction of houses and similar buildings. Prairie style architects built upon the tenets of the Shingle style and applied a design process in which structure followed function and conformed to the contours of a site. They perfected and simplified residential design by using the conventions of landscape architecture, including stairways, terraces, walls, patios, and mantles of vines, to unify site and structure and to integrate indoor and outdoor spaces. Prairie style architects also explored the use of low-pitched overhanging roofs and other features to emphasize horizontality, the predominant characteristic of the midwestern landscape. The collaboration of landscape architect Jens Jensen and architect Frank Lloyd Wright and the work of Walter Burley Griffin, who was trained in both professions, led to important advances in adjusting built structures to natural landforms and in creating a gradual transition between structure and setting. Although these advances were applied most often to structures in suburban settings, they had underlying principles based on naturalism which would be readily applied by others to natural settings, such as parks, mountains, and seashore.

The principles and characteristics of the Prairie style were immediately embraced by the Arts and Crafts movement and were diffused through the publication of pattern books such as Hermann Valentin von Holst's *Modern American Homes* (1913), which featured Prairie style homes alongside works by California architects. Von Holst acknowledged that the back-to-nature movement called for country homes that were part of the scenery and were built of local materials.[7]

The West Coast Work of Greene and Greene

The work of Charles and Henry Greene in southern California provided another essential link between the Shingle style and the design of buildings in national and state parks. Through their influence, the lessons of the Shingle style entered into the mainstream of the Arts and Crafts movement in America and blended with indigenous West Coast building forms, materials, and ideas. They also drew inspiration from the architecture and landscape design of Japan, which they had seen at the Columbia Exposition in 1893, the Japanese Tea Garden in San Francisco, and the Louisiana Purchase Exposition at St. Louis in 1904. Like the Prairie style architects, they endeavored to integrate structure and setting and used terraces, walls, and outdoor features, including plantings, to blend the two and to create a gentle transition between inside and outside spaces. They also adopted the vernacular forms of the Southwest and gave modern expression to traditional styles drawn from the Spanish haciendas and missions. As a result, their work infused the bungalow craze of the first two decades of the twentieth century with innumerable prototypes and design details. The work of Greene and Greene and the many references to their work in the publications and work of others were important sources for the designers of state and national parks through the 1930s.[8]

The Greenes experienced the Shingle style firsthand during their studies at the Massachusetts Institute of Technology, where they graduated in 1891, and their subsequent employment in several Boston firms, including that of Shepley, Rutan, and Coolidge, which had taken over Richardson's practice in 1886. Returning to California, they introduced many innovations in keeping with the burgeoning Arts and Crafts movement. They drew heavily on native rock, particularly the boulders of Arroyo Seco, the natural canyon that passed through Pasadena, to fashion battered piers, raised and battered stone foundations, massive bold fireplaces, and undulating retaining walls. The brothers made great use of undulating stone walls in their efforts to ease the transition of each house with its site. Aged gnarled oaks and walls of cobblestone and clinker brick lined the Arroyo Terrace, which traversed the steep canyon walls and was being developed for homes and studios in the Craftsman style. Walls supporting terraces enabled them to adjust buildings to sloping or even hillside sites. Their affinity for working with the natural topography of each site, their understanding of Prairie style innovations, and their admiration for Japanese landscape design led them to create terraces on gradual slopes with walls that were low and followed naturalistic undulating lines, such as those at the Gamble, Blacker, and Pratt Houses.[9]

In keeping with the Arts and Crafts movement's interest in the past, the Greenes reinterpreted the traditional southwestern hacienda by introducing the U-shaped Bandini House in 1903. The one-story house centered on an open, informally landscaped court. A veranda having simple squared posts, shingle roofs, and exposed beams extended around the court and provided a transition from the interior rooms to the out-of-doors. The U-shaped plan was well suited to California's climate and casual style of living. Distinctive were the vertical board-and-batten walls made of native redwood and the large projecting boulders that formed seats to each side of the living room and dining room fireplaces. The house interpreted the indigenous adobe houses with tile roofs in native materials of redwood and cobblestone. The combination of redwood siding and cobblestone construction was a synthesis that occurred for the first time in the work of Greene and Greene about 1903. These materials and their use would figure prominently in the bungalow movement and would be used in the residences and other buildings built at Yosemite Village in the 1930s. The courtyard plan with its inner veranda would be readapted years later in a number of park service buildings in the Southwest, including the regional headquarters building in Santa Fe.[10]

The mountain house designed for Edgar W. Camp in the Sierra Madres,

California, in 1904 probably exerted more influence on park architecture than any other work by Greene and Greene. The *Craftsman* featured the house in December 1909 as "a mountain bungalow whose appearance of crude construction is the result of skillful design." Although its plan was similar to that of the Bandini House, the Camp House was unique in its low, rambling character that adjusted to the site's sloping topography and boulder-strewn setting. The building's silhouette was created by a series of intersecting and overlapping roofs with broad gables and projecting eaves. The exterior walls were sheathed by vertical boards and battens of native wood. Inside, a massive fireplace with "an appearance of great strength and ruggedness" was formed by piling up giant boulders around an unusually large fire opening with a capacity for huge logs. A heavy board formed a shelf above and to either side of the fire opening; two boulders projected naturalistically to form two fireside seats. Interior beams of Oregon pine were roughly hewn, undressed, and left exposed. Outside, the chimney rose from the ground battered and constructed of stone "as if it were part of nature's magnificent rockpile." It formed a naturalistic surface continuous with the boulder foundation made of rough fieldstone. The east wing of the house extended out at an angle to form a terrace off the dining room which provided views of the valley below, departing from the U-shaped plan.[11]

The article described the location as "deep and restful, rugged with frequent masses of richly-toned stone" and pointed out the native materials and features that helped the building adapt so successfully to its site. These included the low-pitched roof with projecting eaves, the foundations and chimneys built of rough fieldstone, and the rough and undressed timbers. The colors of the finished house blended with the ruddy brown of the hills, and the stonework echoed the large boulders scattered across the grounds. The roughness and random quality of the stone materials echoed the ruggedness and irregularity of the site. Particularly striking was the chimney, which seemed "hardly more than a great heap of rock" and which was planted with ivy that was destined to become "a startling beautiful bit of natural decoration" when in autumn the red foliage contrasted with the gray-brown rock.[12]

The Greenes' chimney and fireplace had many characteristics of those of the Adirondack camps but with greatly exaggerated proportions. The exterior treatment of the stone chimney at the refectory at Palmetto State Park bears a striking similarity in both its massing of stone and its irregular, random, and battered naturalistic appearance. This suggests that New Deal park designers not only revived an interest in Arts and Crafts traditions but also drew strongly from the actual examples that had been published in the *Craftsman* in the first two decades of the twentieth century.

Smaller structures designed by Greene and Greene would also influence park architecture. The entrance portals and waiting station designed about 1905 for the South Pasadena Realty and Improvement Company in Oaklawn Park were constructed of massive boulders fashioned into battered stone foundations and walls. In the walls of the waiting station, small stones were nested into the crevices formed by huge boulders, which decreased in size as they emerged upward and inward from the ground. The waiting station and the entry gate and pier were capped with overhanging tile roofs with exposed beams. The adjoining concrete walls of the reinforced-concrete Oaklawn Bridge were masked by a profusion of climbing vines. This portal with a massive battered pier on one side provided the prototype that would evolve from a pergola-inspired form with support piers of unequal size into a single battered pier with a hanging entry sign by the end of the 1920s. Such entry signs were built to mark the entrances to parks such as Lassen well into the 1930s.[13]

The Shelter for Viewlovers built atop Monks Hill in Pasadena in 1907 provided an even more exaggerated version of the Oaklawn waiting station, one intended for viewing. Here massive battered piers and exposed beams supported a greatly exaggerated overhanging roof. Both these structures provided a precedent for the open-air shelter that would first be directly adapted to the needs of the National Park Service in the scaled-down Glacier Point Lookout in Yosemite in 1924.[14]

Herbert Maier, more than any other park designer, was indebted to the influence of Greene and Greene. This influence was most strongly expressed in his own preference for battered random masonry walls of local fieldstone. He worked with Hull and Vint in 1924 on the design for the Glacier Point Lookout and may have drawn their attention to stone shelters designed by the Greenes. The flexible floor plans of Greene and Greene's designs greatly influenced Maier, particularly the multiangled design of the Rudd and Pratt Houses of 1909, which he adopted for the museum at Norris Geyser Basin in Yellowstone. He freely incorporated terraces around his museums to create a transition between the natural site and the building, and he ingeniously adopted pergolas and a porte-cochère to create a dramatic walk-through entry at the Norris museum. The influence of the Oaklawn portal clearly influenced several designs for entrance signs drawn in 1934 by his district office of the Civilian Conservation Corps.[15]

Another influential work was the oceanside house Charles Greene designed for Dr. D. L. James in Carmel, California, in 1918. Randell L. Makinson, the foremost authority on the work of Greene and Greene, has called this the most creative and ambitious work of Charles Greene's late career and the most significant structure apart from the Greenes' wooden bungalows. Makinson described its effect: "The stone structure seems to have grown out of its site atop the rocky cliffs south of Carmel. At places it is difficult to ascertain just where nature's rock has ended and man's masonry genius has begun."[16]

Here, Charles Greene used a flexible system of stonemasonry to adjust the house to a highly irregular and rocky site. Predominantly Mission Revival in style, the house was built of roughly cut quarried stone and accented with sandstone from nearby beaches and limestone from Carmel Valley. Greene opened up the U-shape in dramatic angles to follow the natural contours of the rocky cliff. Entry was through a single stone arch, and the stone walls imitated the indigenous adobe construction. Curving stairways and a circular overlook of lichen-encrusted rocks were built into the stone walls on the seaside and blended with the natural cliff walls. The site required the setting of walls some forty-five feet down the cliff to secure an adequate footing; this contributed to the sense that the house was integral with the cliff itself (221–26).

Greene supervised the stonework to ensure that the courses would begin and end at random and follow irregular horizontal lines. The joints of the stonework were irregular in thickness and deeply incised to create deep shadows and heighten the textural quality of the walls so that they had the same worn and weathered appearance as the cliffs. The splitting of the stone to expose cut edges and the horizontal coursing gave the walls a stratified appearance not unlike the limestone masonry of the Midwest. The plasticity and irregularity of the walls were repeated in a tile roof that had undulating lines.[17]

Greene's achievement in integrating structure and site was analogous to that of Peabody and Stearns in their Shingle style masterpiece, Kragsyde, built forty years earlier and three thousand miles away at Manchester-by-the-Sea. The park structures most indebted to the James House are Maier's Yavapai Observation Building and the Fred Harvey Company buildings by Mary Colter at Grand Canyon National Park and the CCC-built lodge designed by Guy Carlander at Palo Duro State Park in Texas.

The house designed in 1929 for Walter L. Richardson in Porterville, California, was Henry Greene's last major work. It followed the U-shaped plan of the Bandini House and was built with adobe made on site from natural materials. Natural stone matching that of the surrounding bedrock formed battered foundation walls; the roof was of rough timber and had exposed beams and overhanging eaves. The building also had reinforced concrete headers between stories and above windows. It was built into a gently sloping, rocky hillside. The combined use of concrete and adobe materials was attracting interest from the National Park Service about the same time and would be used increasingly in its parks in the 1930s.[18]

The legacy of Greene and Greene to the designers of national and state parks consisted of techniques to integrate indoor and outdoor spaces, to adjust structures to natural topography, and to achieve a unified design using native materials for both structural and decorative details. Their use of a design vocabulary that drew from traditions in landscape architecture as well as architecture further added to the appeal of their work and the suitability of their solutions for building in a natural area.

The Work of Bernard Maybeck and Bay Area Architects

The distinctive style of architecture which emerged in the Bay Area around San Francisco in the first two decades of the twentieth century also had a lasting influence on the design of park buildings. Bernard Maybeck was the leader of this style, which was characterized by indigenous materials of wood and stone, accommodation of buildings into natural hillsides and forests, use of exposed (and often stained) beams and trusses to vault interior spaces and support steeply pitched roofs, and tall vertical window walls to integrate indoor and outdoor spaces. Maybeck used laminated trusses to vault large interior spaces in his schools, churches, and clubhouses. Although this style drew directly from the English Arts and Crafts movement, it used American materials and followed principles of siting, hand craftsmanship, harmonizing nature and structure, and presenting scenic views that aligned it with the American movement.[19]

Although Maybeck is best known for the Beaux Arts–inspired Palace of Fine Arts built for the Panama Pacific International Exposition in 1915, his versatility and creative expression in a rustic idiom were also demonstrated in his many hillside homes in Berkeley and in his lesser-known exposition exhibit for the Pacific Lumberman's Association, called the House of Hoo-Hoo. This humorous building was a vine-draped Parthenon-like structure whose columns were unpeeled logs of fir, cedar, and pine and whose front portico was flanked by artificial columns, sixteen feet in diameter, which imitated the massive trunks of native redwood trees.[20]

The influence of the Bay Area style was expressed in three Yosemite buildings: LeConte Memorial Lodge (1903 and 1919), Parsons Memorial Lodge (1915), and the Rangers' Clubhouse (1921). These buildings reflected the fusion of Bay Area sources and other influences of the Arts and Crafts movement. Built for the Sierra Club, the LeConte Memorial Lodge in Yosemite Valley was designed by Maybeck's brother-in-law John White, built in 1903, and rebuilt on a new site according to the original plans in 1919. The Tudor Revival building assumed a compact form inspired by the natural setting of the granite-walled valley. Distinctive features were the irregularly coursed ashlar masonry of roughly cut granite, an entry porch in the form of a hexagonal raised terrace paved with flagstone and surrounded by a stonemasonry parapet, a Y-shaped plan, and a steep overhanging wood-shingled roof.[21]

The Parsons Memorial Lodge, built more than a decade later in the harsher mountain environment of Yosemite's Tuolumne Meadows, was built of reinforced concrete with a masonry veneer of rough granite and feldspar gathered from the Sierra high country and set with deeply raked mortar joints. In contrast to the steep roof of the earlier lodge, the Parsons Memorial had a low-lying gable roof with broad overhanging eaves supported on exposed rafters and diagonal braces fashioned from peeled logs. The design for Parsons Memorial Lodge is believed to be the result of the collaboration of architect Mark White, construction engineer Walter Huber, and Bernard Maybeck. The Rangers' Club (1921) in Yosemite Valley was designed for National Park Service director Stephen Mather by San Francisco architect Charles Sumner. Made of redwood shingles, boards, and battens, this clubhouse had a U-shaped plan and entry courtyard; a steeply pitched, wood-shingled roof pierced by dormers of varying lengths; and Swiss-inspired second-story balconies with jigsawn railings (174–78, 200–205).

Several features that distinguished the work of the Bay Area architects from their Pasadena contemporaries Greene and Greene were the steep roofs and the floor-to-ceiling windows, which often became part of the plastic form by creating bays and glazed alcoves. The Japanese and southern Californian traditional influences were replaced by an almost Nordic expressionism drawn from English, German, and Scandinavian sources. Maybeck explored the use of trusses to support steep roofs and create soaring interior spaces and developed a technique for laminating trusses using native wood materials. The exploration of truss systems and use of large windows with small panes opened up new possibilities for the design of national park buildings. The adaptation of the horizontal ribbon windows of Shingle style to a vertical format to provide large expansive views and light-filled interiors influenced and would be further developed by Gilbert Stanley Underwood in his national park lodges of the 1920s.

In 1921, Maybeck redesigned the Glen Alpine Springs resort near Lake Tahoe, which had been destroyed by fire the previous year. Maybeck used natural materials and industrial products to produce an efficient and fireproof structure that blended with its setting in the high Sierras. His design incorporated battered piers and walls of heavy stonemasonry construction and native timber trusses with industrial sash and corrugated iron roofing. Although the building's rough stone walls shared much of the character of the Parsons Memorial Lodge, they took the bolder and more dynamic form of battered buttresses. The pattern of separating buildings in the Adirondacks because of the threat of fire may have influenced Maybeck to design a connected group of low-lying pavilions. The Glen Alpine Springs resort broke new ground in rustic design through its use of modern building materials and its advances in the structural use of stone. Years later when the national park designers were faced with the problem of building harmonious structures for Hawaii Volcanoes National Park, where fire was an ever present concern and timber scarce, the combination of local stone and corrugated iron provided a satisfactory solution. Corrugated iron, industrial sash, and concrete would be used extensively in the garages, shops, and sheds of maintenance facilities. In the late 1920s, Gilbert Stanley Underwood drew heavily from Maybeck's structural system of timber trusses supported on massive battered and buttressed piers in his designs for the Ahwahnee Hotel at Yosemite and the North Rim Lodge at Grand Canyon.[22]

National park designers, those working for concessionaires as well as those working for the government, knew the work of Greene and Greene, Maybeck, and other California architects from published sources and from the works themselves. Certainly the LeConte and Parsons lodges that the Sierra Club had built at Yosemite were inspirational forms. The work of Maybeck and other Bay Area architects was an important link between the Shingle style and national park architecture. These practitioners used forms such as the octagon and hexagon and explored the relationships of space, site, view, and native materials that were in keeping with the Shingle style principles. Maybeck made significant advances in the relationship of interior space, external setting, structural design, and light—advances that would influence national park design.

The Architecture of Park Concessionaires

The earliest hotels in the national parks date from the era before the advent of the automobile, when the transcontinental railroads brought visitors to the parks. These buildings represented a fusion of picturesque European prototypes, the Adirondack style, and an imagery of form and detail suitable to the West. Built at the height of the American Arts and Crafts movement, these buildings integrated the concerns for setting, structure, and decorative arts into a single unified and harmonious form that suited the natural surroundings of the parks where they were located. The Old Faithful Inn (1903) in Yellowstone National Park is considered the first "rustic" hotel built in the national parks in a large-scale effort to harmonize construction with the natural surroundings. Although the Swiss-influenced Adirondack style was adopted for the Northern Pacific Railroad's hotel by architect Robert Reamer, the proportions of structural features such as the imposing gabled roof pierced by window dormers were exaggerated. Logs, wood shingles, and stone were fashioned into structural features. Gnarled and twisted logwork formed interior and exterior decorative details such as railings and brackets, giving it an exuberant decorative appeal and a feeling of the western frontier. Inside were a multistoried lobby and a massive fireplace.[23]

The system of hotels and chalets built in Glacier National Park for the Great Northern Railway in 1913 is based on the European system of hostelries located within a day's hike or ride of each other. Swiss-influenced architectural themes—both the chalet form and details such as sawn-wood balconies and clipped or jerkinhead gables—were carried out in several lodges, mountain chalets, hotels, and a store, built in varying scales. Some of the buildings were built predominantly of log; others were of local stone available at the higher elevations. A similar architectural theme was used in Glacier's Lake MacDonald Lodge (1913), built by proprietor John Lewis and considered to be one of the finest hotels built in the Swiss style in the United States (11, 136–44).

A synthesis of the style of Norwegian villas and the Swiss chalet form inspired the El Tovar Hotel (1905), built at the Grand Canyon for the Fred Harvey Company by Charles Whittlesey. In 1909, a rustic depot of massive log construction with Craftsman period details was built nearby as the terminus of the Atchison, Topeka, and Santa Fe Railway and as a fitting gateway to the resort area that was taking form on the South Rim (10–11).

Mary Elizabeth Jane Colter, the architect and interior designer for the Fred Harvey Company at Grand Canyon, forged her own unique expression of the Arts and Crafts movement. Her work was a synthesis of West Coast and midwestern influences and her study of the indigenous architecture of the Southwest. She was particularly inspired by the pueblo constructions, cliff dwellings, and temples found in the Mesa Verde ruins and living Hopi communities such as Oraibi, Arizona.

Colter was one of the foremost designers to seek harmonious solutions for blending built structures into sites on precipitous canyon rims. Although Colter's Lookout House at Grand Canyon (1914) and Charles Greene's James House at Carmel (1918) differ in scale, an interesting similarity exists between them in the architectural problem of siting a building along a steep cliff and in the solution of using masonry of native rock in a plastic and irregular way to achieve a harmony of site, setting, and structure. Colter continued to explore the relationship of site and setting, drawing inspiration from the indigenous architecture of Southwest cultures and likely Greene's masterful and expressive stonework at Carmel. Her work reached maturity in the Desert View Watchtower of 1932.

Colter's interest in the indigenous architecture of the Southwest led her to study pueblos such as those at Oraibi, Arizona, as models for her own work. Her interest in the distant past extended to the ruins of Mesa Verde and other prehistoric cliff dwellings and temples. Whereas Oraibi influenced her Hopi House, Mesa Verde's Temple to the Sun inspired her design for the Desert View Watchtower. She studied the ruins from aerial photographs and called her designs "recreations" that captured the idea and feeling of the prehistoric models but were built on a scale that served modern-day functions. Colter's work was a fusion of cultural influences of the Southwest which included Spanish colonial and territorial heritage as well as the traditions of contemporary and prehistoric Native Americans. The Spanish influence was visible in details such as the entry wall and bell arch at Hermit's Rest, a stopping point along the Fred Harvey Company's tour route of the South Rim. Pioneer spirit abounded in her arrangement of historic and new buildings in the cabin cluster at the Bright Angel

A Design Ethic for Natural Parks

3.5. Located at the top of Bright Angel Trail on Grand Canyon's South Rim, the Lookout was designed in 1914 by Mary Colter for the Fred Harvey Company. Influenced by the indigenous architecture of the Native Americans of the Southwest as well as the Arts and Crafts movement, Colter created an ingenious solution to harmonizing construction with nature. The random character of the masonry walls, the irregular lines of the rooftop, the outside terraces, and the curvilinear flow of a roughly textured parapet along the canyon walls would influence National Park Service designers for several generations. *(Photograph courtesy National Park Service Historic Photography Collection)*

Lodge complex. Skilled in architecture, landscape design, and decorative arts, Colter was the quintessential practitioner of the Arts and Crafts movement.[24]

   Colter's work — Hopi House (1913), Lookout House (1914), Phantom Ranch (1921), Hermit's Rest (1914), Desert View Watchtower (1932), and Bright Angel Lodge (1933–35) — would have substantial influence on the design of national and state park structures for more than two decades. The first national park landscape engineers, Charles Punchard and Daniel Hull, both met with Colter on several occasions. They studied the architectural precedent set at the Grand Canyon by El Tovar Hotel, Santa Fe Railway Depot (1909), and Colter's Lookout House and determined that the buildings established an architectural theme to be followed by the park service as well as the concessionaire in the park's future development. In his design for the first national park buildings at Grand Canyon, Hull followed Colter's treatment of stone and wood materials at Phantom Ranch on the canyon floor. Herbert Maier had special interest in Colter's ability to site buildings on the edge of natural canyons and to blend harmoniously masonry of native stone with the natural rock formations. A respect for Colter's work is suggested by his design for the observation station at Yavapai Point in Grand Canyon and the designs of structures such as the lodge at Palo Duro State Park in Texas, the refectory at Longhorn Caverns State Park in Texas, and the administration building at South Mountain Park in Phoenix, Arizona—all of which were constructed by the Civilian Conservation Corps under his direction in the 1930s. Maier's Grand Canyon Observation Station and the work of Colter would influence the design of Sinnott Memorial (1929) at Crater Lake, which was the first museum designed by the landscape architects of the National Park Service with funds appropriated by Congress. Colter's anthropological interest in the indigenous architecture of the southwestern Native Americans was shared by Mesa Verde's superintendent, Jesse Nusbaum, and his wife, Aileen, who designed the park's earliest National Park Service buildings in a style that complemented the Anasazi ruins and harmonized with the rugged topography of cliffs and mesas.

Gustav Stickley and the Craftsman

The greatest source of design and detail in the Arts and Crafts tradition was the writings of Gustav Stickley in his periodical, the *Craftsman,* and in his books, *Craftsman Homes* of 1909 and *More Craftsman Homes* of 1912, which were compilations of designs and essays drawn from the *Craftsman* and *Country Life in America.* Stickley frequently displayed the work of Greene and Greene and drew attention to the unity of site and setting displayed by the Edgar Camp House in the Sierra Madre. He showed many examples of homes that used rock as a building material and as a means of joining structures with the earth. Stickley brought together articles on landscape design, architecture, and interior design, many of which illustrated principles and practices that were compatible with the National Park Service's principles for preserving landscape and harmonizing development. The *Craftsman* would have an enduring influence on the park designers of the 1920s and 1930s and would serve as useful pattern books of details, interior and exterior, which could embellish the structures of national and state parks in the 1930s.

Stickley was in many ways a twentieth-century version of Downing in his promotion of diverse architectural styles and types and his insistence on unity of structure and setting. His books functioned much as Downing's *Architecture of Country Houses* had sixty years before. Stickley, however, recognized American influences such as California bungalows and the Prairie style. Moreover, he was the direct link between the Shingle style of Henry Hobson Richardson and twentieth-century bungalow design. Because of the Arts and Crafts movement and the preponderance of Shingle style design in park structures, Henry Hubbard proposed that the National Park Service adopt a Craftsman aesthetic in 1917. This interest in handcrafts would be refined and expanded during the next two decades in national park buildings and would be promoted in the design of state park structures built by the Civilian Conservation Corps and Works Progress Administration in the 1930s.

An article entitled "The Effective Use of Cobblestone as a Link between the House and the Landscape," which was published first in the *Craftsman* in November 1908 and a year later in *Craftsman Homes,* drew national attention to the use of cobblestones in West Coast architecture. Featuring several country homes in California including one by Greene and Greene, the article pointed out the interesting effects achieved by using cobblestones in chimneys, walls, walks, and foundations. The author noted that when big rough stones and cobbles are used with taste and discrimination, "they not only give greater interest to the construction but serve to connect the building very closely with the surrounding landscape." [25]

Such construction was particularly well suited for dwellings in rugged locations, the stone in its natural form being a harmonizing element that could closely connect landscape and building. Readers were told, "In the building of modern country homes there seems to be no end to the adaptability of cobblestones and boulders in connection with the sturdier kinds of building material, for, if rightly placed with regard to the structure and surroundings, they can be brought into harmony with nearly every style of architecture that has about it any semblance of ruggedness, especially if the surrounding country be hilly and uneven in contour and blessed—or cursed—with a plentiful crop of stones" (102).

Stickley attributed the popularity of cobblestone construction in California to the influence of Japanese gardening: "In these buildings the use of stone in this form is as inevitable in its fitness as the grouping of rocks in a Japanese garden." He praised the way the stonework brought "the entire building into the closest relationship with its environment." The rounded, worn character of the cobbles in western homes was attributed to their edges having "worn off during the ages when they have rolled about in the mountain torrents." Wedged "helter-skelter among the irregular, roughly laid bricks of the walls, pillars and chimneys," they differed from the conventional use of stone in a Japanese garden and the typical walks and flower beds of American homes. Such a dwelling was in harmony with its site and surroundings (104–6).

California designers explored the combination of bricks and cobbles and appreciated the picturesque qualities of moss- and lichen-covered boulders.

Stickley described the results: "The effect of this is singularly interesting both in color and form, for the warm purplish brown of the brick contrasts delightfully with the varying tones of the boulders covered with moss and lichens, and the soft natural grays and browns of the more or less primitive wood construction that is almost invariably used in connection with cobbles gives the general effect of a structure that has almost grown up out of the ground, so perfectly does it sink into the landscape around it" (104–6).

Cobblestone construction when applied to walls, piers, chimneys, and terraces harmonized well with rough shingle and timber construction as well as the native trees of a woodland setting. Stickley pointed out how successfully the mountain house was linked to the surrounding landscape and how striking the effect was of native materials against the lacy foliage created by the surrounding trees that had been undisturbed by the construction.

The use of boulders for foundations and chimneys had wide application in the design and construction of park structures. It was commonly used for the foundations of pioneer homes and appeared over and over again in Shingle-style dwellings and Adirondack cabins and lodges. Early on it had been used in the construction of Crater Lake Lodge in Oregon and Bear Mountain Inn in New York; it was adapted by Maier for the lower story of his museum at Yosemite and would appear in diverse variations in the construction of all types of park structures throughout the 1930s.

In his essay "Architectural Development of the Log Cabin in America," Stickley promoted the adaptation of log construction to contemporary housing and upheld the log cabin as a national prototype worthy of emulation: "And so today a house built of wood which has not been metamorphosed into board and shingle, but still bears the semblance of the tree, rouses in us the old instinctive feeling of kinship with the elemental world that is a natural heritage." In *More Craftsman Homes* (1912), Stickley introduced readers to his log house at Craftsman Farms in New Jersey and provided numerous interior and exterior views of an assortment of log homes and cottages that featured vertical and horizontal logwork, rustic stone fireplaces and chimneys, and broad, sloping porches. These would provide numerous models for the designers of national and state parks in years to come.[26]

The Bungalow Craze

The Arts and Crafts movement, particularly through the bungalow craze, forged an appreciation of architectural details influenced by the Shingle style, the Prairie style, the West Coast work of Greene and Greene, and the Adirondack style, as well as native or indigenous forms of architecture. Practitioners used native materials, seeking designs that harmoniously integrated site, structure, and setting. They followed nature, avoided artificial appearances, capitalized on scenic vistas, used picturesque details, and unified interior spaces with the out-of-doors through porches, terraces, and pergolas. Boundaries between inside and outside were softened by terraces, porches, pools, plantings, patios, and gardens. Although the Shingle style brought architects and landscape architects in collaboration with each other, it was only after the Columbian Exposition in 1893 that architects readily adopted landscape features and devices in their architectural designs and collaborated routinely with their landscape counterparts. This was especially true of the work of the Prairie style architects and Greene and Greene. This integration was well suited to the Arts and Crafts philosophy, endeavoring to establish a unity of home and hearth, community and nation, and dwelling and land.

The bungalow movement seized upon a variety of styles and types that were part of the naturalistic, rustic tradition. Of the many bungalow guides and pattern books, *Bungalows, Camps, and Mountain Houses* of 1915 by William Phillips Comstock and architect Clarence Eaton Schermerhorn provides perhaps the most diverse collection of prototypes adapted to outdoor living and natural settings. As an index of period design, the book illustrated prototypes that would be revived twenty years later in the design of buildings in state and national parks.

One example was the home of D. Knickerbacker Boyd at Robbins Point on Grindstone Island in the St. Lawrence River, New York, which emerged from a rocky shore on massive stone piers. The natural weathering of the shingles of the roof and walls, the rusticity of the porch railings, and the character of the porch posts fashioned from tree branches and trunks further added to the inconspicuous nature of the building. Comstock wrote that the outside would weather to a natural gray which, when combined with the natural effect of the porch and the rough stone, would blend the building into the landscape when viewed from the water.[27]

Under the category of camps, lodges, and log cabins, Comstock illustrated with architects' plans and photographs modest four-bedroom log cabins in the woods. Featured in most detail were Stonecliff on the coast of Maine by Albert Winslow Cobb; the William A. Read Camp in the Adirondacks; and Minnewawa on Blue Mountain Lake, New York, by Clarence Eaton Schermerhorn, who wrote the introduction to the book. John Calvin Stevens, preeminent architect of summer homes in the Shingle style, provided designs for a modest log house that had a two-story living room with a massive stone fireplace and a sleeping loft (108–9).

One prototypical West Coast bungalow was the Pitzer Bungalow (1910) in Pomona, California, by Robert H. Orr. It was distinctive for its rambling roof lines and projecting eaves supported on battered piers of cobblestone which rose to form arched openings. Cobblestone construction dominated the whole and characterized the flared walls of the foundation, porch walls, massive porch piers rising to form wide arches, and chimneys. The massive stones of the foundation were planted firmly in the ground and rose inward and upward with decreasing size to emphasize the relationship between the earth and the walls of natural stone. Its most innovative feature was an interior patio vaulted by an open lattice of beams forming a pergola and a framework for hanging protective canvas to keep out the midday sun. The walls surrounding the patio were made of cobblestone masonry, and a naturalistic assemblage of rocks sprang from the center of the patio.[28]

While national park designers Thomas Vint and Herbert Maier had firsthand knowledge of West Coast bungalows by Greene and Greene and others, other designers knew examples only through periodicals such as the *Western Architect* and publications by Stickley, Comstock and Schermerhorn, and others. The greatest manifestation of the bungalow craze was the unprecedented suburban and residential growth that occurred in California from 1900 to 1920. Bungalows lining suburban streets and arranged into bungalow courts provided a lucrative source of income for real estate developers and a slate for creative expression for architects and landscape architects inspired by Greene and Greene and others.

Many designers explored the characteristics promoted by the Arts and Crafts movement in this period. Splayed or flared cobblestone foundations and massive stone piers were characteristic of the Los Angeles work of Arthur S. Heineman. He incorporated these features in the Parsons House (1909) in Altadena, the Los Robles Court in Pasadena, and other works. These characteristics were an important unifying quality of Sylvanus Marston's St. Francis Court (1909) in Pasadena, believed to be the first bungalow court in America. Here rugged, battered rockwork appeared not only in the foundation walls of the court's eleven dwellings but also in the entry gate and enclosing stone walls.

The bungalows of Irving Gill, especially his Mission style bungalow courts, introduced a variation that abandoned the rustic stone construction and details in favor of smooth stuccoed surfaces inspired by the region's cultural heritage. His work influenced the construction of cabins in the Southwest, including the adobe Indian Lodge at Davis Mountains State Park in Texas, as park designers looked to cultural prototypes and pioneer and indigenous methods of construction. The work of Gill and Heineman may have inspired such massing of cabins interconnected with walks, parapets, stairways, terraces, and courtyards to conform to the natural topography and to appear as a single continuous building. Such clusters offered an ideal medium for blending influences of the Mission style and the indigenous architecture of Southwest pueblos.

The ideas of America's Arts and Crafts movement had widespread applications in the development of the bungalow for vacation and suburban living. Followers of the movement shared Downing's concern for the unity of structure and landform, advocated the use of native materials such as log and stone, re-

3.6. Gartz Court, constructed in 1910, is among the oldest bungalow courts in Pasadena, California. Attributed to architects Myron Hunt and Elmer Grey, the one-story cottages exhibit characteristic Craftsman styling, including low-pitched roofs with large overhangs and exposed eaves, prominent stone chimneys projecting through the roof plane, and generous covered porches. The use of native building materials, plantings, and stone-lined walkways further create a sense of harmony and integration between the structures and the site. *(Photograph by Richard J. Sicha, courtesy Pasadena Heritage)*

vived traditional and pioneering arts and crafts, and used naturalistic gardening. This movement carried forward the tenets of the Shingle style of the 1870s and 1880s which had been successfully used in buildings for public parks since the 1880s. The Arts and Crafts movement adapted English gardening practices to the grounds of the middle-class home, particularly Robinson's ideas for naturalizing the homesite with wild plants. It also assimilated Japanese building traditions that used rockwork and organic principles of design to integrate structure and site. Furthermore, it recognized diverse regional features of buildings and landscape which had emerged across the nation in efforts to unify buildings and sites, such as the Prairie style architecture of the Midwest, the open terraces and patios of the Southwest, and the log construction of the pioneers.

Landscape architect Thomas Vint and architect Herbert Maier, having studied at the University of California, Berkeley, and lived in California, were well acquainted with the works of these individuals and the profusion of variations on the bungalow theme that flourished in and around Los Angeles and the Bay Area. Vint himself worked for builders and architects of such homes during his high school and college years in Los Angeles and Pasadena, where the bungalow, inspired by the local work of Greene and Greene, would have its greatest flowering of expression. At age nineteen, he worked for A. S. Falconer, who was developing a portfolio of bungalow designs for a Los Angeles real estate development firm.

By the 1920s, when National Park Service landscape engineers were working out a program of landscape design for national parks, there existed a well-established philosophy for park design drawn from the practices and precedents in landscape architecture and architecture. Architectural forms and landscape treatments coalesced to provide ideas, examples, solutions, and a philosophy for the design of park structures. These trends merged most emphatically in the Arts and Crafts tradition spurred by California's development of the bungalow, the work of Greene and Greene, and the publications of Stickley and others. By 1919, when the National Park Service instituted its first program of landscape design, there existed a firmly rooted tradition of landscape gardening and rustic architecture and a philosophy for landscape protection and harmonization in the development of natural areas. There were established principles of composition, practices for informal and naturalistic designs, and an aesthetic appreciation and a horticultural knowledge of American wild plants, which would be explored in the work of national park designers in the next decade.

PART II

*A Policy and
Process for
National Park Design, 1916 to 1927*

Chapter 4

Scenery Preservation
and Landscape Engineering

*In the construction of roads, trails, buildings, and other improvements,
particular attention must be devoted always to the harmonizing of
these improvements with the landscape. This is a most important item
in our program of development and requires the employment of
trained engineers who either possess a knowledge of landscape
architecture or have a proper appreciation of the esthetic value of
park lands.*

National Park Service, Statement of Policy, 1918

W hen the National Park Service took charge of the parks and monuments in 1917, seventeen national parks and twenty-two national
monuments were being administered by the U.S. Department of
the Interior.[1] The parks covered an area of 9,772.76 square miles, the monuments
143.32 square miles. The service inherited the development of former administering bodies—the U.S. Army, the railroads and concessionaires, and, in the case
of Yosemite, the state of California. A varied assortment of roads, trails, patrol
cabins, and rudimentary ranger stations existed in most parks, but in general
visits to the parks were hampered by poor roads and lack of facilities. By far
the grandest of park architecture were the hotels that concessionaires, often sub-
sidiaries of the western railroads, had built at Yellowstone, Glacier, and Crater
Lake. Concessionaires, too, operated campgrounds and provided touring cars
to transport visitors to the scenic features of the park. In some parks, private
organizations had built lodges, such as the Parsons Memorial Lodge at Yosemite
built in 1915 by the Sierra Club.

In 1914, the secretary of the interior appointed Mark Daniels to the newly
created position of general superintendent of Yosemite National Park and landscape engineer for national parks. To Daniels was entrusted the job of readying

the national parks for the public. Although he could plan building groups with a common architectural theme on paper, there were little or no funds to carry out these plans. Daniels' efforts, however, established the concept of an architectural scheme whereby a type of architecture is determined "in light of a careful study of the best arrangement of the buildings and for picturesqueness."[2]

Mather's Vision

In 1915, Stephen T. Mather, an assistant to the secretary of the interior, assumed leadership of the national parks. He was aided by the superintendent of national parks, Robert B. Marshall, until December 31, 1916. In a pioneering report of 1916, *Progress in the Development of the National Parks,* Mather set forth his early impressions of the conditions and future needs of national parks. Mather's report was the first comprehensive look at the condition of national parks as a system, with common purpose and goals. To many, Mather's appointment was a hopeful sign that park matters would gain increasing attention and that the much needed improvements would receive congressional funding.

Accessibility was the foremost concern. Mather was particularly interested in bringing the public to the national parks. He felt that the federal government had an obligation to pursue a broad policy for the extension of road systems in the parks and to encourage travel by railroad and automobile. Mather put great effort into developing cooperative relationships with the railroads, some of which, like the Santa Fe and Great Northern, already had a strong presence in the parks, and with the automobile associations, or "good roads" associations, which were emerging across the nation as the automobile gained in popularity and Americans began to satisfy their urge to see the country. The parks were not isolated places but rather objectives in large regional and national networks of scenic highways.

Mather wished to open up spectacular areas of parks not previously penetrated by roads. At Mount Rainier, he called for opening up new sections of the park, particularly the northwest, from which Spray and Moraine Parks on the northern slopes of the mountain could be accessible. A road had been surveyed up the Carbon River valley which would provide access to this side of the mountain. He called for public roads in Yosemite and talked of building a road across the Continental Divide in Glacier National Park and expanding that park's western boundaries.

Gateways held particular importance. Mather urged the construction of gateways to mark the entrances to the parks as soon as possible. Gateways were to be simple, dignified, and in harmony with their environments; they were not, however, to be costly structures. The gateways were envisioned not only as

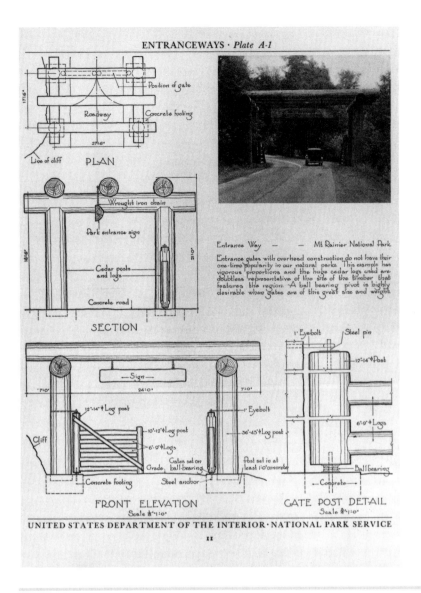

4.1. Built about 1910, the first gateway to Mount Rainier National Park was fashioned from mammoth logs of western red cedar having the same proportions and character as the trees of the surrounding forest. This style of entrance continued to be used for the park's other entrances through the 1930s. It was featured in *Park Structures and Facilities*, a portfolio published by the National Park Service in 1935. *(Reprinted Albert H. Good, ed.,* Park Structures and Facilities, *1935)*

physical barriers marking park boundaries but also as points of transition orienting the visitors to an environment where nature predominated and amenities were rendered inconspicuous through harmonious structures. Mather wrote: "It is with a thrill of pride in our great national playgrounds that the average visitor passes through these gates and beneath the Stars and Stripes waving over them." Most impressive, in Mather's opinion, were the gateways already constructed at Yellowstone's Gardiner Entrance, a great Roman arch fashioned from clinker-style stonemasonry, built by engineer Hiram M. Chittenden in 1903, and the Nisqually Entrance to Mount Rainier built about 1910, with posts made of massive peeled trunks of native western red cedar. No two archways differed as greatly as the Gardiner and Nisqually gates, each reflecting a different method of construction and feeling of the picturesque. The two sites — the grass-covered high plains of Montana and the deep ancient forests of Mount Rainier — boldly contrasted.[3]

The gateways introduced an architectural theme that harmonized with the natural setting of each location and could be carried over into the development of similar areas elsewhere in the park, giving a consistent identity to park structures. Administration buildings, which would give the government an identifiable presence in the park, were likewise needed throughout the park system.

Mather closely examined the concessionaires' facilities in each park. He praised the system of hotels, mountain chalets, and tepee camps built by the Glacier Park Hotel Company, and he exclaimed that proprietor John Lewis's hotel on Lake MacDonald in Glacier was "unique in sylvan architecture." At Glacier, he also praised the recently improved trail system and noted the attractive designs of shelter cabins along the trails (12).

Although most of the parks needed better provisions for water and sanitation, conditions and needs varied from park to park. At Giant Forest in Sequoia National Park, needs included the acquisition of additional stands of giant trees, the construction of hotel accommodations and an administration building, and a water system. Mesa Verde National Park needed a museum to display the many artifacts gathered from the park's prehistoric ruins. And Yosemite needed public roads.

National Park Design about 1915

A series of national park conferences brought together conservationists, park superintendents, and members of private organizations to discuss issues of park administration and development. These were held at Yellowstone in 1911, at Yosemite in 1912, at the University of California, Berkeley, and the Panama Pacific Exposition in San Francisco in 1915, and in Washington, D.C., in 1917. Topics included the construction of roads and trails, the role of concessionaires, fire fighting and forest protection, administrative policies, the development of campgrounds, and transportation issues.

At the third conference, held in 1915, Mark Daniels, the first landscape engineer hired by the Department of the Interior to consult on the development of national parks, outlined some of the Department of the Interior's concerns for national parks. He called for a three-tiered system of accommodations which provided hotels or mountain chalets for overnight lodging, permanent camps where visitors would sleep in tents and take meals in a dining room, and camps where visitors would sleep in tents and cook their own food and where groceries could be purchased at a camp store. He defined the park village as a place where, like Yosemite Valley, five or six thousand people could gather at one time for supplies and lodging. In addition to the roads, lodge, tent sites, dining hall, camp store, and gas station, such a village required utilities in the form of a sanitary system, water supply, a telephone system, and electricity. Park villages, in this way, were comparable to municipalities elsewhere and required careful planning. Daniels planned a village for Yosemite and began the plans for villages at Crater Lake, Mount Rainier, Glacier, and Sequoia. The plans for Yosemite included a study of the architectural character of every building to be constructed over a ten-year period. Locations for buildings were all carefully selected and the type of architecture determined to provide the best arrangement and to be picturesque. Although securing the money to carry out such plans was difficult, Daniels hoped that eventually they would be executed.[4]

Most of the improvements funded in the parks by the United States government until this time had consisted of roads and trails. The proceedings of the 1915 conference provide an idea of the principles and practices that guided this construction. It is clear that at the time the service was being organized a well-rooted philosophy existed which called for development, whatever its function, to be suited to its particular site and to the natural character of the surroundings.

T. Warren Allen, a representative of the Bureau of Public Roads, spoke from his experience in building roads in the national forests. Allen was already involved in making road surveys in Glacier, Sequoia, and Yosemite. Although he had not surveyed roads in Mount Rainier, he recommended a series of radial roads linked with Washington state highways; these would eventually be connected by a rim road.

> The maximum of usefulness and benefit requires preservation and reproduction, which may be successful only if it is possible to reach all points readily. Roads to subserve commercial interests may be so built as to harmonize with the natural features and, without undue extension or circumlocution, make accessible the features of natural beauty. The road as such should be inconspicuous. The cost need usually be no more to construct a road which shall be an harmonious feature of the landscape, though the preliminary study may cost a little more. (26)

Allen outlined the process of building roads in scenic areas. The road should connect features of interest and visitor facilities, as well as link the park with outside routes. The road was first laid out on a topographical map and then examined in the field to ensure that the route was feasible and to make any changes to enhance the view from the road or to take in a waterfall, rock out-cropping, or other scenic feature. The road was staked out in such a way that markers were visible from distant points and then studied from several view-points, including nearby trees, and altered to bring out the most attractive view. Barren areas were enhanced by plantings or by the creation of a small lake or pond. The final survey and preparation of plans and estimated costs followed in a way similar to the construction of country highways. Center-line stakes were placed at hundred-foot intervals, called stations, and cross sections were taken at each station to determine the amount of material to be moved. As each plan was prepared, it was closely examined in the field to "see how it [fit] the ground." In the field, areas requiring cuts and fill to attain a desirable road surface and gradient as well as those requiring culverts and ditches for proper drainage were noted. The final plans were drawn on large sheets of tracing paper, with the road divided into sections, each measuring six to eight miles in length. The plans, which noted all the work to be done, were accompanied by detailed specifica-tions that gave contractors who were bidding on the project instructions on how the work was to be carried out (18, 22–29).

Allen called for a main system of roads of "very light grades" in each park. He praised the road being constructed along the old Flathead River Road in Glacier, which followed easy grades not exceeding 5 percent and passed through pleasant, heavily wooded sections and alongside the creek, crossing it at several points. Allen envisioned park roads as an aesthetic achievement, foreshadow-ing the roads program that would evolve more than a decade later: "I, as a road builder, have dreamed of road development in the various parks, and have dreamed of seeing such roads, lined and banked with flowers which grow wild in the meadows of the parks and upon the mountain sides, winding unassum-ingly along the brook, beneath the waterfall and skirting timidly the majestic mountain" (29, 32).

The construction of bridges was integral to the building of park roads and presented problems in both engineering and aesthetics. Although by 1915 vari-ous methods of construction were being used in the national parks, most park bridges were made from timber cut on site and assembled unhewn. Depend-ing on the diameter and strength of the logs, such bridges could be built to accommodate vehicles as well as pedestrians. At Yosemite, where bridges were fashioned from timber cut nearby and served park visitors as similar ones had pioneers to the area, yellow pine, tamarack, and incense cedar were commonly used. Although log bridges were sturdy, they were subject to decay and had a relatively brief life span (61).

The issue of what types of bridges were most appropriate in the natural setting of a park was discussed at great length. While many applauded achievements such as the Chittenden Bridge, a concrete Melan arch bridge in Yellowstone, others felt that only natural materials of stone and timber should be used. Truss bridges up to 87½ feet long were being constructed in Yosemite. Builders were working on new designs that reduced the distance between the floor and the top chord "so a person could walk over the bridge and get a good view of the scenery without looking through the trusses." Arch construction was preferred because it offered the advantage of raising the elevation of the center point of the bridge and avoiding the interference and vertical dimensions of a trussed superstructure. David Sherfy, Yosemite's resident engineer and one of the national parks' most experienced bridge builders, said he envisioned a day when all park bridges could be made of arch construction and concrete or stone: "We are called upon to build different kinds of bridges, and the condition in each locality must determine the kind or character. Where you have a locality in which you can not use an arch bridge for some reason or another, why, I should say, build a girder bridge or a reinforced concrete bridge" (61, 64–65, 67, 68).

On the construction of trails, one of the most experienced trail builders in the national parks, Gabriel Sovulewski of Yosemite, told the conference that those designing trails needed to be sympathetic to the meaning and intention behind a park's creation. Reflecting the nineteenth-century romanticism of Downing, he said that "diversion from a straight path to points of interest, regardless of expense," was important and necessary.

> I believe it is very important that every feature of natural beauty should be taken into consideration and diversion made to bring such features to the eye of the traveler. It will not be necessary to divert from the course laid out, but it is important that trails be laid out along beautiful streams, through different species of timber and interesting undergrowth, alongside and through rich green meadows and dashing brooks abounding in trout, and not omitting a single interesting feature that will attract the attention of the traveling public in order that the trail taken with these features included will be so delightful that the traveler will forget his fatigue in a review of the panorama unfolding before him at each turn. The trail along brooks and meadows will lead the traveler to many other beautiful views and points of interest, and finally he should be led to a picturesque spot where he can rest and establish his camp for as long a time as he desires. (51–52)

Exploration was the first step in building trails. This required strength, determination, a natural sense of direction, love of work, love of nature, and an ability to sit in the saddle or travel by foot for twelve or fourteen hours if necessary. The location of the trail, once determined on the ground, was marked by leaning limbs against trees or making stone piles that could later be erased.

Trail building required a crew of workers headed by a foreman experienced in woodcraft and knowledgeable about sharpening drills and tools and using explosives. Under favorable circumstances, trails were to ascend long steep hills at a grade between 15 percent and 30 percent. Although usually determined by the importance of the trail, a width of four feet was generally recommended. Trail construction required both cutting into the slope by "benching" and laying and backfilling dry rubble walls on the downhill slope to support the trail. Overhanging limbs and undergrowth beside the trail were to be cut back. Unlike the grade of a railroad, where evenness was desired, the grade of a trail was varied to allow for better drainage and to give the traveler some relief from a continuous uphill climb. Ditches and other forms of drainage such as water breaks made from logs or preferably flat split rocks embedded in the ground were to be included. Culverts and drains were constructed beneath the trail to allow streams to flow in an uninterrupted course downhill (53).

Although the techniques for trail building were well established in national parks and forests by 1915, the condition of trails varied greatly from park to park. Improvements, especially regarding the maximum grade, would be made over the next fifteen years by the National Park Service's civil engineers, and in 1934 the first published standards for trail construction were issued. The civil engineers continually sought new solutions for ascending steep grades, traversing high peaks, and circumventing or crossing deep gorges. By the late 1920s, park engineers who continued to supervise the building of trails met these challenges with suspension bridges, tunnels, high-powered drills, climbing equipment, teams of horses, and daring workmen.

The fourth annual conference, held in January 1917, was a momentous occasion. It brought together individuals interested in the recreational, artistic, inspirational, economic, and other aspects of national parks, including officials of the Department of the Interior, members of Congress, representatives of cooperating clubs and associations such as the American Civic Association and General Federation of Women's Clubs, businessmen, educators, and specialists in forestry, natural science, landscape architecture, and wildlife conservation. It was hoped that the conference would result in a body of expert advice that would help the soon-to-be-organized National Park Service formulate policies for the future of the national parks.[5]

The enabling legislation for the National Park Service in August 1916 had spelled out its twofold purpose of preserving the integrity of the parks while making them accessible. The foremost issue, therefore, was how to develop the parks to attract and accommodate people of all economic circumstances. Among the many topics discussed was the physical development of the parks. In his introductory speech, Enos Mills recalled Robert B. Marshall's advice that the parks be developed for all people and that the buildings be attractive and fit harmoniously into the surroundings. Mills believed that making the parks ready for the public was all the publicity and promotion needed to draw tourists. Being ready meant providing transportation and amenities. Expanding on Mill's introduction, William Welch, the chief engineer for the Palisades Interstate Park, spoke on the "making of a recreational park," while others spoke on recreational activities such as hiking, winter sports, and fishing (39).

A National Park Service

As soon as the service was organized, Director Mather took up the cause of informing the public about the scientific, scenic, and historic values of the parks. As part of his "vigorous educational campaign," the service disseminated thousands of copies of the *National Parks Portfolio,* a pamphlet on parks called *Glimpses of National Parks,* and guide maps to parks. Local chambers of commerce, tourist bureaus, and civic associations set up free auto camps to encourage travelers to visit the national parks.

Automobile travel in national parks greatly increased during the 1917 season, with 22,286 entrance licenses issued in 1917, compared with 455 in 1914, 12,609 in 1915, and 15,536 in 1916. Visitation was heavier than ever before; 487,368 visitors came in 1917, greatly exceeding the 240,193 who had visited parks in 1914, 335,299 in 1915, and 358,006 in 1916. The service was concerned not only with travel within the parks but also with park-to-park travel and highways leading into national parks. Mather sought the cooperation of automobile clubs, highway associations, and other organizations in providing signs and the help of state highway commissions in improving the roads leading to parks.[6]

Mather envisioned a park-to-park highway from Colorado to Washington State, linked to parks in Arizona and California. The National Park-to-Park Highway Association had organized in Yellowstone in 1916 to designate and promote a road system that would link the western parks. The National Park-to-Park Highway Association, located in Spokane, Washington, had designated and posted a route with signs connecting Yellowstone and Glacier with Mount Rainier and Crater Lake parks by way of the Columbia River Highway. Free automobile camps opened in each park. Camps were located in specially cleared areas provided with water, at convenient distances from supplies of fuel. Toilet facilities were provided and cooking grates installed. Shelters for cars were even constructed at Yellowstone (801).

Among the first year's accomplishments at Yellowstone were the opening of a southern gateway at Jackson Hole, Wyoming, the construction of more than one hundred miles of trails and fire roads, and a reorganization of the concessionaires. These improvements were part of a plan to make Yellowstone an important all-summer resort where visitors could stay for several weeks at a time. Arrangements were also made with the U.S. Bureau of Fisheries to stock lakes and streams.

At Yosemite, workers made improvements to the overall road system, including the El Portal Road. The service took over the Wawona toll road and eliminated charges other than the regular park entrance fee. A new hydroelectric power plant began to furnish power for lighting hotels, camps, roads, and footpaths and for heating the buildings in Yosemite Valley. Land along the Big Oak Flat Road was acquired, through exchanges with private owners, to ensure that "splendid forest growths" would be "forever safeguarded" (27).

New concessionaires' facilities were praised for their progress in making parks accessible to various classes of visitors. Paradise Inn on the slopes of Mount Rainier and the Glacier Point Hotel on the rim of Yosemite Valley both opened. Yosemite's new hotel was highly acclaimed; Mather wrote, "It is beautifully located on the very rim of the gorge where a magnificent view may be obtained of all of the great canyons through which the Merced and its tributaries flow. Vernal and Nevada Falls are plainly visible and the panorama of the peaks of the Sierra that may be had from the hotel beggars description. The hotel itself is very attractive from every point of view" (841).

At Sequoia, improvements were made to the roads, trails, and campgrounds, and the water system was extended. In the Giant Forest, private holdings were acquired, and large areas were prepared for camping. A new stairway was built to the summit of Moro Rock, from which the entire park and surrounding mountains could be viewed. The sturdy 364-foot stairway of wood timbers, planks, and railings was a common type of trail improvement built in the early twentieth century to provide safe access to precipitous and spectacular viewpoints, often across steep and rugged ground. These structures consisted of basic cut timbers joined at right angles to form ramps and stairways and led visitors upward in stages to a viewing platform on the summit. Stylistic pretension and the rustic latticework inspired by Downing and the Adirondack style were absent from these functional structures. Mather described the achievement at Moro Rock:

> This stairway was built to afford the best possible opportunity to view the magnificent scenery of the park region and the mountains beyond. Moro Rock, 6,719 feet in altitude, is a monolith of enormous yet graceful proportions. Its summit is nearly 4,000 feet above the floor of the valley of the Middle Fork of the Kaweah below, and the huge granite mass stands apart from the canyon wall in a manner that affords one a marvelous panoramic view. The new steps to the summit were built carefully and are perfectly safe. As the top of the rock is flat, and there is no opportunity to gaze down perpendicularly, it may be enjoyed by most people without fear of dizziness. (27, 88, 852)

4.2. Built and photographed in 1917, the stairway at Moro Rock, Sequoia National Park, illustrates what was then the "state-of-the-art" construction for scenic overlooks. Cut lumber was arranged in rectilinear fashion to form long stairways, bridges, handrails, and platforms. For almost fifteen years, this 364-foot stairway made it possible for thousands of visitors to ascend the monolithic dome to its peak at 6,719 feet and experience one of the most spectacular views of the High Sierras. It was replaced by a less obvious and angular, naturalistic trail of stone and concrete in 1931. *(Photograph courtesy National Park Service Historic Photography Collection)*

To Mather the stairway was magnificent, a fine achievement for service engineers and a demonstration of the fledgling agency's commitment to making park scenery accessible to the general public and not just seasoned mountaineers. Mather proclaimed, "The view from the top of the rock is indescribably wonderful, the panorama of the peaks of the Great Western Divide being the most thrilling scene to greet one as he mounts the summit of Moro" (852).

Statement of Policy, 1918

The need to forge a policy for developing and managing the national parks was great. On May 13, 1918, Secretary of the Interior Franklin Lane approved a statement of policy to guide the administration of the National Park Service. This document set forth broad principles and objectives that would guide the service in its stewardship of the parks and its efforts to make parks accessible and enjoyable to the public. First of all, criteria set for new parks, called park projects, required areas to possess "scenery of supreme and distinctive quality or some natural feature so extraordinary or unique as to be of national interest and importance."[7]

The statement set forth three fundamental principles, echoing the language of the 1916 enabling legislation: "First, that the national parks must be maintained in absolutely unimpaired form for the use of future generations as well as those of our own time; second, that they are set apart for the use, observation, health, and pleasure of the people; and third, that the national interest must dictate all decisions affecting public or private enterprise in the parks" (813–14).

This policy made the public interest preeminent in all national park matters, present and future, raising several practical implications and limitations. Summer homes were prohibited, as were commercial uses not specifically authorized by law or incidental to accommodating and entertaining the public. Sheep grazing was prohibited in all parks. Other forms of grazing were prohibited in Yellowstone National Park but allowed in other parks in isolated areas not frequented by visitors and where it was unlikely to injure natural features. The cutting of timber was allowed only where it was needed to construct buildings or other improvements and where it could be removed without damaging the forests or disfiguring the landscape. Cutting was also allowed to thin forests or clear vistas to improve scenic features or to eliminate insect infestations or diseases common to forests and shrubs (1074–75).

All parks were to be open to automobiles, motorcycles, and other vehicles of all kinds and were to provide a variety of facilities for the comfort of tourists. Outdoor sports were to be allowed and aided as far as possible, except hunting and other activities that would injure park wildlife. Especially favored were mountain climbing, horseback riding, walking, motoring, swimming, boating, and fishing. Winter sports were to be developed in parks that were accessible throughout the year. Parks were to provide opportunities for classes in science and establish museums containing exhibits on park flora and fauna (814, 1075).

Accommodations were to serve various classes of visitors and included low-priced camps as well as comfortable and even luxurious hotels operated by the concessionaires. As funds allowed, the government was to create and maintain a system of free campsites by clearing areas and equipping them with water and sanitation facilities.

Above all, the 1918 statement of policy established the mechanism for a process of park design and planning based on the principles of landscape preservation and harmonization. Responsibility for carrying out such a process was placed under the aegis of a landscape engineer.

> In the construction of roads, trails, buildings, and other improvements, particular attention must be devoted always to the harmonizing of these improvements with the landscape. This is a most important item in our program of development and requires the employment of trained engineers who either possess a knowledge of landscape architecture or have a proper appreciation of the esthetic value of park lands. All improvements will be carried out in accordance with a preconceived plan developed with special reference to the preservation of the landscape, and comprehensive plans for future development of the national parks on an adequate scale will be prepared as funds are available for this purpose. (1075)

Concern for landscape preservation and the harmonization of all built features would guide park development and management for years to come. Through these principles, the 1918 statement aligned park development and natural conservation, thus upholding the dual mission of the National Park Service. Mather's thinking was clearly influenced by the landscape architecture profession's position on the stewardship of natural areas and the growing movement for parks across the nation. Common practices used in country or rustic areas of city parks were immediately adopted. Construction was to disturb the ground as little as possible. Improvements were to be of native materials and rustic in character. Obtrusive development was to be avoided altogether or placed in inconspicuous locations and screened from public view.

Despite the detailed writings of Henry Hubbard and Frank Waugh and the naturalistic intent of numerous parks and parkways that had sprung up in and around American cities, nowhere had the landscape profession dealt with natural character on such a large scale as in the national parks of the West. Never before had there been the need or the opportunity for the federal government to institutionalize a policy for landscape preservation and harmonious design. While practitioners such as the Olmsted firm could design a park and make recommendations for its future, efforts to maintain naturalistic parks as they were designed were often impeded by political power and ambition. To the landscape profession and to the future landscape engineers of the National Park Service, the 1918 statement of policy posed a great challenge and a momentous opportunity to advance the principles and practices of naturalistic landscape gardening.

In the fifteen years following the 1918 declaration of policy and preceding the massive expansion of park development that began in 1933, National Park Service landscape architects and engineers forged a cohesive style of naturalistic park design. This style would be rooted in the fundamental twofold philosophy, first, that landscape be preserved, and second, that all construction harmonize with nature. It evolved as designers encountered landscape problems and arrived at practical and aesthetic solutions. This style—translated into a set of principles and practices—would have lasting influence on the character of national, state, and metropolitan parks and public highways across the nation.

The Role of the Landscape Engineer: Charles P. Punchard

All improvements in the national parks—roads, trails, and buildings—were to be carefully harmonized with the landscape. Accomplishing this, the 1918 policy recognized, required the expertise of "engineers who possessed a knowledge of landscape architecture or appreciated the esthetic value of park lands." Director Mather appointed Charles P. Punchard Jr. to fill the role of the National Park Service's first landscape engineer, as park designers were called at the time. Punchard had studied landscape design at Harvard University and been a partner in the firm of Evans and Punchard. At the time of his appointment, he was working for the Office of Public Buildings and Grounds in Washington, D.C., where he was in charge of the landscape development of all the public parks and reservations in the city.

Punchard's first task, beginning in July 1918, was to make a comprehensive study of the existing conditions and landscape problems of each park. During his first year, he visited seven national parks and four monuments, spending two and a half months in Yellowstone and seven months in Yosemite. He studied the various types of scenery, analyzing in detail landscape problems that required immediate solution and identifying others that needed treatment in the future.[8]

By the end of 1919, Mather reported that Punchard had already made his office one of the "most important influences for the betterment of the national parks." Punchard forged a role that combined stewardship for the park with practical day-to-day management of park facilities. Punchard gave special attention to the entrances to parks, the location and design of park buildings, the layout of campgrounds, and the physical appearance of lakes and roadsides. Punchard also initiated a process of design which involved park managers, engineers, and service officials. He consulted closely with park superintendents and provided advice in the form of consultations, sketches, working drawings, and detailed instructions for improvements. He assisted the public operators, or concessionaires, in designing and improving the physical appearance of their facilities (1175).

In *Landscape Architecture,* the profession's journal, Punchard described his work as one of "control," that is, maintaining a balance between the preservation of natural qualities and purely scenic areas and improvements for the comfort and the accommodation of visitors. Punchard summarized his manifold role:

> The problems of the Landscape Engineer of the National Park Service are many and embrace every detail which has to do with the appearance of the parks. He works in an advisory capacity to the superintendents and is responsible directly to the Director of the Service. He is a small fine arts commission in himself, for all plans of the concessioners must be submitted to him for approval as to architecture and location before they can be constructed, and he is responsible for the design of all structures of the Service, the location of roads and other structures on the ground which will influence the appearance of the parks, ranger cabins, rest houses, checking stations, gateway structures, employees' cottages, comfort stations, forest improvement and vista thinning, the preservation of the timber along the park roads, the design of villages where the popularity of the parks has made it necessary to provide certain commercial institutions for the comfort of the tourist and the camper, the design and location of the automobile camps, and so on through the many ramifications of all these problems.[9]

Maintaining a balance between the preservation of nature and the development of facilities was a twofold challenge. Punchard believed a balance could be achieved over time through careful planning. The secret of successful development lay in following an organized plan as closely as possible and accommodating changing conditions as they were presented. The result of such an approach would be "harmonious, attractive, well organized, and at the same time practicable and serviceable" and would ensure the preservation of the "spirit" of the parks and the "object for which they were created."[10]

Punchard played a key role in translating the landscape policy of the National Park Service into practices that would influence the character and management of the parks. Experienced and well versed in his field, he closely studied each park and skillfully put into action plans that immediately improved its physical character. His reports and designs, furthermore, laid a solid ground, philosophically and functionally, for future landscape work.

Punchard's work followed the state-of-the-art principles for developing natural areas which had evolved out of the American landscape gardening tradition and were set forth in Henry Hubbard and Theodora Kimball's *Introduction to the Study of Landscape Design.* Improvements were many, each requiring a specific treatment stemming from the professional landscape practice of the day. These approaches were in keeping with Mather's vision for the preservation and restoration of the native landscape and the broad progressive thought of an era that advocated conservation of natural reservations and highly acclaimed the nation's diverse native characteristics.

The length of Punchard's service was brief—less than two and a half years. Punchard, who suffered from tuberculosis, died in November 1920. As the National Park Service's first landscape designer, he provided a philosophical framework for future park development and management. His many hours spent pressing the landscape architect's viewpoint would influence the decisions made by park superintendents, concessionaires, and his assistant, Daniel Hull, as well as park service directors Stephen Mather and Horace Albright, for years to come.

Landscape Preservation

Foremost among Punchard's responsibilities was protecting the landscape of the national parks. Mather commented in 1922, "It is in the need for protecting and safeguarding this superb natural scenery, which has been preserved for the world to see, that we have the justification of the landscape division as an integral part of the service."[11]

Preservation meant maintaining existing natural conditions and keeping views free of artificial intrusions. It also meant restoring areas where natural conditions had been lost owing to previous uses or activities. Debris and deteriorated buildings could be removed and the sites of mining or lumber camps or old homesteads cleared. Scenery preservation was the corollary of the governing rule that the national parks be maintained in absolutely unimpaired form for the use of future generations. Mather explained, "In all of our landscape work the guiding principle followed is that the natural conditions of the park must be disturbed as little as possible consistent with the necessary development in the public interest, and where such conditions have been unnecessarily or carelessly or wrongfully changed in the past they must be restored where this can be done, and in any case made less objectionable if restoration to a state of nature is impossible."[12]

Punchard was a troubleshooter. He attacked practices that disturbed the natural appearances of the parks, especially when viewed from park roads, trails, or areas frequented by visitors. He worked with park superintendents and concessionaires to remove or screen unsightly conditions from view. One common problem was the scarring left at borrow pits after fill was gathered for road construction. In his first annual report, Punchard merely suggested that these be located in remote places and that areas burned or cut over for firewood be reforested. A year later, he adamantly called upon superintendents to close old borrow pits alongside the roads and open new ones at points screened from park roads. The removal of these "scars" was the first step toward erasing the evidence that construction had ever taken place.[13]

Punchard drew attention to diverse landscape problems, both major and minor, and provided practical solutions for eliminating unsightly conditions, called cleanup. His solutions set precedents for plans and designs that prevented the future occurrence of unsightly conditions and fostered harmonization. By controlling the numerous details that affected the visual appearance of a scenic feature, roadway, or developed area, the landscape designer could work toward maintaining the overall scenic character of the park. Cleanup entailed the removal of rubbish, dilapidated vacant structures, and even dead or dying timber alongside roads, in lakes, or at scenic features. One of his first projects of this type was the removal of dead wood and debris from the terraces at the Mammoth Hot Springs formation.[14]

In his efforts to correct existing problems, Punchard established a standard for the visual appearance of developed areas of the park. This standard was based upon the naturalistic principles of nineteenth-century landscape gardening, whereby vistas were carefully framed, plantings were used to screen unsightly views, and roadways were laid out for the most scenic effect. It also made practical use of Downing's suggestions for making secondary or service entrances and areas inconspicuous or separate from the main or public entrances. Where it was not possible to plant trees or use natural masses of trees and shrubbery for screening, fences were constructed around service yards. He worked closely with park superintendents and concessionaires to screen unsightly views in developed areas and to improve the overall scenery of campgrounds, roadways, and developed areas. In response to his suggestions, the concessionaire of the Mammoth Camp at Yellowstone redesigned the approach and grounds of the main building. On the east side, the porte-cochère and driveway were eliminated, an ornamental fence was built to enclose the service area, and a lawn was planted so that the "superb" scenic view could be enjoyed without distraction; a new driveway was built at the opposite end of the building (1091).

His solutions to several problems at Sequoia indicate Punchard's concern for the treatment of natural features of great significance. Concerned with the loss of trees in the Giant Forest, Punchard urged a program of reforestation whereby new trees were planted as older ones fell across roadways. The discovery of Crystal Cave at Sequoia presented Punchard with the problem of how to open an underground cave to the public while preserving its natural character. Visitor access demanded an approach trail, an entrance, and interior pathways and lighting. Punchard's suggestions were aimed at creating the most natural development possible, "making it appear to the visitor that he has come upon the cave in the course of a walk along a trail." The entrance and approach were to remain as natural as possible, and a system of indirect lighting was recommended for the cave's interior to create "very beautiful effects." Here he established the precedent of leaving the entrance in its natural condition and building trails that led into and through the cave. The precedent established at Crystal Cave was followed in the later development of larger caverns such as Carlsbad and Mammoth. The natural arch of cave openings was considered such a desirable and picturesque element that it was imitated in the portals of tunnels along park roads and trails (1178).

Punchard's work in Yosemite laid a strong philosophical and practical basis for vegetation management based on scenic values. Punchard spent the winter of 1919 in Yosemite, where he closely studied the landscape from a historical perspective, much as Charles Eliot had studied the Massachusetts reservations. Visualizing the scenic potential of Mirror Lake in Yosemite Valley, Punchard recommended the removal of dead and dying timber and other sediments. He defended his position, saying,

> The lake seems to be such a well-known and well-patronized object of interest in the valley it would hardly be consistent to allow the present condition to continue until the lake had become entirely filled with sediment. It seems that some steps should be taken for the correction of this condition, even though it [may] cover a period of two or three years. The drive to the lake is attractive, the setting is interesting and beautiful, and it is the only body of still water on the valley floor. With the completion of the new road to Mirror Lake its popularity will increase to such an extent that unless something is done the result will be very disappointing. (1176)

Under Punchard's direction, submerged trees were likewise removed from Lake Eleanor, which had been dammed as part of the San Francisco power and water project in Yosemite. He justified this work on grounds that the visual appearance would be improved and that any pollution and danger to fish caused by the decaying timber would be eliminated. Punchard, particularly bothered by the results of artificial projects to dam natural valleys, wrote, "There is nothing more desolate in appearance than trees and underbrush, brown and dead, standing in a body of water; and when the water is withdrawn and they stand on the muddy, barren lake bottom and higher shore lines, this appearance of desolation is augmented to the highest degree."[15]

Concerned about the encroachment of trees and shrubs upon the splendid meadows of Yosemite Valley, Punchard closely studied the natural processes and cultural influences that affected the meadows. He found that during the period of Native American occupation there had been no forests in the valley and only scattered large trees had existed; the present growth had occurred after settlement and under state control. Punchard made several trips by trail to remote areas of the park to study undisturbed mountain meadows and to gain information about the type and nature of vegetation that originally existed in the park. Recommending that trees and shrubs in Yosemite Valley's meadows be thinned and cleared, Punchard argued that such measures were necessary for two reasons, "first, to preserve the health of the larger trees and as a protection against serious fires, and second, . . . to open up and develop very interesting open spaces and vistas on the valley floor." The intention was not to reclaim the meadow floor by entirely reproducing the conditions that existed at the time of the Indians but rather to carry out the work to "make the woodlands safer from the standpoint of fires and also produce a pleasing landscape effect."[16]

Punchard's improvements to enhance the beauty of Yosemite Valley included abandoning the portion of the valley road crossing the meadow and planting the grounds around the new power plant to give it a setting that would "enhance its value as a structure." Punchard praised the superintendent's planting of vines around the base of the concrete walls of the power plant, saying, "When these establish themselves and begin to cover the walls they will soften and break up the barren surfaces, which at the present time are uninteresting." Lawns were to be planted around the residences of park employees along "Army Row" as a first step toward beautifying the area as a village street; staff were encouraged to plant shrubs and flowers around the foundations of park buildings. Punchard designed several new residences in the area proposed for the site of the new village. He recommended that a footbridge be built across the Merced River to connect with paths throughout the valley. He suggested clearing and grading the cemetery "to achieve a more pleasing appearance." He reviewed plans for the new Yosemite Falls Camp, making sure that the development was not visible from trails and the rim of the valley walls. Punchard also worked closely with California's state architect for a fish hatchery that would be attractive and a credit to the state and the park service alike (1176–77).

By successfully drawing attention to the changing character and inherent beauty of the valley's native vegetation, Punchard encouraged a sense of stewardship among park staff and concessionaires for the valley's scenery and native vegetation. In 1920, the Curry Camping Company provided the labor to remove trees that were blocking the vista of the valley and cutting off views of Half Dome and Clouds Rest from the popular stopping points along Black Spring Road locally known as the "Gates of the Valley" and "Bridal Veil Vista." Recognizing the preeminent value of the meadows for their natural beauty rather than as a source of hay and fearing the loss of plants such as the mariposa lily, Yosemite's park superintendent called for an end to the mowing of Sentinel Meadow and other meadows in the valley. In 1921, the Yosemite National Park Company employed a gardener to care for its grounds and to plant native trees and shrubs to screen foundations and other objectionable views, generally improving the appearance of the company's hotels and camps. This action set the stage for the landscape and educational programs of the 1920s and 1930s which would focus on the meadow wildflowers. Punchard's pioneering concerns for the landscape character of the valley were revived in the late 1920s as the park emerged as a laboratory for natural history and landscape naturalization.[17]

Landscape engineers were concerned with the location and appearance of park roads. Ever present were the general problems of opening vistas; clearing fallen timber and brush from roadsides and scenic areas; and locating roads, trails, bridges, and other structures. As new roads and trails were funded, the landscape engineer helped locate them in relation to scenic views and natural features. Mather saw opening new roads or trails and improving existing ones as "exposing delightful landscape heretofore unknown to the public." These were essential in the development of park scenery from a landscape standpoint.[18]

Vistas dominated the landscape architect's concern for scenery preservation, and capturing scenic vistas was one of the primary forces that drove the landscape engineer's recommendations for locating roads and trails. This concern was secondary only to making sure that popular vistas remained unimpaired and free from intrusion. The clearing of timber to improve or expose vistas was an important activity and occupied some of Punchard's time in Yellowstone in 1919. Punchard directed the clearing of timber along the Tower Falls–Mammoth Hot Springs Road to open up a view of Wraith Fall and on the Upper-Basin-Thumb Road to give visitors a better view of Duck Lake, which was considered "a perfect gem in a setting of dense forests." Albright and Mather both recognized the value of this work for park development. The concern for vistas would by the late 1920s result in specific practices for developing scenic viewpoints.[19]

The locations of facilities, whether roads, trails, or buildings, were based either on the desire to select and develop viewpoints that revealed scenic vistas to their best advantage and maximized the viewer's landscape experience or on the desire to protect scenic vistas from any form of artificial obtrusion or interference. In the early years of the National Park Service, the desire to develop vistas and make them accessible to the public was particularly strong. Parks therefore provided access by automobile wherever practical and allowed park concessionaires to develop accommodations at many of the most scenic locations, such as Glacier Point at Yosemite. As park visitation increased and the wear and tear of heavy visitation became more and more evident in places like Yosemite Valley, the Grand Canyon of the Yellowstone, and Sequoia's Giant Forest, the balance between providing access and protecting scenic values shifted, and the character and location of developed areas changed.

In 1919, Mather reported excellent results from the thinning of trees to reveal vistas in certain parks. He saw this as an important part of the landscape engineer's work, related to preserving stands of trees along highways crossing private holdings, clearing brush and down timber along the roadside, and eliminating dead timber in flooded lakes, such as Lake Eleanor in Yosemite Park.

Mather recognized, however, the difficulty of this kind of work. Not only was it costly, but it also required the cooperation of private individuals and corporations who had property rights on park waters or along roads and who were generally reluctant to cooperate. This concern led Mather to urge Congress to enlarge the boundaries of a number of parks so that private land along park roads could be acquired. He also worked out arrangements with the U.S. Forest Service to maintain roadside buffers, one hundred feet in width, to either side of park approach roads that passed through national forests (941).

The concern for preserving park scenery extended to minor details such as signs. Park signs, if they existed at all, took an assortment of rudimentary forms. Frequently they were nailed to trees. At the park superintendents' conference in Denver in 1920, the National Park Service adopted its first system of uniform signs. The system, which was already being developed at Yellowstone, called for metallic signs with green letters upon a white field which were to be mounted on posts.[20]

Even some of Punchard's minor recommendations had lasting applications. Punchard objected to labeling trees with tags and recommended that, where it was desirable to provide labels, the park service use a practice devised by the Sierra Club in its commemorative plaque to Gifford Pinchot in Muir Woods. There, an attractive bronze tablet was placed on a large boulder, which was rolled to the foot of the tree. With this solution, Punchard noted, the sign was "hardly noticeable" and "simple in design," and "the trunk of the tree [was not] injured or disfigured." This method would be followed in the service's own custom of placing plaques dedicated to Stephen Mather's memory in each park beginning in the 1930s.[21]

Although many of Punchard's improvements were in themselves minor, their cumulative effect greatly enhanced the appearance of heavily visited places, such as Yosemite Valley. They moreover established precedents for landscape improvements that would be continued through the years and would be implemented in the Emergency Conservation Work of the 1930s in both state and national parks. These improvements, too, drew heavily upon the naturalistic landscape gardening tradition espoused by Andrew Jackson Downing, Henry Hubbard, Samuel Parsons, and Frank Waugh.

Development of Campgrounds

Campground improvements took a considerable amount of Punchard's time. Most parks needed new or enlarged campgrounds to serve the increasing numbers of motorists that visited the parks in the aftermath of World War I when Mather's efforts to promote parks coincided with the burgeoning popularity of automobile transportation. Punchard's work entailed locating and developing permanent automobile camps or rehabilitating existing camps.

No park experienced a greater increase in motor travel than Yellowstone, where Superintendent Horace Albright called for automobile camps on a "comprehensive scale." Albright envisioned a system of campgrounds that could be "progressively extended and improved year by year" and would make available no less than thirty camps. Much of Punchard's first visit to Yellowstone was spent studying conditions at the permanent camps run by concessionaires, which offered visitors a campsite and a nearby dining hall. He made suggestions to make these places more attractive. He mapped the existing conditions at Mammoth Hot Springs, Old Faithful, and the Grand Canyon of the Yellowstone and during the winter developed plans for rearranging and improving the grounds. The construction of several large camps at Mammoth Hot Springs near the general park headquarters entailed removing stumps and dead wood, installing a water system, constructing toilets and fireplaces, and policing the grounds on a regular basis (960–1179).

By the end of 1919, Punchard had worked out the basic requirements for national park campgrounds. Top priorities were good drinking water and sanitary toilet facilities. Campgrounds were located where there was a supply of water and where they could be screened from the park roads and were reached by graded and surfaced side roads. At areas such as the Upper Geyser Basin at Yellowstone, small dams were built to create small reservoirs. Elsewhere water was piped in from streams and lakes known to be free of pollution. Trees were cut and stumps and dead wood removed to provide space for roads, parking, and outdoor living. Fireplaces with grills for open-air cooking not only provided a welcome amenity but also reduced fire hazards. Seats, tables, and shelters were additional improvements (960).

By 1919, campers at Sequoia National Park had "outrun the whole Giant Forest" to the extent that shrubs and ground cover in the village were completely destroyed. Mather recommended that the area ultimately be reserved only for its scenery and that the hotel be relocated to another part of the forest because the most interesting and the largest trees were in the vicinity of the hotel camp and around the meadows. In the meantime, Punchard made some temporary improvements to achieve a greater harmony of site and setting. He found the store and studio to be harmonious with the forested setting and recommended that the post office be covered with cedar bark "to fit into the general scheme in a very satisfactory manner." He moved the post office closer to the store and studio to complete the "group already begun" and to open up a dangerous corner that could be flattened and regraded. New government buildings were added in designs that established a precedent to be followed in future construction. Old buildings were to be removed and replaced by new buildings on less conspicuous sites. He recommended that the canvas tents be replaced with a new type of structure built of redwood and cedar bark that "would add materially to the attractiveness of the buildings" and "be more in keeping with the spirit of the colony." Despite Punchard's changes, by 1920 the use of the Giant Forest for camping had increased to a point where it was becoming increasingly difficult to preserve the natural conditions and at the same time provide adequate accommodations. Punchard observed that heavy use had taxed the area to its utmost capacity and resulted in the "gradual destruction of the undergrowth, leaving the ground bare and dusty." In 1926, the area was finally closed to camping, the buildings removed, and the ground allowed to recover.[22]

Because of the rapid increase of park visitors equipped for automobile camping at Sequoia and Yellowstone, Punchard recognized campground improvements as his most important work. In 1920, he urged that the "higher development of the automobile camp ground" proceed "with renewed vigor."[23]

Development Schemes

The 1918 statement of policy called for the preparation of comprehensive plans for future development of the national parks. It was many years, however, before funds became available for this purpose. To ensure that when funds became available improvements would be based on a preconceived plan making "special reference to the preservation of the landscape," Punchard began to draw up plans called development schemes. For the most part, these were versions of the village plans having a common architectural theme which Mark Daniels proposed in 1915.

Plans were necessary for all forms of development. In 1920, Mather announced that all future improvements by both the service and the concessionaires were to be based on an organized scheme of development in order "to avoid mistakes in the location and design which the service inherited." Concessionaires were to submit "intelligent, well-prepared plans" for Punchard's review (94–95, 1075).

The first plans took the form of organized schemes of development for areas of the parks called villages where both government and concessionaire's facilities were centered. The planning process involved the director of the National Park Service, the park superintendents, members of the park advisory committees, and the park concessionaires. Each scheme clustered buildings together functionally and aesthetically into an attractive and harmonious "ensemble." This often meant examining the condition and design of existing government and concessionary buildings to determine what should remain, what should be altered, and what should be removed to achieve a unified, harmonious appearance.

The major goal of planning was to uphold the visual attractiveness of these areas, either by designing and arranging new structures, by removing unnecessary buildings, or eliminating unsightly conditions. Such schemes were intended to avoid many of the types of mistakes which the service had inherited and to remedy the previous pattern of development, which was described as "topsy-turvy" (1180).

Park development and operations required maintenance facilities. Equipment was necessary for the construction and maintenance of roads, trails, and buildings. Such activities included ongoing repairs and the annual clearing of debris from winter storms on mountain roads. Some parks were already excellently arranged administratively, but conditions varied widely. In the worst cases, buildings were scattered, inadequate in size, and poorly located, and this lack of organization led to inefficiency. To remedy this situation, Punchard outlined a typical industrial group that included structures essential for park maintenance, including stables, wagon and equipment sheds, a garage, a warehouse, and shops for machinery, blacksmithing, electrical work, painting, plumbing, and carpentry. Housing and mess halls for laborers were included in permanent camps. Buildings were arranged to make maintenance activities more efficient. The industrial group was often located within the headquarters area. Punchard and Hull continued to study these conditions with a view to coordinating these developments in a single area for "most effective administration."[24]

By the end of 1920, development schemes had been formed for several parks. The development of administrative groups and facilities used by the concessionaires was central to most of these plans. In most parks such schemes had to accommodate existing development as well as future needs. An organized plan for the development of the areas, including commercial, industrial, and residential zones, had been formulated at Yosemite. At Mount Rainier, plans were approved for future building at Paradise Valley to accommodate rapidly increasing tourist travel and for the development of the newly acquired land at Longmire as the park's administrative headquarters. The Longmire development called for the removal of old buildings and the development of an open meadow as in Yosemite Village. At Rocky Mountain National Park, plans for an administrative site in the village of Estes Park were developed and the problems of housing park employees and storing park equipment necessary for improvement work reviewed.[25]

General Grant National Park provided a different challenge and opportunity for park development. Although it covered only four square miles of territory, its scenic interest and the possibilities for development, in Punchard's opinion, could make it one of the "gems" of the national park system. Existing buildings were old, deteriorating, and unsuitable for park use. Punchard seized this opportunity to locate and design an entirely new village, removing the old structures and setting new buildings in an artistic arrangement that was both serviceable and harmonious. The location selected was a little meadow that Punchard described as a "delightfully refreshing spot after a long hot climb up the mountain road to the park." The village was to be the "vestibule" of the park and a pleasing place for the visitor to stop for "rest and reflection." An administration building—well constructed, attractive, and well placed—provided a "model and nucleus" for additional structures to be built as the growth of the park demanded. Punchard described the plan for the new village:

> In connection with . . . the administration building, which has already been erected, it is proposed to group the structures about three sides of a square which will open toward the road, the administration building on one side, the store and post office on the rear, and a building for the photographer on the side opposite the administration building. By such an arrangement an orderly, attractive village group may be developed on a site which is suitable for the purpose, unoccupied at the present time and centrally located.[26]

Punchard's solution for clusters of administrative and commercial buildings along three sides of a village square with the road passing along the fourth side would be repeated throughout the western national parks, including Mount Rainier and Yosemite. Punchard's scheme established the precedent for the village plaza having a common architectural character that would occur in national parks throughout the 1920s and early 1930s.

Topographical maps, which provided a record of contours, drainage patterns, and existing built features, were essential to park planning and design. Such maps were central to the process of landscape design as it had evolved in the United States under the influence of the Olmsted firm. Punchard, who had spent much effort surveying existing conditions on the ground, urged park superintendents to prepare maps of their parks showing the location of all buildings; roads; bridges; water and sewer mains; electric light, power, and telephone lines; and other elements in relation to the contours and natural features of the park. This information was essential to planning development areas, to coordinating the engineering and landscape work, and to working with park superintendents, engineers, and concessionaires. Anticipating the development of plans for each park, Hull, in 1926, again urged the preparation of topographical maps. In 1931, the Landscape Division requested that prominent trees and rock formations also be indicated on these maps. Such mapping was generally conducted by park engineers and preceded the layout of roads, utilities, and other facilities in the developed areas of national parks. In the 1930s, much of the mapping was done by crews of Civilian Conservation Corps enrollees before planning and construction (1180).

Locating and Designing Park Facilities

The landscape engineer played an important role in locating all park facilities. Beyond the basic engineering questions of suitability of soil and terrain, provision of water, and accessibility, the location of park facilities involved a number of landscape issues, particularly the effect that facilities had on scenic views. From the beginning, facilities were to be as inconspicuous as possible and situated so that they did not interfere with or intrude upon scenic vistas. The landscape engineer was involved in the decision on where to locate not only government buildings but also those of the concessionaires. Incinerators, power plants, maintenance shops, and garages all were placed where they would not be seen by the visiting public but where they could efficiently serve their essential functions. The location of gas stations was commonly a matter of dispute between the park staff and concessionaires. The landscape architects wished them to be screened and not noticeable, whereas the concessionaires, who wanted to sell their products, wished them to be located in prominent locations on plazas or beside roadways.

The location of buildings within existing park villages posed other considerations. Distance from the rim became an important factor as Charles Punchard negotiated the location for the Kiser Studio at Crater Lake's Rim Village, and twenty-five yards was finally agreed upon as the distance at which the building would not be visible along the rim from distant points. Sites where structures could lie gently and unobtrusively on the land were sought. Where it was desirable to afford a view from the building, the landscape engineers made sure that construction would not impair natural features or interrupt pristine scenic vistas from other viewpoints.

Park designers discovered, however, that location and siting of facilities were only part of the solution, for administration buildings, ranger stations, museums, and the like needed to be visible to the public. Designers therefore began to look to the character of design, materials, and method of construction as ways to achieve harmony with nature. When they constructed buildings that successfully blended into the site and setting, the designers realized that distance from the rim mattered little.

Since forested locations and rising elevations often provided best cover, it was not surprising that screening development by planting stands of trees became a standard practice by the late 1920s, especially in the case of maintenance buildings, comfort stations, and gas stations. Of the many planting conventions practiced by park designers in the early years of the service, screening was the most important and the one that the service continued to practice on a large scale and promoted in its portfolios of the 1930s, *Park Structures and Facilities* and *Park and Recreation Structures*. Where stands of trees did not already exist, they could be planted in masses that followed the species and character of the surrounding area's natural vegetation. In areas of little or scattered tree cover, designers provided other forms of closure and concealment in the form of ornamental fences or walls that complemented the area's architectural scheme. The first of these fences was built at the concessionaire's camp at Mammoth Hot Springs in 1919 to conceal the service yards from public view. In the open subalpine meadow of Yakima Park, a stockaded fence was built in the early 1930s to hide the maintenance shops and motor pool of service vehicles and provided the same pioneer feeling as the blockhouses that served as administration buildings. In the deserts of the Southwest, adobe walls were stuccoed to blend with the natural soil and rock. This concern for concealment led designers such as Punchard and Hull to lay out maintenance areas in quadrangles in which garages and shops were connected to form an enclosed central court where maintenance activities could be screened from the view of the general public.

Increasing numbers of visitors put pressure on the National Park Service to improve and develop new facilities, such as museums, observation stations, checking stations, comfort stations, and administration buildings. Plans made in the early 1920s to move the old village in Yosemite Valley out of the open meadows to a new site under the trees and against the valley walls established the concept of the "plaza" as the center of park business and of locating development under the screen of vegetation. Overcrowding in many parks led designers to identify additional areas for development and to separate the areas for park housing and maintenance. The influx of automobiles into parks created a need for parking areas, campgrounds, gasoline stations, and watering stops. Concessionaires wishing to expand accommodations or develop new ones worked closely with park designers to reach solutions that were appropriate for park use and harmonious with park scenery.

Designing park buildings was another important function of the landscape engineer. Punchard designed employees' cottages, ranger stations, automobile checking stations, comfort stations, and other buildings. Except for Mark Daniels' brief tenure as landscape engineer for the national parks, park superintendents or civil engineers designed the buildings for a park or approved the work of architects or builders hired by concessionaires. In an advisory role, Punchard was now able to critique the plans drawn up by the superintendents and to encourage them to accept his assistance. The locations of buildings, whether built by the government or the concessionaire, were selected by the park superintendent in "conference with the landscape engineer on the ground." The landscape engineers selected and marked all timber to be cut to make way for construction. This was the beginning of the collaboration between park superintendents and landscape engineers in all matters pertaining to park design. This collaboration resembled the professional and client relationship common to the professional practice of landscape architecture and would characterize the process of national park design for years to come (940).

As early as 1917, the landscape engineers recognized that the best approach for designing harmonious park structures was to use native materials. The practical problem of getting building materials to remote locations made this not only desirable but essential. Economics was a factor, too, since the construction of buildings of any type was limited by the fifteen-hundred-dollar ceiling that Congress had placed on the cost of park buildings unless special appropriations were granted. In 1919, Punchard urged that this amount be raised to twenty-five hundred. Mather and Hull continued to make similar recommendations throughout the 1920s. Punchard argued that the high cost of lumber made it impossible to construct facilities of an adequate size under the allotment. In some parks, materials were salvaged as older buildings were dismantled to alleviate the problem, but many parks had no existing structures that could be used for this purpose. Punchard urged the careful dismantling of dilapidated buildings so that materials could be salvaged for lumber suitable for framing or other rough work and to keep construction costs within the limit set by Congress. This amount remained a constant problem throughout the 1920s, despite efforts by Hull and Mather to increase the ceiling or drop it altogether.[27]

A number of the outstanding park buildings were donated to the parks by outside sources. The Sierra Club had built the LeConte Memorial Lodge and the Parsons Memorial Lodge in Yosemite. Mather himself had paid for the Rangers' Club, built in 1920 at Yosemite under direction of Charles K. Sumner, a San Francisco architect and practitioner of the Bay Area style. It was situated on the south side of the valley overlooking the meadow and offered expansive views up and down the valley. Sumner built it in conference with the landscape engineering division. To Punchard, the clubhouse set a standard in national park building design: "A great deal of care was given to the preparation of the plans of this building in order to provide for all the requirements, design a building harmonious in its setting, attractive in exterior appearance and comfortable within. The architecture is original, free, and by the use of logs, stone, and shakes an attractive structure has developed" (337).

Gateways were developed at several parks which were to be "entirely unique, yet harmonious with their surroundings." Mather praised the advantages of the park gateway, "not the least of which are the sense of pride and thrill of pleasure that are inspired in the American tourist as he passes through imposing pillars or arches that announce to him that he is entering a great playground that belongs to him and to all America." The construction of many of these gateways relied upon special appropriations, and plans were often prepared with the hope that funding would follow. In 1919, Punchard designed gateways for Yellowstone's Cody Entrance and Yosemite's Wawona Entrance. It was not until the following year, however, that there were funds to construct the Cody Entrance, which featured a portal of massive local logs which was in scale and character with the surrounding forest and modeled after the Mount Rainier arch.[28]

Although Punchard relied upon the use of local materials as a key to harmonizing park structures, he understood that this practice could potentially conflict with the policy of landscape preservation. In his design for the gateway to General Grant, he resolved this problem and established a sound approach

4.3. The Rangers' Clubhouse (1921), a gift of Stephen Mather to Yosemite National Park, was designed by San Francisco architect Charles K. Sumner in the Bay Area style. On the south side of the valley, it overlooked the meadows and offered expansive views of the valley. To landscape engineer Charles Punchard, the building established a standard for national park design in its harmonious setting, comfortable interior, and attractive exterior of logs, stone, and shakes. When photographed about 1928, the building was surrounded by plantings of native trees and shrubs. *(Photograph courtesy National Park Service, Yosemite National Park)*

for future design and construction by calling for a semirustic effect, in which structures reflected their function but were constructed of natural materials.

> In studying the problem . . . I felt that it should be constructed of materials which could be found within the park or would suggest the interior of the park in some manner. The chief attraction of the park is the General Grant Tree. Therefore, redwood seemed to be the medium to use. To use sections of the trunks of the trees seemed to me a useless sacrifice of these monarchs which we hold so dearly and treasure so carefully. At the same time it did not seem that a satisfactory rustic gateway could be obtained in this manner. Therefore, I suggested the use of redwood from fallen trees, cedar bark, and local stone, all materials which would be found in the park, and instead of working for a rustic effect, I worked for a semirustic

effect, acknowledging frankly that it was a gateway. It should be dignified, perform its function frankly and definitely, and be harmonious and attractive. (1178)

Punchard encouraged the construction of community buildings. Located in the larger campgrounds and accessible to both the government free camps and the concessionaire's complexes, these buildings would contain bathing facilities for both men and women, laundry tubs, a store, and perhaps a post office. They could also house one or more rangers. Of great importance was the large room with table and chairs and fireplaces where campers could enjoy evening lectures on the natural history of the park and find shelter in inclement weather. During 1921, several of these buildings, constructed of logs, were built at the Canyon and Old Faithful campgrounds and another proposed for Lake Junction in Yellowstone. This building type would continue to be a popular feature of park campgrounds in the 1920s and 1930s, and several outstanding examples are those built at Paradise and Longmire at Mount Rainier in the late 1920s.

Under Punchard the architectural program was basic and meager. Unless special annual appropriations were justified, only the most basic and essential structures could be built. Yellowstone, for example, required new ranger stations and needed to replace snowshoe cabins in the backcountry. Mather adamantly pleaded with the secretary of the interior and Congress to fund the most basic park facilities to house park employees. He believed that "the ranger force of every park, considering the nature of its work, should have dry, sanitary quarters and, in winter, the means of overcoming the effects of exposure while on long patrols in below-zero weather." Buildings were primitive in their construction and relied upon natural materials available at each site and tools that could be transported by pack animal or on foot. A standard snowshoe cabin consisted of a single room of twelve by sixteen feet, was built of pole framing and log siding chinked with mud, and had sturdy shutters made of planks to protect the ranger from bears. Many of the cabins at Yellowstone had an earthen roof consisting of a rubberoid base surmounted by six inches of soil.[29]

Punchard established a standard for the functionalism and harmonious construction of park buildings in keeping with the character of other buildings and the natural setting. He explored the use of native materials, from volcanic rock to natural timbers, and worked out solutions for comfort, sanitation, convenience, and pleasure in park campgrounds. Although Punchard's tenure was a brief one, he established a program of landscape review and design which would guide the park service for many years.

Review of Concessionaires' Designs

Another important function of the landscape engineering department was the review of concessionaires' plans and designs. Mather wrote, "It is in connection with the location and design of all new structures by these operators, and their harmonious relation to existing structures and the landscape, that the landscape engineering department fulfills one of its most important functions."[30]

After visiting a number of parks in 1919, Punchard became convinced that the quality of design and construction in the developments of concessionaires greatly needed improvement. He urged concessionaires to employ architects, for his own review of proposals was frequently stymied by inadequate plans that lacked information and made it impossible for him to visualize the finished structures. He also discouraged the construction of temporary buildings, because they tended to become permanent after several years.[31]

Much of Punchard's initial effort was spent encouraging concessionaires to improve the appearances of facilities that included lodges, hotels, campgrounds, stores, and photographic studios. At Yosemite, he spent a great deal of time studying and approving the development plans for an extensive building program for Yosemite Lodge. The plans included sixty-five new cabins and an industrial group. The industrial group consisted of a garage and several repair shops; although the group was centrally located, it was well hidden and constructed in the same architectural style as the company's other buildings. At Yellowstone, Punchard reviewed designs for gas stations, which he praised as attractive and "unique in this field of automobile service, and deserving of the highest commendation from a designer's standpoint." These were constructed of logs and stone and carefully located in relation to their surroundings.[32]

Punchard gathered ideas from the designers hired by the park concessionaires, on whose work he was to make recommendations and give approval prior to construction. He met with Mary Colter and reviewed the Fred Harvey Company's plans for new development after the Grand Canyon was made a park on February 26, 1919. Reviewing proposals submitted by the concessionaires was Punchard's only opportunity to make recommendations and affect the character of the larger buildings being built in the parks. This role would occupy an increasing amount of the interest and time of his successor, Daniel Hull, in the 1920s.

Punchard's suggestions for the design and location of Fred H. Kiser's studio at the Rim Village at Crater Lake illustrates Punchard's approach to locating buildings along a rim and to using landscape features such as terraces to achieve an acceptable and harmonious design. It also illustrates the extent to which Mather and Punchard conferred on these matters. In January 1920, Mather asked Punchard's opinion on the photographer's proposal to build a studio on the rim at Victor's Rock in the form of a log structure with a ten-foot porch extending across the lakeside elevation. Mather questioned the proposed location of the studio on the rim of the crater, disliking as he did the Kolb Studio and several other buildings at the Grand Canyon where the tendency was "to get right down to the rim." Mather felt that the hotel at Crater Lake should have been set back some distance from the rim and that if anything was built at Victor Rock, it should be "simply an open-air observation station for the tourists with the photographic studio being placed back on the other side of the road."[33]

Although Punchard agreed that buildings should be situated well back from the rim, he felt that a distance of seventy-five feet was adequate provided the building did not stand out alone and was inconspicuous. If care was taken to design an attractive building above Victor Rock, noted Punchard, the result could be "pleasing and satisfactory." Instead of log, which the park had used for its entrance buildings, Punchard recommended that the volcanic stone found in the park, which was "so interesting and [worked] up so well in buildings," be used to some degree in the construction of the studio. He further suggested,

> To attract tourists and at the same time have a physical connection with the rim of the crater, Mr. Kiser might work in a terrace effect on the axis of the rim. This terrace might be paved with flat stones and [have] seats and benches placed there. There might be a covering of this terrace if necessary during the heat of the day which could take the form of a log frame supporting a log rafter roof on which could be stretched a dark brown canvas which could be rolled back when not in use. In this manner he would be attracting the tourist and still not be building directly on the rim of the crater.[34]

Punchard's recommendations were followed. The building's lower story was made of random masonry of irregularly cut stone, and the upper story and gable were board and batten. There was an overhanging roof with exposed log purlins. The building reflected the influence of the Arts and Crafts movement and was moreover one of the first buildings built with the recommendations of the service's landscape engineer and incorporating the landscape architect's use of terraces, open pergola-like porch, accommodations for seating to enjoy scenic views, and native stone materials in creating a terrace wall and flagstone floor. Punchard set forth the concept that harmony required the careful selection of location but also the utmost consideration of design and materials. Screening, viewpoint, and vista figured importantly in Punchard's solution. Vista was considered in terms of both the building's conspicuousness and its ability to present a scenic view. Favoring the use of local stone at Rim Village, he wrote, "The volcanic rock which is found close at hand offers unlimited possibilities when used alone or in combination with logs in the design of simple attractive buildings."[35]

Several years later when a promenade was built along the rim from the Crater Lake Lodge to a point west of the studio, the building with its terrace and porch area was readily incorporated into the design. So well did the building suit its site and the emerging ethic of rustic park architecture that when Kiser closed his business about 1930, the park service adapted the building for use as an information center.

4.4. So appropriate was the design for Kiser's Photographic Studio (1919) at Crater Lake's Rim Village that the building was later incorporated into the design of the rim promenade and adapted for park service use as an information office. Landscape engineer Charles Punchard strongly influenced the design of the building, with its lower story of stonemasonry, upper story of logs, and log pergola. Visible in this 1933 photograph are the stone parapet with crenulating piers, picturesque ghost trees, walkway, and views of the lake which characterize the promenade design of the late 1920s. *(Photograph by George A. Grant, courtesy National Park Service Historic Photography Collection)*

Professional Stewardship

While Punchard's work was primarily focused on the problems and details of park development, his professional sense of stewardship led him to raise questions about the boundaries and commercial exploitation of the parks. He urged the expansion of park boundaries in the General Grant and Sequoia parks to include additional areas of big trees, and Sequoia Lake, which, although artificially created for logging operations, had scenic potential and was threatened by the development of vacation homes. Grazing practices and the development of water resources for power and irrigation were timely issues that concerned Punchard.[36]

Although the 1918 statement of policy restricted grazing to particular remote areas, these restrictions had been relaxed during the war and seriously threatened native flora. On the situation in Yosemite, he commented, "The destruction to the small mountain meadows caused by intensive grazing of a large number of cattle will become a very serious matter. In Yosemite the appearance of these meadows after only one year of grazing as a war measure was very disheartening indeed. The forest floor of the Sierra offers very little forage on account of the great areas of rock and the steep canyon walls. Therefore, the small meadows suffer the greatest amount of destruction and their resources are soon depleted by concentrated feeding" (1180).

In 1920, he spoke out against a federal power bill that proposed to remove the control and administration of national parks from Congress and place it under a commission empowered to control all federal land and to develop water resources and irrigation. In his annual report and *Landscape Architecture,* Punchard unequivocally outlined the threats of water projects to parks such as Glacier, Yellowstone, and Yosemite, and he cautioned against placing the control of national parks under a commission whose purpose was to promote and develop water resources for irrigation or power. He recalled the controversy over the damming of the Tuolumne River in Yosemite's Hetch Hetchy Valley earlier and mentioned the destruction of scenery to be caused by several proposed water projects affecting Glacier National Park:

> Although this is not the first time in the history of the national parks that their beautiful valleys, lakes, streams, and scenic areas have been in danger of commercial exploitation, the movement has come at this time with a new vigor and determination to transgress upon these areas and develop them selfishly and for the benefit of a comparatively small number of citizens within the immediate vicinity of the project, compared with thousands and thousands of citizens for whom, and who, through their representatives, have set these areas aside and preserved them forever as national playgrounds for themselves, their children and their children's children.[37]

Following his study of national parks, Punchard was overwhelmed by the many problems and frustrated that only the most urgent could be addressed. Mather recognized that success depended not only on the engineer's training but also on a "clear and practical understanding and appreciation of the relation of these varied problems to the limitations of existing appropriations." The process was in no way aimed at compromising ideals but rather was "simply getting the best possible results out of every situation." Mather commented that much greater effort was spent in advising superintendents and concessionaires on what not to do than on what to do to uphold the natural character of each park (93).

The many small changes recommended by Punchard would have a cumulative and lasting effect on the character of park development. Mather commented on the marked results of the changes at Yellowstone: "Although many of them were of a minor nature, all had a direct bearing on each other and the whole, and obviously their continuance will eventually knit the whole ensemble into a harmonious whole, eliminating many of the unpleasant conditions which we have inherited" (96).

Expert Advice

During Punchard's tenure, the National Park Service forged ties with experts outside the service. Several prominent landscape architects visited the parks and advised on landscape matters. Jens Jensen assisted with plantings and provided advice at Hot Springs in December 1918. Frederick Law Olmsted Jr. visited the newly established Lafayette National Park and gave advice on its future development. He even helped locate some industrial buildings inconspicuously at Annie Springs while visiting Crater Lake in 1921. Charles Moore, chairman of the Commission of Fine Arts, visited Yosemite with Mather, initiating the commission's involvement in planning and designing the new village in Yosemite Valley.[38]

Although decisions were made by the superintendent of each park, Mather kept well informed of issues and proposals for development. The park service landscape engineer faced the challenge of conveying practices that upheld a philosophy of harmonization and landscape preservation to superintendents from various backgrounds. In the parks, advisory boards were important players in decisions on park development; these boards were commonly made up of local businesspeople, representatives of the regional "good roads" associations, members of mountaineering and hiking clubs, leaders of environmental clubs, and other park supporters. Mather was professionally affiliated with many prominent park officials. He regularly attended the annual meetings of the National Conference on State Parks and followed with great interest the progress of state park systems. He sat on the National Capital Park and Planning Commission, and he likely consulted with fellow members on park issues. From time to time, he requested assistance and advice from the federal Fine Arts Commission and its prominent members.

Chapter 5

Accommodating the Public:
Park Villages and Scenic Roads

Daniel Hull as Landscape Engineer

The demand for advice on landscape matters became so great that on August 1, 1920, Mather hired Daniel Hull to assist Punchard. Hull became the senior landscape engineer in November 1920. Hull had studied at the University of Illinois, graduating in 1913 with a bachelor of science degree in agriculture with a specialty in horticulture. He then attended Harvard University, where he received a master's degree in landscape architecture in 1914, the first year that Harvard offered separate degrees for architecture and landscape architecture. Hull likely studied horticulture under Joseph Cullen Blair, a well-known horticulturalist who also laid out several local parks in the Urbana-Champaign area. He may have studied with Wilhelm Miller, who taught at Illinois from 1912 to 1916. At Harvard, Hull was exposed to the ideas of many leaders in the landscape architecture profession, including Henry Hubbard, James Sturgis Pray, John Nolen, and Frederick Law Olmsted Jr.[1]

Hull's contributions from 1920 to 1927, when he left the park service, were varied. He took a leading role in designing park communities and working with concessionaires to develop well-planned facilities. He designed park structures ranging from entrance stations to bridges. It was under Hull's direction that the landscape engineers assumed a leading role in the development of park roads and trails and developed a technique of stonemasonry which incorporated native materials and achieved an informal appearance that harmonized with nature. Under Hull's supervision, the national parks began to develop comprehensive plans to guide all future improvements throughout a park. Hull appears to have had fine drafting and architectural skills, which supplemented Punchard's strong philosophical outlook. Hull's office was first in Yosemite and then in Los Angeles, where he shared an office with Gilbert Stanley Underwood, whom he met at the University of Illinois and who was building a reputation as a designer of concessionaires' facilities. Hull was the National Park Service's principal planner and designer until 1927, when the Landscape Division was moved to San Francisco to become part of the Western Field Office. Paul Kiessig was appointed Hull's assistant in February 1921. Kiessig, also a graduate of the University of Illinois, spent his time in Yosemite, Grand Canyon, and Sequoia before leaving the service in early 1923. In November 1922, Hull hired Thomas Vint, who would take charge of the division in 1927.[2]

Although Hull studied at Harvard, he did not have Punchard's close associations with the East Coast landscape profession. No mention is made in the society's journal of his work or the service's progress in landscape architecture during the 1920s, and he did not even join the ASLA until 1923. Hull's ties were in the Midwest, where he had grown up, and California, where he spent most of his career. Vint also had a California background. He was trained as a landscape architect at the University of California, Berkeley, then the leading school of landscape architecture on the West Coast. Several others from Hull's graduating class at Harvard became involved in the landscape design of national and state parks. One classmate was Frank Culley, who had studied under Frank Waugh at Massachusetts Agricultural College before attending Harvard, later taught at Iowa State College, which had the first curriculum in landscape engineering to prepare students for design work in forests and parks, and was in private practice with former national forest landscape designer Arthur Carhart just before the depression. Another was George L. Nason, who was hired by the National Park Service to supervise CCC work in Texas state parks.[3]

Hull aggressively worked at eliminating unsightly conditions and improving the scenic quality of the parks. Unlike Punchard, he wrote few reports, and those he did write were brief. There is little question, however, of the achievements of the landscape program during his tenure. Likely echoing Hull's own thoughts, assistant Paul Kiessig wrote in 1922, "It is not a landscape engineer's purpose to add anything to nature's achievement, but to restrain the human inclination to desecrate and destroy, and where human construction is necessary, to keep it as unobtrusive or inoffensive as possible."[4]

Much of Hull and Kiessig's effort went into drawing attention to practices that detracted from the scenic beauty of the parks, such as the cutting of swaths through forests to place telephone lines, the unsightly storage of equipment and vehicles by the government or the concessionaires, the intrusion of old structures into scenic views, the cutting of roads in straight lines, and the removal of native vegetation in the vicinity of new buildings.

Hull continued the work of scenery preservation and restoration initiated by Punchard. He continually called for cleanup along roads and in developed areas. He sought ways to improve the appearance of necessary intrusions into the landscape. In 1921, he reinforced Punchard's advice that borrow pits be located

THE IMPORTANT JOB OF HARMONIZING PARK CONSTRUCTION WITH PARK ATMOSPHERE IS UP TO DANIEL R. HULL, NATIONAL PARK ARCHITECT AND LANDSCAPE MAN

5.1. Cartoon of Daniel R. Hull, chief landscape engineer of the National Park Service from 1920 to 1927. *(Illustration from the* Oakland Tribune, *courtesy National Park Service Historic Photography Collection)*

out of sight and introduced the idea that cuts created along roads during construction be graded to form gently sloping banks, rather than abrupt ones, so that they might reseed themselves and thus blend into the natural landscape. Cautioning against easy solutions, he urged that utilities, such as telephone lines, electric service, and sprinkling tanks, be placed where they would be least noticeable. If it was necessary to place wires on poles, Hull recommended that the poles have brackets rather than cross arms to make them less conspicuous. He called for the removal of all abandoned or unnecessary structures by the government or the concessionaires.[5]

The landscape engineer's role in the parks remained varied. Kiessig somewhat sardonically recounted the list of the landscape engineer's many tasks:

Landscape problems are present at every turn of the road or trail; the need for new trails, vetoing of roads projected where scenically undesirable, diversion of traffic to save trees, location of new camp areas, rarely the opening of a vista, the screening of another view, proposing a lake for reflection purposes, preserving meadow vegetation from pack horses and cattle (and others), restraining the human garden maker (this is often embarrassing and difficult), replanning of traffic ways, location or relocation of service units, the shops, the employee dwelling groups, housing of horses and machinery, bridge location, concession sites, location of shelter cabins and comfort stations, advising or restricting tree cutting for scenic or safety purposes, protection of river banks, planning or replanning of villages and the general preservation of the original glory of forest and stream. The landscape engineer never rides without meeting new and interesting problems.[6]

In 1922 Mather praised the landscape engineers' accomplishments as being "of the highest order and of inestimable value." The most important problems in his opinion were locating and harmonizing the design of buildings and villages in relationship to the surrounding natural environment. Vista thinning, locating trails and roads, screening objectionable views, placing utility wires underground, and improving the public campgrounds were other important tasks carried out by the landscape engineers.[7]

Cooperation with Park Superintendents

The role of the landscape engineer was intended as an advisory one, but getting superintendents and concessionaires to accept advice was not always easy. Before 1918, superintendents routinely made construction decisions and often designed park buildings themselves. Punchard began a process of conferring with park superintendents on site and conveying design ideas through rough sketches, finished drawings, and written reports. While major decisions were followed closely by Mather, the landscape engineer and the park superintendent worked out solutions for locating and designing most of the lesser buildings of the park, from ranger stations to utility areas. Consultation frequently involved the concessionaires.

In 1921, Mather still found it necessary to assert the authority of the landscape engineers: "No buildings are permitted to be erected in the parks without the approval as to design by the landscape engineering department with such occasional exceptions in emergency cases as may be directly approved by the director based on their preparation by satisfactory professional talent. It is in this aspect of park development that our landscape engineering department fulfills one of its most important duties."[8]

To encourage park superintendents to accept the advice of the landscape engineer, Mather praised the engineer's accomplishments each year. Still, Kiessig, and likely Hull as well, was of the opinion that one solution to the over-whelming problem of preserving and developing the parks was to appoint super-intendents with landscape backgrounds, who could see that all work was carried out with sensitivity toward the landscape on a continual and regular basis. The landscape engineers felt that their role should be not only advisory but one in which they actually had some authority on landscape matters.[9]

By the end of 1923, the respective roles of the superintendent and land-scape engineer were generally understood and appreciated. That year Mather praised the marked advances in landscape improvements, which he credited partly to the cooperation between park superintendent and landscape engineers. The same year Hull noted, "The whole-hearted interest in the protection of our park landscapes . . . developing from the superintendent down in our various parks has been splendid to observe and has made my work and relationship to the service really enjoyable."[10]

Horace Albright, the superintendent of Yellowstone, contributed heavily to this acceptance. At the superintendent's conference in November 1922, he enumerated the many improvements that had come from his collaboration with Punchard and Hull. These included the organization of new campgrounds and the expansion of old ones, improvements in the design of concessionaires' facili-ties, the construction of the West Thumb and Cody Entrances, the construction of large community buildings at the Canyon and Old Faithful campgrounds, the clearing of vistas along park roads, the construction of new patrol cabins and other buildings, the construction of walkways across hot spring formations and along the Grand Canyon of the Yellowstone, and numerous improvements in developed areas.

From Development Schemes to Town Plans

Under Hull's direction, the landscape program became more and more in-volved with the problems of planning for villages. Grand Canyon and Yosemite received substantial attention in the early 1920s. Hull was called upon to design a variety of new park structures, including administration buildings, commu-nity halls, ranger stations, and lookouts. It was often difficult to achieve har-mony with nature in areas that had been developed in a haphazard fashion or where traffic and demand for visitor use greatly surpassed the capacity of exist-ing facilities.

One of the pressing problems that concerned Mather was Yosemite Village. As early as 1916, he called for the building of a new village, since the old village was subject to flooding. A new site was selected away from the river and under a canopy of trees so that the village was less conspicuous from popular viewpoints on the rim. The federal Commission of Fine Arts, following Chairman Charles Moore's visit in 1918, continued to be interested in the future of Yosemite Village. The new village was planned with the assistance of the commission and the services of Myron Hunt, a prominent Los Angeles architect who had been an associate of Frank Lloyd Wright and Jens Jensen in Chicago earlier in his career. The issue of planning for Yosemite Valley was foremost in the minds of park officials when the superintendents' conference was held at the park in November 1922. Hull attended, as did commission landscape architect James Greenleaf (54).

Hull worked closely with Hunt, and by the end of 1923, a definite plan was finally approved for the future development of Yosemite Valley. This allowed many long-delayed projects to proceed, "thus helping to relieve the congested situation" that had developed. The plan placed the unit on the opposite side of the valley and provided sites around a central parking plaza for an administration building and post office to be built by the government and general stores, studios, and shops to be built by concessionaires. In 1923, with money appropriated for a new administration building and approval for a new post office building, construction got under way. The new village made possible the elimination of many dilapidated structures and improved the valley "from the standpoint of practical operation and landscape effect." The plan called for the careful selection of building sites, the park service's approval of all designs, and adherence to an architectural theme that harmonized construction with the natural surroundings (37, 54).

In 1924, with the construction of a new administration building, plans for the new village center began to take shape. The design of Myron Hunt, the administration building introduced a modest Craftsman structure with a lower story and foundation of concrete faced with boulders, an upper story of shingled walls, and a broad sloping roof supported on exposed log purlins. This building established the particular mode of harmonious "rustic" design to which later buildings in the village would conform. The construction of a post office and museum followed within two years. The three government buildings and the Rangers' Club of 1921 created a nucleus for a civic center to replace the old village.

The Grand Canyon was made a national park in 1919. Here the landscape engineer was presented with the challenge of fitting new government facilities into the scheme already established by the Santa Fe Railroad and the Fred Harvey Company. Punchard met with the Fred Harvey Company's architect, Mary Colter, in 1919. At the Grand Canyon's South Rim, park service buildings had to be coordinated with the large number of prominent buildings already built by the concessionaire. A village character clearly existed, and a distinctive architectural character representing a variety of styles prevailed. Prominent buildings included the stone Lookout House on the edge of the rim, the pueblo-style Hopi House, the El Tovar Hotel with its Swiss- and Norwegian-inspired design and details, a train station of massive log construction, and a number of utility buildings including stables and a power plant. A preliminary plan for an administration or civic group was prepared and a general scheme for the canyon's development worked out. In 1921, Hull designed the park administration building, using a combination of stone and log, establishing a style that would harmonize park service construction on the South Rim with the natural setting and with the concessionaire's buildings.[11]

In 1923, Hull spent two weeks at Grand Canyon, collaborating with Colter. He drew up several development schemes fitting together the needs of the National Park Service and the existing development. Hull sought a solution that would preserve the "wonderful landscape beauty but provide adequately for the large number of visitors there." In 1924, Hull and Vint, the Santa Fe Railway engineers, and Fred Harvey officials worked out a comprehensive plan for future development on the South Rim. Myron Hunt also provided advice and assistance. Mather optimistically reported, "Many complicated problems were worked out to the satisfaction of all interests concerned and structures no longer will be located hit or miss, but with assurance that they will fit in the development scheme for all time to come as far as contingencies can be foreseen. For the first time all parties concerned can build for permanence." The plan called for a new administration building and new superintendent's residence. By the end of 1926, the new village plaza was taking form with a new road leading into it. The new auto camp was praised as one of the finest in the United States, with a community room, delicatessen, comfort station, and other amenities.[12]

Punchard had spent substantial time in Sequoia and General Grant National Parks studying the problems of crowding in the Giant Forest. A summer home for the superintendent and an administration building were built at the Giant Forest, and in 1923 an administrative and industrial headquarters was begun at Ash Mountain to serve the Alder Creek district. By 1926 a new village was taking form at the edge of the Giant Forest, and the old facilities were being removed.[13]

Design of Park Structures

Hull applied his knowledge of landscape architecture and architecture from the beginning of his park service career. He explored native materials from rock to logs and studied pioneer forms such as traditional log cabins and pueblo structures. Hull's career with the National Park Service was a period of experimentation with architectural forms and the use of native building materials and primitive construction techniques that were well adapted to local natural conditions. Although functional and economical, each of his designs was unique in its materials and design. Some of the notable achievements of his park service career were the administration building in Sequoia's Giant Forest, the Fall River

Pass Entrance Station at Rocky Mountain, the administration building at Grand Canyon, the entrance building at Zion, and several community buildings and the Lake Ranger Station at Yellowstone.

His first buildings, designed in 1920 and 1921, included several large community buildings for the Canyon and Old Faithful campgrounds and entrance stations at Yellowstone. The community buildings were built of logs and featured a large room for social gathering and an information center with huge fireplaces and other comforts. The West Thumb Entrance, like the Fall River Entrance at Rocky Mountain, incorporated a porte-cochère and was constructed of logs. In 1921, a checking station was constructed at the Gardiner Entrance as part of a site plan that included the 1903 arch, a comfort station, space for parking, a water fountain, and a flagpole. The building harmonized with the masonry arch, being constructed of basaltic rock laid in cement mortar upon a base of flagstone set in cement. The stone-and-log checking station was designed to house a ranger and measured sixteen by fifteen feet.[14]

Also at Yellowstone, Hull designed a combination fire lookout and shelter. At an elevation of ten thousand feet, the lookout became a popular objective for visitors. The building was constructed of rough native stone and mortar (cement was mixed from melting snow) and cost twenty-five hundred dollars. With rock walls two feet in thickness and a fireplace, the lookout could accommodate a ranger as well as provide visitors with panoramic views. In his design for the Lake Ranger Station, bold in its log construction, at Yellowstone in 1922, Hull explored the idea that the cultural character of a region's architecture could provide appropriate sources for a cultural theme and harmonious construction.

The need for park museums was first recognized in 1920, but it was several years before the park service found sources to fund construction. Starting in 1924, the construction of park museums and interpretive structures was carried out under grants from the Laura Spelman Rockefeller Memorial. This funding provided both the opportunity to plan educational facilities for national parks and the challenge of exploring the principles of harmonious architectural and landscape design for park needs. Herbert Maier was hired by the American Association of Museums to design a museum for Yosemite and several museums and trailside exhibits, called nature shrines, for Yellowstone and Grand Canyon. Maier work closely with naturalist Ansel Hall, who would by the end of the 1920s become chief of the Educational Division, and Carl Russell, the park service's museum expert. A decade later as a district officer for Emergency Conservation Work in state parks, Maier would become the National Park Service's foremost expert on park structures and would have great influence on the design of national and state parks in the Southwest and elsewhere.

In an advisory capacity, the landscape engineers became involved in approving the location and design of the park museums, upholding the landscape standpoint. The collaboration of Thomas Vint and Herbert Maier was fortu-

"FOR THE BENEFIT AND
ENJOYMENT OF THE PEOPLE

5.2. Compatibility with existing architecture was as important as harmony of design with nature. At Yellowstone's Gardiner Entrance, the checking station (1921) designed by landscape engineer Daniel Hull is visible through the massive clinker stone arch designed by Hiram Chittenden in 1903. *(Photograph by George A. Grant, courtesy National Park Service Historic Photography Collection)*

itous, each having similar training and a West Coast orientation in the Arts and Crafts movement. They both understood the principles and practices of naturalistic landscape design and drew ideas from it to harmonize construction with nature.

Maier's design for the museum in Yosemite Valley both suited the architectural style of Myron Hunt's administration building and boldly forged a new standard for the construction of park buildings. Opened in May 1926, the museum was a compromise solution to the architectural problem of integrating the design with that of the newly planned village and the practical problem of building in a national park, where buildings of any type were necessary evils. Furthermore, the service requested that Maier use only indigenous building materials in all visible exterior parts, namely logs, shakes, and stone. With a grant of seventy-five thousand dollars from the Laura Spelman Rockefeller Memorial, a building of substantial size was constructed, providing a fireproof vault for museum collections. Maier called his work a "structural dichotomy." A lower story framed in reinforced concrete and sheathed with rough-hewn granite blocks

5.3. The Yosemite Museum, designed by Herbert Maier in 1924 and constructed with funds from the Laura Spelman Rockefeller Memorial, set a precedent for park museums. The lower story was built as a fireproof, masonry-clad concrete vault; the upper story echoed the redwood shingle siding and exposed log framing of the nearby administration building. Photographed about 1928, the entrance shows the boulder-lined paths, log lampposts, and boulder curbs that characterized the village plaza in the late 1920s. *(Photograph courtesy National Archives, Record Group 79)*

provided a fireproof vault, and an overhanging upper story made of log framing and hand-cut shakes provided offices. He deliberately subordinated the building to its natural setting against the towering granite walls of the valley by emphasizing its horizontality:

> To attempt altitudinal impressiveness here in a building would have meant entering into competition with the cliffs. . . . The horizontal key, on the other hand, makes the museum blend easily into the flat ground; this is restful to the eye, here everywhere drawn upward: and some distance away the building is lost to sight swallowed by the overtopping forest — a point of merit in the light of what has been said of preserving parks undefiled by man's handiwork.[15]

5.4. Glacier Point Lookout, Yosemite National Park, under construction in 1924. Envisioned as a field station of the museum in Yosemite Valley, it was perched on the edge of one of the park's most spectacular monoliths. It featured exhibits, an open viewing window, and an observation terrace. Made of randomly laid native stonemasonry, it was the first interpretive shelter designed by Herbert Maier for the National Park Service and established a model for lookouts, nature shrines, and other shelters in national and state parks. *(Photograph courtesy National Park Service Historic Photography Collection)*

In 1924, the same year the administration building was dedicated, work began on the Yosemite Museum and an interpretive lookout at Glacier Point. Designed by Maier as an extension of the valley museum, the lookout was constructed on the edge of the valley rim and was intended to present and interpret the valley's dramatic natural history at one of the park's most spectacular sites. The lookout represented Ansel Hall and Maier's first collaborative effort in creating an open-air shelter and trailside exhibit. It was a simple shelter with a large rectangular opening for taking in the view; it featured battered stone walls that emerged from the granite outcropping, which served as a natural flooring of stone. With open sides and an overhanging roof, it was a scaled-down and less exaggerated version of Greene and Greene's Oaklawn Waiting Station in Pasadena. With its use of native materials and simple design, it was intended to blend into the surface of the cliff where it was located. Years later, Maier would fault the proportions of its stones and the light appearance of its roof, while landscape architects would criticize its location and call for its removal. Functionally, however, the lookout was the first interpretive shelter built in the park and was a direct link with the shelters that Downing and Hubbard urged be placed at scenic overlooks. It represents the origins of an educational program for national parks which drew visitors' attention outside the village centers and offered an intellectual understanding of the scenic wonders of the park. Despite its lack of architectural sophistication, the lookout was an important prototype that linked park architecture with the nineteenth-century Schoolmaster's Hill shelter of the Olmsted firm at Franklin Park and with numerous lookouts built by the Civilian Conservation Corps in state parks in the 1930s. Such examples as the lookout at Davis Mountains State Park in Texas copied the simple floor plan and basic elevation as well as the use of stone walls and timber rafters.

The design of park service buildings at Mesa Verde National Park by Superintendent Jesse Nusbaum and his wife, Aileen, explored the idea that park buildings should have a cultural theme suited to the prehistory or history of the park area. Like the work of Mary Colter, the Nusbaums' designs drew on the indigenous architecture of the Southwest and achieved solutions that used native stone and traditional construction techniques. The buildings were at once harmonious with the natural setting and suitable in their cultural allusions. The ruins of cliff dwellers and temples at Mesa Verde National Park, which were the subject of continuing excavation in the early twentieth century, offered ideal prototypes for park buildings.

The Mesa Verde buildings—the superintendent's residence (1921), administration building (1923), post office (1923), museum (1923), rangers' building (1925), and community house (1927)—reflected a fusion of indigenous materials and methods of pueblo construction with Spanish colonial influences. Like their prehistoric antecedents, the Mesa Verde buildings were flat-roofed structures whose walls were rough masonry of relatively evenly sized blocks of local sandstone joined with mud mortar. The roof was supported by peeled timbers called vigas that were arranged laterally and protruded through the outer stone walls. A masonry parapet surmounted each building, forming a continuous surface with the load-bearing and slightly battered walls. Distinctive architectural details included corner fireplaces, exposed vigas, *latia* ceilings, corbeled posts, lintels made from adzed timbers, and decorative grillwork.[16]

The Nusbaums' achievements would prove extremely important to the design of later state and national park buildings in the Southwest. This work was the first serious attempt to incorporate the influence of cultural traditions, particularly indigenous ones, into modern buildings for park use. The fact that the work was based on a detailed study of original examples and ethnographic reports distinguished it from other less serious attempts of the early 1920s.

The fifteen-hundred-dollar ceiling on the cost of park structures still limited the design possibilities for park structures. Except for advising on "donated" buildings such as the Rangers' Club or the Yosemite Museum and reviewing the design of the park concessionaires, the landscape engineers had little opportunity to work on larger construction projects.

Hull was eager to improve the building program and recognized that both additional funds and better topographic surveys were needed. In 1925, Hull called for surveys of sufficient scale to indicate all natural features, trees, and rocks. Concerned with the strict limitations on building the much needed park structures, Hull recommended in 1926 that the fifteen-hundred-dollar clause be stricken or doubled, that maps as a base for planning be procured, that more careful data be gathered on the costs of proposed structures, and that five-year comprehensive plans be prepared for each park.[17]

Collaboration with Concessionaires

One of Hull's greatest areas of interest was working with concessionaires on the design of facilities that would provide for visitors' comfort. It seems clear that Hull had avid architectural interests and viewed this work as an opportunity to learn from experienced and creative architects hired by the concessionaires and to work out his own ideas on harmonious construction on a much larger scale than he was able to in the design of simple and functional government buildings. He was greatly inspired by Colter's work at Grand Canyon, directly borrowing her use of log and stone in his own design for the administration building.[18]

About 1923, Hull began to work closely with Gilbert Stanley Underwood, whom he had met at the University of Illinois in 1912. Underwood graduated with a master's degree in architecture from Harvard in 1923 and returned to California, where he began seeking park commissions. Unsuccessful in his bid for the administration building at Yosemite, Underwood did receive the commission for the park's post office. In 1923, Underwood, apparently with Hull's support, began to work as an architect for the Utah Parks Company formed by the Union Pacific Railroad, which was taking a leading role in developing the national parks of southern Utah for tourism. When Hull moved the landscape engineer's operation to Los Angeles in 1923, it was to share Underwood's offices. It seems that Hull and Vint worked directly on designs for some of the smaller buildings associated with the developments in Utah. These working arrangements facilitated the service's review of plans and made it possible for the Underwood firm to work out solutions for the parks. In addition to the Zion and Bryce facilities, Underwood designed the Ahwahnee Lodge in Yosemite Val-

5.5. The lodge at Zion National Park, designed by Gilbert S. Underwood for the Utah Parks Company in the mid-1920s, introduced a new concept for accommodating visitors in national parks—that of a small central lodge or pavilion with outlying cottages and service buildings. In 1926, landscape architect Daniel Hull praised the "comprehensive landscape plan" that was "being carried out in the vicinity of the new lodge." The buildings were sited far back from the canyon rim against a rocky hillside that provided a scenic backdrop for the centrally located pavilion. A one-way curvilinear drive enabled tour buses and automobiles to approach and depart from the two-story pavilion, which featured a lobby, dining hall, and about seventy-five guest rooms. The grounds before the lodge were fashioned into a cactus garden edged with stone boulders and paths leading to the rim. *(Photograph by George A. Grant, courtesy of the National Park Service Historic Photography Collection)*

5.6. Following the concept he developed at Zion National Park, architect Gilbert S. Underwood designed fifteen deluxe cabins and a small centrally located pavilion for the concessionaire at Bryce Canyon National Park. Located in a pine grove and reached by meandering paths, the cabins were built to harmonize with the natural setting. They had log slab siding, rubble masonry foundations and chimneys of locally quarried stone, and porches of peeled log railings and posts. *(Photograph by Laura Soullière, courtesy National Park Service, National Historic Landmarks Survey)*

ley and later the development of the North Rim of the Grand Canyon. Hull and Vint continued to work closely with the Underwood firm until 1927, when the Western Field Office was organized in San Francisco and the landscape engineering function moved again.[19]

About 1923, a major change in concessionaires' facilities occurred, apparently at the urging of Stephen Mather. Underwood's plan for a large hotel at Zion had been approved and highly complimented by the Commission of Fine Arts. Hull praised the project plans, which he said resulted from a study of the site, "having always in mind the necessity of keeping unharmed the splendid scenery of this area." Not only were the buildings of a high quality, but a comprehensive landscape plan was also developed for the entire development. Mather, however, opposed the idea of a large hotel, and Underwood redesigned the plan in the form of a smaller lodge or pavilion with outlying cottages and service buildings, establishing a design precedent that would be followed for many years. By 1926, Hull reported that "a comprehensive landscape plan" was "being carried out in the vicinity of the new lodge" and that the National Park Service had approved a utility group proposed by the concessionaire. Several features distinguished the site plan and the design of the pavilion and cabins. The buildings were sited far back from the canyon rim against a rocky hillside that provided a scenic backdrop for the centrally located pavilion. A one-way curvilinear drive enabled tour buses and automobiles to approach and depart from the two-story pavilion, which featured a lobby, dining hall, and about seventy-five guest rooms. Passengers disembarked and entered the lobby through a porte-cochère made of massive piers of rustic stonemasonry. The roof of the porte-cochère functioned as a second-story observation deck surrounded by a parapet of stone piers and log rails, from which visitors could view the canyon. The grounds before the lodge were fashioned into a cactus garden edged with stone boulders and paths leading to the rim. Standard and deluxe cottages, fashioned from native pine and stone, were nestled in the surrounding woodland and reached by paths leading from the central pavilion. Parking was placed behind the pavilion.[20]

Underwood's designs were in keeping with the National Park Service's program for rustic design and native materials yet advanced the idea of "rustic" into a design idiom that had far-reaching influence on government-built structures and the overall definition of principles of rustic design. Underwood creatively adopted features such as the porte-cochère, jerkinhead gables, bands of small-paned windows, elongated dormers, clerestories, truss roofing, and massive stone fireplaces. He explored many features of the Adirondack style, the work of the Bay Area architects, and the work of designers of the early park lodges. He achieved "rustic" solutions with modern building materials such as stained and textured concrete and plate-glass windows, and he successfully incorporated into his designs landscape features such as terraces, stairways, stone parapets, loop entry drives, and native plantings. The work of Underwood strongly reinforced and expanded the principles emerging from the Landscape Division's own work. Like the collaboration with Maier, the association with the Underwood firm stimulated and enriched the Landscape Division's inventiveness and expression in the design of park structures. This collaboration also enabled them to work out landscape plans for the new developments.

The Development of Park Roads

The development of roads took on major importance during Hull's years with the service. By the end of 1925, a substantial amount of Hull and Vint's time was spent on the construction of roads. The landscape engineers worked with the Civil Engineering Division, then headed by Bert H. Burrell, and the Bureau of Public Roads from the initial on-the-ground inspection of the territory before the road was surveyed to the final approval of the work. A landscape engineer carefully went over the preliminary road lines, suggesting changes to protect landscape features or to take advantage of scenic points previously overlooked. The landscape engineer made a number of visits during construction to review the work and advise on landscape matters, "particularly with the idea of making the finished result the best possible in its relation to the landscape." The landscape engineers also paid considerable attention to the design, construction, and workmanship of the bridges.[21]

Ever since Punchard's tenure, the landscape engineers had collaborated with the civil engineers to develop park roads as scenic routes. Under George Goodwin, the service's first civil engineer, the roles of the civil and landscape engineers were differentiated. Civil engineers were concerned with the technical aspects of road construction, and the landscape engineers were concerned with the protection of significant features and locating the road in reference to scenic vistas. Roads were more than just a necessity leading visitors to scenic points and the comforts of developed areas; they were an integral part of the park experience.

From 1883 until 1917, when the service hired George Goodwin, park roads were built under the supervision of an engineer from the War Department. Built under the direction of the army engineer Major Hiram M. Chittenden, Yellowstone's roads were the best of all the national parks. Among his engineering achievements were the road over Mount Washburn, the 200-foot Golden Gate Viaduct—a series of eleven concrete arches built into a cliff wall, and the Yellowstone River (later Chittenden) Bridge—a 120-foot arch of steel and concrete. Chittenden also built the first road into Mount Rainier, funded by Congress from 1903 to 1906 and involving passage over rough, mountainous terrain. By 1910, a "barely passable" road was built as far as Paradise Valley.[22]

Creating a curving roadway that flowed with and lay lightly on the land had been the goal of park designers even before the creation of the National Park Service. Chittenden believed that the extension of the road system in Yellowstone should be restricted to actual necessities and that the park should be preserved in its natural state to the fullest degree possible. Where roads were necessary they should be made as perfect as possible. Roads were to be well built so they would detract from the natural scenery far less than ones rough and incomplete. The government played an important role in ensuring that roads were limited in extent, met actual needs, and were perfect examples of their class.[23]

Funding for roads remained a problem into the 1920s, particularly in Yosemite, where in 1923 only 8 of the park's 138 miles of road had been constructed under congressional appropriations. Roads were narrow, unsurfaced, and exceedingly steep; there were numerous sharp curves, and frequent accidents were reported. Increasing numbers of visitors came to the parks by automobile, placing greater and greater pressure on the National Park Service to make roads safer and increase visitors' access to various points within the park. New entrances into parks were opened as approach highways were built by state highway departments or the U.S. Forest Service. Throngs of visitors entered the parks, requiring new entrance stations, park roads, parking, and campgrounds. In 1923, when the Naches Pass Highway opened, twenty-five thousand visitors traveled across the Cascades and entered Mount Rainier National Park at the White River Entrance.

Road Design and Construction

Park road designers endeavored to eliminate the hazardous curves, sharp turns, and steep inclines that characterized mountain roads. Switchbacks, where a road changes direction at a tight angle, were common in early roads such as the Fall River Road in Rocky Mountain National Park built early in the century by the state of Colorado. Switchbacks on most roads were gradually replaced by radial curves.

It was the Columbia River Highway, constructed between 1913 and 1922 by Samuel Lancaster, an engineer of the Oregon Highway Department, which established the state of the art for building scenic roads in mountainous areas. The Columbia River Highway, originally seventy-four miles in length, featured a hundred-foot-minimum curve radius, a twenty-four-foot-wide roadway, and maximum grade of 5 percent in its first section. Naturalistic tunnels were carved out of the steep rock embankments that rose from the river; several had arched buttresses that alternated with open galleries to provide the motorist with river views framed by jagged cuts in the natural bedrock. Guardrails in a variety of designs and bridges were incorporated into the design. Particularly well known was the series of radial curves which enabled motorists to ascend the steep banks that rose sharply from the Columbia River near Crown Point. Skirting the edge of the national forests and providing access to popular attractions such as Multnomah Falls, the road provided opportunities for recreational development. The U.S. Forest Service built its first campground at nearby Eagle Creek, and the state of Oregon developed a visitor center and observation tower at Crown Point and visitor facilities including a lodge, trails, and bridges at Multnomah Falls. The aesthetic and engineering achievement of the road would greatly influence the construction of park roads in the next decade.[24]

For the national park roads, the civil engineers focused on the practical and technical details of road construction, including gradient, drainage, excavating, grading, surfacing, and the construction of revetments, culverts, and bridges. Meanwhile, the landscape engineers were interested in aesthetic and scenic con-

5.7. Photographed in 1915, Mitchell Point Tunnel was one of several naturalistic tunnels constructed along the Columbia River Highway by the Oregon Highway Department from 1913 to 1922. Carved out of a steep rock embankment that rose from the river, the tunnel was 390 feet long and had arched buttresses that alternated with open galleries to provide the motorist with river views framed by jagged rock work. *(Photograph courtesy Oregon Historical Society, neg. 3587)*

cerns, such as the location of the road, provisions for viewpoints and vistas, the external character of structures, and the creation of a smooth flowing road that followed the natural contours of the land. As stewards of the park landscape, the landscape engineers also ensured that significant natural features and scenic qualities would be protected from construction damage as well as from damage related to its location and use. Scenic views, especially those from trails, other roadways, and scenic overlooks, were to remain undisturbed by roads or other forms of development. Where such interference was unavoidable, efforts were made to blend the roadway into the natural setting and to conceal any construction scars.

Cut-and-fill techniques were employed to create an even grade by boring into the natural hillsides on one side of the roadway and building up areas of fill on the other. The construction of roads initially relied upon tangents and radial

5.8. The Grand Loop envisioned by Hiram Chittenden for Yellowstone National Park required a segment of road near Tower Falls which traversed the steep canyon walls along the Yellowstone River without disturbing the area's outstanding scenic character and natural beauty. *(Photograph by George A. Grant, courtesy of the National Park Service Historic Photography Collection)*

curves. By the 1920s, tangents gave way to curvilinear stretches interconnected with radial curves. By the end of the 1920s, superelevations were being built into roadways and bridges. As the National Park Service gained experience in designing parkways in the East in the 1930s, smooth transitional curves based on spirals and superelevations were introduced, raising the standard of park roads. The National Park Service endeavored to maintain a maximum grade of 5 percent, although as much as an 8 percent grade was sometimes allowed.[25]

Downing's classification of approach, circuit, and service roads of the nineteenth-century pleasure grounds influenced the character and the classification of national park roads. The idea of the circuit road would be extensively applied at various scales in national park design, from Yellowstone's Grand Loop to campground roads. So well did the circular movement of vehicles serve park designers in creating a flow that loop developments occurred at all scales to control and facilitate the flow of traffic, from the headquarters at Mammoth Hot Springs

5.9. In 1903 Hiram Chittenden directed the construction of the road near Tower Falls in Yellowstone National Park. The road was carefully carved into the base of the famous Overhanging Cliff so that it merged visually with the natural bands of columnar basalt on either side of the canyon. Such park roads required frequent clearing, repair, and restoration. This 1933 view shows log guardrails, a crushed rock surface, and debris left from the one of the area's many rockslides. *(Photograph by George A. Grant, courtesy of the National Park Service Historic Photography Collection)*

to spur roads to scenic overlooks. Although it was never realized, Frederick Law Olmsted Sr. had recommended a circuit road in Yosemite Valley in 1864.

Another convention from the English gardening tradition adopted and commonly used by national park designers was the "wye" intersection, whereby intersecting roads came together at a wide angle. Frequently the wye was used for branch roads leaving or entering a main road. This configuration facilitated the flow of traffic; it eliminated the need for motorists to make sharp turns and allowed traffic to flow in an uninterrupted manner along the curvilinear line of the roadway. The center of the wye often provided an island for rockwork, native plantings, or signs. Wye intersections and loop developments would become major characteristics of the park drives and parkways developed in the East in the 1930s.

Several important developments had occurred in the design of park roads and parkways by the 1920s. Not only had the nineteenth-century parks provided carriage roads separate from bridle and pedestrian trails, but the idea of interconnected parks and parkways which the Olmsted firm had pioneered in Brooklyn and other East Coast cities had spread across the nation, and by 1920, such park and parkway networks were also developing in Buffalo, Essex County (New Jersey), Seattle, the District of Columbia, Kansas City, Memphis, and other cities.

Like the landscape engineers, the civil engineers looked to the nation's experts for advice on park development. Major William A. Welch, the nation's foremost park engineer and general manager of the Palisades Interstate Park in New York and New Jersey, visited a number of the parks in 1921 and provided advice on engineering issues from the construction of roads to the development of sanitary facilities. Featured as a model of park development at the 1917 national parks conference, Welch's work remained in the forefront of state park work through the 1920s. Those attending the 1922 meeting of the National Conference of State Parks saw firsthand Welch's dramatic Storm King Road. Although Welch's work was held in high regard, his designs for stonemasonry guardrails in the Craftsman style would be criticized several years later by national park designers for their quaint, peanut-brittle-like character. The scarring of monolithic Storm King visible from the Hudson River and the nearby Bear Mountain Bridge also disturbed park designers, who sought ways to conceal and subordinate artificial construction.[26]

The civil engineers relied heavily upon the work of the U.S. Forest Service, which, in collaboration with the Bureau of Public Roads, had been constructing wilderness roads for many years. Their technical specifications, including solutions for log bridges and trestles, cribbing, culverts and retaining walls, dry-rubble masonry, riprap, and wooden guardrails, were published annually in *Specifications for Forest Road Construction*. Harwood Frost's *Art of Road Making* (1910) and Arthur H. Blanchard and Henry B. Drowne's *Text-book on Highway Engineering* (1913) were state-of-the-art manuals for road engineering, treating subjects such as road gradients and cross sections.[27]

The Bronx River Parkway, constructed from 1913 to 1925, pioneered in the development of scenic roadways by reclaiming land along the riverfront. This development was an effort to clean up unsightly and unsanitary conditions along the Bronx River and protect the river from further pollution while at the same time creating a pleasure drive and network of cross-county roads. It was the collaborative effort of chief landscape architect Hermann Merkel, superintendent of landscape construction Gilmore Clarke, and engineer Jay Downer. Field trips to see this pioneering work were featured at the 1922 meeting of the National Conference of State Parks. By the late 1920s, Vint and Clarke were well acquainted and had exchanged staff for short periods of time to increase their experience. Stanley W. Abbott and Wilbur E. Simonson, designers of parkways for the National Park Service in the 1930s, had worked under Clarke in Westchester County before joining the National Park Service.

Landscape architects likely heeded the philosophical and practical advice of Hubbard and Waugh. Hubbard described the "good park road" as one that, often following uneven topography, "may be irregular in curvature, shrub-grown at the edges, somewhat steeper in gradient, slightly rough and inconspicuous in surface, sunk below the surrounding surface in places to avoid interruption of a view, even slightly irregular in width if thereby it might carry its traffic to the points intended with less interruption of the natural character of the landscape."[28]

Hubbard stressed the practical necessity of roads in natural areas but upheld their aesthetic value. He recommended the development of circuit roads: "If the park is large, perhaps in several circuits large and small, different in the views that they command. The various scenes which are to be displayed to the visitor by automobile should be revealed to him to good advantage and in pleasing succession, that their characters may enhance one another. The circuit drive should of course be far enough within the park to allow of a sufficient screen between the drive and the outside city: the drive should be in the park, that is, not between the town and the park" (309).

The distinction of roadways for varying purposes and different modes of transportation was an inherent characteristic of nineteenth-century urban parks. Frederick Law Olmsted Sr.'s emphasis on separate systems for different types of transportation was so fundamental to the development of national parks that it is often taken for granted, and the origins of the idea in the principles of landscape architecture are often overlooked. The idea of separation meant that not only would roads for motor traffic be separate from bridle trails or pedestrian trails but that to protect the forests from fire, a separate network of fire or truck trails could also be developed and maintained in an inconspicuous way. This concept would prove to be of great value in national parks, where it was desirable to separate motor roads from trails and scenic roads traveled by visitors from roads serving administrative purposes. Such separation reduced the visual intrusions presented by other forms of construction and ensured that the sequential experience and pleasure of traveling scenic park roads or hiking wilderness trails remained uninterrupted.

By the end of the 1930s, most parks had developed independent circulation networks serving various functions. These were coordinated under each park's master plan. Annual roads and trails appropriations, public works allotments, and Emergency Conservation Work by the Civilian Conservation Corps made construction of the various roads and trails possible. Shenandoah National Park had five different, intersecting systems of circulation. First was Skyline Drive, a scenic road constructed from 1931 to 1942 along the ridge as the linear backbone of the park. Second was a section of the long-distance Appalachian Trail, begun in the late 1920s and relocated during the 1930s to accommodate the ridge drive. The trail followed the ridge from north to south, crossing the drive at various points and intersecting with recreational trails that led to scenic peaks and picturesque hollows. A system of truck trails provided a network of administrative roads used for controlling fires and patrolling the park boundaries. These penetrated distant areas of the park and connected Skyline Drive with local roads in the hollows below. The park also had an extensive network of recreational trails for hiking, which intersected with the Appalachian Trail and Skyline Drive and led to picturesque features such as waterfalls, rock formations, springs, and hemlock groves or to ridgetop outcroppings where spectacular views could be had. Many of these were built by the Civilian Conservation Corps in the 1930s. In addition, there was a network of sturdier bridle trails, which brought visitors on horseback to some of the finest scenic features and, in the late 1930s, connected with stables developed at Skyland, one of the developed areas on the drive. In addition, each developed area had its own system of loop and spur roads. Approach roads, in the form of state highways, crossed or adjoined the park in several locations. These were improved through roadside cleanup, planted medians, wye intersections or grade separations, and attractive park entrances.

Grade separation was an ingenious device developed by Frederick Law Olmsted Sr. at Central Park and adopted at other urban parks including Franklin Park. Park designers were usually able to avoid having trails cross roadways, but not always. At the east entrance to Mount Rainier at Tipsoo Lake, for example, a bridge carrying the Cascade Crest Trail across the approach road became at once a grade separation, a boundary marker between the national park and national forest, and a gateway to the park. In Yosemite Valley in the late 1920s, the separation of pedestrian, horseback, and automobile traffic in what was already a congested valley warranted the development of grade separations, basically stone-veneered bridges that incorporated arched tunnels for bridle and pedestrian trails to pass underneath.

The Landscape Architect's Role

Punchard, Hull, and Vint brought valuable expertise to the road construction program. As stewards of the park landscape, they endeavored to protect the scenery from damage and ensure that all built features harmonized with the natural setting of the park. They were concerned with selecting the route that provided access to major attractions in the park and offered the best views of park scenery along the way. Their challenge was to do this without destroying the inherent beauty of the park. Paramount in designing a park road from a landscape standpoint was locating it in reference to scenery. Downing's principles on creating a sequential experience in which the visitor would pass through spaces of varying character and past picturesque features and then arrive at scenic vistas were central to their recommendations.

One of the first roads resulting from the collaboration of park service civil and landscape engineers was the Carbon River Road on the west side of Mount Rainier. Mather had urged the construction of this road in his report, and in 1921, Goodwin and Hull together located the new road, which was described in the annual report as "being laid out so as to develop and save such scenic accents as individual fine trees and springs gushing from the rocks—in short, to make the most of every scenic detail in making travel over the road enjoyable." This route opened up the particularly beautiful northwest area of the park to motorists. In Hull's opinion, because of its careful preliminary planning, it also promised to be one of the national park system's "finest scenic routes."[29]

The success of many park roads lay in their ability to present the splendors of nature. Vista was of primary importance in locating a road, and selecting viewpoints for visitor enjoyment was an important role of the landscape engineer. Hubbard gave specific rules for the design and planting of roads in natural areas:

> If this enjoyment of views from the road is a matter of considerable importance in the whole design, pains should be taken that the spectators come to the various outlooks and objects of interest without retracing their course, in pleasant sequence, and prepared by each one for the next to come, as where, after passing through a shady wood, a road comes to an outlook over a sunny landscape. Views taken up and down the road must be considered: they are inevitably seen by every one who travels upon it. Where a road changes direction, a view out at the point of change, continuing the line of the road which approaches it and centering on an interesting distant object suitably enframed by the planting about the road itself, is a desirable possibility which the designer should have in mind. Views to be enjoyed from a road, where the spectator looks sharply to the right or left, should of course be enframed by the planting along the road itself, but they should not be enframed with so small an opening that the traveler has been carried by before he has had time to enjoy the view. It is usually desirable also that interesting views should not be seen to the right and left of the road at the same time, if it can be arranged that they be seen alternately.[30]

One of the first to understand and articulate ideas about wilderness roads was Frank Waugh. He wrote in 1917 that the landscape designer should utilize to the utmost all the natural scenery, fully developing every good view. Development required at least three things: "First, the line of the best view must be determined and kept open; second, this view must be framed by suitable plantings; third, inferior views must be blocked out or reduced to mere promissory glimpses." [31]

According to Waugh, vistas were to be open and have a clear focal point such as a mountain, lake, or waterfall. In keeping with Downing's principles, he urged that roads be designed to draw attention to each view: "As a rule such special views require further to be fixed, marked and advertised by placing at the optimum point of observation an appropriate seat, carriage turn, rest house or similar accessory. Thus the stranger is directed unmistakably to the main feature, the desirable vista or the glorious outlook" (121).

Waugh carried out his own ideas in his work for the U.S. Forest Service. His design for Mount Hood Road, a curving mountain road with a panorama of unraveling vistas and parking turnouts to provide scenic views, is the most complete example of his own theory. Waugh also worked at Bryce Canyon in the years just before it was made a national park and may have influenced the design of the scenic road with its spur roads to scenic viewpoints. During the 1930s, Waugh, at the request of his former student Conrad Wirth, then assistant director of the National Park Service, conveyed his ideas on roads, trails, and other aspects of development for natural areas in a manual for the Civilian Conservation Corps entitled *Landscape Conservation*.[32]

Waugh saw roads and trails as the framework for the entire design of a recreational area, providing transit between principal points in the park and a means of "revealing pleasant scenery." The designer's role was to locate the main points of scenic value, such as fine outlooks, stately groups of trees, and objects of local interest, and to lay out trails connecting these. The angle at which hikers approached scenic features was particularly important. In Waugh's theory of trail design, scenic objects or features were to be viewed straight ahead and at proper distances, whereas broad outlooks over valleys, mountains, or water were to be viewed at varying angles to the trail. This was accomplished by giving a "convenient" turn to the trail at the point of view and by widening the trail and providing a stopping place, perhaps with seats facing the outlook. Waugh believed that scenery should be arranged along a trail like a series of themes or motives arranged in "paragraphs" that drew attention to the unique natural features of a variety of landscape types. He drew attention to the desirable effects created at "paragraphic points" where roads or paths changed direction or grade, at prominent overlooks and viewpoints, where the nature of vegetation changed, or where the subject of the primary motive — for example, a panoramic mountain view — came into full view. Waugh, furthermore, cautioned against the use of straight lines and radial curves in building paths or roads.[33]

Henry Hubbard also gave substantial advice for designing roads in natural parks. Roads were to lay gently on the ground, interrupting the natural topography as little as possible. They could be made inconspicuous by concealing them with vegetation and by carefully shaping the roadway and selecting materials. Influenced by the naturalistic gardening techniques that Repton and Downing had espoused and the Olmsted firm practiced, Hubbard wrote,

> In a naturalistic landscape, as far as it is possible, the road should seem to lie upon the surface of the ground without interruption of the natural modeling. The surface of necessary cuts and fills should simulate the natural surface where possible; where this is impossible their modeling should still be as sequential and unbroken a continuation of the natural surface as the designer can arrange. Usually, if the road lies somewhat below the adjoining surface, it will be less conspicuous. Where a road must cross a view over an open area, in a naturalistic scheme, it may be impossible to conceal the road by planting without thereby interrupting the view. It may be still possible to lead the road across the open space in a depression, deep enough at any rate to conceal the road surface, perhaps deep enough to conceal any traffic as well, and in any case so arranged that the line of sight passes from a surface on the nearer side, related to the whole open area, to a surface on the farther side, apparently continuous with it, and the mind is thus led to suppose that the intervening surface, not seen, is of the same character.[34]

Hubbard further suggested that roads be surfaced with gravel and broken stone. If asphalt was to be used, the surfaces and edges of the road should be softened so that the appearance was similar to that of macadam. Hubbard recommended the construction of gutters made of cobblestones to form an irregular line along the edge of the road; along with turf gutters, these could provide adequate drainage (219–20).

Mather and Punchard had both been concerned about roadside conditions. Their first reports expressed their concerns over the problems of park roads passing along private lands and the problems of dead and decaying timber in the woodlands alongside park roads. One solution lay in the acquisition of additional lands for a park, a solution that was realized in a number of parks including Sequoia. Another, often more difficult to justify and thus to fund, was to clean up roads within existing boundaries. The best that could be hoped for was that new work would avoid the unsightly practices that marred roadsides in the past. Hull continued to encourage roadside improvements. Although he first urged that utility wires be placed on poles equipped with brackets that gave an appearance like that of a branching tree, by 1925 he recommended that the telephone lines that commonly followed the roads be placed underground.[35]

Private concern for the appearance of park roadsides emerged in Yellowstone, where fallen and dying trees as well as utility poles and wires disfigured the scenery along the roads. The first work in what became known as roadside cleanup began with private funds in 1924. Roadside cleanup entailed the removal of dead and fallen tress and other debris that accumulated in the woodlands along the park roads and the placing of telephone wire underground. With funds from John D. Rockefeller, workers cleared and beautified ten and a half miles of roadside between Mammoth Hot Springs and Obsidian Creek in the fall of 1924 and spring of 1925. The work generated a favorable response from park visitors, and the following year, at a cost of $9,068, nine miles of roadside were improved between Mammoth Hot Springs and Norris Junction and along Yellowstone Lake on the new route between Lake Junction and Bridge Bay. Rockefeller, pleased with the results, extended his funding of this work for another year and planned to fund similar work at Crater Lake. Hull considered the cleanup of roadsides and other park areas (such as the abandoned area in Sequoia's Giant Forest) to be the most important improvements in the mid-1920s. It was not until the end of the 1920s that this work became an integral part of park service work and was funded under annual appropriations.[36]

Armed with justifications prepared by park superintendents, Mather annually sought increased congressional appropriations for road construction and improvements. Finally on April 9, 1924, "an act authorizing the construction, reconstruction, and improvement of roads and trails, inclusive of necessary bridges, in the national parks and monuments" made possible annual appropriations for park roads and trails (43 Stat. 90). Recognizing the need to reconstruct most of the existing park roads to modern standards, Congress approved the same year a general road program authorizing a total appropriation of $7.5 million over a three-year period. Appropriations for the years 1924 to 1928 amounted to $6.5 million; an additional $2.5 million was appropriated under the Appropriations Act of 1928. By October 1927, 89.385 miles of modern automobile roads had been completed, and 184.65 miles were under construction; 337.75 miles of surveys had been completed and 676.88 miles of surveys authorized. In order to keep up with increasing visitors and provide adequate modern road systems in all parks and monuments, $50 million, at a rate of $5 million annually over a ten-year period, was estimated as necessary in October 1927.[37]

The Leavitt Approach Road Act of January 31, 1931, further authorized the park service to spend funds on construction and improvement of approach roads leading to parks but located outside park boundaries. This made possible the improvement of state highways and roads through national forests. By controlling approaches to parks, the National Park Service was able to provide a graceful transition into the park from the surrounding countryside. Such a transition prepared visitors for the park experience and oriented them to an environment where nature dominated.[38]

With annual appropriations ensured, each park superintendent developed a three-year plan for road improvements. Under this arrangement, superintendents could program the construction of individual roads in segments and develop a well-coordinated system of circulation which met administrative needs, provided visitors access to the key points within the park, and met the demands of a society increasing reliant on the automobile. At the end of 1925, Yellowstone, for example, had 298 miles of roads that included a Grand Loop of 137.4 miles, 79.1 miles of approach and connecting roads, and 81.5 miles of secondary roads, many of which led to points of scenic interest. Here improvements entailed thirteen different projects to be phased over a three-year period and included the reconstruction of entire roads or portions of them, the widening and surfacing of others, and the construction of new sections.[39]

Interbureau Agreement with the Bureau of Public Roads

The increased appropriations for road and trail construction and a solidifying relationship with the Bureau of Public Roads, which was under the U.S. Department of Agriculture, resulted in a cooperative agreement for the construction and improvement of roads and trails. The interbureau agreement was signed by the Department of the Interior and the Department of Agriculture on January 18, 1926. Consequently all contracts and surveys were turned over to the bureau, and the Engineering Division of the National Park Service reorganized. Although the Engineering Division's headquarters were moved from Portland, Oregon, to Yellowstone and the number of permanent engineers was reduced from eleven to three, three resident engineers were hired to reside in the parks and directly supervise road, trail, and other construction. This new system made coordinating all construction and maintenance activities in the parks more systematic and economical and enabled the engineering department to take on special problems and make standardized improvements, such as oiling roads to eliminate dust.[40]

The agreement enabled the National Park Service to use the road-building organization of the Bureau of Public Roads to survey, construct, reconstruct, and improve roads and trails within the national parks. This collaboration ensured that park roads would be built or upgraded to modern standards and reflect state-of-the-art engineering. The agreement called upon the Bureau of Public Roads to make every effort "to harmonize the standards of construction" of park roads and trails with those adopted for the roads of the national forests and others that were part of the Federal Aid Highway System and to "secure the best modern practice in the location, design, construction and improvement" of the roads. This agreement made it possible for the National Park Service to cooperate with state highway departments and the U.S. Forest Service on a general scheme of improvements that would result in an interconnected system of highways.[41]

As part of the initial planning for each project, the National Park Service's landscape engineer cooperated with Bureau of Public Roads engineers in the preliminary investigation of proposed roads and prepared a report on all landscape features of the proposed project. Meanwhile, the bureau's engineer would

5.10. Steam shovel and construction vehicles near the summit of the Going-to-the-Sun Highway in the late 1920s. Collaboration with the Bureau of Public Roads and contracts with private construction companies enabled the park service to "secure the best modern practice in the location, design, construction, and improvement" of wilderness roads. *(Photograph courtesy National Park Service, Glacier National Park)*

report on the location and construction of the project and provide an estimate of the cost. These reports were submitted to the park superintendent, who would in turn respond in the form of another report.[42]

As projects got under way, the bureau's district engineer took charge of the project and with the cooperation of the park superintendent and landscape engineer conducted the survey and prepared plans, specifications, and estimates for the project. These would ultimately be reviewed and approved by the park superintendent, landscape engineer, and National Park Service director. After contracts for particular sections of road and other aspects such as the construction of bridges were announced, the bureau's engineer and the park superin-

5.11. From the protective parapets of native stonemasonry along the transmountain Going-to-the-Sun Highway, visitors could view the spectacular mountain scenery of Glacier National Park. While civil engineers of the Bureau of Public Roads attended to the technical aspects of road building such as grade and width, the National Park Service's landscape engineers attended to locating the road with least injury to the scenery, presenting vistas, and designing guardrails, culverts, and bridges that harmonized with the natural scenery. *(Photograph by George A. Grant, courtesy National Park Service Historic Photography Collection)*

tendent would together tabulate the bids, and the award would be made by the secretary of the interior. The work would proceed according to the plans and specifications written into the contracts. The agreement pointed out that specifications "shall govern all ordinary landscape features of the work, and any minor alterations which are authorized under the specifications could be made during the progress of the work as ordered in writing by the bureau's district engineer with the concurrence of the landscape engineer.[43]

The agreement clearly placed the responsibility for road construction in the hands of the park superintendent and the landscape engineers, giving only minor responsibilities to the civil engineers of the park service. At the time of the agreement, leadership in civil engineering was weak. Goodwin, who had offices at Glacier and then in Portland, Oregon, left the service in the mid-1920s. In 1927, Frank A. Kittredge became the chief engineer of the National Park Service. Kittredge was a former Bureau of Public Roads engineer with extensive experience in building park roads, had been special assistant to L. I. Hewes, one of the chief administrators of the Bureau of Public Roads for several years, and was considered one of the bureau's best locating engineers. Shortly thereafter, the National Park Service expanded Kittredge's role in the national park road program. The landscape architects continued, however, to have primary control over the aesthetic and protective issues related to road construction.[44]

Landscape protection clearly marked the focus of Hull and Vint's work by this time. As the road and trail program steadily grew, the attention of the landscape engineers shifted from planning and developing park villages to developing roads and trails that were harmonious with the natural setting of each park.

Preservation of Park Scenery

About the time of the interbureau agreement, Mather began to call the work of the landscape engineers "preservation of park scenery." The 1920s proved to be a period of experimentation as Hull and Vint adapted the principles of park design and landscape gardening which they inherited from Downing, Olmsted, Hubbard, and Waugh to the special problems of national parks. Such experimentation characterized their role in the design of park roads more than any other aspect of their work.

Increasing road construction brought greater emphasis to the landscape engineer's role as a steward of the national parks: "In addition to seeing that roads are located with the least injury to the chief scenic features of the park, it is important that attention be given to the preservation of the forests and other natural features along the line of the roadbed, the cutting of vistas, and the harmonizing of the necessary culverts and bridges with the landscape."[45]

Protecting natural features and scenic beauty required control over the construction process. The landscape engineers placed restrictions on the burning of debris cleared from the right-of-way, including roots, stumps, timber, and brush. They approved the location of borrow pits, quarries, and crushing plants and required the cleanup of stones cast beyond the toe of filled slopes. They also required that stumps outside the road section be removed and that the ragged edges of cut slopes be rounded to appear naturalistic.

Scenery preservation also required careful attention to the appearance of the roadway and structures such as bridges and guardrails. From the beginning of the roads program, the landscape engineers were responsible for the materials, methods of construction, and external designs for road features. Roads were generally surfaced with crushed stone or macadam using local stone to harmo-

5.12. Christine Falls Bridge (1927) at Mount Rainier National Park achieved a synthesis of naturalistic design, advanced technology, and scenery preservation. The concrete arch, faced with weathered and lichen-covered native stone, carried the curving roadway and perfectly enframed the scenic vista of the falls. *(Photograph by Jet Lowe, courtesy National Park Service, Historic American Engineering Record)*

nize with the soil and rock of the surrounding countryside. All stone, whether to be crushed or to be used in masonry work, was taken from quarries or other sources approved by the landscape engineer. The landscape engineers explored the use of local stone in designing guardrails, the face walls of culverts, and the side walls and arch rings of bridges.

Although the interbureau agreement governed the procedures for planning and executing road projects, it relegated specific landscape concerns and practices to the specifications for each contract. Specifications contained in the earliest contracts varied from project to project, making it necessary for the park designers to draw up each contract with careful reference to the landscape concerns presented by each project.

By 1927, when Hull left the National Park Service, the landscape engineers had made significant strides in advancing the principles of naturalistic landscape gardening. The park service had adapted the tenets and practices of what Henry Hubbard called the Modern American Landscape style and Frank Waugh called the natural style to the practical needs of parks that had to be made accessible to large numbers of tourists in automobiles. Naturalism required that roads and trails follow the natural contours in curving lines and that overlooks be located to take best advantage of scenic views and provide access to outstanding natural features without impairing them. It also called for roadside cleanup. Park roads were built with a minimum of cut and fill, and steep grades, sharp turns, and switchbacks were eliminated. Wherever roads would be visible from a distance, either from other places along the road or from scenic turnouts, viewpoints, or trails, they were blended into the scenery. Roads were located where they avoided damage to significant natural features such as outcroppings of stone, groves of trees, waterfalls, and splendid gorges. On the other hand, they passed close enough to such features to provide vistas from the roadway or turnouts. When artificial structures could not be concealed by vegetation or topography, they were carefully constructed of log or stonemasonry and designed to harmonize with the natural setting. This was true of guardrails along the Going-to-the-Sun Highway in Glacier, where low masonry parapets were fashioned from a random arrangement of irregularly shaped and sized local rock and where the monotony and linearity of form were relieved by crenulations at regular intervals. It was true of the Christine Falls Bridge at Mount Rainier, where stonework blended harmoniously with the natural rocks of the site and the arch perfectly enframed a picturesque waterfall from several approaches. To achieve this effect at Christine Falls and elsewhere, designers perfected the laying of stone, used weathered stone the color and texture of the surrounding rocks, visualized the scene from several points of view, and used graceful arched forms, not only in the elevation of the bridge but also in the design of the roadway across it. At Christine Falls, the flanking walls were curved to flow continuously with the radius curve of the roadway, and a superelevation was built into the side of the deck. This was a triumph of park bridge design, where engineering and the aesthetics of landscape design coincided with superb results.

PART III

Thomas Vint
and the Work of the
Western Field Office, 1927 to 1932

Chapter 6

Principles and Practices
for Naturalistic Roads and Trails

The very character of the work dictated that the organization be composed of a group of men especially trained in planning the use and improvement of conservational lands; schooled in the principles of design and graphic presentation of ideas; acquainted with the fundamentals of architecture and engineering; accustomed to preparing grading plans, planting plans, preliminary architectural plans, specifications, and estimates; with an understanding of forestry, botany, geology, and wildlife; and above all, men who could evaluate scenic resources and recreational possibilities, and then correlate these values in a Master Plan.

Henry Hubbard, "Landscape Development Based on Conservation," *Landscape Architecture*, 1939

Although Stephen Mather's vision for the landscape engineer's role called for a variety of tasks, by 1927 the landscape engineers' efforts were channeled into three distinct areas: locating and designing park roads and trails, designing park structures, and reviewing concessionaires' plans and designs. In the next five years, the size and influence of the Landscape Division would grow as the National Park Service received additional funds for park development and as the need for advance planning increased. On October 1, 1927, Director Mather established a field headquarters in San Francisco to create a centrally located group of specialists whose job was to advise the director and park superintendents on matters related to park development and management. The field headquarters was divided into several divisions, covering civil engineering, landscape architecture, education, forestry, and sanitary engineering.

Under the new organization, the responsibilities of the Engineering and Landscape Divisions were differentiated. Engineers did the preliminary programming of roads and trails funds and provided design and supervisory services to parks without resident engineers. The engineers advised park superintendents on the construction of trails and minor roads and on the development of utilities, including water, electricity, telephone, and sewerage. They also were in charge of purchasing equipment needed for building and maintaining roads and other facilities.[1]

The Landscape Division's responsibilities lay in three areas. First were design services, including the preparation of landscape layouts for developed areas and architectural drawings—both sketches and working plans—for buildings, bridges, and other structures. Next came the preliminary planning and final approval of roads, trails, and pertinent structures in cooperation with park officials and the Bureau of Public Roads in accordance with the "interbureau agreement" adopted on January 18, 1926. And finally, before construction, landscape architects were to review and recommend approval of all building plans by authorized concessionaires, or park operators. All of these projects were to be inspected by the landscape architect to verify that the approved plans and specifications were "faithfully carried out from a landscape standpoint."[2]

Under Thomas Chalmers Vint in the late 1920s, the landscape program expanded into a single, fully orchestrated process of park planning and development based on the principles of landscape preservation and harmonious design. Vint offered the service a varied background of practical skills in architecture and landscape architecture. As Hull's assistant, he had many years of field experience working out practical and aesthetic solutions. He was able to translate the vision of administrators Stephen Mather and Horace Albright and park superintendents such as Owen Tomlinson of Mount Rainier and John White of Sequoia into plans for interconnecting systems of scenic roads, trails, and developed areas and into drawings that fulfilled the functional and aesthetic requirements of park facilities. He developed a highly successful program of training his staff, assembled from several fields of study and areas of expertise: architects, landscape architects, engineers, and draftsmen. He was the "genius" behind a program of master plans on which the National Park Service relied for many years. He devised standards for locating and designing park roads which have had substantial influence on highway construction outside the National Park Service, and he coordinated a servicewide program of landscape preservation and harmonization to meet the park service's difficult twofold mission.[3]

Although primarily a landscape architect, Vint had training in architecture as well. A skilled draftsman and designer, he studied architecture in high school and graduated from the University of California, Berkeley, with a bachelor of science degree in landscape architecture in December 1920. He supplemented these studies with a semester of study at the Ecole des Beaux Arts at the University of Lyon, France, after serving in Europe during World War I and a course in city planning at the University of California, Los Angeles, in 1921.[4]

Vint's early working experience equipped him with a variety of practical skills that prepared him well for his duties as landscape engineer for the National Park Service. Before graduating from high school in 1913 and during summers while in college, Vint worked in the offices of several Los Angeles landscape architects, architects, and builders. These included A. S. Falconer, who at the time (1912–13) was preparing a portfolio of bungalows for the Southern California Home Builders and Standard Building Investment Company. From January to August 1914, Vint worked for W. J. Dodd, an architect whose projects were mostly large residences. Next, from August 1914 through July 1915, Vint worked as a draftsman and only assistant to Lloyd Wright, a landscape architect and the son of Frank Lloyd Wright, who was designing the grounds of large residences and laying out residential subdivisions. The following summer, Vint returned to work for Wright and his new partner Paul G. Thiene, who were working on landscape designs for residential areas in Pasadena. Years later Vint recalled that in Wright's office he had the opportunity to deal with "every problem from many angles" and received "thorough" training and exposure to the landscape profession. It was through these formative experiences that Vint was also exposed to the Arts and Crafts movement, California's burgeoning bungalow craze, the work of architects Charles and Henry Greene, and what Eugene O. Murmann called the California gardening style.[5]

After graduating from Berkeley, Vint worked a variety of short jobs while intermittently accepting contracts to grade and plant residential grounds and supervise construction. While working with a "pick and shovel" for a Los Angeles construction company, he learned about the large-scale planting of trees and shrubs. While working for the architectural firm of Mayberry and Jones from April to October 1921, he observed firsthand the use of concrete for the construction of hotels, garages, and hospitals. As head of the landscape office for Armstrong Nurseries of Ontario, California, Vint advised on planting designs and supervised planting projects. Just before moving to Yosemite to begin work for the National Park Service, Vint also did experimental nursery work for the California Walnut Growers Association at the state's experiment station at Riverside.[6]

In November 1922, Vint became Hull's assistant and architectural draftsman at the office in Yosemite. In 1923, the office moved to Los Angeles, where Hull and Vint shared the offices of architect Gilbert Stanley Underwood, who was working on a number of park lodges for concessionaires. When the office moved to San Francisco in the spring of 1927, Hull left the park service and Vint took charge of the landscape program, and when the field headquarters was organized the following October, Vint was given the title of chief landscape architect. Through this reorganization the landscape architects of the service, and particularly Vint, as chief landscape architect, assumed official responsibility over the location, character, and quality of all park construction.

In the spring of 1927, Vint began to build a staff to assist him with the increasing tasks related to the division's multifaceted work. At that time the office consisted of him and John B. Wosky, an architectural draftsman hired the previous year. Wosky was to remain in the San Francisco office, provide design support, and take care of landscape matters in Yosemite. Vint first hired Ernest A. Davidson, whom he assigned to work in Glacier, Yellowstone, and Mount Rainier. Davidson had worked on road programs and had substantial experience in the planting and transplanting of native plants and trees. He was assigned to the field to work on campground problems, oversee construction projects, supervise road and bridge construction, and advise on general matters pertaining to landscape and landscape protection.

In 1928, owing to increasing appropriations, Vint was able and ready to expand his staff of landscape architects, who would reside in the parks during the summer and work on drawings and plans at the headquarters in San Francisco during the winter. Merel S. Sager was a recent graduate of Harvard University's School of Landscape Architecture and had previously worked in the parks. New to the office, Sager spent a substantial amount of time in the office assisting Vint with plans to expand the staff. Sager also spent time in the field assisting Davidson at Mount Rainier, where he worked on the park's emerging program of native planting and transplanting. Kenneth McCarter and Harry Langley also joined the staff that year and, with little training from Vint, were assigned to the field.[7]

Because there were no civil service standards or examinations, Vint worked out a special list of job responsibilities and qualifications for the staff he wanted. His staff was to be capable in landscape matters, the design of buildings and structures, community planning, and the design of bridges. Designers were to divide their time between the parks and headquarters. Fieldwork included supervising construction of general park development projects, such as communities, tourist camps, buildings, roads, and bridges, and also involved the general protection of the native landscape, tree removal, and screen plantings. Office work included the preparation of working plans, sketches, and perspectives for architectural work and drawings for government buildings, including administrative and utility buildings, living quarters, shelters, and gateways. Designers were also to review and revise plans submitted by concessionaires for the construction of hotels and camps.[8]

Landscape design in national parks called for a unique combination of skills. Vint was looking for staff members who were trained in the general principles of landscape architecture and city planning and had a general knowledge of the fundamentals of architecture. Experience in design and construction of buildings and bridges was desirable, but training in nursery work or horticulture was not needed. He also was interested in individuals trained in architecture and city planning with some knowledge of the general principles of landscape architecture and experience in the design and supervision of the construction of residences, lodges, and resort buildings, particularly in "log, stone, and rustic construction."[9]

Vint described the unique work of his division:

> The work of the Landscape Division . . . is a different character than the general practice of the landscape profession. Although landscape work predominates in the work, it merges into the field of architecture. We have little use for landscape men whose experience is limited to the planting of shrubbery and allied to landscape work. There is little planting done within the National Parks and what is done is limited to the transplanting of native shrubs and trees, so the general commercial stock is not used. The work has to do with the preservation of the native landscape and involves the location and construction of communities, buildings, etc. within an existing landscape.[10]

In June 1928, Vint submitted sample civil service problems to the director to be included in the examination of possible candidates. These problems represented "typical" situations arising in park landscape work and the division's routine work. The first problem was to design, from given floor plans of a park residence, two elevations for each of three types of construction — stone, log, and timber. The second problem was to lay out a small park community having an administrative, residential, and utility area. Buildings, roadways, and walks were all to be located on the topographical map. The third problem asked applicants to design a trail bridge for travel by foot and horseback and to redesign another bridge so that it was suitable for park purposes.[11]

Vint wisely amassed a wide range of expertise in his staff members, who came from different backgrounds and had various strengths. Based on his own experience, with its balance of theoretical study and practical field experience, Vint strived to shape a staff that was equally well rounded and capable. His staff included men experienced in road construction, architectural drafting, landscape architecture, and park engineering. It included graduates of Harvard University and the University of California, Berkeley, who brought with them the most recent design theory from well-known professors, as well as graduates of state agricultural colleges, such as Iowa, Illinois, and Minnesota, which focused on practical applications of design, horticulture, and landscape engineering.

As his staff grew, Vint asked them to submit monthly narrative reports of their progress and problems they encountered in the field. In addition, handwritten notes passed between San Francisco and the landscape architects in the field, often jotted hastily while in transit or in the evening hours. Communication between Vint and his men was constant. Vint, too, spent much time in the parks, examining the work of contractors, Bureau of Public Road engineers, and park landscape architects. He also spent considerable time selecting the sites for museums at Yellowstone and Grand Canyon and cooperating with the Education Division and the advisory committee on the design for the museums.

By July 1929, Vint had transformed the Landscape Division into a design office with an increasing emphasis on general planning. He described its primary purpose as obtaining a "logical well-studied general development plan for each park, which included the control of the location, type of architecture, planting, and grading, in connection with any construction project." The division was involved to some degree in all phases of park development. It prepared the architectural and landscape plans for government projects under the direction of the park superintendents, reviewed the plans for tourist facilities to be built by the concessionaires, and reviewed the plans for roads and prepared the architectural plans for bridges constructed by the Bureau of Public Roads. All field staff returned to the San Francisco office as their field schedules allowed; for many, this was during the winter season. There they prepared and reviewed the plans for each year's construction. Vint preferred to have the men work on the plans that they would supervise in the field. They also developed sketch plans on which the park superintendent could base estimates for requesting funds the following year.[12]

By mid-1929, Vint's staff consisted of six assistant landscape architects and two junior landscape architects. He had established a training process in which each new member of the staff spent a year in the office working on drawings before being assigned to a field position as resident landscape architect. Vint felt that the division had succeeded in making "good landscape men" out of the park superintendents and the engineers of the Bureau of Public Roads and that it took at least a year to make "national park men" out of even the best-trained landscape architects he hired. In June 1929, Vint assigned Wosky to Lassen, Crater Lake, and Yosemite; Davidson to Glacier and Mount Rainier; Sager to Rocky Mountain, Mesa Verde, and Sequoia; Langley to Zion, Bryce, and Grand Canyon; and McCarter to Yellowstone. For the first time, Vint had a team of men with at least one year's experience in park work overseeing the projects in the major parks. New to the staff, Charles E. Peterson remained in the Western Field Office.[13]

Vint clearly envisioned his division as a design office specializing in both landscape and architectural design and his staff as professional advisers. In 1930, he remarked that the San Francisco office operated "much like the usual professional landscape office" except that it had "the ideal condition of having park superintendents for clients."[14]

Design of Park Roads

Building on the years of experimentation in the 1920s, Vint's office made substantial advances in the road-building program and the Bureau of Public Roads work in national parks in the period from 1928 to 1932. During these years, the landscape architects became more and more experienced in the principles of harmonious design and the design of park roads and structures. Their drawings became more and more detailed, and by 1930 they were providing road engineers and contractors with detailed designs for intersections, parking areas, loop developments, guardrails, and the treatment of road banks. Not only did they design the elevations of the bridges, but they also provided detailed diagrams of the arch rings and masonry. Masonry techniques based on standardized principles of construction and adaptable to local stone evolved. Specific practices were developed, such as protecting important rockwork and trees in the vicinity of construction sites and locating work camps in the right-of-way rather than beside the road, where they would disturb the roadside scenery and require restoration. The landscape architects supervised various aspects of road construction, paying particular attention to the effects of construction on scenery and natural features and to the harmonization of all built structures. The landscape architects approved the site of borrow pits, stone-crushing operations, quarries, and work camps. They gave instructions on site to the foremen and work crews on the proper technique for all masonry work, whether for bridges or guardrails. They approved the stone used for construction based on weathered appearance, coloration, and availability and gave careful directions for the shape and size of stones, the width of mortar joints, and the way that stones were laid to ensure the greatest harmonization possible with the natural setting.

As the program expanded, a number of landscape problems arose. Foremost was the destruction caused by blasting and burning. Although in 1928 the National Park Service drafted an amendment to the interbureau agreement inserting more stringent guidelines for the protection of park scenery, the situation was finally settled by a letter clarifying the role of the National Park Service landscape architect in all park road work and by special provisions in the specifications of future contracts. Writing the engineers in charge of park work in October 1928, J. A. Elliot, senior highway engineer for the Bureau of Public Roads, defined this role:

> There are certain features in the construction of roads within the National Parks which require the approval of the Landscape Architect, such as parking areas, loop development, the type of guard rail to be constructed, location and extent of each type of rail, trees to be taken out under advance clearing operations, etc. The Landscape Architect is anxious to receive suggestions from the engineer, realizing

that he is in close contact with the work and cognizant of all the features upon which the particular design depends. The Landscape Architect is responsible to the National Park Service and in order to avoid any misunderstanding on our part and to guarantee construction conforming with the Landscape Architect's ideas you must receive in writing from the Landscape Architect or his representative a statement on the above points before any orders or instructions are issued to the contractor. In the case of the parking areas and loop developments, a sketch will be furnished showing the proposed treatment of the area. Strict compliance with the above instructions is imperative.[15]

In the first several years of park service and bureau cooperation, specifications were carefully worked out for each project, whether a section of road or a group of bridges, and made available to contractors interested in bidding on the work. Vint was determined not only to streamline the process but also to ensure that the advances made in masonry techniques and landscape protection were understood and carried out by road engineers and the contractors. Having become director upon Mather's illness in 1928 and death the following year, Horace Albright gave Vint freedom to make improvements that emphasized the landscape standpoint in the building of roads.

Protection of the Landscape

In 1929, Vint's division developed a standard list of general provisions covering the points that were common to each project and could be translated into specifications for all projects. The provisions were intended to advance the goals of landscape protection and stewardship. They included many of the improvements that had evolved during the landscape architects' experience in road building since the mid-1920s. They emphasized the importance of landscape preservation, prohibited destructive practices of excavation through blasting, and described the standards for masonry work which had been incorporated in the plans for bridges and guardrails. Innovative was the introduction of type B excavation, which provided for careful rock excavation to avoid damage to outstanding natural features at specific sites. In June 1929, Director Albright approved the new provisions.

The general provisions for all park road projects called for the protection of natural features during construction in several ways. Special care was to be given to the protection of natural surroundings and adjacent campgrounds. Any timber or other landscape features scarred or damaged by the contractor's operations were to be removed, trimmed up, or restored as nearly as possible to their original condition at the contractor's expense. Special procedures for excavating earth and rock were incorporated to minimize the destruction and

6.1. Cooperation with the Bureau of Public Roads, better construction methods, and increased funding for public works made possible the improvement of many existing park roads in the late 1920s and 1930s. Built in 1883, the first road along the steep, vertical walls of Yellowstone's Golden Gate was carried on a wooden trestle. About 1900 the road was widened, and a reinforced concrete viaduct replaced the wooden trestle. As shown in this 1939 view, when the road was widened in the early 1930s, the viaduct was rebuilt according to the standards of the Bureau of Public Roads and the National Park Service's Landscape Division. The present-day viaduct was built to yet more advanced standards — in the 1970s. *(Photograph by George A. Grant, courtesy National Park Service Historic Photography Collection)*

casting of debris caused by a blasting process called shooting. Contractors were to remove unsightly rock falling outside finished slopes and limit the development of temporary trails and roads. They were allowed to clear a margin of land only as wide as the road, and trees and bushes were to remain uncut along the shoulders, where they protected the surrounding woodlands or meadows from damage during construction. Trees and shrubs of "value to the appearance of the roads" were to be preserved. All holes left by the removal of stumps and roots were to be backfilled. Borrow pits were to be located in areas not visible from the completed road "in bushy draws adjacent to the road." The provisions also included detailed instructions and requirements for masonry construction of walls, bridges, guardrails, and the headwalls of culverts.[16]

Particularly significant were the new specifications for type B excavation. These specifications clearly prohibited practices such as block holing, in which gopher- and coyote-sized holes were drilled and planted with powerful explosives, which broke apart large masses of rock and earth when detonated, creating extensive rock falls and scarring. During such blasting, engineers had little control over the extent of the blast, the scarring and pitting that would result along the road, or the distance to which harmful debris would be cast, damaging the natural environment and scenery. Several cases gained Mather's attention. The greatest damage had occurred during the construction of the East Entrance Road in Yellowstone and the Transmountain Road in Glacier, where excavation debris was carried far down the slopes. Mather and Vint witnessed similar destruction on the Yakima Park Road when they visited Mount Rainier in July 1928. Mather immediately sent a photograph to Thomas MacDonald, chief of the Bureau of Public Roads, with a letter saying, "There is evidently an advantage in moving as much material as possible at once but when it results in such destruction as this it is entirely away from the principles that you and I have established." [17]

Although the problem was brought to the attention of the bureau and the contractor, heavy blasting continued on the Mount Rainier road. It appeared that the road engineers were not aware of the restrictions on shooting and were little concerned with specifications, preferring to build roads according to "common sense and good engineering." From the viewpoint of economics and maintenance, chief engineer Frank A. Kittredge agreed with the need for stricter requirements and called for their enforcement. He explained the technical problems:

> There is no question but what the coyote or gopher hole shooting is much more practical from the contractor's point of view. Furthermore, these gopher holes are placed clear back against the toe of the slope and there is no question but that in many places the shaking of this gravel formation brings down large quantities of material which would not need to be removed if taken out with a shovel or by other types of shooting. Furthermore, the shaking of the hillside makes it possible for the water to gain access to the back slopes and with the constant freeze and thawing of the next few years after construction there is bound to be a large amount of inflow which must be removed at the park's expense under Maintenance.[18]

Vint and his staff developed the methods for type B excavation in consultation with bureau engineers and a representative of the Dupont Powder Company. The methods called for modified blasting procedures to be used in designated areas to prevent damage to surrounding objects and to eliminate the scattering of rocks, stumps, and other debris outside finished slopes. Gentle, controllable techniques for breaking surface boulders or rock fragments, known in the field as plastering and mudcapping, were approved, and block holing was prohibited. Practices for blasting and sidewall excavation which used "gopher" and "coyote" holes were prohibited.[19]

The provisions were added to each contract in the form of a checklist and were to be incorporated into the 1929 contracts for new work at Lassen, Yellowstone, and Rocky Mountain and all future contracts. The inclusion of this specification in all contracts provided the landscape engineers with a mechanism for giving special protection to landscape features at places where normal methods of excavation were likely to cause considerable damage. Landscape architects were to identify particular locations—in terms of stations and distances—requiring the modified methods of excavation during their preliminary road surveys and note them in the survey reports. Because type B procedures were likely to increase the costs of road building, only work in those areas identified in the contract were affected.[20]

Treatment of Road Banks

One of the most significant advances made by the Landscape Division in the design of park roads was the naturalistic treatment of the earth cuts and filled slopes created during construction. Although Hull had called for the finishing of the banks alongside roads by shaping them into slopes in the early 1920s, it was not until 1929 that a technique for rounding and flattening slopes was developed and institutionalized. That year, Vint's office issued four cross-section drawings for the slopes of earth cuts and fill areas along national park roads under construction by the Bureau of Public Roads. The diagrams introduced a technique to round the tops of cut-and-fill slopes and to flatten the slopes so that they attained a proportion of 3:1. Slopes were not to exceed a ratio of three feet in depth for every one foot of elevation. This technique would become a major characteristic of park roads and parkways. It made it possible to ease the disturbed slopes gradually into the surrounding landscape and helped reduce erosion. Once graded in a graceful slope, the banks would be able to recover vegetation naturally or could be sodded and planted so that they blended into the natural vegetation of the surrounding woodlands or hillsides.[21]

The idea of creating continuity between a roadway and the surrounding landscape by flattening the slopes was first developed by John C. Olmsted in an article in *Garden and Forest* in 1888. Olmsted warned against leaving too steep an incline along roads because of erosion and difficulty in mowing and maintenance. He suggested "lessening the incline to avoid unnatural appearances" by learning from nature how to make an ogee curve by combining concave and convex arcs and by varying their proportions to "produce an undulating surface, graceful if grace is a quality to be desired in the locality, but in all cases informal and natural." He advised his readers to vary the distance and the shape of the slope to take advantage of the configuration of the adjoining ground and to use existing trees or rocks as suggestions for determining "where to widen the slopes and the road or to make them more gentle." In a series of simple diagrams, Olmsted illustrated how the length and height of the concave and convex surfaces of an ogee curve could be manipulated to adjust a roadway to the surrounding topography.[22]

Henry Hubbard encouraged his readers to follow Olmsted's advice and to study natural conditions to create a "sequential and smooth flow of surface." Several considerations would unify and harmonize a designer's work with nature. These included creating variety in the form and steepness of a road's slopes, giving special care when joining new surfaces with old ones, and avoiding symmetrical forms, straight lines, and sharp angles in all aspects of design.[23]

In summer of 1930, Director Albright gave Vint authority to forge ahead with improving the standards for national park roads. By the following spring, Vint had issued more advanced diagrams for the treatment of slopes. These illustrated typical cross sections for rounding slopes, twenty feet in depth or less, and included directions for warping the ends of the cuts to enhance the naturalistic appearance of the slopes. Adherence to the diagrams became a specification in all new contracts. The Bureau of Public Roads readily accepted the designs and put them into use throughout the national parks. Within four seasons of use, the treatment was adopted by several other road-building agencies and was being widely used in national forests and other federal lands.[24]

The Landscape Division's technique for treating slopes had many advantages. First of all, by rounding the edges of cuts, road builders could erase the most conspicuous trace of human intervention — the ragged, unnatural line of the cut. Flattened into proportions more similar to the natural angle of repose, the slopes could provide a graceful transition from the natural woodland or meadows beyond the road to the roadway itself. From a practical standpoint, slopes that had been rounded and flattened were less vulnerable to erosion and more quickly able to recover vegetation by natural means, through wind dispersal of seeds or through propagation from the surrounding woods or meadows.

The treatment of the slopes of park roads continued to be studied and improved. By 1932, the results of the rounding and flattening of cut slopes were apparent from decreasing maintenance costs and improved appearances. The division further examined the treatment of road shoulders, width of slopes, and size and types of ditches. Designs for drop inlets, ditches of crushed stone and loose gravel, and other solutions were introduced in the early 1930s to improve the drainage along park roads. The Landscape Division continued to make improvements in the cross sections for park roads, refining the treatment of rounding and flattening the slopes. When revised specifications were issued in 1938, the ratio had been increased from 3:1 to 4:1, flattening the slope to an even greater degree. These new designs went hand in hand with the advances made, primarily through parkway development, in the use of transitional spirals and superelevations to create graceful curving roadways along steep inclines.[25]

The Naturalization of Road Banks

Although many slopes quickly reverted to natural conditions, erosion on newly cut and shaped slopes was a constant concern. At the same time that Vint's staff was developing ways to blend road banks into the scenery by rounding and flattening the slopes, they became interested in the possibilities of speeding up and controlling the process of revegetation by planting or sodding the finished slopes. Practical concerns about erosion, maintenance, and visibility were coupled with an interest in returning the roadsides to a scenic and naturalistic appearance. Planting roadsides added to their beauty and created a pleasing sequence of effects, particularly where there were no distant views.

The park service's interest in treating the slopes of park roads coincided with a growing interest nationally in planting highways for scenic beauty. Articles on the topic by noted landscape architects P. H. Elwood Jr., Jens Jensen, Warren Manning, and Frank Waugh appeared in *Landscape Architecture* in the late 1920s and early 1930s. Several states had extension programs or state highway programs that performed planting as a form of beautification. Since about 1915, Illinois had promoted planting native trees and shrubs alongside rural roads to improve the beauty of the countryside and "restore" the character of the native prairie. Jens Jensen had designed the planting for the ideal section of the Lincoln Highway in the Midwest, and Massachusetts, Pennsylvania, and several other states were planting flowering shrubs and other plants along highways.

Hubbard suggested that slopes be held in place by the roots of vegetation or by boulders. The final form and slope of road banks were to be determined by the geological composition of the natural site and the physical characteristics of available materials, such as vegetation and boulders. Hubbard preferred plantings that developed the particular character of the landscape through which the road passed. In a naturalistic design, Hubbard recommended informal plantations of trees and shrubs so that the road appeared to run through preexisting groups of foliage.[26]

The most scientific theory on roadside planting was put forth by Frank Waugh in "Ecology of the Roadside," published in *Landscape Architecture* in 1931. Waugh applied the principles of dynamic ecology to the natural growth and planting of roadside vegetation. He praised the diversity existing in the species along a roadside and pointed out that this was due to the varying conditions of light and moisture created by the design of the road. Waugh recognized the potential of studying the natural arrangement of plants along a road and re-creating these zones along other roadways to enhance scenic beauty and preserve local landscape character. He criticized the careless and destructive mowing, slashing, and clearing of roads in the country and forest lands which destroyed the natural order of plant development and sometimes entirely eliminated shrubbery or herbaceous species. He believed that such clearings should be made with great care, respecting the natural order of vegetation and preserving as much as possible the most attractive plant colonies and zones.[27]

National park landscape engineers began to give attention to vegetation along park roads in the late 1920s. Among the first planting efforts were experiments Davidson conducted in 1927 along the banks of new roads in Mount Rainier. In three separate areas, Davidson planted brake ferns, cuttings of salal, and cuttings of thimbleberry and common huckleberry. The expanding interest in roadside planting coincided with the National Park Service's 1930 policy excluding all exotic seeds and plants from the national parks, with the exception of nonnative grasses, which were impossible to control and already abounded in parks. Roadside grading and planting became one of the most important and widespread activities of the Civilian Conservation Corps in national parks. In many parks, experimental plots for grasses, perennial herbs and wildflowers, vines, and shrubs were maintained, some in conjunction with the natural history programs and museum gardens.[28]

In many locations the banks of new roads rapidly recovered a ground cover through natural seeding. In others planting and stabilization were necessary to control erosion. After being flattened and rounded, slopes were planted with the seeds or seedlings of native grasses and herbaceous plants, including wildflowers. Experiments were often conducted before planting, from seeds collected locally in previous seasons. Temporary log cribbing was constructed on particularly steep slopes subject to erosion. To catch runoff, gutters were dug and in some places lined with stones. Rocks were also artistically embedded in slopes for stabilization and erosion control.

At Yosemite, serious erosion problems in the cuts along the Wawona Road and difficulty in getting vegetation to take hold naturally led to a cooperative study with the park's natural history program. Dr. Frederic E. Clements of Carnegie Institution, who had done extensive research on plant ecology and operated a field station in Santa Barbara, California, advised the park service on this program in the early 1930s. Various experiments were conducted involving seeding and sodding slopes, installing wooden cribbing to hold seedlings in place, and planting creeping vines and other plants in the interstices of rocky slopes. Techniques were developed for erasing the line between the natural woodland or meadow and the cut-and-fill slopes by clearing vegetation before construction along an irregular line and replanting likewise with species appropriate to the area. Sections of the Yosemite Museum's garden were set aside for experiments.

Enrollees from one of the park's Civilian Conservation Corps camps carried out the work of collecting seeds and planting the slopes.

By 1930, Vint added planting to an expanded definition of roadside cleanup, which was funded under annual appropriations for roads and trails. Cleanup now assumed great importance as one of the principal means by which the landscape designers could uphold the natural beauty of the park and erase the scars of development. The naturalization of roadsides after construction was added to the already routine practices of screening undesirable views, opening up scenic vistas, clearing dead and decaying timber from the roadside, and placing telephone lines underground. Cleanup also included small-scale improvements at parking turnouts and roadside springs, such as water fountains, curbs and sidewalks, and benches.[29]

By 1931, the preparation of slopes for natural reseeding or for planting was routine. Duff, or the top layer of soil, was removed from the slopes before construction, stored, and reapplied on finished fill slopes. The duff improved the appearance of the soil and helped blend it with the undisturbed duff of the surrounding woodland. Spread on the slopes after construction, it encouraged regrowth of natural vegetation and provided fertile ground for planting seeds or cuttings. In some cases, sod was removed from the rights-of-way and transplanted where needed. Vint reported his satisfaction, saying, "Our efforts toward protection of roadside and natural landscape are also showing encouraging results."[30]

As more and more attention was given to vegetation, so too were ways sought to blend the newly planted banks into the natural surroundings. A technique of bank blending emerged in which trees cleared for the construction of roads were cut in swathes having an irregular uphill or downhill edge. This technique eliminated the artificial appearance of a straight, regular line and created a wavering, curving line that appeared naturalistic. Shrubs, ground covers, and woodland plants could be planted along these edges in a natural succession, further erasing the line between planted areas and natural areas. Hazards from falling limbs and the risk of obscuring the motorist's vision generally made saving trees within the road cross sections impractical. It was far better to clear the trees and replant the new slopes, the location of the road having been selected to avoid trees or rock formations of importance.

Among the many conservation projects carried out in national parks by the Civilian Conservation Corps in the 1930s, the sloping and naturalization of road banks left by cut-and-fill operations during road and trail construction were among the most important and widespread. It had an important role in controlling slope erosion as well as lasting value for beautification. Landscape architect Davidson recognized the practical and aesthetic value of this work in 1934, when he stated that the stabilization and naturalization of the cut-and-fill scars resulting from road and highway construction was the most important work carried out by the Conservation Civilian Corps in the national parks.

> Such erosion control work is not merely an excellent landscape betterment, but will make road and trail maintenance work immensely easier and more economical. We should not consider that Erosion Control work has been completed in the park until every cut and filled slope along all roads or trails has been stabilized to a point where there is no more erosion either from slides, rainfall, or other natural conditions except accidental occurrences. We need not go into the many methods from which the best should be selected to apply to each project, it is sufficient to mention here that any method will result in greatly increased roadside beauty when stabilization is actually accomplished.[31]

The contouring and naturalization of road banks had many useful applications for other aspects of design in both national and state parks. These include the rounding, flattening, and planting of slopes alongside trails, at parking areas and overlooks, and on other embankments where a gradual and naturalistic transition between a developed area and the natural park surroundings was desired. It was particularly valuable where practical necessity required the creation of a flat, level plaza in an otherwise naturally contoured area. This technique would also prove invaluable in stabilizing streambanks and enhancing their aesthetic appeal by reducing erosion and the buildup of debris in snags. It would also add to the beauty and naturalistic character of the shorelines of the newly constructed lakes developed for recreational purposes in state parks and recreational demonstration areas in the 1930s. This contouring technique, combined with plantings of native species, contributed greatly to returning construction sites and other disturbed areas to naturalistic appearances.

The National Park Service was a pioneer in what became in the 1930s a nationwide movement for roadside beautification and soil conservation. Through the efforts of the Soil Conservation Service and many state highway departments, roadside planting with flowering shrubs, perennial herbs, ferns, and ground covers became routine practice nationwide in the 1930s. The park service's work represents an important stage in the evolution from the English gardening tradition to the present-day standards for highway design. By translating John C. Olmsted's and Henry Hubbard's ideas for treating slopes into modern design theory that was institutionalized by the Bureau of Public Roads, national park designers contributed substantially to twentieth-century landscape architecture. Their innovations in treating the banks of roads would have lasting influence on the character of modern highways, as well as on the development of roads in national parks, national forests, and state parks. Because the techniques proved economical and reduced the potential for erosion, they were adopted to control erosion along streams and embankments in park areas other than roads.

6.2. In the mid-1930s, the Civilian Conservation Corps shaped the slopes of the newly constructed North Rim Road in Grand Canyon National Park according to the techniques introduced in the late 1920s for rounding and flattening the slopes of park roads and blending them into the surrounding forest. This work greatly reduced soil erosion along new roads and created the illusion that nature had never been disturbed. *(Photograph courtesy National Archives, Record Group 79)*

By blending and warping slopes and ensuring the regrowth of vegetation, the designers of national park roads also drew attention to the natural character and inherent beauty of native vegetation. The work of the park service in roadside planting and the early work of state highway departments in Illinois, Massachusetts, New York, and Pennsylvania together laid an aesthetic and practical foundation for the recent movement for highway beautification and scenic byways and for such programs as Operation Wildflower, cooperatively run through the Federal Highway Administration and state highway departments.

Scenic Overlooks

The development of scenic overlooks on national park roads grew out of Downing's nineteenth-century romantic notions on viewpoints and vistas. Overlooks were an important feature of park roads, providing a stopping and resting place and affording visitors spectacular, and often panoramic, views. They ranged from simple widened areas along the road where traffic could pull over and stop to larger terraces accommodating sizable parking areas with curbing, sidewalks, and protective guardrails. They could be combined with paths and trails that allowed the visitor to ascend a peak or outcrop for a better view or to descend to a scenic waterfall or gorge.

Overlooks on park roads were derivatives of the terrace form used by landscape architects. Henry Hubbard defined two types of terrace: those that were architectural objects of simple shape fitted to a site as the base of a structure of architectural interest and those that were outdoor areas dominating a view. It was the latter type that park landscape architects incorporated into the design of park roads. Terraces offered designers endless possibilities for presenting views to the best advantage. Hubbard urged landscape designers to explore this form, drawing attention to the retaining wall or bank that created a boundary between the structure and its surroundings and allowed a rise in elevation which could command a view over the surrounding area and "perhaps much further afield."[32]

The first overlooks were designed on existing plateaulike promontories of land. They were bounded by curtainlike parapet walls that conformed to the natural shape of the promontory. One of the earliest overlooks of this type was the Sunrise Ridge Loop (1929–30) on Mount Rainier's Yakima Park Road. It provided both an aesthetic and engineering solution along a steep incline where it was necessary for the road to shift direction to continue smoothly uphill. The overlook was essentially a switchback opened up to form a sweeping loop and afford panoramic views and a stopping point along the incline. The center of the loop was reserved for parking. Visitors crossed the road to the viewing area where a stonemasonry guardrail separated them from the steep slopes beyond the overlook. The monotonous line of the guardrail was relieved by crenulating piers that echoed the majestic form of the nearby mountain peak.

The idea of a walkway with a protective guardrail which followed the natural contour of the land was applied to curvilinear paths and trails along scenic rims such as the South Rim of the Grand Canyon and Rim Village at Crater Lake. Guardrails of masonry piers and log cross timbers were installed as early as 1920 along the Grand Canyon of the Yellowstone. By the late 1920s such structures were called promenades and equipped with viewing bays, water fountains, and dust-free walkways that connected with parking areas, nearby buildings, and nature trails. Masonry and log guardrails, following the specifications used in road projects, were also used in precipitous locations along hiking and bridle trails, such as the tunnel approach along the Ptarmigan Trail in Glacier National Park.

The Wawona Tunnel at Yosemite, constructed in the early 1930s, represents the most ambitious precedent for creating an artificial terrace. Here the terrace was created by fill excavated from the forty-two-hundred-foot tunnel,

6.3. The Loop at Sunrise Ridge on the Yakima Park Road, Mount Rainier National Park, presented spectacular views of the Cascade Mountains, north to Canada and south to Oregon. The loop was an enlarged switchback where the road turned sharply and proceeded upward. Inside the loop was a parking area. Outside, following the shape of the site, were sidewalks flanked by stonemasonry guardrail of the "mountain" type that formed naturalistic viewing bays and a panorama of scenic views. *(Photograph courtesy National Park Service Historic Photography Collection)*

shaped into a naturalistic curvilinear form, and retained by a hand-laid revetment wall of weathered local stone. The terrace was separated from the roadway by an island of plantings which helped control the flow of traffic on and off the road. It was bound by a curtainlike masonry parapet of local rock which was separated from the parking area by curbing of roughly cut stone and a sidewalk. Depending on their location, such artificial terraces would either use a dry-laid retaining wall or be gradually sloped and planted to adjust the fill to the surrounding terrain.

Many variations of the two basic types—those following the natural contours of a site and those naturalistically created from earth fill—were built along roads in both eastern and western parks. The most extensive development of scenic overlooks occurred in the park drives and parkways of the eastern parks, particularly Shenandoah's Skyline Drive and the Blue Ridge Parkway of the 1930s, where scenic overlooks and vistas at frequent intervals became an integral and essential aspect of the park experience and offered visitors a sequential panorama of spectacles and scenery.

Loop Developments, Intersections, and Grade Separations

Although the landscape architects had collaborated on the location of roads and the design of bridges and guardrails since 1920, in 1928 they began to design parking areas and loop developments as well. These loop developments became characteristic of the park road systems and would have many applications in the overall design of national and state parks. Derived from the circular drives of pleasure grounds and estates in the English gardening tradition and functioning like the traffic circles of urban parkways, a loop development made it possible to lead automobiles on and off a main road without altering the flow of traffic and without introducing right angles and tangents into the design of a road. Such a device allowed designers to divert traffic for scenic or other purposes. In the case of parking areas at overlooks or campgrounds, they allowed traffic to return to the main road without stopping, backing up, or making sharp turns. Loops were often developed as side or spur roads leading to important viewpoints or to parking, sidewalks and paths, and comfort facilities. Ernest Davidson incorporated the loop in his design for the Yakima Park Road in order to convert an undesirable switchback into a lovely and spectacular viewpoint on Sunrise Ridge, where in clear weather one could see north to Canada and south to the Cascade Range of Oregon. He further used this device to disperse the visitors to several points at Yakima Park by way of side roads and spurs. Gilmore Clarke used the loop to channel traffic through Mammoth Hot Springs and to form the nucleus of his master plan for this heavily trafficked area of Yellowstone. Park designers adopted it for campgrounds and picnic areas as well as for parking areas adjacent to scenic points of interest, such as Bridalveil Falls in Yosemite and Artist's Point at Yellowstone.

Intersections of roads and trails caused park designers special concern and were deliberately avoided wherever possible. Where unavoidable, they were carefully designed according to the conventions of the English gardening tradition. The "wye" intersection with its divided roadway and central island became the standard for intersections where side or spur roads met a main park road. At these points, travelers needed directions, visibility, and safe passage. Signs, curbing, parking areas, and plantings were incorporated into these designs to provide for safety and to blend the roadway into the surrounding woodlands or meadows.

The wye enabled traffic to leave the main road without coming to a stop and without having to turn at a right angle, interrupting the flow of traffic and slowing forward momentum. Traffic entering the main road was likewise able to merge without making an abrupt turn. This convention had been used on limited-access roads and parkways. Henry Hubbard advocated the wye as a solution for maintaining the flow and safety of travel and reducing the amount of road surface that detracted from the natural scene. He recommended that intersecting roads approach each other by gentle curves and that islands be formed between the branches of the roads and be covered with low plantings to conceal any undue amount of road surface.[33]

Customarily road and trail systems in national parks were developed so that there was little need for intersections or grade separations to carry one form of traffic over the other. Yosemite Valley was one place in the national parks, however, where pedestrian and automobile traffic came into conflict and where it was impossible to route a bridle trail or footpath so that it would not cross a roadway. Here arches were incorporated into bridge designs to allow pedestrians or those riding horseback to pass underneath. Another notable grade separation was the east entrance to Mount Rainier; constructed of stone and large logs, it was built to carry the long-distance Cascade (later Pacific) Crest Trail across the road at Naches Pass. It also served as a boundary marker and entry gate between the adjoining national forest and the park.

Another form of grade separation used in the steep terrain of the national parks was the loop structure. This ingenious viaduct enabled a road to follow a spiral course and pass over itself at a higher elevation, thus facilitating a gradual change in elevation in a steep valley. Such a structure, commonly called the "corkscrew," had been built in the form of a wooden viaduct near Sylvan Pass in Yellowstone National Park in 1906. In the early 1930s when engineers and landscape architects faced a similar problem along the Newfound Gap Road in Great Smoky Mountains National Park, a reinforced concrete structure with an arch of stone voussoirs and stonemasonry-veneered walls was proposed. Designed by the Bureau of Public Roads engineers from a preliminary drawing by Charles Peterson, the loop structure required the construction of massive curvilinear abutments that flanked the arched opening and served as retaining walls for the filled material required to carry the approaches. On the upper deck, inconspicuous log railings served as guardrails, and plantings enhanced the naturalistic effect. Tree wells were constructed nearby to protect and preserve aged hemlocks. Trees and shrubs were planted around the completed structure to disguise artificial appearances and erase the scars of construction.

The Development of Standards for Masonry

The uniform specifications introduced by Vint's office in 1929 included standards for the design of guardrails, bridges, and culverts along park roads and trails. These standards had evolved in the 1920s as Hull, Vint, Davidson, and others endeavored to instruct the engineers and contractors of the Bureau of Public Roads on techniques for stonemasonry which harmonized and blended with the natural setting. Specifications had been written into contracts and were listed on the drawings for bridges and guardrails as early as 1928. The success of harmonization depended on the freehand lines and rusticity of the roughly cut stone, the avoidance of right angles and straight lines, the integration of battered stone walls into the contours of adjoining slopes and rock formations, and the curvature of the roadway and adjoining walls to follow natural contours.

The nature of built stonework directly influenced the extent to which a structure appeared naturalistic and blended harmoniously into the natural setting. The random pattern, variegated natural colors, and irregular lines that resulted from using natural boulders or exposing the weathered surfaces of split stones and from deeply incising mortar joints created a camouflaged surface. When viewed from afar, the stonemasonry was indistinguishable from the natural outcrops from which it emerged. The masonry specifications worked out by Hull and Vint represented a pragmatic twentieth-century application of the nineteenth-century principles for picturesque rockwork which Downing, Hubbard, and Parsons had promoted.

The special provisions for the stonework in guardrails and bridges were in keeping with the general principles that straight lines and right angles were to be avoided in the design of park structures. The provisions enabled the landscape engineer to select the source of stone to be used and prescribe the size and shape of the rocks. They required that finished stonework "present a good architectural appearance" and that rubble masonry be constructed by experienced workmen. Larger stones were to be placed at the base of the guardrail or bridge and extra large ones at the corners. Only weathered and moss- or lichen-covered surfaces were to be visible. The nesting or bunching of small rocks was to be avoided. Stones were to be laid in courses in such a way that no four corners were contiguous, thus ensuring a random, irregular, and informal appearance. Joints were to be angular and no greater than one inch wide. Guardrails were to conform to standard plans, and no joints in the top course were to be parallel with the horizontal line of the structure. The top of exposed walls was to be uniformly even with variations up to one-half inch allowed to avoid the appearance of a straight line. The provisions also required that drainage openings, called weep holes, be included in all stone walls.[34]

Guardrails

In the national parks, both log and stone were used in the construction of guardrails designed to harmonize with the natural setting. Customarily log guardrails were built in forested areas, and masonry ones were built in open, rugged, steep, or mountainous areas.

Several designs for masonry guardrails had been developed in the mid-1920s for work on roads such as the El Portal Road in Yosemite and Going-to-the-Sun Highway in Glacier. Guardrails were also used along trails such as the Ptarmigan Trail in Glacier and the promenade at Crater Lake's Rim Village. These eighteen-inch stone walls were all designed for the protection of visitors, whether in automobiles, on horseback, or on foot. The same attention to detail in masonry which marked the development of park bridges guided the specifications and designs for these walls and ensured both safety and harmonization. The irregularity of the stonework pattern, the avoidance of right angles and straight lines in the setting of stones, and the elimination of parallel joints along the top course provided a camouflage effect whereby native stone blended with the surrounding setting. Functional features for curbing, drainage gutters, and sidewalks were incorporated into the designs for the basic guardrail.

Guardrails were essential for public safety along steep inclines of roadway and also protected visitors at overlooks. They were the counterparts of the parapets described by Hubbard as an essential component of terraces. Of the many types suggested by Hubbard and commonly used in public parks—balustrade, pierced wall, post and panel, lattice log construction, and others—the park service designers settled upon two simple types: a malleable masonry curtain wall of native stone and a more rigid and less permanent log structure of roughly hewn log posts and cross rails.[35]

One of the existing prototypes Daniel Hull examined in the 1920s was the guardrail designed for the Palisades Interstate Park by William Welch. Its use at the Storm King Highway along the Hudson was well known and had been published in the 1924 portfolio *American Landscape Architecture*. It featured a split-stone wall with an irregular crown created by small stones set on end in rows parallel to the face of the wall. This design was rejected for use in the national parks by the Commission of Fine Arts, perhaps because of its dated character. There was much discussion about the character of masonry during the construction of guardrails along Yosemite's El Portal Road in 1926, mainly between commission landscape architect James Greenleaf and Daniel Hull, before a simple linear parapet without any coping was decided upon. The guardrail was made of irregularly shaped and weathered stones having no right angles or straight lines. The lines of the guardrail derived from the irregularity of horizontally laid stones arranged in a random pattern with deeply incised mortar.

Early in 1928, Vint issued standardized designs for six types of stone guardrails and five types of wood-and-log guardrails for national park road projects. These were superseded by new drawings a year later. Drawn by Davidson and approved by Vint, the new sheets included designs for six stone guardrails and seven log or wood guardrails. The designs gave patterns for the arrangement of logs or the placement of stone in measured plans, elevations, and sections. They were based on the successful designs that had been developed in the mid-

1920s for roads such as Glacier's Going-to-the-Sun Highway, Yosemite's El Portal Road, and Mount Rainier's Yakima Park Road.

Rusticity, irregularity, and native materials marked the overall character of stone guardrails. The designs were simple and consisted of a solid wall without the coping, openings, or ornamentation characteristic of their urban counterparts. Masonry was laid in such a way that straight lines and right angles were avoided and the qualities of continuity, irregularity, and randomness dominated. The lines of demarcation between courses were obscured by the irregular shapes and moss- and lichen-covered surfaces of the stones and the deeply incised mortar. The walls retained the random character and rough, irregular forms of naturally found boulders or weathered outcrops. Most of the designs were variations on masonry walls in which the stones were irregular in shape and laid horizontally. The dimensions and arrangement of stones were further refined in 1929 drawings. The basic designs made standardization possible while allowing for a number of variations for different field conditions, uses, and needs. One design even had a space for a walk or for planting between the face of the wall and the curb. Some included combination wall and curbs with pavement for a sidewalk; others had end buttresses or wide crenulating piers, five to six feet in length, spaced at six- or twelve-foot intervals to avoid a monotonous line and add to the overall irregularity of the linear surface. The end walls of others were flared or battered to suit local field conditions. New in the 1929 standards was a stone guardrail having a crenulation in the shape of a peaked mountain every fourteen feet. This was the guardrail Davidson developed for the Sunrise Ridge Loop and Yakima Park Road. The design used for the Cadillac Mountain Road at Acadia, which consisted of unjoined, horizontally laid granite blocks embedded in the earth, was omitted from the 1929 sheet.

Within the standard set of proportions for eighteen- and twenty-four-inch walls, irregularity and variation were encouraged. Certain rules of joining were established to ensure informality of design and harmonization by blending. The standard designs made it possible for Vint and his staff to specify on master plans, contract specifications, and drawings the type of guardrail suitable for particular locations within each park. In the 1930s, it became standard practice to include a sheet in the master plans for each park showing the guardrail designs recommended for the park; these included diagrams for treating the slopes, culvert designs, and various techniques of joining and cutting logs for construction.[36]

To ease the monotony of long linear expanses of guardrail, the national park designers introduced crenulating piers. In this they followed Hubbard's advice that where a long straight run of terrace wall might become monotonous, it be "broken by projections which offer particularly good viewpoints and which serve some subordinate purpose of their own as objects in the design." The crenulating piers became a distinctive aspect of the masonry work of the National Park Service. They appeared along many park roads and varied from Davidson's "mountain" form at Mount Rainier to broader, more lozenge-like horizontal forms along Rocky Mountain's Trail Ridge Road. The design of guardrails allowed for elaboration for functional purposes, such as the incorporation of water fountains, including one at Crater Lake whose bowl formed the shape of Crater Lake with a projecting Wizard Island. In the mountain type used at Mount Rainier, the pier consisted of a single stone shaped to a blunt point imitating a mountain peak. Only the weathered or lichen-covered surfaces of stones were to be exposed, perpetuating an aesthetic quality of the rustic which had come from Downing and was promoted by landscape architects such as Hubbard and Parsons.[37]

In 1942, the Branch of Plans and Design issued simplified designs for standard guardrails, distinguishing between blocky and stratified types to better accommodate differences in stone character (these differences concerned whether the stones were best divided into blocks, like igneous or metamorphic rock such as granite, or into stratified layers, like limestone). More detailed plans for log guardrails were also issued at this time.[38]

When Charles Peterson came east to head the Eastern Office of the Landscape Division in 1930, he adapted the standard plans to the more gentle topography and geology of the Appalachian Mountains. Although the features of the roads of Great Smoky Mountains National Park followed the designs of the Western Field Office, greater variations and more architectural features appeared in the design of the guardrail, bridges, and other road structures that Peterson and his staff designed for the park in 1932 and 1933. These established a "style" of stonemasonry which had greater rectilinearity in the shape of the stones but still fulfilled the requirements that right angles and straight lines be avoided, that workmanship be high, and that stones be carefully chosen to achieve a unified and harmonious appearance.

Stone curbing was an integral part of stone walls, and at overlooks walls were accompanied by sidewalks in a single unified design. These improvements had important applications in the New Deal era, when labor and funds became available to improve park villages and scenic attractions. Made from local materials of stone and log, naturalistic curbing and sidewalks began to appear at parking areas, overlooks, ranger stations, museums, and other park buildings. Curbing of a single type was installed throughout park villages such at Grand Canyon Village and Yosemite Village. Rustic curbing, made from unfinished, peeled, and knotted logs or roughly cut native stone, was installed to bound parking areas. Curving paths were graded and paved with crushed stone and gravel from native rock. Edging of native stone or rough-cut peeled logs laid end to end was installed along many pathways in an effort to keep visitors on the designated pathways. These improvements greatly improved the appearance of park areas and reduced the wear and tear of traffic on the fragile natural environment. At Yosemite Village, boulders embedded in the earth in the mid-1920s to delineate the parking plaza and valley roadways were removed in the 1930s and replaced by continuous sections of partially embedded log curbing which were less conspicuous.

The Design of Bridges

In the early 1920s, the landscape engineers took part in the design of bridges along park roads. By this time, log, concrete, steel, and masonry construction had been used in various parks. Leaving technical aspects of construction to civil engineers, the landscape engineers were concerned with the suitability of materials and design for natural sites, the workmanship of masonry or logwork, and the degree to which each bridge harmonized with its setting.

The form of the stone arch bridge, inspired by the romantic English prototypes and by Hubbard's illustration of the Scarborough Bridge at Franklin Park, went through an important engineering and aesthetic evolution in the 1920s. This transition is evident in a comparison of several examples beginning with the Yosemite Creek Bridge in 1922 and ending with the White River Bridge at Mount Rainier in 1928.

The Yosemite Creek Bridge was one of the earliest masonry-veneered bridges designed by one of the landscape engineers, in this case Daniel Hull. Voussoir stones were dovetailed into the concrete and held in place with crossbars and a central longitudinal bar. It followed a simple arched form with rectangular buttressed piers at the four ends (where the roadway flared). Stones were rectangular in shape and varied in size so that an irregular pattern of horizontal and vertical joints resulted. The parapet was surmounted by a coping of regularly sized and placed stones that were tied into the buttress ends, which had lanterns.[39]

Two Mount Rainier bridges, those at Christine Falls and nearby Narada Falls, illustrate the milestone achieved by the Landscape Division in the design of bridges about 1926. These were among the first park bridges to follow the radial curve of the roadway and to incorporate the guardrails, buttresses, spandrels, and arch into one continuous and slender curvilinear form. Not only did the stone-faced bridge blend physically and visually into the natural rocky site, but the Christine Falls arch also enframed the nearby falls and created a scenic and spectacular downhill approach. This bridge incorporated a superelevation and was at once a part of the natural scene and a harmonious constructed element.

The simplified and streamlined form of these bridges indicated a design intent based on function and harmonization. The bridges lacked any decorative elements or amenities such as coping and piers. The size and shape of the stones used in the arch ring and in the masonry veneer of the walls were essential to the successful harmonization of the bridge with the surrounding wooded gorge. On the construction site, landscape architect Ernest Davidson carefully supervised

6.4. Designed in 1928, the White River Bridge on the Yakima Park Road in Mount Rainier National Park reflected the high standards of stonemasonry which the Western Field Office had worked out by the late 1920s. A concrete arch, the bridge was faced with lichen-covered, locally quarried stone carefully placed according to size, color, and shape. Masons worked from an elevation drawing, written specifications, and a sample wall built on site—all of which were prepared by landscape architects of the Landscape Division. *(Photograph courtesy National Park Service, Mount Rainier National Park)*

the masonry work on each bridge to make sure that it was crafted according to specifications to achieve a unified naturalistic appearance. The resident landscape architect's schedule and the numerous road projects, however, allowed only brief and infrequent visits to each road project, sometimes spaced a month or more apart. On several occasions, completed sections reviewed and found unsatisfactory on Davidson's next visit were pulled out and relaid. Davidson's frustration led to several improvements in the Landscape Division's approach to bridge design in 1928 which were first realized in the construction of the White River Bridge on the Yakima Park Road at Mount Rainier.

In 1928, the Bureau of Public Roads assigned the design of bridges to its San Francisco office, making it easier for the Landscape Division to collaborate on the architectural features of road projects. At this time, Vint's office began incorporating architectural sheets and detailed specifications for the stone facing, arch rings, masonry, and other architectural features in the working plans for each bridge project. Engineers and foremen could work closely from these detailed drawings.[40]

Such a detailed drawing was made for the White River Bridge at Mount Rainier National Park. Engineers were given a drawing of the elevation showing the approximate size and shape of the facing stones. The drawing also included "extracts" from the written specifications for the work. So important were the size and shape of the voussoirs that the Landscape Division made large-scale drawings of the arch ring. Voussoir stones were to be quarried to the approximate face dimensions shown on the drawing. Three edges of the wall face of voussoir stones (top edge excepted) and four edges of the soffit face were to be cut to a true line. One-inch holes were drilled five inches deep into the side of each voussoir stone for the placement of steel clamps that anchored the stone to the concrete core.[41]

Specifications for the facing stones and railings required that at least 28 percent to 50 percent of the wall be formed by stones with weathered or quarried surfaces. Individual stones were to have heights between twelve and twenty-two inches and lengths between thirty and seventy inches. Extra large stones were to be placed at all corners. All stones were to be laid with their major axis horizontal. Mortar joints were to be one to one and a half inches wide. The largest stones were to be laid first with courses of smaller stones laid above, making a gradual transition from large to small in each successive course. Stones were to be laid so that four corners were contiguous. The top row of stones was to contain only stones as wide as the wall so that no joints running parallel with the wall appeared.[42]

The elevation drawing specified that large stones be placed along the bottom of walls to each side of the arch in areas abutting the natural slopes, middle-sized stones be placed above larger stones to each side of the arch, and smaller stones be placed in the center above the arch. Stones were to diminish in size gradually from large to small, with the smallest placed in the center of the elevation above the arch. On site during the construction of the White River Bridge, Davidson, with Sager's help, erected a sample wall to which workmen could refer throughout construction.

These changes resulted in much more satisfactory results in the workmanship and appearance of the bridges. The drawings for the Klickitat Bridge (1931), a similar stone-faced concrete arch designed the next year, included a large-scale diagram for the arch ring, specifying the shape and size of each stone to make up the arch ring. By 1931, Vint considered his office's best bridge designs to be the Christine Falls, Frying Pan, Klickitat, White River, and Tahoma Creek Bridges in Mount Rainier; the Happy Isles, Clarke's, and Trail Bridges in

6.5. Laying the keystone in the arch ring of the Baring Creek Bridge in Glacier National Park about 1932. The design of the arch ring was such an important element of the naturalistic design of park bridges that starting in 1931 the Landscape Division drew diagrams indicating the size and shape of each voussoir stone. Irregularly cut stones were laid so that rough, weathered, and lichen-covered surfaces were exposed, causing the structures to blend into the natural setting. *(Photograph courtesy National Park Service, Glacier National Park)*

Yosemite; the Swiftcurrent Bridge (designed by Fine Arts Commission member Ferruccio Vitale) in Glacier; the Log Bridge in Rocky Mountain; and the Lower Pine Creek and Virgin River Bridges in Zion. When Vint assembled a portfolio of representative park structures in 1932, he included only one design for a bridge—Mount Rainier's White River Bridge.[43]

Each vehicular bridge in the national parks was designed as a unique project, although by the end of the 1920s, a number of standard types and common characteristics began to emerge. Designers based the plans for each bridge on its specific site and location in an effort to meet its functional needs and to harmonize it with its natural setting. Not only did topography and setting vary, but the distances spanned to carry roadways also varied. Arched bridges of stone-faced concrete construction abounded but were not always appropriate given the demands of function, engineering, or landscape. Designs using steel, logs, and even stained concrete were developed for special sites. Modifications occurred as bridges were designed to transport bridle trails or allow foot or bridle trails to pass underneath the roadway. As they did for other structures, landscape engineers made great efforts in the design and workmanship of logwork or stonework to make the bridges appear to emerge naturalistically from the earth or natural bedrock and to harmonize with the natural setting.

In the East, Charles Peterson and his landscape architects were strongly influenced by the nineteenth-century Olmsted parks, the eastern parkways under Gilmore Clarke's direction in Westchester County in New York, and the George Washington Memorial Parkway being constructed in Virginia at the time. Peterson was also designing the Colonial Parkway between Jamestown and Yorktown, where he introduced brick stonemasonry and details such as molded coping rails, stringcourses, and buttresses following the brickwork and historical prototypes found at Williamsburg and the Tidewater region. The stonemasonry of the bridges and similar road structures in Great Smoky Mountains National Park built under his direction exhibited a greater proportion of rectilinear shaped stones laid horizontally and mortar joints that roughly followed horizontal and vertical lines. Design features such as stringcourses and buttressing piers were also introduced. Despite these differences, the structures achieved harmony with the surroundings of boulder-laden streams, forests, and steep rocky slopes and met the specifications set by Vint's office several years earlier.

Culverts

Culverts were an essential feature of park roads. Carrying streams underneath roads and trails without interrupting the natural flow of water, they abounded in mountainous and canyonlike areas. Important in protecting the natural landscape, they also required designs that harmonized with the natural setting. In 1928 Vint's office issued "Standard Architectural Details for the Headwalls for Culverts," a sheet of drawings that could be followed in most situations. The sheet included eight designs for masonry headwalls. The four principal designs based on arched openings had detailed specifications. Weathered stones were to be used, and no freshly broken stones were to be exposed. Stones were to be six to eight inches high and eighteen to forty-eight inches long. All stones were to be laid with their larger dimension horizontal, and no four joints were to come together. For arch rings, the keystone was to be at least twenty-two inches in height, and all arch ring stones were to be shaped to the approximate face dimensions shown on the drawings. Mortar joints were to be roughly one to one and a half inches wide; they were to be pointed to a depth of one inch to give the appearance of a rough and irregular surface. These specifications clearly drew special attention to the depth of mortar, irregular lines, and weathered surfaces. Like the landscape designers of the late nineteenth century, Vint and his staff recognized the naturalistic qualities that came from such attention to details and careful masonry work.[44]

Variations on the culvert headwall used both arched and stepped parapets and jack, pointed, elliptical, and round arches. The headwalls of several designs were battered to fit into adjoining slopes. In addition to arched forms, several designs showed simple headwalls of post and lintel construction with rectangular openings. The simplest was a stone housing for the extended end of the pipe. Specifications were included on the plans. They called for the use of weathered stones and prohibited the use of round stones or the exposure of freshly cut stone. Stones were to measure five to twenty-four inches high and nine to forty-two inches long. The specifications for pointing the masonry conformed to the general masonry requirements of bridges and guardrails.[45]

Tunnels

Tunnel construction in the national parks where slopes were too steep to carry a road drew heavily from nineteenth-century railroad engineering. Of concern to the landscape engineers was the character of the portals, which visually connected the tunnel with the natural surroundings of the park. The earliest tunnels in the national parks imitated the arched openings of caves or rock outcrops that formed natural bridges. Such natural features held great romantic appeal for nineteenth-century travelers and were absorbed into the picturesque imagery of the wilderness. Formations such as Arch Rock in Yosemite and Crystal Cave in Sequoia were subjects of popular interest. It is not surprising that the naturalistic arched form was introduced in the portals for artificial tunnels along the Columbia River Highway in Oregon. Here motorists traveled through rough arched openings carefully blasted out of the natural bedrock and cliffs to simulate nature's handiwork. Longer tunnels had a gallery of openings through which travelers could catch glimpses of scenery.

From a landscape standpoint, by creating tunnels through buttresses of hard rock, road designers could avoid extensive blasting and the resulting disfigurement of the rock cliffs. By giving the openings the naturalistic character of a cave entrance, the designers harmonized the tunnel with the natural scenery and enhanced the picturesque qualities of the road.

Tunnels were common on steep rock inclines such as the transmountain roads in Glacier. Park road builders carved such tunnels to avoid extensive excavation and to keep down the amount of material that once removed would have to be placed nearby or transported away. Portals were hewn out of the natural rock, adding to the picturesque character of the landscape. In the 1920s, tunnels with natural rock portals were incorporated in early park roads, such as the Going-to-the-Sun Highway in Glacier National Park, and on park trails, such as

Glacier's Ptarmigan Trail. They appeared at the approaches to the Hetch Hetchy Dam in Yosemite and the Kaibab Suspension Bridge (1928) in Grand Canyon. Even after masonry portals were introduced in the late 1920s, the idea of viewing galleries remained popular. The Zion–Mount Carmel Tunnel (1930) in Zion National Park was built with a gallery of viewing bays from which motorists could view the spectacular scenery.

As tunnels increased in length and were excavated from various types of rock, the desirability of leaving an exposed rock arch at the entrance was ruled out by practical factors such as the nature of the local stone or difficulty in attaining a naturalistic arch. Techniques for staining concrete portals or facing them with stonemasonry to appear rustic or naturalistic emerged. The portals of the Wawona and Zion–Mount Carmel Tunnels were among the first to incorporate new techniques.

The aesthetic approaches to stonework which had been explored in the construction of bridges and culvert headwalls were carried over into the construction of tunnel portals. Weathered stone was used to form arch rings for the portals and was laid up in random, irregular, and rough courses to abut the surrounding earth and natural rock. One of the most successful set of portals to achieve a harmonious synthesis between the natural outcroppings and stonemasonry by merging the stonemasonry into the surrounding rock was in the lower tunnel on the Newfound Gap Road in Great Smoky Mountains National Park. Designed from a preliminary sketch (1933) by Charles Peterson, the portals featured stonemasonry veneer walls and an arch ring of native stones each cut to a specific shape and size.

The exposed rock lining of tunnels would, for practical reasons, give way to concrete linings and carefully designed drainage systems. Problems with water seepage causing serious freezing of roadways inside the tunnels in the winter necessitated the installation of concrete liners.

The Wawona Tunnel and Overlook

Yosemite's Committee of Expert Advisers became involved in the planning for a route to connect Yosemite Valley with Glacier Point by way of the new Wawona and Glacier Point Roads, which intersected at the Chinquapin Intersection. Although the committee recommended that a road of a reasonable grade be built without any tunnels, such an approach was not feasible. Plans for the construction of the forty-two-hundred-foot Wawona Tunnel proceeded, posing many problems from the landscape standpoint. The result was not only an engineering feat but also a design solution that would influence the design of other areas where the construction of a tunnel was inevitable. The desire to create a dramatic overlook at the end of the tunnel and the practical problem of disposing of the extensive amount of fill excavated from the tunnel led to a solution

6.6. Mary's Rock Tunnel on Shenandoah National Park's Skyline Drive was constructed in the early 1930s. The tunnel was blasted through 610 feet of granodiorite. Portals were cut out of the bedrock to form naturalistic arches. The temporary shelter and construction materials in front of the south portal were part of the construction camp, which was placed in the right-of-way to avoid damage to areas surrounding the road. Steep barren areas on the slopes above the portal were later planted with black locust, laurel, and other native plants. *(Photograph by Allan Rinehart, courtesy National Park Service Historic Photography Collection)*

whereby the excavated material was retained by a hand-laid embankment to create a terrace for parking and viewing. A simple curvilinear terrace was formed beside the roadway at the end of the tunnel, and an island was graded to separate the overlook from the road and to control the flow of traffic on and off the road. The overlook provided a parking area bounded by a curb, sidewalk, and ribbonlike parapet wall. Upon exiting the tunnel, visitors would get their first expansive view over the valley and would be able to pull aside and leave their automobiles to contemplate or photograph the scene.[46]

Committee chairman Frederick Law Olmsted Jr. reported that from the "landscape standpoint" the most serious issue of the plans for the tunnel and road into the valley was the "great width and height of the permanently barren rock-fill" in the steeper parts of the valley east of the tunnel. Rock excavated from the tunnel would have to be shattered to relatively small stones (one-man size or less) and would have to take a slope of repose of about 1 1/2 to 1. The bank produced below grade would taper eastward varying from about 200 feet in height and 300 feet in width near the east portal of the tunnel to about 100 feet in height and 150 feet in width at the end of the overlook. The bank would diminish in size as it reached the lower end of the road. Any fill would have to be coarse to prevent any growth of trees or bushes on the slopes, and because the scattering of rocks at great velocity along such a slope threatened existing trees and vegetation, a hand-laid rock embankment would have to be built (1–3).

The committee was interested in efforts to darken artificially, and thereby disguise, the fresh granite dumps left on the hillside and the scars left by the excavation at the tunnel portals. Experiments were made by spraying oil with various chemicals on exposed rock cuts to create a stain that would blend with the natural rock and rockfalls of the surrounding topography. The color was too "warm" or brownish when bituminous spray was used, and the time required for a slow, natural darkening of the granite by lichens was too long when oil alone was used. The idea of staining may have been influenced by the successful artificial coloration of concrete on the Ahwahnee Hotel and the staining of the new suspension bridge across the Colorado River in Grand Canyon. Olmsted analyzed the problem from a visual perspective:

> But at best such camouflaging of the whitish color of the newly fractured granite will not prevent the form of any large area (visible as a unit) of dumped bank of "run-of-the-mine" rock from showing up under many conditions of changing light as conspicuously different from any natural feature of the Valley. So far as it can possibly be accomplished, any definite interruption of visible continuity and uniformity, reducing the scale of what is recognizable by the eye as a single continuous unit of dump, is even more important than a general toning down of color contrast. (6)

Lampblack and oil was finally found to give the desired effect, and in the 1930s, the Wawona Camp of the Civilian Conservation Corps used spray guns to apply this to the exposed rock cuts along the roads and around the tunnel portals.

Westchester County Parks Exchange

The National Park Service collaborated with Gilmore Clarke as early as 1929, when he consulted on a new plan for Mammoth Hot Springs. This collaboration continued through an exchange of personnel for several summers between the Landscape Division and the Westchester County Park System in New York. Highly regarded by the landscape architecture profession, Clarke's work in Westchester County would have continuing influence, as would Clarke himself, who was an adviser to the construction of the George Washington Memorial

6.7. Inspiration Point at the end of the Wawona Tunnel completed in 1933 was one of the first successful efforts to integrate engineering and landscape concerns in the development of a scenic overlook. Fill excavated from the tunnel was used to create an overlook complete with a parking area, island, sidewalk and curb, protective guardrail, and one of the most spectacular and memorable views of Yosemite Valley (Bridalveil Falls is in the distance at the right). *(Photograph by Ralph H. Anderson, courtesy National Park Service Historic Photography Collection)*

Parkway and a member of the Commission of Fine Arts in the 1930s. Wilbur E. Simonson, who directed the work on the George Washington Parkway, and Stanley W. Abbott, who became the designer of the Blue Ridge Parkway, both worked under Clarke in Westchester County. Abbott brought the latest aesthetic and engineering principles to national park work and went on to create a scenic parkway innovative in the use of spiral transitional curves and its sequence of views of the rolling hillsides, farmlands, and forests.

In the winter of 1930–31, John Wosky and Kenneth McCarter, assistant landscape architects on Vint's staff, spent two and a half months at Westchester County parks. There they studied the methods of highway design which had been developed by the Westchester County Park Commission and the operations of the commission and organization of the county park system. On their return trip to San Francisco they were to visit the National Capital Park and Planning Commission to observe its planning process and to observe the development of the Mount Vernon Boulevard and Potomac Parkway portions of the George Washington Memorial Parkway. In exchange, Clarke sent his assistant, Allyn R. Jennings, to the field office in San Francisco. Although a similar exchange was planned for the following year, in which Vint was to send either V. Roswell Ludgate from the Eastern Office or Davidson to New York, it is unclear whether the exchange actually took place.[47]

Park roads took on new direction in the 1930s with the development of linear park roads and parkways in the East, including the Colonial Parkway between Jamestown and Yorktown, the Mount Vernon Parkway (1930), Skyline Drive (1931) in Shenandoah, and finally the Blue Ridge Parkway (1935). These roads represent the fusion of the Landscape Division's experience in designing the roads of national parks in the West, the advancements made by Westchester County under Clarke's direction, and the National Park Service's expanding definition of recreation.[48]

The Significant Landscape Design of National Park Roads

By 1929 the road and trail program was energetically being carried out under an appropriation of five million dollars a year. A ten-year program was under way calling for the reconstruction of existing roads to modern standards, the construction of new roads, and the improvement and extension of trail systems. At the end of 1931, the National Park Service considered several of its road projects "outstanding." These were the Wawona Road and Tunnel in Yosemite, Generals Highway joining Sequoia and General Grant parks, Trail Ridge Road in Rocky Mountain National Park, Rim Drive encircling Crater Lake, Going-to-the-Sun Highway in Glacier, Colonial Parkway between Yorktown and Jamestown in Virginia, and Skyline Drive along the crest of the Blue Ridge in the proposed Shenandoah park. In 1932, the first part (central) of Skyline Drive in Shenandoah had been graded, the Wawona Tunnel completed, and construction of a road from Chinquapin Intersection to Glacier Point in Yosemite begun. In 1933, both the Wawona Tunnel and the Going-to-the-Sun Highway were dedicated.[49]

Viewing the role of the Landscape Division as central to the conservation of national parks, the secretary of the interior remarked in 1929, "Preservation of primitive landscape conditions, adequate protection of wild life, and the safeguarding of forests and watersheds can not be carried out if a reasonable balance between accessibility and wilderness values is not maintained. A group of landscape architects pass on all plans for improvements in the park system and roads and trails are built to designs that will give least injury to natural features."[50]

By the end of 1930, the results of the division's efforts to protect the roadside and natural landscape were visible. Vint credited this to the accumulation of completed work of several years of road construction, the success of the new specifications from both aesthetic and economical standpoints, and the enforcement of type B excavation practices: "The results accomplished were the real test, yet it is noteworthy that their acceptance, by engineers and contractors was accomplished with little effort. Further, the bid prices were not as high as expected and, finally they have made for a proper understanding of what is desired."[51]

Director Horace Albright praised the progress made by the roads and trails program: "1930 is important in the annals of this division as the year in which the fruits of its labors to protect the roadside and the natural landscape generally during road and trail construction became definitely apparent, to the casual visitor as well as to the specialist. There is now a distinct contrast between carefully planned park roads and others planned on a strictly engineering basis. The cooperation of the road engineers aided greatly in achieving this result" (30).

By 1931, the division was providing architectural sheets for bridges, parking areas, intersections, and overlooks to the Bureau of Public Roads. Specifications covered such points as the rounding and flattening of slopes, removal of form marks, and methods of blasting less injurious to the surroundings. Quarries, borrow pits, and abandoned contractors' camps were left in a condition that could be naturalized. Embankments necessary to keep boulders, soil, and rubble from falling upon the roads or to reinforce a substantial area of fill to carry a road or support an overlook were being built by hand by dry-laid methods without mortar.

Recognition and praise also came from the Bureau of Public Roads. At the twelfth conference of national park executives, in 1932, Dr. L. I. Hewes, the deputy chief engineer of the Bureau of Public Roads, estimated that the bureau had built about twenty-five million dollars' worth of park roads in the West. He called the National Park Service's Landscape Division "pioneers" in road landscape work and urged the park service to expand the planting program:

> When the history of this period is written, we are going to have to admit that the beautification of highways started as an offspring of this marriage of the Bureau of Public Roads to the National Park Service. Pennsylvania and Massachusetts have done conscious landscaping; that has been mostly planting. I think the Park Service could do more planting. I think the planting along the slopes could come out of the road funds. . . . It is a wonder to me [national park landscape architects] find so many different ways of giving the landscape effect because they are strictly limited; their manner of expression is very narrow. . . . The way to landscape a highway hasn't yet been found and there are no books about it, so this landscape division in the Park Service is doing pioneer work and we are learning with them and perhaps they are learning a little about roads from us.[52]

The achievements of the road-building program evolved from the technical and aesthetic experiments of the 1920s, the collaboration of the landscape architects and civil engineers, and the adoption of specific principles of design and practices of construction which emerged from Vint's office in the years from 1928 to 1932. Improvements continued during the 1930s, building upon the lessons of the 1920s and the groundwork of Vint's staff in the late 1920s. Road building in national parks was funded on a scale never before imagined. Through public works allotments and the efforts of the Civilian Conservation Corps, the construction of roads and the finishing of slopes to a naturalized condition created efficient, safe, and naturalistic systems of roads in each national park and many monuments. The achievements of the roads program were seen primarily in the parks of the West before 1932. In the 1930s, the focus shifted to the parks of the East, where the park service assumed leadership in the development of scenic and historic parkways, thus realizing portions of Mather's vision for a park-to-park highway system. The early lessons and the advances worked out in the 1920s and 1930s continued to guide park road development. They were inherent in the intent, principles, and philosophy underlying the design standards for modern park roads which the National Park Service published in 1968.

The road program, perhaps more than any other aspect of national park development, endeavored to merge the disparate missions of the National Park Service—to make the parks accessible to the public while leaving them unimpaired for future generations. Recognizing the power of illusion inherent in the principles and practices of naturalistic landscape design in 1939, Henry Hubbard remarked on the success of the National Park Service's roads: "How much effort has been bent [*sic*] toward preserving in the scene that they represent the effect that *man has done nothing.*"[53]

The developments of park road construction would have lasting effects on the history of road building in America. In 1963, Christopher Tunnard and Boris Pushkarev, in *Man-made America: Chaos or Control?*, recognized the contributions of the National Park Service work to the development of the modern highway. Certain characteristics that the park designers had worked out and adopted proved valuable. The slopes of roads blended naturally with the space of the surrounding topography when cut or filled slopes were flattened and rounded and the edges warped. Among the lessons that the highway designer could learn from the English garden landscape Tunnard listed asymmetry, "casual" continuity, a sensitivity to landform, and a skillful use of architectural as well as natural features in the landscape.[54]

The widespread application of the techniques pioneered by national park designers was evident in the 1944 report of the National Interregional Highway Committee, which described the value of flattened slopes and well-rounded cross-sectional contours. These were essential to prevent soil erosion and to minimize the injury and damage caused by vehicles accidentally leaving the roadway. They also helped mold the highway into the terrain, making it a harmonious feature of the natural landscape. The flattened side slopes also favored the growth of vegetation, thereby making it easier to maintain the road's drains, gutters, and culverts. Overall the techniques appealed to the committee because "design for utility and economy" went "hand in hand with sound landscape design."[55]

Construction of Trails

Both civil engineers and landscape architects were involved in the development of trails. The problems of trail building mirrored those of road building but on a smaller scale. As in road design, the landscape architects helped to locate the trails, capturing scenic features and views and protecting significant vegetation, rockwork, and other natural features. The civil engineers were responsible for the construction of trails, which was often undertaken by staff within each park rather than outside contractors. The engineers were concerned with the gradient of the trails, attempting to maintain a varied grade not exceeding 8 percent and to use switchbacks only where a gradual curving uphill trail was impossible. The engineers also addressed practical issues such as constructing a solid base for a flat, even path free of rocks, tree stumps, and roots. The landscape architects, however, viewed the problems of trail building from the perspective of visual and scenic character. Upholding the principle of harmonious construction, they recommended that structures along the trail and the surface of the trail be as inconspicuous as possible. Structures included the dry-laid rock benches that carried trails; stonemasonry parapets, culverts, and bridges; and trailside improvements such as signs, benches, springs, and lookouts.

As in road construction, the creation of trails in mountainous or canyon-like areas challenged engineers to find a feasible route and often required drilling and blasting. Equipment was transported by horse or mule, and workers relied on safety lines. The landscape architect's challenge in such cases was to ensure that the excavation did not mar the natural beauty of the area and that scars were inconspicuous, especially when viewed from popular viewpoints. The Ptarmigan Wall Trail in Glacier, the Four-Mile Trail in Yosemite, and the New River Trail at the base of the Grand Canyon all posed such challenges.

By the end of the 1920s, the Landscape Division was becoming more and more concerned about the visual compatibility of trails with their surroundings and significant natural features. The timber constructions that led visitors up Moro Rock in Sequoia, to scenic viewpoints along the Yellowstone River, and across fields of thermal geysers in Yellowstone were considered outmoded and intrusive, and more naturalistic solutions were sought.

In 1926, while visiting Yellowstone to provide a professional opinion on the

6.8. The foot and bridle trail, stonemasonry parapet, and entrance to the Ptarmigan Wall Tunnel in Glacier National Park illustrate the advances made in trail construction by the civil engineers and landscape architects of the National Park Service in the late 1920s. The tunnel was blasted through 180 feet of solid limestone and had enough clearance to carry a person on horseback. *(Photograph by George A. Grant, courtesy National Park Service Historic Photography Collection)*

boundary dispute along the Bechler River, landscape architect Harold Caparn made a number of recommendations to improve the landscape character of the parks. One of these concerned the observation decks along the Grand Canyon of the Yellowstone. Caparn urged that the wooden stairways, ramps, and railings that had been installed about 1920 be replaced with earthen paths and masonry parapets of native stone. Such a system could be modeled and colored to blend into nature's surrounding rockwork. Hull and Vint had designed similar walls the year before for Yellowstone's Apollinaris Spring, a heavily visited natural spring that had become a problem from both a sanitary and an aesthetic standpoint and was rehabilitated into an appealing natural garden.[56]

In 1927, Davidson conferred with Ansel Hall on the potential development of an interpretive program at Artist's Point, Grandview, Lookout Point,

6.9. In keeping with the 1930s master plans for the Grand Canyon of the Yellowstone, the wooden overlooks constructed about 1920 were rebuilt with flagstone terraces and naturalistic stonemasonry guardrail shaped to blend with the irregular, curvilinear contours of the natural cliffs. Viewed from a distance, the built walls were indistinguishable from the walls of the natural gorge. *(Photograph courtesy National Park Service Historic Photography Collection)*

and Inspiration Point along the Grand Canyon of the Yellowstone. In anticipation of Hall's obtaining private funding to carry out the development, Davidson sketched out plans and elevations for the existing and proposed development of trails, walkways, observation platforms, and shelters. Old guardrails and steps made of two-by-fours and wooden lookout platforms on stilts had been built at the scenic overlooks about 1920, and Davidson and Hall worked out plans to replace these structures with rockwork along the lines of that developed at Apollinaris Spring. Hall also wanted to construct an interpretive lookout shelter at Artist's Point similar in function to that at Glacier Point in Yosemite.

Davidson's sketches and their recommendations for masonry guardrails, stone steps, and flagstone flooring for the observation platforms and stairways at the various scenic points along the Grand Canyon of the Yellowstone were the first consideration of the area from a "landscape standpoint." In the next few years and throughout the New Deal, this area received considerable attention as some of the concessionary and National Park Service facilities were removed from the canyon and the observation points, trails, and access roads were slowly redeveloped to replace wooden stairways and platforms with more naturalistic and harmonious constructions of masonry walls and flagstone. The master plans continued to encourage the improvement of this area.[57]

The 1932 master plans for the redevelopment of points such as Artist's Point recommended a number of variations for curvilinear stonemasonry and steel guardrails all intended to blend into the natural scenery. It was not until the mid-1930s, however, that improvements of this type began to occur. After heavy snow destroyed the old wooden platforms overlooking the Upper Falls in 1936, public works money was used to build a new overlook with curvilinear masonry walls, stone steps, and a bridge of sturdy logs. This type of improvement continued to be made at other overlooks on Yellowstone's Grand Canyon through the 1950s.[58]

Meanwhile, naturalistic solutions were worked out elsewhere in the national parks. One of the first viewpoints to receive naturalistic treatment using stonemasonry and a combination of concrete and crushed native stone was Moro Rock, which had been developed with a wooden framework in 1919. Built in 1931, the new stairway was a series of stairs and ramps 798 feet in length which ascended the granitic dome on the southern rim of the Giant Forest Plateau. The stairway was designed to fit the natural contours of the ridge as closely as possible. From the base of the dome, it followed a natural ledge for about 100 feet and then ascended through a natural crevice to an observation platform at 6,645 feet. The trail then climbed a steep stairway along the crest of the ridge and crossed the eastern wall of the rock on a series of ramps supported by masonry retaining walls, before reaching another natural crevice. After continuing to pass through natural crevices along the crest, the trail then followed a series of switchbacks to reach the summit at 6,715 feet. The trail made extensive use of massive masonry walls and was surfaced with concrete that was mixed to blend in with the natural granite bedrock.[59]

Landscape architect Merel Sager and engineer Frank Diehl had selected the route and the building materials to blend the new stairway into the natural scenery to the greatest degree possible. The new stairway avoided the rectilinear lines and angles of the old stairway, which perched awkwardly upon the dome. Instead, it curved naturalistically and was shaped to fit into the natural crevices and along the natural ridges. Retaining walls and protective guardrails were made of randomly coursed rubble masonry of local granite. Ramps led over natural bedrock or were surfaced with concrete mixed with crushed stone matching the coloration of the granite. The result was a durable, safe, and harmonious stairway that could handle the large amount of traffic the site attracted.[60]

6.10. View of the Old Faithful area of Yellowstone National Park in 1929 shows the open terraces surrounding the geyser to the left, the Old Faithful Inn in the center, and the recently completed trailside museum and amphitheater just visible beneath the canopy of trees at the lower left. *(Photograph by George A. Grant, courtesy of the National Park Service Photography Collection)*

The Landscape Division drew heavily on its experience in road construction in making improvements along trails. Although trails differed from roads in scale, the functional and design problems of trail building were similar to those of road building, particularly in popular areas. Concern for visitor safety as well as access necessitated, for example, the grading and surfacing of trails and the construction of sturdy bridges, stairways, and protective barriers, which in turn called for harmonious and inconspicuous solutions. In some areas, such as Sunrise Ridge on the Yakima Park Road at Mount Rainier, the installation of walks and protective parapets was integrally linked to the development of park roads. In other areas, such as the promenade at Rim Village in Crater Lake, trails were developed independently from the road program but adopted many of its solutions.

The lessons of surfacing roads with macadam of crushed gravel taken from native stone and constructing masonry walls of native stone with exposed weathered surfaces were readily applied to trails. Not only could these improvements be made on site with existing local materials, requiring the portage of only essential equipment, but the improvements themselves could also be fashioned to achieve naturalistic curvilinear lines that at once followed nature and blended inconspicuously with the natural setting. One of the most remote developments of this type was the Ptarmigan Wall Trail and Tunnel constructed at Glacier in the late 1920s. Here a tunnel was necessary to pass through 180 feet of solid limestone at an elevation of 7,400 feet. The tunnel was approached along a trail carved into the side of the cliff and protected by an irregular stonemasonry guardrail that blended with the surrounding rock. The achievement was a remarkable engineering feat and a notable success in blending constructed improvements and natural scenery to fulfill the goals of landscape protection and accessibility.[61]

Building trails across geyser formations in Yellowstone demanded a different solution. The story behind the design of the Formation Trail at Old Faithful indicates the designer's varied concerns, from public safety to visual appearance. Earlier trails had been laid out in the 1920s. In some areas, logs eight or ten inches in diameter had been placed end to end along the ground in parallel rows to form an unsurfaced path about six feet wide. Kenneth McCarter, the park's resident landscape architect, felt the trails closest to Old Faithful should be at least ten feet wide to handle the foot traffic, including guided tours, which the site needed to accommodate. He also argued that concrete and masonry were inappropriate materials for constructing paths because they permanently defaced the formations. Therefore, he suggested that although the use of log curbing should be continued, it should be topped with planks to form a wooden boardwalk above the surface of the open grassland.

Hot pools were a hazard to public safety at Yellowstone's several geyser basins. At Old Faithful there were six such pools, and McCarter doubted the adequacy of the log trails to serve as a safeguard. He recommended that curbing be installed six to eight feet away from each hazardous pool and that low signs marked "dangerous" be placed around the pools. He felt these would "serve the purpose of warning the tourists and would not seriously interfere with the natural beauty of the pools or the landscape."[62]

McCarter's idea was followed at Old Faithful and again at Norris Geyser Basin in the mid-1930s when the Civilian Conservation Corps, following the area's master plan, constructed a system of naturalistic trails that led into the basin and wound around the geysers in a loop before returning to the trailhead and ascending the hillside to the parking area, trail museum, and comfort stations.

The achievements of the late 1920s and early 1930s established precedents that were followed and modified to suit local conditions during the New Deal. Trail improvements were slated for the most popular scenic attractions in other

6.11. Photographed in 1939, the nature trail across Norris Geyser Basin, in Yellowstone, inconspicuously guided visitors safely among the geysers, fumaroles, and hot springs. The curvilinear, elevated boardwalk was built by the Civilian Conservation Corps in the summer of 1936. The curving walk created a loop around the geyser basin and connected with a footpath that led in sweeping arcs to the trailside museum, parking area, and other facilities on the hill. Interpretive markers supported on slender poles identified the features. The flagpole and jerkinhead gable of the museum roof are visible midway along the line of trees on the hill. *(Photograph by George A. Grant, courtesy National Park Service Historic Photography Collection)*

national parks, including the Grand Canyon of the Yellowstone with its many viewpoints, the South Rim of the Grand Canyon, and Carlsbad Cavern. The advances in masonry guardrails and the development of surfaces that used natural materials made it possible to adjust construction and appearances for local topography, conditions, and setting and at the same time construct sturdy and durable improvements that could sustain adverse weather conditions and heavy visitor use. Many of the trail improvements funded by Public Works Administration allotments followed the principles and incorporated the methods of blending and harmonization which the Landscape Division and Engineering Division had worked out by 1930. The Civilian Conservation Corps working in both national and state parks perpetuated these principles and practices to an unprecedented extent.

6.12. Photographed in 1934, the naturalistic system of footpaths atop Cadillac Mountain in Acadia dispersed visitors from a parking loop at the end of the mountain road to numerous panoramic viewpoints of Frenchman's Bay. Designed in 1931 by Charles Peterson, head of the new Eastern Field Office, the paths successfully blended with the summit's natural character and coloration. The paths inconspicuously wound among the gentle contours of the granite summit. The paths followed the surface of the natural pink-colored bedrock, and, wherever needed, naturalistic rockwork provided coping and steps. *(Photograph by Allan Rinehart, courtesy National Park Service Historic Photography Collection)*

By 1930, improvements were taking place in the construction of trail bridges. Designs and materials depended on the site, setting, and function of the bridge. Bridle trails, for example, required bridges of greater strength, width, and clearance than foot trails. Simple cross-plank bridges were sufficient to carry hikers across streams, but more elaborate solutions were sought for deep precipitous gorges. Log bridges were generally preferred, and by the end of the 1920s, efforts were being made to fashion them from logs similar in size to those in the surrounding forests. While a few bridges, such as the suspension bridge carrying the Kaibab Trail across the Colorado River at the base of the Grand Canyon, were particularly notable as engineering achievements and were de-

6.13. This foot and bridle trail in Yosemite Valley was built to the standards followed by the Engineering Division in the late 1920s. A bench of dry-laid stones was constructed to carry a meandering path and allow for drainage without disturbing the natural slope. The path was easy in grade and had a flattened, earthen surface. Trees left in place to either side of the trail preserved the woodland setting and screened the trail from a nearby utilities facility. *(Photograph courtesy National Archives, Record Group 79)*

signed by national park engineers, they heralded advances in landscape design as well. Like road bridges, trail bridges were designed to fit into their sites and harmonize with their natural settings. The Kaibab bridge was built in the late 1920s to replace an earlier one. The approaches were tunnels carved through the canyon walls with naturalistic cavelike portals. The bridge, constructed of steel cables and girders, was stained a special color to blend in with the canyon walls and river sediments. This was the first major application of staining to match metal surfaces with natural scenery.

In the late 1920s, the park service focused increasingly on designing and building sturdy trails that could serve those on horseback as well as those on foot. Considered outstanding were the five-foot-wide Kaibab Trail of the Grand Canyon, the trails to the East and West Rims of Zion, the High Sierra Trail from the Giant Forest toward Mount Whitney in Sequoia, and the Four-Mile Trail from Yosemite Valley to Glacier Point.[63]

In October 1934, the Engineering Division published its first standards for foot and bridle trails. These would be used by the builders of national park trails for several decades. The standards developed by chief engineer Frank Kittredge and his staff were instructions for trail building in the form of a large sheet with diagrams that could be folded into a pocket-size reference guide for use in the field. These standards ensured that foot and bridle trails were durable, safe, and pleasurable to use.

Specifications for building trails called for a standard width of 4 feet, which could be accommodated by cutting into the slope or by benching the supporting ground with a dry-laid wall of large stones. Dry random rubble walls could be built downhill to retain soil and rocks on a steep slope or uphill to retain material above the trail and prevent slides. All walls were to be battered. The rate of grade was limited to 15 percent except in extreme cases, and grades of less than 15 percent were recommended wherever possible without unduly extending the length of the trail. To avoid excessive construction costs, grades of 18 percent and 20 percent were allowed in short stretches of not more than 150 feet. The grade was to vary at intervals, in order to "avoid all the strain being confined to a certain few leg muscles."[64]

Detailed instructions and diagrams were given for the construction of drainage features, switchbacks, and dry rubble walls. For drainage, dips and water breaks were to be built into the trail at regular intervals, and culverts and bridges were to be built only where simpler solutions were inadequate. The precipitation and runoff characteristics of a locality were assessed to determine the type and spacing of drainage features best suited to the conditions. Although a curving alignment was preferred throughout the trail, switchbacks could be introduced on steep slopes provided the turn itself could be built upon level ground. In building dry rubble walls, attention was to be given to the slope of the footing and joints and the batter of the inner and outer walls to ensure that the stones were laid firmly in place.[65]

The landscape architects of the Branch of Plans and Design (formerly Landscape Division) reviewed and approved all phases of trail location, the construction of culverts and walls, and the removal of large trees. Trail builders were asked to make sure that all evidence of construction outside the trail prism was held to a minimum to preserve the natural setting. The ground was to be cleared to provide a ten-foot clearance above the trail, and no more than one foot to either side of the trail or the cut or filled areas. The trail was to be routed around large trees, and no large trees were to be cut unless this was impractical. The walls, culverts, and other features were to be constructed to harmonize with the natural setting and to avoid the destruction of natural features.[66]

Chapter 7

Park Architecture, Landscape Naturalization, and Campground Development

Expanding the Building Program

From 1927 to 1932, the building program of the National Park Service made substantial progress in providing each park with administrative buildings that were functional and harmonious in design. Utilitarian industrial buildings such as garages and workshops were arranged to form enclosed compounds where their activities did not interfere with visitors' use of the park. At campgrounds, community buildings served a number of functions, including quarters for rangers, central showers, and gathering places for relaxation and evening lectures. Each building, whether an administration building or an employee residence, was designed for its site and setting, fitting the development scheme determined for the area. Each reflected an architectural theme based on native materials and method of construction and sometimes a cultural theme drawn from the region's pioneering or indigenous architecture. Designers often created buildings to match the style of preexisting structures felt to be in keeping with the natural character of the park.

The idea of an architectural theme for all park structures in keeping with a park's natural character had been promoted by Daniels, Punchard, and Hull. In the late 1920s, Thomas Vint, chief landscape architect, realized that architectural themes could be imposed on standard plans that met the broad functional needs of parks in general. The designs for new buildings were therefore standardized according to type, providing model floor plans and elevations that could be adopted elsewhere in the park. The materials, type of construction, and details of park structures, on the other hand, were determined by the natural qualities of each site, including climate, weather, presence of local stone or timber, topography, and the scale of surrounding forests. While larger structures, such as administration buildings, were generally unique designs, structures such as patrol cabins or comfort stations could follow a common design that was repeated throughout the park. The same design might be used again and again in one park, provided the external characteristics of the structure fit harmoniously into the natural setting.

For this reason, a number of successful designs developed in the late 1920s reappeared in the public works and emergency conservation programs of the New Deal era. For example, about 1928 an efficient design for a duplex comfort station was developed. The building was divided into separate sections for men and women, which were entered by screened doors and porches on opposite ends. A central utility room separated the two sections. The prototype for this design appears to be the Union Point comfort station at Yosemite, which was repeated several years later at Tuolumne Meadows and whose floor plan and utilities layout appeared in many forms throughout the 1930s. With separate paths and screened entrances, the solution proved efficient for utilities and still maintained the privacy of separate structures.

Also important was the development of standards for the construction of housekeeping cabins. In the mid-1920s, housekeeping camps were first introduced in the national parks as an experiment. They proved particularly popular among tourists and profitable for concessionaires. Soon concessionaires were demanding that they be allowed to build large numbers of such facilities, preferably laid out in rectangular grids so that their allotted space could be filled with as many cabins as possible. Because of the increasing demand, Director Horace Albright requested that Vint's division make a special study of housekeeping cabins and draw up plans for a cabin suitable for the automobile tourist in the national parks.

In consultation with the service's sanitary engineer, the division developed Standards for Housekeeping Cabins to be followed by both the government and park operators. Issued in November 1929, the standards took the form of three sheets of drawings that specified physical requirements such as equipment, size of cabin, and number of windows, rather than preferred floor plans or designs. The study proved useful to the development of concessionaires' facilities and to the service's landscape program. Albright recognized the effect that large units of housekeeping cabins would have on the national parks. Perceiving the study's far-reaching value, he remarked, "The question developed a great deal of thought on the development of all tourist facilities. The benefits will bear fruit in all future programs."[1]

Within the next few years, the demand for cabin development and housekeeping accommodations increased, and the standards enabled the park designers to review the adequacy of concessionaires' plans. By 1932, these lower-priced accommodations had become increasingly popular, and a definite trend toward housekeeping camps became apparent and continued into the 1940s.

The Landscape Division reviewed many plans submitted by concessionaires to meet this demand by modernizing their existing complexes or by constructing entirely new ones. Unlike the lodges at Zion and Bryce, which offered accommodations in several types of cottages that were spaciously arranged in keeping with the natural contours and blended harmoniously into the wooded areas, the new housekeeping camps called for large numbers of uniform cabins situated closely together, replacing what previously would have been a tent platform. In their best configuration, the camps were laid out in courts with curving walkways and roads; in their least desirable form, they were densely clustered in a rectangular grid with only enough space for parking a car alongside. Whatever the configuration, the Landscape Division did require that wiring for utilities be placed underground to avoid the spiderweb effect of typical cabin camps.

Mount Rainier's concessionaire sought approval for developments of this type at Yakima Park and Paradise. The camp at Paradise illustrates the scale of these developments. Located in the upper half of the free public campground, the camp included a large service building, containing a cafeteria, salesrooms, shower-baths, comfort stations, and forty bedrooms. It also served as a winter lodge for one hundred guests. In the fall of 1930, 275 cabins had been completed, and an additional 250 were slated for construction the following year. The old tent camp was abandoned, and the cold storage building was converted for summer offices and a dormitory and dining hall for employees. A new warehouse was constructed to house a laundry, an ice cream plant, and supplies.

Keeping pace with the government development of the northeastern side of the mountain, the Rainier Park Company opened a similar but less ambitious housekeeping cabin camp in the summer and fall of 1931 at Yakima Park. A service building, referred to as the lodge, had a cafeteria, salesroom, and about forty bedrooms. There were two hundred housekeeping cabins.[2]

Rather than artlessly massing standard cabins, several concessionaires developed communities that provided model solutions for maintaining a harmony between the accommodations and the natural setting. The two most noteworthy were the North Rim development of the Utah Parks Company, designed by Gilbert Stanley Underwood, and, several years later, Mary Colter's Bright Angel Lodge and cabins for the Fred Harvey Company at Grand Canyon.

The standards made it possible for the park designers to draw up model designs useful in other aspects of park architecture. They would have the strongest influence in the development of recreational cabin areas in state parks through the work of the Civilian Conservation Corps and later the Works Progress Administration. In 1934, Conrad Wirth compiled a portfolio of the variations on housekeeping cabins which had been developed by the Landscape Division, by then called the Branch of Plans and Design, and the Resettlement Administration. These plans served as models for conservation work and other relief work in state parks and in recreational demonstration areas. Architect Cecil Doty of

Herbert Maier's District III office for New Deal Emergency Conservation Work in the state parks developed blueprints for a number of standard cabin designs that were used extensively in Texas, Oklahoma, Arkansas, and other southwestern states. Unlike the crowded communities built by the concessionaires, the cabin clusters built in state parks were constructed and arranged to harmonize with the natural site and setting. Outstanding early examples were the cabins in the Virginia state parks, which illustrated how a standard plan could be varied by altering materials, methods of construction, and features such as porches. Also noteworthy were the cabins designed by state park architect Arthur Fehr at Bastrop State Park in Texas, which strongly resemble and may have influenced the prototypical designs issued by Herbert Maier's district office.[3]

From the early years of the National Park Service, designers had recognized pioneer and traditional forms of construction as suitable prototypes for park structures, for several reasons. Such forms used native materials such as timber or stone that blended with forests, boulder-strewn rivers, or canyons. These forms offered an economical and practical approach to harmonization in keeping with the 1918 policy. Furthermore, pioneer traditions used construction techniques yielding irregular lines, roughened textures, and handcrafted finishes that were compatible with the character of nature.

Within these requirements, there was a great deal of latitude. Vint's early experience as a draftsman working on bungalows and residences in Los Angeles and Pasadena was formative for integrating building and landscape. He continued to draw on Bungaloid and Craftsman motifs, designs, and plans. Park buildings constructed by the concessionaires, the creative achievements of the Underwood firm and Mary Colter, the work of Jesse and Aileen Nusbaum at Mesa Verde, and Herbert Maier's highly individual and successful designs for park museums provided a wealth of inspiration and a climate of free expression. While Vint's staff perfected the design of log and stone structures, they also studied other cultural and indigenous traditions and explored new materials and methods. In 1929, Vint asked Colter for copies of her photographs of the cave dwellings and temples at Mesa Verde which had inspired her own work at Grand Canyon. In 1930, Vint began to examine the possibilities of adobe construction, which had been traditionally used in the Southwest, and Charles Peterson gathered notes on the method of construction and the various uses of adobe in the buildings of Santa Fe.

To Vint, the lodges at Glacier and Zion represented the best of park architecture. He was extremely satisfied with the developments at Bryce and the North Rim of the Grand Canyon as well. In December 1930, the Department of the Interior issued a press release that praised the variety of facilities at the North Rim and named the development the "best all-around public utility development in the national parks."[4]

If the early 1920s were a period of experimentation with forms, materials,

7.1. Sinnott Memorial at Crater Lake National Park was the first museum funded by Congress and designed by the National Park Service's Landscape Division. Intended as an observation station and an interpretive center, it was built into the steep slopes below Rim Village. In 1933, shortly after the museum's completion, park service photographer George A. Grant captured the animalistic form of the head of an eagle as depicted in Native American art. Mountain hemlock and other native specimens were later planted to stabilize and naturalize the steep, exposed slopes in the foreground. *(Photograph by George A. Grant, courtesy National Park Service Historic Photography Collection)*

and architectural themes, then 1927 to 1932 were the years when principles and practices borrowed from Downing, Vaux, Olmsted, and Hubbard and a variety of architectural styles coalesced to form a mature ethic of rustic and naturalistic design which would be carried over into the 1930s and affect the character of national and state parks nationwide.

In 1932, Vint compiled a portfolio of representative administrative buildings and structures which was circulated to various parks. Today this document indicates what Vint considered the most successful and representative designs that emerged from his office from 1927 to 1932. Illustrated in the portfolio are the administration buildings at Longmire (1928) and Yakima Park (1931), the comfort stations at Union Point in Yosemite (1928) and Logan Pass in Glacier (1931), the Tioga Pass Entrance at Yosemite (1931), a ranger dormitory at Crater Lake (1932), a community building at an unidentified location (1927), the fire lookout at Crane Flat in Yosemite (1931), and checking stations at Sequoia and Mount Rainier (1926). Residences were drawn from the work at Yosemite Village, where there had been a serious shortage of housing in the late 1920s. Among these were a dentist's residence (1931), a four-family residence (1930), and a cabin designed for the new Indian Village. Other examples of housing included a staff residence built at Mount Rainier (1930) and the superintendent's residence and ranger dormitory built at Crater Lake (1932).[5]

The buildings selected for the portfolio reflect not only the maturing architectural vision of Vint and his staff but also their collaboration with other programs of the National Park Service. By this time, several other programs had reached maturity, such as engineering, sanitation, and forestry, and had become a permanent part of the administration of national parks. As these programs demanded facilities and made changes in the park landscape, the Landscape Division collaborated with them. Moreover, one of the advantages of the Western Field Office was that it brought together the park service's various programs. It was also possible to forge a stronger link with the Educational Division, headed by Ansel Hall, whose office was nearby in Berkeley.

Designs for the Educational Division

Under the leadership of chief naturalist Ansel F. Hall, the Educational Division grew in the 1920s. This division offered myriad programs to teach visitors about the natural history of the parks, including interpretive trails and waysides, museums, gardens, nature shrines, and amphitheaters. Since many of the division's programs involved building structures or trails, the Landscape Division had worked closely with the division since 1924, when the Yosemite Museum and the Glacier Point Lookout were being planned and constructed in Yosemite.

Herbert Maier, the designer of these buildings, collaborated closely with Hall and a special committee of outside experts to work out the final design of the buildings and their exhibits. Maier went on to design a number of museums funded by the Laura Spelman Rockefeller Memorial for various national parks. He created a series of museums for Yellowstone and expanded the idea of the trailside museum devoted to the interpretation of a single aspect or particular area of a park, such as Old Faithful Geyser. By 1930, he had also designed the Yavapai Observation Building and Museum on the South Rim of the Grand

Canyon. The government landscape designers, particularly Vint, collaborated with Maier and the museum committee in selecting the sites for the museums and reviewing Maier's designs.

The first museum to receive special congressional funding was the Sinnott Memorial at Crater Lake. Designed by Vint's office, the building closely followed the solutions for a rimside observation-type building which Maier had worked out for the Yavapai Observation Building. It was also influenced by Colter's Lookout and Hermit's Rest at Grand Canyon. Rather than being located at the top of the rim, however, the stonemasonry building fit closely into the steep slope of the crater high above the lake and assumed the form of an eagle's head.

By 1930, the concept of natural history interpretation had expanded to encompass trails, trail hubs, wildflower gardens, trailside nature shrines, branch museums, naturalist residences, and outdoor amphitheaters. The education programs expanded and made use of the natural and scenic features for on-site interpretation. As these structures developed to serve the expanding interpretive programs, they assumed a distinctive stylistic character that placed them in the traditions of both rustic architecture and naturalistic landscape design.

Most ambitious was the education program at Yellowstone, where the Old Faithful Museum was accompanied by branch museums at Madison Junction, Norris Geyser Basin, Yellowstone Lake, and Mammoth Hot Springs. The museum concept thus grew from the idea of a central museum with an outlying lookout, as built in Yosemite in 1924, to a parkwide system of branch museums, each containing a museum, residence, amphitheater, trails, parking areas, paths, and comfort stations. They could be connected with a nearby concessionaire's complex and campground to provide visitors convenient access at all times of the day.

Amphitheaters and interpretive waysides were additional structures that emerged from the work of the Educational Division in the late 1920s. In 1927, Ernest Davidson, the resident landscape architect assigned to Yellowstone, discussed various improvements and installations of exhibits at the major overlooks at the Grand Canyon of the Yellowstone, including Artist's Point and Inspiration Point. Davidson made sketches on site incorporating both Hall's and his own ideas. Although he sent them to Wosky in the San Francisco office to have finished drawings made, there is no evidence that the final drawings were ever made. The collection, however, illustrates the vision the Landscape Division had for developing interpretive viewpoints in the late 1920s. Although Hall's plans for redeveloping the paths and overlooks along the canyon never materialized, the ideas were further expanded in the master plans of the 1930s and laid the groundwork for future interpretive developments incorporating trails, walkways, observation platforms, and interpretive shelters, called "nature shrines." Although such features were being developed in a number of parks, Yellowstone's interpretive program led the service in integrating these features into the

7.2. At the Lake Museum in Yellowstone National Park, a flagstone observation terrace with a compass rose and stonemasonry parapets provided a viewpoint that immersed visitors in panoramic views of Yellowstone Lake and glacier-capped Mount Sheridan. Trailside museums were designed to interpret a park's natural history and enhance the visitor's inspirational experience. *(Photograph by George A. Grant, courtesy National Park Service Historic Photography Collection)*

design and operation of museums throughout the park. These structures drew heavily from the traditions of rustic architecture and naturalistic gardening.

The first interpretive wayside at Yellowstone was the Obsidian Cliff Nature Shrine. Built in 1931, it explained to the public the site's natural formation, a mountain of volcanic glass approximately two miles long. Designed by Herbert Maier, the nature shrine was the idea of Carl Russell, the park naturalist who had become an expert in museum exhibits. Built on the west side of the Grand Loop Road twelve miles south of Mammoth Hot Springs, the nature shrine measured

7.3. Ideas about park architecture, landscape architecture, and the interpretation of natural history coalesced in Herbert Maier's designs for trailside museums in Yellowstone National Park. At Fishing Bridge, curving rock-edged paths planted with native species led from the Lake Museum to a naturalist's residence and a woodland amphitheater. *(Photograph by George A. Grant, courtesy National Park Service Historic Photography Collection)*

six by sixteen feet and was set twenty-five feet from the road at the edge of a parking lot and at the base of the cliff. The walls were constructed of clusters of basaltic columns that had been carefully selected from a nearby formation and moved to the site. A wood-shingled, overhanging roof was carried on exposed log purlins. The open-sided structure housed exhibit panels that were originally placed behind glass. Flagstone paving, a curb of basaltic stone blocks, and native plants surrounded the shelter. A number of smaller trailside nature shrines were constructed of native logs and stones in Yellowstone at the same time. Several of these structures were illustrated in the National Park Service's portfolios published in the 1930s.[6]

The amphitheater was first incorporated into the design of Yellowstone's Old Faithful Museum in the late 1920s and similarly appeared at the Lake Museum at Fishing Bridge. The idea of an amphitheater in a national park, how-

7.4. The Obsidian Cliff Nature Shrine in Yellowstone National Park was one of several wayside exhibits designed by Herbert Maier for the National Park Service in the early 1930s to interpret points of interest by providing on-site exhibits. The design illustrated the converging principles of rustic architectural design and landscape naturalization. Photographed just after construction, the shelter sat upon a flagstone terrace and was planted with native spruces and other plants. The raw, unfinished slopes of the parking lot and road are visible beyond. *(Photograph by George A. Grant, courtesy National Park Service Historic Photography Collection)*

ever, was not new. In 1920 at Yosemite, a simple outdoor auditorium seating 250 people had been constructed in a natural amphitheater surrounded by trees using funds provided by the Sierra Club and M. Hail McAllister of San Francisco. The seats were in three rows of twelve-foot pine logs about eighteen inches in diameter with the bark left on. They had backs of canvas inserted over one-inch iron pipe frames and were arranged on a slope facing the speaker's stand. Charles Punchard praised this design as "attractive, unique, and comfortable" and recommended the development of outdoor amphitheaters in other parks.[7]

Outdoor theaters and amphitheaters appeared across the nation in the early twentieth century; they were a popular feature in parks, college campuses, and private estates. The grandest was the great Greek Theater (1903) at the Uni-

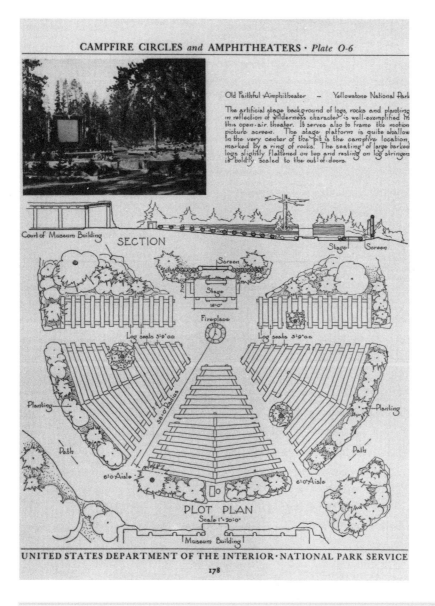

7.5. The amphitheater at Yellowstone's Old Faithful Museum was featured in the National Park Service's portfolio *Park Structures and Facilities* of 1935 as a design ideal for a woodland setting and having a wilderness character. *(Reprinted Albert H. Good, ed.,* Park Structures and Facilities, *1935)*

versity of California, Berkeley, a prototype with which Maier and Vint were familiar. National park designers likely also knew of Myron Hunt's design for Pomona State College in California. Articles appeared in *Landscape Architecture* and other journals in the 1920s on the construction of outdoor theaters. Frank Waugh had a continuing interest in amphitheaters and published *Outdoor Theaters: The Design, Construction, and Use of Open-Air Auditoriums* in 1917 and several articles in the 1920s. He wrote on natural amphitheaters and the relationship of the amphitheater and the campfire. In his own landscape work, he adapted the more traditional forms to the natural setting of national forests.[8]

The semicircular amphitheaters at the Old Faithful and Lake Museums in Yellowstone were rustic versions of the traditional Greek theater form built into a hillside with radiating aisles and rows of seating rising evenly from a center stage. Maier's semicircular designs with their log materials were better suited to the intimate woodland surroundings and use for evening lectures and slide shows than the massive stone and concrete prototypes. While he clearly drew from the Berkeley example, he developed it on a much smaller scale and in a naturalistic manner befitting its forested location. Screens of trees hugged the theater's edges and created a backdrop for the stage, and scattered trees within the theater were left in position, with seats built to either side of them. Roughly hewn logs were laid vertically in progression with height decreasing from the center outward to create a backwall for the stage, echoing the verticality of the surrounding forest and framing the slide screen.

Benches were also fashioned from split logs. The amphitheater incorporated the traditional campfire in the form of a stone ring placed before the stage. As Maier's amphitheater, with its radiating aisles and arcs of seating descending the slope toward the stage, was adopted in other parks, this campfire circle was moved to one side of the stage, so that smoke from the campfire would not obscure the audience's view of the slides being projected on the screen or activities occurring on stage.

By 1932, the amphitheater had become an important and regular feature of park campgrounds where evening ranger talks could be heard. Many were adaptations of Maier's woodland theater. Variations included outdoor theaters at Zion and Mesa Verde, where the theater was situated in a depression along the rim of a canyon to present a scenic view that could be interpreted by a ranger or simply contemplated in a type of open-air temple.

By the end of 1932, the expansion of the education program was reflected in the design of new kinds of structures and features in the parks. Amphitheaters, nature trails, lookout shelters, nature shrines, and campfires were built in conjunction with campgrounds and other developed areas. Park designers at Paradise experimented with a centralized trail hub from which interpretive trails could lead to scenic areas and special features of the park in conjunction with the new landscape work around the community building and housekeeping cabins.

This idea was later recommended for the terminus of trails at Tuolumne Meadows in Yosemite.[9]

Forestry and the Protection of Park Forests

Another growing function of the National Park Service was the protection of park forests carried out under the Forestry Division, part of the Western Field Office headed by fire-control expert John Coffman. Coffman had developed detailed surveys of fire hazards in a number of parks and comprehensive plans for the prevention and suppression of forest fires in those areas. A number of serious fires, including the Half Moon fire at Glacier Park, called for liaisons and collaborative effort with other agencies. In 1929, the Landscape Division collaborated with Coffman to develop standard designs and specifications for forest lookout towers.[10]

In 1931, the collaboration resulted in two lookouts: the Watchman at Crater Lake and the Shadow Mountain Fire Lookout at Rocky Mountain. A year later, Lassen's Harkness Peak Lookout was added to the repertoire of successful designs. These designs used stone and timber materials fashioned into functional two-story structures that included a large viewing platform on the upper story entirely surrounded and enclosed by large windows and an outside balcony. The fire lookout posed a dilemma for designers: in order to perform their essential function, these structures needed to be situated on prominent peaks; they needed to provide visibility in 360 degrees; and they could not be concealed or screened by vegetation. The use of native stone and timber and the simple, rectangular form with hipped roof contributed greatly to the ability of these structures to blend inconspicuously into their setting, even when viewed from a neighboring peak or nearby trail. Towers such as the Watchman not only helped detect fires in remote areas but also were open to visitors for the enjoyment of scenic views. These basic designs would be repeated in appropriate local materials in many variations throughout the parks in the 1930s.

A Program of Landscape Naturalization

The naturalistic landscape gardening practices that had evolved in the 1920s called for the planting of groupings of native trees, shrubs, and grasses along roadways, construction sites, and eroded areas and the removal of vegetation for fire control and beautification. As construction took place in the parks, trees and shrubs were removed from the construction sites of buildings, roads, overlooks, and parking areas and transplanted in temporary nurseries or on the sites of completed construction. This process of transplanting and replanting became known as "landscape naturalization" by 1930. At this time, the National Park

Service under the leadership of Harold C. Bryant adopted a policy banning the introduction of exotic plants into the parks and encouraging the elimination of exotics already growing in the parks. This change occurred at the same time that park service landscape architects were developing a process of flattening and rounding slopes to curb erosion and naturalize park roadways.

National park designers recognized the benefits of planting in the early years of the landscape program. Charles Punchard had encouraged Yosemite's park superintendent and concessionaires to use techniques of the Arts and Crafts movement to conceal artificial surfaces with a mantle of vines and other native plants. He had drawn attention to the need to replant the giant sequoias of Sequoia National Park in 1919. In 1925, Hull called for reforestation to screen or mask unsightly objects or burned-over areas. That year, in cooperation with the Public Health Service, Hull had used plantings to rehabilitate the Apollinaris Spring in Yellowstone, making the area more attractive and sanitary, and recommended that springs in other parks be studied with the idea of "increasing their usefulness and beauty." It was not until the end of the decade, however, that planting was done in a routine or serious manner either as a consequence of construction or as an effort to add to the scenic beauty of the park.[11]

In spring of 1927, Vint hired Ernest Davidson, who had substantial experience in planting and transplanting trees and shrubs. Davidson's first assignment was to supervise the planting of trees at the Gardiner Gate at Yellowstone. Here the year before, Vint and the concessionaire had discussed plans to redesign the approach to the Gardiner Gate and build new company garages. Davidson drew up a planting plan that screened the company garages from public view and restored a natural appearance to the area in front of the entry arch where a reflecting pool had been filled in. Concerned by the loss of vegetation, he transplanted trees and shrubs in the Mammoth Hot Springs and Canyon campgrounds. By September, Davidson's plantings had taken hold with only a few having died. Davidson believed that if proper care was given to transplanted materials for two months, one could successfully transplant even late in the season when the leaves were fairly well developed. Vint's decision to hire Davidson may well have been influenced by the recognition that a planting program could solve many of the park service's landscape problems.[12]

Later that year at Mount Rainier, Davidson began the first serious planting program in a park village. He and a small crew planted evergreen trees, shrubs, and ferns and constructed some rockwork near the grand log arch at the Nisqually Entrance. By planting alders, vine maples, and evergreens, they also screened the old switchback road from the view of the new Nisqually Road. Davidson's projects for Longmire Village included planting plans for four new employee cottages, which called for simple foundation plantings that the residents could plant and care for. At the campground, soil was hauled in to grade the grounds around the new community building, and small evergreens, maples, alders, and similar shrubs were planted around the building. Ferns were planted about the foundation and the entry walk, which was outlined by rock cobbles embedded in the soil. This work improved the visitors' access to the site, erased the scars of construction, and created the illusion that the woodland had never been disturbed. The thick forests at Longmire consisted of a canopy of mature trees that consisted predominantly of western hemlock (*Tsuga heterophylla*), Douglas fir (*Pseudotsuga menziesii*), western red cedar (*Thuja plicata*), and Alaskan cedar (*Chamaecyparis nootkatensis*) and an understory of herbaceous plants and shrubs that included salal (*Gaultheria shallon*), sword fern (*Polisticum munitum*), Oregon grape (*Berberis nervosa*), and vine maple (*Acer circinatum*). Davidson also conducted several experiments with the planting of sloped banks of the new roads, by planting the root cuttings of various shrubs and plants including brake ferns (possibly the cliffbrake fern, *Pellaea glabella*), salal, and huckleberry (*Vaccinium* spp.).[13]

Davidson continued his planting program at Mount Rainier in 1928, taking special interest in the new administration building, which was taking form on the village plaza according to his designs. A year with the park service had shown Davidson that planting was not considered a serious part of park development and needed funding: "It seems extremely difficult to establish the fact that landscape planting is work and must be handled on the same plans as any construction and that it is *important work,* if we expect to make a material change for the better in some of our most prominent park community appearances. This does not especially apply to any park, but to all in which I have had experience."[14]

Mount Rainier's superintendent, Owen Tomlinson, favored the planting program and would become one of the strongest advocates of such work. He issued a memorandum to all park residents encouraging them to use native flowers, shrubs, and trees and offering them Davidson's services in preparing planting plans for their residences. Tomlinson praised many of Mount Rainier's native plants for their ornamental purposes.[15]

Davidson and Merel Sager spent a substantial amount of time at Mount Rainier in 1928 working on landscaping projects, in addition to supervising the construction of roads, guardrails, and bridges along the Yakima Park Road. At Paradise, Sager planted the entrance to the new community building with fir trees and other evergreens six to eight feet high. These plantings apparently included subalpine fir (*Abies lasiocarpa*), Pacific silver fir (*Abies amabalis*), and Alaskan cedar, which came through in "splendid condition" and "greatly improved the appearance of the building." In this subalpine terrain on a ridge with sparse vegetation, the trees were planted in small groups along the front of the building and created vertical accents that echoed the massive vertical timbers of the building which repeated across the facade. Davidson and Sager also assisted the concessionaire in planting the grounds of the Paradise Inn with trees transplanted from the construction site for the new lodge and housekeeping cabins.[16]

The new administration building, the centerpiece of the plaza at Longmire, was near completion and ready for grading in October 1928, when funds ran out. Davidson scraped together enough money and labor to plant a screen of six- to fourteen-foot evergreens, including western hemlock and Douglas fir, at the northeast corner to block the view of park housing from the plaza. These supplemented the few trees untouched during construction, the most prominent of which was the stalwart Douglas fir on what was to become the front lawn.[17]

In 1929, with the grading and development of the plaza, the grounds of the administration building were graded, and a lawn was seeded. At the same time, landscape improvements were made throughout the village. Over a two-week period in November 1929, several hundred trees and shrubs were transplanted by a crew of four men supervised by Davidson. Stone curbs consisting of large and medium-sized boulders were placed around the plaza according to the plan for the Longmire Plaza development. Several large Douglas firs on the grounds of the residences were cut down because they were damaged or hazardous to residents.[18]

Davidson's estimate for the November 1929 planting called for 112 evergreen trees two to twelve feet in height, 441 deciduous trees and shrubs one to ten feet in height, 149 small perennial plants, and a large number of ferns. Evergreen trees likely included the western hemlock, Douglas fir, western red cedar, silver fir, grand fir, and western white pine. Deciduous trees were likely red alder, Douglas maple, vine maple, bitter cherry, Sitka alder, Sitka willow, creambush, western serviceberry, red elderberry, Indian plum, Pacific ninebark, and western hazelnut. Shrubs likely included red flowering currant, black twinberry, evergreen huckleberry, salmonberry, goatsbeard, Cascades azaleas, gooseberry, salal, snowberry, and Douglas spirea. Various ferns, ground covers such as pipsissewa and bunchberry, and perennial herbs such as wood violets and twinflowers were likely planted as ground cover.[19]

Changes to the road leading past the administration building caused the removal of several cottonwoods and evergreens on the building's south side. Davidson was determined to restore the effect after the roadway was fixed because, in his opinion, they formed a natural terminus to the plaza and helped frame the new building. By 1932, a grouping of evergreens, predominantly western red cedar, were planted at this location.

For several seasons, Davidson worked individually with residents in the village in planting newly completed dwellings, where tall evergreens had been thinned to provide light and air and space for yards. He also provided the concessionaire with a plan for planting the newly constructed cabin court. Winding cobble-edged paths and understory and foundation plantings of sword ferns, salal, and other low-growing plants throughout began to give the village the unified appearance of a sylvan garden. A rock garden shaped from native boulders was planted with ferns at the entry of the administration building, and

7.6. In 1929 a four-man planting crew at Mount Rainier National Park transplanted several hundred trees and shrubs to the plaza around the recently completed Longmire Administration Building. Directed by resident landscape architect Ernest Davidson, the work led to a servicewide program of landscape naturalization in which native species were used to reestablish lost vegetation, erase the scars of construction, and blend built structures with a park's natural setting. *(Photograph courtesy National Park Service, Mount Rainier National Park)*

small rock gardens appeared throughout the village in the yards of park staff. Davidson's work received Superintendent Tomlinson's praise and recommendation that such work be encouraged through year-to-year appropriations.[20]

It appears from historical photographs and the physical evidence of the hardier of plantings in the park landscape that Davidson and Sager followed Henry Hubbard's advice on planting around buildings from the *Introduction to the Study of Landscape Design*. Hubbard had written that "in its relation to architectural structures, planting bears its part in landscape composition in these ways: it enframes, limiting the composition of which the structure is the dominant object and concentrating attention upon the structure; it leads up to the structure as a subordinate mass to a dominant one, — 'tying the structure to the ground,' as the phrase goes; and it decorates, perhaps paneling the face of a structure with chosen patterns of green, perhaps changing the texture of parts of the facade from that of stone to that of leaves." [21]

Hubbard recommended that trees and shrubs be planted at the corners of buildings to create a foreground for the facade, to enframe the building with vegetation, and to make the main entrance more prominent. The shadows cast by trees placed at the corners could furthermore relieve an otherwise monotonous expanse by creating a "tracery of winter branches or the dappling of summer shade" (188).

Hubbard also urged the planting of low-growing plants in naturalistic scenes. Ground cover was an artistic medium that gave the designer an opportunity to model the ground, add interest to a particular area, or differentiate one area from another by choosing different ground-covering plants. Hubbard wrote, "A bed of ferns may grace the foot of a rock or a mat of partridge vine run over it, the darkness of a dell may be made deeper by a carpet of blue-green myrtle, a sunny open space may be made still brighter by the yellow green of moneywort." The choice of ground cover was to depend on suitability to growing conditions and landscape character. Native ferns were an ideal material for foundation plantings and ground cover in temperate climates and moist woodland settings. They were commonly planted along the foundations of Adirondack lodges and were well suited to the forested setting of Longmire Village at Mount Rainier.[22]

Using the example of the Scarborough Bridge in Franklin Park, Hubbard stressed the compositional value of planting the areas abutting newly constructed bridges: "The span of a bridge is necessarily somewhat bounded and enframed by its abutments when it is looked at along the reach of water which it crosses, but the compositional strength of the masses on each side between which the bridge springs can be much increased by planting which rises well above the level of the bridge. . . . The best outlook from the bridge is presumably up or down the stream from well out upon the bridge span, and these same plantations will give some sense of enframement to this view as well." [23]

Planting could be used to enhance architectural structures and to blend them visually into their surroundings. Park designers had previously recognized the value of plantings as screens to hide monotonous or unpleasing surfaces, such as the power plant in Yosemite Valley. And park designers encouraged concessionaires to incorporate plantings and walks and drives into their own projects. But until 1927, it does not appear that the park designers had used planting to blend new structures to their site after construction in any routine way.

Davidson documented his work in an illustrated report in 1929, and Vint used Davidson's successful results to encourage landscape work and help justify the costs for transplanting and planting projects in other parks. Upon seeing this report, Director Albright immediately became committed to making this work a routine aspect of park construction:

7.7. Photographed in 1932, the "naturalized" plaza at Longmire in Mount Rainier National Park reflected the manifold achievements of the National Park Service's Landscape Division on the eve of the New Deal. Completed in 1928 and constructed of massive native boulders and stout logs, the administration building was the focal point of the village. It resulted from a synthesis of rustic design principles, including the use of native materials, pioneer building methods, and elements that stressed irregular lines and horizontality. Native firs, hemlocks, and cedars were left in place or planted around three sides and at the corners of the building. Ferns and other low-growing native plants were planted in the rock garden by the entry porch and along the foundation. A flagstone walkway and curbing composed of horizontally laid, lichen- and moss-covered stream boulders further unified the village setting. The plantings and rockwork represented the beginnings of a servicewide program of landscape naturalization intended to provide village improvements and blend built structures with a park's natural setting. *(Photograph by George A. Grant, courtesy National Park Service Historic Photography Collection)*

Mr. Davidson has kindly given me an opportunity to read his report on "Land-scape Naturalization (transplanting and planting)" within the national parks. I am writing this letter to tell you that this report has made a profound impression on me and for the first time has brought me to full realization that we have not been giving enough attention to planting in the national parks. . . . I am disposed at the present time to take an unusual interest in this sort of thing and would like to take steps as soon as possible to make this so-called "naturalization" work a definite feature of National Park Service activity.[24]

The report—brief, concise, and illustrated with photographs—also established a model that would be followed in the reports of landscape architects to Vint and, later, the narrative reports for Emergency Conservation Work in both national and state parks. Davidson's work illustrated how natural vegetation could be planted in conjunction with grading the grounds of new buildings and making naturalistic improvements, such as curvilinear walkways, parking areas, and rock gardens.

Encouraged by Albright's interest, Vint asked his staff to develop cost estimates for similar work in other parks. Davidson's cost estimates for the 1929 planting at Longmire were circulated to park resident landscape architects and superintendents in the fall of 1929 as an example of how similar naturalization work could be included under budget requests for 1931. Vint's intention was to convince superintendents to include an item for landscape naturalization each year to improve existing conditions as well as to naturalize the sites of new construction. Because few work crews were trained in this kind of work, Vint recommended confining efforts to one or more buildings or groups of buildings, "doing a complete and finished job," that is, one that included grading, flagstone paving, and the construction of "furniture and fixtures," such as drinking fountains and stone seats.[25]

Vint's definition of landscape naturalization was "grading around buildings or elsewhere for better topographical effects; filling and fertilizing of soils; transplanting or planting of trees, shrubs, lawns, flowers, to make artificial work harmonize with its surroundings; erection of outdoor furniture such as stone seats, drinking fountains, flagstone walks, etc.; vista clearing and screen planting and cleanup in areas not included as Roadside Cleanup."[26] Vint distinguished this work from roadside cleanup, which was funded under annual appropriations for roads and trails and included restoring natural conditions along highways by clearing dead timber and debris, repairing construction damage, planting slopes, screening the traces of old roads, clearing vistas, and planting old roadways and borrow pits.[27]

Under landscape naturalization, Vint grouped much of the work that had been the responsibility of park designers since Punchard's tenure, such as the clearing of vistas and campground development. Realizing, however, that landscape harmonization required much more than locating and constructing rustic structures whose design and materials blended with the natural setting of a park, he added planting and transplanting and the construction of small-scale landscape features, such as water fountains and walkways. These improvements were essential to the village concept, making the village setting more attractive and the visitor's stay more comfortable. Such improvements also enabled park designers to better manage pedestrian and motor traffic, ensure safety and sanitation, and alleviate some of the wear and tear of visitor use.

Decades of increasing visitation and use were already affecting the natural character of parks. The low-budget expedients such as wooden-frame stairways and boulder-edged drives were wearing out and could no longer accommodate the increasing numbers of park visitors. Improvements in the roads and trails program had demonstrated the value of stone curbs and sturdily built trails, walkways, and guardrails. Walkways and curbing allowed park designers and managers to channel pedestrian and automobile traffic and thus minimize the wear and tear of visitor use on park resources, and guardrails ensured safety at precipitous points. The transformation of springs into pipe-fed pools and lush rock gardens ensured sanitation and provided places of appealing beauty. In short, the park designers faced the challenge of solving urban-scale problems without sacrificing natural features and scenic qualities. The program of landscape naturalization enabled park designers to create or maintain the illusion that nature had experienced little disturbance from improvements and that a stone water fountain or flagstone terrace was as much at home in a park as a stand of hemlocks or meadow of wildflowers.

Large-scale revegetation programs were instituted in several parks. One of the earliest was Rocky Mountain National Park. In 1930, Vint and Charles Peterson visited the park with ASLA representatives Gilmore Clarke and Charles W. Eliot II to examine the park boundaries and make recommendations for restoring the natural landscape in areas, such as Aspenglen, which had been heavily grazed or logged. Later that year, twelve hundred three-year-old western yellow pine trees were planted near the Aspenglen campground. Local hiking and conservation organizations commonly assisted in some of these early efforts.[28]

Trees were now protected during the construction of buildings; afterward they became the screens to hide development or were blended with new plantings in naturalistic groupings. Provisions were entered into the wording of contracts for the construction of buildings that required contractors to protect trees in the vicinity of their work. Not only did landscape architects confer on the location of sites for buildings, but they also identified the trees that were to be retained. This process also applied to the clearing of selected trees and vegetation in campgrounds or picnic areas. Construction scars were erased as native grasses, ferns, and shrubs embraced battered stone foundations. Tall trees were planted individually or in small clusters at the ends of bridges and corners of buildings to blend the construction with the natural setting.

Landscape naturalization revived many of the planting practices that Downing, Repton, Robinson, Hubbard, and Parsons had promoted. Several of these techniques, including the planting of climbing vines to disguise concrete and stone walls and ferns around foundations, had been favored by the Arts and Crafts movement and accompanied the use of native wood and rock as construction materials to harmonize a structure with its natural setting. Naturalistic devices such as rock gardens, fern gardens, vine-draped walls, curvilinear paths and stairs, and boulder-lined walks had been popular in the Adirondacks and had regional equivalents in California gardening.

The expanding natural history programs of the parks provided a wealth of information about the plant ecology, natural features, and native species of each park. With this information, landscape architects could readily apply Waugh's ecological approach of grouping plants, shrubs, and trees according to their associations in nature. Such work was often done informally as landscape architects and foremen on site drew materials and ideas for species composition from the surrounding woodlands and meadows. In other places, efforts were made to recreate lost plant colonies, such as wildflowers in the meadows of Yosemite. These plantings were motivated by the need to naturalize an area whose vegetation had been destroyed by construction, erosion, excessive use, or the elimination of old roads and trails. It was also motivated by the need to create an artificial screen or windbreak.

By the early 1930s, the aesthetic value of landscape naturalization was well recognized, and this kind of work became the focus of village "beautification" programs and accompanied other village improvements such as the installation of curbs, parking areas, and sidewalks and the construction of signs, lights, and water fountains. Beginning in 1933, many landscape naturalization projects were carried out with the labor and technical expertise of the Civilian Conservation Corps; this was the case with improvements carried out in Yosemite Village from 1933 to 1936.

An extensive program of naturalization occurred at Crater Lake's Rim Village, where decades of use, poor soil of ash and pumice, and harsh winter weather had contributed to the loss of natural grasses and trees. In 1930, a half-mile promenade marked by a masonry parapet wall of native rock with observation bays was constructed along the rim. Following the natural undulations of the caldera, the promenade connected the information center located in the former Kiser Studio, the Sinnott Memorial, parking areas, and the Crater Lake Lodge. Along with the walk, a fully orchestrated program of rustic and naturalistic design was planned. Experiments with native grasses were made to determine the most appropriate cover for the area before a sod mixture of wildflowers was selected. Mature trees of several native species—white fir (*Abies concolor*), sub-alpine fir (*Abies lasciocarpa*), noble fir (*Abies nobilis*), and mountain hemlocks (*Tsuga mertensiana*)—were transplanted from construction sites in other parts of the park. The density and arrangement of the trees followed the natural distribution and clustering found in similar areas of the park and allowed vistas of the lake from many points. The careful attention to detail even extended to the creation of water fountains imitating the crater rim in a pier of the wall and the retention of ghost trees along the slopes of the caldera.[29]

Merel Sager's program of restoration for the Rim Village was inspired by the park's primeval natural character. Sager believed that the rim area had originally had the same appearance as Sun Notch, an unspoiled and undeveloped region of the park which offered one of most attractive views of the lake. Sager wrote of Sun Notch, "Here, we find trees in abundance along the Rim, with open areas covered with grass, sedges and wild flowers. Here, in spite of sandy soil and extreme climatic conditions, nature has seen to it that beauty flourishes." Interestingly, Sager claimed this view was supported by a professor of fine arts at the University of California, Wirth Ryder, and an artist of national park scenery, Gunnar Widfores, indicating the extent to which such projects were, in 1930, considered a matter of aesthetic, and not merely ecological, concern.[30]

Sager's report indicated that the work of restoration would be twofold. First, it was necessary to install walks, parking areas, curbs, and parapets to eliminate the trampling of the area by automobiles and pedestrians. Although parking restrictions imposed in 1928 had helped somewhat to remedy the situation, the soil was in such poor condition and pedestrian traffic so heavy that it was unlikely that the vegetation would recover on its own. Second, an aggressive planting project was necessary. The plan, beginning in 1930, was to recondition the soil, plant sod, and transplant evergreen trees. The trees were to be arranged in small groups to "lend variety" but not in great enough numbers to obstruct the view of the lake from the road. This planting program was to be accompanied by the installation of a system of pathways linking the parking areas and lodge with the promenade, trails, and key viewpoints.

In 1931, Congress suspended funding for capital improvements, and the work of the landscape architects was redirected to compiling development plans for the parks. It is unclear whether Albright ever approached Congress for additional funding for landscape naturalization work. What is clear, however, is that naturalization projects were funded and carried out in a number of parks that year, including Crater Lake, where the multiyear landscape restoration project got under way, and Yosemite, where meadows were cleared. The landscape naturalization program gave the landscape architects control over the many small details that could affect the scenic character of a developed area. It expanded their responsibility as protectors of the landscape to the design of the landscape itself. The program, occurring just as the park service was making major advances in park planning, set important precedents for the Emergency Conservation Work by the Civilian Conservation Corps, which would begin in spring 1933.

The Prohibition of Exotic Seeds and Plants

In 1930, the National Park Service established a policy excluding all exotic seeds, plants, and animals from the national parks. This policy drew greater attention to the emerging program for landscape naturalization, which dealt primarily with transplanting native plants, shrubs, and trees from one location in a park to another. In November 1930, Albright issued a "set of ideals" for the use of native flora and the elimination of exotics already planted around hotels, lodges, and private dwellings. Harold C. Bryant, assistant director for education, had prepared these ideals after consulting with Thomas Vint, chief landscape architect, and the park superintendents.[31]

Set of Ideals

It is the consensus of opinion that national parks should stress the protection and conservation of native plants and animals, and . . . the introduction of exotic species endangers the native forms through competition and destroys the normal flora and fauna, and . . . it is the duty of the National Park Service to protect nature unchanged for the benefit of this and future generations. . . .

1. It is important that a serious attempt be made to exclude all exotic seeds and plants from the national parks and monuments. Concessionaires and residents are asked to cooperate in following carefully this endeavor to hold closely to a fundamental national park principle. (Grass seed for lawns will have to be an exception to the rule.)

All concerned should avoid looking at this plan as a curtailment of personal liberty. Rather should it be regarded as an opportunity to make a garden which is unique and more difficult, therefore indicative of real achievement, certainly one more fitted to park ideals.

2. Constant endeavor should be made to eliminate exotics already planted around hotels, lodges, and private dwellings, and energy directed to the replacement of these with native shrubs and flowers. (The Landscape Division will cooperate in every way with suggestions as to the most suitable plants for replacements.)

3. As far as is possible, the same ruling shall apply to all forms of life: birds, animals, reptiles, insects. In the case of fish planted, efforts should be made to allocate exotic species (Loch Leven, Eastern Brook, etc.) to certain restricted localities.

Wider planting of native species should be encouraged, with the hope that eventually non-native forms may be largely eliminated.

—Harold C. Bryant, Assistant Director for Education, National Park Service, 1930

This policy was by no means sudden or unprecedented. Many park superintendents already had set forth similar rules for concessionaires and park residents. Joseph Grinnell and Tracy Storer of the University of California, Berkeley, had called for the elimination of exotic plants and animals from the national parks in an article in *Science* in 1916. In 1921, the American Association for the Advancement of Science had issued a resolution strongly opposing the introduction of nonnative plants and animals into the national parks and all other unessential interference with natural conditions. The association presented this resolution at the Second National Conference on State Parks in May 1922, urging the National Park Service to prohibit such introductions and interferences on the basis that one of its primary duties was to pass on to future generations natural areas where native flora and fauna might be found undisturbed. Planting nonnative trees, shrubs, or other plants, stocking waters with nonnative fish, and liberating nonnative game animals impaired or destroyed the natural conditions and native wilderness of the parks.[32]

The set of ideals offered the first servicewide guidelines for the management of vegetation. It was of particular importance to the work of both the Landscape Division and the Educational Division. Bryant's statement excluding all exotic seeds, plants, animals, and insects and strongly emphasizing the use of native plants in all landscape work was motivated by the serious ecological damage done by introduced species in various parts of the world. He described how "escaped" plants, such as Europe's St. John's wort, had harmed the landscape and hindered sheep raising in Australia, how the uncontrolled growth of lantana in the tropical jungles of the South Pacific had made many areas impenetrable, and how the introduction of the American prickly pear to Australia had made large areas useless for cattle grazing and resulted in a quarantine between North and South Australia.[33]

Grasses were not prohibited because, by 1930, the parks had little control over the many exotic species that already existed. At Yosemite, numerous exotic grass species had entered the park through the feed for the horses used in patrolling the park and in construction work. Furthermore, the artificial moisture conditions created by road construction and banking made it necessary to use nonnative grasses for stabilizing slopes in some cases.

In formulating the statement of ideals, Bryant requested the opinions of park superintendents on the issue of exotics in the parks, an issue raised by

Yosemite's superintendent, C. G. Thomson. Speaking from his experience at Mount Rainier, Superintendent Tomlinson replied,

> There is a fundamental national park principle involved in this question, and it is my opinion that it is mandatory for the National Park Service to prohibit, or at least greatly restrict the planting of exotics of all kinds in the national parks if we are to pass them on to future generations in an unmodified condition. I do not see how the Service can very well permit the introduction of exotics without infringing on a vital park policy. . . . With proper care and the expert assistance of the Landscape Division, I believe there will be no great difficulty in properly beautifying residences, camps, hotels, and other "modified" areas by planting and transplanting native flowers and shrubs.[34]

Vint supported Bryant's statement but was concerned with the reaction of park residents to the prohibition:

> In order to help sell the idea it might be well to point out in the memorandum the advantages of having a garden of native plants rather than one of exotics. In a way it is an opportunity that few people get in their efforts at building a garden for personal enjoyment. It is a more difficult task than making a garden of commercial bulbs and flowers, yet when it is done is a far greater achievement. . . . Not many park employees look at this problem in that light. They look at it as a restriction of their personal liberties rather than as an opportunity to do something that cannot be done outside. I think it might be well to add a paragraph or so to your memorandum expounding the advantages of a native garden over an exotic one. Otherwise I think it is perfectly satisfactory and not a bit too strong.[35]

The prohibition on introducing exotic species into the parks was upheld by a 1932 study on what policies Congress expected would govern the national parks based on the 1916 enabling legislation, stating that "proper administration will retain these areas in their natural condition sparing them the vandalism of improvement" and "exotic animal or plant life should not be introduced." This policy would become one of the basic guidelines for Emergency Conservation Work in the national parks.[36]

Grounds of the Concessionaires

In keeping with the growing interest in gardening with native plants, concessionaires began planting natural gardens, many of which were already in place when Bryant issued the set of ideals. In the early 1920s, Yosemite's Curry Camping Company hired a wildflower expert, Carl Purdy, to establish wildflower meadows around Camp Curry. Although plants commonly grazed by deer were avoided, the project was abandoned after three years of unsuccessful attempts to keep out the deer. Longer lasting, and of far-reaching influence, was the Olmsted firm's development of the grounds for the Ahwahnee Hotel in Yosemite Valley in the late 1920s.[37]

Required by the park superintendent to use only native species, Olmsted Brothers developed a landscape plan in 1927 which preserved and enhanced the existing vegetation in the form of a wild garden and native plant reserve. The building was located so that the greatest number of trees would screen the building and shelter the grounds. The Ahwahnee was sited to provide superb views of Glacier Point, Half Dome, Yosemite Falls, the Royal Arches. It also offered an ideal all-year site because it afforded a maximum amount of sunshine in winter and had sufficient forests surrounding it to relieve the extreme heat of the north wall of the valley (2).

In 1927 the Yosemite Park and Curry Company reported on the public's favorable reaction to "landscape development." The Ahwahnee was ideally situated for natural gardening, offering a location where the meadow and forest would gradually merge with the meadowlike lawn and where the plant life of several life zones could be restored. The company remarked, "Perhaps no where else in the valley could the combination of dry granitic rock plants (usually found in altitudes from 500 to 2,000 feet), wet meadow plants (commonly found in altitudes from 4,000 to 6,000 ft.) and shade-loving plants of the woods be grown with such a degree of success and in such close proximity to each other" (2).

The plan was to create a plant reserve that could be enjoyed by visitors from the windows of the lodge and by those who strolled the grounds:

> It was our general thought, therefore, to create a plant refuge at The Ahwahnee and restore the area to the condition it was in ten and fifteen years ago. It is well remembered that the meadows many years ago were filled with Evening Primroses, Godetias, Mariposa Lilies and countless other wild flowers which have practically disappeared, owing to the grazing of the deer. We plan to restore this condition gradually, working from the hotel outward and attempting no more in a year than we could handle. It was also planned to give the Nature Guide Service free access to the area, in order that the nature classes could study many of the wild flowers that have practically disappeared from the floor of the Yosemite. (2)

Many of the first plantings were destroyed by grazing deer and elk. The elk were particularly destructive, grazing on manzanita, cascara, wild rose, and other plants and actually pulling great branches to the ground and killing entire trees. As a result the concessionaire requested permission to erect "fences, ditches and wire entanglements" to "be an absolute barrier against deer and elk." In November 1927, Frederick Law Olmsted Jr. visited the Ahwahnee site with Donald Tressider, president of the Yosemite Park and Curry Company, and Eldridge T.

Spencer, a San Francisco architect. Olmsted's purpose was to locate twenty-five cottages on the grounds and to consider the location for an eight-foot fence to keep out deer and elk. He recommended grading the lawns on the south, east, and west sides of the hotel so "that the hotel appeared to rest on a natural knoll." This was worked out in cross sections on site. He also suggested "bouldering" the slope cut into the east side of the brook and planting it with ferns and rock-growing flowers. As an interim measure until the fence could be built, he recommended planting only those plants that deer would not eat, such as ferns, bay trees, azalea, spruce, and pine. His assistant further suggested planting ferns and vines of the native California grape about the bases of the hotel's stone piers, noting that the grapevines would need to be protected by wire screens.[38]

By 1929, with the fence constructed and thousands of dollars having been spent for replanting by the Yosemite Park and Curry Company, the garden provided a splendid display of azaleas and was reported by Albright to be "the only place in the valley where native flowers" could "be seen in any profusion." [39]

There is little question that the landscape work at the Ahwahnee greatly interested Vint and his staff, and they drew on this splendid example of a naturalistic landscape in the wilderness. By 1933, resident landscape architect John Wosky likely had drawn up a naturalization plan for the government area of Yosemite Village. The planting of California azalea, California wild grapes, ferns, manzanita, cascara, and other native plants was part of a village beautification program. Other improvements included the construction of curbing and new paths, the repair of many old oak and apple trees, and the removal of a number of dilapidated buildings, borrow pits, and dumps. This program would be carried out through Emergency Conservation Work from 1933 to 1936. Ferns were planted along the boulder foundations of Lewis Hospital, wild grapevines were staked to climb up and cover the boulder walls of the museum and administration building, and azaleas and other shrubs were planted throughout the village around new residences. And a wildflower garden representing several life zones was developed in the yard of the Yosemite Museum. These plantings were largely in the same spirit as the grounds of the Ahwahnee. Furthermore, the work of the Yosemite concessionaire in wild gardening encouraged other concessionaires to plant displays and borders of wildflowers and other native plants.

Museum Wild Plant Gardens

Under the leadership of Ansel Hall, who headed the Educational Division in the Western Field Office, and with the support of the Laura Spelman Rockefeller Memorial and the American Association of Museums, programs interpreting the natural history of the parks expanded in the late 1920s. By this time, they included flora studies, ranger talks and tours, museum exhibits, institutes, and the publication of "nature notes" in many parks. The educational program provided abundant information that could be used in the landscape naturalization program. Each park had a rich palette of native specimens that included herbaceous plants, shrubs, and trees, which could be used to naturalize the grounds of museums, wayside exhibits, amphitheaters, and trail hubs. Native plants and curving paths edged with natural cobbles and boulders drawn from nearby streambeds became an important characteristic in the landscape design of these new facilities. By 1930, outdoor "zone" gardens had become a popular interpretive feature of national park museums.

The first wildflower garden was planned around the lookout at Glacier Point in Yosemite as a collaborative effort between the Educational and Landscape Divisions in 1925. It was not until the end of 1929 that wild gardens were considered a regular feature. That year, gardens were planted at the newly completed museums at the Old Faithful formation in Yellowstone and Yavapai Point at Grand Canyon. In Sequoia, a wildflower garden was established at Giant Forest in an area approximately forty by sixty feet, adjacent to the museum and administration buildings. About seventy species of wildflowers were transplanted and labeled with metal signs; many of the specimens were carried from Alta Peak and other timberline habitats many miles distant, and others were brought up from lower elevations (171).

A moist rock garden had been planted as a student experiment behind the Yosemite Museum, and the Castle Crest Garden was taking form near the headquarters at Crater Lake. At Yellowstone, naturalist Carl P. Russell integrated interpretive gardens and natural plantings into the design of branch museums at Fishing Bridge, Norris Geyser Basin, and Madison Junction and the trailside exhibits, nature shrines, and lookouts that were being developed throughout the park with the assistance of funds provided by the Laura Spelman Rockefeller Memorial and representatives of the American Association of Museums. The gardens were generally situated on one or several sides of the building and were laid out among shrubs and trees preserved during construction. Trees were planted at the entrances and corners of the buildings much as Davidson and Sager had done at Mount Rainier. What was different, however, was the integration of plants and labels along the paths leading to the museum's entrance and to the outdoor garden, amphitheater, or naturalist's residence (171).

In his annual report, Horace Albright commended the new nature gardens. In his opinion, they enabled visitors who, through lack of time or physical strength, were unable to visit all parts of the park to "see and enjoy as many varieties as possible of the exquisite wild flowers that abound[ed] in out-of-the way places." The Landscape Division, however, was not altogether in agreement with the Educational Division on the appropriateness of interpretive gardens. Throughout the 1930s, Davidson, with Vint's backing, opposed the development of a garden at Longmire:

A "wildflower garden" is one of the most difficult of all gardening feats. To be successfully done it must have constant care and attention of an exceptionally good gardener. The entire park is a "wildflower garden," and an attempt to condense species and varieties into a small area for tabloid consumption, is partially defeating one main objective of the park, i.e. to get visitors to move about and enjoy the park—its scenery and its floral decorations. "Wildflower gardens" are artificial, unconvincing and more or less depressing in effect.[40]

Museum gardens were a direct result of the park service's expanding interest in natural history. Not only had Harold Bryant been appointed to the service's new position of assistant director for education in Washington, but parks had also begun to hire resident naturalists to direct the interpretation programs. Interpretation relied upon both plantings of native vegetation and the preservation of the natural ecology of the park. The advances and discoveries made by the naturalists contributed to the specialized horticultural knowledge of park landscape engineers and architects, who grouped native, wild species based on climate, elevation, soil, and water as they developed a palette appropriate to each location within a park. Selection of appropriate plants, the dynamics of natural revegetation, methods for transplanting, and the necessary conditions for propagating were all areas in which the park naturalist could help the landscape architect. Although no formal procedures existed for this interaction, the presence of landscape architects on site in the parks to oversee grading, sloping, and planting activities would have provided many opportunities for collaboration.

Unlike buildings, which could be constructed in a single season, it took several seasons to establish life-zone gardens and achieve splendid displays of park flora. Donations of time, labor, and funds contributed to the development of many park gardens. At Grand Canyon in the area surrounding the Yavapai Point Observation Building, an extensive garden of native wild plants was begun as soon as the museum was completed in 1929. By 1931, plants from the Canadian Zone of the North Rim and from the Lower Sonoran Zone within the canyon were installed in defined plots along tightly curving paths studded with local boulders. The rest of the area was landscaped with plants of the Upper Sonoran Zone, which is the natural habitat at the South Rim. The Boy Scouts of America, which made a naturalist expedition to the park in 1930, contributed the initial planting for the garden. Later, plants were added by park naturalists.[41]

The development of interpretive gardens extended to the national monuments as well as the parks and became increasingly popular features in the 1930s. Casa Grande, which was also the headquarters for the southwestern monuments, had installed an interpretive desert garden in the late 1920s. By 1930, a garden of southwestern plants and cacti had been planted at the entrance to Carlsbad Cavern, attracting visitors and furnishing an excellent opportunity for interpretation by nature guides. By 1931, there were plans to reestablish lost flora at Muir

7.8. When photographed in November 1936, the zone garden at the Yavapai Point Observation Building in Grand Canyon National Park was laid out in tightly curving, rock-edged paths and had gardens that displayed the native flora of the park's several zones. Begun in 1930, the planting occurred over several years and was carried out under the supervision of the park naturalist. *(Photograph by George A. Grant, courtesy National Park Service Historic Photography Collection)*

Woods, including the azaleas, dogwoods, and other flowering plants that were almost exterminated in the past. Many of these gardens were plotted in the master plan for each park (137).

The Wild Garden at the Yosemite Museum

The interaction of the natural history and landscape design program was probably its greatest at Yosemite, which had the oldest and most extensive interpretive and educational programs in the national park system. Herbert Maier's design for the park museum completed in 1926 included a back porch for open-air exhibits, including one depicting the living plants of the region. The first flower exhibits consisted of freshly cut flowers displayed in individual vases on a pyramid-shaped stand on the rear porch during the summer months. The stand was especially designed so that fresh water constantly circulated through the vases. Once a week, a nature guide would travel to different parts of the park to collect flowers, including meadow pennyroyal, yarrow, Queen Anne's lace, giant hyssop, yawning penstemon, St. John's wort, Indian hemp or dogbane, tiger lily, knotweed, buckwheat, calycanthus, wild ginger, alumroot, asters, azalea, columbine, clarkia, broadiae, pinedrops, and evening primrose. This type of exhibit, however, presented several difficulties. Keeping specimens fresh during the journey from distant points of the park was not easy. Many plants could survive only for brief periods, and the numbers of rare plants, such as snow plants, which could be exhibited were limited. The exhibits were especially popular with park visitors, and by 1928, efforts began to create "live" gardens in the area behind the museum.[42]

The museum garden evolved in several stages. It began in the summer of 1929 as an experimental student project in the form of a moist rock garden behind the museum on a section of the alluvial fan at the mouth of Indian Canyon. The following year, a dry, or moraine, garden, requiring special soil, sun, and watering conditions, was added. A well-drained bed of soil imitating the dry soil and rocky crevices of the glacial moraines was prepared, and plants were gathered from various locations among the cliffs of the valley. In 1932, with a gift of four thousand dollars from Marjorie Montgomery Ward, a two-acre area was fenced, a flagstone path was laid out, and more than one hundred different types of wildflowers were planted. An "ancient" spring was revitalized, and a stream and several pools of fresh water were created. Faucets were installed and hoses supplied. The area was the warmest section of the valley and had been a hot and dusty area before being cultivated. Naturalist Enid Michael recognized the value of the garden as a valuable interpretive tool, and by September 1932 the National Park Service was committed to maintaining the garden. Additional native species were to be added to the collection each year to represent the park's various life zones, so that the visitor could observe wild flowering plants of the valley floor, the trailside and roadside, meadows, and even the higher elevations of the park. The Civilian Conservation Corps overhauled the garden and grounds of the museum beginning in the spring of 1934 and continuing over several work periods. The enrollees improved the soil, constructed paths and log benches, and planted many trees and flowering plants.[43]

Yosemite's natural history program provided a ready-made palette for planting the recently completed Wawona Road. Ranger naturalist Enid Michael observed that native flowering plants were taking hold in the raw road cuts along the three-year-old Wawona Road. Prominent were several species of the genus *Lupinus,* members of the pea family, and creeping lotus. Shrubs of the ceanothus group also made good cover for the slopes, but best was the tough, crawling cuneatus, which formed dense, leafy clumps. Michael noted the plants that grew most readily, recognizing the value of such information for the planting of park roads. The roadside planting program began as the conservation work of the Cascades Camp of the Civilian Conservation Corps beginning in the spring of 1933. One of the most important projects in the National Park Service's Emergency Conservation Work program, the work was directed by the renowned plant ecologist F. E. Clements of the Carnegie Institution. The project included collecting seeds and planting them in the cut-and-fill slopes of the new road. An experimental plot was set aside in the museum garden to cultivate many of the seeds collected.[44]

Propagation Nurseries

Landscape naturalization required a readily available source of native plants. In reviewing the location for new facilities, the landscape architects carefully identified the trees that were to be saved and protected during construction. Other plants, trees, and shrubs were dug up and transplanted to other locations where they were needed for naturalization. The road construction program provided large numbers of trees and shrubs for this purpose. In many cases, however, the number of native plants was insufficient to fill the demand, especially for the mass plantings of large areas or the replanting of special species such as the giant sequoia. The demands of a landscape naturalization program for plant materials exceeded the available supply.

Sequoia was one of the first parks to establish a nursery for the holding of transplanted materials. The idea to reseed the giant sequoias as they died had originally been Punchard's. In the mid-1920s, after the forest pathologist E. P. Meinecke made the startling discovery that the presence of humans in the Giant Forest was the prime reason for the dying trees, a nursery was started at the Ash Mountain headquarters. By 1930, the nursery provided stock for reforesting trampled areas in the Giant Forest, planting in the administration area, and furnishing sequoia seedlings to selected institutions and organizations. The seeds of many native plants were gathered to increase the variety of planting stock. In 1930 the nursery was enlarged, and by 1935 it had outgrown its space and was moved outside the headquarters area.[45]

Although the main purpose of the park nurseries was to provide large numbers of native trees and shrubs for mass plantings in areas whose native cover had been destroyed by forest fires and previous destructive uses, the nurseries also became useful places to hold plants removed from construction sites which were not immediately planted elsewhere in the park. Moreover, construction sites rarely provided sufficient numbers of plants and trees for large reforestation projects; in these cases the nurseries became important centers of propagation and cultivation. A nursery for reforestation was established in Acadia before 1930. At Yellowstone, the Game Ranch located near Gardiner was developed as a nursery and propagating center, making use of irrigation and the area's low elevation, sunshine, and iron gauge fencing, which kept out wild predators. Here in specially prepared beds, sheltered by rows of locusts, plants such as Douglas firs and roses were started and nurtured, transplanted, and moved as needed.[46]

Another source of trees was the U.S. Forest Service. Public Act 319 (71st Congress, approved on June 9, 1930), which authorized the Department of Agriculture to enlarge the tree-planting operations of national forests, also authorized the Forest Service to provide seedlings and young trees for the replanting of burned-over areas in any national park, upon the request of the secretary of the interior. Although the Civilian Conservation Corps was assigned to clean up areas burned by forest fires in Yellowstone and Glacier, the extent to which the National Park Service used this authorization to restore burned areas is unclear.[47]

In the 1930s, the National Park Service became a partner in a larger movement that was occurring in various state institutions. State agricultural experiment stations, and consequently the state extension services and nursery programs, were the main promoters and practitioners of the use of native vegetation for roadside and forestation purposes. These institutions were also sources of native plants used in Civilian Conservation Corps projects in state and national parks. In her 1939 book on California's flowering shrubs, Lester Rowntree noted the pioneering nature of this work, saying that work in the field was new and little was known about the cultural treatment of native shrubs. She praised the experimental work done by botanic gardens, government departments, and individuals, who collected seeds for propagation. In California this work was being performed by the Rancho Santa Ana Botanical Garden, the California Forest and Range Station at Berkeley, and the CCC camps, especially the nursery at La Purissima Mission in Santa Barbara under the direction of the National Park Service.[48]

As the National Park Service took the leadership of Emergency Conservation Work in state parks in the 1930s, it became apparent that most state parks, especially those developed from submarginal farmland, were in need of planting stock. Nurseries were established at some parks—for example, Virginia Kendall Park, near Akron, Ohio. In parks such as Ludington State Park in Michigan, native trees, shrubs, and other plants were trucked in from other state parks or state nurseries. At Palmetto State Park, materials were donated by an adjoining landowner, and in many other parks commercial sources were used.

E. P. Meinecke and Campground Planning

The modern campground resulted from marked changes in theory and policy which occurred in the early 1930s. The National Park Service, like the U.S. Forest Service and several state park systems, was concerned with the impact of heavy use and trampling on the vegetation of camping areas. After studying the problem in Sequoia National Park, the California Redwood State Parks, and other places, the eminent plant pathologist E. P. Meinecke identified the destructive effects that the compaction of roots and other injury to natural vegetation were having on campgrounds and other heavily used areas. In response to the problem, he formulated a theory of camp planning and reconstruction which has ever since influenced the design of picnic areas, campgrounds, and waysides in national and state parks and forests.

In the 1920s, campgrounds were located in open meadows or forests where the understory had been cleared to make way for a loop road and areas for parking and camping. Campgrounds provided water, fireplaces, and a comfort station. Campers parked their cars randomly on open meadows or in cleared areas; they hung tents from the sides of vehicles and set up portable tables.

In Sequoia National Park, giant sequoias planted in the 1920s as older ones were lost failed to regenerate. In 1926, Mather called in E. P. Meinecke to study the problem. Human trampling and construction, Meinecke found, had caused the loss of the great trees and other native plants. He urged that a program of reforestation be introduced to restore these species. The shallow roots of the giant sequoias made the trees especially susceptible to soil compaction and damage during construction. Damage had occurred to the trees during the construction of the Generals Highway and, in the Giant Forest, through years of heavy occupation and visitation. Immediate efforts were made to limit future construction in the Giant Forest. Discussion about removing development altogether from the Giant Forest began shortly thereafter and has continued for many years. Later in the 1920s, Superintendent John White established a nursery at the Ash Mountain headquarters.[49]

Meinecke's 1928 report on similar problems in the California state parks brought widespread attention to the impact that heavy concentrations of tourists in certain areas had on the surrounding vegetation. Compaction of soil and roots by constant trampling and automobile traffic was a serious threat to the native ground cover, trees, and shrubs and thus meant "a slow but steady destruction of the very features that [made] these localities attractive." The problem lay in the constant repetition of the injurious action, day after day and year after year. Nationwide, campgrounds had become unappealing places and were being abandoned. Not only was vegetation dying, but car tracks, the cutting of wood for fuel, and remnant ashes added to the decay.[50]

Meinecke considered foot traffic a minor threat in comparison with the havoc the automobile created:

> If unregulated foot travel was responsible for noticeable damage, it is not to be wondered at that the machine causes far greater injury. Man, in walking, makes a narrow path and compresses the soil at points a pace apart with about 140 lbs.

on the average. The car with its ton and a half of weight makes a continuous wide track on its four tires. Man injures only those smaller plants he actually tramples under foot. The car, much clumsier to handle, crushes shrubs and sideswipes trees, tearing off living bark and severely injuring them. Oil, a deadly poison to plants, drips from the parked automobile. (2)

To remedy the problem, Meinecke urged greater regulation of camping areas and recommended revolutionary changes in campground design and management. In 1932, the Forest Service issued *A Camp Ground Policy,* which set forth Meinecke's ideas. Foremost was the selection of sites based on the type of soil. Preference was to be given to areas with light sandy soils and to places such as Longmire at Mount Rainier where the ground was richly strewn with round boulders from an old riverbed and whose interstices were filled with rich soil that could support tall trees. Length of seasonal use was another important consideration. At high elevations, where use seldom exceeded three months, the probability of compaction was less than at lower elevations in mild climates, where use was longer and where frost heaving and snow cover to break up the compaction did not occur. Type of vegetation was important for a campground's desirability and usefulness. Designers were to consider the composition and density of the vegetation as well as its distribution to determine which plants and trees were to be saved, which were to be cleared, and which were to be given special protection by stone or log barriers. Some trees, including quaking aspens, lodgepole pines, sugar pines, and thin-barked species, were particularly endangered by campground use. The final consideration was the type of camper. Meinecke described the typical tourist in a park or forest as one having little knowledge about the woods but a willingness "to conform . . . to what he is supposed to do in the forest." Seeking "release from the restrictions of town and city life," this type of camper needed a carefully planned campground and a minimum of signs with prohibitions and demands (8–9).

Equally important was the campground plan, according to Meinecke: "Camp planning does not end with the setting aside of a campground. Instead of permitting the campers to do their own haphazard planning, the ground must be gone over and divided up into individual campsites of legitimate sizes, each one offering approximately as much privacy, shade, and other advantages as the other, based on the vegetation on the ground and on the preservation of its essential features throughout the life of the camp site" (10).

Meinecke's plan minimized the chances that cars would leave the road and damage vegetation. The campground was reached by a well-planned system of one-way roads from which "garage" spurs extended at angles. One-way roads worked best because new roads could be added as the demand for more spaces increased; they were narrower, requiring less space, and they encouraged a smooth flow of traffic. Individual campsites were delineated, each consisting of a

7.9. Emilio P. Meinecke, the founder of the modern campground, was a plant pathologist who made the startling discovery in the 1920s that human activity in the forests of California was killing the giant sequoias and redwoods. He later applied his understanding of plant ecology to the problems of campground planning and design. *(Photograph courtesy National Park Service Historic Photography Collection)*

parking space and a clearing equipped with a fireplace and a camp table fixed in place and a tent site. Logs, stones, or vegetation defined each camping site; large logs or boulders marked roadways, road spurs, and parking areas. Vegetation interfering with or unlikely to survive under camp use was cleared. Remaining trees and shrubs, however, were protected from the automobile by placing large boulders at the corners of intersecting roads and where parking spurs branched off the main road. Trees and shrubs between campsites were to be retained. As screens, they enclosed each campsite and afforded campers privacy; they also provided the natural setting that visitors had come to experience (10–13).

The garage spur was Meinecke's most important innovation. Cleared of vegetation and clearly marked by heavy rocks or posts imitating boulders at strategic points, the spur offered several benefits, which Meinecke described: "Since the moving *automobile,* winding in and out among the trees, is by far the most destructive element, it must be fixed at the entrance to the camp site and not be permitted to enter the latter at all. This is easily accomplished by providing for each site a definite garage in the shape of a short spur leading off at a suitable angle from the one-way road. The car easily moves off the road into the spur and backs out again without turning" (11).

Meinecke viewed the campsite as the visitor's "temporary home" but a permanent feature of the campground. As long as the fireplace, table, and tent site were logically and permanently placed, visitors would have no desire to rearrange them. Natural and permanent trails could then be developed between car, table, tent, and fireplace, thereby eliminating any destructive trampling of vegetation within and around the campsite (12).

Restoring old campgrounds, a problem the park service had been working on in Yellowstone for many years, was a far more difficult task. Meinecke reiterated his recommendations to introduce one-way roads, garage spurs, and fixed fireplaces and to protect key trees by placing boulders along roadways, at corners, and around garage spurs. In 1932, Meinecke encouraged planting trees in campgrounds temporarily withdrawn from use to restore vegetation: "By the planting of native trees at strategic points in close imitation of the natural type the site can slowly be brought back again for future use. Landscaping in the usual sense of the word has no place in the mountain camp where the visitor seeks at least the illusion of wildness." By 1932, the overall condition of existing camping areas in public forests and parks was dismal. Meinecke recommended a system of camp rotation, whereby new grounds were opened and older ones closed until the vegetation could recover by natural processes or planting (14).

Meinecke also recognized the effects of climate on camp planning and restoration. Semiarid regions, such as southern California, were especially problematic. Meinecke suggested artificially creating a naturalistic setting for such campgrounds by systematically planting on suitable sites long before actually using them. In the West, cottonwoods could be planted in land irrigated by nearby

7.10. The Paradise Camp Ground at Mount Rainier was reconstructed in the early 1930s according to E. P. Meinecke's principles of camp planning and landscape protection. Parking spurs were laid out on one-way roads and marked with boulders and log barriers. Each campsite was equipped with a table, fireplace, and tent clearing. *(Photograph courtesy National Archives, Record Group 79)*

streams or springs. Cottonwoods grew quickly and provided a thick canopy for shade. Meinecke explained, "The success of such planting depends on the judicious selection of sites, on the choice of suitable native species, on the amount of care that can be given the young plants until they become self-supporting and last, but not least, on a clear and sympathetic understanding of the ultimate objective, namely the creation of green and shady camps where the American lover of the out-doors can feel happy and at home" (16).

The National Park Service shared the forest service's concern for deteriorating campgrounds. The loss of trees was a foremost concern, and in addition to efforts to close the Giant Forest campground in Sequoia, planting projects had been attempted at several campgrounds in Yellowstone in the 1920s. About 1928, the park service began urging the construction of fixed fireplaces. At this time at Grand Canyon a model stove was devised; it was only ten to fourteen inches in height and fashioned in local stone to give the camper the effect of being around an open camp fire.[51]

Meinecke's policy on campgrounds was circulated among park designers in the National Park Service, and major changes began to appear in the camp-grounds. As a result, park campgrounds began to incorporate defined roads, paths, and campsites and provided barriers of stone and log to control traffic and parking so that heavy use of the grounds would not damage the root systems of surrounding shrubbery and trees. Meinecke's advice on using irrigation and spring sites to plant cottonwoods to prepare shady campgrounds was followed at Zion and other places in the Southwest. The term "meineckizing campgrounds" became common among landscape designers and CCC supervisors in the 1930s and continued to be used into the 1950s.

Meinecke's theory applied to the development of picnic grounds as well. He urged that picnic areas be separated from campgrounds and recommended a similar one-way road system leading to parking spurs that accommodated a group of cars and were arranged in a herringbone fashion to alleviate traffic problems and use the space most economically. Fixed fireplaces, for either indi-vidual or community use, were also essential to regulating picnic area use.

Several years later Meinecke expanded his theory in *Camp Planning and Camp Reconstruction*. Here the campground was viewed as a community of roof-less cabins. The grounds were subdivided into individual sites, or "lots," off per-manent one-way service roads. As before, the essential components of each site were the garage spur and the permanent hearth or fireplace, table, and tent site. The later manual was a more comprehensive guide to planning campgrounds, treating vegetation in greater detail and offering a flexible system that could be adapted to different conditions and enlarged over time.[52]

Camp planning combined two objectives—the "fullest utilization of the limited space compatible with increased convenience and comfort of the camper" and "the permanent protection of the woodland character of the camp ground." The type and distribution of natural vegetation therefore governed the arrangement of campsites:

> The natural, untouched vegetation in the forest is irregularly and unevenly dis-tributed so that no two camping areas are alike. Each one has to be planned and arranged on its own merits. A similar variety exists with regard to the composition of the forest cover. At lower elevations wide-spreading oaks, with shrubs, make excellent camps. Higher up there are pines, firs and cedars, with scattered broad-leaf trees in the openings, and at still greater elevations the camp grounds may be located in aspen groves and among subalpine pines. The varying sizes of the trees and shrubs, their mass effects, and even color and different shades of green, have a strong bearing on the character of pleasantness and power of attraction. (6)

Meinecke's idea of laying out service roads to create tiers of varying shapes had great applicability for the National Park Service, whose campgrounds de-manded an increasing number of campsites within a compressed space and whose role of stewardship called for minimum disturbance of the landscape. His advice on creating barriers to guide traffic by using rocks was now extended to the use of substantially sized logs. Unlike in other park structures, rocks were to be selected for their ability to contrast with the surroundings rather than their ability to blend and then were to be embedded in the ground. Barriers were intended to replace signs as forms of communication. Meinecke described the ideal configuration of roads and movement of automobile traffic:

> The best utilization of the whole camp ground is secured by a one-way road which is lined on both sides by campsites. In the simplest case, that of a relatively narrow strip, the road leads through its middle, serving lots on either side. On larger grounds the road may swing back at the end to serve another single or double tier, parallel to the first. In broader camp grounds of rectangular or square outline connecting roads break up the area into smaller units, each laid out in individual lots. These connecting roads run back into the main road at such an angle that the driver is forced to continue in the one direction, and large rocks or other obstacles are placed so that he will not attempt to turn against the one-way travel. . . . The distance between two paralleling connecting roads is determined by the size, and more particularly by the depth, of the lots making up the two tiers lying back to back between the roads. (8–9)

The community of the campground was expanded to include natural areas and features that could be shared by all. The manual reflected a greater awareness of landscape and ecological concerns, the treatment of vegetation, and the possibility of reintroducing vegetation through transplanting (perhaps based on Waugh's guidance or Meinecke's knowledge of the park service's experience). It expanded upon the environmental hazards faced by certain trees and plants that were susceptible and sensitive to invasion by humans:

> The large old oaks of the lower country, with the broad open stretches of grass under and between them, are less endangered by public use than are the dense groves of short aspens and high-altitude pines of the mountains. Even a road slashed through the aspen and pine thickets upsets the natural balance of life on their borders, and when openings for campsites are cut into the groves the entire physiological setup under which the trees, with all the many associated plants, have grown into a natural association is profoundly disturbed. The sudden letting in of strong sunlight and of winds in itself effects changes from which trees suffer and to which they have difficulty in adjusting themselves. (6)

Greater attention was given to the arrangement of campsites in relation to sunlight, privacy, and prevailing winds. The screening and shade provided by existing trees and shrubs were important in the arrangement of each site. Meinecke wrote of "neutral zones" between adjoining sites and along roads to afford campers privacy and to protect the campsites from the dust and noise of nearby roads. Ideally, these zones were to consist of a strip of green shrubs or young trees or a correspondingly broader belt of open land if no such vegetation was present (9).

The clearing of plant growth and timber to make way for the campsites required care and selectivity. Sites were to be carefully fireproofed so that overhanging limbs and shrubbery would be clear of the fireplaces, particularly highly flammable plants such as sage. The best boundaries between campsites were natural ones afforded by stands of tall trees or thick shrubbery. Meinecke urged that the greatest care be exercised in the choice of trees and shrubs to be removed and that the work be done only by trained men. This kind of work required in his opinion "careful weighing and a good deal of creative imagination." He wrote that "each tree or shrub to be cut should be designated, and the cutting should be strictly confined to these plants. No greater mistake can be made than to cut out all lower growth indiscriminately. A screen of shrubs or young reproduction between camps is a valuable asset, and its preservation must be made an integral part of any subdivision plan" (10).

Planting was expensive, and it took several years for its effects to become visible. The planting of exotics was discouraged on the grounds that "even if they adapt[ed] themselves to their new site they [would] always be felt as strangers in the native plant community and [would] detract from the natural beauty of the landscape." Meinecke now found it often "necessary to help out the natural vegetation" and advocated transplanting to fill in the gaps in screening from camp to camp and create barriers along the highway:

> With careful balling and the usual precautions in transfer and planting, these native young trees and shrubs, grown under the same climatic conditions, will have the best chance to survive. As for their placing, the same rule should be followed that governs the distribution of obstacles. They should be planted only where needed. . . . Intelligent planting, therefore, makes high demands on imagination. The landscape gardener must visualize the ultimate effect of his planting as it will appear in the future. The final proof of good planting comes to light only after ten or twenty years have elapsed. (21)

Meinecke encouraged the inclusion of picturesque details: "An old log overgrown with green moss is an asset in the landscape, a thing of beauty, and therefore to be protected." In addition, particularly beautiful spots along a creek, small waterfalls and islands, rocks, and vegetation were to be reserved in the camp plan for common enjoyment (20–21).

Although park designers followed Meinecke's manual, campgrounds continued to be one of the service's most serious problems. The National Park Service secured Meinecke's services as a consultant in the 1930s to advise on problems in Yellowstone, Grand Canyon, Yosemite, Mesa Verde, and other parks. Improvements continued to be made in the design and standardization of the designs for campground layouts, camp tables, and fireplaces. Meinecke's recommendations revolutionized camping in the national parks and forests in the 1930s and also determined the design of campgrounds in state parks and forests by the Civilian Conservation Corps. In addition, his findings shed greater light on the damage caused by automobiles and pedestrians on the natural vegetation of national parks, prompting park designers and managers to reassess the accessibility of automobiles to forested areas and consider the need for defined footpaths across fragile areas of vegetation, such as the alpine meadows at Yakima Park. His ideas also fueled the Landscape Division's request for funding for improvements such as sturdy curbs, graded paths, and delineated parking areas.

Yosemite's Committee of Expert Advisers

While Vint's ideas on landscape naturalization were taking shape, an expert committee was conferring on the long-term questions of protecting the landscape of Yosemite Valley. Its concerns were not far removed from those of Punchard a decade earlier, and its philosophical, if not practical, message seems to have had a far-reaching impact on the park landscape work of the 1930s. That the concerns and the issues are still viable today indicates the universal character of the thought and wisdom of Frederick Law Olmsted Jr. and the other members.

In a 1930 report, Yosemite's expert committee set forth its observations on the "nibbling" process through which Yosemite Valley was gradually being eroded. It perceived its duty and that of the National Park Service to be to approach the problem from two directions. The first was to envision a long-term ideal that could be achieved barring any adverse conditions and obstacles. The second was to meet the immediate practical needs of increasing visitation while striving to advance the more distant objectives of the first approach.[53]

Overall, the committee members agreed that the built improvements in the valley were superficial, temporary, and relatively inconsequential when compared with the geological forces that had created the valley. Nature would outlast any constructed changes. The members believed, however, that removing "certain effects caused by human use of the Valley" would accelerate the process of returning to natural conditions and largely increase the public's enjoyment of the valley's scenic qualities. The report, written by Olmsted, stated, "Looking ahead in terms of those coming centuries of human resort to the Yosemite Valley, it is only by constant repair and renewal that the changes thus far made by man in the Valley could be indefinitely perpetuated, and by far smaller exertion of energy it is possible to accelerate very greatly nature's obliteration of such of them as are recognized to have upon the whole an adverse effect on human enjoyment of the Valley" (13).

Concerned by the cumulative effect of artificial changes, the committee identified several areas that could be returned to a more natural condition. One of these was the meadows, which were considered vital elements of scenery because they created open foregrounds from which the enclosing walls for which the valley was famous could be viewed. The committee commented:

> This injury has been effected in places by the encroachment of new tree growth, encouraged by prevention of fires and in other ways; in others by the establishment of orchards and other artificial plantings, and at innumerable places by the construction of roads, ditches, fences, and other artificial constructions, far more conspicuously artificial and distracting where they intrude into and interrupt the simplicity of the meadows than under almost any other conditions in the Valley. (13, 15)

Of particular concern was Leidig Meadow, where an oval racetrack had been branded by use of the meadow for Indian Field Day events. Also illustrative of the "nibble" principle was Stoneman Meadow, where embankments, roadways, and parking areas for Camp Curry were built.

The committee applauded the service's efforts to move back the limits of the camping areas from the edges of the meadows and river. They saw the beginning of a systematic obliteration of the scars of abandoned roads, borrow pits, and dump heaps as "hopeful signs of an effort to reverse the nibbling process of encroachment and artificialization" (20).

More controversial, however, was the construction of a cableway connecting the valley with Glacier Point, which offered one of the most spectacular views of the valley. The committee strongly opposed the construction in 1930:

> The first point is that the cableway . . . would be visible throughout most of its length, under many conditions of lighting and background and from important points of view, as a consciously artificial element, vast in scale of length and height even though very tenuous in transverse dimensions, adding a new kind of evidence to the many now existing that the scenery is in process of progressive and cumulative alteration away from its original natural condition toward a condition more and more conspicuously man-handled, more and more expressive of subordination to human conveniences and whims, with no limit to that process yet apparent. The second point is that the great landscape in which the proposed cableway would be situated is precisely that part of the entire Park which is its most distinctive, most famous, and most precious natural feature — the very heart of the Yosemite Valley proper, extending from El Capitan to the Half Dome. (8)

Although the committee was seriously concerned with providing better access between the valley and the rim, it recognized that some problems must remain unsolved and that restraint was necessary where irreversible harm might occur:

> If we of today have not skill enough to solve to our practical satisfaction the utilitarian problems of transportation and so forth, involved in the resort of great numbers of people to the Yosemite, without continuing indefinitely the process begun by our predecessors of progressively weakening and nibbling away the natural impressiveness and natural beauty of this *great central unit of the Valley*, it were better to admit our limitations and leave some of these problems unsolved pending the discovery of solutions clearly and certainly free from this fundamental objection. (9–10)

The committee recommended that a landscape map of the valley be prepared, recording the existing areas occupied by each of several distinctive types and subtypes of landscape conditions, such as forest woodland, chaparral, and meadow; the distribution of these and other natural landscape types in the past as far as was ascertainable from photographs and records; and observations on the apparent relation of these differing units of landscape to the impressiveness and beauty of the valley as enjoyed by visitors to it. The committee recommended that a member of the Landscape Division be assigned to coordinate this study and develop a systematic plan for controlling and guiding the continuing human influences on the landscape. To some extent, a study of the landscape conditions and some of committee's ideas were incorporated into the master plans for the valley and areas on the valley rim, such as Glacier Point (21).

The work that ensued in the 1930s was a measurable result of both the committee's recommendations and the park service's expanding program of landscape naturalization. Envisioning the great benefit of this work to future visitors, Director Albright reported in 1931,

> The encroachment of forests into El Capitan Meadow and a few other areas was partially corrected by cutting out pine and oak trees under 6 inches in diameter. Many denuded areas on the valley floor which had needed treatment for years were restored by plowing, harrowing, fertilizing and the planting of native grass and flower seed. Areas from which several houses were removed were treated similarly. A general program along these lines is continuously underway in all areas.[54]

Beginning in 1933 and continuing for several years, the Civilian Conservation Corps carried out a number of projects that removed obsolete structures and returned parts of the valley and meadows to a more natural appearance. Borrow pits and dumps were eliminated, trees were planted to screen campgrounds from the road, and numerous improvements made artificial intrusions inconspicuous, giving the meadows a more naturalistic appearance. Most traces of the old village were removed. Extensive work was undertaken to beautify the new village by planting native trees, shrubbery, and wildflowers; maintaining the existing vegetation; and replacing curbs and walks.

The 1932 Study on Park Policies

In 1932, Louis C. Cramton, special attorney to the secretary of the interior, conducted a study of the *Congressional Record* and all other legislative documents relating to Yellowstone National Park to determine what Congress, in establishing the park system, intended the national parks to be and what policies it expected would govern the parks. Formerly a member of Congress and chairman of the Interior Subcommittee of the House Appropriations Committee, Cramton had been instrumental in building the financial structure of the national park system. Albright believed Cramton's contributions were second in importance only to the great achievements of Stephen Mather in developing the fundamental organization and policies of the National Park Service.[55]

Cramton's findings resulted in a statement of policy that was published in the 1932 annual report. The statement clarified and codified the various policies that had evolved since 1916 concerning the establishment, preservation, protection, maintenance, use, and enjoyment of the national parks. First, the statement clarified the issue of criteria for national parks, stating that preservation should depend alone on the outstanding scenic, scientific, or historical quality and the resulting national interest, regardless of an area's location or proximity to population centers or the financial capacity of a state. National interest was defined as widespread interest and meant that a park should appeal to many individuals, regardless of where they lived, because of its outstanding merit.

The statement upheld the twin purposes of parks: they should be accessible to the public for enjoyment and use, and they should remain unspoiled for future generations. Toward these ends, the statement upheld the 1930 policy excluding exotic plants and wildlife from the parks and prohibited the capture of fish and game for commercial purposes and the destruction of animals except those "detrimental to the use of the parks." Timber was to be cut only when necessary to control attacks of insects and disease or to otherwise conserve the scenery or significant natural or historic objects. The removal of dead timber was allowed where it was necessary to protect or improve park forests. Laying the burden of stewardship on National Park Service officials, the policy stated, "Proper administration will retain these areas in their natural condition, sparing them the vandalism of improvement" (7).

Many aspects of park administration which had been mentioned in the

1918 statement of policy were expanded and given new emphasis. These included the role of education, the role of a civilian ranger and administrative force, the provision of tourist accommodations of various types, the provision of suitable roads and trails for safe travel, the prohibition of commercial activities other than those essential to the care and comfort of the visitor, and the prohibition of private ownership and leasing. Under the preeminent principle that national parks were established for the permanent preservation of areas and objects of national interest and were intended to exist forever, the principles of landscape protection and harmonization merged into one single concept: "Roads, buildings, and other structures necessary for park administration and for public use and comfort should intrude upon the landscape or conflict with it only to the absolute minimum" (9).

Forestry, road building, and wildlife conservation were recognized as special problems, and park administrators were called upon to define the objectives for these programs "in harmony with the fundamental purposes of the parks." In issues related to forestry, the National Park Service was to consider scenic values and the goal of preservation. In the building of roads, the service was to ensure that "the route, the type of construction, and the treatment of related objects" contributed to "the fullest accomplishment of the intended use of the area." In wildlife conservation, the "preservation of the primitive" was to be sought rather than the "development of an artificial ideal" (8).

The report also addressed the topic of recreation, which would have increasing importance in the 1930s:

> Recreation, in its broadest sense, includes much of education and inspiration. Even in its narrower sense, having a good time, it is a proper incidental use. In planning for recreational use of the parks, in this more restricted meaning, the development should be related to their inherent values and calculated to promote the beneficial use thereof by the people. It should not encourage exotic forms of amusement and should never permit that which conflicts with or weakens the enjoyment of these inherent values. (8)

The 1932 statement of policy has greater meaning in view of the controversies over park boundaries which had occurred at Yellowstone and elsewhere, the increasing concern that all states should have a national park, and the development of civil service standards and examinations for park rangers. It also broadened the scope of national parks to include historical parks and wilderness areas.

The 1932 statement forced the realization that in many parts of the country, particularly the East, pristine, undisturbed lands were not to be found to form national parks and that gradual efforts might be necessary to reach permanent objectives for conservation. New parks, including Shenandoah, Great Smoky Mountains, and Mammoth Cave, required the acquisition of land from numerous private owners; the removal of homesteads, farms, and previous land uses; and the restoration of natural conditions and scenic character. It addressed the issue of existing encroachments on lands of outstanding significance:

> When, under the general circumstances such action is feasible, even though special conditions require the continuance of limited commercial activities or of limited encroachments for local or individual benefit, an area of national-park caliber should be accorded that status now, rather than abandon it permanently to full commercial exploitation and probable destruction of its sources of national interest. Permanent objectives highly important may thus be accomplished and the compromises, undesired in principle but not greatly destructive in effect, may later be eliminated as occasion for their continuance passes. (9)

Albright applauded the study, stating that Cramton's findings reduced "to concrete form the policies of the National Park Service as they [were] established by Congress in laws enacted during the [previous] 60 years, and [would] be of invaluable assistance in keeping to the course mapped out by the far-sighted men who laid the foundation of [the] national-park system." Coming on the eve of the New Deal, Cramton's report would serve as a blueprint for landscape preservation and stewardship during a period of unprecedented development and program expansion.[56]

Chapter 8

A Process
for Park Planning

*The development of a national park or a national monument requires
no specific magic. It is like any other job of planning the use of land
for human enjoyment. It is necessary to know the land involved
thoroughly, to know how people are to use it, and about how many
will use it at one time. That information should state the problem;
however, it is too frequently incomplete. Next, it is necessary to work
out a design, that is satisfactory to those in authority. Then to make it
a reality, all that is needed is to finance and build.*

Thomas Vint, "National Park Service Master Plans," *Planning and Civic Comment,*
1946

The 1918 statement of policy of the National Park Service called for planning before design and construction. The early development schemes
and the town plans for Yosemite Valley and Grand Canyon Village were
efforts to fulfill this requirement. In 1925, however, the National Park Service
began to give serious attention to comprehensive park planning that coordinated the development of roads and trails with the development of park villages,
ranger stations, and maintenance areas. For the first time, planning was applied
to the park as a cohesive unit with interconnecting circulation systems and designated areas to serve administrative and other needs. The impetus for planning
came from the increased funds for roads and trails and the need to schedule
projects over a five-year period. In 1925, Daniel Hull, then the park service's
chief landscape engineer, began working with Mount Rainier's superintendent
to plan for the park's future and coordinate the development of much needed
roads and trails with a vision for opening additional areas of the mountain to
visitors. At the superintendents' conference that year, superintendents were directed to draw up five-year plans to meet the future needs of their parks.[1]

The park superintendents initiated the plans, working closely with Hull and Thomas Vint. The first plans outlined five-year programs for the expansion and improvement of developed areas of the parks, such as administrative centers and park villages. Park superintendents drew up separate plans for road and trail construction, which was being funded on a larger scale and was phased in over several years.

The first five-year plan was developed for Mount Rainier National Park and was submitted to Director Stephen Mather in September 1926. A plan for Crater Lake was developed in 1927. These plans listed the existing facilities alongside an itemized list of improvements needed within a five-year period. Although most improvements called for the construction of buildings such as sheds, comfort stations, or residences, a number called for extensions to campgrounds and landscape improvements. For example, the 1927 Crater Lake plan called for a dustless promenade with rustic seats to be laid along the rim from the lodge to the Rim Road and for nineteen "picturesque" stone troughs and drinking fountains to be placed along park roads and trails.[2]

Park superintendents could use these plans to develop a strategy for meeting the demands of increasing visitation over a period of five years and to justify requests to fund improvements and new construction. The five-year plans enabled the park superintendent to identify the areas within the park requiring development for various purposes, such as ranger stations, "village" services, maintenance, park administration, educational facilities, fire protection, and shelter for hikers in remote, backcountry areas. These were plotted in relationship to existing and proposed roads and trails within the park and to approach roads outside. Furthermore, the plans enabled the superintendent to coordinate the administrative needs of the park with the concessionaire's services.

The superintendents' concerns in the planning process were numerous: the location of park facilities; the function and form of park structures; the circulation of traffic to the park and to key points within the park through roads, trails, and, in some cases, railroads; the provision of safe access to points of scenic beauty and outstanding natural features; the management and protection of the park through patrol trails, patrol cabins, fire roads, fire equipment, and fire lookouts; maintenance facilities; and the comfort of visitors, primarily through concessionaires' services such as food, lodging, and gas. These concerns could easily come into conflict with the goal of preserving the parks' natural character. Ever present, therefore, was the concern that the park landscape be left unimpaired and that the service's dual mission be upheld.

Planning required accurate and current information. At the request of park superintendents, the service's civil engineers carried out surveys and made updated topographical maps that recorded not only natural features, contours, waterways, and existing structures but also important trees and rock formations.

Although park planning was viewed primarily as the responsibility of the Landscape Division, it involved coordination with a number of programs. Coordination with the Engineering Division entailed receiving accurate topographical information and also working out the details for water, electricity, sewerage, and telephone systems and for minor roads to serve the developed areas. As programs for interpretation expanded through the development of museums, exhibits, nature gardens, and trails, the Landscape Division began to cooperate with the Educational Division and Herbert Maier, the principal architect for the museums being funded through the Laura Spelman Rockefeller Memorial. As concern for the protection of park forests increased, collaboration became necessary between the Forestry Division and the Landscape Division. The need to build safe systems for sewage and garbage disposal involved the Sanitation Division.

As more money became available and planners realized the diverse kinds of facilities that were needed, they discovered that they required a stronger planning process than that provided by the five-year plans. They needed a process that simultaneously solved the immediate pressing problems of park management and called for long-range vision. They required plans that viewed the park holistically in terms of geography, visitation, and landscape protection, all in relation to the service's many developing programs: fire control, interpretation and natural history, and engineering. Engineering was particularly important because it provided the infrastructure of essential utilities such as sanitation, water, sewerage, power, and communications. Plans needed to foresee the cumulative impact that small-scale improvements would have over time. As the number of park visitors grew on the one hand and the number of parks increased on the other, the direct involvement of the park service director and the chief landscape architect diminished. A formal system for planning, design, and review was imperative. Under Thomas Vint's leadership, therefore, the five-year plans evolved into a program of comprehensive planning which coordinated the service's growing programs and brought together the divergent interests of landscape preservation and park development into a single, fully orchestrated vision for the future.

From Development Outlines to Master Plans

In 1929, park development plans were made mandatory. The purpose of this change was as follows:

> Such a plan will give the general picture of the park showing the circulation system (roads and trails), the communication system (telephone and telegraph), Wilderness areas and Developed areas. More detailed plans of developed areas (villages, tourist centers, etc.) will be required to properly portray these special features.

These plans being general guides will naturally be constantly in a state of development and should be brought up to date and made a matter of record annually. Their success depends upon the proper collaboration of study and effect on the part of the Park Superintendent, the Landscape Architect, the Chief Engineer, and the Sanitary Engineer. The resulting plan will not be the work of any one but will include the work of all. Since Park Development is primarily a Landscape development, these plans will be coordinated by the Landscape Division.[3]

By 1929, therefore, the preparation of plans dominated the work of the Landscape Division. In his annual report, Vint described the division's primary purpose as obtaining a "logical well-studied general development plan for each park, which included the control of the location, type of architecture, planting, and grading, etc., in connection with any construction project." The division was involved in all phases of park development from the location of incinerators to the design of fire lookouts. Landscape architects strongly influenced decisions on where park development was to occur by participating in reconnaissance surveys; identifying and calling for the protection of scenic vistas and significant natural features; and reviewing proposals by superintendents, concessionaires, and other divisions. These proposals included the plans for road and trail projects, tourist facilities, museum developments, administrative centers, and maintenance facilities. The division was responsible for developing all architectural and landscape plans for government facilities and all projects involving the Bureau of Public Roads. It was also responsible for coordinating concessionaires' developments with government facilities.[4]

The plans now contained three parts to be developed in sequence over a three-year period. First was the park development outline that listed the various areas of the park and their components. Next was the general plan, a graphic representation of each particular area. Third was the six-year plan, which was a list of the various projects required to complete any portion of the plan. Projects included the construction of new facilities and the removal of obsolete ones.

Superintendents were responsible for the development outline and were asked to include what they needed to develop an area properly over several years, assuming funds were available. The park development outline was intended to be a written statement of all items necessary for the development of the park and was organized according to geographical areas and within each area according to use. A standard format ensured that the outline for each park covered the same items and gave an overall view of the park's current condition and future needs. The new format combined the items previously covered under the five-year plan and the road and trail plans. The plan enabled each superintendent to translate his vision for the park's development into written and graphic form, incorporating the interests of the director as well as the specialists in landscape, educational, and engineering matters.[5]

With the outline, the superintendent could schedule construction and improvements progressively over six years while maintaining a single vision for the interrelationship of various aspects of development. Maps accompanied the outline and were to be updated annually as the construction of roads and trails progressed. The outline made it possible to orchestrate the essential infrastructure of park development, that is, to coordinate roads and trails with campgrounds and other facilities and to plan utilities to serve the building program. It also provided an opportunity to advance the landscape standpoint in the location of facilities, the protection of scenic and natural features, and the provision of facilities to enjoy the park scenery. Proposals for underground wiring, scenic turnouts and overlooks, and the removal of dilapidated buildings were included alongside proposals to build bridges and comfort stations. While the plans called for development in keeping with the directive to make parks accessible to the public, they served the corollary directive for landscape protection as well by indicating the limits of development beyond which the park was to be left undisturbed.

Mount Rainier's first plan outlined development in five categories: a general road system, a general trail system, development areas, entrance units, and miscellaneous development. The road and trail systems were divided into units by names and linear miles. Each development area was divided into eight sections: administrative unit, residential unit, utility group, public auto camp, water supply, sewage disposal, garbage disposal, and concessionaires' facilities. Under each section there was an item-by-item description of "existing facilities" and "present and future needs." Entrances were simply named for their location, and component features such as entrance arches, comfort stations, storage sheds, checking stations, ranger quarters, stables, water fountains, and water systems were classified as "existing" or as "present and future needs." Under "miscellaneous developments" were fire-fighting stations that included water-pumping facilities, caches of tools at patrol cabins, and an assortment of equipment in the developed areas. Also listed in this category were road maintenance camps housing about ten men, shelters for trucks and road-clearing equipment, and a 115-mile telephone system that encircled the park and needed overhauling.[6]

Mount Rainier's park road system was designed to connect with state highways at four entrances and to form, with the state roads, a complete circuit that would encircle the park and allow travelers several points of entry. Six areas of development were planned in relation to the interconnecting network of state and park roads. The park road system was divided into units identified by name and distance, for example, the twenty-one-mile Nisqually Road on the south side of the park extended from the park's southwest entrance to Paradise Valley, and the fourteen-mile Yakima Park Road connected with the Naches Pass Highway near the northeast entrance and extended to Yakima Park.

The maps showed the interconnecting system of park roads and their relationship to state highways or roads through adjoining national forests. A de-

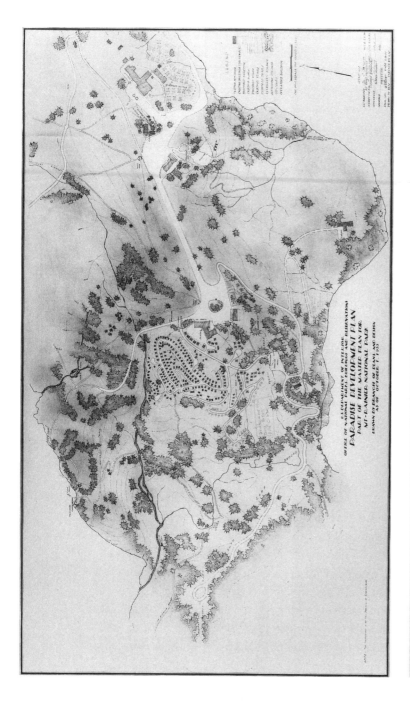

8.1. The 1933 development plan for Paradise, a major developed area in Mount Rainier National Park, incorporated a combination of existing government and concessionaire's facilities. Centrally located was a traffic circle, the 1927 community building, and a "hub" for trails leading up the mountain and to overlooks above Nisqually Glacier. To the northwest lay the concessionaire's lodge and cabin village, to the southwest Paradise Camp Ground, and to the east Paradise Inn. The plan called for the removal of several structures, including the dormitories for the concessionaire's staff near the inn. (*Plan courtesy National Archives, Record Group 79*)

scription of the construction program for each two-year period followed. The Nisqually Road, which was reconstructed and surfaced between 1925 and 1927, was to be paved during the 1928–30 construction program. The one-way road to Ricksecker Point, which was one of the park's most scenic stretches of road and had been closed to traffic in 1922 because of heavy landslides, was to be reconstructed and surfaced. The scenic and congested Narada switchback was to be reconstructed and surfaced, and three concrete bridges were to replace wooden ones. While improvements were being made on the park's most traveled route from the southwest entrance to Paradise Valley, work was to begin on the West Side Road and the Yakima Park Road to the east. As part of the third construction program, from 1931 to 1933, the twenty-five-mile Stevens Canyon Highway was to be constructed, creating a link between the Nisqually Road to the west and the Naches Pass and Yakima Park Roads to the east. This would make it possible for motorists to enter the park from state highways to the east, northwest, southwest, and southeast and travel in a circular manner around the park.

Not only did the park outline call for the construction of buildings and utilities, but it also included items related to landscape protection and naturalization: small parking areas accommodating five to fifteen cars were to be constructed at points of scenic interest along all roads, and guardrails, retaining walls, and roadside slopes were to be constructed to National Park Service standards. Natural features, springs, and trees were to be conserved and protected during construction.

The trail system envisioned for Mount Rainier consisted of one main loop called the Wonderland Trail, which encircled the mountain, and various trails and footpaths connecting the loop with important scenic features and areas. In the mid-1920s, the park's trail system had twenty-five different units covering a total of 241 miles. Many of these had been constructed hurriedly to open up fire patrol routes; to be safe for visitors or for mounted patrols on horseback, they needed to be relocated and improved. Additional trails were needed "to open up important scenic and patrol routes" as roads were constructed and automobile camps developed. The funding for trails included the construction of fourteen patrol cabins on the Wonderland Trail and other trails (4–8).

Of the six development areas proposed for the park, only two had begun to take form: Longmire Springs, a mountain resort predating park acquisition on the south side of the park, and Paradise Valley, also on the south side of the park, where a lodge had opened in 1917 and which was envisioned as a center for mountaineering and winter sports. The remaining four areas—Yakima Park, Spray Park, Ohanopecosh Hot Springs, and Sunset Park—were to be developed with government buildings for administrative purposes, free public auto camps, hotels, pay camps, and other concessionary facilities. Of the new areas proposed, Yakima Park received the greatest attention in the years 1929 to 1932. A similar development—to help relieve the crowding at Paradise and open up views

8.2. Master plan for the Yakima Park Development Area, Mount Rainier National Park, 1933, shows the concentration of buildings around a village plaza and the layout of spur roads and trails that led to outlying scenic overlooks, picnic areas, special natural features, the power station, and a reservoir. (*Plan courtesy National Archives, Record Group 79*)

of considerable grandeur and access by trails to remote areas of the park—was planned for Spray Park on the western side of the mountain. Dependent on the construction of the West Side Road, it never materialized and was dropped from the plans in the early 1930s (9).

Many improvements were proposed for Longmire Springs. A larger administration building, a new comfort station, an assembly hall, a museum building, post office, service buildings, and a one-mile system of underground wiring for telephone and electricity were needed for administrative purposes. Additional housing, a community garage, a variety of work and repair shops, a stable, a general warehouse, and several sheds for equipment were also required. The public auto campground needed to be enlarged, and variety of buildings, including four comfort stations, a bathhouse and laundry, and a community house, were needed. Picnic grounds were also needed. The government facilities relied upon the concessionaire's water system, and designers therefore proposed an independent water system that could accommodate present and future growth. A sewage disposal plant was proposed to replace a primitive system that was both inadequate and unhealthy. An incinerator to dispose of garbage and can-crushing facilities were also needed. Although the concessionaire's facilities were substantial, improvements and additions were proposed (12–18).

The construction of the Yakima Park Road was intended to make Yakima Park, a scenic subalpine plateau in the northeast section of the park, accessible to visitors during the summer months. The land was completely undeveloped in 1926 and was one of the first areas to be designed through the advance planning process. The plan called for the following administrative and residential facilities: a two-story administration building measuring twenty-four feet by forty-eight feet to serve as the district ranger headquarters, information office, and living quarters for four rangers; a public comfort station; a branch museum building; and one mile of underground wiring for electricity and telephone. Utilities required were an equipment shed, twenty by sixty feet, a bunk and mess house, and a stable for four horses. The auto camp was to serve at least one thousand cars and required six comfort stations, one combination bathhouse and laundry, one community building, a water system with pipes, and about fifty water faucets. In addition to a water system, a sewage disposal plant and garbage disposal plant were needed for government use. The concessionaire was allowed a large hotel accommodating at least five hundred people, staff dormitories, a guide and hiking building, a camp service building with a lunch counter and store, bathhouse, repair and workshops, a stable for thirty horses, and a hydroelectric plant (30–36).

The Employment Stabilization Act of 1931

The preparation of plans accelerated substantially. In 1931, Congress passed the Employment Stabilization Act, requiring all government bureaus to prepare six-year advance plans on which federal appropriations for construction could be based should an economic emergency occur or should the depression continue. Agencies were to provide cost estimates for carrying out plans to the Employment Stabilization Board.

In 1932, the Landscape Division undertook the work of future planning on an unprecedented scale. Vint's staff made substantial progress on the general development plans based on the development outlines superintendents had prepared the previous year. The plans at this time showed the development scheme for an entire park and covered road and trail systems, fire-control plans, and the general layout of all developed areas including utilities, buildings, and roadways. In some cases, drawings were included in the plans to illustrate a special type of wall, guardrail, or other detail to be used at a certain place in the park.[7]

Landscape architect Gilmore D. Clarke of the Westchester County Park Commission influenced the form that general development plans assumed in 1931. In June 1930, Clarke spent ten days in Yellowstone National Park preparing a general plan for the Mammoth Hot Springs area. He represented the New York chapter of the American Society of Landscape Architects, which was helping the National Park Service solve problems related to the development of the park headquarters. This area posed a serious problem in park planning. It had previously been used as the headquarters for the U.S. Army during the period when the military managed the park. The village, a popular destination for tourists because of its location at the edge of the famous terraces of hot springs, was marked by a discordant array of structures and buildings and a system of congested roads which contradicted the naturalistic principles that the national park designers sought to uphold.

In 1927, Vint and Ferruccio Vitale of the federal Commission of Fine Arts had visited the area with members of the museum committee to choose a location for the headquarters museum. They abandoned their search for a suitable location, however, and instead began efforts to redesign the area. In 1930, Clarke and his assistant, Allyn R. Jennings, studied the area and drew up a plan that was reviewed by National Park Service director Horace Albright, Superintendent Roger Toll, and Vint. This plan, which was eventually approved and incorporated into Yellowstone's comprehensive plan, appears to be one of the first general development plans to take the large-scale, hand-colored format that was to characterize the master plans until the late 1930s. Clarke's plan showed all existing features based on Jennings' survey of the area and indicated the roadways and structures that were to be removed, alongside those proposed as new con-

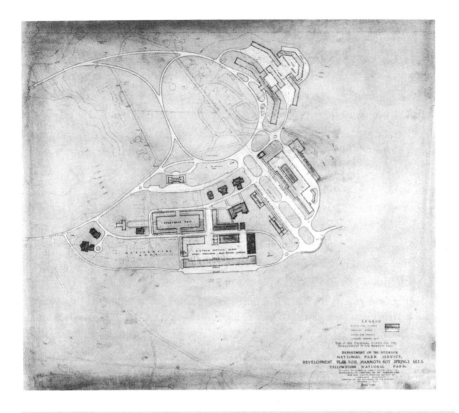

8.3. The 1931 general development plan for the headquarters village at Mammoth Hot Springs, Yellowstone National Park, reflects Gilmore Clarke's recommendations for the removal of many army-era buildings and the centrally located hotel and the construction of new roads, a central elliptical lawn, a main street divided by circular islands of plantings, a concessionaire's development of a lodge and cabins, and numerous smaller buildings spread out according to function. *(Plan courtesy National Archives, Record Group 79)*

struction. It called for the removal of most of the former army buildings and the hotel and its related buildings but retained recently built park buildings such as the superintendent's residence, a barn, and a ranger's residence. The entire area was redesigned, changing the circulation system to one of curving streets around an open elliptical lawn on the site of the old hotel. The new concessionaire's development was situated to the east in a radiating pattern, and the park administration area, residential area, and utility complex were located to the south in several tiers along curving roads. A road with diagonal parking and a median of several planted islands joined the park and concessionaire's business areas.[8]

The term "master plan" was applied to the general development plan in

1932, when Director Albright spoke before the twelfth meeting of National Park Executives in Hot Springs, Arkansas. Albright spoke of these plans as the domain of architecture and landscape architecture and stated that the primary function of the Landscape Division was to prepare the plans for all parks in the East and West. The Engineering Division was to provide technical information on construction details and furnish estimates. Vint's staff would coordinate plans and update them annually according to appropriations and changing conditions. By the end of 1931, development outlines and general plans had been prepared for every park, for a moratorium on building had freed up the landscape architects' time and allowed them to work on plans.[9]

For Albright, each plan was more than a breakdown of needed facilities that could be funded through annual appropriations. It was a legacy for the future—a final and decisive vision of how each park should fulfill its dual purpose of preserving outstanding scenery and natural features and providing for public enjoyment: "What we have here are more than year plans. They are not the stabilization plans; they are the permanent plans for the park. The program set forth in these plans can not be carried out in a period of six years on any basis of appropriations that we can expect" (94).

Park Development Outline

1. Circulation
    a. Road System (outlined on Park Topographic Map)
       1. Project plans for each unit of road system
    b. Trail System (outlined on Park Topographic Map)
       1. Project plan or report of field work for each unit of trail system
2. Wilderness and Sacred Areas (outlined on the Park Topographic Map or Park General Plan)
    a. Wilderness Areas—large areas to be generally protected as undeveloped wilderness
    b. Sacred Areas—small areas to be protected against all development for the protection of a special natural feature—e.g. 1/8 mile radius around Old Faithful Geyser. Similar areas around important waterfalls, a special group of trees, or geological features.
3. Developed Areas. Includes building group units such as villages or tourist centers. Each should have all or part of the following according to the use of each area:
    a. Circulation System
       1. Roadways
       2. Parking Area

3. Bridle Paths

4. Foot Paths

b. Public Utilities (General layouts by Sanitary Engineer or Chief Engineer).

1. Water System

2. Sewerage System

3. Garbage Disposal

4. Telephone System

5. Power System

c. Government Building Units

1. Administrative Group (administration building, museum, post office, etc.)

2. Residential Group (all employee housing)

3. Utility Group (shops, equipment housing, barns, etc. possibly laborers mess and bunk houses.)

d. Tourist Facilities

1. Hotel Areas

2. Lodge Areas

3. Housekeeping Camp Areas

4. Govt. Auto Camp Areas

5. Retail Areas (only in larger parks)

e. Park Operators' Non-Tourist Units.

1. Administrative Area (often in hotel and not a distinct unit)

2. Residential Area (residences and dormitories)

3. Utility Area (warehouses, shops, etc.)

4. Transportation System Area (usually is part of Utility Area)

SOURCE: "General Planning," Tentative Outline, 2–3, February 1929, Record Group 79, National Archives, Washington, D.C.

At the 1932 meeting, the nearly completed general development plan for Mount Rainier was displayed, and Vint described the design process. Working from a photostatic enlargement of the U.S. Geological Survey topographical map for each area, the landscape architects had an enlarged view from which they traced streams, mountain peaks, and other important features. The scale of the finished plans was either the same or one and a half or two times that of the topographical map. The landscape architects made various tracings so that separate maps could be used to plot different kinds of information, such as roads, trails, or developed areas. They also made numerous copies, some of which would be shaded with colored pencils (96).

By the end of 1932, the plans for all national parks and monuments were complete, with a park development outline, a general plan, and a six-year program. The completed plans took the form of a series of large color drawings and an accompanying narrative, the development outline. The five-year plans for trails and roads which had been developed since 1926 were incorporated into what was now called the master plan for each park. Plans were organized in several sections: major roads, trail systems, major development areas, and minor development areas.

Each plan began with a statement of the park's purpose taken directly from the legislation establishing the park. The location of the park and its relationship to state highway systems and nearby population centers were described. The roads and trails were broken into sections and distances that required either improvement or construction. The major development areas were the park villages, having many functions, and both concessionary and government facilities, such as the valley floor at Yosemite. Plans for major development areas included buildings and structures related to park administration; concessionaire facilities; utilities such as power, telephone, sewerage, and water systems; minor circulation systems of paths and roads; vistas; and in some cases, existing vegetation or natural features that should be protected or retained. The minor development areas were outlying areas such as ranger stations, park entrances, and campgrounds. They included a range of areas in which several types of development or clusters of buildings and structures were situated, including important intersections that posed particular design problems or were of particular importance in park design, such as Chinquapin Intersection at Yosemite.

Areas serving only a few functions and having a relatively simple layout—such as patrol cabins, hiking shelters, parking overlooks for scenic views or trailheads, and fire lookouts—were generally located on the master plan sheets for the fire protection plan, system of trails, or system of roads. Although not the subject of detailed attention in the master plan, these were commonly treated in site plans and architectural drawings prepared once funding was available.

From 1932 to 1942, master plans were revised annually. They plotted existing construction and recommended changes in the form of new construction and the removal of existing features. They also noted important vistas, areas of vegetation, and individual trees or rock formations that merited preservation. The plans reflected an integrated approach to park planning and management. Each master plan was based upon an understanding of the significance and purpose of the particular park. Vint described its function: "The Master Plan of a national park fills the same function as a city plan or a regional plan. Its use is to steer the course of how the land within its jurisdiction is to be used. Nothing is built directly from it. Each project, whether it be a road, a building, or a campground, must have its construction plan approved. In the course of approval it is checked as to whether it conforms with and is not in conflict with the Master Plan." [10]

Although the landscape architects were responsible for preparing the plans, they made no administrative decisions. They were employed in an advisory and professional capacity. Plans were drawn up as recommendations for the approval of the park superintendent, the division chiefs from the Western Field Office, and the director. Later the regional directors and the regional landscape architects, architects, and engineers became involved in the decision-making process. The plans also facilitated the review of concessionaires' plans for expansion, by spelling out the extent of development which was considered reasonable to accommodate public use and comfort.[11]

Drawings for individual projects plotted on the plans were made as funds became available for construction, reviewed for consistency with the master plans, and approved separately. Planning made it possible to program the funds and phase projects according to funding, personnel, and needs.

When employment stabilization and relief funds became available in 1933, the National Park Service was equipped with comprehensive plans and, in many cases, actual drawings. The service was ready to begin construction. The efforts that park service officials and Vint's staff put into advance planning brought immediate results through public works funding and emergency conservation projects by the Civilian Conservation Corps.

During the 1930s, capital improvements in the form of roads and buildings were funded through Public Works Administration allotments or regular park funds and used private contractors and skilled labor. The coordination of public works projects with Emergency Conservation Work enabled parks to make substantial progress on the master plans. From April 1933 to March 1936, resident landscape architects worked closely with the landscape architects and architects assigned to the Civilian Conservation Corps camps. In 1936, design services were consolidated in the regional offices set up for state park Emergency Conservation Work. These offices became the National Park Service regional offices when the service was regionalized a year later. As park development proceeded, the plans were updated. The annual plans visually charted the impact of New Deal construction and conservation programs on national park development. The completion of many plans believed unattainable in 1932 was realized within a decade.

What had been conceived as advance planning for the construction of roads, trails, and facilities by the end of the 1930s encompassed all aspects of park administration. To a large extent, the plans addressed issues of interpretation, forestry, fire control, engineering, scenery preservation, automobile traffic, pedestrian circulation, and concessionaires' operations. During the 1930s, the development plans included, in addition to site plans, sheets on vegetation, fire control, utility layouts, geological formations, and wildlife areas and provided housing and road inventories and interpretive statements to guide the service's growing programs.

One of the most important advantages of developing an outline and a plan was that areas could be developed as a functional unit with a carefully predetermined set of structures. Standard approaches to making certain kinds of facilities inconspicuous could be devised. A ranger station serving as a checking point was located where it could control incoming and outgoing traffic and provide ample space for parking for visitors seeking information, water, and comfort. Water fountains, signs, curbs and sidewalks, paths, and flagpoles were conveniently placed at these points. Comfort stations were located behind screens of existing vegetation and in inconspicuous places and reached by curving footpaths from the parking area. Directions were given by simple and carefully placed signs. Maintenance facilities, including garages, sheds, workshops, dormitories, and mess halls, were located on side roads out of the view of the public. The components of these developed areas were standardized so that visitors could anticipate the provision of certain services at given points within a national park.

Within the general formula for developing certain types of areas, designers were able to coordinate functions such as trails and paths with the broader circulation system and the natural features of a particular park. They were also able to develop floor plans and specifications for specialized buildings that, while meeting functional requirements, could be adapted to the natural conditions and character of each site. Furthermore, the plans enabled designers to develop a unifying architectural theme for each park or for similar areas within larger parks. These themes were related, through materials and form, to the natural setting and cultural history of the park.

Plans as a Tool for Landscape Preservation

In 1942, ten years after the term "master plan" was introduced, park service spokesperson H. T. Thompson stated that "in parks, master planning may mean development—it may also mean purposeful refusal to develop." Mount Rainier's park development outline of 1929 demonstrated the role of park plans in landscape preservation when it recommended six areas as the maximum number of developments in the park and urged that all other regions be left undisturbed except for the construction of trails and patrol cabins. The concept of wilderness areas was relatively new to the park service. The previous year, Director Mather had designated the glacial zone and particular areas of outstanding natural beauty at Mount Rainier as wilderness areas. They were accessible only by foot or on horseback and were otherwise to remain undeveloped. By 1929, large areas in each park had been set aside to be left in their natural condition.[12]

Secretary of the Interior Ray Lyman Wilbur saw Glacier National Park as an excellent example of a park in which certain areas should be preserved in primitive conditions. Furthermore, he saw no reason to modify the plans for wilderness areas in order to open new country in the older and more developed parks such as Yellowstone and Yosemite. The secretary viewed the role of the

Landscape Division as central to the conservation of national parks: "Preservation of primitive landscape conditions, adequate protection of wild life, and the safeguarding of forests and watersheds can not be carried out if a reasonable balance between accessibility and wilderness values is not maintained. A group of landscape architects pass on all plans for improvements in the park system and roads and trails are built to designs that will give least injury to natural features."[13]

Under the 1929 planning outline, any area not identified as a developed area was considered a wilderness area. This was in keeping with the idea that the master plan was a blueprint for the future. Plans also identified "sacred" areas, which were to be protected from development or other forms of disturbance. Selected for their pristine condition, sacred areas were small zones or designated features, such as the one-eighth-mile radius around the Old Faithful Geyser at Yellowstone, a geologically important rock formation such as Yosemite's Sentinel Rock, a group of trees, a margin of land along the Grand Canyon of the Yellowstone, or an island in the river at Tuolumne Meadows in Yosemite. Such areas were inviolate and to remain unimpaired. In fact, the park service saw these designations as equally important to park management as development plans. In the 1930s, research areas were added to the list of areas specially designated for preservation. Research areas were reserved for the scientific study of plants, animals, and other natural features and were accessible only by trails. Examples of these were a seventy-five-acre biotic succession area at Gregory's Bald in Great Smoky Mountains National Park and a four-thousand-acre area between Tuolumne Meadows and White Mountain in Yosemite.[14]

The plans also served as a tool for landscape preservation. Important viewpoints and vistas, stands of trees, and rock formations were identified on the plans and designated for protection. The plans served as a guide for cleanup operations by calling for the elimination of unsightly or deteriorated buildings and structures that, in many cases, predated the organization of the National Park Service.

The Grand Canyon area of Yellowstone National Park—one of the park's most scenic—posed one of the most perplexing problems to park designers. In 1927, Vint recommended that no camping be allowed within one hundred feet of the brow of the hill. The master plan was used to alleviate the deterioration and destruction of scenery which had been caused by overdevelopment and overuse. A sacred area was designated along the two rims above the Yellowstone River. Citing the intention of the legislation founding the park, the master plan summarized the dilemma faced by park designers:

> The present Canyon area development has violated, and continues to violate this
> Act to a considerable degree, to the detriment of the area and to the exclusion of
> thousands of tourists enjoying the area to the greatest possible degree. The present

concentration of development about the Upper and Lower Falls is gradually breaking down the natural conditions so that within a comparatively short while the area will be barren. Except for those who visit the lodge, it is not readily accessible to the other tourists without the intimate knowledge of the area or without a guide. . . . The circumstances are such that it would seem wise to try to correct these mistakes, and justify the effort for a number of reasons. *Conservation* is primary and that point is readily conceded. *Aesthetically* the present development is beginning to compete with the Canyon for attention. Gradually it becomes more prominent as the vegetation dies or is done away with. This alone should be reason enough for restoring it to its original state if possible. . . . *Economically* it is advantageous to concentrate this development at some other location. Under the present setup there are three separate and unrelated water and sewer systems. . . . The administration of the area would be facilitated if a well-organized scheme were carried out. . . . The object of such improvement would be eventually to remove all of the development away from the edge of the Canyon to an area better suited to such development and yet allow expansion on a well ordered scale.[15]

Recommendations for restoring the scenic beauty of the area were several. All development except for trails, paths, and observation points was to be removed from the edge of the canyon. Trails, roads, and parking were to be improved. Concessionaires' facilities, including a lodge, more than 300 cabins, and a campground with 173 tent cabins, were to be removed and similar facilities built at a new village site set back from the north side of the canyon. At the new site, the government would establish a campground based on the system of individual campsites and an amphitheater. The existing government campground had been laid out by Charles Punchard and improved in the early years of the landscape program. It had been heavily used and was the site of some of Davidson's first work in transplanting during the summer of 1927. By 1930, the Landscape Division resolved that the only way of saving the campground area was to move the campground elsewhere and allow the natural vegetation to recover. Eventually, all the frame platforms and stairways along the canyon were replaced with observation bays made of stonemasonry walls and flagstone terraces. Despite the strong wording of the master plan, it was many years before all the concessionaire's facilities were removed from the canyon rim and reestablished at Canyon Village.

Glacier Point was another area that the Landscape Division believed had been developed beyond the public interest. Yosemite's superintendent strongly argued that Glacier Point road should end at the campground, thereby eliminating any encroachment on the scenic point itself. He viewed Glacier Point as a spectacle to be developed by pathways and educational exhibits, not by road traffic. The landscape architects asserted that the ideal plan was to remove the hotel and the nearby lookout and provide a terminus at the rim with radiating paths and trails to various scenic overlooks. The master plans from 1932 on called for the redevelopment of this area as a pedestrian promenade having a rustic log guardrail along the edge of the rim, a new lookout, and connecting trails to various viewpoints, including the famous overhanging rock. Although the removal of the buildings was never approved (the hotel burned in the 1960s), the plan made it clear that such development as had already occurred was undesirable given the extreme importance of the point. Here the plan became a "tool" to visualize an ideal based on the principle of landscape preservation. The plan described the promenade:

> Glacier Point is perhaps the most superlative location in Yosemite National Park from which an unsurpassed view may be secured of the High Sierras. Under the present setup it is difficult for transient visitors to grasp or appreciate the magnitude of the vast panorama spread before them. With the adequate development of this promenade and observation point the visitors may be more eager not only to view the glorious scene, but also to learn a little of the forces of nature that brought about these gigantic transformations, and they will be impressed and pleased with the facilities the Park Service has provided for their utilization and enjoyment.[16]

The plans became a vehicle for putting forth the landscape architect's point of view, either in opposition to development proposed by superintendents or others or in favor of cleaning up or in other ways improving the scenic character of the parks. At Mount Rainier, the Landscape Division used the plans to object to the park concessionaire and engineer's proposal for the construction of a scenic road extending into Paradise Valley: "The Landscape Division has consistently opposed construction of this road on the grounds that it will generally depreciate landscape views from the Paradise area to have moving automobiles and a roadway between Paradise and the mountain, and because of the addition to existing scars which its construction will necessitate. Furthermore, it is believed that no real need will be met by its construction."[17]

Although the landscape architects opposed the project from a landscape standpoint, they were willing to cooperate with the park engineer to stake out a line of a "least objectionable nature." Similarly, they felt that the construction of a spur road between Narada Falls and the lower campgrounds at Paradise should be put off until it became "indispensable for traffic reasons," because of scarring from cut-and-fill operations and because the road would destroy much of the forest screen in an area already scarred by development.[18]

Aboveground telephone poles and wires were a continual annoyance to the landscape architects, who urged superintendents to relocate them underground for scenic effect and economical reasons. Mount Rainier's master plan carried the following argument:

The Landscape consideration of getting all wires out of sight is the main point, and surely worth the cost. . . . The idea that exposed wires must clutter the landscape, ruining views, detracting from the natural simplicity of the scenery and even preventing the taking of good kodak pictures from many points, is one thing which draws condemnation from every visitor. . . . But waiving all these esthetic values, the absolute impossibility of keeping lines in operation in the winter and the great cost of maintaining them through the summer, makes the economic angle of underground wires an appealing one.[19]

As ultimate plans for the development of the park, master plans were linked on the one hand to the purpose for which the park had been set aside. On the other hand, they were to uphold the broad policies of stewardship and management stemming from the 1918 and 1932 statements of policy. The ever present concern for justifying development is indicated in the following summary of progress included in Mount Rainier's 1938 master plan:

In order that this enjoyment and education may be available, the park must be accessible and developed areas must be built and maintained. The road system as described in the following pages will allow such accessibility and yet will make available to the automobile but one-fifth of the area of the park or less than 50 square miles. . . . Five developed areas, three major and two minor projects, with free auto campgrounds, comfort stations, water and sewerage systems, hotel and cabin facilities, and the proper quarters and equipment necessary for the maintenance organization are planned. The connecting road system is now 40% complete and the free camping facilities at Longmire and Paradise areas are about 90% complete and those at Yakima about 70% complete. . . . The completed development of the park contemplates leaving at least 80% of the entire area of the park in its primitive state and the north side has been set aside as a "Wilderness area" to have no roads or other man-made features within its boundaries, excepting the minimum number of trails for its protection and preservation. . . . A trail system is planned of approximately 300 miles, one-third of which will be standard tourist trails in the vicinity of the developed areas and the remaining two-thirds forest trails for the more adventurous nature lovers, but primarily for the proper protection of the park. This trail system is now about 70% complete. . . . The roads, trails, telephone systems, developed areas and other items of the park program are all in keeping with the organic law creating the National Park Service; to make available to the present generation and preserve for future generations the wonders and beauty of Mount Rainier National Park.[20]

Master plans became the guiding tool for the operation of the National Park Service. In 1942, one service spokesperson summarized their value:

They help the parks to preserve the scenery so that in their final development it will still appear that man has done nothing to alter the natural landscape. They keep constantly before planners and construction men the original concepts of the National Park Service—that provision for public use must not alter the natural beauty of parks and that developments must be harmonized with the typical character of the area. They caution the park administrator against permitting unwise building or use which might destroy the very thing the visitor comes to admire. They provide for adaptation to ever changing conditions while providing loyalty to the fundamental responsibility—the conservation of the park areas.[21]

In 1939, the park service issued *Master Plans: A Manual of Standard Practice for Use in the National Park Service,* to be used in developing the plans for 1941. This was the first comprehensive manual for completing plans, which after 1937 had been drawn up by the design staff of the regional offices. By this time, the process for developing plans was extensive and required data and preparation by specialists outside the Branch of Plans and Design (formerly the Landscape Division). The plans mirrored the expanding programs of the park service and the increasing numbers and types of parks entering the park system in the 1930s.[22]

The master plan had become the "controlling document for all development." The plan retained the format of a general development plan and a development outline. The general development plan, sometimes called a zoning plan, graphically illustrated all existing and proposed elements of the park's ultimate development and indicated the ownership and use of adjoining lands. The development outline now called for detailed sheets for each program area and served as a working tool to coordinate the thoughts and efforts of the various offices needing facilities. The superintendent was responsible for coordinating the field activities of the various specialists, and the Branch of Plans and Design was responsible for compiling the information and interpreting it graphically.

The road and trail systems were covered by separate drawings and narratives. Plans for each developed area continued to be prepared by the resident landscape architect and regional architect; in addition to all buildings, bridges, trails, and roads, plans were to include minor features, such as flagpoles and drinking fountains. Plans for telephone and radio systems and utility layouts, which were the responsibility of the Branch of Engineering, appeared on separate detailed maps.

One program to gain in importance and make use of the planning process during the 1930s was forest protection. Plans called for a map indicating the various types of vegetative cover present in the park. This map was used to rate fire hazards, indicate areas needing insect control or suffering from tree diseases, develop campgrounds, assess conditions for wildlife, plan for reforestation, control erosion, and chart plant succession. Reforestation maps were included when large-scale planting was being considered to correct erosion or restore primeval or historical forest conditions. Forest fire control maps charted existing and proposed improvements such as firebreaks, lookout stations, fire guard cabins, communication systems, caches of fire tools, sources of water, roads, and trails (B.1, 82).

Additional plans concerned the diverse issues facing different kinds of park units. Historical maps and interpretive statements, for example, became part of the planning for the historic sites, battlefields, and monuments such as the Statue of Liberty which had come into the park system in 1933.

Henry Hubbard wrote of national park plans in 1939, "The Master Plan is the essential machinery by which this planning is accomplished. . . . The Master Plan presents a complete graphic record of the designer's conception of the ultimate development, and its many parts represent the combined effort of all who are concerned with the policies governing the future use and protection of the park." [23]

Through annual revisions, year-to-year accomplishments were recorded and the ultimate plan refined as time progressed, "thus providing an outline of the existing conditions and a constantly improved statement of future policies." Hubbard recognized the value of the plans during the New Deal:

> The advance planning program set forth in the Master Plan is carried into execution through a long-range work program, based on the desired priorities of construction, allocation of funds required, and the personnel available to complete the work. The value of advance planning, with respect to the service rendered to the various administrators of park lands has been especially well demonstrated during the past few years of emergency activity when the Service was found ready with plans and prepared to offer immediate employment on worthwhile projects. (109)

As the United States entered World War II, the Civilian Conservation Corps ended and public works funding ceased. The preparation and revision of plans slowed dramatically during the war, and, except for new areas such as Big Bend, planning virtually ceased. Most staff had gone into the armed services or were working for the war effort. Those who remained spent their time working on "unsettled problems and policies that influence[d] park development," since no funds were available for construction. The process of master planning which Vint had spearheaded in 1930 withstood the test of time and was revived as the essential planning tool following the war. Vint reported in 1946,

> The continuity of the planning process has been maintained although the thread became very thin for a time. The machinery is intact and as personnel return and programs get under way, Master Plans will be brought up to date. Many park facilities, like our cities, are adequate for 1930 conditions. All indications are that

people will come in greater numbers than before and facilities to accommodate them are inadequate. There is much to be done on many new problems.[24]

The Planning Process in Action: The Story of Yakima Park

Yakima Park on Mount Rainier was one of the first national park villages to be developed entirely through the process of comprehensive planning established in the late 1920s by the Landscape Division. The development of Yakima Park illustrates how the plans were created and used as a tool for coordinating various park service activities and for protecting the landscape.[25]

In the mid-1920s, plans were made to open Mount Rainier to automobiles from the east and develop visitor facilities at Yakima Park. Also called Sunrise, the area was a subalpine plateau overlooking the moraine of Emmons Glacier, the mountain's largest glacier, and the White River valley. Stephen Mather himself was enthusiastic about this project, seeing it as a way to relieve crowding at Paradise on the mountain's southern flanks and to encourage greater visitation by connecting the park with cities east of the Cascade Mountains.

The road leading to the village was one of the first park roads to benefit from the improvements and innovations in landscape protection and design made by the San Francisco office in the roads program at this time. It was also the laboratory for developing new specifications and procedures for the design of bridges. The park service's varied landscape concerns and the emerging role of the Landscape Division in planning coalesced as Yakima Park took form. Here advances were made in several programs—from the rustic architectural design of buildings by the park service and concessionaire to community development. The plan included a circulation system of loop and spur roads and trails to give the visitor access to spectacular mountain scenery.

As early as 1915, Mather had envisioned opening up the east side of Mount Rainier to visitors. He had corresponded with local groups interested in a Cascades parkway that would join the new Naches Pass Highway, a state highway that crossed the Cascades and connected the Puget Sound area with the southeastern part of the state. The highway passed through the national forest adjoining the park to the east and was to travel along the east side of the mountain and connect with a road to Yakima Park.

The development of Yakima Park was just one part of a plan for the east side of the mountain and represents one of the service's first efforts in comprehensive planning. On his last trip to the western parks in July 1928, Mather traveled by horseback to view the site and consider the proposed plans. Accompanying him were Thomas Vint; Superintendent Owen Tomlinson; Henry Rhodes of the Rainier Park Company; Asahel Curtis, chairman of the park's advisory committee; and several other officials.

Yakima Park was located on a high plateau in the northeastern corner of the park, which was characterized by rolling terrain, subalpine vegetation, and two lakes, Shadow and Frozen Lakes. For a country broken by such extremes of high mountain peaks and deep canyons, the plateau was comparatively large and level, making it an ideal village site and destination for visitors. The park measured less than one mile long and one-half mile wide. It was bordered by Sunrise Ridge (or Sourdough Ridge) to the north and the White River Canyon to the south. The topography lay in a "concave sweep, very steep near the ridge and flattening to perhaps an eight per cent grade in the most level section adjoining the canyon rim." [26]

Given the pressing need to relieve crowding at Paradise, Superintendent Tomlinson noted that the area was "one of the extremely few within the park which could be reached by a highway without prohibitive cost, and which was large enough, and with topography accommodating enough, to make possible adequate facilities to care for crowds of people. Again the people of the surrounding country and others who [knew] something of Mt. Rainier Park were calling for a new 'playground' on the mountain." [27]

Several years later, landscape architect Ernest Davidson recalled, "The entire development was one within virgin territory, therefore, it was decided that every possible means be taken that it be well planned in advance. In this manner one of the most interesting of landscape architectural problems within any of the National Parks got under way." [28]

Davidson enthusiastically greeted the challenge of developing the east side of the mountain: "The views and scenery are so exceptionally fine that adequate description is difficult. This will be a wonderful development and I would like to help push it, with the hand in its building."

The construction of the Yakima Park Road was part of a long-term planning effort to open the east side of Mount Rainier to public traffic and entailed coordination with roads of the adjoining national forest and the state highway system. In 1926, the Bureau of Public Roads completed the preliminary survey for a sixteen-mile road connecting Yakima Park and the Naches Pass Highway. Construction of the park road began on August 26, 1927, through the cooperative agreement with the Bureau of Public Roads. The construction coincided with the Landscape Division's efforts to improve park roads by inserting clauses in construction contracts which required special attention to the preservation of scenery and landscape values. Landscape architect Ernest Davidson was assigned the job of supervising the road's construction from the landscape standpoint.

Builders encountered several problems in the construction of Section 3B, which extended from White River Crossing to Yakima Park, and Vint's office responded with a number of innovations. One of these was the development of rubble masonry walls and walkways at Station 55 in what became known as the Sunrise Ridge Loop. Replacing a line of switchbacks, the loop was an outgrowth

8.4. In July 1928, Director Stephen Mather (*right*), Mount Rainier's Superintendent Owen Tomlinson (*middle*), and Henry Rhodes, the president of the Rainier Park Company, inspected Yakima Park, a subalpine plateau on the Mount Rainier's eastern flanks, and made plans to develop the area for visitor use and enjoyment. *(Photograph by Asahel Curtis, courtesy Washington State Historical Society)*

of a single switchback at the eastern end of Sunrise Ridge. From this point at an elevation of 6,120 feet, on a clear day visitors could enjoy views south to the Oregon mountains and north across the Cascades to Canada. Constructed over two seasons in 1929 and 1930, the loop featured a native stone guardrail of the "mountain" type. Especially designed for this point, this type of rail could be used on other open, precipitous stretches of the Yakima Park Road where log guardrail was not suitable. The loop was immediately praised: "There can be no question that this scenic point is destined to become one of the best known in our country." Parking accommodated at least fifty automobiles, and walks and curbs were installed. The guardrail alone was described as "interesting" to the tourists and as having evoked "favorable comment" for being "in keeping with the surroundings."

The entrance to Yakima Park near the end of the road presented a technical and aesthetic problem. The original survey indicated a series of switchbacks along the steep incline just below the plateau. Preparing plans in winter of 1928–29, Vint's office found a solution for a more graceful and inviting entrance that eliminated the switchbacks and provided access to special points of interest. The result was described: "It follows, in long easy curves, a routing near the canyon rim which had no tendency to seemingly bisect the open parklike area, and which affords excellent and unobstructed views." The route was staked and special arrangements were made with the Bureau of Public Roads to preserve the scenery along the route by using modified procedures for blasting and by end hauling the excavated fill.

Four bridges were built along the Yakima Park Road from 1928 to 1931. As a group, these bridges represent the range of types created by the park service to meet the varied needs presented by topography and natural surroundings. The ninety-foot White River Bridge (1928) was a stone-faced concrete arch that replaced an old log-and-sawn-timber truss bridge built many years before. This was the first bridge to be designed and constructed along the road and the first to benefit from the masonry specifications introduced at the time by the Landscape Division. In addition to written specifications in the contract and on the plans, a "sample wall" was made and remade before any stonework was begun on the bridge. In the summer of 1928, Davidson placed assistant landscape architect Merel Sager in charge of building the sample wall and was greatly pleased with the results. The sample wall showed the type of masonry and the desired sizes, shapes, color, and textures of the stone to be used, giving the foremen and the workers on site a model to follow. The stone for the bridge was cut from a designated quarry near the bridge. Special attention was given to integrating the guardrail coping into the spandrel walls so that they appeared as one continuous and unified surface.

The sixty-foot Shaw Creek Bridge (1929) was constructed of huge logs. The stringers were cut from trees that Davidson had selected on site. Davidson described the design intent of the bridge: "We felt that this would impart a feeling of solidity, strength and durability, as well as being really in better proportion, considering the long span for a log structure." The road engineer reported, "Its rustic appearance lends charm to the primeval setting of this attractive little bridge."

The 132-foot Frying Pan Creek Bridge consisted of a steel arch with masonry abutments. Steel was used when local conditions made concrete spans impractical. The masonry abutments, however, helped create a smooth transition between the natural setting and the construction. Vertical jointing of the steel panels of the arch somewhat relieved the smooth steel surface.

The eighty-foot Klickitat Bridge (1931), like the White River Bridge, was a stone-faced arch that required the training of masons. This bridge was placed fifty feet above the water between the precipitous solid rock walls of the creek in a dense forest. Noted for its exceptional beauty, the site was located just above the White River Entrance Station. For these reasons, special care was given to the clearing of the site and the construction of the bridge. All operations, including the construction of a temporary bridge, were confined to the right-of-way, and no tote roads were allowed. A stone-faced arch ideally suited the site and setting, and detailed drawings were made by Vint's office for the masonry headwalls and the arch ring. Workmen were able to cut the ring stones for the arch from a nearby granite ledge following the shapes and sizes of stone indicated on the large-scale details provided by Vint's office. Davidson said the bridge "admirably fit its site and contains some of the best masonry work in Mt. Rainier Park."

The White River Entrance Station was situated near the park's eastern boundary in the late 1920s. In 1931, the boundaries of the park expanded to include the territory east to Naches Pass and the Tipsoo Lake area, where westbound travelers through the national forest got their first view of the ice-capped mountain. The station remained the principal administrative facility in the northeastern section of the park. A minor developed area with a combined ranger station and checking point, it included a parking area and comfort stations situated below the grade of the parking area and behind the screen of the trees. The site's natural vegetation of dense trees was preserved and cleared only to the edge of the building sites and parking area. A service road connected to an area for housing road crews and storing equipment. Like the station built at the Nisqually Entrance several years before, the station was constructed of logs and had a porte-cochère for weather protection. The contours of the site allowed for enlargement if necessary.

Several precautions were taken to minimize the effects of the road construction on the natural features. Construction camps were placed on the right-of-way to prevent damage to the surrounding landscape. A "log protection rail" was designed as a movable guardrail "to prevent damage to landscape values" and was placed about all tree groups in danger of being damaged by construction. It was also placed along stretches of highway where motorists were apt to drive off the road upon the soft volcanic soil but where heavy log guardrail was not needed for safety. The log rails were also used as barriers to limit parking in the picnic grounds and double as park benches. To prevent stones and soil from rolling beyond the toe of fill slopes, road engineer W. T. Utz developed a technique of creating windrows along the toe of the slopes with smaller trees cleared from the right-of-way. The windrows blocked the fall of the earth and debris during construction and prevented any damage to the vegetation beyond the slope. Two quarries providing crushed stone for surfacing the roads were located; one was inside and the other outside the park. Areas where stone was removed along the roads, called quarry banks, were shaped and sloped to a naturalistic form after construction.

During his visit in July 1928, Mather became concerned with the destruction caused by extensive dynamite blasting. Careless excavation at Yakima Park

Road in Mount Rainier and along Going-to-the-Sun Highway in Glacier led to increased supervision of road construction by the park service's landscape architects. Soon after, provisions designating certain areas for special excavation procedures appeared in all road contracts. Particular concern arose over the destruction that blasting methods such as sidecasting and "shooting" had on the landform and surrounding trees and vegetation. Likewise, when the burning of cleared timber got out of control, stricter regulations were placed on burning.

Landscape architects recognized the fragility of the subalpine meadows from the beginning and made efforts to transplant sod after grounds were graded. Native shrubs and trees were transplanted. Wood guardrails were placed along forested sections of the road where stone would have been out of place. Logs of Douglas fir and western red cedar were used for posts measuring fourteen to sixteen inches in diameter and eighteen inches high and for rails ten to eleven inches in diameter.

Engineer Utz reported, "Autumn paints the mountain maple, ash, and huckleberry vivid red, orange, and yellow. The sheer beauty of it all is startling enough to make even the most languid sit up and take notice: Nor is this all. Man has contributed his bit in the bridges Deadwood, Klickitat, Shaw Creek, Frying Pan and White River, and in the rustic station—all fit their environment perfectly." [29]

Since the earliest planning of Yakima Park, it had been understood that the hotel would occupy a prominent site on the rim overlooking the White River valley. When Davidson's first four plans, presented in January 1929, showed the hotel group (which now called for six hundred cabins and a lodge) in this position, Vint immediately opposed them on the grounds that they limited public access to the most scenic viewpoints and barred automobiles from reaching the Shadow Lake and Burroughs Mountain areas. Two plans drawn by Davidson in March 1929 moved the development away from the rim and across the plaza. Davidson laid cabins out in a curvilinear fashion and spread development out to the east or to the west of the administrative center. The Rainier Park Company, however, insisted on space for six hundred cabins in the center of the village. Vint's office offered a compromise plan in September, but it was unacceptable to the concessionaire. In all, Davidson drafted eight plans before one was finally agreed upon by the concessionaire and the park service in April 1930.

Vint commented on the version preferred by the concessionaire: "From a landscape point of view we are disappointed in the development of Yakima Park because the size of the developments that must be provided are of such large scale that they cannot be submerged sufficiently to preserve the original beauty of the park. Further, due to loose soil and thin ground cover, artificial planting will be necessary in the most used areas to stabilize the soil." [30]

It was finally decided to place the lodge and cabins on the north side of the village plaza away from the rim, "thus removing all construction away from

8.5. The view of Yakima Park in the 1931 General Development Plan for Mount Rainier National Park shows the results of the initial construction. Visible are the concession-aire's cabin cluster, the park administration and maintenance buildings, and the layout of roads and campsites for the new campground. *(Photograph courtesy National Archives, Record Group 79)*

that area between the road and the canyon rim." An area to the northwest of the plaza well beyond the administrative group was reserved for future develop-ment. Davidson remarked that "the plan was adopted, followed and [proved] satisfactorily workable with a smaller amount of landscape damage to natural conditions than such development usually involves."[31]

The government buildings were laid out on two sides of a triangular park-ing plaza. As with previous village developments, native materials were used and an architectural theme sought for the buildings. The most prominent and first to be built was the administration building, or park headquarters, called the block-house. Davidson sketched the design for the building in the winter of 1929, and A. Paul Brown, a new draftsman in Vint's office, completed the working draw-ings in February 1930. Davidson described his sources:

> Some time was spent on consideration of a suitable type of Government headquar-ters building. . . . We wished to build into the structure as much of local or his-

torical interest as might be secured without sacrificing other values. Yakima Park was known as a summer rendezvous of Yakima and other Indian tribes. Since their "architecture" offered no possibility of adaption, the next step was taken to the time when white pioneers of the locality erected buildings for protection against Indians or other enemies. The Historical Museum at Tacoma was searched for pictures of old structures, with a log blockhouse type in mind, which seemed quite adaptable.[32]

The log blockhouse thus established the architectural theme for the village. Davidson then worked out what he called a "modified" form of this "rustic architectural treatment" for the government utility structures. He remarked, "The combination of local stone with logs and shakes provides a touch of similarity which identifies the Government structures and makes a harmonious development."[33]

Details for locating the buildings, grading the area, and laying out walks and trails were worked out on a plan of the village drawn to a scale of one inch for every forty feet. Davidson staked out the roads and all foot and bridle paths. The government campground was located beyond the village on its own loop road. To provide parking and picnic areas for two to three thousand Sunday cars, roads beyond the entrance road and plaza were built. Spur roads ended in loops for parking and turning. The spur to the Shadow Lake area was developed for picnicking and provided trails to points of scenic beauty, and several lookouts were developed with observation terraces having naturalistic stonemasonry walls.

Numerous engineering and landscape problems were solved in the development of Yakima Park. Telephone and other wiring was placed underground. A power plant operated by turbine engines (in keeping with the policy for the noncommercial development of streams) was placed out of sight along a spur road. A gravity-driven system of water was installed throughout the area providing water from the reservoir at Frozen Lake by underground pipes to the village and to outlying picnic areas and campgrounds. A system of sewers was also installed connecting comfort stations and buildings throughout the park. Government and concessionaire's facilities around the plaza included a lodge, a multitude of cabins, a check-in station, an auto camp, a comfort station, headquarters buildings, a gas station, and several garages. Davidson had staked out the trails to scenic overlooks and spur roads to the outlying picnic areas and had located observation lookouts, trail bridges, and comfort stations outside the village. The campground was laid out in loop fashion on several tiers and was located just north of the administration building.

By 1930 the road was complete, including an extensive scenic overlook at Sunrise Point, which afforded views east to the mountain, north to Canada, and south to the Oregon Cascades. The concessionaire's lodge and cabins and the

8.6. Lookout Point on the loop trail above Yakima Park, as it appeared in 1932, was developed as a curvilinear observation bay with a battered masonry retaining wall and parapet. Walls were backfilled and surfaced with gravel from local rockwork to provide a safe, flat terrace that could accommodate large groups of visitors on foot or horseback. *(Photograph by George A. Grant, courtesy National Park Service Historic Photography Collection)*

park administrative building were in place. By July 1931 Yakima Park had sufficient camping, sanitary, and other facilities. It was ready to be opened.

The innovations that occurred during the development of Yakima Park reflected the extent of the evolution of the National Park Service's planning process and policies for integrating roads, trails, buildings, and scenic values in planned developments. The concessionaire's lodge and cabin court were built away from the rim of the canyon overlooking the Emmons Glacier, the White River outflow, and the ridge to the north. The plaza was defined by a large parking area bounded on two sides by space for park buildings and visitor services to be built in phases. Telephone lines were placed underground. A modern power plant was located away from the village screened by trees. A network of foot and horse trails with scenic overlooks connected the village with the canyon rim to the south and the ridge to the north.[34]

8.7. Photographed on a Sunday afternoon in the early 1930s, the picnic loop outside the Yakima Park village was the "end of the road" and attracted thousands of visitors the first season. A trail led to alpine trails and a nearby overlook offering splendid views of Emmons Glacier and Burroughs Mountain. *(Photograph courtesy National Park Service, Mount Rainier National Park)*

Although Davidson considered the development of Yakima Park to be one of the service's most interesting architectural problems and every possible means had been taken for its careful planning, he had reservations about the final result:

> It is true that, purely from a landscape viewpoint, the whole development might be classed as a failure since the area is far less attractive than it was before the first idea of development took root. On the other hand, from a purely landscape viewpoint, the project may be considered one of the greatest successes since the general appearance and result is far superior to those other developments with which comparison may be made, and 'just grew' like topsy.
>
> Hundreds of thousands may now easily see and enjoy the beauty of Yakima Park. Their spontaneous exclamation of delight, their almost universally expressed approval of the development, their manifest enjoyment and benefit of the area and the park are sufficient indications that good work has been accomplished.[35]

The construction of Yakima Park required the collaboration of engineers and landscape architects. The engineering feat was accomplished under extreme difficulty, for all supplies were hauled over fifty-five miles of mountain road still under construction. Resident engineer R. D. Waterhouse, who had worked in the park for four seasons and was well acquainted with the problems of terrain and climate, directed construction. Two assistant engineers with crews of five men each were employed on the Yakima Park development project. Superintendent Tomlinson praised the work of this team for its speed and efficiency "in the face of many difficulties." By the end of 1930, $97,150 had been allocated for the Yakima Park development. Of that, $3,000 was allotted for comfort stations, $15,200 for a sewer system, $14,000 for the water-supply reservoir, $19,350 for campground development, $5,000 for the administration building, $15,000 for parking areas, $15,000 for subsidiary roads, and $10,000 for foot trails. Additional money in 1931 extended the roads, trails, and water system and built a generating plant and electrical system.

Vint had visited the park several times during the year. He and Davidson directed all landscape matters in connection with the location and construction of roads and trails and the construction of bridges, buildings, and other improvements, including the extensive improvements of the Rainier Park Company. The work of landscape naturalization, village improvements such as stone stairways and curbs, and the construction of campstoves and an amphitheater for the campground were accomplished after 1933 by the Civilian Conservation Corps.

PART IV

Park and
Recreation
Progress since 1933

Chapter 9

A Decade of
National Park Development

*In any area in which the preservation of the beauty of Nature is
a primary purpose, every modification of the natural landscape,
whether it be by construction of a road or erection of a shelter, is an
intrusion. A basic objective of those who are entrusted with the
development of such areas for the human uses for which they are
established, is, it seems to me, to hold these intrusions to a minimum
and so to design them that, besides being attractive to look upon, they
appear to belong to and be a part of their settings.*

Arno B. Cammerer, *Park Structures and Facilities,* 1935

Beginning in the spring of 1933, New Deal programs made possible the
development and improvement of national parks at an unprecedented
speed. In the early 1930s under the administration of President Herbert
Hoover, the construction of Skyline Drive in the newly authorized Shenandoah National Park had begun through emergency appropriations for drought-
affected areas which had been instituted as the nation's concern for economic
stabilization grew. The programs implemented by President Franklin D. Roosevelt to boost employment in early 1933, however, provided the impetus for a
massive expansion of park development nationwide, from the construction of
roads and administrative facilities to forest preservation, landscape naturalization, roadside cleanup, campground construction, and recreational development. Above all, the programs of the 1930s put into operation and proved the
value of the master planning process spearheaded by the Landscape Division,
later renamed the Branch of Plans and Design, under Thomas Vint.

The two major programs to affect the development of the national parks
were (1) federal projects funded by emergency appropriations and administered
through the Public Works Administration (PWA) and (2) Emergency Conserva-

tion Work (ECW) carried out by the Civilian Conservation Corps (CCC). The PWA channeled special allotments to fund capital improvements in the national parks, such as roads and buildings. The work itself, including the clearing, grading, and surfacing of roads and the construction of bridges, culverts, and guardrails, was carried out according to National Park Service standards and designs with skilled labor provided by private contractors. ECW, on the other hand, was an interagency effort involving the Departments of Labor, Army, Interior, and Agriculture and administered by an interagency advisory board. From the beginning, the program was intended as a temporary emergency measure and required reauthorization periodically. In 1937, the program became an independent agency and was extended for several more years. At this time, the program was officially renamed the Civilian Conservation Corps, and all references to Emergency Conservation Work were dropped.

ECW was carried out by camps of CCC enrollees assigned to each park; it consisted largely of forest protection, cleanup, landscape naturalization, trail construction, village improvements, roadside planting, and the construction of small park structures such as trail bridges. It later included the construction of larger projects. All conservation work was under the direct supervision of the resident landscape architect for each park; other park specialists, such as naturalists and foresters, directed work related to their programs. The CCC technical staff—architects, landscape architects, and engineers—were actually employed by the National Park Service through ECW funds.

In addition to this influx of funds and labor, the National Park Service acquired responsibility for a number of new sites in this period. Several other administrative actions and relief programs had turned over new areas such as monuments, historic sites, parkways, and national seashores to the park service. Under Executive Order 6166 of June 10, 1933, the monuments and public grounds of the nation's capital, an assortment of national monuments previously under the U.S. Forest Service, and many battlefields and military cemeteries previously under the War Department were brought under the stewardship and management of the National Park Service. Moreover, in 1934, in cooperation with the new Federal Emergency Relief Administration (FERA), the National Park Service assumed leadership for nationwide recreational planning and began to develop model parks called recreational demonstration areas on land considered submarginal for agriculture. Once developed, these parks were to be turned over to state park systems. This role was strengthened by subsequent legislation solidifying a cooperative partnership of national and state park officials begun initially through the National Park Service's supervision of ECW in state parks. In addition, grants through the Works Progress Administration, established in 1935, added substantially to facilities in national, state, and metropolitan parks.

Public Works Administration Projects

The PWA was created by Executive Order 6174 on June 16, 1933, under the authority of Title II of the National Industrial Recovery Act (48 Stat. 200). The order called for a comprehensive program of public works "to increase the consumption of industrial and agricultural products by increasing purchasing power, to reduce and relieve unemployment, to improve standards of labor and otherwise to rehabilitate industry, and to conserve natural resources." President Roosevelt appointed Secretary of the Interior Harold L. Ickes administrator of the new agency.[1]

The PWA administered the program of federal and nonfederal works through allotments. Federal projects received funding based on their value to national planning and their role in fulfilling comprehensive plans prepared in advance. As a result, the National Park Service received funding for greatly needed capital improvements in all the parks and monuments. Projects ranged from the development and improvement of trails, roads, and water systems to the construction of a wide range of park buildings and structures, the most common of which were comfort stations, ranger stations, patrol cabins, fire lookouts, garages, residences, and maintenance shops. Some parks received funds for administration buildings and museums. Others received funds for campground development. Existing buildings in many parks were added to, improved, and adapted for new uses using PWA funds. Restoration projects were undertaken in national monuments, such as Casa Grande.

In the West, the influx of funds enabled the park service to build long-needed facilities and add to the administrative infrastructure required to meet the demands of increasing visitation. The development of facilities in the national monuments, such as Casa Grande, Petrified Forest, and Tumacacori Mission, received for the first time a regular source of funding. In the East, PWA funds made possible the development of facilities in the numerous memorials, battlefields, and reservations that had come into the system in 1933, as well as eastern parks such as Acadia, Shenandoah, and Great Smoky Mountains. PWA funds also made possible the acquisition of important land areas for the Blue Ridge Parkway and the construction of the Department of the Interior Headquarters in Washington, D.C.

During the first year of the PWA, the National Park Service received approval for roads and trail work valued at $17,059,450 and other physical improvements valued at $2,145,000. The master plans prepared by Vint's office during the preceding two years provided a ready-made outline of work projects that could be put into action immediately to provide relief to the unemployed. Work was done under contract with skilled labor subject to specifications drawn up by the Landscape and Engineering Divisions. Resident landscape architects reviewed the progress of each project and approved the completed work.[2]

Although the public works programs emphasized construction, this work had a strong relationship to the landscape design of the parks. First, all projects were based on master plans and as such shared the larger concern for site development and conformed to the principles for landscape protection and harmonization which underlined all park development. In addition, projects such as the stockade around the service area at Mount Rainier's Yakima Park and the fence and entry gate at Tumacacori Mission, although structural in nature, were important landscape features.

In 1933, the Landscape Division, renamed the Branch of Plans and Design, was given full responsibility for producing building plans, specifications, and estimates. As the demand for working drawings and updated master plans increased dramatically in summer of 1933, the design process and training program that Vint had instituted in the late 1920s changed. In July 1933, when the first public works allotments became available, Vint (who was now called chief architect) had a staff of fifteen, which included a structural engineer, as well as many landscape architects with varying degrees of experience. Most of these were resident landscape architects assigned to one or more parks in the West and were directing the landscape work of the CCC. Both the men assigned to the parks and those who worked in the office created plans, drawings, and specifications under the process Vint had set up in 1928.

Within two months, however, Vint's office had expanded dramatically. New members included architects and engineers as well as landscape architects with the skills to carry out the drafting and engineering required by the accelerated construction program. By November 1934, twenty-four additional designers had joined Vint's staff in San Francisco. Although this corps enabled Vint to meet the immediate demand for designs for public works projects in the parks, this new generation of designers lacked firsthand familiarity with the parks and direct contact with park superintendents. All design of working drawings for the western parks was now done by staff assigned to the San Francisco office. The resident landscape architects continued, however, to revise the master plans and review all drawings for their parks. These changes resulted in a loss of the informality and free exchange of ideas which had marked the late 1920s. There emerged the need for a well-defined approval process involving the park superintendents, the resident landscape architects and engineers, the chief architect, the chief engineer, the chief forester, the sanitary engineer, and the director of the park service.

Vint's own status changed as well. In late 1934, he moved to the park service headquarters in Washington, D.C., to head the Branch of Plans and Design. William G. Carnes was placed in charge of the Western Division, and Charles Peterson remained in charge of the Yorktown office, which became the Eastern Division. At this time, the Western Division was divided into geographical

9.1. The entrance to King's Palace in Carlsbad Cavern in 1934 illustrates the lighting and trail improvements made possible by Public Works Administration funds. The trail formed a loop that followed an undulating line among the cave's principal features. A smooth trail surface was made from earth and stone that had been removed from the cave floor during cleanup. Larger rocks formed a coping along the paths as well as the dry-laid walls that supported the trail. *(Photograph by George A. Grant and Herbert Kennicott, courtesy National Park Service Historic Photography Collection)*

districts headed by Ernest Davidson, Merel Sager, Harry Langley, John Wosky, Howard Baker, Herbert Kreinkamp, and Kenneth McCarter.[3]

All designers in the service were consolidated into the western and eastern offices, where the architect, structural engineer, mechanical engineer, specifications writer, and estimator could work together and efficiently complete the massive volume of public works projects. This arrangement was successful, building on Vint's idea for a professional design office. Recounting the achievement of the Western Division from 1933 to 1937, architect E. A. Nickel wrote, "It was due to this complete organization that the entire Public Works Building Program was brought up to a satisfactory conclusion, despite many unknown factors at the time, and the continuous change in building conditions and prices of labor and materials in the National Park and Monument areas."[4]

The national parks used PWA funds to build a wide variety of structures, from administrative and utilitarian projects such as patrol cabins, fire lookouts, and blacksmith shops, to landscape structures such as gates and steps, to utility systems and facilities for visitor use. The Western Division received a total of 185 PWA allotments from 1933 to 1937. These allotments covered projects as diverse as steps to the cliff at Montezuma Castle National Monument, the naturalist's residence at Lassen Volcanic National Park, the superintendent's residence at General Grant, barns at Sequoia's Redwood and Ash Mountain headquarters, innumerable snowshoe cabins at Mount McKinley (later Denali), picnic ground improvements at Muir Woods, an administration building at Crater Lake, a pump house and water system at Canyon de Chelly National Monument, and repairs to the lighthouse at Cabrillo National Monument (2–7).

At Mount Rainier, public works projects included the construction of a stockaded fence at Yakima Park to screen the maintenance sheds, garages, and equipment from public view, thus enclosing the work yard of the park village. Screens of vegetation were impractical in this subalpine terrain, where wind, temperature, and soil conditions hindered tree growth. The design of the stockaded fence was in keeping with the pioneer theme introduced by the blockhouse-style administration building. Public works funds were also used for the construction of log-and-stone comfort stations at the camping and picnic grounds at Yakima Park and a log ranger station and frame warehouse at the White River Entrance. Constructed elsewhere in the park were four fire lookouts, several fire patrol cabins, a number of fire guard cabins and caches, and even an icehouse. PWA funds were also used to develop campgrounds.

At Yosemite, housing demanded much of the designers' attention, and a number of residences were built, in the form of individual homes, apartment houses, and duplexes. There the funds also went toward developing a campground at Tuolumne Meadows, building cabins for the Indian Village, and constructing the Henness Ridge Fire Lookout. In Yellowstone, at the Mammoth Hot Springs headquarters, a large apartment house was built for rangers, and utility

9.2. During the 1930s, funding from the Public Works Administration made possible the construction of much-needed housing for park employees in Yosemite National Park. Single-family residences took the form of Craftsman-style bungalows and had redwood siding, wooden shingles, stone foundations, an entrance porch with peeled log railings, and a stone chimney. Each house had a living room, dining room, kitchen, three bedrooms, and two baths. The Civilian Conservation Corps removed dangerous limbs from the surrounding oaks and planted ferns, azaleas, and other native plants as part of a program to beautify and naturalize Yosemite Village. *(Reprinted National Park Service, "Report on the Building Program from Allotments of the Public Works Administration, 1933–1937")*

buildings were constructed. At Grand Canyon, a community building was built, in addition to many maintenance shops and residences. At new parks, such as Grand Teton, an administration building, entrance stations, and a superintendent's residence were constructed. At Glacier, sorely needed backcountry patrol cabins and fire caches were built, as well as many snowshoe cabins and several boathouses.

In all of these projects, emphasis was placed on principles of landscape protection and harmonious design. In the 1930s, the Branch of Plans and Design relied heavily on the standards and specifications developed in the late 1920s and benefited greatly from the experience of Punchard, Hull, Vint, and the service's first resident landscape architects, including Ernest Davidson, John Wosky, Merel Sager, Kenneth McCarter, and Charles Peterson. Practices well established by the 1930s were readily incorporated into the public works building program. Designers endeavored to harmonize structures with the natural surroundings by using native materials. Road building adhered to the specifications drawn up by Vint's office and maintained the characteristics that were recognized as hallmarks of national park roads. The landscape designs for bridges, which routinely included elevations and details for arch rings, were increasingly prepared by engineers in the Western and Eastern design offices. The standards for trail construction which had been developed for western parks by chief engineer Frank Kittredge in the late 1920s were published as a circular for the parks in 1934 and, through the substantial PWA funds available for trail building, were applied to parks nationwide, including the Great Smoky Mountains and Shenandoah National Parks in the East. The concern for naturalism and harmonization which determined the construction of surface trails was also applied to underground trail construction and improvements in parks such as Carlsbad Cavern. As the National Park Service inherited the parkways in the East, including the Mount Vernon Parkway near the nation's capital, and as the Eastern Division gained experience in building linear park roads and parkways, such as Skyline Drive in Shenandoah and the Colonial and Blue Ridge Parkways, major advances were made in the aesthetics, kinetics, and engineering of park roads.

Although the principles and practices for park development were standardized, their applications were highly individual based on the unique character of each park and the site and setting selected for construction. The western parks, for example, covered many types of areas, such as forested and wilderness areas, deserts, barren mountainous areas, rocky and treeless areas, areas of heavy rain and snow, and areas of no rain. The Western Division adopted a specific type of building for each location, such as flat-roofed adobe or pueblo structures in the Southwest and log or heavy timber constructions in heavily forested areas. As they adopted these forms, designers acknowledged the cultural influence of Spanish and Native American traditions in the Southwest and the pioneer traditions of covered-wagon days in other parts of the West.

The designs were simple and functional but remained consistent with the architectural themes that had been developed for each park or, in new parks, took on appropriate characteristics drawn from pioneer, indigenous, or other local forms. Designers of utilitarian buildings endeavored to find obscure locations out of the sight of park visitors and simple functional and economical designs that harmonized with the natural setting. Because of the rapid production of drawings and the cost limitations placed on construction, new designs frequently lacked the careful attention to detail which marked the late 1920s and early 1930s.

Specific objectives guided the work of the Branch of Plans and Design during the 1930s. In a 1937 report on the achievements of the Western Division, E. A. Nickel summarized six basic principles. First, buildings should be in harmony with the natural surroundings and should be secondary to the landscape, unlike the buildings in a city or town. Second, all buildings in any one area should be in harmony with each other, having similar materials and elements of design—for example, roofs of the same type built of the same material and having the same slope. Third, horizontal lines should predominate. Fourth, stones and logs used in construction should be in scale with each other and their surrounding natural counterparts, providing a well-balanced and unified design. Fifth, where large trees and rock outcroppings were likely to dwarf buildings, giving them the appearance of being under scale, stones and logs used in construction were to be slightly oversized. Finally, rigid, straight lines were to be avoided wherever possible, "creating the feeling that the work was executed by pioneer craftsmen." This last principle applied to the adze-hewn ends of logs, stonemasonry, ironwork and hardware, and the numerous architectural details that made up a park building (12–13).

Before starting a building project, designers carefully studied the field conditions of each site, based on information generally provided by the park superintendent or the resident landscape architect. Designers considered the available natural materials and transportation, the proximity of the site to park headquarters, and any unusual factors that might affect the cost and design of the structure. Certain types of structures were more problematic and costly than others. Fire lookouts, snowshoe cabins, and outlying ranger stations required that materials be transported to remote locations, often on mountaintops. Hauling in supplies for the work crew and construction materials such as cement, lumber, glass, hardware, and water added substantially to the cost of backcountry construction. Materials were often carried on muleback, making it impossible to transport materials larger than eight feet long. The cost of construction in a large park such as Grand Canyon varied from location to location. Costs on the South Rim were lowest because of proximity to the railroad and park headquarters. On the North Rim, materials had to be transported two hundred miles from the railroad terminal, and at Phantom Ranch on the floor of the canyon, materials were transported by mule requiring a one-day trip. At Yosemite, construction occurred in three principal sites of varying distances from the railroad: the park headquarters area in Yosemite Valley, fourteen miles from the railroad; Glacier Point and Wawona, one-half day's trucking time from headquarters; and Tuolumne Meadows, approximately one day's trucking time from headquarters. At Yellowstone, the distance between park headquarters and building sites varied from five miles to a full day's trucking time, and some sites were accessible only by mule (13–14).

Because of their functions and the need for sturdy construction, many of the structures built with public works allotments entailed a substantial amount of concrete work. This work, whether in the form of concrete footings or walls, was carried out in a very different manner from that in cities or towns, where sacks of cement and aggregate stone were delivered by truck to a site and water was piped in by public utility. In national parks, concrete materials were gathered from nearby gravel and sand beds, and water was collected from nearby streams and springs and sometimes brought to the site by mule. Not surprisingly, at Mount McKinley National Park, where cement cost four dollars per sack, compared with seventy-five cents to a dollar in most other parks, construction costs were the highest of any park (14–15).

PWA projects fostered an increasing reliance on modern materials that were long lasting and durable and simple and functional designs that were adapted to the topography and character of their setting. In locations where rustic log-and-stone construction was out of place, where there was little supply of native building materials, or where the scale or utilitarian purpose of a structure made construction with native wood and stone impractical, designers experimented with substitute materials. Concrete was the most common choice, and efforts were made to stain concrete walls a natural color or give them a texture, often by imprinting the natural grain of carefully selected form boards. Climate and the character of nearby vegetation were important factors in the selection of materials, and culturally inspired designs were used whenever possible. Volcanic rocks, for example, formed the walls of overlooks at Hawaii, while corrugated iron provided a practical material for roofing.

Emergency Conservation Work

On March 31, 1933, President Roosevelt signed the Federal Unemployment Relief Act, calling for Emergency Conservation Work on public lands and the creation of a body of unemployed and generally unskilled men called the Civilian Conservation Corps (CCC). Emergency Conservation Work was immediately organized, and in mid-May 1933 the National Park Service was prepared to open 63 camps accommodating 12,600 men for work in national parks and monuments. Chief forester John Coffman was placed in charge of ECW in national parks. Headed by Robert Fechner until his death on December 31, 1939, the CCC included camps for work not only in the national parks but also in national forests, wildlife reserves, and state parks and forests, as well as camps working on soil conservation projects. The work of the state park camps was under the direction of the National Park Service, which hired skilled technicians, using ECW funds,

9.3. While the Bright Angel Trail in Grand Canyon was rebuilt to the advanced standards of the National Park Service's Engineering Division, shelters along the trail were constructed by the Civilian Conservation Corps. Perched above the trail and fashioned from native stone and juniper thatching to blend with the natural setting, the first shelter was located two miles below the canyon rim. It offered visitors traveling on foot or mule-back a shady spot to rest and enjoy the scenery. *(Photograph by George A. Grant, courtesy National Park Service Historic Photography Collection)*

to assist in the development and planning of state parks systems. Conrad L. Wirth of the National Park Service was placed in charge of the state park ECW program. During the first enrollment period, which extended through September 1933, 105 camps were assigned to state park projects in twenty-six states. By the end of 1933, those working in state and national parks included 35,000 enrollees and approximately 2,300 men in supervisory and advisory capacities.[5]

From the beginning, the National Park Service fully supported the social program of the CCC. Superintendent Owen Tomlinson of Mount Rainier acknowledged the moral and spiritual value of conservation work in the parks:

> In all our plans for carrying out the Emergency Conservation Work in this park, the training of these young men in woodsman craft and an appreciation of honest

labor go hand in hand. We shall expect them to do a fair day's work to contribute to the improvement and security of the park. In turn we want to contribute to their self-respect and to give them a wholesome outlook on life that comes about from honest labor amid inspiring scenic surroundings. We hope to send them back to their homes better mentally and physically to carry throughout their mature years a love of nature and active desire to help protect and perpetuate the nation's most valued scenic area, the national parks.[6]

As many as six or seven camps were assigned to the larger national parks at one time. Each was composed of two hundred men involved in work projects that would last six months. The park service was allowed to hire a small number of skilled local experienced men, called LEMs, who brought a knowledge of local climate, vegetation, building materials and practices, and environmental conditions. At first enrollees were housed in canvas tents rigged upon wooden platforms arranged in orderly rows. Thomas Vint visited some of the parks and helped to select locations for the first camps. As the CCC became more firmly established, these tent colonies were replaced by sturdier wooden structures, such as temporary army barracks and other facilities, arranged in a quadrangle around a parade ground and flagpole. Evidence of some camps remains today in the form of concrete pads, paths and plantings, and isolated buildings. Once skilled in landscape work, CCC enrollees laid out paths and beautified the grounds of their camps with transplanted trees and shrubs.[7]

Emergency Conservation Work in the national parks made possible work that the park service had been trying to justify under ordinary appropriations, including the landscape naturalization program under Vint's Landscape Division and the forest protection work under John Coffman's Forestry Division. Work undertaken in the first year included forest improvement projects, construction and maintenance of firebreaks, clearing of campgrounds and trails, construction of fire and recreation-related structures, road and trail building, forest fire suppression, survey work, eradication of exotic or disease-causing plants, erosion control, flood control, tree disease control, insect control, campground construction, and general landscape work. Although forest protection and fire control were envisioned as the primary purposes of Emergency Conservation Work, scenery preservation and improvements in landscape design were viewed as complementary activities. The director's summary of the first year's work stated that not only was fire hazard reduced, but the appearance of forest stands was greatly improved by cleanup along the park highways:

Many acres of unsightly burns have been cleared and miles of fire roads and truck trails have been constructed for the protection of the park forest, and excellent work was accomplished in insect control and blister rust control and in other lines of forest protection; improvements have been made in the construction and development of telephone lines, fire lookouts and guard cabins; and landscaping and erosion control have been undertaken.[8]

Emergency Conservation Work was envisioned as a temporary relief measure and continued to be reauthorized through the 1930s. By October 1934, with the expansion of the program and the relaxing of rules regarding the hiring of LEMs, there were 102 camps in national parks and 263 camps in state parks. On September 25, 1935, Roosevelt called for the reduction of enrollees to 300,000 by June 1, 1936, but he modified the figure to 350,000 in response to public opposition. The number of national park camps was reduced from 446 to 340. The number of camps in state parks was also reduced in 1936. The size of camps was cut from 200 to 160 men at this time.[9]

On June 28, 1937, Congress passed new legislation officially changing the name of the program to the Civilian Conservation Corps, giving it status as an independent agency, and extending it three more years. At this time, park service assistant director Conrad Wirth was in charge of the CCC program in both national and state parks and was designated to represent the department in meetings of the CCC advisory council. This coincided with the authorization for the National Park Service to undertake a nationwide recreation study in cooperation with state and municipal authorities to determine regional recreational needs and inventory existing and potential park and recreation areas.

Prior to 1937, the supervision of ECW in national parks was entrusted to the Branch of Forestry, under the direction of John Coffman, the chief forester in the Western Field Office. ECW focused on projects such as the construction of truck trails and telephone lines for fire control, protection of trees against white pine blister rust through the eradication of ribes species, road clearing and planting, prevention of soil erosion, and beautification projects (many of which would now be considered ecologically harmful) such as the clearing of dead trees from Jackson Lake in Grand Teton and the sites of destructive forest fires in Glacier.

National park policies, including the preservation of scenic values and natural features and the ban on exotic plants and animals, were upheld in the CCC work in national parks from the beginning. They were strongly stated as "fundamentals and policies" in Superintendent Tomlinson's letter welcoming CCC camp superintendents to Mount Rainier as temporary members of the National Park Service:

> The national parks are the most beautiful and interesting scenic spots in our country selected by the Congress and supported by Federal appropriations for the benefit and enjoyment of the people. The use of these national parks is unique in the history of the administration of the Nation's land areas. All other lands are used primarily to serve man's economic needs, but in the national parks the law requires that nature shall be supreme and that man must conform to the natural processes.

The twin purposes of the establishment of a national park are its enjoyment and use by the present generation, with its preservation unspoiled for the future; to conserve the scenery, the natural and historic objects and wild life therein, by such methods as will ensure that their present use leaves them unspoiled for the future. The administration aims to retain these areas in their natural condition, sparing them all vandalism and disturbance by improvements and developments. Exotic animal and plant life shall not be introduced. There shall be no commercial enterprises of any nature except those necessary for the comfort or convenience of visitors in their enjoyment of the area. Timber shall never be considered from a commercial standpoint but may be cut only when necessary in order to control the attacks of insects, or diseases, or otherwise to conserve the scenery or the natural or historic objects. Trees may be removed in limited number only for the purpose of providing access to outstanding scenic objectives or when necessary to provide shelter or other minor facilities that aid in the enjoyment of the region.[10]

CCC camp superintendents were to cooperate closely with national park staff, including the chief ranger, the park engineer, the general foreman, the park fiscal agent (who was the assistant superintendent), and the naturalist. Service specialists, including the chief architect, the fire-control expert, and the chief engineer from the Western Field Office, were also to be involved in camp projects. During the first six periods, which extended from April 1933 to March 1936, the park resident landscape architects, who were employed by the Branch of Plans and Design, worked closely with the architects and landscape architects hired by the park and assigned to one or more CCC camps within the park.

At Mount Rainier, resident landscape architect Ernest Davidson would have "full charge" of all matters pertaining to the protection of the landscape and important natural features. Tomlinson told camp superintendents that their "cooperation with Mr. Davidson" would be especially required, as this official had "full responsibility" for carrying out the fundamental policies of the National Park Service for the protection and preservation of the natural features, and it was this work that he desired to emphasize as "second in importance only to protection against fire and other destructive elements."[11]

Work was broken into jobs that could be completed during a six-month period, beginning in April 1933. Some parks had active camps all year round; those in colder, more rugged climates operated camps only from April to October. Camp superintendents and park landscape architects filed quarterly and semiannual reports of the work completed. Progress was measured in terms of the number of men and days spent on each project. Each job received a number based on a classified system of work tasks. This approach favored small projects that could be completed in a relatively short time. Large projects were broken down into a series of smaller ones that could be carried out consecutively. A single project, such as the landscape development at the mouth of Bright Angel

9.4. The landscape architect's concern for naturalism extended to the construction of stepped earthen and rock dams to impound water for wildlife and fire suppression. With the help of teams of mules in the backcountry of Grand Canyon National Park, enrollees from the Powell Camp built several dams of dry-laid native rock masonry which were backfilled with earth and blended with the natural surroundings. *(Photograph courtesy National Archives, Record Group 79)*

Creek in Grand Canyon near Phantom Ranch, would consist of many jobs frequently extended over several enrollment periods.

Jobs were classified according to numbers assigned to different types of conservation work. Landscape projects fell into several categories and frequently overlapped with engineering, architectural, or forest protection work. For example, Job 4 covered roadside cleanup for fire prevention, while Job 11 covered general cleanup not related to fire prevention. Job 46 covered erosion control and included clearing debris from streambanks and sloping and planting them. Job 14 covered the construction and maintenance of trails. Job 27 covered "other public campground facilities" and included items such as the construction of a swimming pool adjacent to the public campground at Phantom Ranch. Job 38 covered the collection of seeds; Job 11 covered the planting of trees, shrubs, seeds, and sod. Job 132 covered the construction of guardrails along roadways, at scenic overlooks, and along rim trails. Job 53 was a general category for landscaping and included numerous small-scale improvements, such as the grading of parking areas, the installation of curbs and walks, and the construction of seats and water fountains, which were important aspects of the development of park villages, campgrounds, overlooks, trails, and roads.

Distance, natural conditions, and a lack of tools made many projects difficult and time consuming. One of the most extensive cleanup projects was at Jackson Lake in the newly created Grand Teton National Park. When National Park Service director Horace Albright announced the emergency conservation program for national parks, he specifically cited artificial lakes, such as Jackson Lake, as areas that would greatly benefit from the efforts of the CCC. Large-scale clearing projects were also planned for several locations in Glacier where forest fires had ravaged the landscape and left much timber dead and dying.

The condition of Jackson Lake had been a continual source of concern for Albright, who, as the former superintendent of Yellowstone, had for many years advocated and worked toward making Grand Teton a national park. His advocacy had been fueled partly in recognition of the lake's scenic potential.

Cleanup projects were guided by a concern for both scenery preservation and the elimination of fire hazards. Punchard had established the precedent for clearing for scenic reasons at Lake Eleanor in Yosemite about 1920, following Charles Eliot's ideas for improving the beauty of public reservations in Massachusetts. As superintendent at Yellowstone, Albright had been a champion of roadside cleanup and had successfully undertaken the first large-scale work of this type in the national parks with private funds donated by John D. Rockefeller.

The cleanup of Jackson Lake took several years. Two separate CCC camps, each with two hundred men, were employed over several periods to clear the lake and surrounding shore. Thousands of acres were eventually cleared, and the lake achieved a scenic character that would draw visitors for decades to come. Work entailed removing debris by cutting it and hauling it to places where it could be piled and eventually burned when weather conditions allowed. Camps were set up in remote places. Conditions were primitive, equipment lacking, and the work extremely tedious. The area needing cleanup greatly exceeded the early estimates. One particularly difficult section was the far shore of the lake. Here, at the beginning of the third period in April 1934, an estimated 500 acres were to be cleared by Camp NP-2. A survey of the area after work began, however, indicated that 1,760 acres needed clearing. By October 1, 1,300 acres had been cleared. Meanwhile Camp NP-3, working on the other side of the lake, had piled up 16,300 cords of wood, ready to be burned when autumn weather permitted and when there was little hazard of forest fires. The superintendent of Camp NP-2 described the difficulty his men encountered in this project:

9.5. Depicted in August 1933, the cleanup of Jackson Lake in Grand Teton National Park was slow and tedious, requiring more than three years' labor by several camps of the Civilian Conservation Corps. Enrollees hauled dead and submerged timber, cut debris, and stacked it up to be burned in the autumn. This work created a beautiful lake that has attracted and inspired visitors ever since. *(Photograph by George A. Grant, courtesy National Park Service Historic Photography Collection)*

In this cleanup work there was a considerable area of standing timber — large trees which have been killed by the water — and thousands of cords of loose logs, trees, brush that had been washed into drifts by the waves of the lake and piled in almost inextricable masses. This coupled with wet and boggy ground made an almost impossible task. . . . In addition, this camp is short on tools and equipment. No power other than hand has been used in this work, with the exception of two or three weeks when an engine hoist was put into service to clean an old river bed and six teams were used the past two months. The lake shore is so steep and the camp is situated as to make it impossible to use trucks to transport the men to and from work making it necessary . . . for them to walk some three to four miles each way to work.[12]

At the beginning of the ECW program, park superintendents had been asked to outline the work that the CCC could accomplish in their park. The prospectus for CCC work at Yosemite listed work under the following categories: roads or fire motorways, fire buildings or structures, fire lanes, fire trails, bridle paths and other trails, insect-control projects, blister rust control projects, type-mapping projects, forestry projects, proposed telephone construction, planting operations, roadside cleanup and landscaping, cleanup operations in cut-over areas, reclamation of meadows, and miscellaneous operations. Conservation work was dominated by projects for fire control and forest protection. Planting operations included the reforestation of approximately 320 acres in the vicinity of the Crane Flat fire lookout and small planting projects for landscape purposes in Yosemite Valley and other places. Roadside cleanup planned for approximately 28 miles of the new Wawona Road called for the removal of snags, dead trees, and trees felled during insect-control work. Especially important were the "flattening, rounding, and planting of cut banks for erosion control." Cleanup operations were slated for areas that had been logged near Chinquapin, Eleven Mile Meadow, Wawona, Crane Flat, and Merced Grove. Old lumber camps were to be removed, dangerous trees cut, underbrush thinned, and old shacks, fences, and trash removed in various areas. Sixteen hundred acres of meadow at Wawona, Tuolumne Meadows, and Yosemite Valley were to be reclaimed by clearing the small growth that was "choking out" the beautiful meadows. Miscellaneous operations included erecting a 12-mile fence along one side of the park boundary to eliminate grazing, allow reforestation, and prevent erosion. They also included campground construction, the painting of exposed surfaces of fresh rock cuts along the Wawona Road, drainage of meadowland for mosquito control, selective clearing for vistas, and collection of survey data for conservation work.[13]

Although the majority of work concerned forest preservation, it was the work called cleanup or intended for "landscape purposes" which most directly affected the appearance of areas frequented by visitors. ECW covered many of the activities that Vint had included under landscape naturalization. It also covered many projects that called for a combination of supervision and unskilled labor, such as the construction of minor roads, particularly truck or fire roads, which were constructed to lay gently upon the land but often allowed steeper grades than public roads. As the CCC program proceeded, more and more attention was given to landscape projects, community improvements, recreational development, and the construction of visitor facilities.

Transplanting and planting wild vegetation was an important activity in most camps, and CCC work followed the best nursery practices of the day. Great care was required in transplanting trees and shrubs from construction sites or obscure parts of the park to areas where screens were needed or construction scars naturalized. Trees and shrubs were dug and balled, wrapped in burlap, and transported either to a site in need of screening or naturalization or to a nursery where they could be held until needed. In some cases, trees were boxed to hold soil intact and prevent damage to roots. The box could then be hoisted onto a truck and transported to a suitable place for planting. Before planting, it was necessary to prepare the soil. In many cases this meant hauling in loam and soil and fertilizing it. Mulch was spread on the ground around new plantings and areas watered regularly for several months to ensure the survival of transplanted materials. The resident landscape architect for each park directed this work, selecting sources for both loam and plants and ensuring naturalistic and successful results. In some parks, trucks were rigged with tanks from which water could be sprayed onto the roadside and other newly planted areas.

Collecting seeds was also an important ECW activity and entailed gathering seeds from plants and trees in the proper season and propagating the seeds in prepared soil at a later date. At Sequoia and Yellowstone, where large nurseries were developed, evergreen seeds were collected mechanically from cones, planted, and grown under careful supervision. Within several seasons, seedlings could be transplanted to parks where needed.

As a result of master planning and the supply of funds and labor for work at various scales, it was possible for the first time to coordinate large-scale and small-scale projects and treat development in a comprehensive way, from the selection of locations to the grading and planting of building sites to conceal construction scars and blend the final development harmoniously into the surrounding environment. Through this process, park designers achieved an illusion that nature had never been disturbed. Trees and shrubs selected for protection and preservation during the siting process became indistinguishable from transplanted plants. Sod, grasses, and perennial wildflowers were equally important to achieving naturalistic scenery, whether around a residence or administration building or alongside a road. So successful was landscape naturalization that, in most parks, it is impossible today to distinguish the planted vegetation from the natural and the construction site from its undisturbed setting.

Mount Rainier

Emergency Conservation Work made possible the further development of Longmire Village, Paradise, Yakima Park, and other areas of Mount Rainier according to the master plans. Five CCC camps were located in various areas of the park in June 1933. During the first six-month period, 172 miles of telephone lines were maintained and another 14½ miles constructed. Twenty miles of firebreaks were cut and 700 cubic yards of channel cleared. For fire protection, 656 acres of timber were cleared. CCC enrollees cleared underbrush from 47 miles of roadside to a depth of 200 feet for scenic purposes; constructed twelve horse trails totaling 25 miles and improved an additional 114 miles; built three footbridges; cleared campgrounds; constructed 6 miles of power lines between the headquarters at Longmire and the Nisqually Entrance to the park; erected 2,000 feet of cribbing along the Nisqually River to form a dike to keep the bank from washing away and to protect the buildings downstream at Longmire; controlled white pine blister rust in 254 acres; planted native trees, ferns, sod, and shrubs at the Carbon River ranger station, Longmire, and Yakima Park; and constructed several trailside shelters.[14]

Landscape naturalization received immediate attention on the east side of the park in the vicinity of Yakima Park. During the first enrollment period, enrollees of the White River CCC camp planted eighteen thousand square feet of meadow sod, constructed stone steps and walks, and planted fir trees and shrubs around the front of the new blockhouse and comfort station. At Sunrise Point, trees and shrubs were planted around the observation terrace. Along the Yakima Park Road, road banks were flattened and rounded to control erosion.[15]

Naturalization on the east side of the park continued for several years. In 1934, more than two hundred trees, varying in height from three to six feet, and hundreds of shrubs were planted around the village plaza at Yakima Park. Sod, heather, and shrubs of mountain box, huckleberry, and mountain ash were interspersed with subalpine firs and other evergreens to imitate natural groupings of plants. Low shrubs and sod were planted at Emmons Glacier Overlook, one of the observation terraces of native stone constructed high above the White River drainage several years before. Trees and shrubs were also planted at the trail intersection just above the point to impede trampling and prevent trail erosion. Additional sod and heather were planted at Sunrise Point, where walks were being surfaced with crushed rocks and topsoil.[16]

At Yakima Park, an amphitheater for naturalists' lectures and activities was constructed. Based on an octagonal design by ECW landscape architect Halsey M. Davidson, it featured thirty log seats arranged to seat 220 persons around a bonfire pit and before a viewing screen. Hauled nine miles from the White River, the logs were peeled, cut to length, leveled, and smoothed to form low, flat benches. The seats were arranged in five sections around the pit with aisles between the sections and rear seats slightly elevated above those in front. Topsoil was placed behind the projection screen to raise the grade, and a thick backdrop of evergreens was planted. A dense coppice of whitebark pine (*Pinus albicaulis*), mountain hemlock (*Tsuga mertensiana*), subalpine fir (*Abies lasiocarpa*), and Engelmann spruce (*Picea engelmannii*) was planted around the amphitheater, "protecting it from winds as well as beautifying the popular spot." Most dominant on the open plateau were clusters of spire-topped subalpine firs. The arrangement of trees allowed for unobstructed views of the mountain to the west, the screening of nearby campsites, and passage by narrow footpaths.[17]

The windswept, subalpine plateau with its extreme climate, short growing

9.6. As this 1940 view shows, many changes occurred in Yakima Park on Mount Rainier during the New Deal era. A lodge and additional cabins were added to the concessionaire's housekeeping camp. A stockaded fence was built around the maintenance yard, and a second blockhouse and community building (under construction) were added to the government buildings. Walkways and steps were constructed between the parking area and administration buildings, and numerous trees and shrubs were planted in the campground and around the plaza. *(Photograph by George A. Grant, courtesy National Park Service Historic Photography Collection)*

season, and dry, pumicelike soil was far from an ideal site for planting. Halsey Davidson described the problems:

> The planting done last year at this site, which was to serve as a windbreak, came through the winter in good shape with the loss of only half a dozen trees, but its capacity as a protection against wind is practically nil. Tree growth is so slow in this area that a windbreak would have to be transplanted thick enough and large enough to serve the purpose at once if any good is to be obtained. Special equipment for moving larger trees should be provided as it is useless to try to move them without boxing the roots. This, of course, makes them too heavy to move by hand. Trees up to ten feet in height were moved to the rear of the movie screen but

there will likely be considerable loss in transplanting trees of this size by hand. All trees used at Yakima Park were brought four miles by road, the nearest available source of supply.[18]

At Tipsoo Lake near the park's east boundary, the scars of an old road and fishing camp were obliterated and the area restored to a natural condition in the first few years of the ECW program in Mount Rainier. Sod was transplanted from road construction sites nearby and from "hidden" sites up to three miles away. The old road was replaced by a four-foot-wide foot trail that followed a meandering course around three sides of the lake. It was raised slightly above the ground, surfaced with sand from the lake bed, and connected with the parking area and picnic area. The road construction camp was erased by the planting of two groups of fifty-four trees following the composition of the area's natural vegetation, which, like that of Yakima Park, was dominated by subalpine fir. Where the park bounded the national forest, a grade separation of log and stonemasonry was built across the entrance road. This structure was designed to function as a boundary marker, an entrance sign and gateway, and an overpass for the Cascade Crest Trail (later Pacific Crest Trail). The CCC also built stonemasonry campstoves for the picnic area and outlined the parking area with partially embedded rocks to serve as barriers. The work extended over several enrollment periods and was broken down into projects. For example, during the fifth enrollment period, between April and October 1935, 201 man-days were spent on planting a total of 532 shrubs and trees and 1,944 square feet of sod.[19]

Planting and transplanting native trees and shrubbery at Yakima Park continued to be an important project. During the fifth enrollment period in 1935, 4,537 trees and shrubs were planted at Mount Rainier, the majority at Yakima Park.[20]

By 1935, park administration and visitor use had outgrown the existing facilities, necessitating expansion of the village at Yakima Park in keeping with the master plans. A community house would provide shelter from the cold winds that prevailed during the entire summer season. This building would be a center for educational programs and provide a lecture hall, replacing the outdoor amphitheater. Also needed was a second administration building. The two administration buildings, in the form of blockhouses, were to be connected by the community house, with an equipment shed and back area enclosed by the stockade fence, completing the administrative group for the village. The development at Tipsoo Lake required a water and sewer system, two comfort stations, and a ranger station to replace the tent quarters that had been in use for several years.[21]

Landscape naturalization projects occurred elsewhere in the park during the first five periods of ECW. At Paradise, village improvements were made in the area adjoining the community building and concessionaire's new lodge, which had become the village center. Here a wide flagstone terrace with sod joints was

9.7. When the boundaries of Mount Rainier National Park were extended in 1931, Tipsoo Lake became the site of the park's eastern entrance. Through the work of the Civilian Conservation Corps, as this 1940 view illustrates, the area was developed according to the park's master plan as a naturalistic park entrance and recreational area. The master plan designated scenic views of Mount Rainier which were to remain open and stands of trees which were to be protected. Scars of old roads and former fishing camps around the lake were returned to a natural condition as sod and native trees were planted. A recreational trail was built around the lake, and a picnic area with campstoves of native rock was developed in a grove of subalpine firs adjacent to the highway. *(Photograph by George A. Grant, courtesy National Park Service Historic Photography Collection)*

built across the front of the community building, and a six-foot-wide flagstone walk was built from one end of the terrace to connect with the nearby lodge. A large drinking fountain was built of massive native stone piled into a six-foot-high conical formation, in a design strongly influenced by the Arts and Crafts movement.

At Christine Falls, where large slides and erosion had caused considerable damage over several years, a dry retaining wall of native rock was built. Large boulders formed the wall at the base of the slide. Topsoil was hauled in and placed behind the wall to create a ledge on which native alders (*Alnus rubra*) and other trees were planted which in time would screen the unsightly scar of the long slide.[22]

Campgrounds at Paradise, Longmire, White River, and Ohanopecosh were constructed or improved in keeping with the Meinecke system, in which campsites and road spurs were defined and trees protected by logs and, in some cases, boulders. At the campground at Longmire, a strip of small cedars (*Chamaecyparis nootkatensis*), hemlocks (*Tsuga heterophylla*), fir (*Pseudotsuga menziesii*), huckleberry (*Vaccinium* spp.), vine maple (*Acer circinatum*), and other shrubs and trees was planted along the river to keep campers from trampling the area and to give the entrance to the campground a more inviting appearance. Trees and shrubs were planted at the campgrounds at White River.[23]

Extensive planting and transplanting took place at Longmire, continuing the work Davidson had begun in the late 1920s. Planting was seasonal and required preparation of soil beforehand and careful maintenance and watering afterward. It was often carried out with other projects such as laying curbs, parking, and paths. In an area of about ten acres of the residential village, boulder curbs were laid, new lawns planted, parking rearranged, and trees, shrubs, ferns, and herbaceous materials planted. Landscape foreman H. J. Cremer described the numerous problems he and a crew of twelve men encountered during the first two months of work at Longmire:

> The community of Longmire is built on an old river bar and practically all the soil has to be brought in from outside. Every hole dug for planting must first have all rock debris removed and then be bedded with soil to insure safe transplanting. The very short planting season makes transplanting quite difficult. Large trees and shrubs which are dug and planted in the latter part of June can only survive when given the most expert handling. In this respect, proper balling and transportation are necessary. Most of the plants for this area are hauled a distance of 20 miles early in the morning to prevent the soil from drying out and falling away from the roots. The holes for transplanting are dug and prepared the previous afternoon, so that the planting can be carried out with the greatest dispatch.[24]

Chinquapin Intersection, Yosemite

The development of Chinquapin Intersection, where the Wawona and Glacier Point Roads come together, illustrates how the National Park Service's programs for road construction, building construction, and landscape naturalization were coordinated through the New Deal programs.

Chinquapin was an important stopping point on the road between the valley and Wawona. It was a convenient place to provide comforts and information to the public and to patrol a portion of the park boundary needing deer protec-

9.8. Through the Civilian Conservation Corps, village improvements occurred in the developed areas of most national parks and monuments in the 1930s. Before the Paradise Community Building in Mount Rainier National Park, enrollees laid a naturalistic flagstone walk with sod joints. *(Photograph courtesy National Archives, Record Groups 79)*

tion during hunting season. A concessionaire had built a store and gas station here in the 1920s, but the buildings had burned.

Completion of the new Wawona Road in 1933 made possible the construction of the new Glacier Point Road. With increasing traffic and visitors along the Wawona Road and to Glacier Point, park officials decided that "a complete administrative unit" was necessary at the junction. The construction scheme prepared by the Landscape Division called for a ranger station, a comfort station, and a gas station with a small refreshment stand arranged around a plaza area connecting the two roads. The Wawona Road at this point followed a wide sweeping curve, and the Glacier Point Road dissected the arc and extended uphill behind the gas station.[25]

The design for the ranger station drawn up by resident landscape architect John Wosky called for a one-story frame structure measuring 38.5 feet by 46.5 feet and containing two apartments. One apartment consisted of a bedroom, kitchen, lavatory, and shower, and the other had a living room, bedroom, lavatory, and shower. A porch, 8 feet in width, extended along the full length of the building and led to a small hall for public use. The building was set back from the road and was separated from it by an island. It offered a view off the back porch and parking at the front. The foundation was concrete with a 9-inch stone veneer, and the walls were redwood painted white with a touch of gray. The roof was made of royal cedar shingles, each measuring 24 inches long and having a random width to add to the irregularity of form. Two telephones were installed, and lighting was provided by the gas station's gasoline-driven power generator. Work began in September 1933 and finished in December of that year, for a total of $4,960. Workers hired by the Civil Works Administration, a short-lived program that created jobs in the winter of 1933–34, were detailed to paint interior walls and varnish floors the following February.

The design for the comfort station likewise was drawn up by Wosky. It was a one-story frame structure with a stone-veneered concrete foundation fit into the hillside, so that the rear wall became a retaining wall of reinforced concrete which extended along the ends of the building in a stepped fashion. Begun in September 1933, it was completed in December and cost $3,469. It was located beyond the ranger station at the far end of the intersection on the corner where the Glacier Point Road branched off and proceeded uphill. On the two ends of the building, entrances were covered by simple gabled porches with lattice screens. Both the ranger station and the comfort station, with their shake roofs and painted horizontal siding, were influenced by the nineteenth-century homes and hotels of the region.

The projects were carried out under the supervision of the park's engineering department, with the assistance of Wosky, the park's resident landscape architect. The gas station and refreshment stand, located on the Wawona Road across from the ranger station with the steep slope of the Glacier Point Road rising behind it, was built by the concessionaire under private contract with the approval of Vint's office. This building, too, reflected the horizontal painted redwood siding, steeply sloped overhanging shake roof, and stone-faced foundations of the nearby government buildings. It had two connecting sections, one serving the gas station, the other the refreshment area. Here a pair of overhanging porches echoing that of the ranger station became a porte-cochère for the gas station and an entry porch for the restaurant.

9.9. Chinquapin Intersection, Yosemite National Park, where the Glacier Point Road (*left*) and Wawona Road (*right*) came together, was developed by the National Park Service in the 1930s. By September 1934, when this photograph was taken, a ranger station (*distant right*) and comfort station (*far left*) had been built with public works funds, the concessioner had built a combination gas station and lunch room (*center foreground*), and the Civilian Conservation Corps had begun to install log curbing and plant dozens of trees, shrubs, and herbaceous plants. The intersection was named for the native chinquapin (*Castanopsis sempervirens*), a flowering shrub that dominated the site's natural vegetation. (*Photograph courtesy National Park Service Historic Photography Collection*)

In the spring of 1934, enrollees from Wawona Camp set to work on the landscape improvements that were part of Wosky's overall design for the plaza. The area was graded, the steep hillsides behind the gas station and comfort station were flattened and sloped, and log curbing was installed along the roadway, islands, and parking areas. Beside the ranger station, a view was cleared and a viewing area designated by the flagpole and plantings. Trees, shrubs, and flowers were planted throughout the site. Thirty-eight loads of black soil, measuring fifty-six and a half square yards, were hauled in from the woods to prepare the site, and twelve cubic yards of rock were removed and hauled away. By July 1934, 213 holes (moving one cubic yard of dirt each) had been dug and the following planted: 27 willows (*Salix* spp.), 134 chinquapins (*Castanopsis sempervirens*), 14 cherry (*Prunus* spp.), 12 manzanitas (*Arctostaphylos mariposa*), 17 ceanothus (*Ceanothus* spp.), 27 buckthorn (*Rhamnus californicum*), 6 ferns, and 2 mountain currants (*Ribes* spp.). One enrollee spent 15 days watering, and the total project required 494 enrollee and 50 civilian man-days.[26]

Planting continued in the fall with 384 chinquapins, 18 manzanitas, 2 sugar pines (*Pinus lambertiana*), 3 willows, 2 buckthorn, 5 cedars (*Libocedrus decurrens*), and 5 white firs (*Abies concolor*). Thirty-two cubic yards of black soil were hauled in for planting purposes, and twenty-five cubic yards of poor soil were hauled away. This work, performed over a three-month period, required 688 enrollee and 51 civilian man-days.[27]

During 1935, enrollees from the Cascades Camp installed 852 linear feet of log curbing, requiring thirty-three truckloads of logs. Logs measuring about 14 inches in diameter were fitted end to end and embedded partially in the ground. The logs were the snags and old logs being cleared under a separate job by other members of the camp and piled up along the old Wawona Road. Two hundred feet of road surface previously treated with oil were removed from the area and 80 cubic yards of dirt hauled in to create a naturalistic slope behind the curbs.[28]

The work was finally completed in early 1937. More shrubs were planted than had been originally estimated, and the loss of plants was greater here than in Yosemite Valley, owing to poor soil conditions and an inexperienced foreman. The plantings around the ranger station included chinquapin shrubs in great abundance at all corners, manzanitas and cherry trees at each end of the station, and white firs and cedars on the slopes behind the gas station to create a screen for motorists ascending the Glacier Point Road. Islands in the plaza were planted with chinquapins and other low-growing shrubs. The slopes behind and beside the comfort station were planted with shrubs, predominantly chinquapins. At the end of the parking area for the comfort station, where the road began its ascent, pines were planted to blend the plaza with the roadside vegetation. Recognizing that the results of the planting were not immediately obvious to observers, the camp superintendent advised, "Give the trees and plants a chance to spread out and in another year or two this plot will be one of the beauty spots on the Wawona Road."[29]

Of particular importance is the comprehensive nature of the intersection's development, embracing road design and construction, the building of park facilities, and the finishing touches of landscape naturalization that included village improvements such as curbing and grading as well as plantings that erased construction scars, beautified the area, controlled erosion, and blended the development into the natural setting.

The dominant use of chinquapin, a native shrub characteristic of the intersection's natural setting, was significant. The chinquapin (*Castanopsis sempervirens*) is a flowering shrub whose height varies from one to six feet depending on elevation; the average is three feet in height and six in width. It has smooth gray bark and "stiff, narrow, pointed, two-inch leaves shining rich deep green on top and underneath first green-gold and later rich dark gold." When in flower, the shrub is arrayed with "long, creamy catkins of bloom—picturesque against the dark leathery foliage, rather dreadfully fragrant, and pervading the whole locality with over-powering sweetness." Bright, golden brown, chestnut-like burrs follow the flowers, holding clusters of small round nuts. Calling the chinquapin an endearing shrub, Lester Rowntree in 1939 told readers of *Flowering Shrubs of California and Their Value to the Gardener* that the best place to see the chinquapin was at the Yosemite Park intersection named for the plant.[30]

Nowhere else in the national park system had an intersection received so much attention. This special treatment was due in large part to the importance that surrounded the construction of the Wawona Road and the many difficulties it encountered. No other road received such scrutiny by national park landscape architects, officials, and the Yosemite Board of Expert Advisers. Elsewhere the advances in park design made by the park designers by 1933 were developed and expanded upon. The principles of naturalistic design were reinforced with full force, and many practices were rediscovered and innovations made, from the rehabilitation of springs to the naturalization of roadsides and newly constructed buildings.

Roadside Naturalization

Vint's program for landscape naturalization and roadside planting received an immediate boost in 1933 when Emergency Conservation Work began in the national parks. Interest in the "finishing" work of landscape naturalization had arisen, and park designers were just beginning to understand the aesthetic and economic advantages to planting the flattened and rounded slopes along new park roads. In 1931 the first funds for this work were programmed. Now, suddenly, a strong body of labor was available and ready. Through the Civilian Conservation Corps, the service also had an opportunity to hire many well-trained unemployed landscape architects to supervise the work.

Roadside naturalization was a twofold process requiring that slopes be graded naturalistically to form concave and convex curves at a ratio of depth to height of at least 3:1, and preferably 4:1. Revegetation was accomplished either through the natural process of recovery or through the planting of native sod, grasses, ground cover, perennial plants, shrubs, and other forms of vegetation. Duff removed before construction was placed on the slope in either case. Planting also often required stabilization of seeded slopes by embedding rocks in the slopes or building temporary wooden cribbing to keep the soil in place until roots could take hold.

The naturalization of banks after road and trail construction became one of the most important and widespread of all CCC projects. It played a vital role in controlling slope erosion as well as having lasting value for beautification. Great effort was taken to blend the planted vegetation into the natural setting of the roadside. Techniques were developed for what became commonly known as bank blending. Resident landscape architect Harold Fowler of Sequoia, where a planting program was undertaken along the Generals Highway, reported,

> The steep cut slopes and hills form an ugly scar that has been slow to encourage plant growth. This planting project will help materially to hasten a naturalistic roadside planting. . . . It is not intended that this planting should look like a formal border mass. The object has been to blend the new slope planting into the existing growth above the cut slopes. If the growth is shrubby material above the cut slope, the same type of planting should be carried down on the slope. Care should be taken, of course, not to decrease sight vision on curves. . . . In the cases where there are only grass and flowers above the slopes similar planting should be carried down on the slopes. An extreme planting of shrubbery would give the border mass effect, which, as stated before, is not desired.[31]

Many rock-loving and creeping plants had already started naturally on the slopes. Fowler recommended that this type of planting be encouraged and carried out to a greater extent with the occasional use of shrubbery material. Approximately eighty thousand plants were used in eight miles of roadside planting, consisting largely of native plants such as ceanothus (*Ceanothus* spp.), yerba santa (*Eriodictyon californicum*), bush poppy (*Dendromecon rigida*), lupine (*Lupinus* spp.), manzanita (*Arctostaphylos* spp.), yucca (*Yucca whipplei*), and flannel bush (*Fremontia californica*). Because most of the plants were in the form of cuttings and had been transplanted, Fowler expected that a considerable loss would occur and that it would take several years to create a significant effect.[32]

At Yosemite, as a result of the cooperation between the Landscape and Educational Divisions, a successful planting program got under way along the newly completed Wawona Road in the early 1930s. The program began as an experiment but would have lasting success and would influence the design of park roads for years to come.

In summer 1934, enrollees from one of Yosemite's CCC camps collected numerous seeds of native flowers, shrubs, and trees for planting cut banks and fill slopes. They gathered 291 pounds of seed and twenty-two grain sacks of chinquapin burrs. Species included were sugar pine, incense cedar (*Calocedrus decurrens*), white fir, manzanita, chinquapin, aster (*Aster adscendens*), dock (*Rumex* spp.), pennyroyal (*Monardella lanceolata*), white yarrow (*Achillaea millefolium*), senecio (*Senecio lugens*), bear clover (*Chamaebatia foliolosa*), phacelia (*phacelia heterophylla*), pentstemon (*Pentstemon* spp.), coffee berry (*Rhamus californica*), goldenrod (*Solidago elongata*), azalea (*Rhododendron occidentalis*),

9.10. Renowned ecologist Frederic E. Clements supervising the work of the Civilian Conservation Corps along the Wawona Road in Yosemite National Park in November 1934. When serious erosion threatened the recently completed Wawona Road, Clements provided advice on techniques for growing plants on the steep eroding slopes. He also provided the plant list of native species suitable for the slopes of the park's roads. *(Photograph courtesy National Park Service, Yosemite National Park)*

wild rose (*Rosa californica*), gilia (*Gilia aggregata* and *G. capitata*), wyethias (*Wyethia angustifolia*), lessingia (*Lessingia leptoclada*), elderberry (*Sambucus cerulea*), mountain mahogany (*Cercocarpus ledifolius*), potentilla (*Potentilla* spp.), mullein (*Verbascum thapsus*), godetia (*Godetia* spp.), bitter cherry (*Prunus emarginata*), lupine, California black oak (*Quercus kelloggii*), shield leaf (*Streptanthus tortuosus*), and others.[33]

In spring 1935, under the direction of ecologist Dr. Frederic E. Clements of the Carnegie Institution, a new method of planting seeds was attempted along the Wawona Road. Previous efforts to stabilize slopes by digging pockets for seeds to germinate had failed. Under the new method, small trenches were dug laterally along the slopes, seeded, and then filled with duff and topsoil. The following were among numerous shrubs, trees, wildflowers, and ground covers planted: California poppy (*Eschscholtzia californica*), lupine (*Lupinus nanus*), baby-blue-eyes (*Nemophila menziesii*), clarkia (*Clarkia elegans*), globe gilia (*Gilia capitata*), tarweed (*Madia elegans*), fiddle-neck (*Phacelia tanacetifolia*), agoseris (*Agoseris heterophylla*), yerba santa, columbine (*Aquilegia truncata*), spice bush (*Calycanthus occidentalis*), owl's clover (*Orthocarpus purpurascens*), Indian pink (*Silene californica*), collinsia (*Collinsia bicolor*), eriophyllum (*Eriophyllum confertiflorum),* nightshade (*Solanum xantii*), blue-eyed grass (*Sisyrinchium bellum*), meadow foam (*Floerkea douglasii*), fivespot (*Nemophila maculata).*[34]

Landscape architect Russell L. McKown viewed roadside planting as the Wawona Camp's most important work: "By the installation of small trees, shrubbery, native flowers and grasses, and the banks covered with forest litter and duff, the picture along the Wawona Road is very pleasing, and former scars have been practically obliterated." [35]

Writing in *Ecology* in July 1935, Clements, who had been involved with the planting of the Wawona Road since 1933, described the road and the experimental work being done there in natural landscaping and soil erosion:

> To reduce the steep grades, [the Wawona Road] has been carved out of the mountain sides in such a manner as to produce a continuing series of cuts for thirty miles . . . forming an unsightly scar from a distance. These have been organized by sites and units in accordance with terrain and soil, and a detailed plan for preparation and planting worked out for each. One example of each kind has received the necessary reduction or rounding of slope, with protective trenching above and terracing on the face, and has been sown and planted to yield natural patterns in general harmony with the vegetation present. . . . In addition, the plan contemplates the enhancement of the original stretches of forest and the many recesses and dells, where soil and water permit installing final compositions without the preliminary successional modification of raw slopes.[36]

9.11. Landscape naturalization took several forms. Civilian Conservation Corps enrollees stained the tunnel entrance and rock embankments on the Wawona Road using spray guns, a compressor, and a mixture of linseed oil, mineral oil, and lampblack. This work was intended to give an aged and weathered appearance to the large rocks that were blasted in carving out the road. *(Photograph courtesy National Archives, Record Group 79)*

Overlooks, Truck Trails, and Trails

Another important development of the roads program during the 1930s was the design of overlooks for scenic roads. Using naturalistic practices in landscape design, the CCC developed numerous scenic overlooks in the early 1930s

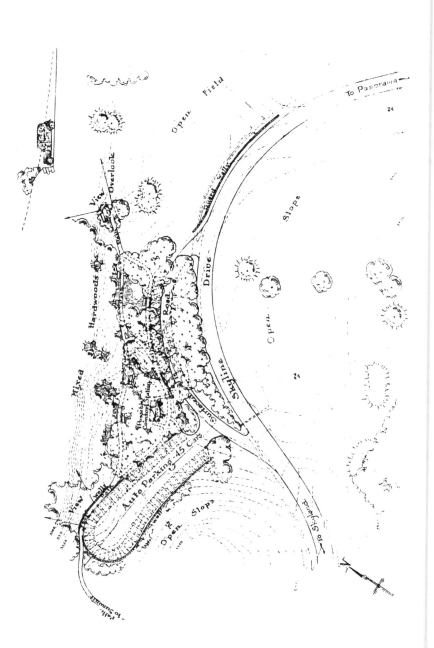

9.12. Jewell Hollow Overlook on Skyline Drive in Shenandoah National Park was designed by the Eastern Field Office in 1933 and built by the Civilian Conservation Corps. The site was selected for its valley views, natural outlooks, and interesting rock formations. The overlook conformed to the natural contours of the hillsides; the parking area was partly built upon a terrace created by a dry-laid and backfilled random-rubble wall. CCC labor and the naturalistic principles of national park design coincided in the 1930s to advance the construction of naturalistic overlooks on park roads and parkways. (*Drawing courtesy National Park Service, Technical Information Center*)

on Skyline Drive, a scenic drive along the crest of the Blue Ridge Mountains in Shenandoah National Park. Overlooks such as Jewell Hollow, Crescent Rock, Hogback Mountain, and Hazel Mountain were unique solutions, each fully developing the scenic potential of spectacular vistas, natural topography, and the region's dramatic geological features. Skyline Drive, built with relief funds through the cooperative agreement with the Bureau of Public Roads, would become the backbone of the new park. As an integral part of the design, the overlooks reflected the increasing influence of motoring as a form of outdoor recreation.

Hazel Mountain Overlook (1935), sited along the natural contours of the east side of the ridge, provided views across the Piedmont Plateau. The overlook was developed around a picturesque outcrop of granodiorite having a dramatic pattern of jointing. Curvilinear stone walls sprang from each side of the outcrop to provide a barrier for cars and a guardrail for visitors. Stone steps built by the CCC into the outcrop led to a summit where one could view the dark hollows and farmlands below. The parking area was separated from the drive by an island, edged in stone and densely planted with native pines, oaks, and an understory of mountain laurel (*Kalmia latifolia*) to screen the sight and noise of traffic on the drive and to blend the overlook with the natural slopes beyond the drive.

Under the direction of Charles Peterson and resident landscape architect Harvey P. Benson, the landscape architecture of Shenandoah was characterized by a blending of natural rock and native plants which links it with the romantic gardening tradition espoused by Downing, Parsons, Hubbard, and others. The park's natural outcrops of rock with their inherent picturesque character were accentuated wherever possible, in picnic areas, at overlooks, along roads and trails, and in developed areas. Artificial assemblages of moss- and lichen-covered rock were also created, as old stone walls from the period of mountain settlement and farming which preceded the park's establishment were dismantled and the stones scattered. At the picnic grounds at Dickey Ridge, such stones were embedded in the ground and scattered in a random arrangement to build an informal rock garden and to screen and make the comfort stations beyond less conspicuous.

Roadside cleanup was another common activity of CCC camps. This work entailed clearing dead and decaying brush and fallen trees along park roads and removing trees and vegetation that made roads unsafe. This work had begun in Yellowstone in the mid-1920s with donated funds and by 1930 was covered by appropriated funds as a cost of maintaining and improving roads. Extensive cleanup occurred along Skyline Drive in Shenandoah, where the chestnut blight had left numerous dead stumps and fallen timber. Cleanup also occurred along the Wawona Road in Yosemite and in parks where the white pine blister rust had already taken its toll on native pines.

Emergency Conservation Work developed many truck trails, the service

9.13. An important activity of the Civilian Conservation Corps in Yosemite National Park and elsewhere, the construction of truck roads served a variety of administrative purposes, including fire control and backcountry patrol. Although visitors seldom used these roads, care was taken in construction to make them inconspicuous, to protect natural features, to avoid erosion, and to blend them into the natural setting using native vegetation and boulders. *(Photograph courtesy National Archives, Record Group 79)*

roads that provided administrative access to various parts of the park often passing through nonpark land. Although these were not traveled by the general public, some park superintendents felt they should receive the same treatment of cleanup and the flattening and rounding of slopes as public roads. Fire trails were six-foot lanes cut through brush and undergrowth generally following ridges, ascending to mountain summits, and penetrating deep forests. These two types of roads together formed the system of fire suppression for a park and as such were an extremely important part of CCC work. Their construction, however, often left scars upon the natural landscape which could be seen from popular viewpoints. Consequently, the roads were situated with concern for landscape protection and screening. They were constructed in ways that would minimize scars and help them blend into the natural scenery. One of Sequoia's resident

Park and Recreation Progress since 1933

9.14. Daunted by snow and sleet in May 1934, enrollees from Yosemite's Cascades Camp rebuilt the stairway ascending the eastern face of Half Dome. They replaced the nine-hundred-foot cable, refastened iron posts, and repaired wooden treads. While using hammers and chisels to drill new holes, enrollees were held by lifelines tied to the posts above. The slender but strong iron cables and lacelike design enabled the stairway to blend with the gray granite walls of the monolithic dome. *(Photograph courtesy National Park Service Historic Photography Collection)*

landscape architects observed that when trails followed wavy lines rather than straight clean-cut ones, they were less conspicuous and blended more readily into the natural setting when viewed from a distance.[37]

Substantial progress was made on the improvement of trails, particularly in popular places. At Yosemite, the cables on Half Dome which had been installed about 1920 by the Sierra Club were now replaced and strengthened by the CCC. This work involved replacing 429 feet of 3/8-inch cable with 7/8-inch galvanized iron cable and thirty-nine pipe posts with stronger 1-inch pipe. One section had to be removed every winter so that it was not torn out in the spring by snowslides. Workers drilled forty-one holes averaging 7 inches in depth by hand in the rock for the new pipe posts. Each man was tied with a piece of rope to the pipe posts while he was drilling to prevent slipping or falling. New wooden steps were installed at the base of each pair of posts, so that hikers could rest at these points. The hemp rope leading to the saddle of Half Dome was retightened and respliced. This trail work was done from a stub camp located at the base of the dome. Although the weather had been perfect before work began, when enrollees set up camp and started the task, it suddenly changed. Every afternoon a storm blew in with either rain, hail, or snow combined with high winds, and work was discontinued. During this time, the men worked on the rehabilitation of nearby Iron Spring. Finishing the trail required forty-one enrollee man-days and five civilian man-days.[38]

Several other cases illustrate the way special kinds of trails were built following the advances worked out by the Engineering and Landscape Divisions in the late 1920s. A naturalistic footpath was constructed across the geyser basins at Norris Geyser Basin in Yellowstone in the summer of 1936. It followed the construction methods that Kenneth McCarter had recommended for the Old Faithful walk in 1929 and took a circular route as indicated on the master plan for the area. It consisted of three stages of construction: the installation of parallel rows of log curbing, the building of a boardwalk of planks supported on two-by-fours, and a final surfacing with concrete and gravel that blended with the natural coloration of the basin. In 1936, the Upper Falls Overlook at the Grand Canyon of the Yellowstone was damaged by falling snow and ice. In keeping with the master plan, the stairways were rebuilt, and a new overlook was built in the form of a terrace that featured a naturalistic rock guardrail and was accessible by a sturdy log stairway and a log bridge.[39]

Headquarters Area, Sequoia

Construction and landscape naturalization projects were coordinated throughout the national parks and monuments during the 1930s. An ECW project at Sequoia's Ash Mountain in the fourth enrollment period, from October 1934 to April 1935, enlarged the administration building, which had been constructed in 1923 in a form typical of California bungalows. For the addition, builders used a technique called California box framing, which had been used in the original construction, and gave it an exterior of split shakes and false exposed framing. The new addition changed the public entrance to a covered flagstone patio, where rustic rafters were supported on masonry piers of schist. Planting areas were left in the joints of the stone floor and walk to allow grass and moss to grow. Ferns were planted at the base of the porch piers, and shrubs of California laurel (*Umbellularia californica*) were planted on the slopes leading to the building from the parking area. A new stone stairway gracefully curved from the parking area to the new entrance. It was built of heavy rounded boulders that formed the steps and a coping to either side, and reflected a high degree of craftsmanship and an understanding of the naturalistic mode derived from the Olmsted firm's work at Franklin Park. The redesign of the headquarters' principal building added greatly to the appearance of the area.[40]

The improvement of the grounds included the construction of a dry rock base wall around three sides of the administration building and low border walls set along the walk. An eighteen-inch-thick curb wall of schist rock masonry set fourteen inches below the surface of the ground and extending eight inches above the ground was constructed along the approach road and the road leading to the parking area. Similar curbing surrounded the checking station island. The old parking area was enlarged to accommodate twenty-two cars and improved with a sidewalk and curb combination to serve as a barrier for cars. Five-foot-wide paths leading to the building were paved with a mix of oil and crushed stone and edged with flat schist rock, a type of construction economical to place but rustic in appearance. Curving lines replaced the rectilinear lines and corners of the earlier walks, adding an informal appearance and allowing more direct passage.[41]

A new entrance sign featuring a massive hand-carved profile of a Native American was built at Ash Mountain during the following enrollment period. Logs three and one-half feet in diameter were set in stone-faced concrete bases to form columns on each side of the road, one of which was nine feet in height, the other fifteen. Carved in relief by enrollee George Muno of Camp NP-1, the signboard was made from a massive slab of redwood. The sign contained the name of the park in bold letters and was fastened to the taller post with wrought-iron braces and fasteners.[42]

Yosemite Village

Emergency Conservation Work made possible improvements in many national park villages. At Yosemite Village, these community improvements took the form of an extensive program of beautification. CCC enrollees removed deteriorated buildings in the old village and through grading, soil improvement, and plantings returned the area to a naturalized condition. They installed log curbing and new paths, repaired existing trees, and planted trees, shrubs, ferns, and other plants. The boulders that had been placed along the roads and parking areas in the 1920s were removed and replaced with ditches or curbs made of logs laid horizontally end to end and partially embedded in the earth. Planting occurred around the plaza, administration building, new hospital, residences, and museum. Ferns, trees, and shrubs were planted along foundations and at entrances and corners, and grapevines were planted in Craftsman fashion to climb up the boulder walls of buildings and give them a more naturalistic appearance. The museum garden, set aside in the late 1920s as an interpretive exhibit of park flora, was expanded and improved.

Transplanting projects were carried out in several enrollment periods. In the spring of 1934, native plants dug at various places outside the valley were transplanted around both old government residences and new ones that had been constructed with PWA funding. The plants covered a wide variety of species native to Yosemite Valley. They included 41 azaleas, 104 ferns, 10 spice bushes, 10 woodwardias (*Woodwardia radicans*), 12 manzanitas, 21 spireas (*Spirea* spp.), 10 lungworts (*Mertensia ciliata*), 2 yellow flowers, 5 chinquapins, 2 willow trees, 14 black-eyed Susans (*Rudbeckia hirta*), 7 clumps of daisies (*Bellis perennis*), 8 alumroot (*Heuchera* spp.), 3 ceanothus, 2 Washington lilies (*Lilium washingtonianum*), 1 cedar (*Libocedrus decurrens*), 8 quaking aspens (*Populus tremuloides*), 2 syringa (*Philadelphus lewisii*), 22 coneflowers (*Rudbeckia californica*), 6 mountain mahogany, 2 lupines, 3 dogwoods (*Cornus nuttallii*), 4 forget-me-nots (*Myosotis sylvatica*), 3 monkeyflowers (*Mimulus* spp.), and 1 fifteen-foot maple tree (*Acer macrophylum*). This project took 237 enrollee and 50 civilian man-days and was carried out under the supervision of Cascades Camp's landscape architect and landscape foreman.[43]

Plantings continued in subsequent seasons, and the variety of species expanded. The inventory of trees, shrubs, and other materials planted in the village in the fall and winter of 1934–35 included 1 Douglas fir (*Pseudotsuga taxifolia*), 4 red firs (*Abies magnifica*), 36 redbuds (*Cercis occidentalis*), 94 spice bushes, 2 elderberries (*Sambucus velutina*), 12 mock oranges (*Philadelphus lewisii*), 19 toyons (*Photina arbutifolia*), 6 wild roses (*Rosa californica*), and 12 scrub oaks (*Quercus dumosa*), as well as additional ferns, azaleas, dogwoods, and miscellaneous shrubs and herbaceous plants. Ninety-six cubic yards of topsoil were hauled in for this planting. Wildflower seed was broadcast over 3,090 square yards of the area. The work took 458 enrollee and 53 civilian man-days.[44]

In 1935, planting continued around the government residences. Native shrubs and trees were taken from various places outside the valley floor and were transplanted around the new and old government residences. CCC enrollees from the Cascades Camp continued to plant trees, shrubs, and herbaceous

9.15. Although unique in its craftsmanship and subject, the sign at the Ash Mountain Entrance to Sequoia National Park illustrated the typical 1930s construction of entrance signs in many western parks. Posts were made of tall, single or clustered logs of native timber embedded in a rock-faced concrete base; the signboards were roughly cut boards of native wood, were hung on metal straps or brackets, and had the name of the park carved in relief or burned into the wood. *(Photograph courtesy National Park Service, Sequoia National Park)*

plants similar to those planted in previous seasons. The planting was considered a success, "the residences beautified to a great extent." [45]

CCC crews also maintained trees in the valley which had been neglected or become hazardous. In the spring of 1935, dead limbs were removed from 223 oak trees around the government residences in the village. A total of 250 apple trees in the valley were trimmed and repaired; this work entailed cutting out suckers and draining cavities. The apple trees, located near Yosemite Falls and Camp Curry, were the remnants of orchards planted by some of the first settlers in Yosemite Valley. [46]

Village improvements accompanied the planting program. In the winter of 1933–34, workers removed border stones lining the sidewalks of the plaza and in the spring filled the remaining holes and planted sod. At the same time flagstones were placed around the telescopes in front of the museum. In April 1935, large border stones were removed from the new village plaza, with the help of a gasoline shovel, and were hauled to the old borrow pit or set aside for fireplace construction.

With the planting in the village under way, efforts turned to the beautification of other parts of the valley. Over a six-month period beginning in April 1935, 1,973 pine and cedar trees and 36 quaking aspens were planted in semibarren areas fronting on the road at Camps 7 and 15, "greatly enhancing the appearance of these camp grounds and adding to the general scenic beauty." Twenty-eight trees were transplanted to the cemetery. This work was labor intensive and required 1,258 enrollee and 105 civilian man-days.[47]

By the end of the seventh enrollment period, the project to screen campgrounds from the road was substantially completed at Campgrounds 7, 11, 12, 14, and 15, and similar planting was planned for Camp 16 during the eighth period. "The many rather unsightly conditions ever-present in any public campground will now be nicely screened so that the numerous wash-lines of campers and unkempt conditions in the individual camp sites will not be so noticeable." In addition, 3,771 feet of log railing was constructed around Camp 12 in 1935. The railing consisted of pine logs measuring 9 to 14 inches in diameter, which had been taken from pine thickets, peeled, and hauled to the valley. They were bolted to concrete posts made from sheet metal forms.[48]

Yosemite Museum's Wild Garden

In 1935, CCC enrollees from the Cascades Camp, under the direction of the park naturalist, carried out the largest planting project that had yet taken place at the Yosemite Museum. During the year, the two-acre garden was substantially overhauled. Enrollees watered, cleared out weeds, collected seed, hauled soil, prepared walks, transplanted trees and shrubs, and carried out other routine tasks. Superb records were kept of the plants transplanted from other parts of the park. The plantings around the museum building included 32 grapevines (*Vitis californica*), which were planted along the museum's boulder foundations and intended as climbing vines across the boulder walls of the lower story. Primroses (*Oenothera hookeri*) were planted in the garden, where they were protected from browsing deer and created a collection that, blooming in the early evening, became the object of popular evening walks in the museum garden. The inventory of plants added to the museum garden and grounds in 1935 included 23 spice bushes (*Calycanthus occidentalis*), 27 redbuds, 2 cedar trees, 12 manzanitas, 4 Douglas firs, 4 mock oranges, 3 toyon bushes, 42 lupines, 5 azaleas, 2 dogwoods (*Cornus californica*), 2 everlastings (*Anaphalis margaritacea*), 12 grass clumps, and 200 miscellaneous plants. Enrollees also prepared thirty seed boxes, eighteen inches square, for the experimental planting of seed in conjunction with the planting along the Wawona Road. To prepare the soil for planting, enroll-

9.16. As part of a beautification program for Yosemite Village, Civilian Conservation Corps enrollees planted azaleas, ferns, and other native plants at the entrances and along the foundations of buildings. Plantings, such as those at Lewis Hospital, helped erase the scars of construction and eliminate the lines of demarcation between constructed boulder walls and the natural setting. *(Photograph courtesy National Archives, Record Group 79)*

ees hauled in fifteen cubic yards of topsoil and scattered it around the garden. Twenty-six cubic yards of rock were dug out of the garden and hauled to the old borrow pit; an additional twenty-two cubic yards of debris were hauled to the Curry Dump.[49]

The garden paths were also replaced at this time, requiring the removal of 343 square yards of old walk and the installation of new walk made from rock removed in the cleanup of streambeds along the Merced River and crushed rock hauled in from elsewhere. Twelve cubic yards of pine needles were hauled to the area of the garden occupied by an outdoor exhibit interpreting Native American life which had been part of the museum since the 1920s. In the fall additional flowers and shrubs were removed from construction sites at Crane Flat and along the Wawona Road and trucked to the valley for transplanting around the museum.[50]

9.17. The Wild Garden at Yosemite Museum in the late 1930s abounded with wildflowers from the park's several zones. Under the direction of the park naturalist in 1935, the Cascades Camp of the Civilian Conservation Corps transformed the garden, which started as a student project in 1929, into a wildflower meadow with a spring and stream. Enrollees hauled in rich soil and mulch, installed new walks of crushed rock from nearby streambeds, and transplanted trees, shrubs, and other plants from construction sites throughout the park. *(Photograph courtesy National Park Service, Yosemite National Park)*

While waiting for fire calls, one CCC fire-suppression crew built log benches for the entrance and garden. Materials came from insect-damaged trees felled for insect control. Hewn from single logs measuring as much as twenty-four inches across, the benches were given a weathered appearance by scorching them with a blowtorch and rubbing them with linseed oil.[51]

These projects had long-lasting results that are still visible today. The clinging vines and the sequoia planted in 1935, for example, continue to grace the museum entrance. This work also showed how the landscape and educational programs of the National Park Service could interact and mutually enhance each

9.18. The rehabilitation of springs provided a perfect opportunity for creating quiet resting spots and graceful rock gardens using naturalistic gardening practices. At Iron Spring in Yosemite National Park, Civilian Conservation Corps enrollees diverted the naturally flowing spring through pipes into a rock-lined basin and planted more than a hundred ferns and other native plants, including heathers, alumroot, raspberry bushes, and mountain ash. *(Photograph courtesy National Archives, Record Group 79)*

other and at the same time assist the road construction projects being carried out through PWA and roads and trails funds.

Rehabilitation of Springs, Yosemite

CCC work in Yosemite included rehabilitating springs and making them safe sources of drinking water. Landscape architects saw this work as an opportunity to develop beautiful rock gardens, following the precedent established in 1925 at Apollinaris Spring at Yellowstone. In the mid-1930s, the Cascades Camp transformed several of Yosemite's springs from unsightly and muddy spots into appealing places of tranquil beauty.

At Iron Spring, the upper spring was boxed and covered with soil, and water was piped to the lower spring, which had been dug out and lined with rocks. Eight log steps were built from the road down to the spring. Sod, moss-covered rocks, and various plants and trees were planted around the spring. Plantings included eighty ferns, seventy grass clumps, six raspberry bushes (*Rhubus leucodermis*), thirty heathers (*Phyllodoce breweri*), six mimulus (*Mimulus* spp.), twelve alumroot, one wild spirea (*Spirea* spp.), six calycanthus, twelve mountain ash (*Fraxinus dipetala*), seven red firs, one azalea, and one cedar.[52]

Several seasons later, enrollees turned Fern Spring into an attractive naturalistic rock garden by artistically arranging rocks at the site and planting a variety of ferns, wildflowers, azaleas, and ground covers. A log guardrail was placed to define the parking area, and log seats were placed in the woods about the spring to improve the popular spot.[53]

Designers developed naturalistic solutions for providing water in the form of fountains. These projects involved connecting natural sources of water to places accessible by the public. In the early days of motoring, watering spots along highways, especially in mountainous terrain, provided motorists with refreshment and water for overheated automobiles. The Cascades Camp installed several roadside fountains along the Wawona Road. The fountains were made from cut and hauled gnarly canyon live oak sections approximately twelve inches in diameter and three feet in length. A bowl was chiseled out of the log for the drinking fountain, and pipes were fitted into holes bored for the water line and drain. The water line was connected by a one-inch pipe eight hundred feet in length to a small reservoir built by a rock-and-earth dam on Grouse Creek.[54]

Such projects served a combination of important purposes. First, they sanitized popular watering spots. Second, they protected spring areas from the compaction of soil and erosion which resulted from trampling and a constant flow of water. Finally, they offered park designers an opportunity to create rock and water gardens with native plants and local rocks in the tradition of William Robinson's wild gardens and the naturalistic waterfalls and fern gardens of American practitioners such as Henry Hubbard, Samuel Parsons, and Ferruccio Vitale.

The Development of Campgrounds and Picnic Areas

In 1932, one year before the founding of the CCC and the organization of ECW, the U.S. Forest Service introduced the Meinecke plan for campground development. The Meinecke plan called for the extensive rehabilitation of existing campgrounds, closing of many old campgrounds, and construction of new ones according to Meinecke's principles of camp planning. ECW was immediately seen as a means to carry out this reform, and the work of the CCC became closely associated with campground construction.

The CCC's campground work included the construction of loop roads with tiers and parking spurs. It entailed clearing, grubbing, and thinning underbrush for roads and campsites. Flammable vegetation was cleared from each campsite, while tall trees and screens of shrubbery between campsites were marked for preservation. Barriers in the form of boulders or logs embedded in the earth were installed to mark roadways and parking spurs and to protect vegetation. Comfort stations, amphitheaters, water fountains, campstoves, signs, and picnic tables were constructed, and a system of footpaths was laid out. Enrollees commonly planted trees and shrubs in existing campgrounds.

Advances were made in the design of items such as campstoves, which needed to be safe enough for public use and to eliminate the threat of forest fires. Amphitheaters and campfire circles became basic features of campgrounds. And in parks where climate necessitated more sheltered gathering places, community buildings were built adjacent to campgrounds.

In response to the increasing popularity of trailer camping in the 1930s, the National Park Service created numerous schemes for trailer and car camping which were developed in national parks and published in *Park and Recreation Structures* in 1938. These schemes were intended to suit most locations and conditions and allowed for parking along one-way loop roads in parking spurs, drive-through lanes, and several other configurations that could accommodate the automobile with and without trailers. Campgrounds were to be developed in tiers off the main loop road. Additional one-way roads with camping sites could be developed as more facilities were needed.

Recreational Development

The 1918 and 1932 statements of policy encouraged certain kinds of recreation in the national parks, particularly winter sports, which would encourage people to come to the parks at times when there were no crowds. This policy created opportunities for the construction of facilities such as ski slopes, toboggan slides, and golf courses.

The Badger Pass area in Yosemite, the Lodgepole area in Sequoia, and Paradise at Mount Rainier were all envisioned as centers of winter recreation. At the Lodgepole and Badger Pass areas, CCC camps constructed recreational ski trails and other landscape features related to winter recreation. Sensitive to the effects of recreational development, landscape architect Russell L. McKown reported that at Badger Pass, although it was necessary to construct ski runs and an area for the ski school, the development was not objectionable. He also noted that a small ski jump had been constructed with a minimum of destruction to timber and existing slopes.[55]

Near Phantom Ranch at the base of the Grand Canyon, where Bright Angel Creek flowed into the Colorado River, recreational development by the CCC took the form of a series of coordinated projects to enhance existing facilities. Phantom Ranch had been designed by Mary Colter for the Fred Harvey Com-

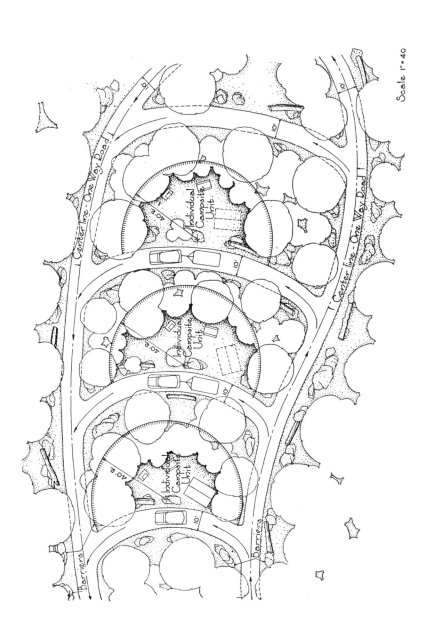

9.19. Trailer Campsite Unit K, illustrated in *Park and Recreation Structures* (1938), was one of several solutions by the National Park Service for accommodating automobiles with trailers in park campgrounds. Automobiles turned from one-way roads onto spur roads leading to single campsites. The spur roads were arranged in tiers and enabled motorists to drive in, park, and drive out without reversing direction. (*Reprinted Albert H. Good, ed., Park and Recreation Structures, 1938*)

9.20. On the floor of the Grand Canyon near Phantom Ranch in winter 1933–34, Civilian
Conservation Corps enrollees from the Walcott Camp cleared massive boulders to make
way for a naturalistic swimming pool to be used by visitors to Phantom Ranch and the
nearby campground. Outlined by the park's master plan, the recreational development
of the canyon floor called for campground improvements, riprapping along Bright Angel
Creek, an irrigation system, packers' cabins, a corral and shelter for mules, a new trail
along the river, and plantings of cottonwoods and other plants for shade and erosion
control. *(Photograph courtesy National Archives, Record Group 79)*

pany and was a popular overnight stopping point for riders and hikers making
the trip from the rim to the floor of the canyon. The Walcott Camp NP-3 was
established here in 1933 and carried out many improvements over several enrollment periods. To protect the area from erosion, the banks of Bright Angel
Creek were stabilized with riprapping made from boulders excavated from the
campground and from what was to be a new swimming pool. The campground
was leveled, boulders removed, and cottonwoods planted for shade. Because this
area was used by hikers and anglers who arrived by mule or on foot, there was no
need to organize the campground according to Meinecke's principles, although
his advice for planting cottonwoods was followed.

In the winter of 1933–34, using 2,043 man-days of labor, the CCC constructed a swimming pool for both campground and ranch visitors. The design of the pool exhibited the naturalistic intent and creative spirit that guided the resident landscape architects at the beginning of the CCC period. An area beside the existing recreational building was cleared of soil and boulders to make way for the pool. Although constructed of concrete, the pool took the form of a naturalistic pond inspired by Japanese landscape design. It was curvilinear in design and lined with stream boulders taken from the site. Water entered the pool through a pipe fashioned like a naturally flowing stream, trickling in over the boulders. Around the pool, Bermuda grass sod and about four hundred shrubs and trees were planted, and a fence of stone pylons and log rails was constructed.[56]

The development of this area was coordinated with trail construction and improvements carried out by members of the same camp. One project was the construction of the new River Trail, which connected with the Kaibab Trail and crossed the Colorado River on the suspension bridge built by the Engineering Division in 1928. This trail work was particularly hazardous and challenging, for the trail was literally carved out of the natural bedrock with a jackhammer and compressor. It required constant drilling through the sheer walls of the canyon with little space for equipment and machinery, and progress was slow. The Walcott Camp also repainted the suspension bridge in colors that blended into the natural coloration of the canyon walls and constructed cabins for packers and the trail caretaker.[57]

As recreational motoring gained in popularity in the 1930s, park service designers explored the development of waysides to provide services and amenities along park roads and facilities for camping and picnicking. In conjunction with the development of Skyline Drive in Shenandoah, Jens Jensen's scheme for waysides at periodic intervals to provide amenities to travelers was revived. Small recreational areas had also been integrated into the design of the Westchester County parkways under the direction of Gilmore Clarke. In Shenandoah, waysides were created at Dickey Ridge, Elkwallow, South River, Big Meadows, and Lewis Mountain. Along the Blue Ridge Parkway, similar areas were developed at Pine Spur, Smart View, Cumberland Knob, Bluff Park, and Rocky Knob.

Wayside areas provided many of the same facilities as park villages did in the large western parks, including gas stations and stores run by concessionaires, but with new emphasis placed on recreational motoring and its demand for picnic areas and campgrounds equipped with tables, water, and comfort facilities. Wayside areas often provided access along foot trails to scenic viewpoints, picturesque waterfalls, or groves of aged hemlocks, thus adding to the recreational program of the park road. In the larger areas, a lodge, cabins, and a campground were provided. Government and concessionary facilities were generally separated, sometimes located on different loops that extended off the main road

9.21. Constructed of concrete, the pool at Phantom Ranch in Grand Canyon National Park took the form of a naturalistic pond inspired by Japanese and Craftsman-era landscape design. The pool was curvilinear in design and lined with stream boulders taken from the site. Water entered the pool through a pipe fashioned like a naturally flowing stream trickling in over boulders. Construction of the pool alone required 2,043 mandays. Around the pool, Bermuda grass and about four hundred shrubs and trees were planted, and walls of stonemasonry piers and log rails were constructed. *(Photograph by George A. Grant, courtesy National Park Service Historic Photography Collection)*

or parkway. A one-way loop road drew travelers off the main road at gracefully placed wyes and led them around the grounds where sites for picnicking were located on either side of the road. Parking occurred off the road in areas widened for this purpose. The picnic loops allowed designers to adapt the naturalistic principles and practices of landscape gardening to a contemporary recreational use. Often, locations with natural hills and rolling topography or scenic views were selected. Curving paths and stone steps and stairways built into natural rock outcroppings led picnickers to hillside sites furnished with rustic tables and stone fireplaces. Comfort stations were centrally located, and water fountains, fashioned from boulders, hollowed logs, or stonemasonry, were placed at cross paths and other locations. Shelters offered cover and massive stone fireplaces. Paths led from the picnic grounds to scenic viewpoints or hiking trails.

The various relief programs of the 1930s made possible the development of park roads and the expansion of recreational motoring in national parks. The construction of Skyline Drive was initially funded through drought relief funds under the Hoover administration and was continued and finally completed in the late 1930s through public works allotments. Federal Emergency Relief Administration (FERA) funds earmarked for the conversion of lands having low productivity to recreational use made possible the acquisition of land along the Blue Ridge Parkway for development as recreational areas. Although park administration and maintenance facilities were often PWA projects, a number of concessionaires' facilities were built as Works Progress Administration projects. It was the Civilian Conservation Corps, however, which carried out the extensive conservation and landscape naturalization work associated with recreational development and built facilities for picnicking, camping, and hiking, following the landscape design principles and practices laid down in the previous decade by the National Park Service's Landscape Division.

The Development of Parkways

A major advancement in the landscape program of the National Park Service during the 1930s was the development of scenic parkways. This work was planned and carried out by the landscape architects of the Eastern Division of the Branch of Plans and Design, which had evolved from the Yorktown field office staffed in 1930 and headed by Charles Peterson. It was established primarily to plan and design the Colonial Parkway between Yorktown and Jamestown, Virginia. This office was responsible for the development of parks in the East in the 1930s, which included Acadia, Shenandoah, Great Smoky Mountains, and many of the historic sites, battlefields, and encampments that came into the national park system in 1933 and thereafter. It was also in charge of the park service's first historic preservation projects at George Washington's birthplace and the Revolutionary War sites at Morristown, New Jersey. The partially completed George Washington Memorial Parkway outside the nation's capital was also added to the park system in 1933.

The five-hundred-mile Blue Ridge Parkway, the genius of resident landscape architect Stanley W. Abbott, was an essential link in the plan for a park-to-park highway connecting Shenandoah and Great Smoky Mountains National Parks. It brought together the aesthetic and engineering influences of the Westchester County parkways and the National Park Service's Western Field Office. Furthermore, it reflected the ideas coalescing in the 1930s about regional planning, natural resource utilization, and recreational development. The parkway also set forth a new standard of scenery preservation based on cultural history as well as natural beauty. Unlike Skyline Drive, which was a linear park road within a large national park, the Blue Ridge Parkway was a narrow linear corridor dependent on the acquisition of a narrow right-of-way, intermittent recreational areas, and scenic easements to protect vistas of scenic beauty and interest and preserve cultural and natural features.

In 1939, Henry Hubbard defined a national parkway as "an elongated park, featuring a developed highway solely for the passenger car and recreational purposes, bordered by adequate buffer strips on which occupancy, commercial development, and access are restricted." Parkways were "a recent development of a recreational and conservation nature which offer[ed] a means of injecting park values into automobile travel."[58]

National parkways preserved scenes of beauty and interest along a route selected to avoid unsightly developments, such as distracting advertising, dilapidated structures, monotonous stretches of farmland, and other discordant elements. Parkway development was based on the idea that the motorway was part of a larger area having natural attributes, such as forests, lakes, and streams, which were to be preserved or restored to their pristine state. The parkway was furthermore a linear refuge or sanctuary for the protection of wildlife and flora (120–21).

In the late 1930s, the National Park Service established standard requirements for the design of parkways to assure safety and pleasure in recreational motoring. The roads were intended for the use of passenger vehicles primarily for recreational use. They were to be laid out along a wide right-of-way in undeveloped areas so that the land immediately abutting the roadway could be preserved as parkland. Parkways were to be designed with the intention of making the best scenery accessible to the motorist. Dangerous grade crossings and intersections with main highways and railroads were to be avoided, and points of entering and leaving the parkway were carefully selected and designed, at spaced intervals, to eliminate unnecessary interruptions in the flow of traffic along the parkway. The exclusion of private property from fronting the parkway and the limiting of access roadways greatly enhanced the continuity and pleasure of recreational motoring. Scenic easements were to be used to secure the greatest protection of the scenic character of adjoining land without increasing the amount of land to be purchased through fee-simple acquisition, thus allowing the park service control of the natural surroundings along the entire length of the parkway. The high standards of road design, including well-studied alignment, gradient, and landscape naturalization techniques, made it possible for designers to take advantage of scenic features, thus adding to the enjoyment and ease of driving over the completed parkway.[59]

Transportation conventions — naturally curving alignments, grade separations, tunnels, stone-veneered bridges, wye intersections, loop roads, overlooks, and flattened and rounded embankments — which had been adopted in the western parks in the late 1920s ideally suited the needs of a national parkway. Technical innovations such as superelevations and spiral transitions in highway design and advances in bridge construction further added to the experience and pleasure of recreational motoring.

Parkways were to provide facilities for travel and recreation at regular intervals, as well as access to nearby areas having unusual scenic features or offering recreational opportunities. The location and distribution of developed areas along the parkway was a primary consideration in designing the parkway. Foot trails, bridle trails, campgrounds, and picnic areas were to be developed in some areas and facilities for boating, swimming, and other outdoor sports in others.

New Deal programs gave impetus to the development of the national parkway idea. Funding from the PWA and FERA was used to acquire land for parkways and adjoining recreational areas and to construct the roads. Meanwhile, the CCC built trails and overlooks, developed campgrounds and picnic areas, cleared vistas, graded road embankments, and installed the many plantings that naturalized the area after construction. Their work even included turning deteriorating log cabins and homesteads into interpretive displays.

The construction and extension of parkways had national interest and importance, particularly within the context of national recreational planning. State parks, national forests, and national parks became interconnected along parklined highways, serving national as well as regional goals for outdoor recreation and natural resource utilization. By the close of the New Deal, park designers envisioned an extensive system of national parkways to connect important state and national recreational areas.

Chapter 10

A New Deal for State Parks

These relatively nearby wonderlands where people are finding themselves in the highest forms of recreation have been increased and opened to fuller use by the Civilian Conservation Corps. They offer the best there is in the field of recreation—nature itself. Wherever one may live, and whatever his tastes in recreation may be, he can fulfill his requirements for outdoor play in a state park or recreation area.

National Park Service, *The CCC and Its Contributions to a Nation-Wide State Park Recreational Program,* 1937

In the 1930s, the National Park Service's programs for master planning, rustic design, and landscape naturalization extended to the development and improvement of state, county, and metropolitan parks. Emergency Conservation Work (ECW) by the Civilian Conservation Corps (CCC) provided the National Park Service with its first opportunity to give direct assistance to states in developing scenic and recreational areas. This assistance took the form of the supervision of conservation activities carried out by each CCC camp and the dissemination of information about park planning, the construction of park structures, and the design of recreational facilities. Supervision occurred through state park inspectors, who were employed by the National Park Service and who worked directly for the ECW district officer. These inspectors traveled to the parks to oversee and make recommendations on the master plans and the design and construction of park roads, trails, buildings, and other facilities. Technical specialists employed by the park service, including landscape architects, architects, and engineers, were assigned to each CCC camp and closely supervised the work of the CCC foremen and enrollees. The specialists developed plans and drawings under the direction of the state park inspectors. Each camp was headed by a superintendent and had several foremen who directly supervised the CCC enrollees carrying out the National Park Service plans.

As public recreation took on major importance in the 1930s, the National Park Service assumed leadership in developing state parks, surveying the recreational resources nationwide, and encouraging state recreational plans. In states having no state parks, such as Virginia and Tennessee, state parks and park systems were developed with the aid of the park service and other federal programs, including the Tennessee Valley Authority, U.S. Department of Agriculture, and the Resettlement Administration. With the increasing emphasis on national recreational planning, National Park Service designers found themselves designing facilities for swimming, golf, fishing, skiing, boating, and other outdoor activities.

The relationship with state parks was not new. In 1921, National Park Service director Stephen Mather had convened the first meeting of what became the National Conference on State Parks, and park service officials had been involved in meetings with state park officials throughout the 1920s. Mather and Harold Ickes, who became the secretary of the interior in 1933, were both among the founding members of the Friends of Our Native Landscape founded by Jens Jensen in the Midwest in 1913. In his annual reports, Mather traced the development and progress of the state parks movement. By 1933, there was a strong union among the oldest and more established state park systems, including California, Indiana, Iowa, Minnesota, New York, and Pennsylvania.

State Park Emergency Conservation Work

Emergency Conservation Work brought major changes to the administrative organization of the National Park Service. Conrad L. Wirth was selected to head the National Park Service's new State Parks Division in Washington, D.C. Wirth had grown up in Minneapolis, where his father, Theodore Wirth, had been head of the Minneapolis parks for many years. He studied landscape architecture at Massachusetts State College under Frank Waugh, who was to have a substantial impact on his work for the National Park Service from the 1930s until 1964, when Wirth retired from the directorship of the National Park Service. Herbert Evison, who had been the executive secretary for the National Conference on State Parks, became the supervisor for state park Emergency Conservation Work.

Under the first organization of state park ECW, the nation was divided into four districts, each headed by a district officer. J. M. Hoffman, the former director of Pennsylvania's state parks, and later Melvin B. Borgeson headed District I, which covered the East Coast and the adjacent states of Alabama, Mississippi, Pennsylvania, Vermont, and West Virginia. Paul V. Brown, who had worked closely with Colonel Richard Lieber in the Indiana state parks and directed the Bureau of Parks for Allegheny County, Pennsylvania, headed District II, which covered Illinois, Indiana, Iowa, Kentucky, Michigan, Minnesota, Missouri, Ohio,

Tennessee, and Wisconsin. Architect Herbert Maier was put in charge of District III, which covered Arkansas, Colorado, Kansas, Louisiana, Montana, Nebraska, New Mexico, North Dakota, Oklahoma, South Dakota, Texas, Utah, and Wyoming. Lawrence C. Merriam, a forester and administrator, headed District IV, which covered the western states of Arizona, California, Idaho, Nevada, Oregon, and Washington. In 1934, District I was divided into two districts, with H. Earl Weatherwax heading the new district for the southern states. By 1935, the organization had evolved into eight areas called regions, headquartered in Springfield, Massachusetts; Bronxville, New York; Richmond, Virginia; Atlanta; Indianapolis; Omaha; Oklahoma City; and San Francisco.[1]

So dominant a role did state park work play in National Park Service activities in the 1930s that in 1936 the emergency conservation program in the national parks was transferred from the Branch of Forestry to the Branch of Planning and State Cooperation under Conrad Wirth and administered through the state park ECW districts, and the eight ECW regions were consolidated into four. In August 1937, the National Park Service reorganized and decentralized its operations into four regions based on the ECW regions. In addition to staff assigned to CCC camps and a small regional or district staff, the CCC program relied upon itinerant inspectors who traveled from park to park, carrying ideas about design and practice from the central district office to field staff and camp personnel. These men communicated the principles of naturalistic park design and provided assistance and critiques for improving and perfecting the work in the state parks. The program also relied upon the architects and landscape architects employed by state or county park departments.[2]

State park ECW was organizationally independent of the emergency work in the national parks, but groups working in the two areas communicated and collaborated closely. Both groups shared a philosophical foundation advocating landscape preservation and development that harmonized with nature. State park work was guided by the principles and practices that had been adopted and refined by National Park Service designers from 1918 to 1933, many of which evolved from the mid-nineteenth-century English gardening tradition and Downing's ideas about naturalistic gardening, pleasure grounds, wilderness, and rustic architecture.

Before CCC projects for the state parks were approved, the preparation of advance plans was required. Master plans for state parks took varied forms depending on the process already in place in the states and the involvement of National Park Service designers in the actual planning and design. In Virginia, where National Park Service landscape architects were closely involved in the design of parks, the plans were developed on many sheets in a format similar to that of the national parks. In other states, such as Michigan, a single map identifying the name, location, and type of project in relationship to the park's boundaries, roadways, and trails was sufficient. Plans were prepared before any

10.1. Sited to offer scenic views of the lake, the cabins at Bastrop State Park in Texas were built of native stone arranged to give the appearance of having emerged from the natural outcroppings. Civilian Conservation Corps enrollees planted native yaupon (*Ilex vomitoria*) and other shrubs on the surrounding slopes to stem erosion and to further the illusion that the natural landscape had never been disturbed. Curving paths with stone steps and coping led to each cabin, and boulders were embedded along the road to form a naturalistic curb. *(Photograph by Ralph H. Anderson, courtesy National Archives, Record Group 79)*

major construction projects commenced, and they were updated periodically. Once national park designers and officials had roughly agreed on a plan, work was broken down into six-month work projects that the CCC could complete over one or several enrollment periods.

In 1937, with the authority granted by the Park, Parkway, and Recreational Area Study Act, the National Park Service established a formal review process for state park plans. Plans were developed by the state park authorities with the assistance of the inspectors and National Park Service specialists. The master plan was the essential link between the conservation work of the CCC in a state or metropolitan park and the statewide plan for recreation. It simultaneously gave firm direction to the immediate work of park development and fulfilled

10.2. The success of Civilian Conservation Corps projects, such as this stone stairway in Turkey Run State Park, Indiana, resulted from the concerted effort of technicians who advised on design matters, landscape foremen and skilled artisans who supervised stone-masonry or planting, and the numerous spirited and able-bodied young men who provided the manpower and strength to achieve tasks that sometimes seemed monumental. *(Photograph by Ralph H. Anderson, courtesy National Archives, Record Group 79)*

the broader goal of coordinating recreational areas regionally, statewide, and nationally.

The objective of park planning for state parks was similar to that of national parks. The National Park Service designers preparing and reviewing these plans were responsible for ensuring that the entire park area was used to its fullest extent without impairment of natural features and that natural phenomena and historical sites were protected. As a 1937 National Park Service pamphlet stated, "The object is first to conserve and protect the entire area . . . then to develop necessary facilities for the enjoyment of each park feature without interfering with the use of other features. The cardinal principle governing all . . . is that the park areas are to be kept in as natural a state as possible."[3]

Like the national park plans, state park plans were to outline the "existing and ultimate desirable development of the area." They consisted of general development plans laid out graphically on large topographic sheets and a development outline in narrative form explaining the program of proposed work. Layout plans were then drawn up for each area of the park. These plans indicated roads, trails, buildings, and other features and were the basis for determining individual items of construction work to be carried out by the CCC during each enrollment period. Wirth's office offered the following advice:

> All plans should be prepared by someone having first-hand knowledge of ground conditions and therefore the responsibility of their preparation wisely lies with the park authority. All problems should be approached from broad viewpoints, particularly as to how they influence and are influenced by the State and regional park and recreation system. Every possible assistance and cooperation are offered by National Park Service technicians and inspectors in these matters.[4]

Although CCC work in state parks followed the general approach to landscape preservation and harmonization set by the national park designers, less stringent standards were applied to the recreational development of state parks. More freedom existed for creative landscape gardening. Since many state parks were being created out of submarginal land, natural features needed enhancement or creation. Although certain practices that had occurred in the urban parks of the nineteenth century, such as moving earth to form beaches or dams and creating forests, lakes, waterfalls, and streams, conflicted with the mission of national parks, they were commonplace in the development of state parks.

In many parks, the construction of recreational dams was considered the foremost work. In others, the cleanup of dead wood, including blighted chestnut timber in much of the Northeast, was most important. Selective forestry, tree and plant disease control, removal of fire hazards, and other such work predominated in forested parks. In areas not previously mapped, topographical maps were prepared before plans for "orderly development" were drawn up. The construction and improvement of roads and trails were the first building projects begun in many parks. This work sometimes entailed improving sections of old roads, building new roads, and eliminating traces of roads no longer needed. Other common activities included the development of picnic areas and campgrounds, stream improvement, the construction of picnic shelters and comfort stations, and the development of a water supply. In all of these projects, the keys to conveying National Park Service principles and practices were the landscape inspectors, who traveled from park to park in their assigned region, and the camp foremen and technicians, including architects, landscape architects, and engineers, who had day-to-day supervision of conservation work.[5]

Although state park work was similar to work in other types of parks, there were notable differences. While the landscape inspector for the parks in New Jersey and eastern New York in 1933, Norman T. Newton described the tasks

10.3. At Virginia Kendall Park outside Akron, Ohio, cleanup took the form of clearing dead and blighted chestnut trees from hundreds of acres of forest. Civilian Conservation Corps enrollees used hand tools and teams of horses for this work. The wood was stockpiled and later used in the construction of comfort stations, picnic shelters, a boathouse, and a lodge. A nursery was established in the park, and by the end of March 1936, 57,600 native trees and shrubs had been planted throughout the park. (*Photograph courtesy National Archives, Record Group 79*)

to members of the landscape profession as "rough work." Among this work, he listed

> the clearing of park roads, trails, and bridle paths, in which fire protection [was] automatically coupled with improved appearance; the rough construction and alignment of new fire-lines and roadways for access, thus opening up new areas not only for more efficient fighting of fires but also for the use of campers, picnickers and hikers; the selective thinning and cutting of overgrown wooded areas; the clearing of swampy areas and their rehabilitation as lakes for both recreation and water supply; the regrading and planting of slopes as a measure of erosion control, an operation in which the practical and esthetic [went] hand in hand; the construction of park buildings of simple character for both present and future

10.4. At Gooseberry Falls State Park in Minnesota, the Civilian Conservation Corps constructed a swimming beach and a terraced picnic area on the shores of Lake Superior at the confluence of the Gooseberry River. *(Photograph by Ralph H. Anderson, courtesy National Archives, Record Group 79)*

use; and many other types of work normally associated with the development and maintenance of State Parks and Reservations.[6]

As for the social value of the program, Newton wrote,

For the enrolled men, many of whom had never before seen Nature at close hand, the experience is one not only of personal reconstruction and training in the manual arts, but also of contact with those basic properties inherent in nature that we, as landscape architects, recognize as the very reason for the existence of these great State Parks. In the process of educating the public to a true appreciation and a proper use of facilities offered by State and National parks, the experience of these thousands of young men will be a factor of compelling importance. (29)

Emergency Conservation Work attracted large numbers of educated and experienced landscape architects to fill positions of inspectors, camp techni-

10.5. Through a great deal of rockwork and native plantings, the Civilian Conservation Corps transformed this spring into an attractive water garden that blended with the surrounding parkland. Other landscape naturalization work at Palmetto State Park in Texas included rechanneling the creek through a series of rock falls and lining the banks with weathered stone to give the appearance of having been there for years. *(Photograph courtesy National Archives, Record Group 79)*

cians, and landscape foremen. The hiring of local experienced men (LEMs) also added knowledge and experience pertinent to the camp's locality. Typically LEMs were skilled artisans — masons, carpenters, blacksmiths, and builders. They brought an understanding of the local climate and weather conditions, the forestry and woodsmanship of the surrounding countryside, the use of local building materials for construction, and the planting and transplanting of native vegetation.

Herbert Maier's Influence

Perhaps the most successful of the regions from the viewpoint of consistent, imaginative, and successful application of national park principles and practices was ECW District III, which later became Region Seven and was eventually folded into the National Park Service's Southwest Region. Administered first from Denver and then Oklahoma City, the district was headed by Herbert Maier. When the National Park Service was reorganized in 1937, Maier became the director of the Southwest Region. Soon afterward the headquarters moved to Santa Fe.

Maier, an architect who had worked out numerous solutions for the design of park structures in his work for the American Association of Museums for almost a decade, brought experience, wealth of sources, and an amazing ability to express clearly the qualities of naturalistic architecture and landscape design. Maier developed an effective process for translating national park principles and practices to the CCC camps responsible for developing state and metropolitan parks. This process involved strong design leadership in the central district office and an effective network of state park inspectors who served as liaisons between Maier and the state park authorities on the one hand and Maier and the camp superintendents on the other.

Although an architect and a specialist on park structures, Maier had a fundamental understanding of the landscape principles and practices for park planning which Vint's office had developed in the late 1920s and early 1930s. He passed these principles and practices—whether relating to the sloping and planting of road banks, the construction of guardrails, or the layout of campgrounds—on to his inspectors through photographs, drawings, and simple explanations. The inspectors then translated these to the field, where they conferred with CCC technicians and landscape foremen about ongoing work. Maier himself visited the parks frequently, taking interest in special problems.

Maier was identified as the park service's expert on the principles for designing park structures. He not only drew from his own experience in designing park museums and educational exhibits but also assimilated the complete range of the Landscape Division's concerns, from road building to campground development. Maier's commissions from the American Association of Museums had brought him in close contact with the Landscape Division as it was formulating an approach to design and a repertoire of major park buildings and with the scientific and educational experts of the national parks as they were developing a coherent program of park interpretation. Maier used the concept of "design by example," circulating ideas and techniques for rustic construction and naturalization work. He had compiled his own Library of Original Sources, which he shared with those working for him. He developed a photographic inspector's handbook with photos that outlined principles to be followed in park work rather than designs to be copied.[7] He relied greatly on the talents of Cecil Doty, an architect who worked closely with Maier at the district headquarters, became involved in design problems throughout Maier's district, and, by the end of the 1930s, was regional architect for the Southwest Region of the National Park Service.

Maier's understanding of the relationship of site, setting, and structure matured in the late 1920s through his work at Yellowstone. Probably more than any other park designer, Maier assimilated and perpetuated the principles of the Arts and Crafts movement. Although an architect by training and experience, he understood the lessons of Henry Hubbard and readily applied conventions of landscape architecture such as winding walks, native plantings, flagstone terraces, and open foyers to his work. The Yellowstone museums and nature shrines enabled him to develop a common architectural scheme suitable for the park as a whole which could be applied to the specific purposes and characteristics of each individual site. What resulted were interpretive structures, trailside museums, amphitheaters, naturalist residences, and nature shrines that had a common identity but varied in scale, function, materials, and surroundings.

Taking full advantage of the widespread unemployment within the landscape architecture profession, Maier in 1933 assembled an outstanding team of state park inspectors. He drew experts from schools of landscape architecture and public practice. Among his first team of inspectors were landscape architects of considerable experience and acclaim in the profession, including Frank H. Culley and P. H. Elwood Jr., both former professors at Iowa State; George L. Nason, who was a Harvard classmate of Daniel Hull and had been the superintendent of the parks in St. Paul, Minnesota, since 1924; and S. B. de Boer of the Denver metropolitan parks.[8]

Maier assembled drafting expertise in his district office and as a result was able to circulate blueprints of standard designs for cabins, entrance signs, community buildings, and even campground layouts to inspectors and CCC camp technicians and foremen. These drawings were executed by Cecil Doty and show the direct influence of Maier and also park architects such as Arthur Fehr of Bastrop State Park in Texas, whose designs for ECW were considered exemplary. The drawings illustrated representative structures in floor plans, elevations, and details. Depicting a community building, Sheet 13-A drawn by Doty included the side and front elevations, a cross section of the interior with fireplace, a floor plan, and a detail of fireside seats that doubled as wood boxes. Sheet II-C for weekend cabins carried designs for an L-shaped cabin with an open porch and an octagonal cabin. Both featured immense chimneys that emerged majestically from the rocky, uneven ground and walls battered in a similar exaggerated fashion. The blueprint also carried a detail of a wrought-iron and glass lantern called a "light bracket" and an interior light fixture made of cattle horns with two hanging lights with wood and iron fittings and designed to hang from an exposed cross beam. Both in their form and in their details, these buildings bore great similarities to the cabins at Bastrop State Park.[9]

Because many state parks in the Southwest shared similar dry conditions and an abundant supply of local rock, the same methods of construction and similar designs could be repeated from park to park, with variations allowing for local topography and cultural influences. Standard plans provided several basic designs that could be varied, adapted to local conditions, and elaborated upon. District III's designs called primarily for stone construction that could be adapted to the rocky terrain and natural materials of many western parks. Maier's work on the Yavapai Point Observation Building at Grand Canyon provided him with extensive experience in working with canyonlike terrain and rocky soil. The lodge designed by Guy Carlander, a CCC architect, and constructed on the canyon rim at Palo Duro State Park was the direct heir of Maier's Grand Canyon observation station and closely resembled the James House at Carmel by Charles Greene and the Grand Canyon work of Mary Colter.

Maier became the National Park Service's spokesman on the subject of park structures. In 1935, he addressed the conference of state park officials, instructing them in principles of site selection, harmonizing design, and other aspects of construction. Many of Maier's ideas were incorporated in the three-volume work *Park Structures and Facilities,* edited by Ohio architect Albert H. Good and published by the service several months later as a comprehensive statement of the design principles and practices of the National Park Service at that time.

Today, Maier's speech to the state park officials is an important key to understanding the source of the many ideas that Albert Good put forth in *Park and Recreation Structures* and is perhaps the most detailed explanation of park service design. It is an index of practical and aesthetic principles that had evolved out of the formative years of the National Park Service's program of landscape design and Maier's own development as an architect of park structures. These principles emerged from commitments to providing stewardship for park scenery, preserving parks as inviolate places, and assimilating construction to natural conditions. State park architects, landscape architects, and inspectors in Maier's ECW district were the direct heirs of these principles and played an important role in perpetuating them in state park development.

The principles were open ended, fostered creative expression, and allowed for great variation and diversity based on each park's unique cultural and natural history. They allowed for designs that were unique yet unified by principle. The idea of an open-ended process based on principle rather than architectural prototype was itself central to the landscape architect's method inherited from Repton and Downing. Park design therefore encouraged experimentation, innovation, refinement, and, above all, a steadfast search for sensible, simple, and pragmatic solutions that followed function on the one hand and nature on the other.

These principles explain the strength of national park design and the success of the nationwide development of state parks through the leadership of the National Park Service. When it came to state park development, however, the principles were a point of departure for a full flowering of expression which

Concession, Palo Duro State Park, Texas

The difficult problem of a building on the rim of a canyon can only be well met by a low structure, skillfully blended to the character of the canyon wall. There is large measure of successful accomplishment in this example.

UNITED STATES DEPARTMENT OF THE INTERIOR · NATIONAL PARK SERVICE

101

10.6. A rimside location was selected for the lodge at Palo Duro State Park in Texas because of its spectacular view of the canyon. Concrete and native stone materials were shaped to blend with the undulating contours of the canyon. Built with a low profile and skillfully modeled in rough stonemasonry, the lodge reflected the principles of design followed by Mary Colter and Herb Maier at Grand Canyon National Park, while achieving its own unique expression of naturalistic design. *(Reprinted Albert H. Good, ed.,* Park Structures and Facilities, *1935)*

Arno B. Cammerer, then director of the park service, praised in his opening words to *Park Structures and Facilities*. One of the greatest fears shared by Maier, Wirth, Evison, and other administrators of ECW in state parks was the threat of standardization—that park structures in state parks would be copies of national park structures and that park structures nationwide would look alike. National park designers had used native local building materials and adapted indigenous and frontier forms and construction methods to diversify structures from park to park. The fundamental philosophy and versatility of the principles resulted in vastly different results. Herein lay the strength and unity of New Deal park development, particularly for state parks. By 1935, as *Park Structures and Facilities* would demonstrate, great vigor and variety abounded in state park work.

While national park design had originated primarily in the West, in mountainous and forested areas in the Rockies, Sierras, and Cascades, the state parks spanned a greater variety of topography, climate, and native character. The true test of the park service's design principles lay in their applications to the varied environmental conditions and recreational uses of state parks. Maier pointed out in his speech the "extreme varieties" of wilderness and semiwilderness parks operated by the various states. They ranged from the woods of Maine and Minnesota to the semiarid mesas of the Southwest, from the heavy conifer forests of the Rockies to the dunes of the Gulf Coast. This variety made it necessary first and foremost to determine a character appropriate for each park. Maier summarized the National Park Service's principles for the harmonization of park structures. Structures were to be inconspicuous and their number limited by combining several functions under one roof, if practical. Large numbers of small structures interrupted scenic vistas and views that should remain free of built structures. Shelters, so popular in parks, were justifiable only at particular vantage points at the termination of long walks and, unless needed for fire protection, should not occur on every peak.[10]

Maier began his speech with a philosophical perspective on stewardship of natural areas. His thinking in the 1930s mirrored his thoughts of the mid-1920s, when he had just completed the Yosemite Museum. Aside from roads, he believed, park buildings were the "principal offenders in an activity designed to conserve the native character of an area." The concept of "improvement" was an anomaly in park development. The answer to the dilemma for park designers lay in the simple concept of blending, whether in constructing roads, laying out picnic sites, or building structures for use and comfort. The principles of architectural design and landscape architecture offered simple measures for making structures inconspicuous. By following these, park architects and landscape architects could create structures that harmonized with each particular environment and served the demands of visitor use (83).

Structures could be made inconspicuous in six basic ways: screening, the use of indigenous and native materials, adaptation of indigenous or frontier

10.7. Naturalistic stonemasonry, a stepped parapet, and an arch ring of irregularly shaped native stones distinguish this stone culvert built in Longhorn Cavern State Park in Texas. The designs and specifications for bridges and culverts which were developed by the National Park Service's Landscape Division in the late 1920s were readily adopted for Emergency Conservation Work in state parks. *(Photograph by Ralph H. Anderson, courtesy National Archives, Record Group 79)*

methods of construction, construction of buildings with low silhouettes and horizontal lines, avoidance of right angles and straight lines, and elimination of the lines of demarcation between nature and built structures.

Structures were to be located "behind existing plant material or in a secluded nook in the terrain partly screened by some natural feature." If sufficient natural plant material did not exist at the site otherwise best suited to the building's function, an adequate screen should be planted by repeating the same plant material that existed nearby. It was best, however, to locate and adapt structures so that "planting them out" was unnecessary. A building with a low silhouette in which horizontal lines predominated was easier to screen (84, 89).

Using indigenous or native materials was the "happiest means of blending the structure with its surroundings" and was the characteristic that popularly defined "rustic architecture." Maier traced this precedent to the frontiersmen: "Whether he set up his abode on the forest, or sod or adobe covered plains, or in a rock-strewn country, he was forced to adopt the natural material immediately at hand, and when the structure was completed it consequently echoed the identical materials and color from its surroundings" (85).

The adaptation of indigenous and frontier construction included the use of primitive tools which led to a "freehand architecture with an absence of rigidly straight lines, and a softening of right angles." This principle had been an important one in designing the patterns of masonry and the character of guardrails, bridges, and culverts of National Park Service roads. It was likewise a principle that Maier had incorporated in his Yellowstone museums: "And so we find that construction which is primitive in character blends most readily with primitive surroundings and is thereby less outstanding and has intriguing crafts-manlike appearance." It was this characteristic that linked park structures with the American Arts and Crafts movement and made that period's prototypes in-spirational to park designers. Wirth had just authorized a survey of indigenous frontier architecture of America with plans to publish this compilation, making it "available to designers of structures for wilderness areas with a view toward adapting them to modern needs." The intention of the park service was not to restrict modern park buildings to a primitive form of construction but to "fore-stall a threatened standardization of park architecture throughout the country."[11]

Maier recommended that designers use colors that blended structures with the immediate surroundings. For instance, he suggested that designers choose colors for the exterior of wooden buildings and the wooden portions of build-ings which were commonly found immediately around the site of the new struc-ture. Warm browns and driftwood grays were particularly recommended; green was discouraged, being difficult to match with natural greens. Maier recounted that Yosemite designers had attempted several years before to make buildings inconspicuous from Glacier Point by staining them green to blend into the sur-rounding foliage. This plan was abandoned when they discovered that the roofs in fact "screamed," because the planes of the roofs reflected the light whereas the surrounding foliage absorbed it. They found that brown blended into the color of the ground beyond and was least conspicuous (86).

Buildings with low silhouettes and horizontal lines were considered the most inconspicuous. Maier recommended a low roof with a pitch of no more than one-third. He felt that in most locations such a roof was adequate to with-stand the weight of annual snowfall. Roofs, in his opinion, too often dominated the design of park structures and were conspicuous from long distances. Straight lines and right angles were to be avoided. This could be achieved through archi-tectural details and finishes—for example, by selecting logs that were knotted

10.8. Naturalistic stonemasonry fireplace at Bastrop State Park in Texas. The Civilian Conservation Corps in state and national parks in the 1930s fashioned utilitarian objects such as fireplaces and water fountains into handcrafted, naturalistic rockwork that blended with the natural setting. *(Photograph by Ralph H. Anderson, courtesy National Archives, Record Group 79)*

and by allowing the knots to protrude. Maier criticized the "gingerbread" style for its sawn look, the precision of its lines, and its subsequent effect on the architectural features in which it was used (90).

Lines of demarcation were to be erased. If possible, structures were to be designed and located so that it was not necessary to plant them out. Vegetation could be introduced along the foundations to obliterate the too common line of demarcation between building and ground. Rough footings and foundations made of large local boulders at the base of structures to give the impression of natural rock outcroppings was another method for erasing the lines of demarcation. Buildings were to be in scale with their surroundings. Maier recommended buildings of a "heavy rustic scale" for mountainous areas where forests abounded. The structural elements, such as logs, timbers, and rocks, were to be considerably oversized to be in scale with the nearby trees, boulders, and other

10.9. The concession building at Palmetto State Park was built of reddish brown sandstone, native to the area, and reflected Herb Maier's naturalistic principles of rockwork. Among the special features were the raised terrace with its stonemasonry parapet, the battered stone walls that flared as much as ten feet at the corners of the building, and the massive boulder chimney of stones carefully removed from nature and reassembled at the construction site to appear naturalistic. Lichen-covered stones were carefully arranged throughout to give the building the appearance of having grown out of the ground. *(Photograph by Ralph H. Anderson, courtesy National Archives, Record Group 79)*

natural features. Lighter construction was appropriate for less mountainous regions as long as designers steered cleared of "twig" architecture that flourished under the name of "rustic" (88–89).

Maier's greatest contribution to park design was his mastery of rockwork, assimilating both the landscape gardener's emphasis on naturalism and the architect's vision of the construction potential of this material. He recommended the use of naturalistic and natural rockwork to eliminate lines of demarcation:

> One of the principal phases of park development which may be an indicator of appreciation of good installations is rockwork in general. The rock selected should first of all be proper in scale, that is the average size of the rocks employed should

10.10. In keeping with the romantic rustic tradition that A. J. Downing had popularized in the nineteenth century and the American Arts and Crafts movement had applauded in the early twentieth, the roof of the concession building at Palmetto State Park in Texas was thatched with fronds of native palmetto (*Sabal minor*) to contrast with the hanging Spanish moss that hung from the surrounding elm, pecan, and cottonwoods trees. The roof required thirty-two thousand leaves, many of which were gathered outside the park. Since nine leaves alone weighed ten pounds, the roofing turned out to be quite an undertaking. *(Photograph by Ralph H. Anderson, courtesy National Archives, Record Group 79)*

be sufficiently large to justify the use of masonry. In rockwork it is better, due to the scale of the nearby natural features, to oversize rather than undersize. Whether in retaining walls or in buildings, or bridges, it is usually better to employ rough rockwork or rubble, if properly done, than cut stone, and the weather faces of the rock should, of course, be exposed. Rock should be selected for its color, and for the lichens and mosses that abound on its surface as well as its hardness. (91)

Maier's instructions echoed Henry Hubbard's advice that to be in a "geologically correct" position, rocks were to be placed on their natural beds with strata or bedding planes horizontal. Rocks were never to be placed on end or laid in courses like bricks, and the horizontal joints were to form an irregular pattern. Maier encouraged variety in the size of stones and advised,

> In a wall larger rocks should be used near the base, but this does not mean that smaller ones should be used exclusively in the upper portions, rather a good variety of sizes should be common to the whole surface. I like to see a rock wall splay out near the base and especially at the corners so as to give a feeling of natural outcropping and to prevent a fixed line of demarcation at the ground. The terminating of the top of a wall by creating it with a row of rocks set on end gives a "peanut brittle" effect and is always in bad taste. (92)

Maier stressed the importance of all elevations in park buildings because the public would view and approach these buildings from various directions. Maier was particularly aware of this in his work at Yellowstone and Grand Canyon. At Yellowstone, he ingeniously made the Lake Museum the centerpiece of a larger complex, with a naturalist's cottage to one side, the lake before it, an amphitheater in the woodland behind, and footpaths to parking areas, comfort stations, a nearby concessionaire's development, and trails. The building had several entrances and housed several exhibit rooms.

Maier used landscape techniques and features to blend museum buildings and structures with the natural setting they were intended to interpret. He attempted to integrate interior exhibits with exterior areas such as gardens, amphitheaters, viewing terraces, and trails. Uniting viewpoints within and around the building with surrounding scenic vistas demanded a solution that fused both architectural and interpretative considerations. Maier looked to the terrace, rock-edged walks laid out in irregular curves, and screens and displays of native vegetation to unite the indoor and outdoor activities and the principal and auxiliary functions of the museum. At the Fishing Bridge and Old Faithful Museums, Maier and the park naturalists worked at incorporating landscape concerns on a small scale in architectural solutions. As a result, the terrace became part of the park designer's repertoire of devices, and the amphitheater was elevated to an architectural form in its own right.

The Role of the District Inspector

The itinerant district inspector was the essential link between the National Park Service and the state park authorities and CCC camps. Working directly for the district officer, inspectors reviewed applications for CCC camps and visited sites proposed for new parks. Once camps were established, they inspected the work carried out by the enrollees under the direction of the camp foremen and superintendent, giving foremen directions and reporting progress and problems

10.11. At Big Bend State Park (later national park) in Texas in 1934, one of the first Civilian Conservation Corps projects was the construction of trails among the Chisos Mountains. *(Photograph courtesy National Archives, Record Group 79)*

to the district officer. The inspectors ensured the high workmanship and consistent adherence to principles of naturalistic and rustic design. They offered critiques of the naturalistic treatments of lake projects, trail construction, and plantings. Initially, the inspectors coordinated the production of plans and drawings developed by draftsmen in the state offices and transmitted instructions for their execution to camp foremen. Then, in the spring of 1934, the park service assigned specialists in architecture and landscape architecture to each camp. These technicians produced the plans and drawings, with the inspector's assistance and approval, and provided routine supervision of ongoing work. As a result, the selection and training of capable camp technicians were crucial to achieving good park design. The need for technicians opened up innumerable opportunities for recent graduates as well as experienced professionals in landscape architecture, architecture, and engineering to engage in creative work and apply practical skills and knowledge. This collaboration of park technicians and district inspectors worked successfully until the late 1930s, when major reductions occurred in the number of CCC camps and the National Park Service's allotments for technical assistance.

Inspectors traveled extensively, often stopping in one park for only one or two days before driving on to the next, which might be several hours or an entire day's journey away. Although they were usually assigned to one geographical region, for example, west Texas or the combined states of South Dakota and North Dakota, parks were generally far apart and sometimes located in remote areas. Assignments changed and varied as the program grew and peaked in the mid-1930s. The inspectors maintained close contact with the state park organizations and with Maier, who himself traveled extensively to the state parks and state park offices and became involved in issues varying from the state acquisition of land to cooperation with the army, which constructed the camps and managed the men. The inspectors regularly returned to the district office and traveled to state offices to meet with state park authorities.

In the first enrollment period, May to October 1933, much of each inspector's time was spent visiting proposed sites for camps and preparing plans for work in parks that had already received camps. In 1934, the district inspectors played a key role in inspecting submarginal lands and selecting areas to be developed as recreational demonstration areas. The opinion of each district inspector on important matters of site selection and park development was backed up by Maier, additional inspectors who would visit the sites, and traveling inspectors of extensive experience and knowledge, such as P. H. Elwood, who were brought in to make critical judgments or to suggest solutions to difficult problems.

District inspector George Nason and district officer Maier played a key role in the establishment of Big Bend National Park through their initial inspection of the territory in 1933, their approval of the early plans for its development as a state park, and the early work of the CCC carried out there under their direction. In fact, Maier's office prepared the report documenting the area's superlative geological and biological features and outlining a plan for its development as a national park, which resulted in congressional authorization for the park in 1935. This report included essays by national park officials who examined the area according to the criteria for parklands set by the 1918 statement of policy and noted botanists and other scientists who had studied the area. It also included sketches for park buildings suitable to the natural character and cultural traditions of the region, as well as maps showing a system of park roads and hiking and bridle trails to reach the area's most spectacular features and viewpoints. This report was later published under the title *Big Bend National Park Project, Texas* in an effort to stimulate public and political support for acquisition of the land, which was the responsibility of the state of Texas if the national park was to be realized.

Park development required a sense of planning and a command of the naturalistic, or informal, ideas of landscape design. By the end of the first period,

10.12. Admiring the rose-colored porphyry spires and emerald slopes of live oaks, state park inspector George Nason remarked that the Chisos Mountains presented an opportunity in park design greater than any he had seen before. As the state of Texas acquired land, the Civilian Conservation Corps built a park road through Green Gulch, a natural gateway in the mountains, alongside the old ranching road and began developing the park in 1934 and 1935. For its splendid collection of biological species, its dramatic geological features, and its outstanding scenic character, the state park became Big Bend National Park in 1944. *(Photograph by Ross A. Maxwell, courtesy Big Bend National Park)*

it became clear to Maier and the inspectors that the key to successful park design lay in the hands of camp technicians who could both plan designs for the sites and supervise the work on a day-to-day basis, giving instruction to the men and approving work as it progressed. Park development required engineers, who directed trail and road construction; architects, who designed buildings; and landscape architects, who attended to landscape issues such as locating sites for construction, protecting natural features, presenting views, designing structures that were inconspicuous and harmonized with nature, and naturalizing disturbed areas after construction. These three groups were key in the overall development of a park and had the skills needed to ensure naturalism and quality of workmanship. Other camp technicians were geologists, foresters, archeologists, and wildlife biologists hired by the National Park Service to direct special studies and conservation activities.

The ECW state park program was enriched as men with national park experience accepted assignments in state park work. One such individual was Halsey Davidson, who was the ECW landscape architect at Mount Rainier in 1933 and 1934 before becoming a state park inspector. Since assignments in camps were only for six-month periods and many northern camps closed for the winter months, landscape architects and architects frequently changed positions. There was a great deal of movement from national park work to state park work and from one area of the country to another. Over time experienced camp technicians became qualified for inspector work.

Assignments were often political in nature, too, with local congressmen and senators appointing people from their districts. For example, a U.S. congressman from El Paso recommended local architect William Wuehrman for appointment to Big Bend in May 1934. The CCC program was not as politically motivated, however, as the civil works projects that were administered through state offices and provided vast numbers of jobs for skilled workers in local areas. Although a number of recreational facilities, such as artificial lakes and park refectories, were constructed in state parks in 1934 under the brief Civil Works Administration program, it was not until 1936 with the establishment of the Works Progress Administration that such projects came under the review and supervision of the National Park Service. Informal occasions arose, however, where park inspectors traveling in the vicinity of a project or inspecting CCC work in the same park where a dam was under construction would review the work in progress and offer technical advice.

By 1933, some states had organized park systems and established positions for park designers, while others had few developed parks and no statewide system. It was necessary, therefore, that the state park ECW program adapt to the existing state park structure and coordinate activities with state park authorities. As a result, the landscape architects or architects already employed by some states or local governments were involved in planning parks and designing park structures under Emergency Conservation Work. Wherever possible, the park service had designs drawn up by designers or private practitioners working for the state or local park organization. In this way, the ECW program gained the service of experienced park designers such as Arthur A. Shurtcliff, who was designing buildings and developing plans for Blue Hills Reservation near Boston, and the firm of Hare and Hare, which worked on the Fort Worth Park in Texas. The diffusion of ideas coming from experienced state park designers enriched the overall program and was viewed by Maier, Good, and others as essential to maintaining the vitality and individuality of state park design.

Speaking before state park officials in 1935, Maier called upon the use of landscape designers in private practice to broaden the character of park structures: "While the National Park Service under this program assists to a major extent in furnishing landscape architects and architects as inspectors and technical foreman, it also encourages the States in securing competent professional service from private practice. We are most anxious that State park officials engage professional technical service on a fee basis to cooperate and even take a

10.13. New Deal programs elevated the design of picnic shelters to a fine art. The shelter at Iowa's Backbone State Park reflects the fusion of National Park Service principles, Civilian Conservation Corps craftsmanship, and the talent and ingenuity of state park architects such as Ames B. Emery. *(Photograph courtesy National Archives, Record Group 79)*

major hand in the development under the State Park Emergency Conservation Work. And this should be an integral part of the program and will tend to lessen the threat of standardization."[12]

In *Park Structures and Facilities* of 1935, Albert Good noted the need for professional designers of "consummate skill" and "rare good judgement" in adapting designs to the conditions of a particular location. These persons were considered to have "the best judgement available" to determine the style most appropriate to an area:

> The most completely satisfying subjects included herein are so, not as a result of chance, but because training, imagination, effort and skill are conjoined to create and fashion a pleasing structure or facility appropriate to a particular setting. Who then, but those of professional training and experience are equipped to decide that a perfect structural interpretation for one setting will sanction adaptation

for another, and in what detail or degree modification will make the most of the conditions presented by another environment?[13]

Davis Mountains State Park was one of the early parks to show the direct influence of national park experience. Creative, spacious, and well-hidden picnic grounds were developed, in which each unit was a rustic grotto or alcove reached through natural rock outcrops, offering views, natural shade, and the amenities of campstove, table, and benches. Even the comfort station was camouflaged by design, stone material, and vegetation. The "premier" picnic site, with an eighteen-foot banquet-sized table, was an outdoor alcove reached by stone steps inserted into the narrow space between two rock outcrops and descending to an earthen terrace made flat by large flagstones laid against the natural rock outcrop. Natural rock walls and thickets of vegetation enclosed the site on three sides, revealing a spacious view north and east of the valley and hills beyond. Carefully screened from view by vegetation were the road below, a "gateway" cut through the rugged outcrops of the mountaintop, and the naturalistic stone comfort station fit into the hillside one hundred yards away. Also at Davis Mountains, a lodge in the pueblo style was constructed using adobe blocks made on site by traditional methods.

Principles and Practices

Maier's office aggressively sought ways to convey the park service's principles and train his inspectors and camp landscape architects, architects, and engineers. Although experienced in the principles of design and construction for park structures, he also understood and instructed his inspectors in the principles of park road design, guardrail construction, and campground and picnic area development.

Sometime in 1934, Maier's office produced a photographic handbook for district inspectors. The handbook presented the practices and principles of good park design in the form of twenty-two numbered plates that were linen-backed photographs. Each photograph was accompanied by a simple principle or instruction placed on the back. Included were illustrations of Maier's earlier work in Yosemite, Yellowstone, and Grand Canyon; early ECW work in Oklahoma; and national park work in the campgrounds and along park roads at Rocky Mountain National Park. This handbook represented Maier's ideas about the basic principles of park design. They reflected his own growth from an architect of museums to a park designer, planner, and administrator. By 1934, Maier had assimilated ideas drawn from the professional fields of architecture and landscape architecture, as well as the principles and practices formulated by the Landscape Division for the design of park roads, trails, and campgrounds.

The inspector's handbook illustrated museum buildings, nature shrines,

Park and Recreation Progress since 1933

amphitheaters, campgrounds, picnic sites and shelters, road banks, guardrails, dams, footbridges, culverts, and water crossings. It provided basic instructions for building park structures, constructing roads, and designing campgrounds and picnic areas.

Maier stressed basic principles of design, which he then translated into specific practices that enabled structures to blend inconspicuously into their natural surroundings. Similar to those he summarized in his address to state park officials in 1935, these principles were the use of indigenous materials, use of freehand lines, horizontal emphasis, commonality of scale among all members and the whole structure, elimination of right angles and rigid lines, and architectural blending. Maier used his work at Yellowstone, Yosemite, and Grand Canyon National Parks from 1924 to 1930 to illustrate principles and practices of good architectural design.

Using his museum at Norris Geyser Basin with its central open foyer, Maier urged designers to use freehand lines and allow horizontal lines to predominate. He explained how park structures could be made less conspicuous and more readily screened when their silhouette was low and horizontal lines predominated. He encouraged the use of rock along the base of the building and showed how the lines between earth and building could be erased by splaying the lower courses and by placing plant material along the line of demarcation.[14]

Grand Canyon's Yavapai Point Observation Building illustrated the elimination of right angles and rigid lines. Maier drew attention to the absence of sharp right angles and straight lines in the building's overall shape, masonry walls, and details such as windows and doors. He pointed out the treatment of stone lintels supported by rock corbels so that openings closely resembled the irregular recesses in the nearby rock formations. He said that sharp right angles and rigid straight lines were to be avoided in buildings in wilderness areas and that irregularity lent a feeling of primitiveness to the workmanship, as well as one of age to the structure (plate 20).

The Yavapai Point building presented a vastly different design problem from that of the Yellowstone museums. Here not only did Maier explore the use of rough local rock as a material of inherent beauty and interest, but he achieved variations of form, texture, and line which assimilated the character of the surrounding canyon. Although the use of flat roofs was generally discouraged in wilderness areas, Maier felt justified in incorporating one in the design of the Grand Canyon museum. "In this particular case," he said, "on the rim of the Grand Canyon, the building is silhouetted against the sky and a gable roof would have been too conspicuous. Also, the flat roof here is in keeping with the extreme flatness of the Canyon rim area and, of course, there is the historical precedent in Pueblo architecture" (plate 19).

Maier coupled principles with practices and offered detailed advice. Stone pylons and walls were to be splayed near the base. Exposed log members were to be selected for their knotty character, and log trusses were to be supported on stone corbels. Chimneys were to be stepped back as close to the ridge as possible to become "a more intimate part of the building." Although many of his terraces at Yellowstone were made of cement, he preferred flagstone as flooring for terraces, lookouts, and shelters. He drew attention to how planks and logs were cut and joined to form doors and stressed that stones forming walls should be in a variety of sizes to lend a structure "interest." Roofs were to be shingled with shakes one inch thick. Each course was to have a wavy appearance, adding to the freehand character. Every fifth course was to be doubled to add to the appearance of a roof's weight. In keeping with pioneer prototypes, windows were to be relatively small in size and contain small panes of glass. Maier felt glass was out of harmony with rough rockwork. Because glass was "a scarce article" to the pioneer builder, he further believed large, single-paned windows were out of character in a natural park. Although he claimed no precedent for clipped or jerkinhead gables in pioneer America, he recommended their use because they eliminated "what might otherwise be too prominent a point."

The handbook contained numerous suggestions for the details of rustic construction and design. For example, illustrating the Madison Junction ranger station at Yellowstone, Maier pointed out how a cap log placed along the top of a rock base could join together the rock and shakes. Interior logwork, including the rafters and purlins of the exposed roof and the posts and lintels framing doorways and windows, was to be in scale and have an irregular knotty appearance. The scale of doorways, too, was important, with the width exaggerated in proportion to the height. The shingle courses for roofing or walls were to be laid in wavy freehand, rather than rigid, lines. Decorative details included a cutout of an evergreen tree backed by green cathedral glass.

Maier was a critic of his earliest work. Illustrating the fireproof features of Yosemite Museum, he said that from a design standpoint it would have been better to carry some of the lower-story rockwork up through the second story to avoid the appearance of two horizontal halves, one stone and the other frame. He suggested that the arch rocks of the entrance arch should have been "a trifle larger . . . in better scale with the adjoining rocks." Similarly, he was critical of the proportions and stonemasonry of the Glacier Point Lookout (1924), saying the walls should have been twice as thick and the stones of the lower courses should have been larger "to give the appearance of growing out of solid rock." He advised that such a roof be given a heavier appearance by using thicker shakes or doubling the courses. He criticized the uniformity of rocks in the walls of the Yavapai Point building (1929) at Grand Canyon. In the Bear Mountain Museum (ca. 1925) in the Palisades Interstate Park, he found the shingle roof too light and rigid in appearance for the heavy stonemasonry walls and the change in the size of stones in successive courses to be too sudden.

Coloration was important. In selecting colors for paint or stain, he said,

"Warm browns have been found to be the best medium for lessening the importance of a structure. Green roofs are difficult to handle. It is most difficult to harmonize this color with nearby tree foliage and . . . green pigments usually fade to unpleasant hues. . . . It is frequently desirable to paint window muntins a lighter color than the walls in order to take advantage of their architectural value" (plate 6).

Maier's lesser works, such as Yellowstone's nature shrines and amphitheaters, would prove particularly influential in state and national park ECW. Nature shrines at Obsidian Cliff, Tuff Cliff, and Firehole Canyon in Yellowstone and amphitheaters from Yellowstone National Park and Boulder Mountain Park were illustrated in the handbook. Amphitheaters were to be located in naturally occurring bowls and screened from view by encircling trees that also served to shade the audience. Usually the stage was to be oriented to the east so that the audience would not face the afternoon sun. Masonry seats were preferred because they could be modeled into curvilinear benches that fit inconspicuously into the bowl-shaped theater. Log seats resulted in a more definite geometric pattern and were considered more conspicuous.

Maier emphasized the importance of vegetation and edging stones in woodland theaters. At Old Faithful in Yellowstone, rows of Engelmann spruce were planted before and behind the log parapet of the stage. An edging of irregularly sized and shaped boulders outlined planting beds that separated the stage from the aisles and seating. Natural trees were left between seats. A campfire circle of stone was constructed in front of the stage. Trees were planted or left in place around the amphitheater to screen it from outside activities.

To accommodate the presentation of lantern slides, which had become a popular evening program in national parks by the 1930s, Maier suggested building a log frame into a palisaded parapet of vertical logs which served as a back wall of the stage and mounting a canvas screen that could be removed in winter. A lantern house—a miniature house rendered in rustic principles—was to be located on center axis to the stage.

What Maier could not draw from his own experience as a park designer he drew from the principles and practices of the Landscape Division and the first experiments in ECW work in state and local parks under his jurisdiction. Building roads was the first stage of development in any park and, as a result, was a particularly important type of conservation work. Maier looked to the work being done on the Trail Ridge Road in Rocky Mountain National Park not far from his Denver office. This road was one of the first to be built entirely according to the improved specifications for excavation, masonry, and landscape protection which Vint's office had introduced in 1929. Illustrating various views of the newly constructed road, the handbook gave instructions for building guardrails, shaping road banks, naturalizing the roadside, and developing scenic turnouts.

Following the standards worked out by the Landscape Division, Maier explained the techniques for sloping road banks:

> The primary purpose of bank sloping is to return the bank to as near its original condition as possible, thereby removing the scars which have resulted from road building. . . . The degree of slope will depend on the natural terrain and on the character of the soil. Where possible the slope should be low enough to hold grass and to prevent erosion. As a rule a three-to-one slope is desirable but a four-to-one slope is preferable. . . . The cross-section of a sloped bank should be an O.G. curve with the lower part forming the gutter. It is a common fault that this lower part is omitted so that the bank enters the gutter at a sharp angle. . . . It is most essential that the top of the bank be well rounded into the natural grade so that root cornices will not develop later. One of the common mistakes is to direct the workmen to work to a series of stakes beyond which they do not go thereby leaving a line of demarcation along the top of the bank. (Plate 26)

Where a steep rock bank was exposed, Maier suggested leaving it in place and rounding it off at various points to give it the appearance of a natural rock outcrop. He pointed out the desirability of adjusting the degree of the slope to the natural terrain and avoiding a constant degree of slope. A common question facing road builders was whether or not to preserve the trees on road banks. Where trees were plentiful, Maier advised, "their retention, unless in the matter of outstanding specimens, should be secondary." He felt that it was usually "better to develop the bank to its proper slope and introduce seedlings than to retain the trees at the expense of the proper ground form" (plate 25).

On naturalizing the roadside after construction, Maier recommended that slopes be allowed to recover naturally and that sodding be attempted only where cuts were too steep "to give promise of natural restoration." Rocks could be embedded in the slopes for naturalistic effect. "Where vegetation is fairly profuse and the bank has been properly sloped, the natural vegetation will frequently restore itself. . . . However, it is sometimes necessary to seed the bank. In such cases only grasses that are natural to the region should be used" (plate 25).

Combining principle and practice, the handbook showed how a steep road cut could be resodded by introducing board strips and wooden pegs to hold the sod in place. Existing rocks were to be left in place and others introduced to hold the sod further and break up the monotony of the slope. Camp foremen and technicians were reminded that slopes were to be watered for a considerable period after planting.

Illustrating the newly constructed guardrail along the Trail Ridge Road, Maier translated the Landscape Division's standards into simple instructions. He said that rock guardrails were preferred in wilderness areas because they were permanent and blended readily into the landscape. He drew attention to the proportions of the walls and to the spacing of the crenulating piers that occurred at intervals and broke the monotony of a continuous horizontal line. His instructions recommended dimensions for walls and piers and the irregular placement of stones outside courses to give the effect of a continuous and naturalistic parapet. Maier warned against practices such as troweling off the top of the walls with mortar or placing wafer-shaped rocks along the top course (plate 23).

Maier offered two designs for culverts, one of stonemasonry, the other of dry rock. These were built for Wintersmith Park in Oklahoma and followed the standard designs and masonry specifications worked out in the late 1920s by Vint's office.

To illustrate campground construction, Maier drew on Meinecke's theory and again looked to projects under way in nearby Rocky Mountain National Park. He recommended Meinecke's idea for using logs and boulders as barriers to control traffic and protect valuable vegetation. Using logs was much cheaper than hauling in boulders and embedding them in the earth but "much less permanent." Logs were to be considerable in size. Cedar was the best material, being more durable than pine, and fir the least desirable. Maier encouraged naturalism: "The plain natural log placed in such a way that it gives the appearance of having fallen where it lies, is without doubt the most preferable" (plate 23).

Where trees were most endangered—at sharp corners, on the outside of the road curve, and at the entrance to parking spurs—boulders offered the best protection. Rockwork was to appear naturalistic:

> When boulders are used they should be large and should be partially embedded in soil so that they will appear natural and solid. Small rocks should not be used because they are easily overlooked and can be moved. The visibility of the boulders is important. Use dark ones against light colored soil and light boulders against dark soil or a green background. Do not outline roads or spurs with regular rows of rocks—these look unnatural. Boulders need not be placed closer than to prevent the driver from attempting to go between them. Parking spurs should be located in the shade. . . . Spacing of boulders should neither be regular nor in a straight line. Make the arrangement appear as natural as possible. (Plate 27)

In Maier's region, where rock outcrops and boulder-strewn hillsides abounded, the naturalistic development of picnic areas offered creative possibilities. In the Southwest, the early picnic areas were large, with a small number of sites developed as individual and private units. Built into the hillside on a terrace of natural rock and flagstones or concealed behind a rock outcrop or thicket of trees, each picnic site was designed as a naturalistic grotto. Some were designed to accommodate a single family; others were designed for larger groups. Maier illustrated one at Oklahoma's Turner Falls Park where stonemasonry was the principal method of construction for fireplaces, benches, and tables. Maier found fireplaces were frequently unsightly and recommended naturalistic designs that blended with the terrain, using rock where it was available. Maier called for standard proportions in the measurements for seats (eighteen inches wide) and tables (thirty-one inches high) but encouraged variations in the size of tabletops to create banquet tables as well as family-and even children-sized versions:

> Naturalistic picnic units built up of rocks blend into the surroundings more readily than do those constructed of logs or sized lumber. . . . It is more difficult, however, to satisfactorily execute tables and benches of rock since, due to their freehand lines, workmen find it difficult to execute them accurately from a blueprint. . . . There are several other factors which militate against the use of masonry tables and benches. They must be located in almost permanent shade since otherwise they become thoroughly heated and radiate heat for a long period. Furthermore, only the smoothest stone slabs serve satisfactorily as seat tops and table tops and these are not always readily obtainable. (Plate 37)

The inspector's handbook illustrated a number of other naturalistic structures and landscape features. A footbridge made of oak logs, peeled to eliminate insect damage, blended with the surrounding forest. A low-water crossing built at Turner Falls Park in Oklahoma was both a dam and a bridge made naturalistic by the irregular placement of stones along the lower courses. Highly successful was a low, naturalistic dam from Wintersmith Park in Oklahoma, which created a scenic lagoon for fishing and boating while giving the illusion of a natural waterfall by the stepped progression of lower courses laid to imitate natural ledges.

Also at Wintersmith, a stairway of naturalistic steps showed the direct influence of Olmsted's stairway at Franklin Park, illustrated in Hubbard and Kimball's *Introduction to the Study of Landscape Design*. It was built into natural ledges and had heavy coping walls along both sides.

> Few landscape units are so difficult to execute satisfactorily as are naturalistic steps. . . . The primary object is to give the appearance of having utilized natural ledges. It is most important that the width of treads should not be kept constant but should vary. . . . The rocks forming the coping walls at either side of the steps should not be placed in a row but should vary in height. . . . The stairway should be blended into the surroundings by occasionally carrying additional rocks some distance to either side into the adjoining vegetation. . . . No mortar should be evident—steps of this type are usually laid entirely by dry construction. . . . Width of treads and height of risers vary with the natural slope. Treads should be as wide as possible and risers should not exceed six inches. (Plate 32)

10.14. The "Inspector's Photographic Handbook" for Civilian Conservation Corps District VII gave advice on the construction of naturalistic picnic units, such as this one at Turner Falls Park, Oklahoma. Tables and benches were to be built of rock so that they readily blended into the naturalistic surroundings. *(Photograph courtesy National Archives, Record Group 79)*

Attention to detail contributed greatly to Maier's success as an architect and was a key concept that he endeavored to pass on to his inspectors and to the ECW architects and landscape architects designing facilities in state parks. Maier's rigorous and methodical approach resulted in structures that, although derived from his designs or those of the Landscape Division, exhibited freedom of expression in their own right.

Maier's advice was focused on the climate, natural conditions, and topography of the southwestern states, but it reflected the overall principles of park design adopted and advanced by the National Park Service. Above all, the inspector's handbook upheld the critical role of inspectors in state park Emergency Conservation Work and pointed out the specific principles and practices that the park service advocated and endeavored to communicate to the foremen and technicians of the CCC camps.

Submarginal Lands and Recreational Demonstration Areas

Although a number of federal programs provided funds and labor for the development of state and county parks, few provided funds for the acquisition of land to create the parks. State parks were developed in areas already owned by the state or in the process of being acquired by the state. Roosevelt, who had become interested in land-use issues and the utilization of natural resources, saw submarginal lands that had limited agricultural value as having great potential as future public parks and recreational facilities. In 1934, as a preliminary step toward affecting land use, the Federal Surplus Relief Administration provided twenty-five million dollars for the purchase of low-productivity or poorly used lands, called submarginal lands; five million of the total allocation was for the acquisition of lands to be converted to recreational use. Later that year, the funds were transferred to the Federal Emergency Relief Administration (FERA), directed by Harry Hopkins. Conrad Wirth, designated as coordinator for the Interior Department's participation, immediately developed a program for acquiring submarginal land suitable for park development and recreational activities. The Civilian Conservation Corps and other forms of relief labor could be used to restore these areas to a natural condition and develop recreational facilities for hiking, boating, swimming, skating, skiing, picnicking, and camping.[15]

On May 1, 1935, the land program was transferred to the Land Utilization Division of the newly designated Resettlement Administration headed by Rex Tugwell. On November 14, 1936, however, responsibility for the recreational development area (RDA) program was returned to the National Park Service. By the end of 1936, the park service had drawn up general development plans for many of the projects and was developing the areas with labor and funds provided by the Emergency Conservation Work program, the Works Progress Administration, and the Resettlement Administration.[16]

Beyond the primary goal of reclaiming submarginal lands, the program had two additional purposes. It was both an effort to meet the need for increased recreational facilities, particularly among lower-income groups, and a demonstration of how recreational facilities could be planned and developed. Each project was considered an experiment, and the resulting park, wayside, or park extension was viewed as a model for recreational development having important social and humanitarian value for the nation as a whole. The experience of the National Park Service in comprehensive planning, in building park roads and trails, in constructing rustic buildings and structures, and in naturalizing and reforesting the landscape was put to use for the first time, on a massive scale, in developing parks from submarginal lands for primarily recreational purposes. From the beginning, the intention was to turn most of the areas over to state park or highway departments after development and to encourage state and local governments to develop similar kinds of park areas.

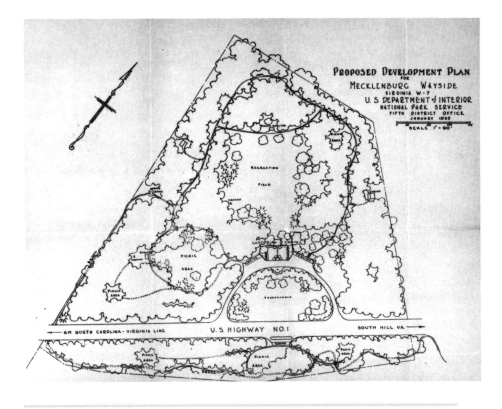

10.15. In Virginia and South Carolina, recreational demonstration areas took the form of waysides along main highways. RDAs were designed by the National Park Service and constructed by the Civilian Conservation Corps. The wayside on U.S. Highway 1 outside Mecklenburg, Virginia, included parkland on both sides of the highway and featured picnic areas, a playing field, a caretaker's residence, and several picnic shelters. Although most RDA's were eventually turned over to state park systems, the waysides were transferred to state highway departments. *(Plan courtesy National Archives, Record Group 79)*

The program identified four kinds of recreational demonstration areas: (1) vacation areas fifteen hundred to two thousand acres in size located near major population centers and providing a variety of facilities for daytime recreation and overnight camping; (2) waysides twenty to fifty acres in size along principal highways where motorists could rest, picnic, play sports, and enjoy the outdoors; (3) extensions to national parks and monuments developed for recreational activities such as camping, picnicking, and swimming; and (4) areas adjoining state scenic areas which could be redeveloped for recreational uses.[17]

In the first year of the program, more than four hundred areas of land were investigated and twenty-five projects approved. By 1936, forty-six projects had begun in twenty-four states. By 1941, the forty-six recreational demonstration projects covered approximately 400,000 acres and consisted of sixty-two separate areas. Most popular were the thirty-one vacation areas, which included children's camps, family camps, and industrial and social organization camps — all of which offered opportunities for low-income groups, public and semipublic organizations, and others to enjoy low-cost vacations in the out-of-doors. These areas also provided facilities for picnicking and daytime use. In addition, thirteen waysides were developed along highways in Virginia and South Carolina. Approximately 77,294 acres in eleven separate areas were added to national park areas, including the Manassas National Battlefield, Kings Mountain National Military Park, Badlands National Monument, and White Sands National Monument. Approximately 41,841 acres were added to five existing state parks: Alex H. Stephens State Park and Pine Mountain State Park in Georgia, Custer State Park in South Dakota, Fall Creek Falls State Park in Tennessee, and Lake Guernsey State Park in Wyoming. The program made possible the development of recreational areas along the Blue Ridge Parkway and the acquisition of land authorized but not yet acquired in Acadia National Park and Shenandoah National Park. The newly acquired land in these parks was developed for recreational purposes: waysides for picnicking and camping were built along the Blue Ridge Parkway, and campgrounds, scenic viewpoints, picnic areas, bathing beaches, and boating facilities were developed at Acadia.[18]

Vacation areas were designed to supplement existing state parks, which most commonly had been set aside and developed for their scenic features. They were modeled closely on state parks, with particular emphasis on the development of organization camps, particularly the Harriman section of the Palisades Interstate Park, which had begun a program of organization camps about 1910. The requirements for vacation areas stipulated that they were to be from two thousand to ten thousand acres in size and located within approximately fifty miles of a major center of population. In Pennsylvania, which had five such areas — the most of any state — these areas were accessible to seven urban centers: Reading, Philadelphia, Scranton, Wilkes-Barre, Altoona, Johnstown, and Pittsburgh. The acreage was to be adequate to provide separate sections for day and overnight uses and to accommodate several organization or group camps that would be separated from each other and from the public camping and day-use areas. Because swimming was the most popular sport, it was desirable for each demonstration area to have a natural or artificial body of water. Camps were often located out of sight among the trees bordering the shoreline. The park service promoted as a model the fifteen-thousand-acre Chopawamsic RDA outside Washington, D.C., in Virginia's Prince William County, one of the first areas opened for public use. In 1936, the service published *Recreational Demonstration Areas, As Illustrated by Chopawamsic, Virginia* as a basis for the development of other RDAs, state parks, and metropolitan parks, partially fulfilling the objective that the RDAs be demonstrations of public recreational areas.[19]

Organization camps were one of the most significant features of these areas. The U.S. government constructed facilities for several separate camps in each RDA for use and management by private and semiprivate social, educational, and welfare organizations, such as the Campfire Girls or a local board of education. Such camps provided an experience in nature and the outdoors for youth and families from nearby cities and rural areas. Each camp was divided into an administrative center and small outlying units, each housing twenty-four campers. Central dining and recreation halls, an infirmary, a director's quarters, and other administrative buildings were located in the administrative center. Radiating out from the center were the various camping units, located so that each was out of sight and hearing of other areas of the camp. Each unit consisted of sleeping cabins for campers and leaders, a washhouse and latrine, and a lodge with an outdoor attached kitchen. The arrangement of the camp made it possible for each unit of cabins to operate independently of the larger camp. The design of the lodges, with fireplaces and ample space, made it possible to house groups for winter activities.[20]

The educational and recreational value of such camps had long been recognized, but until 1934 only a few state parks provided such facilities. One highly acclaimed program was in the Harriman section of the Palisades Interstate Park in New York, which had begun about 1910 and by the 1930s had more than ninety camps providing low-cost vacations annually to more than six hundred children. On the West Coast, several cities had developed similar camps for children and families in nearby public forests.[21]

The success of the RDA program was measured immediately in the accessibility of the areas to population centers and the popularity of the areas themselves. In 1936, it was projected that the forty-six demonstration areas would serve an estimated thirty million people. In 1937 alone, the completed areas received one hundred thousand days of use by overnight campers and one million days of use by daytime visitors. The project employed significant numbers of men through the CCC and Federal Emergency Relief Administration (FERA). By 1938, eight thousand relief workers and twenty-three hundred CCC enrollees had been put to work developing a total of 352,874 acres of land for recreational purposes.[22]

Acquisition called for the purchase of land possessing some degree of scenic character and topographical qualities that made it possible to develop a body of water, a system of roads and trails, and several separate areas for daytime use, overnight camping, and organization camps. The National Park Service directed all planning and development of the new parks, and the Resettlement Administration moved the displaced residents to areas outside the parks. The social and administrative aspects of organized camping had been the subject of state park meetings in the 1920s, and the National Park Service drew from the experience and knowledge of the nation's leaders in the fields of camping and organized camping, such as Fay Welch, who headed the camping program at the Palisades Interstate Park.

Developing an RDA posed planning and design problems that called for the use of the principles and practices formulated by the landscape architects of the National Park Service. Since these areas were not primarily scenic in nature, they provided the opportunity to use techniques for landscape naturalization, from cleanup to replanting. The task of redeveloping the land for its scenic and recreational potential was not unlike that encountered by the state of Virginia and the National Park Service in developing Shenandoah National Park from former fields and pastures. This work had called for the removal of structures and buildings, the planting of road traces, the clearing of dead and down timber and old stone walls, and the recovery of natural vegetation. RDAs, however, called for the blending of recreational development with naturalistic gardening on a scale not encountered by park designers previously. Wildlife and forest protection studies and measurements were made, and each area was carefully planned before development. Emphasis was placed on the development of all-year recreational facilities, especially the creation of lakes and ponds for swimming, fishing, boating, and skating. Within this context, Frank Waugh wrote *Landscape Conservation* for the park service in 1935, emphasizing the importance of studying and reproducing natural conditions when creating artificial landscape features. Waugh's instructions for naturalizing the shores of newly created lakes by re-creating naturally occurring zones of vegetation and by locating cabins, lodges, and buildings other than boathouses away from the water's edge had important applications.

The development of RDAs challenged park service designers to expand their repertoire of park facilities to accommodate a full range of recreational activities from boating to winter sports and new kinds of structures called for by the organization camps. Although the actual number of areas developed by the National Park Service was limited, the resulting design ideas had widespread applications for state and metropolitan parks in general.

RDAs had a lasting impact on public recreation and the design of state and metropolitan parks. Organization camps and artificial bodies of water were developed for recreational purposes throughout the nation's state parks and forests during the CCC era. Moreover, other federal agencies called upon the National Park Service to develop recreational areas. These agencies included the Tennessee Valley Authority, which had incorporated several large parks in its plans for the region, and the Bureau of Reclamation, which controlled Lake Mead, the largest artificial lake in existence at the time and the result of the construction of Boulder Dam on the Colorado River. Recreation took on broad meaning,

10.16. The Park, Parkway, and Recreational Area Study Act of June 23, 1936, upheld the physical, social, and educational values of outdoor recreation and urged that recreational facilities be within reach of every American. The bathhouse and swimming beach on Lake Cleawox in Oregon's Jessie M. Honeyman Memorial State Park, photographed here about 1940, represent the burgeoning interest of state governments in the 1930s to utilize natural resources for recreational purposes. Named for the leader of Oregon's movement for roadside beautification and scenic conservation, the park was developed by the Civilian Conservation Corps from 1936 to 1941. *(Photograph courtesy Oregon Historical Society, neg. 68663)*

and a definite shift in emphasis occurred from the conservation-minded goals of those who had advocated scenic areas as state parks in the early decades of the twentieth century to the creation of multipurpose recreational parks in a natural setting. The experience of the National Park Service—in master planning, landscape preservation and naturalization, and rustic architectural design—was coupled with a philosophy that called for creativity and diversity of expression based on harmonization with natural conditions and adherence to common principles and practices.

The New Deal programs allowed the National Park Service to take a leading role in the development of state and local parks and to help fulfill the broad vision for the use of natural resources for public outdoor recreation which had been emerging among state park advocates and public officials since the 1920s. As new and improved state parks opened their gates to increasing numbers of Americans in the 1930s, the idea that outdoor recreation should be affordable and accessible to every American became firmly ingrained in the national conscience. Organization camps, more than any other facility built during the New Deal, embodied the new park ideal. Those built as RDAs and those modeled after the RDAs have continued to fulfill their social, educational, and recreational purposes.

Although the National Park Service took leadership in promoting organized camping and developing model camps, such camps were developed only in areas to be turned over to state park systems. The issue of building organization camps in national parks was debated in the late 1930s, but such camps were viewed as conflicting with the official park service policy forbidding special uses by certain groups. National Park Service policy determined that all camping areas within national parks should be open to the general public and that no special privileges should be granted to private or semiprivate organizations to operate camps on national parklands. As a result, organized camps were not developed in national parks, including the RDAs that were extensions to national parks and provided campgrounds, picnic areas, bathing beaches, and other recreational facilities for the general public.

Works Progress Administration

Another source of funding and labor for state and local park development was the Works Progress Administration. The WPA was established by executive order by President Roosevelt in 1935 and headed by Harry Hopkins until 1939. This program paid wages for skilled labor in a variety of fields, including art, theater, architecture, writing, and engineering. WPA funds helped create reservoirs and lakes for recreation such as Lake Murray in Oklahoma, amphitheaters for public entertainment, lodges in state parks and national forests, murals for public buildings, public highways, and utility systems. Administered through state agencies, the funds were given to local governments and were designed to increase the purchasing power of paid workers on WPA projects and thereby stimulate the economy. In December 1935, the National Park Service began to cooperate with the newly created WPA by assuming responsibility for the technical supervision of the work programs of forty-one WPA work camps operating in state, county, and municipal parks.

The National Park Service's involvement was prompted by the state, county, and municipal agencies sponsoring the camps, who saw the program as an extension of the CCC program to conserve natural resources and develop public recreational areas as well as the emergency relief program for recreational demonstration areas. As a result, state park inspectors and National Park Service designers reviewed applications, commented on construction designs, and supervised progress in conjunction with their review of CCC work. WPA projects adhered to the same basic principles that guided Emergency Conservation Work and public works construction.

The first year, projects took place in three federal, twenty-two state, and thirteen municipal park areas. WPA projects included large facilities built in state parks, such as refectories, lodges, museums, dams and artificial lakes, large amphitheaters, swimming pools, and even golf courses. This program also made possible the expansion of concessionaires' facilities in both national and state parks; one example was the Big Meadows Lodge and Cabin Development in Shenandoah National Park. In addition, through the WPA the National Park Service took charge of a program to stabilize the North Carolina shoreline through the construction of sand fences and the planting of dunes. The park service continued to review and oversee WPA recreational improvements in state and local parks until the program ended in 1943 as the wartime economy eliminated the need for relief work.[23]

The Park, Parkway, and Recreational Area Study

Support for state park development and the leadership of the National Park Service in surveying and fostering recreational resources nationwide increased in the early 1930s. This support went beyond the development work of the CCC through Emergency Conservation Work and the creation of RDAs and resulted in a cooperative effort between the National Park Service and state governments to formulate a national recreational policy. By executive order of June 30, 1934, President Roosevelt established the National Resources Board "to prepare . . . a program and plan of procedure dealing with the physical, social, governmental, and economic aspects of public policy for the development of land, water, and other national natural resources." The board was to submit a report on land and water use by December 1, 1934. The National Park Service set up a Recreation Division headed by George M. Wright to study the topic of national and state parks and related recreational activities and prepare the chapter on the recreational use of land in the United States. This preliminary report showed the need for an exhaustive nationwide survey of recreational activities. The proposal for such a study immediately gained the support of the Department of the Interior.[24]

In 1935, an advisory committee was appointed to help the park service formulate policies and programs relating to state park work. This committee included the retired head of Indiana's parks Colonel Richard Lieber, former park service director Horace Albright, and several planners, park promoters, and association representatives. By this time, CCC work in state parks was being planned and supervised by experienced architects, landscape architects, engineers, foresters, wildlife specialists, geologists, and archeologists. By mid-1935, approximately 150,000 workers and 6,000 technicians had been involved in Emergency Conservation Work in both national and state parks. The park service cooperated with the National Recreation Association at this time to conduct a study that resulted in the publication of George Butler's *Municipal and County Parks in the United States, 1935*.[25]

It was not until passage of the Park, Parkway, and Recreational Area Study Act of June 23, 1936, that the National Park Service was authorized and given funding to make a comprehensive study of the public parks, parkways, and recreational area programs of the nation. The study was to assess the legislative provisions for recreation and conservation at all levels of government and examine the existing resources. The act also authorized the park service and other federal agencies to aid states in planning, establishing, improving, and maintaining parks, parkways, and recreational areas. Other important features of the act were its recognition of the principle of regional planning and the provision that two or more states could enter into agreements with one another to develop recreational areas. The act, although limited in its scope, codified the cooperative relationship that the National Park Service had with state parks informally since 1921 and through Emergency Conservation Work since 1933. For the national parks, it extended the meaning of "recreation" as used in the National Park Service policy statements of 1918 and 1932 to include intellectual and aesthetic pursuits that more closely embraced scenery preservation, study, and interpretation. It also broadened the scope of national parklands to encompass the diverse types of parks managed by the service in the mid-1930s — the large natural parks, monuments, historic sites, battlefields, military parks, and parkways — and made way for new areas such as seashores and lakeshores.

State surveys of recreational areas were conducted as a basis for the national study. Recreation was classified into five broad types: physical, aesthetic, creative, intellectual, and social. Parks were divided into four types: primitive, modified, developed, and scientific. The state surveys resulted in reports, many of which were individually published. They functioned as comprehensive plans and as guides to recreational resources which coordinated the activities of parks, forests, wildlife refuges, and reservations at all levels of government into a single recreational system for each state. These studies were later incorporated into re-

10.17. Built into the slopes of the lake in the limestone-rich region of eastern Wyoming about 1935, the museum at Lake Guernsey State Park exhibited the principles of naturalistic rockwork and the methods of stonemasonry followed by the Civilian Conservation Corps. Particularly distinctive is the stonemasonry of the gable, consisting of roughly cut native rock, carefully selected for its color, size, and weathered textures and laid in irregular courses. *(Photograph by Ralph H. Anderson, courtesy National Archives, Record Group 79)*

gional and national studies. In 1941, the National Park Service published *A Study of the Park and Recreation Problem in the United States*. By this time, thirty-four states had completed detailed studies assessing the condition of their parks and their needs for recreational areas. The momentum for state and national park cooperation continued despite the war, and the first grants-in-aid bill was introduced in 1945. The bill was unsuccessful, and it was not until 1964, with the passage of the Land and Water Conservation Fund Act, that a grants-in-aid program for park development was realized.[26]

The concept of the nationwide state park recreational program was set out in a brochure published by the National Park Service in 1937. Entitled *The CCC and Its Contributions to a Nation-Wide State Park Recreational Program,* the brochure emphasized the accomplishments of the CCC in state park work and in RDAs. Not only had ECW made possible the development of existing parks, but it was a catalyst in the acquisition of new lands: thirty-seven states had acquired a total of 350 new park areas covering 599,091 acres, and eight states — Colorado, Mississippi, Montana, New Mexico, Oklahoma, South Carolina, Virginia, and West Virginia — established their first parks as a result of the stimulus provided by the CCC. This promotional brochure upheld the physical, social, moral, and educational value of outdoor recreation and called for state and regional planning to ensure that recreational facilities were within reach of every American. It called for planning at all levels — in the park itself and in the selection and co-ordination of recreational resources across a state or among a group of states.[27]

In 1937, the National Park Service began publishing an annual yearbook on park and recreation progress, which brought together articles by noted experts on a range of topics related to the federal relief work in public recreation. Over the next seven years, articles appeared on park planning, sports, park structures, landscape architecture, and park administration. In the first issue, Wirth proclaimed, "The greatest resource of any nation is its human wealth, and in the conservation of the human wealth recreation plays a major part." He set out the three components of a nationwide park and recreation program: (1) the park and recreation system, (2) access and travel, and (3) use and direction. He wrote, "It is through properly directed use that the physical, mental, and spiritual benefits of outdoor recreation are produced with equal emphasis to achieve social adjustment of the individual in order that he may live a full, useful, and complete life." Wirth and other park service officials saw their work as a social-humanitarian effort. They were laying the foundation of a federal and state partnership in recreation which would significantly contribute to the human wealth of the nation.[28]

Chapter 11

Portfolios for
Naturalistic Park Design

Early Portfolios of Park Structures

Designs and ideas for every aspect of park development were circulated in several publications of the National Park Service. These included the *Portfolio of Comfort Stations and Privies* and *Portfolio of Park Structures* in 1934, *Park Structures and Facilities* in 1935, and the three-volume *Park and Recreation Structures* in 1938. The first of these was begun immediately after the formation of the State Parks Division, headed by Conrad Wirth, who had studied under Frank Waugh at Massachusetts Agricultural College and had been working for the National Capital Park and Planning Commission. Wirth hired Dorothy Waugh, a capable illustrator and draftsperson and the daughter of his mentor, Frank Waugh, to gather information on park facilities and develop an illustrated manual with instructions for the construction of basic park structures which could be used by the CCC. The 1935 and 1938 volumes were edited by Albert "Ab" Good, an architect from Akron, Ohio, who was experienced in the design of park and recreational structures.

The first two portfolios took the form of loose-leaf binders that could be circulated immediately and expanded as new designs became available. The idea was to get designs and technical information out to the CCC camps, where work was proceeding and guidance needed, as quickly as possible. The first portfolio included an assortment of designs for comfort stations and privies and covered technical details of sanitation and construction. The most basic of park structures, comfort stations and privies were distinguished on the basis of whether they employed plumbing or more primitive arrangements in their sanitary design. The comfort stations that Vint's office had designed for Union Point in Yosemite and Logan Pass in Glacier were published, alongside those built by the Westchester County parks in New York and the designs of Albert Good for Virginia Kendall Park in Akron, Ohio.[1]

The second loose-leaf portfolio incorporated the designs for privies and comfort stations and added sections on fireplaces, picnic tables, park benches and seats, entranceways, barriers, bridges, lights, bathhouses, administration buildings, picnic shelters, cabins, community buildings, service buildings, museums, and lookouts. As new designs became available, they were distributed to the district offices and state park camps, where they were added to the corresponding section of the binder. The portfolio would eventually become a compendium of park and recreation structures, from substantial buildings to small elements such as log guardrails and stone fireplaces. Dorothy Waugh's selections represented the state of the art of park construction in 1933 and 1934.

All of Waugh's designs were based on actual examples. She included only structures that provided practical prototypes that could be adapted or reproduced by the CCC. Working from blueprints and architects' drawings, Waugh developed simple floor plans and elevations in the form of line drawings that could easily be grouped by structural type, numbered, and reproduced in the form of pages to be inserted in binders. Designs were credited to the state or local park and in some cases to specific designers, such as Ames B. Emery, the architect of Iowa state parks. The plans and drawings were basic and simple, with no "unnecessary" details. Not intended as a substitute for the services of an architect or engineer, the plans were designed to give park officials a "better grasp of the problems of developing facilities" and to present "concrete" ideas that could be "used and worked out" by their technical staffs.[2]

Waugh drew heavily from the work in state and county park systems to represent the full range of recreational buildings. She collected blueprints and drawings of picnic shelters, bathhouses, boathouses, and other buildings from state and county park systems that were part of the mainstream park movement, including the Westchester County Parks Commission and other regional commissions in New York; municipal parks of Akron, Ohio; state parks of Indiana, Iowa, and Pennsylvania; and Forest Preserve District of Cook County, Illinois. Many of these likely came from the files of the National Conference on State Parks, which Herb Evison had directed before becoming the National Park Service's supervisor for state park Emergency Conservation Work. Waugh also considered designs used by the U.S. Forest Service, particularly for outdoor fireplaces. She drew heavily upon the designs for the park structures that were built by the CCC during the first two or three enrollment periods, particularly relying on districts headed by Herbert Maier and Paul Brown. Her sources included the blueprints for signs, cabins, and a community building which Cecil Doty had prepared in Maier's district office for use in state park Emergency Conservation Work. Among these drawings, which became the first prototypes for park construction, were a basic comfort station with battered walls that could be rendered in stone or log and had been developed for Virginia state parks, a roof-covered picnic table developed by the Pennsylvania Department of Forests and Waters,

STATE PARK EMERGENCY CONSERVATION WORK

11.1. From transplanting trees to building picnic shelters, the various landscape improvements and conservation work of the Civilian Conservation Corps in state parks were depicted in the frontispiece of the *Portfolio of Park Structures,* drawn by Dorothy Waugh in 1934. *(Reprinted National Park Service,* Portfolio of Park Structures, *1934)*

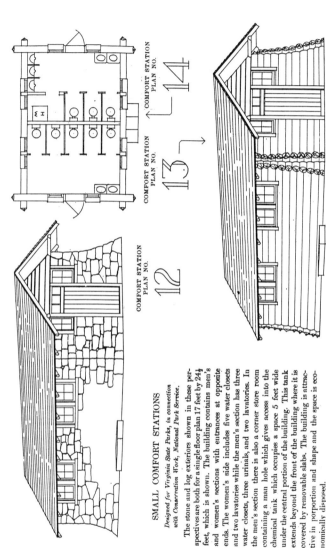

COMFORT STATION
PLAN NO.

12

COMFORT STATION
PLAN NO.

13

COMFORT STATION
PLAN NO.

14

SMALL COMFORT STATIONS

*Designed for Virginia State Parks, in connection
with Conservation Work, National Park Service.*

The stone and log exteriors shown in these perspectives are both for a single floor plan 17 feet by 24½
feet, which is shown. The building contains men's
and women's sections with entrances at opposite
ends. The women's side includes five water closets
and two lavatories while the men's section has three
water closets, three urinals, and two lavatories. In
the men's section there is also a corner store room
containing a man hole which gives access into the
chemical tank which occupies a space 5 feet wide
under the central portion of the building. This tank
extends beyond the front of the building where it is
covered by removable slabs. The building is attractive in proportion and shape and the space is economically disposed.

11.2. Published in 1934, the National Park Service's first portfolio of designs for emergency conservation projects in state parks included plans, drawings, and instructions for constructing privies and comfort stations. A small comfort station, designed for Virginia state parks, could be constructed in several variations using local materials of stone or log. It was praised for its attractive proportions and shape and economical use of space. *(Reprinted National Park Service, Portfolio of Comfort Stations and Privies, 1934)* an adobe cabin group that was designed for Davis Mountains State Park in Texas, a tourist cabin from Minnesota's Itasca State Park, a lodge for Giant City State Park in Illinois, a museum and administration building for South Mountain Park in Phoenix, an observation tower from an Alabama state park, and a bridge from Enfield State Park in New York which closely resembled Franklin Park's Scarborough Bridges and the White River Bridge at Mount Rainier. This group included a number of building types, such as bathhouses, which had no counterpart in national park work. Waugh included bathhouses from Indian Lake in Michigan and open picnic shelters such as one for Allegheny County parks in Pennsylvania.[3]

In 1934, work on the portfolio was abandoned in favor of a volume consolidating photographs, drawings, and plans of successful CCC, PWA, and WPA projects, as well as national and state park work. Dorothy Waugh became a member of the advisory committee whose job it was to collect and recommend plans and designs of merit, and her ideas and research, but not her drawings, were absorbed into the new volume. She continued to work for Wirth designing posters that promoted recreational activities, including winter sports, in national and state parks.[4]

Park Structures and Facilities

The new volume, *Park Structures and Facilities,* was intended as an honor roll of outstanding examples of park structures, many of which had been constructed through Emergency Conservation Work. It was edited by Albert "Ab" Good, the designer of buildings for Virginia Kendall Park, a new Akron park being developed through ECW. His earlier work was at the nearby Boy Scout camp, Camp Manatoc, and featured a stockaded entrance with carved totem pole pylons, which was illustrated in Waugh's portfolio. Good's other buildings included a Swiss chalet-style dining room and numerous cabins and cottages.

Other members of the editorial board were Thomas C. Vint; Paul V. Brown; Herbert Maier; Oliver G. Taylor, the deputy chief engineer of the Eastern Division of the Branch of Engineering; and Norman T. Newton, the landscape architect for ECW Region Two. Although Good wrote the apologia and comments throughout the book, the ideas set forth represented the thinking of the committee as a whole. These ideas were principles and practices that Vint and Maier especially had formulated in the late 1920s and early 1930s. Herb Evison, the supervisor of the State Park Division and the former executive secretary of the National Conference on State Parks, also offered "helpful counsel" based on his broad experience in state park work.[5]

The volume stands as a comprehensive index of national park principles and practices for naturalistic landscape design and rustic architecture. Although the book focused on construction methods and materials of park structures, it provided some general guidelines on locating and planting facilities to harmonize with the natural landscape. The park service published 2,350 copies of *Park Structures and Facilities* in 1935. The popularity of the work led to the much larger distribution of an expanded three-volume set in 1938, entitled *Park and Recreation Structures.*

Both editions included drawings of floor plans and elevations carefully delineated in the same neat hand, presumably that of Good himself. Photographs were drawn from many sources; most of those depicting national park work were taken by George A. Grant, who had begun working as a park service photographer out of the Western Field Office in the late 1920s and had created a visual record of newly completed work of the Education, Engineering, and Landscape Divisions. A number of photographs were from Maier's own portfolio. The majority of photographs, however, came from the illustrated narrative reports submitted by CCC camp superintendents, landscape inspectors, and resident landscape architects.

Although the books primarily depicted state park construction, they did include some of the earlier rustic structures built in the national parks. A number of park buildings designed by Vint's office and Herbert Maier were shown, perhaps drawn from previous portfolios and their own "libraries" of successful designs. Included were the administration buildings at Longmire and Yakima Park and the community buildings at Paradise and Longmire in Mount Rainier; park housing at Yosemite; museums at Fishing Bridge, Madison, and Norris Geyser Basin in Yellowstone; the Yavapai Point Observation Building at Grand Canyon; and the entrance station at Tioga Pass in Yosemite. Views of the Trail Ridge Road in Rocky Mountain illustrated the masonry techniques of the Landscape Division. Nonetheless, the experience of the national park designers was limited in view of the full range of structures needed in state parks, many of which were being developed primarily for recreational uses.

The books omitted a number of the outstanding national park structures because they were not considered practical models for CCC work given the capabilities and resources found in state park camps. Those works left out included the Ahwahnee Hotel at Yosemite, the Golden Gate Bridge at Yellowstone, and the Kaibab Trail Suspension Bridge at Grand Canyon.

Diverse examples of state park structures dominated the books, and Good praised the ingenuity of their designers, who remained nameless throughout the books. For example, Iowa was noted for its shelters and entrance stations, Texas for its entrance pylons of native stone, and Virginia for its cabins. Sometimes the work in a particular park was highlighted—for example, the cabins in Bastrop State Park in Texas, where Arthur Fehr, the park architect, developed a prototypical set of cabins. These became standard drawings that were circulated in the form of blueprints and copied in other parks of the Southwest, such as Lake Murray in Oklahoma.

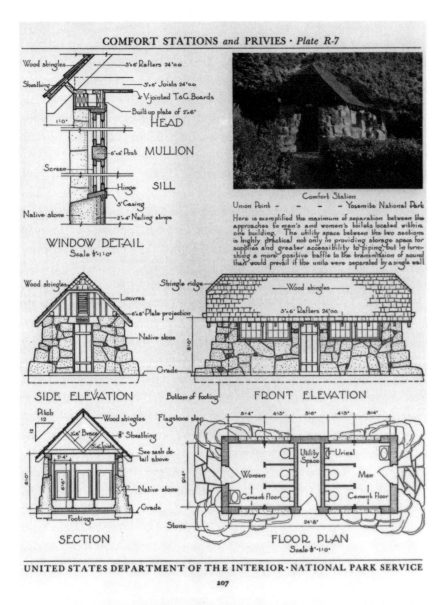

COMFORT STATIONS *and* PRIVIES · *Plate R-7*

Comfort Station

Union Point – – – – Yosemite National Park

Here is exemplified the maximum of separation between the approaches to men's and women's toilets located within one building. The utility space between the two sections is highly practical not only in providing storage space for supplies and greater accessibility to piping but in furnishing a more positive baffle to the transmission of sound than would prevail if the units were separated by a single wall

WINDOW DETAIL
Scale ¾"=1'0"

SIDE ELEVATION

FRONT ELEVATION

SECTION

FLOOR PLAN
Scale ¾"=1'0"

UNITED STATES DEPARTMENT OF THE INTERIOR · NATIONAL PARK SERVICE

207

11.3. *Park Structures and Facilities* illustrated the comfort station developed for Union Point and several other sites in Yosemite National Park in the late 1920s. The book offered details, elevations, sections, and floor plans with photographs of the completed structures, providing instructions for simple, commonplace structures that could be adapted to many sites and local materials. *(Reprinted Albert H. Good, ed.,* Park Structures and Facilities, *1935)*

Exemplary structures were drawn from natural parks, as distinguished from naturalistic or formal city parks. Although most depicted work in national and state parks, the committee selected examples from metropolitan and county parks which members felt "would be equally at home in a completely natural environment." These included examples from the Blue Hills Reservation near Boston, the Virginia Kendall Park near Akron, and the parks of Boulder, Chicago, Denver, and Oklahoma City, as well as the parks in Essex County, New Jersey, and Reading, Pennsylvania (7).

The illustrations were intended to show not prototypes to be copied but examples to foster imaginative harmonious solutions adapted to the needs and character of each situation. The Landscape Division had compiled a volume on representative park buildings in national parks in 1930 and one on cabins in 1934–35. The idea of portfolios was not new, and its use in promulgating principles of design was highly successful. Vint had worked many years before illustrating plans and drawings of bungalows for a Los Angeles real estate development firm. Maier had compiled his own personal Library of Original Sources. And in format the 1935 and 1938 volumes most closely resembled Augustus Shepard's *Camps in the Woods,* a portfolio of Adirondack architecture, which was published in 1931 and familiar to Vint and Maier.

In the introduction to *Park Structures and Facilities,* Director Arno Cammerer recognized the efforts of the National Park Service, state park authorities, and other agencies in achieving a "constantly improved technique of design and execution for the structures . . . required for safe, convenient, and beneficial public use of these parks." He emphasized the fact that construction of any type was an intrusion into a natural landscape and that the basic objective of designers in such areas was to "hold these intrusions to a minimum" and design them so they appeared "to belong to and be a part of their settings." He credited the work of the architects of the Emergency Conservation Work program, with its emphasis on recreational facilities, for the marked progress in this field. He stated that the purpose of the book was to present some of the successful structures of natural parks and to stimulate "still further improvement in this special field of design" (1).

Good wrote of the committee's goal: "It is firmly of the opinion that the aim should be toward a comprehensive presentation of structures and appurtenances in which principles held in esteem by park planners, landscape designers, engineers, and architects, have been happily combined in adequate provision for man's need with minimum sacrifice of a natural setting" (6).

The book was not intended as a primer, an encyclopedia, or a handbook but as a record and honor roll of good practices in designing park structures and facilities. The examples were intended to illustrate principles and stimulate new designs. The examples selected fit into one of three categories:

1. Minor facilities that were "developed to a pleasing and thoroughly satisfying expression" and were illustrated in sufficient detail so that they could be duplicated and closely adapted to other localities.

2. Designs "eminently suited to particular locations" that, illustrated in limited detail, were intended to portray "the spirit" of structures in a natural setting and inspire ideas and further examples for harmonizing design and setting.

3. Outstanding solutions to highly individual problems that were unlikely to occur elsewhere. These were intended "to inspire in those to whom the more complex park structures may be entrusted in the future, a high purpose to approach their specific problems with equally refreshing individuality, ingenuity, and forthrightness" (7).

Designers were to subordinate construction to the park plan, which determined the size, character, location, and use of every structure. In addition, park structures were to be subordinated to the environment and located to take advantage of any natural screening that existed on the site. Where natural screening did not exist, the site was to be "planted out" to integrate structures and natural setting. Signs played a particularly important role in natural parks, marking the way to buildings that were concealed behind vegetation. Little advice was given on planting other than the suggestion to plant around foundations to erase the line between the ground and structure. Good explained "naturalization" in simple terms of following nature's lead in the selection of plants for vegetative screens:

> The subordination of a structure to environment may be aided in several ways. One of these is to screen the building by locating it behind existing plant material or in some secluded spot in the terrain partly screened by some other natural feature. In the absence of such screening at a site otherwise well suited for the building's function an adequate screen can be planted, by repeating the same plant material which exists nearby. Preferably, structures will be so located with reference to the natural features of the landscape that it is unnecessary to plant them out. (4)

Adaptation rather than imitation was the preferred approach for designers using *Park Structures and Facilities.* Good particularly discouraged the copying of the more elaborate and complex buildings in the third category. The more involved and extensive a structure, Good explained, "the more evident that it is the result of an altogether unique interplay of needs, topography, traditions, materials and many other factors." What was unique to one location and set of circumstances could hardly be successfully duplicated in another place (7).

Good noted that *rustic* was the term generally used to refer to the style widely used in the forested national parks and in other wilderness parks but felt the term was misused and inaccurate to describe the greater meaning of the style practiced by park designers in state and national parks. Although he hoped a more apt and expressive term for the style would evolve, the term *rustic* endured. Good defined rustic design as a style that "through the use of native materials in proper scale, and through the avoidance of rigid, straight lines, and over-sophistication, gives the feeling of having been executed by pioneer craftsmen with limited hand tools. It thus achieves sympathy with natural surroundings and with the past" (3–4).

Park Structures and Facilities explained and illustrated the basic principles of design as developed by Vint, Maier, and others. The striking similarity between Maier's 1935 speech and Good's text makes it impossible to discern the originality of either author and supports the idea that they represent the consensus of the committee and the contributions of the committee's varied members.

The book gave advice on the orientation of park buildings and the importance of all sides as facades: "It should be remembered that park buildings will be viewed from all sides, and that design cannot be lavished on one elevation only. All four elevations will be virtually front elevations, and as such merit careful study. Admittedly, one side of major park buildings will always provide for service, and while enclosures on park areas are to be deplored and only installed where necessary, a palisade or some other suitable enclosure on this side of the building should completely screen all service operations" (5).

On the principle of horizontality, Good wrote that park structures were less conspicuous and more readily subordinated to their settings when horizontal lines predominated and the structure's silhouette was low to the ground. Horizontality called for roofs that were low in pitch, perhaps no greater than one-third (5).

The volume upheld the use of native materials. Good claimed that it was character, not the fact of "nativeness," which gave rocks or logs their value as building materials. He cautioned against cutting stone or forming concrete blocks to a regular size and surface and shaping logs like rigid telephone poles or commercial lumber. Rockwork was to be proper in scale. The average size of the rocks employed was to be large enough to justify the use of masonry.

> Rocks should be placed on their natural beds, the stratification or bedding planes horizontal, never vertical. Variety of size lends interest and results in a pattern far more pleasing than that produced by units of common or nearly common size. Informality vanishes from rock work if the rocks are laid in courses like brick work, or if the horizontal joints are not broken. In walls the larger rocks should be used near the base, but by no means should smaller ones be used exclusively in the upper portions. Rather should a variety of sizes be common to the whole surface,

Backbone State Park, Iowa

Boulder Mountain Metropolitan Park, Colorado

Rock Barriers

  Surrounding are varied examples of rock contrived to serve as guard or barrier along the outer edge of mountain and hillside roads and trails. The curb shown in connection with the rock wall at lower right serves to keep parked cars far enough from the barrier to permit pedestrians to pass between cars and wall.

Rocky Mountain National Park

Turner Falls State Park, Oklahoma

Rocky Mountain National Park

UNITED STATES DEPARTMENT OF THE INTERIOR · NATIONAL PARK SERVICE

35

11.4. *Park Structures and Facilities* (1935) illustrated designs for naturalistic rock barriers and guardrails in state and national parks. Many of these came from Herbert Maier's collection and appeared in the "Inspector's Photographic Handbook" produced by his office for Emergency Conservation Work in state parks. *(Reprinted Albert H. Good, ed.,* Park Structures and Facilities, *1935)*

Drinking Fountain

Lake Guernsey State Park – – – Wyoming

Here certainly is the peak accomplishment in naturalistic masking of a provision for bubbler and tap. It is a temptation hardly resistible to state that the rock was smitten with a rod and that the water gushed forth in the best biblical tradition. However the section drawing below evidences too plainly to the contrary – a laborious business of drilling and pipe fitting. Smiting with a rod would have been easier.

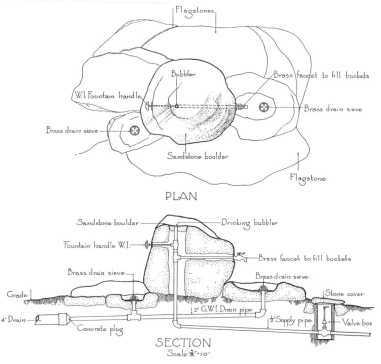

PLAN

SECTION
Scale ⅜"·1'·0'

UNITED STATES DEPARTMENT OF THE INTERIOR · NATIONAL PARK SERVICE

86

11.5. The water fountain designed for Lake Guernsey State Park in Wyoming was adopted in other state and national parks where large boulders existed in the natural landscape.
(Reprinted Albert H. Good, ed., Park Structures and Facilities, *1935)*

11.6. Reflecting principles of naturalistic design, the Log Bridge in Pine Creek State Park, South Dakota, was built by the state highway department in the form of a circular chord. *(Photograph courtesy National Archives, Record Group 79)*

the larger predominating at the base. Rock should be selected for its color and hardness. (5)

Logs were to be carefully selected. Most desirable were those "pleasingly knotted." Knots were not to be removed by saw but left to add texture and character to the log. Good addressed the debate on using unpeeled logs:

> Strong as may be the immediate appeal of structures built of logs on which bark is left, we do well to renounce at once this transitory charm. If the bark is not intentionally stripped, not only will this process naturally and immediately set in, but the wood is subjected to aggravated deterioration through ravages of insects and rot. It is in the best interests of the life of park structures, as well as in avoidance of a long period of litter from loosening bark, and of unsightliness during the process, that there has come about general agreement that the bark should be entirely sacrificed at the outset. (5)

Good encouraged designers to seek inspiration from pioneering and primitive expressions of the surrounding region or from Native American practices: "In fitting tribute he graces his encroachments by adapting to his structures such of their traditions and practices as come within his understanding. . . . Over the covered wagon routes the ring of the pioneer's axe is echoed in the efforts of today. The habits and primitive ingenuity of the American Indian persist and find varied expression in park construction over wide areas. All these influences contribute to a growing variety in expression promising eventual high attainment" (3).

The harmonious relationship of component architectural features was essential to good design. Foundations were the key to uniting land and structure and fostering harmony with nature. In this Good echoed the writings of Hubbard and Waugh, the philosophy of the Arts and Crafts movement, and the work of Herbert Maier: "Rough rock footings artfully contrived to give the impression of natural rock outcroppings, are a means of blending the structure to the site. A batter to a stone wall, with skillful buttressing of the corners, if done with true finesse, will often bring to the building that agreeable look of having sprung from the soil. Park structures giving that impression are of the elect" (5).

Roofs were to exhibit the quality of weight to be in character with the heavy walls of rock and timber which they crowned. This quality was achieved in several ways: verge members in gables were to be oversized, eave lines were to be thick, and the roofing material was to appear correspondingly heavy and durable. Where wood shingles or shakes were used, they were to be a full inch in thickness if possible, with the doubling of every fifth course or so, unless the building was quite small. This would bring the roof texture into more appropriate scale with the rest of the structure. Good advised his readers, "The primitive

11.7. Civilian Conservation Corps enrollees at Gooseberry State Park, Minnesota, in June 1936 used hand tools to peel and assemble native logs into a naturalistic guardrail for the parking concourse and overlook constructed near the Gooseberry River on U.S. Highway 61, which passed through the park. The retaining wall for the concourse alone required about 646 cubic yards of native granite and contained stones weighing as much as three tons. *(Photograph courtesy National Archives, Record Group 79)*

character we seek to create is furthered tremendously if we shun straight rigid eave and course lines in favor of properly irregular, wavering, 'freehand' lines. The straight edge as a precision tool has little or no place in the park artisan's equipment" (6).

Good built upon Maier's concept of overscaling, recommending that in high, mountainous, and forested regions the various structural elements of rustic construction were to be reasonably overscaled to surrounding large trees and rough terrain. For pleasing harmony, he suggested that the scale of structural elements be reduced proportionately as the ruggedness and scale of the surroundings diminished (4).

Structures were to incorporate the colors that occurred in nature and were dominant in the immediate surroundings. In general, warm browns were recommended for "retiring a wooden building in a wooded or partly wooded setting." Another "safe" color was driftwood gray. Where contrast was desired for architectural accents, such as window muntins, a light buff stone color could be used sparingly. Good discouraged the use of green: "Strangely enough, green is perhaps the hardest of all colors to handle, because it is so difficult to get just the correct shade in a given setting and because it almost invariably fades to a strangely different hue." He pointed out that a green roof, while expected to blend with surrounding trees, did not result in harmony because foliage was an uneven surface, mingling with other colors and broken up into patches of deep shadow and bright openings, whereas a roof was a flat plane that reflected a solid continuous color. Good recommended brown or weathered-gray roofs to blend with the colors of earth and tree trunks (4–5).

Promoting the basic concept of architectural unity, Good recommended that in one park a single style and a limited range of materials and construction methods be used for all structures. This meant harmonizing new buildings with older ones or abandoning discordant old styles in favor of a new, more suitable, and unified scheme (6).

Good urged designers to keep down the number of buildings in any one area and to combine functions in one structure wherever practical. The book illustrated examples of lodges that combined concessionaire operations, such as dining rooms and stores, with administrative uses and community rooms for social gatherings and lectures. Bathhouses, boathouses, and overlook shelters were commonly combined with other functions. "The grouping of two or more facilities under one roof tends to bring welcome variety to park structures generally. The limited range of expression of any simple, one-purpose building is vastly widened as other purposes are combined with it" (6).

One issue that the committee disagreed on and which, as a result, was left unresolved was the "long debated" question of honesty in the use of materials in the rustic or pioneer style. One opinion held that park buildings "should not appropriate the semblance of primitive structures without appropriating as well all the primitive elements and methods of the prototypes." Others argued that there were "not at hand today the seemingly inexhaustible resources of pioneer days" and that to insist on the use of logs might waste those resources whose conservation was at the "very root of the impetus toward park expansion." Another point of view advocated the use of pioneer log construction for the more important park structures so that they could allow the observation and study of "fast-disappearing frontier construction methods." Minor and often commonly duplicated units, such as cabins or comfort stations, could utilize a "more economical, even though picturesque and durable, method." In the administrative facilities being built in national parks with PWA funds, economy and accessibility of materials had already dictated the use of alternative materials such as concrete and corrugated iron. In the state parks, concrete was used to a great extent in the construction of bridges, buildings, dams, and culverts but was generally faced with locally available stone. The latitude given park designers in experimenting with alternate materials led to other techniques to achieve naturalism. These techniques included the creation of naturalistic rockwork and

11.8. The overscaling of logs and an irregularity in the axe-hewn ends gave this guest cabin at Minnesota's Itasca State Park a rustic informality and exaggerated sense of pioneer architecture. Describing the building as "almost humorous" in scale, *Park Structures and Facilities* assured readers that the logs, the result of windfalls and not cut timber, were a reminder of "magnificent forests all but extinct." *(Photograph Ralph H. Anderson, courtesy National Archives, Record Group 79)*

steppingstones of concrete in parks such as Palmetto State Park in Texas and the covering of concrete abutments of dams and bridges with mantles of climbing vines in parks such as Ludington State Park in Michigan (7–8).

Park and Recreation Structures

In 1938, the service published an expanded six-hundred-page version called *Park and Recreation Structures*, which was issued in three separate volumes. Individual sections on, for example, cabins or signs were also printed separately. Volume 1 covered facilities for basic services and administration such as entranceways, signs, bridges, culverts, and comfort stations. Recreational and cultural facilities, the subject of volume 2, included picnic shelters, fireplaces, tables, boathouses, campfire circles and amphitheaters, refectories, dams and pools, and miscellaneous sports facilities such as toboggan runs and docks. Volume 3 covered overnight and organized camp facilities, including tent and trailer campsites, cabins, lodges, campstoves, washhouses and laundries, and facilities for cooking, dining, social activities, and sleeping in organization camps.

The expanded range of structures and facilities reflected the growing programs for state park development and recreational demonstration areas and the increasing involvement of the National Park Service in planning areas where recreational activities rather than scenic and natural features were of primary importance. The inclusion of trailer campsites indicates visitors' increasing interest in carrying their "temporary home" with them and the demand for longer, drive-through parking spurs, circular loop roads, and tiers with wider turning radii. The 1938 volumes also included a number of examples drawn from historic sites and parks, where new facilities were being coordinated with historic structures and in some cases reconstructions.

The development of RDAs was probably the most important factor influencing the expansion of *Park Structures and Facilities.* Volume 3 of *Park and Recreation Structures* was entitled "Overnight and Organized Camp Facilities" and presented for the first time designs for a full range of camp buildings: dining halls, recreation halls, infirmaries, washhouses, latrines, laundries, and sleeping cabins—all of the components that made up a self-sufficient camping unit. It also provided layouts for organization camps of varying sizes and settings. Common to all the layouts was the division of the camp into small social units and the informal arrangement of buildings across the natural topography. In their designs for organization camps, the National Park Service designers drew heavily not only from examples at the Palisades Interstate Park and the successful cabin camps in state parks but also from the great camps of the Adirondacks, which featured clusters of buildings having specialized functions and arranged in relation to the shoreline, forest, and natural topography. Not surprising is the similarity of the camp layouts in *Park and Recreation Structures* to an Adirondack camp illustrated in 1931 in Augustus D. Shepard's *Camps in the Woods.*

In RDAs as well as many metropolitan and county parks, there was an increasing emphasis on winter activities and the need for facilities for sledding, skiing, skating, and ski jumping. The park service looked to parks such as the Forest Preserve District outside Chicago and Bear Mountain in the Palisades for models of winter facilities. It looked also to the design of ski areas in the national parks such as Yosemite and Sequoia. These kinds of facilities were included in volume 2 of *Park and Recreation Structures,* which covered recreational and cultural facilities.

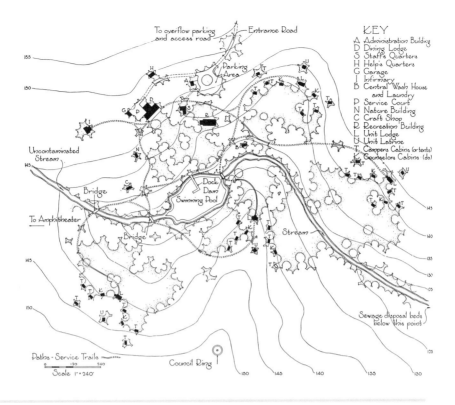

KEY
A Administration Building
D Dining Lodge
S Staff's Quarters
H Help's Quarters
G Garage
I Infirmary
B Central Wash House
     and Laundry
P Service Court
N Nature Building
C Craft Shop
R Recreation Building
L Unit Lodge
U Unit Latrine
T Campers Cabins (or tents)
K Counselors Cabins (do)

To overflow parking and access road — Entrance Road

Parking Area

Uncontaminated Stream

Bridge

To Amphitheater

Bridge

Dock
Dam
Swimming Pool

Stream

Stream

Sewage disposal beds below this point

Paths - Service Trails
0   120   240
Scale 1" = 240'

Council Ring

11.9. The plan for a large organized camp along a dammed stream, from *Park and Recreation Structures,* featured a central administrative center with a dining lodge, offices, staff housing, infirmary, and garage, and several outlying camp units, each having a lodge, latrine, and cabins for campers and counselors. *(Reprinted Albert H. Good, ed.,* Park and Recreation Structures, *1938)*

Landscape Conservation

While the portfolios gave thorough information on designing park structures and facilities, *Landscape Conservation: Planning for the Restoration, Conservation, and Utilization of Wild Lands for Parks and Forests* by Frank A. Waugh, first published in 1935, covered the larger issue of land reclamation, the development of lakes for recreation, and the creation of trails and campgrounds. This booklet was a compilation of Waugh's principles for recreational development in natural areas, which he had practiced in national forests, and his theory on the natural style of gardening, which was first published in 1917. Waugh's ideas on the use of native vegetation in landscape design expanded in the 1920s, and a series of his articles — "Ecology of the Roadside," "Natural Plant Groups," and

"The Physiography of Lakes and Ponds"—appeared in *Landscape Architecture* in 1931 and 1932.

By the 1930s, Waugh had a long-established career in the recreational development of forest lands. Through seasonal contracts with the U.S. Forest Service at Grand Canyon, Mount Hood, Bryce, and Kings Canyon, Waugh had put into practice his early ideas on the "natural style" of landscape gardening. His work on the Mount Hood Road illustrated his ideas about sequence of motives, change of direction, and overlooks at the climax of scenic vistas. Waugh was indebted to Downing's principles and had several years earlier published a revision of Downing's theory of landscape gardening. Waugh's work set forth ecological principles and a zonal approach to re-creating vegetation based on the study of natural conditions and plant associations. These principles were particularly important for the mass plantings that were to occur in submarginal lands and the creation of artificial lakes for recreational use.

Published first in a typescript form at Conrad Wirth's urging, *Landscape Conservation* was an effort to get practical and technical information on park building to the CCC camps in national parks, national forests, and state parks and forests. It set forth principles and practices for the Civilian Conservation Corps to follow in varied aspects of conservation work.

Eight principles, according to Waugh, were to guide the development of wild lands for public use and enjoyment: human use and enjoyment, order, cleanliness, beauty of scenery, conservation, restoration, economy, and circulation. The achievement of human use and enjoyment called for the construction of structures built in good proportions, agreeable in appearance, and lacking in ornamentation. Echoing the National Park Service's dictum on harmony with setting, Waugh maintained,

> Artificial structures in wild park lands should be made as inconspicuous as possible, should be harmonious with the landscape as fully as possible, and should be constructed of native materials such as local stone, peeled logs, etc. Nevertheless, the general principle is true that what is practical and useful, simple, direct, and straightforward, is agreeable to the human eye. This fact, fully grasped, leaves us free to pursue our primary purpose of developing the land under our charge for the fullest and freest human use.[6]

The principle of order called for the simple and orderly arrangement of groups of buildings or structures into clusters. Cleanliness required that easy maintenance and proper disposal of waste be included in the planning from the beginning. Economy could be achieved through simple, solid construction and provisions for easy and economical maintenance.

The principle of beauty of scenery called upon planners to study the landscape by going alone to experience all kinds of landscape in all kinds of weather, at all times of day, and in all seasons. This firsthand experience of landscape was the best preparation for planning the development of wild places. "The absolute foundation of all inspirational outdoor recreation," Waugh claimed, "lies in the beauty of the landscape" (5).

The principle of conservation upheld the preservation of native flora and fauna as a fundamental but complex requirement, calling for long and serious study. Where native species were already depleted or lost, Waugh called for their restoration: "Such favorite plants as mountain laurels, rhododendron, trailing arbutus, azalea, and many others are to be considered in this category. Amongst animals special attention will usually be given to game birds and fish" (6).

An adequate system of circulation, Waugh pointed out, was the first problem in all physical planning and included main roads, side roads, trails, footpaths, bridle trails, and water suitable for canoeing. He cautioned against overdoing circulation systems and suggested that designers should begin the development of any area with meager roads and trails, enlarging old roads if necessary, but improving construction and extending fresh trails in new areas only when positively demanded by use (6–7).

Waugh outlined the types of sites needed for developing wild lands: administrative sites, service sites, sites for hotels and accommodations, sites for water conservation and supply, sites for sewage disposal, clubhouse sites for special recreational purposes, campsites for permanent group camps, sites for temporary tent camping, playing fields, tennis courts, golf courses, bathing beaches, and fishing areas. He stressed the need to plan for these and select the best location for each even if they were not to be developed right away.

Roads and trails were the framework of the entire design of a recreational area, providing transit between principal points in the park and "revealing pleasant scenery." The planner's role was to locate the main points of scenic value, such as fine outlooks, stately groups of trees, and objects of local interest, and to lay out trails connecting these. According to Waugh's theory of trail design, trails were to be laid out so that the most spectacular views were seen at turning points against a rising grade. Scenic objects or features were best viewed straight ahead and at a distance, whereas broad outlooks over valleys, mountains, or water were to be viewed at varying angles to the trail. This was accomplished by giving a "convenient" turn to the trail at the point of view and by widening the trail and providing a stopping place, perhaps with seats, facing the outlook. Waugh introduced his ideas of arranging the scenery along a trail as a series of themes or motives arranged in "paragraphs" that could draw attention to the unique natural features of a variety of landscape types:

> If the trail leads up a narrow valley with a pleasant stream in its bed, there will be repeated pictures of the brook which will be the subject of principal interest. The stream supplies the motive to be developed. View after view, picture after picture,

will be shown at the most effective points. It is desirable that these views should present considerable diversity. In one place the water will be singing over the rocks, in another there will be a quiet pool with reflections, in another the brook will drop over a cliff forming a fine waterfall. (10)

Trails were to offer a variety of scenes. Waugh wrote, for example, that a trail along a pond shore "should not be kept directly on the bank all the way but from time to time should run back into the woods and out of sight of the lake." The grade of a trail was to be varied to avoid tiring the hiker and to ward off monotony (11).

Although Waugh's instruction on siting campgrounds was practical and basic, he elaborated on the construction of two types of features to which he had given considerable attention in his career: the bonfire and the outdoor theater. In *The Natural Style in Landscape Gardening* Waugh had written that the bonfire was a social and communal gathering place requiring an ash pit or paved area for the central fire with room about it for people to congregate in concentric circles, perhaps on low seats of sawn or split logs. Waugh gave instructions for transforming the campfire into an outdoor theater designed to harmonize with the surrounding woodlands. He called for a good location: "The perfect ideal is formed by a river terrace where the curvature has a moderate radius. Such sloping concave banks make the best sites, but a simple outdoor auditorium can be made upon a plane slope or even on level ground" (19).

Outdoor theaters could be circular with a central bonfire, or, for performances, they could be semicircular with a stage at the front, aisles radiating outward and upward, and seats forming the arcs of the circle between the aisles. He called for a stage raised two or three feet from the ground and a blank wall for the back of the stage. Seating could be either on the ground or on sawn planks or halved logs. Waugh's description clearly reflected the solutions that Maier and the national park designers had developed at the Old Faithful and Lake Museums in Yellowstone National Park. These solutions, however, were probably initially inspired by Waugh's treatise *Outdoor Theaters,* published in 1917, and a corresponding article, "Notes on Outdoor Theaters," which had appeared in *Landscape Architecture* in the 1920s. Waugh's interest in outdoor theaters was inspired by the examples he found in Dresden, Germany, and led him to develop the form for use in national forests, integrating it with the American image of the pioneer campfire.

A large portion of Waugh's booklet was devoted to the ecological principles of "dressing" the margins of forest plantations and the lakeshores that were being created in many wild parks through mass planting of hardwood species and the damming of streams for recreational purposes. Waugh's instructions, unknown in general silviculture, enabled the CCC to shape the boundaries of tree plantations to fit pleasingly into the landscape, to suit the topography, and

11.10. A trailside shelter and overlook at Gooseberry Falls State Park in Minnesota provided scenic views of Lake Superior, reflecting both the nineteenth-century ideas of A. J. Downing and Frank Waugh's instructions for locating trails and presenting scenic views. *(Photograph by Ralph H. Anderson, courtesy National Archives, Record Group 79)*

to blend forest into meadow or prairie. Waugh cautioned his readers that "a genuinely naturalistic planting was excessively difficult to achieve" and that training and a close observation of natural conditions were necessary. Using the example of the "mountain laurel" admired by Downing and adopted for roadside plantings in his home state of Massachusetts, Waugh expounded:

> Occasionally it will become necessary to make new plantations of native shrubs, either for game cover or for frankly ornamental purposes. In New England and along the Appalachian range, for example, rather extensive plantations of mountain laurel have been undertaken. Many other native species are deserving of similar consideration, as flowering dogwood, azalea, trailing arbutus, and several of the viburnums. It is highly important, when such planting is undertaken, to give the new colonies the similitude of nature. Yet this is a very difficult ideal to achieve. It can be reached only by extended and critical study. The formation of large solid

masses of mountain laurel, for example, is palpably unnatural. Laurel grows by preference in half-shade, under a fairly thick forest canopy and mixed with other species. Each species has its own way of spreading and of forming colonies; and unless artificial planting copies these forms meticulously the results are not natural. (28–29)

Waugh recommended dividing the landscape into a series of zones in which dominant species and associated species of trees, undergrowth, and ground covers could be identified. He illustrated his point using plant associations from the forests of western Massachusetts, with which he was familiar. His principles, however, could be applied to any climatic zone, geographical region, and grouping of vegetation. Cross sections of the plant composition and lists of the plants in each zone could be developed from field observations of natural areas similar to that being created or restored.

Waugh pointed out that the "grading out" of the natural forest growth was much like the "facing down" done by landscape architects in park planting, though it was "apt to be more free and easy, more natural and more agreeable to the eye." He also recommended "selective cuttings" of "interlopers" or plants that did not belong to the natural groupings or were unduly aggressive and invasive. He noted the effect that common aspen had in crowding out better species such as dogwood or viburnum. His recommendations (like Meinecke's) on selective clearing of campgrounds and picnic grounds called for the supervision of experienced workmen (33).

On preserving natural rock formations, sand dunes, and other physiographic features, Waugh said that these were often of "great scientific interest" or "surpassing beauty": "Where roads or trails must be carried over ledges, outcrop or talus, there is always danger of marring or completely destroying some of the choicest items of natural scenery. Moreover, these features, once lost, cannot be replaced as can trees and shrubs" (34).

Waugh's empirical method for studying and re-creating the vegetation zones found in nature was applied to lakeshores in state, county, and metropolitan parks across the nation. The artificial development of lakes and ponds, which accompanied the increasing utilization of natural resources for public recreation in the 1930s, presented two problems for naturalistic design. On the one hand, it altered the relationship between the lake and the surrounding topography, sometimes radically, and, on the other, it completely displaced the vegetation along the shoreline. Waugh was particularly concerned with the readjustment of flora:

Nearly all natural lakes and ponds are bordered by masses of trees, shrubs, vines, sedges, and herbaceous plants peculiar to the lake shore. This bordering zone of vegetation is of the utmost significance. It is important in several ways, but above

11.11. The lakeshore plantings at Butler Memorial Park, Kentucky, reflected Frank Waugh's advice that around the edges of artificial lakes and ponds native species be planted in concentric zones and in the same conditions of light, soil, and moisture as they occurred in nature. *(Photograph Ralph H. Anderson, courtesy National Archives, Record Group 79)*

all else it determines the landscape character of the lake or pond. It constitutes an integral part of the lake regarded as scenery. Its removal or alteration profoundly changes the looks of the pond; these changes always mean that the pond becomes obviously less natural, more artificial. (40)

Waugh pointed out that lakeshore vegetation always grows in concentric zones, some of which might be narrow bands dominated by a single species. For example, he wrote, "Out in the water there may be water lilies, nearer shore rushes or pickerel weed, at the edge of the water cattails or irises or buttonbush and back a little from the water's edge, alders or willows" (41).

Landscape architects needed a complete knowledge of the species inhabiting a particular area and of the peculiar habits of each. Shrubs were of particular importance, but trees also required careful attention. Waugh recognized that the clearing of considerable stretches of lakeshore was necessary for recreational development of beaches and other uses. He cautioned designers about creating artificial lines when delineating clearings, and he especially deplored the cement coping that encircled the ponds of city parks. Shores developed for recreational purposes were to be kept clear of campsites and buildings except for a boathouse that might also be a clubhouse or refectory and serve as an outlook for viewing the lake (45).

On the creation of artificial ponds, Waugh urged designers to study natural ponds existing nearby. "The new lake should be made as nearly like the natural prototype as is humanly possible. This imitation begins with location, includes conformation of the shores and especially the pattern of the natural border of vegetation." Although Waugh realized that it might take many years to achieve the desired bordering flora, he urged the "planting of critically chosen native shrubs in considerable quantities" with strict regard for "the patterns locally provided by nature." Waterlines against natural rock outcrops were to follow closely those in nature, and standing timber below the waterline was to be removed before flooding. Timber several feet above the waterline was also to be cleared and replanted in naturalistic zones (46–48).

Other Publications

In 1937, as part of its expanding educational program, the Civilian Conservation Corps published a series of manuals known as the Project Training Series. Edited by Guy B. Arthur, the series covered many of the vocational skills that enrollees needed for conservation work under fourteen topics, including concrete, lumber, brick and stone work, carpentry, lawns, common range plants, and forestry. The last four of the series covered management and training skills for project supervisors and foremen. Arthur compiled the information for many of the manuals by consulting with specialists in the U.S. Forest Service and other agencies. Several manuals reprinted materials already being used; consequently Frank Waugh's *Landscape Conservation,* which was written for the National Park Service in 1935, was republished as number 6 of the series.

Construction of Trails, number 7 in the Project Training Series, was a manual of trail-building techniques that had been originally compiled by the Landscape and Engineering Department of Great Smoky Mountains National Park for work in that park. Based on the standards worked out by the National Park Service's engineers and landscape architects, the manual was a general guide to trail-building procedures such as staking, clearing, benching, bank sloping, constructing water breaks, and building stream crossings. Although the park service's specifications for location, grade, width, and drainage were given,

11.12. A hand-hewn trail marker, bench, and fern garden marked the trail entrance at the edge of the North Beach Area parking lot in Deception Pass State Park, Washington. *(Photograph courtesy National Archives, Record Group 79)*

they were recommendations that could be varied for use in other parks and forests.[7]

Signs and Markers, number 9 in the series, examined the design and construction of a variety of naturalistic park signs and markers. Drawing heavily from the CCC work in state and national parks, it provided numerous models and styles of lettering and illustrated practical techniques such as burning, carving, embossing, and engraving. The manual stressed the concept of "fitness," whereby a sign was suited to its purpose and its setting.[8]

The End of the Civilian Conservation Corps

Although there were several attempts to establish the Civilian Conservation Corps as a permanent agency, they failed, and with the entry of the United States into World War II, the CCC ended. The CCC program had experienced a steady decline with greater and greater cuts each year after 1936. By 1938, the National Park Service had 77 camps in national parks and 245 camps in state parks. In

1939, the CCC lost its status as an independent agency and was consolidated with other federal relief programs into the Federal Security Agency on July 1, under the Reorganization Act of 1939. At the end of 1939, when faced with still more cuts to the supervisory force, Conrad Wirth created central service units within the National Park Service regional offices to handle design and technical matters and abolished the positions within the individual camps. Designers became further detached from the natural sites and settings for which they were to design harmonious structures. As the United States became more involved in preparation for war in 1941, the work of many camps was redirected for wartime preparation and training, and the National Park Service lost 133 CCC camps between September and November 1941. On December 24, 1941, the Joint Appropriations Committee for Congress recommended that the CCC be terminated by July 1, 1942, and subsequent efforts by President Roosevelt to extend CCC funding failed.[9]

A number of administrative changes had occurred by the end of the CCC period. Diminishing funds and staff at the regional level meant that regional landscape architects and architects spent less time in the parks and had less familiarity with the parks. Marked changes occurred in the attitude of park designers and advocates by the end of the CCC period, and the Craftsman ethic and attention to detail which had guided the design of structures gave way to a functionalism in design which advocated modern materials, streamlined forms, and mechanized technology.

In 1956, with the implementation of Mission 66, the National Park Service once again gained congressional and presidential support and the funding to develop facilities on a large scale. But the hiatus between 1942 and 1956 had been too great, economics too drastically changed, and the trends of park visitation too different to recapture the spirit and character of park design in the 1920s and 1930s. Although adherence to principles of naturalism such as avoiding straight lines and right angles in all aspects of design continued, the character of park structures, roads, and trails changed without the craftsmanship, primitive tools, training, and carefully worked out specifications that had been such important aspects during the New Deal. The design of park roads perpetuated the lessons of Hull, Vint, and the parkway builders of the 1930s, but the treatment of bridges, culverts, overlooks, and tunnels received increasingly less individual attention and succumbed to modern materials and solutions deemed appropriate for a particular park but not necessarily a particular site. Practices of planting and transplanting native trees, shrubs, and other plants continued, but on a smaller scale without the massive labor force once provided by the CCC. While stonemasonry with native rock continued to be practiced, concrete surfaces were often left unfaced and the lines of masonry joints and the shape and size of stones became more regular. Stone for curbs, guardrails, and structures was now cut by machine and lacked the surface textures and irregularity of hand-cut stone. Although vistas continued to be a driving force in design, the most important view became that seen through the large window of plate glass and metal sash of the modern visitor center. Master planning continued to guide the development of national parks for many years, but the ideas about the location of buildings and roads had changed. Mission 66 would forge its own expression. The legacy of the period of landscape design of the National Park Service, from 1916 to 1942, has endured. Numerous rustic and naturalistic buildings, bridges, and other structures built in the 1920s and 1930s still serve visitors today. And countless miles of park roads and trails and hundreds of scenic overlooks continue to present visitors with the pictures of nature.

Chapter 12

National Park Design
since 1940

B y 1940, the value of recreation to American life and the relationship of conservation and recreation were well established in the minds of public administrators, park designers, and landscape architects. By constructing roads and trails, building campgrounds, and fighting forest fires, the CCC had opened up millions of acres for public use and enjoyment in national and state parks, recreational demonstration areas, national and state forests, wildlife reserves, and areas created by public reclamation projects. The development of recreational areas by state park agencies, the Tennessee Valley Authority, and the National Park Service had proved the value of natural resources for public recreational use and demonstrated a process of recreational planning. Visitation in national parks had grown tremendously in the late 1930s in response to the increasing number of parks, greater accessibility, better visitor services, and the increasing popularity of recreational motoring.

Administrator Paul V. McNutt of the Federal Security Administration summarized the relationship of conservation and recreation in *Landscape Architecture:* "Conservation for recreation is conservation in its broadest aspects, for it involves not only preservation of the intrinsic values of areas of scenic, scientific, and historic importance, but planning and development for the proper use of these values to meet human requirements. Through it, human lives are made richer and more abundant in experiences which readjust and broaden the perspective, amid surroundings offering relief from the dull, everyday scene."[1]

The experience of landscape architects in recreational planning was substantial. McNutt and others clearly recognized the present and future role of landscape architects as technical advisers to the work of the CCC in state and national parks. Planning was critical to successful park design, and natural areas required that design be subservient to the natural character of an area and that the work of the landscape designer be simple, understated, and naturalistic.

Former CCC state park inspector George L. Nason summarized the components of park planning and recognized the self-effacing character of a park designer's work in the *1940 Yearbook: Park and Recreation Progress:*

> A good landscape plan molds and advances the heritage of values germane to the park area; it provides and preserves breadth, repose, simplicity, and fitness; it strives for harmony in the several parts and for the stimulus of man's imagination. Working with the materials of nature, many of the effects will be those that nature in time could well have produced herself. From this follows that disappointing anomaly of landscape architecture, which is: the greater the perfection of design the more likely man will forget that the designer has been at work.[2]

Park designers began to question the principles and practices that were shaping facilities in national and state parks. Although all agreed that development was to be in harmony with nature, a trend was emerging against the picturesque and Arts and Crafts–inspired prototypes that had been promoted by Herbert Maier and Albert Good and circulated widely through *Park and Recreation Structures.* Forward-looking designers such as Nason advocated the use of indigenous materials to create structures having "sturdy permanence" but viewed pioneer and indigenous methods of construction as outmoded, impractical, costly to maintain, and not suitable given the diminishing resources of the Civilian Conservation Corps. Nason called upon architects to create simple, honest park structures that considered "people in the present natural state of progress" and in which "modern man" belonged:

> It should be remembered that we are heirs of the past, that we live in a high state of civilization and inherit the attitudes and tastes of generations of skilled builders. . . . The precedent of the past decade may be already outmoded, unnatural, and inappropriate to modern man. . . . Park buildings should be as permanent as the progress of the arts and funds can make them. Well conceived, well built, modern buildings are milestones in the progress of architecture. (57–58)

Although there was general agreement on the various roles of the landscape architect, architect, and engineer in park development, opinions differed on the degree to which parks should be developed. In 1940, the American Society of Landscape Architects (ASLA) published a statement of policy for national parks calling for the limitation of constructions to those necessary to make the parks useful and accessible without serious damage to their scenic character. The ASLA further recommended that the forms of recreation allowed and the kinds of construction undertaken should be consistent with the preservation of natural beauty and with recreational purposes incidental to the enjoyment of that beauty for which the parks were created.[3]

Writing on nature's balances the same year, Richard Lieber, the renowned state park administrator from Indiana, expressed his concerns for the overdevelopment of state and national parks. "To protect and preserve our magnificent heritage of scenic wonders," Lieber called upon park designers "to find better and more fitting methods for concessions" in the parks. Urging a radical departure from the Mather-era philosophy of park development, Lieber urged that large service areas be constructed outside existing parks and that facilities for new national parks be built on the outer edge of parks or outside park boundaries. Park highways were to be replaced by simple park roads, and traditional pack trains were to be used to transport visitors to isolated camp centers. Such changes would, in Lieber's opinion, give nature an opportunity to "restore her own balances."[4]

The Contribution of the CCC to National Defense

Although hope that the Civilian Conservation Corps would become a permanent program diminished, the program gained the attention and interest of leaders concerned with preparing for the emergency of war. In July 1940, CCC director James J. McEntee announced the redirection of the CCC to train young men for the specialized work of military service and occupations essential to defense industries. This action recognized the value of the work that the CCC accomplished and moreover the skills and training that had prepared a generation of young men for defense work. McEntee commented:

> All of us know what the CCC has been doing, and doing well, most of the things which we are now being called upon as a national defense contribution. . . . For seven years the Corps has been contributing to national defense by increasing national health, by building up natural resources wealth, by teaching skills to enrollees, and by giving millions of youngsters opportunity to become better and more useful American citizens.[5]

Already organized, trained, and equipped, CCC companies provided ready-made units to provide the leadership, training, and skills for military service and wartime industries. Having provided Army Reserve officers with experience in supervising CCC camps, the CCC was viewed as "a proving ground for leadership training." Above all, the experience of camp life with its emphasis on "training through work" provided young men with skills and knowledge of the kind useful for military recruits, including first aid, safety, sanitation, personal hygiene, discipline, the ability to operate equipment, and the ability to perform a variety of practical trades.[6]

Within months, following the axiom that "conservation is preparedness," the CCC was mobilized to train young men for various roles in the national defense program. The experience of the CCC in felling and sawing timber and operating and maintaining trucks, tractors, power shovels, jackhammers, road machines, and pile drivers was put to use by military engineers. By spring 1941, twelve thousand enrollees were assigned directly to military forts and reservations, where they cleared land, built roads, installed water and sewer systems, and developed target ranges, drill fields, tank maneuver grounds, and airplane landing fields. Like the work in national and state parks, the work was directed by skilled foremen, met blueprint specifications, and underwent critical inspection (1–2).

A 1941 pamphlet entitled the *Civilian Conservation Corps: Contributing to the Defense of the Nation* applauded the contributions of the CCC and the hardiness and determination of CCC enrollees: "The work of the CCC has increased the natural wealth of the Nation by hundreds of millions of dollars. These young men have made our land a better place to live; more worth protecting and defending; and in terms of reserve resources and reserve manpower, more able to protect and defend itself. . . . Fighting forest fires and floods, building roads and trails through rough country, connecting outposts with wilderness by telephone — such typical CCC jobs have produced men able to use their heads and hands under difficult circumstances" (1, 5).

Park Design and Park Designers during World War II

Despite the recognized value of the CCC as a tool for defense preparation, the entry of the United States into World War II brought an abrupt end to the Civilian Conservation Corps. By July 1942, the thirty-nine CCC camps remaining in national and state parks were disbanded, and within a year equipment and property were transferred to the War and Navy Departments. Many former CCC enrollees found themselves readily enlisted as noncommissioned officers in the armed forces because of their CCC training and experience. In several parks and recreational demonstration areas, CCC-camp buildings were left on site and adapted for administrative and maintenance use.[7]

Progress in recreational planning nationwide halted in 1942 after the United States entered World War II. Many park staff were dispersed to fulfill defense occupations, and there were few funds or resources for development and maintenance. A small number of conservation camps for conscientious objectors did operate in several parks, including Shenandoah and Big Bend, to continue the work of forest protection, trail building, and soil erosion control.

World War II caused an exodus of landscape architects and architects from the civilian to armed services. Men with state and national park experience—state park inspectors, camp technicians, and others—sought useful and relevant wartime defense work. While Conrad Wirth and Thomas Vint temporarily relocated their National Park Service offices to Chicago, a small number of the older and experienced landscape architects, such as Ernest Davidson, remained in the regional offices. By the end of 1942, many former National Park Service landscape architects and architects found work related to the war effort. For example, former Texas state park inspector B. Ashburton Tripp became the chief of landscape design for the new War Department headquarters, the Pentagon; Russell L. McKown, a CCC landscape architect from Yosemite, became an infantry officer at Fort MacArthur, California; Harvey P. Benson, the resident landscape architect at Shenandoah National Park, became an officer with the Corps of Engineers at the Richmond General Depot, where he was occupied with construction of quartermaster facilities; former CCC landscape architect at Shenandoah National Park Lynn M. Harriss became the post beautification officer at Fort Bragg, North Carolina.[8]

With the advent of aviation defense, camouflage emerged as a new field of design in World War II—one that was well suited to the skills and knowledge of landscape architects, many of whom had worked in the woods and had spent almost a decade designing constructed improvements that blended into the natural scenery of state and national parks. The increasing use of airplanes and high-magnification optics in World War II brought about the need to design installations—camps, housing, industrial complexes, airfields, factories, and other facilities—in ways that concealed them and blended into natural surroundings so that they would be poor targets for military attack from the air and the sea. Like the design of natural parks, the success of camouflage relied heavily upon site selection, adherence to principles of design which concealed form and detail, and the selection of appropriate materials often including natural vegetation. Camouflage required that development conform to the general character of the site and fit into the immediate surroundings, thereby following the natural contours of the land and avoiding raw scars of cuts and fills. Buildings were to be arranged in irregular groupings, and trees were to remain at the edges of construction.[9]

Camouflage research and development drew upon the skills and experience of several former park designers. At the offices of the Engineering Board of the Corps of Engineers at Fort Belvoir, Virginia, George Nason became the chief of the camouflage design office. His varied staff of designers—architects, landscape architects, illustrators, engineers, model makers, and site designers—included V. Roswell Ludgate, who had been the regional landscape architect for the National Park Service's Eastern Region, and Merel S. Sager, who had been a resident landscape architect for the Western Region since the late 1920s. Former Massachusetts state park inspector Edward B. Ballard served as an Air Corps officer for camouflage research at the California Institute of Technology in Pasadena, and regional landscape architect Norman T. Newton served as an intelligence and camouflage officer for the Air Corps at Pendleton Field, Oregon.[10]

World War II renewed pressures upon the natural resources of the national parks. Recalling their concern over the use of park resources during World War I and fearing that the wartime emergency would once again threaten the national parks, the ASLA passed a resolution in 1942 which called for the preservation of natural and scenic resources in national parks and forests and urged members of the profession to be vigilant against any attempts to damage the natural resources of the parks.[11]

Strong leadership to protect the national parks from the pressures of defense interests to use the timber, mineral, and grassland resources of the parks came from National Park Service director Newton B. Drury. Drury was one of the nation's leading conservationists and had headed the Save-the-Redwoods League before coming to the National Park Service. Especially threatened were the forests of Sitka spruce in Olympic National Park, stands of virgin red spruce and hemlock in Great Smoky Mountains National Park, the grasslands and meadows of Yosemite National Park, and mineral deposits in Death Valley and Organ Pipe Cactus National Monuments. Maintaining a firm stance that activities destructive to national parks should be allowed only if "absolutely essential" and "only as a last resort," Drury succeeded, with the support of Secretary of the Interior Harold L. Ickes, in arguing in each case that the resources were not essential to victory and that alternative materials were available outside the parks. Drury attributed this success to the support of conservation-minded organizations and the "cooperative, open-minded approach" of the war agencies.[12]

By the end of 1944, the National Park Service was concerned that the trend of increasing visitation to national parks which occurred before the war would resume in the postwar period. Planning had continued with a small staff through the war years, mostly in preparation of master plans for new parks. The hiatus created by the war, however, created a backlog of urgently needed construction, and Director Drury urged the resumption of public works funding after the war in the form of a three-year program of planning and construction. A conservationist in principle, Drury called for a program of construction which allowed sufficient time for planning and design so that the natural beauty of the native landscape would be retained.[13]

Drury proposed to correct several problems that in his view conflicted with the National Park Service's dual purpose of protecting the natural features of the parks while contributing to public enjoyment. He called for measures to control visitation to western parks so that "perishable features" could be protected. He proposed removing concession facilities from areas of the greatest natural beauty, curbing the encroachment of campgrounds on the natural landscape of

Yosemite National Park, and relocating the Longmire headquarters at Mount Rainier to a more suitable site at a lower elevation. Drury believed that discouraging resort-type development was one way to meet the objective of keeping the perishable features of parks unimpaired. Drury challenged the need for overnight accommodations in Great Smoky Mountains National Park, calling upon park planners "to envision only such facilities as necessary for daytime use" and look to "nearby communities to furnish sleeping accommodations" (217–18).

Although Drury failed in his efforts to raise money for park construction, work on park master plans proceeded during the postwar years. Special attention was given to the design of new parks such as Big Bend National Park, established in 1944, and Everglades National Park, established in 1947.

The planning for the park headquarters for Big Bend National Park reflected the changing attitudes of park administrators and planners in the postwar era. The development of Big Bend State Park by the CCC from 1934 to 1936 and 1940 to 1942 was centered in the natural basin formed by the Chisos Mountain. The CCC built an eight-mile road into the basin through Green Gulch with foot and bridle trails leading into the surrounding mountains. In the early CCC period, architect William Wuehrman and landscape architect Paul Pressler had developed several grandiose designs for a large hacienda-style hotel; this idea was abandoned when the CCC resumed development in 1940, and a small cluster of Mexican-inspired stone and stucco cabins were built on a spur loop road in the upper basin.

Sentiment for making the basin the centerpiece of the new park because of its scenic beauty and moderate summer temperatures lingered. In 1942, park planner Paul Brown saw the basin as the focal point of summer use with a lodge and cabins, park headquarters, and a hub for foot and bridle trails that led visitors to scenic overlooks and outlying camping areas at the South Rim, Oak Spring, Blue Creek, and Lost Mine Peak.[14]

In 1944, however, Director Drury opposed plans to make the basin the permanent park headquarters, and the search began for a permanent site for the park administrative facilities, which were temporarily housed in the buildings of the former CCC camp in the lower basin. The search was complicated by the vastness and remote location of the park, scarcity of water, and extreme summer temperatures. Harvey H. Cornell, the regional landscape architect from Santa Fe, first proposed the sites of the former Daniel and Graham Ranches near the Rio Grande, where park and concessionaires' facilities could be built and, owing to irrigation, shade trees could be planted while causing little damage to the parks' superlative natural features.[15]

Distance from the entrances to the park and extreme summer temperatures ruled out the development of sites along the Rio Grande, and in 1946 Cornell proposed a site near the center of the park, north of the Chisos Mountains near the entrance to Green Gulch Road. Cornell successfully argued: "Any loss of natural values in this area, would I believe be more than compensated for in the administrative and protective control gained. Here headquarters would be accessible to all visitors, its central resources and reserves could be thrown with equal facility to any part of the area that emergency might require. The location being at intermediate elevation would not be subject to the seasonal climatic extremes." In 1948 this site, known as Panther Junction, was approved for the new park headquarters, which was constructed in the 1950s.[16]

Mission 66

It was more than a decade after the end of World War II before large-scale funding for new construction in national parks was realized. Only a small number of projects were funded in the early 1950s, including some of the first park facilities for the Everglades National Park. The National Park Service became increasingly alarmed by the upsurge in park visitation spurred by the postwar economy, the expansive popularity of automobiles, and a population explosion of recreation-seeking Americans. In 1955, 50 million visitors had come to national parks that were equipped to accommodate half that number. Both government and concessionaires' facilities were woefully inadequate to meet the needs of the number of visitors and automobiles arriving in the parks. The park service was faced with the growing dilemma of maintaining parks unimpaired while accommodating the tremendous influx of visitors. The Federal Highway Aid Act of 1954 alleviated the problem somewhat through a three-year program for funding park road construction. A backlog dating from 1942 continued to exist, however, for campgrounds, museums, administration buildings, staff housing, and maintenance buildings. A study in 1953 by the wives of park superintendents had revealed the inadequacy and substandard conditions of government housing for park employees. Many concessionaires' facilities were outmoded and deteriorated; the grand hotels of 1910–20 no longer appealed to the modern visitor, and the cabins of the 1920s and 1930s failed to meet modern-day visitor expectations for comfort and privacy. In 1955, *Reader's Digest* carried an article, "Shocking Truth about Our National Parks: A Report on the Use of Park Areas and Supporting Funds," which exposed substandard conditions in the concessionaire-operated hotels and cabins, litter in the heavily visited geyser sites of Yellowstone, and inadequate housing and maintenance throughout the national parks.[17]

The National Park Service's response was Mission 66, a multimillion-dollar program designed "to meet the needs of a much greater number of visitors and at the same time safeguard fully the wilderness, scenic, scientific and historic resources entrusted to the National Park Service." The program was ardently promoted by Director Conrad Wirth, a landscape architect by training who had spearheaded the National Park Service's programs for CCC state park development, recreational demonstration areas, and the nationwide park, parkway, and recreational area study in the 1930s. The Mission 66 program was intended to improve and expand visitor services by funding greater staff, improving the interpretation program, constructing modern facilities, and upgrading existing roads, trails, campgrounds, and other facilities in national parks. The program was to be phased over a ten-year period culminating in 1966 to correspond with the fiftieth anniversary of the legislation establishing the National Park Service.[18]

Mission 66 was justified on the basis of the rapidly increasing visitation to the parks. The number of national park areas and the number of visitors had manifoldly increased from 1916. Parks had increased in number from 33 in 1916, to 51 in 1926, 132 in 1936, 173 in 1946, and 181 in 1956. The number of visitors annually had dramatically increased from 358,000 in 1916 to 2,315,000 in 1926, 11,990,000 in 1936, 21,752,000 in 1946, and 50,000,000 in 1955. Visitation to national parks for 1966 — the fiftieth anniversary year and the end of Mission 66 — was estimated at 80,000,000 visits.[19]

The program was designed to bolster park staffs, catch up on the backlog of facility construction and maintenance, and "move ahead of the rising tide of public use." The Mission 66 program called for reconstructing and realigning park roads to modern standards, increasing overnight accommodations in campgrounds and concessionaires' facilities, improving the sanitary conditions of parks, building better housing for park staff, and expanding the interpretive program of the parks through new facilities and increased staffing. The goal was to equip the parks to meet the visitation figures projected for 1966.[20]

Mission 66 proposed to take "a fresh look at the problems and the future of the National Park System," "retain the best from the past," and forge new policies and practices to "most effectively serve the needs of the future." In reinterpreting the 1916 act in "the light of present and future conditions," the Mission 66 program unequivocally emphasized use over preservation and endeavored to enhance the quality of the visitor's experience through the development of modern facilities. Wirth stated in the foreword to the Mission 66 prospectus:

> In saying "conserve" the Act of 1916 recognized that the cultural and inspirational products of parks are supplied by the natural or historic scene undamaged, unmodified, and unimpaired. To change the character of a park area in any important way destroys a part of its ability to yield those benefits to the human mind and spirit. Protection, then, while an absolute requirement, is not an end in itself, but a means to an end — it is requisite to the kind and quality of enjoyment contemplated in the establishment and perpetuation of parks by the Nation. Thus, we complete our concept of park purpose: The primary justification for a National Park System lies in its capacity to provide enjoyment in its best sense, now and in the future. [21]

Mission 66 endeavored to plan facilities that would bring visitors in direct contact with the significant values of the park while preserving the resources. In Wirth's thinking, plans for the development of the new Everglades National Park in Florida, a large subtropical wilderness, "should permit the visitor to approach and observe at close range the resources of the 'glades' in order to understand the basic ecological relationships and the relationships of man to the Everglades." Facilities for meals and boat services, a service station, store, a campground, picnic area, comfort stations, parking areas, walks, roads, a utility area, a ranger station, employee quarters, and interpretive and information services were proposed for the development of a shoreline site, Flamingo, on Florida Bay so that visitors could be transported by water to "various points to experience and enjoy close contact with the living resources of the area." [22]

Envisioned as a bold and forward-looking initiative, Mission 66 adopted modern methods of landscape and architectural design and rejected the picturesque prototypes that had characterized park design in the 1920s and 1930s. Changes were already apparent in the park structures designed in the early 1950s for the Everglades, Dinosaur National Monument, and Big Bend National Park. Economics as well as the intent to create facilities that conformed to "the travel and recreational habits of park users" brought an end to the pioneer and indigenous models, handcrafted appearances, and subtle naturalistic harmonies that marked the park architecture of the 1920s and 1930s. The Mission 66 staff, headed by William G. Carnes, was instructed to "disregard precedent, policy, present operating and management procedures, traditions, and work habits." Remembering "only the fundamental purpose of national parks," the staff was to develop operating and development plans that best met the problems of present and future park use. As a result Mission 66 was a period of experimentation with new structural forms, modern materials—glass, concrete, and steel—and machine-driven methods of construction for sturdy, low-maintenance, permanent structures that could serve the modern-day needs of the traveling public on a large scale. Calling for intensive and rapid construction, Mission 66 promoted the "packaging of projects to get the greatest benefit economically and save labor costs, materials, and equipment" (9).

The National Park Service designers at both the Eastern Office of Design and Construction (EODC) and the Western Office of Design and Construction (WODC) were quickly put to work on the design of overlooks, campgrounds, and other facilities. Private architectural firms, some having national and international reputations, were hired to design innovative facilities such as the visitor center in Rocky Mountains National Park and the Clingman's Dome Tower in Great Smoky Mountains National Park.

The landscape architecture profession figured prominently in the Mission 66 program. Wirth called upon landscape architects and others of the National Park Service "to see that, through the techniques of designing, constructing, and

12.1. Mission 66 funding made possible the development of the Everglades National Park for visitor use and enjoyment in the late 1950s. In addition to a fifty-four-unit campground equipped for trailers as well as automobiles, the development at Flamingo on Florida Bay featured a boat marina to enable visitors to travel offshore by boat to view closely the region's coastal ecology. *(Courtesy National Park Service Historic Photography Collection)*

managing parks," it was made possible for all the people of the United States to obtain the "supreme enjoyment" of the country's great scenic areas. The primary function of the landscape architect was "to steer the course of how the land [was] to be used" through "the creation, maintenance, and growth of the Master Plan" and by translating the studies of park professionals — historians, geologists, archeologists, naturalists, architects, and engineers — into "an orderly and well-conceived development plan" (13–14).

Education and interpretation took on particular importance in Mission 66. Through new visitor centers, information stations, publications, exhibits, campfire talks, conducted trips, roadside displays, and audiovisual presentations, Mission 66 endeavored to develop the informational and interpretive programs of the parks to help visitors enjoy the parks and use them wisely. For natural parks the role of interpretation expanded from the communication of a park's natural history to become an important tool for park preservation.[23]

Innovative was the concept of the modern visitor center. Strategically placed at centers of primary interest, the visitor center was designed as the hub of each park's interpretive program. A staffed information desk with maps, schedules of activities, and informational panels oriented the visitor to the park, its significant features, its layout, and its visitor services. Museum exhibits, dioramas, relief models, recorded slide talks, and other graphic devices meanwhile informed visitors about the meaning of the park and its features. Larger visitor centers also provided an auditorium and bookstore and housed the park's museum collections, workrooms, and a library. Basic necessities, such as rest rooms, drinking fountains, telephones, and parking, were incorporated into the design of each center.[24]

The design of these facilities required the collaboration of museum specialists, architects, and landscape architects. Architects called for open design in the form of spacious lobbies and wide, floor-to-ceiling windows of plate glass from which the natural landscape could be viewed and interpreted. Museum specialists designed protected, light-controlled areas for displaying artifacts and historical items. Landscape architects closely working with architects made use of traditional devices of landscape design — one-way loop roads, parking lots, paved walkways, terraces, stairways, and naturalistic plantings — to make the facility and grounds attractive and accessible. Modern landscape devices were explored, including the use of gradually graded ramps and wide entry walks to accommodate the movement of large numbers of people and the design of broad elevated terraces with aggregate stone surfaces and protective walls to provide safe, uncrowded viewpoints.

Campgrounds were viewed as a "compelling necessity" in large national parks. In 1955, the National Park System had approximately twelve thousand campsites and anticipated a demand for twenty-five thousand by 1966. In adherence to the Meinecke principles for campground planning, additional tiers and campsites were added to existing campgrounds, and new campgrounds designed to accommodate large numbers of visitors and automobiles, some hauling trailers, were established and equipped with modern fireplaces, tables, comfort stations, and, in the case of the Basin Campground at Big Bend National Park, ramadas made of concrete clad in stonemasonry with metal shed roofs. As a result, the number of campgrounds within national parks and the number of campsites within existing campgrounds dramatically increased during the Mission 66 period. The number of picnic areas, based on modified Meinecke plans and models taken from the 1930s development of picnic waysides in Acadia National Park, in Shenandoah National Park, and along the Blue Ridge Parkway,

12.2. Visitor centers, such as this one photographed at Great Smoky Mountains National Park in 1961, were an essential part of the Mission 66 program. Large, centrally located, multipurpose facilities designed through the cooperation of architects, landscape architects, and museum designers, visitor centers became the hub of the park's interpretive program. Walls of native stone and neutrally toned siding commonly gave naturalistic accents to modernistic designs fashioned from steel, glass, and concrete. *(Photograph by Jack E. Boucher, courtesy National Park Service Historic Photography Collection)*

also substantially increased as Mission 66 recognized the value of daytime picnic areas to concentrate daytime visitor use and thus minimize the impairment of the landscape, the danger of fire, and the cost of providing water and sanitation.[25]

Mission 66 upheld the campfire as the quintessential national park experience and encouraged the widespread construction of campfires and amphitheaters near campgrounds and other overnight facilities. Although those constructed under Mission 66, such as the one at Big Bend's Basin Campground, lacked the handcrafted log benches and palisaded stages that distinguished those of the 1920s and 1930s, park amphitheaters remained simple, secluded rustic theaters naturalistically sited under a "canopy of the skies" with an arrangement of seating in concentric semicircles, a speaker's platform, and a projection booth. The Mission 66 prospectus echoed the sentiments of Frank Waugh a generation before: "The evening gathering of visitors around the campfire typifies the national park idea—that concept so uniquely American and so truly democratic. The informal campfire gathering with a naturalist conducting group singing and question and answer sessions, and telling of the lore of the particular area's wildlife, forests, geology, Indians, pioneers, and of those struggles of the growth and development of the thriving America we know today—these are experiences dear to the hearts of park visitors" (31–31, 94–96).

Road improvements were intended to bring existing park roads up to the same standard as the modern park roads that had been built under the three-year program authorized by the 1954 Federal Aid Highway Act. This meant reconstructing, realigning, and relocating park roads to eliminate steep grades and sharp curves and constructing turnouts, parking areas, and overlooks to increase the park visitor's enjoyment and appreciation of the surrounding natural scenery. Roadside markers and exhibits, which were first introduced at Yellowstone National Park in the early 1930s, became a standard feature of park roads of the early 1950s and were promoted as an important aspect of Mission 66's interpretive program for trails and roads (87–88, 99).

Improvements to park trail systems during Mission 66 were intended to enable visitors "to savor the wilderness" constituting "all but a small percentage of the area of any of the major parks." Much attention was given to close-in trails, those leading from parking areas to nearby features of special interest, such as waterfalls, stands of virgin forest, and scenic viewpoints. Safety was paramount in the Mission 66 program, and popular features, such as overlooks on the Grand Canyon of the Yellowstone and Acadia's Thunder Hole, were equipped—some for the first time—with walkways and protective railings fashioned from standardized stonemasonry and tubular steel. Raised wooden boardwalks similar to those developed in the early 1950s for the Anhinga Trail in Everglades National Park were particularly popular because they provided access to areas not reachable by traditional trails and caused little harm to the natural features over which they passed. Improvements made to backcountry trails created links between

12.3. The safety of ever increasing numbers of park visitors was a prime concern of Mission 66 designers. In 1955 new platforms of textured concrete and tubular steel were built at Inspiration Point overlooking the Grand Canyon of the Yellowstone. *(Courtesy National Park Service Historic Photography Collection)*

existing trails to permit shorter loop trips, scatter use more evenly through the backcountry, avoid overuse of strategic camping spots, and add to the interest of hikers (86, 88–89).

Congress endorsed the Mission 66 idea, and National Park Service appropriations increased 39 percent the first year and 11 percent the next year. The initial construction program to set up Mission 66 contained 1,150 projects valued at $75 million. Accomplishments by the end of June 1957 included 7 visitor centers, 9 modern park headquarters buildings, 56 comfort stations, 146 improved or new housing units for park staff, 24 repair and work shops, 83 wayside interpretive exhibits, parking for 7,500 cars, the reconstruction and improvement of 130 miles of existing routes, the construction of 47 miles of new roads, the improvement of 33 miles of trails, the construction of 25 miles of new trails, 51 new water systems, and 38 new sewer systems. With $7.5 million in private capital investment, rooms for 2,300 additional visitors and 930 new and 1,300 improved campsites were added to overnight accommodations within national parks.[26]

Although Mission 66 was envisioned as a comprehensive program affecting all aspects of park operations, it was the aggressive construction program that included the development of recreational facilities (including ski lifts and boat marinas) which attracted criticism from conservationists and conservation organizations such as the Sierra Club, National Parks Association, and Wilderness Society. Director Conrad Wirth adamantly defended Mission 66, upholding the visitor's right to visit the parks and to do so in large numbers. Well-designed facilities were needed to direct and control visitor use, and, in Wirth's opinion, design and construction offered effective means of preserving the natural resources of the parks. Landscape improvements such as boardwalks in Yellowstone's thermal areas kept people from wandering over the formations and served to safeguard the visitor while protecting the natural environment. Wirth argued that "there is no surer way to destroy a landscape than to permit undisciplined use by man; and roads, trails, campgrounds, and other developments are one means, perhaps the most important one, of localizing, limiting, and channeling park use."[27]

Wirth argued that Mission 66's purpose was not to extend developments farther into the heart of a park but to make better use of what was already accessible, and, where possible, remove undesirable development. This was the case, he claimed, with the new Canyon Village at Yellowstone, a modern village designed to accommodate four thousand visitors in campgrounds and motel-type cottages and provide facilities for stores, a photographic studio, food concessions, and gas stations. Designed by the Los Angeles architectural firm of Welton Becket and Associates and constructed for the concessionaire at a cost of more than eight million dollars, Canyon Village opened in 1957 and met the urgent demand for comfortable accommodations meeting modern-day standards. Meanwhile, plans proceeded to demolish the hotel that had occupied the site overlooking the Upper Falls since the 1880s, remove the campground and other facilities, restore the area's native vegetation, and develop trails and overlooks to make the area's spectacular scenery accessible to all park visitors. Wirth wrote: "In a short time the Canyon Rim will be restored to use for esthetic enjoyment, understanding, and appreciation. To devote a very few of the more than a million acres of lodgepole forest to development is a small price indeed to pay for the restoration and preservation of the far more valuable, far more significant values of Yellowstone."[28]

The most serious concerns arose over the reconstruction of roads in the Mission 66 program. Roads were widened, realigned, and, in many cases, relocated to meet modern highway standards and accommodate increasing numbers of automobiles. Although no new roads were to be built under Mission 66, the improvements, especially the reconstructed roads that dramatically flattened the grades and widened the curves, markedly changed the character of park roads and the surrounding countryside. Automobiles were now able to travel safely through parks in greater numbers but also at higher speeds. The great-

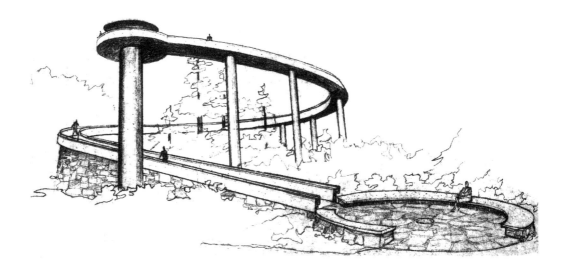

12.4. Nicknamed the "Skypost," the Clingman's Dome Tower in Great Smoky Mountains National Park broke with the naturalistic tradition of constructing lookouts from native stone and timbers. Designed by the firm of Bebb and Olson from nearby Gatlinburg, Tennessee, the tower consisted of a 375-foot-long, 6-foot-wide ramp that emerged from a stonemasonry veneered base, formed a concrete spiral, and led visitors to an observation deck 45 feet above the Fraser fir forest of the natural summit. There visitors could enjoy a 360-degree panorama of the southern Appalachians. *(Copy negative by Glenn Peart, courtesy National Park Service Historic Photography Collection)*

est furor arose over the reconstructed portion of the mountainous Tioga Road at the edge of Lake Tenaya in Yosemite National Park and the conversion of the simple road across Mount McKinley (now Denali) National Park to a modern highway with extensive, irreparable swathes of cut and fill.[29]

Symbolic of the overall purpose of Mission 66 and the inherent conflict between visitor use and preservation is the Clingman's Dome Tower built for Great Smoky Mountains National Park in 1959. The skypost-observation tower on Clingman's Dome (elev. 6,643 feet) replaced an outmoded wooden frame structure of the 1920s and was designed as an open-air tower to bring the visitors up above the treetops where they could view a 360-degree panorama of the Great Smoky Mountains. Designed by the firm of Bebb and Olson, Architects, from nearby Gatlinburg, Tennessee, the tower was enthusiastically approved by the National Park Service's Eastern Office of Design and Construction. Following the modernistic idiom of ramps and spirals, the tower was designed to enhance visitors' enjoyment of the high peak by bringing them upward above the treetops along a 375-foot-long, 6-foot-wide ramp to a point 45 feet above the natural summit. This extended the trail above the natural peak to present a panoramic view not otherwise visible without clearing away vegetation. To the architects, the tower was a simple and direct solution using readily available contemporary materials. The architectural form of a ramp following the gradient of the trail and supported on vertical "trunks" of concrete was, in their opinion, appropriate and in keeping with the beauty of the mountains. The park service praised the structure, noting its "sweeping free-flowing lines of contemporary architecture," "graceful, graded spiral," and ability to move people quickly and safely, "making it possible for visitors to enjoy the view as they moved up and down." [30]

Viewed within the context of the landscape design of the National Park Service, the Clingman's Dome Tower is a modern equivalent of the stairway and platforms built upon Moro Rock in Sequoia National Park in 1917 and rebuilt to the Landscape Division's naturalistic designs in 1931. The tower made a modernistic statement in its architectural design but also in its interpretive purpose. Visitors gradually ascending the spiral ramp on a comfortable 12 percent grade experienced the unraveling beauty of the surrounding stand of Fraser fir. Arriving at the top, they were awed by a spectacular panorama of the Great Smoky Mountains. The tower offered a kinetic experience not unlike that created by the transitional spirals of park roads and parkways of the late 1930s or described a generation earlier by Frank Waugh as the objective of a naturalistic trail.

Even though it was an achievement in park landscape design, the skypost was ridiculed by conservationists for its modernism and its creation of an artificial viewpoint. The tower did little to harmonize visually with the natural setting, and it was viewed as an unnecessary park structure. Although not significantly higher than the Watchman at Crater Lake and other observation towers built in the national parks in the late 1920s and 1930s, the tower was not needed or used for fire surveillance. Furthermore, it broke with the tradition of naturalistic design based on native materials and indigenous methods of construction which conservationists felt suitable for the design of park structures. Anthony Wayne Smith of the National Parks Association criticized the tower as "flashy," "conspicuous," "unnecessarily large," "extravagantly expensive" ($57,000), "eccentric," and "lacking in feeling" for the "frontier" and "wilderness." He called it "noisy architecture" and derided its expression of speed, motion, and technical power.[31]

The case of the Clingman's Dome Tower points out the diverging views of park designers and conservationists on the subject of park preservation and visitor use which were emerging in the late 1950s and would lead to a sweeping reevaluation of park policy in the 1960s. As an era of scenery preservation gave way to an ecologically based system of environmental protection in the 1960s, such reactions against modernism would be replaced by concerns for ecological disturbance. Within the context of park landscape design, Mission 66, despite its modernism, perpetuated and gave renewed expression to the philosophy of park

12.5. As the construction of Clingman's Dome Tower in Great Smoky Mountains National Park in July 1959 illustrates, Mission 66 embraced the materials and methods of modern construction. Built to an easy grade of 12 percent and supported on pylons of steel and concrete, the spiral ramp was constructed of reinforced concrete poured in place and shaped by temporary forms and scaffolding. *(Photograph by Jack E. Boucher, courtesy National Park Service Historic Photography Collection)*

building promoted by Stephen Mather in the formative years of the National Park Service and the practices and principles of park landscape designers of the 1920s and 1930s.

The Wilderness Movement and the Environmental Era

Criticism of Mission 66 was widespread among conservationists who, focused on the wilderness issue, equated the trend for accommodating increasing numbers of park visitors with the destruction of wilderness values. From their standpoint, Mission 66 was a retreat from the mandate of the 1916 act to preserve the parks unimpaired.

The gathering momentum of the wilderness movement to a large extent explains the outcry from conservation-minded individuals and organizations over the results of Mission 66. The wilderness movement originated in the early twentieth century over concern for the preservation of outstanding areas within national forests which were to remain uncut and undisturbed by economic use. This led the U.S. Forest Service to identify wilderness and primitive areas in national forests. The wilderness movement gained substantial momentum in the 1930s with the founding of the Wilderness Society by Aldo Leopold and Robert Marshall in 1935.

To wilderness advocates, the increasing demand for recreation and the upsurge of recreational development by public agencies using relief funds and labor threatened the last remnants of undisturbed land. Writing on wilderness values in the *1941 Yearbook: Park and Recreation Progress,* Aldo Leopold called upon public agencies to seek a higher level of administering wilderness. He protested against what he perceived as "the wholesale and needless sacrifice of wild elements in the landscape" which occurred as parks and forests were developed for public recreation. To Leopold, the administrators of public lands having remnants of wilderness had a double responsibility to the future: "to keep some wilderness in existence, and to cultivate its qualitative enjoyment." Leopold's concerns went beyond the damage created by "road-builders" and "motor-minded promoters" to the imminent ecological threat posed by the loss of wildlife, especially the grizzly bear of the western parks, which he claimed had "no sure citadel for the future" despite the millions of acres dedicated to wildlife conservation.[32]

The National Park Service began designating specific areas within national parks as wilderness areas in 1928 with the designation of the glacial region and undeveloped northern section of Mount Rainier National Park. Such designations were to be made as park master plans were developed. By 1932 this approach proved difficult, and the park service redefined wilderness as any area not identified as a road, trail, or development area on the park's master plan. Such areas were to be left unimpaired by human improvements other than trails and simple shelters. Speaking at the 1938 Conference on National Parks, chief architect Thomas C. Vint explained: "Rather than approach the problem from the angle of setting aside wilderness areas within the national parks, we must approach it from the other direction—that is, we must restrict the limits of developed areas and apply the protection that would be given to the wilderness area to *all* of the area within the boundaries of the park that is not a developed area." At the same meeting, Superintendent Jesse Nusbaum upheld wilderness preservation as the essential purpose of the National Park Service: "The perpetuation and preservation, unimpaired, of wilderness values of national parks continue as its most potent ideals and functional objectives."[33]

Wilderness advocacy strengthened in the late 1940s and 1950s as a result of the Bureau of Reclamation's proposal to build a dam at Echo Park within the boundaries of Dinosaur National Monument as part of the Colorado River Storage Project. Conservationists and conservation organizations successfully urged Congress to oppose the construction of the dam, but the threat of further attempts to exploit the wilderness values of national parks and other public lands lingered. Environmental concern grew as the public became aware of the quickly retreating boundaries of primeval landscape across the West and the impact of America's increasing population and urbanization. In the late 1950s, Congress began debating the need for a national wilderness preservation system that would encompass the remaining undeveloped lands under federal management — national parks, national forests, rangeland, wildlife refuges, and reclamation lands.

The National Park Service was opposed to the wilderness proposals on the premise that its 1916 enabling legislation already charged the service with stewardship of the nation's wilderness. Apart from those areas slated for development in master plans, national parks retained extensive areas that were roadless and void of other constructed improvements. In 1958, the park service published a large, thirty-seven-page brochure entitled *The National Park Wilderness,* in which the concept of national park wilderness was equated with the principles of preservation and use set forth in the 1916 enabling legislation. To a large extent the brochure, which detailed the National Park System's eighty-five-year record, was written to define the concept of national park wilderness and justify the Mission 66 program in the light of wilderness concerns.[34]

The Wilderness Act (P.L. 88–577) became law on September 3, 1964, requiring the National Park Service and other federal agencies to identify areas to be included in a national wilderness preservation system. The Wilderness Act of 1964 defined a wilderness as "an area where earth and its community of life are untrammeled by man, where man himself is a visitor who does not remain." Wilderness was further defined under the act as an area of "undeveloped federal land retaining its primeval character and influence, without improvements or human habitation, which is protected and managed so as to preserve its natural conditions and which 1) generally appears to have been affected primarily by the forces of nature, with the imprint of man's work substantially unnoticeable; 2) has outstanding opportunities for solitude or a primitive and unconfined type of recreation; 3) has at least 5,000 acres of land or is of sufficient size as to make practicable its preservation and use in an unimpaired condition; and 4) may also contain ecological, geological or other features of scientific, educational, scenic, or historical value."[35]

For the National Park Service, the wilderness legislation caused a fair degree of confusion about the essential meaning of parks and the differentiation between developed and undeveloped areas of the parks. The Wilderness Act required the agency to define a new kind of wilderness, propose boundaries that would carry the legislatively mandated designation and protection, and devise a policy to protect wilderness values. All units of the national park system having five thousand acres or more without roads were to be reviewed for suitability as wilderness. Congress would ultimately approve all areas within national parks to carry the special designation. By 1966, the park service established the National Park Service Wilderness Management Criteria for areas of parks to be designated wilderness areas within the National Wilderness Preservation System authorized by the Wilderness Act. The National Park Service resolved to maintain a high standard of preservation throughout the national parks and devised a system for zoning parkland into categories depending on significance, natural character, and wilderness qualities. In addition to "wilderness," there was a category for "wilderness threshold lands" where visitors could experience the mood of wilderness before venturing forth into wild country beyond.[36]

Above all, the preservation of wilderness values determined the limits of development and types of facilities within park wilderness areas. Primarily, these areas were to remain roadless and inaccessible by automobiles. Primitive, narrow foot and bridle trails that blended into the landscape were allowed, and simple footbridges and horse bridges could be constructed where needed for visitor safety. Certain kinds of structures—patrol cabins, trailside shelters, and stock-holding corrals—were allowed where they protected wilderness values. Improvements for the comfort and convenience of visitors, such as developed campgrounds and picnic facilities, were strictly prohibited.[37]

As the wilderness idea was gaining popular and legislative support, so too was the movement for national recreational planning. The 1962 report of the Outdoor Recreation Resources Review Commission (ORRRC) resulted in the creation of a separate Bureau of Outdoor Recreation to coordinate national outdoor recreation policy in 1962 and the passage of the Land and Water Conservation Fund Act (P.L. 88–578) in 1964, which provided for funds for the acquisition of land for recreational purposes by federal, state, and local governments and called for the development of a national recreational plan. Although the role of the National Park Service in coordinating national recreational planning ended, its preeminence in protecting the superlative natural features of the national parks was wholeheartedly confirmed. In 1967, at the request of the President's Council on Recreation and Natural Beauty, the National Parks and Conservation Association drafted a statement of governmental policy on comprehensive recreational regional planning which acknowledged the special problems facing the national parks from overcrowding, the need to provide greater opportunities for outdoor recreation outside national parks, and the overarching recognition of the protection of natural conditions as the highest priority of the National Park Service.[38]

Ecological concerns began to dominate the discussion of national park preservation, and scenery preservation, which had been promoted by park designers earlier in the century, waned in importance. The 1963 report of the Advisory Board on Wildlife Management, chaired by A. Starker Leopold, the son of wilderness advocate Aldo Leopold, had considerable influence on the National Park Service's changing policy. Commonly known as the "Leopold Report," it upheld the vital importance of native flora and fauna to park preservation. The report made the connection between expanding development of the parks and the loss of the ecological scene. It set forth the idea that "the goal of managing the national parks and monuments should be to preserve, or where necessary to recreate, the ecologic scene as viewed by the first European visitors." To achieve this end, the report advocated a program of habitat manipulation to maintain and restore natural communities of plants and animals in the parks.[39]

The Leopold Report called for changes in park design and construction. Planning was to be biologically informed. Parks were to contain permanently zoned roadless wilderness areas, and the design and extent of a park's road system were to be rigidly prescribed. Restrictions were to be placed on road use rather than encouraging new programs to upgrade and expand park roads. Golf courses, ski lifts, and motorboat marinas were "extraneous developments" and were viewed as contradicting management goals for national parks. Parks were to "represent a vignette of primitive America." Above all, the report stated, "the maintenance of naturalness should prevail" (104).

Conservationists began to develop a strong role as advocates for environmental policy in national parks. In 1962, the Conservation Foundation sponsored a study to examine the impact of humans on the national parks, which resulted in the 1967 report *Man and Nature in the National Parks: Reflections on Policy,* by renowned ecologist F. Fraser Darling and geographer Noel D. Eichhorn. The authors drew attention to the dangers facing parks from within by increasing numbers and crowds of people spending more of their increasing leisure time in the parks. They pointed out that not all park environments were equal in their capacity to endure human use without losing significant values and that while Skyline Drive created minimal damage to the recovering deciduous forest of Shenandoah National Park, the alpine environments of Rocky Mountain, Mount Rainier, and Mount McKinley National Parks were especially fragile, requiring a review of the ecosystem's balance and carrying capacity before locating trails and campsites. Eichhorn and Darling warned that more and more facilities needed to be moved outside park boundaries. They viewed the period 1935 to 1940 as optimum in the management of national park resources in the United States, wherein a balance existed between nature and human use. They called the architectural principles and ideals of the era "impeccable," noting the high standard of national park architecture, which achieved a "fitness" with the varied environments of the parks and exhibited "sensitivity in the design office." In the postwar period, as a result of increasing popularity and visitation, the balance between humans and nature was lost, and Mission 66, in their opinion, increased visitation by making it easier for the public to visit the parks and making their stay more comfortable. The authors were especially critical of the great increase in the number of drive-in campsites which resulted during the ten-year period, and they called for systems of advance reservations and increased user fees to control overcrowding instead of expanding campground development. As for the construction of Canyon Village with its suburban-type plaza and cabin-motel accommodations, they commented that the proximity to points of high scenic value in the park was the prime reason why Canyon Village should not have been located where it was. The authors conceded that, although gas stations, restaurants, and 250 miles of roads were inevitable in a park the size of Yellowstone, such facilities were not appropriate for smaller parks, where commercially owned facilities could easily be located outside park boundaries.[40]

Environmentalism in the 1960s, with its emphasis on wilderness and ecology, dramatically altered the management and development policies of the National Park Service under the leadership of Director George B. Hartzog Jr. In 1964 the national parks, which had become increasingly diverse since 1933, were classified into three types—natural areas, historical areas, and recreational areas—and a set of administrative policies was developed for each type. The guidelines for natural areas were derived from the park service's 1916 legislative mandate, 1918 statement of policy, and other pivotal documents, including the Leopold Report and Wilderness Management Criteria. The administrative policy for the development of natural areas stated: "Physical developments within natural areas should be limited to those that are necessary for adequate management and appropriate park use and enjoyment. . . . The location, design, and materials, to the highest practicable degree, should be consistent with the preservation and conservation of the grandeur of the natural environment."[41]

To a large extent, the guidelines for development reexamined the philosophies and practices of the 1930s in the light of the environmental era. Master planning continued to be the guiding document for park development. Although the use of naturalistic, native materials was encouraged, the quarrying of such materials within the parks was ordinarily restricted to that available within a construction site. The idea of an architectural theme reappeared, and a statement of design philosophy was to be prepared for each park. Renewed emphasis was given to harmonizing such developments with their natural environment: "In all cases, maximum creativity in design and materials—preferably those native to the region or locality—shall be used to insure that the manmade facility is subservient to and not competitive with, or dominant of the natural features of the area" (60).

One of the most significant documents to emerge was the 1967 *Park Roads Standards,* developed by a special committee in response to the growing environmental concern over road building in national parks. The result was a comprehensive statement of park road planning and design. Reinterpreting the 1916 legislation against the background of environmentalism, the standards adopted an overriding philosophy of preservation over use: "Preserving the integrity of the landscape, respecting ecological processes, insuring a fully rewarding visitor experience—these are the elements which dictate the means of visitor access and the development of design standards." [42]

The administrative policy for roads in natural areas echoed the philosophies and practices of the early designers and builders of park roads: "An esthetically pleasing road is one which lies lightly upon the lands utilizing natural support wherever possible. Moreover, heavy cuts and fills must be avoided. In effect, the road is molded to the terrain through which and upon which it is passing. Monotony is avoided, and maximum advantage taken of park values, by eliminating long tangents, by changes in elevation, and by developing viewpoints and overlooks, as well as by providing close-range views of local scenes. The road should, in fact, strive to maintain a continuing sense of intimacy with the countryside through which it is passing." [43]

Although the 1967 road standards reflected the traditional concerns for accessibility, presenting nature, and constructing in harmony with nature, they acknowledged the potential environmental damage that roads caused under certain conditions and emphasized traffic management over road construction. While upholding traffic safety and the value of roads for interpretation, the standards called for measures that could meet the demands of increasing use through management. The standards cautioned that new roads be "considered the last resort in seeking solutions to park access" and encouraged the exploration of alternative, nonintrusive methods of transportation. [44]

The new standards went beyond the concerns for scenery preservation to address ecological and interpretive issues. First of all, a "professional ecological determination" was to ensure that the effect of construction on park values—including wildlife habitat and mobility, drainage, stream flow, and the climatic effects of paved areas—was minimal. The construction and improvement of roads could only be justified after "a thorough and thoughtful determination" was made that they provided "the most meaningful way" for people to experience a park (131, 135).

Measures to reduce the impact of roads and road construction in the natural environment of the park were introduced. The design speed within natural areas was to fit the terrain and was limited to twenty-five miles per hour. A 7 percent standard was recommended for a road's alignment, but short stretches of 8 to 10 percent grade were allowed to avoid excessive cuts and fills. Two-way roads were to be converted to one-way roads to increase visitor safety. In mountainous areas, retaining walls were recommended to reduce the height and extent of cut-and-fill slopes, and trestles, bridges, tunnels, and half-viaduct sections were suggested to reduce scarring and permit movement of wildlife. The construction of turnouts, overlooks, and trail connections was encouraged to allow visitors opportunities to enjoy natural features and scenery. Borrow pits and quarrying within a national park were prohibited except where economic factors made it totally impractical to import road materials or where natural factors would eradicate the scars.[45]

The new road standards built upon the techniques for grading and planting roadsides first developed by Vint's Landscape Division in the late 1920s, giving special emphasis to blending roads with the natural setting and controlling soil erosion. In forests, the clearing of timber was to be limited and controlled through selective cutting so that sufficient variation and indentation could occur in the treeline along the road to achieve a naturalistic effect. After being rounded and warped, cut-and-fill slopes were to be seeded, fertilized, and mulched to encourage revegetation and control erosion.[46]

The administrative policies and road standards of the 1960s were a reaction to the boldness, modernity, and "use over preservation" philosophy of Mission 66. They were a conscious return philosophically to the principles of the 1920s and 1930s but also a step forward in the evolution of land-use policy from the preservation of scenic values to overall environmental protection. When the standards were revised and expanded in 1984 in preparation for the massive program of park road construction and rehabilitation funded under the Federal-Aid Highway Act of 1982, the basic philosophy and principles of the 1967 version were retained.[47]

More than any other road-related feature constructed in national parks in the last fifty years, the Linn Cove Viaduct on the Blue Ridge Parkway exhibits the synthesis of ecological protection, naturalistic principles of landscape design, and modern materials and methods of construction. The section of the parkway along the slopes of Grandfather Mountain required special environmental sensitivity. So as not to harm the natural scenic beauty of the site, Figg and Muller Engineers designed a 1,243-foot-long, S-shaped viaduct using the technology of prestressed segmental concrete. Conventional methods of construction would have done irreparable damage to the mountain's vegetation, geology, and streams, as well as scarred the natural scenery. Cast-in-place abutments and piers anchored the bridge to the natural outcrops, requiring minimal clearance of trees and little disturbance of the natural outcroppings. The use of precast segments, each unique in dimension and curvature, enabled the designers to contour the structure to the natural topography and erect the superstructure from the already assembled portion of the bridge, causing little destruction to the surrounding mountainside. The award-winning design for the viaduct, which was

12.6. Completed in 1983, the Linn Cove Viaduct on the Blue Ridge Parkway heralded a new era of park road design marked by the synthesis of ecological protection, naturalistic principles of landscape design, and modern materials and methods of construction. By employing the technology of prestressed segmental concrete, the engineering firm of Figg and Muller was able to create a 1,243-foot-long, S-shaped viaduct that caused minimal disturbance to the natural beauty of Grandfather Mountain. *(Courtesy National Park Service, Blue Ridge Parkway)*

completed in 1983, was an achievement for both its advanced technology and its environmentally sensitive solution.[48]

In the early 1970s, the master plans began to reflect ecological issues, indicating a shift in the thinking of park planners and landscape designers from scenery preservation to environmental planning. The master plan proposed for Yellowstone in the early 1970s was one of the first to reflect the wilderness thinking and new environmental concerns. A sense of urgency and utmost importance pervaded the prologue, which upheld the increasing value of Yellowstone as an "island of serenity in the midst of a world suffering from the pollution of air, water, and land; from the destruction of animal and plant life; and from overpopulation" and warned that if the park was to survive the next one hundred years, "a new equilibrium" had to be achieved: "the irreplaceable park resources must be weighed against the human impact upon them and a new balance struck."[49]

Yellowstone's plan endeavored to restructure visitor use within the park and to "pioneer in the evolution of a new kind of program-oriented wilderness threshold community." The plan questioned the traditional modes of visitor accommodations in multipurpose park villages that were designed for large numbers of people visiting the parks in automobiles; the plan found such accommodations inefficient, lacking harmony with contemporary visitor needs, and wasteful of the park's finite resources. The "wilderness threshold community" was envisioned as a new "design idiom" focused on interpretation and intended to get the visitor off the road and into the park. Such communities to be developed at Grant Village and Lake were to be "tightly knit developments creatively interspersed with plazas or green spaces" and organized on the principles of pedestrian orientation and minimal encroachment on park resources (16).

The Yellowstone Master Plan of the early 1970s proposed substantial changes to existing facilities within the park. From an ecological standpoint, the long-established facilities at Fishing Bridge on Yellowstone Lake occupied land claimed by the park's grizzly bear population. Located east of the Yellowstone River, Fishing Bridge was also a superb ecological environment for fish and birds. The 1973 master plan called for the elimination of existing overnight accommodations, which included the concessionaire's cabins and campground, in order to restore the area's wildlife habitat. A system of walking paths and overlooks and a visitor center were to be developed west of the river to enable visitors to view and enjoy the area's wildlife. For many developed areas, the master plan recommended that ceilings be established on the number of available overnight accommodations. For the newly constructed Canyon Village, also a location where the park's grizzly bears and the public were in conflict, the plan recommended such a ceiling and advised that the area be left alone, allowing "unstable soils as well as peripheral regional developments" ultimately to decide the area's fate. Continuing concern for the Grand Canyon of the Yellowstone led to the recommendation that vehicular traffic be removed from the north rim of the canyon and that alternative methods, such as shuttle buses, be studied to bring visitors to canyon viewing points (17–18, 31).

National environmental laws have substantially affected the planning process since the 1960s. The National Environmental Policy Act of 1969 (P.L. 91–190), which called upon federal agencies "to create and maintain conditions under which man and nature can exist," reinforced the ecological basis of national park preservation and established a process for ecological impact assessment and compliance. A series of acts to protect endangered species substantially affected the planning for Yellowstone and other national parks as knowledge of wildlife habitats and lifeways and the number of threatened and endangered species within national parks increased. Such legislation has helped fuel the efforts by the National Park Service and national and international conservation organizations to reverse the habitat destruction that has occurred in Everglades National Park as Corps of Engineers projects in southern Florida have substantially curtailed the natural passage of water through the grassy glades. The National Historic Preservation Act of 1966 (P.L. 89–665) drew attention to the value of the historic structures throughout the national park system. This has encouraged the National Park Service to inventory, evaluate, and protect historic facilities and other cultural resources within its boundaries. This had led to the restoration of historic hotels, villages, fire lookouts, and other structures within natural units of the park system; the recordation of historic roads and bridges prior to their improvement or reconstruction under the Federal-Aid Highway Act of 1982; and a process of review and compliance for projects such as the removal of the historic buildings from Fishing Bridge in Yellowstone.

Changes have occurred in the planning and design process for national parks since 1970. In 1971, the former Eastern and Western Offices of Design and Construction were consolidated in the Denver Service Center, which continues to provide the National Park Service with multidisciplinary expertise in planning and design. The system of planning through comprehensive master plans, which had evolved under Thomas Vint from the late 1920s to his retirement in 1961, was abandoned in the mid-1970s and replaced by a series of planning documents, in which an overall "general management plan" for each park is supplemented by "development concept plans" that examine the design and environmental issues for specific areas within the park. The management of natural and cultural resources has become the subject of specialized guidelines and plans tailored to the needs of each park. Reflecting to a large extent the complexity of park design in the late twentieth century, the new system of park planning more easily accommodates the increasing provisions for environmental protection and compliance, the public participation requirements of the recent era, and the multidisciplinary concerns that must be incorporated into the design of national parks.

A design ethic for harmony with nature prevails today in the landscape design within natural park units. This has occurred despite the high cost of labor, restrictions on quarrying stone and cutting timber within national parks, and the adaptation of modern building methods and materials. New construction is modest and functional, often relying on painted siding in neutral tones of earthen brown, sandalwood, and driftwood gray for naturalistic blending. Concerns for landscape naturalization continue in the plantings of native shrubs and trees that grace the entrances of modern visitor centers, form shaded islands in parking lots, and frame the views from scenic overlooks. Rusticity is expressed in the cinnamon-colored, oxidized steel guardrails along park roads and the truss bridges on wilderness trails which were prefabricated from similar material and moved on site with little disturbance to the natural environment. Today, a sense of natural harmony persists in the quiet, woodland amphitheaters at park campgrounds and in the many former campgrounds, drawn to Meinecke's principles, which have been converted for daytime use as picnic areas. Landscape conventions—overlooks, loop roads, and grade separations—continue to bring visitors safely and gracefully through the park landscape to present both the pictures of nature and lessons of park preservation.

The Vail Agenda—1991

The Seventy-fifth Anniversary Symposium, "Our National Parks: Challenges and Strategies for the Twenty-first Century," held in October 1991, brought together a wide range of professionals and interest groups inside and outside the National Park Service to discuss present conditions and future directions. Central to the discussion was the park service's 1916 legislative mandate to preserve the parks unimpaired while making them accessible for public use and enjoyment. The symposium resulted in a series of strategic objectives and recommendations, commonly called the *Vail Agenda,* for steering the National Park Service into the twenty-first century.

The working group that examined the question "How will the national park system be used and enjoyed?" recommended that the development of visitor facilities within park boundaries be restricted to those absolutely necessary and encouraged the development of well-planned gateway communities. The working group urged the park service to use whatever authority it had to remove unnecessary existing facilities. Emphasizing the protection of each park's unique values, the group called for an innovative program of facility planning, design, and maintenance to prepare the "front country" of each park for visitor needs, while protecting the unique features of each park. This meant the development of "a new generation of state-of-the-art designs" for trails, overlooks, transportation systems, visitor centers, and campgrounds based on "the unique values of each site, sustainable and wise use of resources, visitor needs, and a full accounting of environmental impacts." Facilities for natural areas were to be designed so that visitors to the front country could gain an appreciation of the area's unique values and "glimpse" enough of the backcountry to be encouraged to leave their automobiles to explore it further by trail. On road planning and development, the Vail Agenda gave renewed emphasis to transportation systems and called for innovative alternatives to the passenger vehicle and the coordination of in-park systems with public transportation in gateway communities.[50]

To a large extent the Vail Agenda's position on park development revisited the concerns of Darling and Eichhorn in *Man and Nature* in the 1960s and the Yellowstone master plans of the early 1970s. New emphasis, however, was placed on sustainable design and renewable resources as environmentally responsible approaches for the twenty-first century. The Vail Agenda called for new kinds of communities within parks to disperse visitors to outlying centers on the "threshold" of wilderness, thus departing from the traditional park village, which concentrated rather than dispersed visitors and automobiles. In calling for increased visitor services in gateway communities and the regions surrounding national parks to relieve development pressures within parks, it acknowledged the threat of sprawl, which already existed outside parks such as Yellowstone, Great Smoky Mountains, and Rocky Mountain, and proposed technical assistance programs for local communities to develop private sector visitor services and strategies for long-term land-use planning and sustainable economic development at ecosystem, landscape, and regional scales (84–86).

As the twentieth century comes to an end, it is clear that national park design today extends far beyond the professional stewardship and skills of the landscape architect and land-use planner. Rapidly increasing park visitation and a growing concern for the carrying capacity of natural areas have radically changed the attitudes and practices of park development in the past forty years. External threats on park preservation have proved to have far-reaching consequences, sometimes at a global level. In comparison with the complex legal battle that has raged over the preservation of the vast and unique ecological region that makes up the Everglades National Park, the quest for scenery preservation which occupied landscape architects Charles Punchard and Daniel Hull in the National Park Service's first decade may seem simple and insignificant. Yet the philosophy and practices advocated in the pioneering years—1916 to 1942— have engendered in each rising generation a sense of natural wonder and have succeeded in preserving the national park legacy.

The mandate of the 1916 legislation establishing the National Park Service calls upon each generation to interpret anew the dual mission that the national parks be accessible for public enjoyment, appreciation, and use, while being preserved unimpaired for future generations. Ever changing is the challenge to strike a balance between humans and nature amidst the ever increasing demands of visitation on the one hand and resource protection on the other. The history of national park design in the twentieth century is a testament to the wisdom and universality of the 1916 charter, but it is also the springboard from which a new ethic of combined environmental protection and landscape design must emerge in the next century.

Registering Historic Park Landscapes
in the National Register of Historic Places

Properties related to the subject of this book may be listed in the National Register of Historic Places under the multiple property listing entitled "Historic Park Landscapes in National and State Parks," which was entered in the National Register on October 4, 1995. Section F, Associated Property Types, of the documentation form for the multiple property listing is reproduced here to assist those interested in evaluating and nominating properties for listing in the National Register. This section covers methods for historical research, identification, and evaluation and describes the physical and associative characteristics that qualify associated properties for National Register listing.

Associated Property Types

Historic park landscapes under the context "The Historic Landscape Design of the National Park Service, 1916 to 1942," are defined as any natural or scenic area established by the federal, state, or local government for the conservation of natural resources and the enjoyment, appreciation, and recreation of the public. Associated property types are entire parks or areas within parks which were developed or improved under the supervision of the National Park Service during the period 1916 to 1942. Park landscapes include national parks, monuments, and parkways, as well as state and local parks that were developed or improved by the Civilian Conservation Corps (CCC) and Works Progress Administration (WPA) during the New Deal era, 1933 to 1942.

Historic park landscapes fall into two general property types: (1) national parks, parkways, and monuments, and (2) state parks, county parks, and recreational demonstration areas. An entire park based on boundaries dating from the period of significance, 1916 to 1942, may be eligible for listing in the National

Register of Historic Places as a historic district. Smaller landscapes within parks may also be eligible as historic sites or smaller historic districts; these may be classified in the following landscape types: park road systems and parkways, trail systems, major developed areas and park villages, minor developed areas, designated natural areas, day-use areas, overnight areas, recreational facilities, scenic overlooks and pull-offs (along park roads), scenic resources and overlooks, entranceways, waysides (for parkways and recreational demonstration areas), campgrounds, picnic areas, organization camps (for state parks and recreational demonstration areas), and Civilian Conservation Corps camps. With special justification, individual resources—buildings, structures, sites, and objects—may be individually eligible for listing, for example, a bridge or building that exhibits fine workmanship of naturalistic stonemasonry or logwork.

The multiple property group, Historic Park Landscapes in National and State Parks, covers landscapes within natural parks or recreational parks where natural resources and features predominate. Historical sites, battlefields, archeological sites, memorials, national forests, and urban parks having similar characteristics or associations with the New Deal programs of the 1930s, including the CCC, WPA, and Public Works Administration (PWA), are not included in the multiple property group. They may be nominated to the National Register on individual registration forms or in other multiple property groups.

Historic park landscapes in national and state parks meet the definitions of designed and rural landscapes. These are designed historic landscapes because they have been legally designated as parks having definite boundaries, were created for the purpose of conservation and/or outdoor recreation, and were developed according to the principles of landscape architecture and planning. Because of their rural location, extensive acreage, mixed uses, and natural character, they are also rural historic landscapes and can be documented using the landscape characteristics outlined in McClelland, Keller, Keller, and Melnick, *Guidelines for Evaluating and Documenting Rural Historic Landscapes* (1990). Circulation networks, response to natural environment, land uses and activities, vegetation related to land use, clusters, and small-scale features are particularly useful characteristics to consider when evaluating historic park landscapes. For example, the design of roads, trails, and buildings was directly influenced in response to the natural topography, climate, and vegetation and the presence of native building materials such as stone, adobe, or timber.

The following section addresses selected methods and sources for research and fieldwork, including a discussion of how the landscape characteristics outlined in *Bulletin 30* apply to historic park landscapes. Descriptions and registration requirements for associated property types follow. This information is intended to assist those using the NRHP multiple property documentation form, "Historic Park Landscapes in National and State Parks," to examine the historic development of a national or state park and to identify historic park landscapes that may be eligible for listing in the National Register for Historic Places.

Researching the Historic Development of a National or State Park: Methods and Sources

A study of the historic development of a national or state park requires a combination of historical documentation and fieldwork. Researchers and field surveyors should be familiar with the historic context in Section E of the multiple property documentation form, "Historic Park Landscapes in National and State Parks," and have a general understanding of the techniques for evaluating and documenting historic landscapes set forth in *Bulletin 30*. They should also have a preliminary understanding of the reasons the park under study was designated for conservation or recreation and be able to identify the park's primary natural and recreational resources.

A bibliography of secondary sources should be compiled and examined for the park under study prior to conducting any research of primary sources or a field survey of a national park landscape. A familiarity with these sources will help the researcher develop a strategy for further research and fieldwork. The bibliography should include park administrative histories, historic resource studies, List of Classified Structures (LCS), Cultural Landscape Inventory (CLI), cultural landscape reports, historic structures reports, National Register multiple property documentation forms and nomination forms, and general histories of each park as well as regional studies for the area where the park is located. For state park landscapes, similar reports, studies, and inventories may be available and should be consulted; the State Historic Preservation Office can provide information about state planning contexts, state surveys, and other documentation relating to state parks. An explanation of the National Park Service philosophy for naturalistic park design and exemplary examples of state and national park development appear in *Park Structures and Facilities* (1935) and *Park and Recreation Structures* (3 vols., 1938) published by the National Park Service.

Primary sources should be consulted to fill gaps in the secondary literature. The following provide information useful in documenting historic park landscapes.

Master Plans

The statement of 1918 establishing a policy for the development and management of national parks called for a comprehensive plan prior to developing facilities that might impair or damage the natural qualities for which the parks had been designated. Early park development was guided by the development of plans for park villages. This was carried out by the park service's landscape engineer with the advice and consultation of park service officials, park superintendents, civil engineers, park concessionaires, and members of the Commission on Fine Arts. At Yosemite and Grand Canyon, professionals from private practice played a leading role in the design of village plans.

The Landscape Division began working with park superintendents to develop five-year plans in the late 1920s, with the earliest plans being developed for Mount Rainier National Park and Crater Lake National Park. In 1929, the Landscape Division took on the task of developing plans for all parks over a three-year period. The plans had three parts: a park development outline covering the existing condition of the park and proposals for future development; a general plan, graphically represented on scale drawings; and a six-year plan for development. By the end of 1932, comprehensive plans, then called "master plans," were completed or in process for all park units. They continued to be updated annually until 1942, when, because of World War II, national park development was drastically curtailed. The revision of master plans resumed after World War II and received renewed impetus in 1956 with the congressional authorization of Mission 66, an extensive ten-year building and acquisition program for national parks.

National park master plans covered road systems, trail systems, major developed areas such as park villages, and an assortment of minor developed areas such as park entrances, ranger stations, or scenic attractions. A chronological study of plans enables a researcher to trace the physical evolution of the park and to understand the factors determining the park's development. The narratives that accompanied the plans began with a summary of the legislative history of the park, the reasons the park was designated a national park, and a description of the park's significant characteristics. The plans were intended simultaneously to plot existing conditions and to propose an ultimate or ideal plan for future development. The six-year plan enabled park superintendents to move toward the ideal by scheduling short-term projects with funds that were available or likely to become available.

The early master plans for many national parks can be found in the collection of the Cartographic Branch of the National Archives at College Park, Maryland, Record Group 79 (Preliminary Inventory 166, entry 32). Complete and partial sets of the plans also exist in the engineering office, library, or archives of many parks. Copies of individual sheets, in some cases, may also be ordered from the Technical Information Center of the Denver Service Center. Master plans for state parks were developed through the CCC program and may be found in state archives or state park offices.

Drawings

Preliminary and final drawings for individual projects were drawn up by park service engineers, landscape architects, and architects as projects proposed on the development outline received funding through public works allotments or park appropriations or were approved as CCC projects. These drawings contain the dates of design and construction, the names of designers and authorizing officials, illustrations and specifications for the proposed design, and notes on the source of funding. For CCC projects, the plans may also note the camp assigned to carry out the project and the date the work was completed. Copies of many drawings may be ordered from the Technical Information Center of the Denver Service Center. Many historic drawings are on file in park offices. Bureau of Public Roads plans and drawings can also be found in Record Group 30 of the National Archives.

Different types of drawings provide information about design and construction in national parks.

Preliminary and Final Drawings by the National Park Service's Landscape Division and Branch of Plans and Design. These depict the architectural design of bridges, culvert headwalls, and guardrails; the layout of parking areas, overlooks, village clusters, picnic areas, and campgrounds; and the design of small-scale items such as water fountains, signs, and trail bridges. National Park Service drawings often reflect the principles of landscape preservation and harmonious design and sometimes include detailed planting plans, stonemasonry details, and architectural details. The Landscape Division developed standard designs for the slopes of road embankments, stonemasonry and log guardrails, and culvert headwalls in the late 1920s. These designs were revised periodically, and the specific designs recommended for a particular park appeared on specialized sheets in the park's master plans.

The National Park Service's Engineering Division Drawings. The division produced topographical maps, standard designs for foot and bridle trails, site plans, and drawings and plans related to the development of utilities (water, electricity, sewerage, telephone) for major and minor developed areas. Park engineers were also responsible for the design and maintenance of fire roads, truck trails, and minor roads within developed areas.

Drawings by the Engineers of the Bureau of Public Roads. These provide detailed technical information about the engineering and construction of park roads, tunnels, and bridges. Drawings with topographical elevations depict each section of the road, identify station numbers, and indicate areas to be cut and filled. Other drawings contain the technical details and designs for the construction of bridges, culverts, drains, retaining walls, guardrail, and other structural features.

Narrative Records

The historical records maintained in the national parks and the National Archives contain several different types of narrative reports that provide valuable information about the design and development of historic park landscapes. They include landscape architects' reports, preliminary surveys for roads and trails, progress reports of the CCC, and superintendents' monthly and annual reports. Many of these are richly illustrated with photographs showing work in progress.

The records of the National Park Service (Record Group 79) are described in the *Preliminary Inventory of the Records of the National Park Service* by Edward E. Hill (Preliminary Inventory 166, National Archives, 1966). Additional narrative materials may be found in the National Archives under Record Group 30 for the Bureau of Public Roads (Preliminary Inventory 134) and Record Group 35 for the Civilian Conservation Corps (Preliminary Inventory 11).

Records relating to the work of the CCC in state parks and recreational demonstration areas may also be found in Record Group 79. They include applications, the reports of state park inspectors, and illustrated progress reports (monthly, bimonthly, semiannual) submitted to the CCC district offices by the camp superintendents. Many of these are richly illustrated with photographs of work in progress and completed jobs. Copies of these reports may be found in state archives and park offices.

Historical Photographs

The National Park Service Historic Photography Collection at the Harpers Ferry Center includes several collections of national park photographs, including those taken by National Park Service photographer George Grant for the Landscape and Educational Divisions beginning in the late 1920s. Many parks, including Yosemite, Yellowstone, and Great Smoky Mountains, maintain extensive collections of historical photographs. Historical photographs may also be found in the Audio-Visual Division of the National Archives under the Records of the National Park Service (Record Group 79) and Records of the Bureau of Public Roads (Record Group 30). The National Archives also maintains several collections of photographs showing WPA and CCC work in state parks and recreational demonstration areas.

Fieldwork: Documenting the Landscape Characteristics for Historic Park Landscapes

The landscape characteristics outlined in *National Register Bulletin 30* provide a framework for organizing the information gathered during research and fieldwork. The first four characteristics are processes—natural and cultural—

which shaped a landscape during the historic period and link it to significant themes in history. The remaining characteristics are physical components that are evident upon the land and define the landscape's historic character. The primary objective of a field survey is to document the characteristics present within a landscape. The landscape characteristics can be used to gather and organize information about historic park landscapes and their physical and associative characteristics. This information can then be used to classify a landscape by property type and thereby evaluate its historic significance and integrity using the registration requirements for the property type.

A familiarity with the historic master plans and drawings for a particular area before beginning a field survey will help surveyors understand the physical evolution of a park and prepare them to identify and interpret significant landscape features. This knowledge will also help them distinguish contributing from noncontributing resources and determine the amount of change which has occurred since the historic period. These sources may indicate spatial organization, circulation systems, intended land uses, the presentation of scenic views, the preservation of natural features, the planting of native vegetation, and other aspects of design or design intent which may not be recognizable in the existing landscape.

Land Uses and Activities

The land uses and activities of a historic park landscape can be considered on several scales. At the broadest scale is the primary purpose or use of the park. Many parks have been designated through legislation and the administration of government for the purpose of conserving natural areas containing outstanding natural systems, geological features, wildlife habitats, groves of trees or meadows, or other scenic features. While the first national parks in the West were withdrawn from the inventory of undeveloped federal lands — many primeval in condition — later parks, especially in the East, were the product of reclamation, where deliberate efforts were taken to remove the traces of earlier land uses and to promote the natural regeneration of former fields and pastures, burned or cut-over forests, and other disturbed areas. Recreation was a corresponding use and, in the broadest sense, meant the enjoyment and appreciation of the natural scenery through activities such as hiking, horseback riding, mountain climbing, motoring, picnicking, and camping. State parks and recreational demonstration areas (and some national parks) also offered more active forms of recreation such as swimming, skiing, boating, fishing, tobogganing, and golf.

Within a park are smaller areas having specific activities or functions, such as roads, trails, a park entrance, an administrative headquarters, a scenic overlook, a maintenance area, or a campground. Park villages usually have multiple uses, including commercial activities, administrative functions, and housing.

Some parks, particularly state or local parks, and former recreational demonstration areas have areas designated for active sports, such as swimming, boating, skiing, golf, and softball. Certain areas within a park such as a museum with an outdoor theater, observation terrace, nature trail, native plant garden, and exhibits may have interpretive and educational functions. Others may be the site of patrol cabins or fire lookouts important in protecting the park's natural resources. Each park also contains facilities that provide essential utilities — telephone, electricity, water, and sewerage — for visitor and administrative use.

Within the comprehensive master plan, the various land-use areas within a park are classified as roads, trails, major developed areas, and minor developed areas. The functions of these areas are frequently interconnected and interdependent. Some areas may relate directly to the visitors' experience in the park, others only to the park's administration and maintenance.

Patterns of Spatial Organization

The spatial organization of a national or state park is primarily dictated by natural systems and topographical features including mountains, valleys, canyons, rivers and streams, ponds and lakes, ridges, plains, forests, prairies, bluffs, and buttes. The location of roads and consequently park villages was historically dictated by natural topography and climate. Determining factors included concerns for scenery preservation, the ability to traverse mountainous terrain, the availability of water, and the feasibility and costs of maintaining roads in extreme weather conditions. The location of roads was also dictated by the circulation networks existing outside the park and the corridors along which visitors approached the park from urban centers or railroad connections along state highways or roads through national forests. The location of trails depended on automobile access along park roads but moreover on scenic features and ideas about how the parks' splendors could be best presented to hikers or riders on horseback.

Master plans graphically and in narrative form represented the relationship of all built improvements to the natural topography of the park. They provided a "complete" view of the park's geographical location and natural topography, the park's relationship to regional transportation networks, and the improvements existing or proposed for the park at a specific date. They also indicated the relationship of developed areas to wilderness areas, which were to be left undisturbed by motor roads or settlements. Principles of naturalistic landscape design drawn from the design of nineteenth-century urban parks and pleasure grounds to a large extent influenced the spatial organization of roads, trails, and developed areas within natural parks.

Response to the Natural Environment

This is the most salient landscape characteristic applying to natural parks. It relates primarily to the presence of natural features and systems and the over-arching purpose to preserve the natural environment and make it accessible for the appreciation and enjoyment of the general public. Topography, climate, and natural features, first of all, dictated the designation of these places as parks and, second, influenced the location and design of all constructed improvements. Roads, trails, and developed areas were located in response to these features, often in an effort to present the most scenic views while preserving the natural beauty. Moreover, the importance of the natural environment led to the develop-ment of principles and standards for the design and construction of roads, trails, and other facilities which called for harmony with nature, minimal disturbance to natural features, and a blending of constructed and natural features. For ex-ample, roads were built to disturb the natural topography as little as possible by minimizing the amount of cut and fill, by constructing culverts to accommodate the drainage of natural streams, and by flattening, rounding, and planting road embankments so they blended into the surrounding setting.

Scenic considerations guided the location and character of development in natural parks. Park museums, overlooks along park roads and trails, observation lookouts, fire lookouts, and other facilities were typically located and oriented in relationship to the natural environment. The intent to present nature at its best without impairing the view influenced the development of overlooks, loca-tion of roads and trails, clearing of vegetation (vista clearing), the planting and transplanting of native vegetation, and the preservation or planting of vegetative screens.

Cultural Traditions

Cultural traditions have influenced the design of national and state parks in several ways. Evidence of cultural traditions exists in (1) the use of accepted practices and principles of American park design and landscape architecture in developing parks for visitor use and enjoyment; (2) the influence of pioneer-era, ethnic, and indigenous building types, construction methods, and materials in the construction of buildings, walls and fences, and bridges; and (3) adherence to a Craftsman ethic of construction, design, and planting.

Circulation Networks

Parks typically contain several independent circulation networks that may or may not interconnect: motor roads, administrative roads, fire roads and truck trails, foot trails, and bridle trails. The principal motor roads connect the park at park entrances with state highways and roads through national forests. Truck trails are used administratively to protect the park against poachers and to control fires and are usually inaccessible to visitors except those on foot or horseback. Trails—foot and bridle—were intended to provide the visitor access to the parks' outlying features and scenic wonders, including wilderness areas undisturbed by motor roads. Each developed area of the park had its own circulation network of paths, minor roads, parking, and connection to motor roads and trails. In parks such as Acadia, transportation by water was also a significant factor in planning the park's circulation network.

Motor roads led to the principal centers of scenic interest and visitor facilities such as campgrounds, scenic areas, and park villages. Built through a cooperative agreement with the U.S. Bureau of Public Roads, major park roads were designed to present the scenic beauty of the park through unraveling panoramic views and to provide access to trails that penetrated the backcountry. Motor roads were designed to follow the contours of the natural topography, accommodate natural patterns of drainage, and blend into the surrounding scenery.

Boundary Demarcations

The boundaries of parks were determined legislatively, and land was acquired through the transfer of ownership from one government to another, through purchase or donation, and, in some cases, through condemnation. Park boundaries are not necessarily marked by physical barriers such as fences or walls, although the boundaries along highways or motor roads are marked by signs, entrance stations, or gateways. In keeping with the naturalistic intent of a park's design, boundaries tend not to have recognizable boundary demarcations. In some cases, where fences were deemed necessary, they took the form of unobtrusive enclosures.

Vegetation Related to Land Use

Park landscapes typically include three kinds of vegetation:

1. Naturally occurring trees, shrubs, and plants create the park's setting and, in many cases, contribute to the natural significance for which the park was designated.

2. Native trees, shrubs, ground covers, and other plants were planted or transplanted for a variety of purposes: to naturalize areas disturbed by construction, to eliminate the traces of old roads and homesteads, to beautify park roads and villages, to screen facilities from view, to enframe scenic views, and to control erosion.

3. Native trees, shrubs, and other plants were introduced on a large scale to re-vegetate burned, lumbered, or eroded areas or reclaim submarginal agricultural and mining land.

Vegetation on the embankments of park roads typically resulted from either a natural process of revegetation or from planting projects to control erosion. During construction in minor and major developed areas, mature trees were preserved wherever possible. Vegetation—in the form of native ground covers and understory shrubs—was afterward reintroduced to erase the scars of construction and to enhance the natural setting. Planted and transplanted vegetation commonly took the form of foundation plantings around buildings or bridge abutments, planted islands at overlooks and parking areas, and interpretive wild gardens. Because plantings were native species and were intended to be naturalized, it is often impossible to discern planted or transplanted vegetation from the naturally occurring vegetation of the park.

Buildings, Structures, and Objects

Various types of buildings, structures, and objects serve the needs of visitors, concessionaires, and park staff. These vary in type and are constructed and operated by the park or a concessionaire. Many facilities—comfort stations, museums, lodges, cabins, and picnic shelters—are intended to accommodate park visitors for safety, comfort, and pleasure. Others, such as the backcountry patrol cabins, ranger stations, and maintenance shops, serve administrative purposes. Buildings with particular functions were developed to meet the specialized needs of outdoor recreation, for example, community buildings built at campgrounds to provide ranger quarters, a room for public lectures, rest rooms, and showers for bathing. Buildings range in size and complexity from simple patrol cabins and comfort stations to administration buildings and museums. Structures include bridges, tunnels, culverts, road structures, guardrails, observation terraces, and stairways. Objects include features such as signs and water fountains.

The buildings, structures, and objects within a park commonly exhibit similar principles of rustic design, native building materials drawn from the natural environment, and methods of construction derived from the vernacular, indigenous, and pioneering prototypes of the surrounding region. Although floor plans, dimensions, and structural aspects of park buildings and structures may reflect standard servicewide designs, the external design of structures differs from park to park based on local geography and climate and the talents of the resident landscape architects, architects, and engineers. Buildings and structures within a park generally follow a common architectural scheme based on the unique natural character and history of the region where the park is located.

Clusters

Major and minor developed areas are the typical clusters found in national parks. They serve a variety of functions, such as entrance stations, campgrounds, park villages, park housing, maintenance, and fire protection, and they typically contain buildings, structures, objects, vegetation, and other landscape features. Day-use areas, overnight areas, organization camps, and recreational facilities are the typical clusters found in state parks and recreational demonstration areas. Master plans provide detailed descriptions of the arrangement and composition of buildings, structures, roads, and trails within these areas and can help surveyors identify clusters and trace their evolution.

The built features within clusters follow a common architectural scheme using native materials, pioneering or indigenous methods of construction, and principles of design which harmonized with the natural setting and adapted to the local climate. Clusters within parks frequently incorporate native vegetation and scenic views and interconnect with hiking and bridle trails and motor roads. Developed areas of parks were typically arranged according to naturalistic principles of landscape design which called for curvilinear roads and trails, including loop roads, and the naturalistic siting of buildings and structures in relationship to scenic views or screens of vegetation.

Several other kinds of facilities found in state and national parks may be examined as clusters. The development of a scenic overlook consists of a roadway, parking area, and observation terrace with a guardrail, sidewalk, and curbing; there may also be signs, interpretive exhibits, comfort facilities, benches, and water fountains. Museums with observation terraces, nature trails, outdoor amphitheaters, nature gardens, and exhibits form clusters that may also encompass nearby natural features for interpretation purposes.

Archeological Sites

Remnant sites of CCC camps, fishing and hunting camps, abandoned and reclaimed homesites, millsites, remnant orchards, mining and lumbering operations, and quarries are some of the historic archeological sites that may be found in state and national parks. Because the National Park Service made efforts to eliminate the traces of old roads, homesites, and camps through landscape naturalization and reclamation projects, the sites of historic activities predating a park's founding or associated with road construction or CCC occupation may have little or no surface remains. Sites used by Native American or prehistoric cultural groups are likely to remain intact in the undisturbed natural areas of a park.

Small-Scale Elements

These are the small-scale built features found along roads or trails or in developed areas. They include curbs, minor signs, fireplaces, benches, markers, foot bridges, and picnic tables and often contribute strongly to the historic character of historic park villages and other clusters. These elements are likely to reflect the craftsmanship, native materials, and naturalistic principles of design found in the larger built features of the park.

Classifying and Evaluating Historic Park Landscapes by Property Types

The Secretary of the Interior's Standards for Identification, Evaluation, and Registration call for the identification of property types and characteristics—physical and associative—in evaluating the historical significance of a historic property. The landscape characteristics typically found in state and national parks can be organized into the general property types and landscape subtypes listed below. Keep in mind that landscape characteristics, whether processes or components, are integral to all of these property types but the extent to which they may be present differs. The characteristics for land uses and activities, spatial organization, response to the natural environment, cultural traditions, vegetation related to land use, circulation networks, and clusters are particularly relevant to the history of state and national parks and should be discussed when documenting properties belonging to the multiple property group.

General Property Types

National Parks, Parkways, and Monuments.   This landscape type includes significant natural areas that have been designated by the United States Congress as national parks, national monuments, or national parkways for the purposes of conservation and public appreciation and enjoyment. Properties of this type must have been administered by the National Park Service during all or part of the period 1916–42. The first plans for national parks called for the development of roads, trails, and centralized park villages housing administrative functions and visitor services. Gateways were placed at park boundaries, and ranger stations, fire lookouts, and patrol cabins were constructed in outlying areas. Popular scenic attractions, such as hot springs and rimside overlooks, were developed with walks, stairways, and protective railings. As the master planning process evolved from 1926 to 1942, park facilities were classified in several categories: road system, trail system, major developed areas, and minor developed areas. Special kinds of facilities could be constructed under one or more categories, for example, a campground might be situated along a major park road or in a minor developed area that also contained a park museum, concessionaire's lodge and cabins, and interpretive trail. Areas not traversed by major roads or designated as developed areas were considered wilderness areas.

Entire national parks, monuments, or parkways based on historic boundaries or smaller areas within such parks may be listed in the National Register of Historic Places under the Historic Park Landscapes in National and State Parks multiple property group. For a list of the landscape types and physical characteristics constituting this property type, see the sections that follow for:

Park road systems and parkways	Scenic resources and overlooks
Trail systems	Waysides (parkways and recreational
Major developed areas and park villages	demonstration areas)
Minor developed areas	Campgrounds
Designated natural areas (national parks)	Picnic areas
Entranceways	Civilian Conservation Corps Camps
Scenic overlooks and pull-offs (in conjunction with roads)	

State Parks, Country Parks, and Recreational Demonstration Areas. This landscape type includes natural areas established by state or local governments for the conservation of natural resources, the enjoyment of scenery, and outdoor recreational use by the public. Country parks are defined as natural areas established by county, metropolitan, municipal, and other local governments for conservation and outdoor recreation and possessing many of the physical and associative characteristics common to state parks. Recreational demonstration areas form a finite group of parks that were developed from submarginal agricultural and mining lands in the 1930s by the National Park Service; most of these were later transferred to state park systems.

Landscapes of this type were typically developed with facilities—roads, trails, and buildings—which gave access to scenic points of interest and provided for the comfort, recreation, and enjoyment of the public. These types are more likely to contain naturalistic constructed features, such as lakes and waterfalls, intended to enhance the park's scenic character and recreational use. These parks also contain facilities related to the park's administration. Function, recreational use, and natural character distinguish various areas of these parks. Many state parks have separate areas for day use, overnight use, organization camps, and special kinds of recreation (e.g., golf courses or ski areas.) Entire parks based on historic boundaries or smaller areas within such parks may be listed in the National Register of Historic Places under the Historic Park Landscapes in National and State Parks multiple property group. For a list of the landscape types and physical characteristics constituting this property type, see the sections that follow for:

Park road systems and parkways
Trail systems
Entranceways
Scenic overlooks and pull-offs (in
    conjunction with roads)
Scenic resources and overlooks
Waysides (parkways and recreational
    demonstration areas)

Day-use areas (state parks)
Picnic areas
Overnight areas (state parks)
Recreational facilities
Campgrounds
Organization camps (state parks and
    recreational demonstration areas)
Civilian Conservation Corps Camps

Subtypes of Historic Park Landscapes

Park Road Systems and Parkways.   This landscape type covers the motor roads making up the circulation system of a park and reflecting the principles of naturalistic park road design developed by the landscape architects and engineers of the National Park Service. It includes the major park roads designed or improved through the cooperation of the National Park Service and Bureau of Public Roads to provide entry to a park and access to the park's scenic features and recreational areas. It also includes minor roads designed by National Park Service engineers to provide circulation within park villages and other developed areas, as well as roads serving administrative purposes such as fire protection. It may include early roads constructed in parks by the U.S. Corps of Army Engineers or state highway departments, which were later improved by the National Park Service. This landscape type also includes parkways designed by the National Park Service in cooperation with the Bureau of Public Roads to connect parks and other scenic areas and to provide recreational and scenic pleasure. This type may also include approach roads developed by state highway departments and the National Forest Service outside national parks to provide a scenic approach to national park areas. In state parks, this includes roads constructed by the CCC, state highway departments, and Work Progress Administration crews.

Major roads (constructed by Bureau of
    Public Roads)
    Systems of loop and circuit roads
    Parkways
Minor roads
    Circulatory roads in developed areas
    Fire roads
    Truck trails
    Spur roads
    Loop development
Approach roads
    U.S. Forest Service and other
        government agencies

    State and U.S. highways
Road characteristics
    Protection of natural features
        (trees, outcrops, topography,
        drainage)
    Clearing with minimal impact
        (destruction and removal of trees,
        transplanting vegetation, saving
        duff, supervised burning, low-
        impact blasting to minimize scars
        and casting of materials)
    Alignment following topography and
        presenting natural beauty

(curvilinear, tangents, radius curves,
complex curves, transitional
spirals, coordinating views and
turns)
Gradient (varied, not to exceed 5%)
Cut and fill
(borrow pits and quarries to be
located out of sight or outside
park)
Cross sections
(crown, width of roadway, gutters,
cut and fill, rounding and
flattening of slopes, superelevation, sight lines)
Surfacing (local stone)
Treatment of slopes
(rounded and flattened at a ratio of
3:1 or 4:1)
Bank blending
Plantings
(sodding, seeding, planting for
erosion control, harmonization,
and beautification; soil preparation: duff; ground covers: grasses,
wildflowers, vines; shrubs:
flowering and other shrubs)
Overlooks (see overlooks below)
Loop developments
Grade separations
(bridges, tunnels, viaducts,
clover-leaf)
Wye intersections
Roadside cleanup
(removal of dead and decaying trees,
stumps, and brush for fire
protection and beautification)
Spring developments
Structures associated with roads

Bridges
Low-water crossings
Tunnels
Guardrails and barriers
Culverts and drains
Revetments
Curbs and sidewalks
Gutters
Tree wells
Loop structures
Grade separations
Developed areas and buildings associated
with park roads
Entrance stations, arches, and gates
Ranger stations
Caretakers' residences
Park headquarters
Maintenance areas
Concessionaires' developments
Waysides (see section below for
waysides)
Picnic areas
Campgrounds
Comfort stations
Gas stations
Interpretive exhibits, such as historic
cabins or mills
Former CCC camps
Small-scale elements
Parking areas
Viewpoints and vistas
Steps and stairways
Trail heads
Signs (directional and interpretive)
Mileposts
Nature shrines
Water fountains and springs
Curbing and coping

Trail Systems.   This landscape type covers the footpaths, hiking trails, and
bridle trails that make up the circulation network of a national, state, or local
park and were designed to provide visitors with access to scenic vistas and natural features. These reflect the naturalistic principles of trail construction practiced by the National Park Service. They may interconnect with park roads and
link park roads, park villages, museums, and other developed areas with scenic
and natural features such as waterfalls, rivers, streams, springs, forests, canyons,
meadows, lakes, and mountain peaks. This landscape type also includes seg-

ments of long-distance scenic trails that pass through national, state, and local parks, such as the Appalachian Trail from Maine to Georgia and the Pacific Crest Trail from Washington to California.

Foot trails	Switchbacks
Bridle trails	Guardrails
Nature shrines	Steps and stairs
Signs and markers (directional and interpretive)	Signs
	Benches
Shelters	Overlooks
Stables	Parking areas
Corrals	Viewpoints and vistas
Bridges	Springs and watering places
Tunnels	Comfort stations
Revetments	Patrol Cabins
Culverts	

Major Developed Areas and Park Villages. This landscape type includes centers of park administration and visitor facilities. They were designed to provide essential commercial services, such as food and gasoline, and overnight accommodations; they often include facilities built and operated by both the government and park concessionaires. They include above-and belowground utilities, a general circulation network for pedestrian and motor traffic, and one or more clusters of park buildings and facilities. Administrative facilities, concessionaire's developments, residential areas, maintenance areas, and campgrounds may be combined to form a single park village, or they may be separated by function and location to form specialized developments. The term "Major Developed Area" was used in the master plans for national parks. For state parks, see "Day-Use Areas" and "Overnight Areas."

Plazas (parking)	Stores
Sidewalks, paths, curbs, stairways, guardrails	Cafeterias
	Gas stations
Roads and bridges	Water towers
Water fountains	Pump houses
Administration buildings	Power plants
Museums (also includes amphitheaters, gardens, and nature trails)	Parking areas
	Curbs, sidewalks, and paths
Park staff housing (houses and dormitories)	Signs
	Steps and stairs
Concessionaire's housing	Trees, shrubs, ground covers, and foundation plantings
Lodges and cabins	
Campground (also includes amphitheaters)	Stables
	Water supply
Community buildings	Utility systems

Telephone
Sewer
Incinerators
Electricity
Industrial groups and maintenance camps
  Dormitories
  Mess halls

Garages
Shops (blacksmithing, metal work,
    woodworking, and other)
Storage buildings and sheds
Work yards
Roads and parking areas

Minor Developed Areas. This landscape type covers outlying areas of a park which were developed to serve one or a small number of purposes, such as maintaining a park entrance, protecting the park against fire, or managing a remote area of the park. The term "Minor Developed Area" was used in the master plans for national parks to indicate the development of facilities such as entrance stations, ranger stations, campgrounds, fire lookouts, and waysides. In state parks, these areas were likely to be named for their function (e.g., "entrance station," "campground," or "ski area"); they may also have been combined with other facilities to form a day-use area.

Entrance gates and stations
Ranger stations
Fire lookouts and caches
Museums (including amphitheaters,
    gardens, and interpretive trails)
Patrol cabins
Trail shelters
Campgrounds
Picnic areas/waysides
Spring developments
Developed intersections
Scenic features (viewpoints and vistas)
Water supply
Recreational areas
  Ski slopes
  Toboggan runs
  Skating rinks

Beaches
Swimming pools
Playing fields
Docks and piers
Trails
Waterfalls
Fish hatcheries
Nurseries
Stables
Curbs, sidewalks, and paths
Trees, shrubs, and ground covers
Utility systems
  Water
  Sewer
  Telephone
  Electricity

Designated Natural Areas (national parks and monuments). This landscape type includes significant landforms, topographical features, areas of native vegetation, and other natural resources within a national park or monument which were to be conserved and remain in a primitive, undeveloped condition. These include (1) wilderness areas, which applied to all areas not traversed by public roads or designated for development on the park's master plan; (2) sacred areas, which were specific zones or natural features that were to remain unimpaired; and (3) research areas, which were reserved for scientific study. Historic wilderness areas should not be confused with the legislated wilderness areas on public lands subsequent to the enactment of the Wilderness Act of 1964.

Wilderness areas
  Trails
  Shelters
  Fire lookouts and caches

Truck trails
Patrol cabins
Sacred areas
Research areas

Day-Use Areas (state parks). This landscape type covers the administrative, commercial, and recreational center of a state park, country park, or recreational demonstration area. This area was generally separated from the overnight area having campgrounds and overnight cabins.

Roads, paths, and parking areas
Picnic areas
  Shelters
  Comfort stations
  Water fountains
  Community kitchens
Refectories and concession buildings
Water towers
Custodian's residences
Pump houses or springhouses
Bathhouses
Boathouses
Dams

Lakes or ponds
Recreational facilities
Spring developments
Museums
Observation towers and lookouts
Water supply
Utilities
Bridges
Trails and stairways
Parking areas
Overlooks
Trees, shrubs, and ground covers
Signs

Overnight Areas (state parks). This landscape type covers the areas of state parks, country parks, and recreational demonstration areas developed to provide accommodations in the form of campgrounds, cabin groups, and lodges. This area was separated geographically from the day-use area but was connected to it by motor roads, footpaths, bridle trails, and, sometimes, a lake or river.

Roads, paths, and parking
Campgrounds
Comfort stations
Community kitchens
Water fountains
Water towers
Check-in stations
Pump houses
Organization camps

Cabin courts
Lodges
Beaches
Docks
Trails and paths
Playing fields
Water supply
Utilities
Overlooks

Recreational Facilities. This landscape type includes specialized facilities developed for outdoor recreation in state and country parks. These may be found in combination with day-use and overnight areas. They frequently include parking, paths and trails, minor roads, plantings, water fountains, walls, shelters, overlooks, and associated buildings.

Lakes, ponds or other water features
    Dams
    Channels
    Beaches
    Bathhouses
    Boathouses
    Boat launches
    Spring developments
    Parking areas
    Fishing and boating docks
    Ice skating shelter
    Picnic shelters
    Overlooks
Winter sports and ski areas
    Ski slopes and trails
    Ski jumps
    Ski lifts

Toboggan runs
Parking areas
Skating rinks
Ski lodge
Playing fields
Swimming pools and bathhouses
Golf courses
    Holes
    Fairways
    Caddy houses
    Clubhouses
    Ponds
    Vegetation
Tennis courts
Trails (foot and bridle)
Stables and corrals

Scenic Overlooks and Pull-offs (along park roads). This landscape type covers scenic overlooks and pull-offs developed along major park roads and parkways for the purpose of providing (1) viewpoints from which visitors could enjoy scenic views or (2) access to nearby scenic resources, such as waterfalls, rock outcroppings, and springs. The landscape type includes overlooks developed on natural points of land and those constructed from fill as naturalistic terraces. Some overlooks and pull-offs are equipped with water fountains, comfort stations, and interpretive exhibits. Overlooks may contain paths leading to other viewpoints, scenic resources, trails, or comfort stations.

Roads and parking areas
Curbs, sidewalks, retaining walls, and
    guardrails
Grading and bank sloping
Viewpoints and vistas
Scenic resources
Trails and paths
Steps and stairways
Bridges
Shelters
Observation towers/lookouts
Signs and exhibits (interpretive and
    directional)

Memorials (e.g., Stephen Mather
    memorial)
Trail markers
Water fountains and supply
Spring developments
Comfort stations
Picnic sites
Trees, shrubs, ground covers, and
    foundation plantings
Benches

Scenic Resources and Overlooks.   This landscape type covers (1) scenic re-sources, such as waterfalls, lakes, promontories, springs, and mountain peaks, which have been developed with minor roads, parking areas, trails, paths, bridges, benches, and other facilities for public use and enjoyment, and (2) over-looks that have been similarly developed along trails or minor roads for the purpose of presenting scenic views to visitors.

Paths and trails	Viewpoints and vistas
Steps and stairways	Benches
Guardrails	Parking areas
Terraces	Comfort Stations
Bridges	Water fountains
Shelters	Trees, shrubs, ground covers, and
Signs and exhibits (interpretive)	foundation plantings
Spring developments	

Entranceways.   This landscape type covers the area where motor traffic along state highways and other roads entered the park. Typically the park en-trance was marked by a sign, a gate, and/or a check-in station where entrance fees were collected and visitor information provided; park roads began at these points. These areas were often equipped with interpretive exhibits, water foun-tains, and comfort stations. In national parks these were classified as a minor developed area.

Roads	Comfort stations
Arches, gates, and walls	Trees, shrubs, ground covers, and
Check-in stations	foundation plantings
Ranger stations	Flagpoles
Parking areas	Signs
Curbs and sidewalks	Water Supply
Paths and trails	Utilities
Water fountains	

Waysides (parkways and recreational demonstration areas).   This land-scape type covers the recreational wayside developed in the 1930s for picnick-ing and simple recreational activities in conjunction with motor touring. Way-sides were developed along parkways developed by the National Park Service and along approach roads and scenic highways outside parks. Several were con-structed as recreational demonstration areas in South Carolina and Virginia.

Roads and parking areas	Concessionaire: stores and gas stations
Curbs, steps, stairs, and sidewalks	Comfort stations
Picnic areas	Picnic shelters

Water fountains   Fireplaces
Trails   Trees, shrubs, and ground covers
Playing fields   Signs
Caretaker's residences   Water supply
Nature gardens   Utilities
Picnic tables

Campgrounds. This landscape type covers campgrounds in national, state, and local parks developed according to the principles of campground planning and reconstruction formulated by E. P. Meinecke and practiced by the National Park Service designers.

Entrance gates   Steps and stairs
Entrance stations   Trees and shrubs
Road system (one-way loop with tiers)   Signs
Parking spurs   Community kitchens
Barriers   Comfort stations
Tent sites   Amphitheaters or campfire circles
Fireplaces   Stores
Picnic tables   Viewpoints and vistas
Water fountains   Lakes, ponds, canals, or other bodies of
Water towers and pump houses   water
Shelters   Water supply
Trash receptacles   Utilities
Paths and trails

Picnic Areas. This landscape type covers picnicking grounds in national, state, and local parks. These were typically developed according to the principles of campground planning and reconstruction formulated by E. P. Meinecke and practiced by the National Park Service designers. They were also an important feature of a wayside.

Road system   Shelters
Parking areas   Community kitchens
Barriers   Comfort stations
Paths   Pump houses
Picnic sites   Water system
Fireplaces   Viewpoints and vistas
Picnic tables   Lakes, ponds, streams, or other bodies of
Water fountains   water
Water towers and pump houses   Overlooks
Trash receptacles   Recreational areas
Trails   Water supply
Steps and stairs   Utilities
Signs

Organization Camps (state parks and recreational demonstration areas). This landscape type covers the overnight camps set aside for use by private and semiprivate social, educational, and welfare organizations in recreational demonstration areas and state parks. These areas were self-sufficient clusters that were geographically and visually separated from other park facilities and operated independently. Each camp was divided into an administrative center and small outlying units that housed campers. A park might have several separate organization camps in outlying areas, for example, on opposite shores of a lake.

Administration buildings/offices
Recreation halls
Dining halls
Infirmaries
Staff quarters
Craft shops
Nature buildings
Water towers
Washhouses and laundries
Comfort stations and latrines
Counselor cabins
Camper cabins

Unit lodges
Paths and trails
Campfire circles
Council rings
Roads and parking areas
Lakes, ponds, or other bodies of water
Dams
Beaches
Docks
Playing fields
Water supply
Utilities

Civilian Conservation Corps Camps. This landscape type covers the camps built to house the CCC in national and state parks. The canvas platform tents that accommodated the first CCC camps were quickly replaced by army-style barracks arranged in an orderly fashion. The buildings could be assembled quickly on site where needed and easily dismantled and moved to a new site once the camp's work was completed. Because of their temporary nature, few of the buildings associated with these camps remain intact. Many are identifiable only by the landscape improvements, such as planting or irrigation, made by the CCC enrollees during their occupation.

Entry roads
Parade grounds
Flagpoles
Headquarters buildings
Dining halls (mess hall)
Dormitories and barracks
Chapels
Workshops (woodworking, metal work,
        blacksmithing, etc.)
Sheds

Sawmills
Educational buildings
Recreational buildings
Garages
Oil houses
Shower houses
Plantings
Paths
Water supply
Utilities

Registration Requirements

A park landscape meeting the requirements listed below may be listed in the National Register of Historic Places. Entire parks based on their historic boundaries or any combination of park landscape subtypes within a park may be listed as a historic district. A single resource within a landscape—such as a picnic shelter, bridge, lookout, or water fountain—may be listed individually as a building, structure, site, or object if it is significant for its landscape or architectural characteristics under Criterion C and the historic landscape to which it was historically associated no longer possesses historic integrity. A building or structure possessing particular importance for its role or design may also be listed individually, for example, a museum important in the educational and interpretive program of a park, a fire lookout reflecting a particular design, and an arched rock-faced concrete bridge having a high degree of workmanship. All properties eligible under the multiple property listing Historic Park Landscapes in National and State Parks will date from a period of significance which includes all or a portion of the New Deal era (1933–42). Many will also include significant park landscapes and resources that predate the New Deal and relate to the origins and early development of these parks prior to 1933; this includes local parks that became state parks and state parks that have become national parks. Landscapes or resources predating the establishment of parks and not possessing the qualities of park landscape design and architecture may be eligible for listing and should be evaluated under other appropriate themes and historic contexts, for example, frontier settlement, ranching, or agriculture.

Ideally, it is desirable to identify and register the largest unit having significance and integrity as a historic park landscape, for example, an entire state park, a park village, a complex of a lodge and cabins, a trail or road, or an artificial lake with a dam, bathhouse, boathouse, and beach. The coordinated development for parks during the historic period through a comprehensive planning process and the development of master plans provides a strong argument for this approach.

Realistically, however, preservation planning and compliance activities may make it necessary to nominate for individual listing and to consider the eligibility of smaller elements within a landscape. Many of the structural features of parks—stairways, overlooks, comfort stations, culverts, dams, springhouses—were unique or one of a small, finite group of similarly designed and constructed features. They were designed for their location and, in many cases, a specific building site, and they resulted from intense workmanship and labor and adhered to a set of naturalistic principles of design and construction rather than standardized models or plans. Many are in remote or isolated places, accessible only by trails and footpaths. Cumulatively they represent the rich and manifold legacy of the New Deal programs to public recreation, social welfare, and conservation. Individually each represents some aspect of the diverse artistry, craftsmanship, structural types, and methods of a program of design and construction suited to the climate, natural topography, available natural materials, and cultural traditions of each park's locality or region. This program resulted from the National Park Service's supervision of such programs as the CCC, WPA, FERA, and PWA and a wealth and abundance of creative talent and energy nationwide by architects, landscape architects, and engineers. Because of the highly individual nature of these features, their finite number, their reflection of a national style of landscape and architectural design, and the high quality of artistic design and workmanship, many are individually eligible. Not eligible by themselves are single examples of redundant features such as ordinary culvert headwalls, retaining walls, and guardrails along park roads or trails (these, however, may contribute to a district based on the entire road or road system, a scenic trail, or a developed area).

The outstanding significance of the programs with which these features are associated and the tremendous importance of these resources to the localities and states to which this legacy was entrusted and to the American public as a whole make a strong argument for the eligibility collectively and individually of associated features. The construction of these features affected the lives of those who created them and those who benefited from their use. These programs—intended to provide economic relief and training—altered the course of history in recreation, conservation, social history, and economics. They left a rich legacy characterized by individuality, creativity, and diversity which can never be replicated.

Properties eligible for listing in the National Register of Historic Places as members of the multiple property group Historic Park Landscapes in National and State Parks meet Criteria A and/or C in any of the following areas: Landscape Architecture, Architecture, Community Planning and Development (park), Conservation, Engineering, Politics/Government, Entertainment/Recreation, and/or Social History. Properties must:

1. be associated with the twentieth-century movement to develop national parks for public enjoyment, to conserve natural features and scenic areas as public parks, to organize statewide systems of state or local parks, or to develop natural areas, including submarginal lands, for public recreational use;

2. retain several or all of the physical characteristics listed above which were developed for that area during or before the New Deal era (1933–42);

3. reflect the following principles and practices of park landscape design developed and used by the National Park Service in national parks from 1916 to 1942 and in state and national parks through ECW, CCC, PWA or WPA projects from 1933 to 1942:

    a. protection and preservation of natural scenery and features

    b. prohibition of exotic plants and wildlife

c. presentation of scenic vistas through the location of park facilities and development of overlooks

d. avoidance of right angles and straight lines in the design of roads, trails, and structures

e. use of native materials for construction and planting

f. use of naturalistic techniques in planting, rockwork, and logwork to harmonize constructed development with natural surroundings

g. adaptation of indigenous or frontier methods of construction

h. transplanting and planting of native trees, shrubs, and ground covers to erase the scars of construction and earlier uses of the land;

4. possess historic integrity of location, setting, design, materials, workmanship, feeling, and association and overall reflect the physical appearance and condition of the landscape during the period of significance. Changes and additions to the landscape since the period of significance, including new campgrounds, buildings, trails, roads, lakes, and recreational areas, diminish historic integrity and are considered noncontributing. Historic park landscapes containing such changes are eligible for listing despite these changes if the overall historic plan is intact and a substantial number of historic characteristics possessing integrity of design, location, materials, and workmanship are present.

Local parks, including metropolitan and county parks, may also qualify for listing under this context if they possess naturalistic characteristics and natural components and if they were partially or entirely developed under the direction of the National Park Service through the CCC or WPA.

Park landscapes having national significance under this multiple property listing are those pivotal in introducing and advancing the principles and practices of national park landscape design and those maintaining a high degree of artistic quality and historic integrity. Such properties should be considered for designation as National Historic Landmarks under the themes Transforming the Environment, Expressing Cultural Values, and Developing the American Economy.

Park Landscapes in National and State Parks—Associated Listings in the National Register of Historic Places

National Park System

(Note: "MPS," "MRA," and "TR" are abbreviations for multiple property submission, multiple resource area, and thematic resource study, which are multiple property designations in the National Register.)

Acadia National Park
    Carriage Paths, Bridges, and
        Gatehouses
    11/14/79   79000131

Bandelier National Monument
    Bandelier CCC Historic District
    5/28/87   87001452

Bryce Canyon National Park
    Bryce Canyon Lodge and Deluxe
        Cabins
    5/28/87   87001339

    Bryce Canyon National Park MPS
    Old Administration Building
    4/24/95   95000430

    Bryce Canyon Historic District
        (Boundary Increase)
    4/25/95   95000434

Bryce Canyon National Park Scenic
    Trials Historic District
4/25/95   95000422

Bryce Inn
4/25/95   95000425

Horse Barn
4/25/95   95000433

Loop C Comfort Station
4/25/95   95000428

Loop D Comfort Station
4/25/95   95000429

Old National Park Service Housing
    Historic District
4/25/95   95000424

Rainbow Point Comfort Station and
    Overlook Shelter
4/25/95   95000427

Riggs Spring Fire Trail
4/25/95   95000431

Under-the-Rim Trail
4/25/95   95000423

Utah Parks Company Service Station
4/25/95   95000426

Buffalo National River
  Buffalo River State Park
  10/20/78   78003461

Carlsbad Caverns
  Rattlesnake Springs Historic District
  7/14/88   88001130

  The Caverns Historic District
  8/18/88   88001173

Casa Grande National Monument
  Casa Grande National Monument
  10/15/66   66000192

Catoctin Mountain
  *ECW Architecture in Catoctin Mountain
    Park MPS*
  Camp Greentop Historic District
  10/11/89   89001583

  Camp Misty Mount Historic District
  10/11/89   89001582

Cedar Breaks
  Visitor Center
  Cedar City 8/04/83   83004386

Colorado National Monument
  Colorado National Monument MPS
  Devil's Kitchen Picnic Shelter
  Grand Junction 04/21/94   94000309

  Rim Rock Drive Historic District
  Grand Junction 04/21/94   94000310

  Serpent's Trail
  Grand Junction 04/21/94   94000307

Crater Lake National Park
  Crater Lake Lodge
  5/05/81   81000096

  Crater Lake Superintendent's Residence
  5/28/87   87001347

  Crater Lake National Park MRA
  Munson Valley Historic District
  12/01/88   88002622

  Sinnott Memorial Building No.67
  12/01/88   88002623

  Watchman Lookout Station No. 168
  12/01/88   88002626

  Comfort Station No. 68
  12/01/88   88002624

  Comfort Station No. 72
  12/01/88   88002625

Denali National Park and Preserve
    (formerly Mount McKinley
    National Park)
  Mount McKinley National Park
    Headquarters District
  10/23/87   87000975

  *Mount McKinley National Park Patrol
    Cabins TR*
  Lower Windy Creek Ranger Cabin
    No. 15
  11/25/86   86003229

  Upper Toklat River Cabin No. 24
  11/25/86   86003211

  Igloo Creek Cabin No. 25
  11/25/86   86003208

  Sanctuary River Cabin No. 31
  11/25/86   86003206

  Sushana River Ranger Cabin No. 17
  11/25/86   86003227

Riley Creek Ranger Cabin No. 20
11/25/86   86003225

Moose Creek Ranger Cabin No. 19
11/25/86   86003231

Lower Toklat River Ranger Cabin
    No. 18
11/25/86   86003222

Upper Windy Creek Ranger Cabin
    No. 7
11/25/86   86003219

Toklat Ranger Station — Pearson Cabin
    No. 4
11/25/86   86003207

Ewe Creek Ranger Cabin No. 8
11/25/86   86003217

Lower East Fork Ranger Cabin No. 9
11/25/86   86003214

Upper East Fork Cabin No. 29
11/25/86   86003209

Frederick Law Olmsted National Historic
    Site
    Olmsted, Frederick Law, House
    Brookline 10/15/66   66000780

George Washington Memorial Parkway
    Mount Vernon Memorial Highway
    5/18/81   81000079

Glacier National Park
    Lewis Glacier Hotel
    5/22/78   78000280

    Lake McDonald Lodge
    5/28/87   87001447

    Sperry Chalets
    8/02/77   77000115

    Many Glacier Hotel Historic District
    9/29/76   76000173

Granite Park Chalet
6/27/83   83001060

Great Northern Railway Buildings
5/28/87   87001453

Going-to-the-Sun Road
6/16/83   83001070

Glacier National Park MRA
Fielding Snowshoe Patrol Cabin
2/14/86   86000341

Ford Creek Patrol Cabin
2/14/86   86000342

Huckleberry Fire Outlook
2/14/86   86000346

Loneman Fire Lookout
2/14/86   86000353

Numa Ridge Fire Lookout
2/14/86   86000357

Nyack Ranger Station Barn and Fire
    Cache
2/14/86   86000359

Quartz Lake Patrol Cabin
2/14/86   86000361

Scalplock Mountain Fire Lookout
2/14/86   86000363

Skyland Camp — Bowman Lake Ranger
    Station
2/14/86   86000365

Upper Kintla Lake Patrol Cabin
2/14/86   86000374

Upper Logging Lake Snowshoe Cabin
2/14/86   86000376

Belly River Ranger Station Historic
    District
    2/14/86   86000329

Logan Creek Patrol Cabin
2/14/86   86000348

Lower Nyack Snowshoe Cabin
2/14/86   86000356

Ptarmigan Tunnel
2/14/86   86000360

Slide Lake–Otatso Creek Patrol Cabin
   and Woodshed
2/14/86   86000370

Upper Nyack Snowshoe Cabin
2/14/86   86000377

Heaven's Peak Fire Lookout
12/19/86   86003688

Pass Creek Snowshoe Cabin
12/19/86   86003689

Logging Creek Ranger Station Historic
   District
12/16/86   86003697

Walton Ranger Station Historic District
12/16/86   86003700

Upper Park Creek Patrol Cabin
12/16/86   86003702

Mount Brown Fire Lookout
12/16/86   86003693

Lower Logging Lake Snowshoe Cabin
12/16/86   86003692

Upper Lake McDonald Ranger Station
   Historic District
12/16/86   86003699

Sherburne Ranger Station Historic
   District
12/16/86   86003698

East Glacier Ranger Station Historic
   District
12/16/86   86003696

Swiftcurrent Ranger Station Historic
   District
12/19/86   86003690

Apgar Fire Lookout
12/16/86   86003695

Lower Park Creek Patrol Cabin
12/16/86   86003701

Swiftcurrent Fire Lookout
12/16/86   86003694

Kintla Lake Ranger Station
2/14/86   86000332

Gunsight Pass Shelter
2/14/86   86000344

Saint Mary Ranger Station
2/14/86   86000367

Two Medicine General Store
2/14/86   86000372

Bowman Lake Patrol Cabin
2/14/86   86000340

McCarthy Homestead Cabin
12/16/86   86003691

Kishenehn Ranger Station Historic
   District
2/14/86   86000335

Polebridge Ranger Station Historic
   District
2/14/86   86000337

Grand Canyon National Park
   Desert View Watchtower Historic
   District
1/03/95   94001503

Hermits Rest Concession Building
8/07/74   74000335

Grand Canyon Inn and Campground
9/02/82   82001872

Grand Canyon North Rim
Headquarters
9/02/82   82001722

Water Reclamation Plant
9/06/74   74000348

El Tovar Stables
9/06/74   74000336

Superintendent's Residence
9/06/74   74000450

O'Neill, Buckey, Cabin
10/29/75   75000227

Ranger's Dormitory
9/05/75   75000219

El Tovar Hotel
9/06/74   74000334

Grand Canyon Railroad Station
9/06/74   74000337

Grand Canyon Village Historic District
11/20/75   75000343

Grand Canyon Lodge
9/02/82   82001721

Grand Canyon Power House
5/28/87   87001411

Grand Canyon Park Operations
Building
5/28/87   87001412

Mary Jane Colter Buildings (Hopi
House, The Lookout, Hermit's
Rest, and the Desert View
Watchtower)
5/28/87   87001436

Tusayan Ruins
7/10/74   74000285

Grand Teton National Park
Leek's Lodge
9/05/75   75000216

Grand Teton National Park MPS
Old Administrative Area Historic
District
4/23/90   90000621

AMK Ranch
4/23/90   90000615

Brinkerhoff, The
4/23/90   90000622

Jackson Lake Ranger Station
4/23/90   90000620

Jenny Lake Ranger Station Historic
District
4/23/90   90000610

Leigh Lake Ranger Patrol Cabin
4/23/90   90000618

Moose Entrance Kiosk
4/23/90   90000619

String Lake Comfort Station
4/23/90   90000617

White Grass Ranger Station Historic
District
4/23/90   90000614

Hawaii Volcanoes National Park
Ainapo Trail
8/30/74   74000290

Kilauea Crater
7/24/74   74000291

Puna-Ka'u Historic District
7/01/74   74000294

Old Volcano House No. 42
7/24/74   74000293

Jewell Cave National Monument
Jewel Cave National Monument MPS
Historic Trail and Cave Entrance
4/19/95   95000337

Ranger Station
4/05/95   95000336

John Muir National Historic Site
John Muir National Historic Site
10/15/66   66000083

Lassen Volcanic National Park
Prospect Peak Fire Lookout
3/30/78   78000295

Warner Valley Ranger Station
4/03/78   78000364

Horseshoe Lake Ranger Station
5/05/78   78000292

Loomis Vistor Center, Bldg. 43
2/25/75   75000177

Nobles Emigrant Trail
10/03/75   75000222

Summit Lake Ranger Station
4/03/78   78000296

Park Headquarters Building
10/03/78   78000294

Mammoth Cave National Park
Mammoth Cave National Park MPS
Great Onyx Cave Entrance
5/08/91   91000490

Colossal Cavern Entrance
5/08/91   91000491

Three Springs Pumphouse
5/08/91   91000492

Bransford Spring Pumphouse
5/08/91   91000493

Maple Springs Ranger Station
5/08/91   91000494

Superintendent's House
5/08/91   91000495

Crystal Cave District
5/08/91   91000500

Maintenance Area District
5/08/91   91000501

Residential Area District
5/08/91   91000502

Mammoth Cave Historic District
5/08/91   91000503

Mesa Verde National Park
Mesa Verde Administrative District
5/28/87   87001410

Mount Rainier National Park
Paradise Inn
5/28/87   87001336

Yakima Park Stockade Group
5/28/87   87001337

Longmire Buildings
5/28/87   87001338

Mount Rainier National Park MPS
Nisqually Entrance Historic District
3/13/91   91000172

Paradise Historic District
3/13/91   91000174

Camp Muir
3/13/91   91000176

Huckleberry Creek Patrol Cabin
3/13/91   91000178

Indian Bar Trail Shelter
3/13/91   91000179

Indian Henry's Patrol Cabin
3/13/91   91000180

Ipsut Creek Patrol Cabin
3/13/91   91000181

Lake George Patrol Cabin
3/13/91   91000182

Mowich Lake Patrol Cabin
3/13/91   91000183

North Mowich Trail Shelter
3/13/91   91000184

Summerland Trail Shelter
3/13/91   91000185

Sunset Park Patrol Cabin
3/13/91   91000186

Sunset Park Trail Shelter
3/13/91   91000187

St. Andrews Patrol Cabin
3/13/91   91000188

Three Lakes Patrol Cabin
3/13/91   91000189

White River Patrol Cabin
3/13/91   91000190

Gobbler's Knob Fire Lookout
3/13/91   91000191

Mount Fremont Fire Lookout
3/13/91   91000193

Shriner Peak Fire Lookout
3/13/91   91000194

Tolmie Peak Fire Lookout
3/13/91   91000195

Christine Falls Bridge
3/13/91   91000196

Narada Falls Bridge
3/13/91   91000197

South Puyallup River Bridge
3/13/91   91000198

St. Andrews Creek Bridge
3/13/91   91000199

White River Bridge
3/13/91   91000200

Edith Creek Chlorination House
3/13/91   91000201

Chinook Pass Entrance Arch
3/13/91   91000202

Ohanapecosh Comfort Station No.
    O-302
3/13/91   91000203

Ohanopecosh Comfort Station No.
    O-303
3/13/91   91000204

Tahoma Vista Comfort Station
3/13/91   91000205

Tipsoo Lake Comfort Station
3/13/91   91000206

Sunrise Comfort Station
3/13/91   91000207

Narada Falls Comfort Station
3/13/91   91000208

Longmire Campground Comfort
    Station No. L-302
3/13/91   91000209

Longmire Campground Comfort
    Station No. L-303
3/13/91   91000210

Longmire Campground Comfort
    Station No. L-304
3/13/91   91000211

White River Mess Hall and Dormitory
3/13/91   91000328

White River Entrance
3/13/91   91000177

Longmire Historic District
3/13/91   91000173

Sunrise Historic District
3/13/91   91000175

National Capital Region
  *Parkways of the National Capital Region
    MPS*
  District of Columbia
  George Washington Memorial Parkway
  6/02/95   95000605

  District of Columbia
  Suitland Parkway
  6/02/95   95000604

National Park Service Southwest Region
  Santa Fe County
  National Park Service Southwest
    Regional Office
  10/6/70   700000067

North Cascades National Park
  *North Cascades National Park Service
    Complex MRA*
  Sourdough Mountain Lookout
  2/10/89   88003449

  International Boundary U.S.-Canada
  2/10/89   88003450

  Swamp — Meadow Cabin East
  2/10/89   88003456

  Swamp — Meadow Cabin West
  2/10/89   88003455

  Sulphide — Frisco Cabin
  2/10/89   88003459

  Copper Mountain Fire Lookout
  2/10/89   88003446

Gilbert's Cabin
2/10/89   88003453

Bridge Creek Cabin — Ranger Station
2/10/89   88003458

Beaver Pass Shelter
2/10/89   88003448

Backus — Marblemount Ranger Station
  House No. 1010
2/10/89   88003463

Backus — Marblemount Ranger Station
  House No. 1009
2/10/89   88003462

Deer Lick Cabin
2/10/89   88003452

Desolation Peak Lookout
2/10/89   88003451

Rock Cabin
2/10/89   88003457

Perry Creek Shelter
2/10/89   88003447

Flick Creek Shelter
2/10/89   88003444

High Bridge Shelter
2/10/89   88003461

High Bridge Ranger Station Historic
  District
2/10/89   88003443

Bridge Creek Shelter
2/10/89   88003445

Purple Point — Stehekin Ranger Station
  House
2/10/89   88003460

Oregon Caves National Monument
  Oregon Caves Chateau
  5/28/87   87001346

Oregon Caves Historic District
2/25/92   92000058

Petrified Forest National Park
Painted Desert Inn
5/28/87   87001421

Prince William Forest
*ECW Architecture at Prince William
Forest Park 1933–1942 MPS*
Pleasant Historic District,
Chopawamsic RDA Camp 4
6/12/89   89000459

Orenda/SP-26 Historic District,
Chopawamsic RDA Camp 3
6/12/89   89000458

Mawavi Historic District,
Chopawamsic RDA Camp 2
6/12/89   89000457

Goodwill Historic District,
Chopawamsic RDA Camp 1
6/12/89   89000456

Redwood National Park
Redwood Highway
12/17/79   79000253

Rock Creek Park
Boulder Bridge and Ross Drive Bridge
3/20/80   80000348

Rock Creek Park Historic District
10/23/91   91001524

Rocky Mountain National Park
Rocky Mountain National Park MRA
Timber Creek Road Camp Barn
7/30/87   87001134

Willow Park Patrol Cabin
7/20/87   87001144

Willow Park Stable
7/20/87   87001145

Fall River Road
7/20/87   87001129

Milner Pass Road Camp Mess Hall and
House
7/20/87   87001130

Glacier Basin Campground Ranger
Station
7/20/87   87001143

Wild Basin Ranger Station and House
1/29/88   87001126

Wild Basin House
1/29/88   87001125

Timberline Cabin
1/29/88   87001136

Fern Lake Patrol Cabin
1/29/88   87001142

Fall River Pass Ranger Station
1/29/88   87001140

Fall River Entrance Historic District
1/29/88   87001139

Grand River Ditch
9/29/76   76000218

Holzwarth Historic District
12/02/77   77000112

Shadow Mountain Lookout
8/02/78   78000279

Trail Ridge Road
11/14/84   84000242

Moraine Lodge
10/08/76   76000206

Rocky Mountain National Park Utility
Area Historic District
3/18/82   82001717

White, William Allen, Cabins
10/25/73   73001944

Thunder Lake Patrol Cabin
1/29/88   87001124

Timber Creek Campground Comfort
     Station No. 247
1/29/88   87001133

Timber Creek Campground Comfort
     Station No. 246
1/29/88   87001132

Timber Creek Campground Comfort
     Station No. 245
1/29/88   87001131

Bear Lake Comfort Station
1/29/88   87001137

Bear Lake Ranger Station
1/29/88   87001138

Twin Sisters Lookout
12/24/92   92001670

Vaille, Agnes, Shelter
12/24/92   92001669

Sequoia National Park
  Pear Lake Ski Hut
  5/05/78   78000285

Ash Mountain Entrance Sign
4/27/78   78000367

Cabin Creek Ranger Residence and
     Dormitory
4/27/78   78000368

Hockett Meadow Ranger Station
4/27/78   78000369

Moro Rock Stairway
12/29/78   78000283

Quinn Ranger Station
4/13/77   77000118

Redwood Meadow Ranger Station
4/13/78   78000289

Generals' Highway Stone Bridges
9/13/78   78000284

Giant Forest Lodge Historic District
5/05/78   78000287

Giant Forest Village–Camp Kaweah
     Historic District
5/22/78   78000311

Tharp's Log
3/08/77   77000117

Smithsonian Institution Shelter
3/08/77   77000119

Shenandoah National Park
  Camp Hoover
  6/07/88   88001825

National Park Service Southwest Regional
     Office
  National Park Service Southwest
     Regional Office
  10/06/70   70000067

Tumacacori National Monument
  Tumacacori National Monument
  10/15/66   66000193

  Tumacacori Museum
  5/28/87   87001437

White Sands National Monument
  White Sands National Monument
     Historic District
  6/23/88   88000751

Wind Cave National Park
  Wind Cave National Park MPS
  Beaver Creek Bridge
  8/08/84   84003254

  Wind Cave National Park Historic
     District
  7/11/84   84003259

Pig Tail Bridge
4/07/95   95000344

Yellowstone National Park
   Old Faithful Historic District
12/07/82   82001839

   Norris, Madison, and Fishing Bridge
      Museums
5/28/87   87001445

   Lake Hotel
5/16/91   91000637

   Northeast Entrance Station
5/28/87   87001435

Yellowstone National Park MRA
Roosevelt Lodge Historic District
4/04/83   83003363

   Lamar Buffalo Ranch
12/07/82   82001835

   Obsidian Cliff Kiosk
7/09/82   82001719

   Lake Fish Hatchery Historic District
6/25/85   85001416

   Old Faithful Inn
7/23/73   73000226

   Madison Museum
7/09/82   82001720

   Norris Museum/Norris Comfort
      Station
7/21/83   83003362

Yosemite National Park
   Tuolumne Meadows Ranger Stations
      and Comfort Stations
12/18/78   78000370

   Tuolumne Meadows
11/30/78   78000371

Tioga Pass Entrance Station
12/14/78   78000372

Camp Curry Historic District
11/01/79   79000315

Acting Superintendent's Headquarters
6/09/78   78000362

Yosemite Valley Chapel
12/12/73   73000256

Yosemite Village Historic District
1/12/95   78000354

Jorgenson, Chris, Studio
4/13/79   79000280

Mariposa Grove Museum
12/01/78   78000381

Merced Grove Ranger Station
6/15/78   78000358

Glacier Point Trailside Museum
4/04/78   78000357

Le Conte Memorial Lodge
3/08/77   77000148

Parsons Memorial Lodge
4/30/79   79000283

Ahwahnee Hotel
2/15/77   77000149

Rangers' Club
5/28/87   87001414

Yosemite Village Historic District
3/30/78   78000354

Yosemite Valley Bridges
11/25/77   77000160

Zion National Park
   Zion Lodge Historic District
8/24/82   82001718

Zion National Park MRA
East Entrance Checking Station
2/14/87   86003711

Museum — Grotto Residence
2/14/87   86003721

South Campground Amphitheater
2/14/87   86003717

Zion Nature Center — Zion Inn
2/14/87   86003719

Grotto Camping Ground South
    Comfort Station
2/14/87   86003704

South Entrance Sign
2/14/87   86003713

South Campground Comfort Station
2/14/87   86003708

Canyon Overlook Trail
2/14/87   86003722

Oak Creek Historic District
7/07/87   86003706

Zion Lodge — Birch Creek Historic
    District (Boundary Increase)
7/07/87   86003753

East Entrance Sign
7/07/87   86003710

East Entrance Residence
2/14/87   86003712

Angels Landing Trail — West Rim Trail
2/14/87   86003707

Grotto Camping Ground North
    Comfort Station
2/14/87   86003705

Hidden Canyon Trail
2/14/87   86003731

East Rim Trail
7/07/87   86003723

Gateway to the Narrows Trail
7/07/87   86003726

Pine Creek Residential Historic District
7/07/87   86003736

Zion–Mount Carmel Highway
7/07/87   86003709

Pine Creek Irrigation Canal
7/07/87   86003734

Emerald Pools Trail
2/14/87   86003725

State and Local Parks

Arkansas

*Facilities Constructed by the CCC in
    Arkansas MPS*
Conway County
    Petit Jean State Park — Blue Hole
        Road District
    Winrock 5/28/92   92000513

    Petit Jean State Park — Cedar Falls
        Trail Historic District
    Winrock 5/28/92   92000514

    Petit Jean State Park — Lake Bailey-
        Roosevelt Lake Historic
        District
    Winrock 5/28/92   92000515

    Petit Jean State Park — Office
        Headquarters
    Winrock 5/28/92   92000516

    Petit Jean State Park — Water
        Treatment Building
    Winrock 5/28/92   92000517

Petit Jean State Park—Culvert No. 1
Winrock 5/28/92   92000518

Petit Jean State Park—Concrete Log
    Bridge
Winrock 5/28/92   92000519

Petit Jean State Park—
    Administration Office
Winrock 5/28/92   92000520

Petit Jean State Park—Mather Lodge
Winrock 5/28/92   92000521

Petit Jean State Park—Cabin No. 16
Winrock 5/28/92   92000522

Petit Jean State Park—Cabin No. 1
Winrock 5/28/92   92000523

Petit Jean State Park—Cabin No. 6
Winrock 5/28/92   92000524

Petit Jean State Park—Cabin No. 9
Winrock 5/28/92   92000525

Greene County
    Crowley's Ridge State Park—Dining
        Hall
    Walcott 5/28/92   92000536

    Crowley's Ridge State Park—
        Bathhouse
    Walcott 5/28/92   92000537

    Crowley's Ridge State Park—
        Comfort Station
    Walcott 5/28/92   92000538

    Crowley's Ridge State Park—Bridge
    Walcott 5/28/92   92000540

Hot Spring County
    Lake Catherine State Park—Cabin
        No. 1
    Shorewood Hills 4/20/95   95000455

Lake Catherine State Park—Cabin
    No. 2
Shorewood Hills 5/28/92   92000526

Lake Catherine State Park—Cabin
    No. 3
Shorewood Hills 5/28/92   92000527

Lake Catherine State Park—Bridge
    No. 2
Shorewood Hills 5/28/92   92000528

Lake Catherine State Park—Nature
    Cabin
Shorewood Hills 5/28/92   92000535

Pulaski County
    Boyle Park 9/22/95   95001119

Washington County
    Devil's Den State Park Historic
        District
    Winslow 7/27/94   92000071

Yell County
    Mount Nebo State Park—Pavilion
    Dardanelle 5/28/92   92000542

Colorado

Denver Mountain Parks MPS
Douglas County
    Daniels Park
    Sedalia 06/30/95   95000795

Jefferson County
    Bear Creek Canyon Scenic Mountain
        Drive
    Morrison 11/15/90   90001706

    Bergen Park
    Evergreen 11/15/90   90001707

    Colorow Point Park
    Golden 11/15/90   90001712

    Corwina Park, O'Fallon Park, Pence
        Park
    Evergreen 12/28/90   90001708

Craig, Katherine, Park
Morrison vicinity 06/30/95
95000797

Dedisse Park
Evergreen 11/15/90   90001709

Genesee Park
Golden 11/15/90   90001710

Lariat Trail Scenic Mountain Drive
Golden 11/15/90   90001711

Lookout Mountain Park
Golden 11/15/90   90001713

Red Rocks Park District
Morrison 5/18/90   90000725

Starbuck Park
Idledale vicinity 06/30/95   95000796

Pueblo County
Pueblo Mountain Park
Beulah vicinity 12/06/94   94001343

Connecticut

*Connecticut State Park and Forest
Depression-Era Federal Work Relief
Programs Structures TR*
Hartford County
Massacoe Forest Pavilion
Simsbury 9/04/86   86001731

Shade Swamp Shelter
Farmington 9/04/86   86001746

Tunxis Forest Headquarters
Hartland 9/04/86   86001759

Tunxis Forest Ski Cabin
Hartland 9/5/86   86001761

Litchfield County
American Legion Forest CCC Shelter
Barkhamsted 9/04/86   86001725

Cream Hill Shelter
Sharon 9/04/86   86001727

Paugnut Forest Administration
Building
Torrington 9/5/86   86001736

Peoples Forest Museum
Barkhamsted 9/4/86   86001737

Red Mountain Shelter
Cornwall 9/4/86   86001745

Middlesex County
Oak Lodge
Killingworth 9/04/86   86001734

New Haven County
Sleeping Giant Tower
Hamden 9/04/86   86001754

State Park Supply Yard
Madison 9/04/86   86001757

New London County
Avery House
Hopeville 9/04/86   86001726

Rocky Neck Pavilion
East Lyme 9/04/86   86001745

Windham County
Nautchaug Forest Lumber Shed
Eastford 9/04/86   86001732

Georgia

Taliafero County
Stephens, A. S., Memorial State Park
Crawfordville vicinity 6/22/95
95000764

Idaho

Benewah County
Chatcolet CCC Picnic and Camping
Area
Heyburn State Park

Chatcolet vicinity 2/01/95
94000632

Plummer Point CCC Picnic and
Hiking Area
Heyburn State Park
Chatcolet 2/01/95   94001587

Rocky Point CCC Properties
Heyburn State Park
Chatcolet vicinity 2/01/95
940011588

Illinois

*Illinois State Parks Lodges and
Cabins TR*
Jackson County
Giant City State Park Lodge and
Cabins
Makanda 3/04/85   85002403

Grand Tower Mining,
Manufacturing, and
Transportation Company Site
Devil's Backbone Park
Grand Tower 4/13/79   79000839

Pere Marquette State Park Lodge and
Cabins
Grafton 3/04/85   85002405

White Pines State Park Lodge and
Cabins
Mount Morris 3/04/85   85002404

Rock Island County
Black Hawk Museum and Lodge
Rock Island 3/04/85   85002402

Indiana

*New Deal Resources in Indiana State
Parks MPS*
Owen County
Recreation Building — Nature
Museum
McCormick's Creek State Park
Spencer 3/18/93   93000176

McCormick's Creek State Park
Entrance and Gatehouse
Spencer 3/18/93   93000175

Stone Arch Bridge over McCormick's
Creek
McCormick's Creek State Park
Spencer 3/18/93   93000177

Pulaski County
Tepicon Hall
Tippecanoe River State Park
Winamac 4/03/92   92000189

Steuben County
Combination Shelter
Pokagon State Park
Angola 4/03/92   92000190

Henderson County
Audubon, John James, State Park
Henderson 3/10/88   87002220

Iowa

*CCC Properties in Iowa State Parks
MPS/Conservation Movement in
Iowa MPS*
Clay County
Wanata State Park Picnic Shelter
Peterson 11/15/90   90001677

Delaware County
Backbone State Park Historic District
Strawberry Point 12/23/91   91001842

Backbone State Park, Cabin —
Bathing Area (Area A)
Dundee 11/15/90   90001681

Backbone State Park, Picnicking,
Hiking, and Camping Area
(Area B)
Dundee 11/15/90   90001682

Backbone State Park, Richmond
Springs (Area C)
Dundee 11/15/90   90001683

Dickinson County
  Gull Point State Park, Area A
  Milford 11/15/90   90001661

  Gull Point State Park, Area B
  Milford 11/15/90   90001662

  Pikes Point State Park Shelter and
    Steps
  Spirit Lake 11/15/90   90001675

  Pillsbury Point State Park
  Arnolds Park 1/12/93   90001674

  Trappers Bay State Park Picnic
    Shelter
  Lake Park 11/15/90   90001676

Franklin County
  Beeds Lake State Park, CCC Area
  Hampton 11/15/90   90001672

Greene County
  Squirrel Hollow County Park
    Historic District
  Jefferson 12/23/91   91001835

Guthrie County
  Springbrook State Park, CCC Area
  Guthrie Center 11/15/90   90001671

Hancock County
  Pilot Knob State Park, Observation
    Tower (Area 2)
  Forest City 11/15/90   90001686

  Pilot Knob State Park, Picnic Shelter
    (Area 3)
  Forest City 11/15/90   90001687

  Pilot Knob State Park, Amphitheater
    (Area 4)
  Forest City 11/15/90   90001688

  Pilot Knob State Park, Portals
    (Area 5a)
  Forest City 11/15/90   90001689

Pilot Knob State Park, Portals
  (Area 5b)
Forest City 4/17/95   95000362

Pilot Knob State Park, Trail Area
  (Area 6a–6c)
Forest City 11/15/90   90001690

Henry County
  Geode State Park, CCC Area
  Danville 11/15/90   90001673

Jackson County
  Maquoketa Caves State Park Historic
    District
  Maquoketa 12/23/91   91001843

Mahaska County
  Lake Keomah State Park,
    Bathhouse—Lodge Area (Area A)
  Oskaloosa 11/15/90   90001666

  Lake Keomah State Park, Erosion
    Control Area (Area B)
  Oskaloosa 11/15/90   90001667

Sac County
  Blackhawk State Park, Wildlife
    Preserve Area (Area A)
  Lake View 11/15/90   90001678

  Blackhawk State Park, Black Hawk
    Preserve (Area B)
  Lake View 11/15/90   90001679

  Blackhawk State Park, Denison
    Beach Area (Area C)
  Lake View 11/15/90   90001680

  Lakeside Park Historic District
  Lake View 12/23/91   91001841

Van Buren County
  Lacey—Keosauqua State Park, Lodge
    and Picnic Area (Area A)
  Keosauqua 11/15/90   90001668

Lacey—Keosauqua State Park, Picnic
and Custodial Group (Area B)
Keosauqua 11/15/90   90001669

Lacey—Keosauqua State Park,
Bathing Area (Area C)
Keosauqua 11/15/90   90001670

Warren County
Lake Ahquabi State Park, Picnic Area
(Area A)
Indianola 11/15/90   90001663

Lake Ahquabi State Park, Bathhouse
Area (Area B)
Indianola 11/15/90   90001664

Lake Ahquabi State Park, Refectory
Area (Area C)
Indianola 11/15/90   90001665

Webster County
Dolliver Memorial State Park,
Entrance Area (Area A)
Lehigh 11/15/90   90001684

Dolliver Memorial State Park, Picnic,
Hiking and Maintenance Area
(Area B)
Lehigh 11/15/90   90001685

Massachusetts

Norfolk County and Suffolk County
Olmsted Park System
Brookline/Boston 12/08/71
71000086

*Blue Hills and Neponset River
Reservations MRA*
Norfolk County
Blue Hills Headquarters
Milton 9/35/80   80000654

Brookwood Farm
Milton 9/25/80   80000655

Comfort Station
Milton 9/25/80   80000658

Eliot Memorial Bridge
Milton 9/25/80   80000662

Great Blue Hill Observation Tower
Milton 9/25/80   80000661

Great Blue Hill Weather Observatory
Milton 9/25/80   80000665

Massachusetts Hornfels-Braintree
Slate Quarry
Milton 9/25/80   80000653

Old Barn
Milton 9/25/80   80000660

Redman Farm House
Canton 9/25/80   80000664

Refreshment Pavilion
Milton 9/25/80   80000659

Minnesota

*Minnesota State Park CCC/WPA/Rustic
Style MPS*
Beltrami County
Lake Bemidji State Park
Bemidji 10/25/89   89001674

Blue Earth County
Minneopa State Park
Mankato 10/25/89   89001663

Brown County
Flandrau State Park
New Ulm 10/25/89   89001658

Carlton County
Cooke, Jay, State Park
Carlton 6/11/92   89001665

Cooke, Jay, State Park Picnic
Grounds
Carlton 6/11/92   92000640

Cooke, Jay, State Park Service Yard
Carlton 6/11/92   92000642

Chisago County
   Interstate State Park
   Taylors Falls 6/11/92   89001664

   Interstate State Park Campground
   Taylors Falls 6/11/92   92000638

Clay County
   Buffalo River State Park
   Glyndon 10/25/89   89001671

Clearwater County
   Itasca State Park
   Park Rapids 5/07/73   73000972

Douglas County
   Lake Carlos State Park
   Carlos 7/02/92   89001654

   Lake Carlos State Park Group Camp
   Carlos 7/02/92   72000776

Itasca County
   Scenic State Park
   Bigfork 6/08/92   89001670

   Scenic State Park CCC/Rustic Style
      Service Yard
   Bigfork 6/08/92   92000595

Kandiyohi County
   Mount Tom Lookout Shelter, Sibley
      State Park
   New London 1/22/92   91002030

   Sibley State Park
   New London 1/22/92   89001673

Kittson County
   Lake Bronson State Park
   Lake Bronson 10/25/89   89001659

Lac Qui Parle County
   Lac Qui Parle State Park
   Montevideo 8/19/91   91001055

Lake County
   Gooseberry Falls State Park
   Two Harbors 10/25/89   89001672

Lyon County
   Camden State Park
   Lynd 4/19/91   89001669

Marshall County
   Old Mill State Park
   Argyle 10/25/89   89001667

   Lindbergh, Charles A., State Park
   Little Falls 10/25/89   89001655

Murray County
   Lake Shetak State Park
   Currie 7/02/92   92000777

Nicollet County
   Fort Ridgely State Park
   New Ulm 10/25/89   89001668

Rock County
   Blue Mounds State Park
   Luverne 10/25/89   89001657

Swift County
   Monson Lake State Park
   Sunburg 10/25/89   89001666

Winona County
   Whitewater State Park
   Elba 10/25/89   89001661

Missouri

   *ECW Architecture in Missouri State
      Parks 1933–42 TR*
   Barry County
   Camp Smokey/Company 1713
      Historic District
   Cassville 2/26/85   85000513

   Roaring River State Park Bathhouse
   Cassville 3/04/85   85000500

   Roaring River State Park Hotel
   Cassville 3/04/85   85000501

   Roaring River State Park
      Dam/Spillway
   Cassville 2/28/85   85000518

Roaring River State Park Deer Leap
Trail
Cassville 2/26/85   85000519

Roaring River State Park
Honeymoon Cabin
Cassville 2/26/85   85000520

Roaring River State Park Shelter
Kitchen No. 2 and Rest Room
Cassville 2/26/85   85000521

Buchanan County
Sugar Lake State Park Open Shelter
Rushville 2/28/85   85000522

Camden County
Camp Hawthorne Central Area
District
Camdenton 2/28/85   85000526

Lake of the Ozarks Recreational
Demonstration Area Barn/Garage
in Kaiser Area
Camdenton 2/28/85   85000523

Lake of the Ozarks Recreational
Demonstration Area Rising Sun
Shelter
Camdenton 2/26/85   85000524

Lake of the Ozarks Recreational
Demonstration Area Shelter at
McCubbin Point
Camdenton 2/26/85   85000525

Lake of the Ozarks State Park Camp
Clover Point Recreation Hall
Camdenton 3/04/85   85000502

Lake of the Ozarks State Park Camp
Rising Sun Recreation Hall
Camdenton 3/04/85   85000503

Pin Oak Hollow Bridge
Lake of the Ozarks State Park
Pin Oak Hollow 9/13/85   85002737

Dallas County
Bennett Spring State Park Shelter
House and Water Gauge Station
Bennett Spring 2/28/85   85000527

Dent County
Dam and Spillway in the Hatchery
Area at Montauk State Park
Salem 2/26/85   85000528

Montauk State Park Open Shelter
Salem 2/28/85   85000529

Old Mill at Montauk State Park
Salem 6/27/85   85001478

Franklin County
Meramec State Park Lookout
House/Observation Tower
Sullivan 2/28/85   85000530

Meramec State Park Pump House
Sullivan 2/28/85   85000531

Meramec State Park Shelter House
Sullivan 2/26/85   85000532

Grundy County
Crowder State Park Vehicle Bridge
Trenton 3/04/85   85000505

Howard County
Boonslick State Park
Boonsboro 12/30/69   69000104

Johnson County
Camp Shawnee Historic District
Knob Noster 3/04/85   85000506

Montserrat Recreational
Demonstration Area Bridge
Knob Noster 3/04/85   85000507

Montserrat Recreational
Demonstration Area Dam and
Spillway
Knob Noster 3/04/85   85000508

Montserrat Recreational
Demonstration Area Entrance
Portal
Knob Noster 3/04/85   85000509

Montserrat Recreational
Demonstration Area Rock
Bathhouse
Knob Noster 3/04/85   85000510

Montserrat Recreational
Demonstration Area Warehouse
#2 and Workshop
Knob Noster 3/04/85   85000511

Laclede County
Bennett Spring State Park Hatchery–
Lodge Area Historic District
Bennett Spring 3/04/85   85000504

Lincoln County
Camp Sherwood Forest Historic
District
Elsberry 3/04/85   85000512

Cuivre River State Park
Administrative Area Historic
District
Elsberry 3/04/85   85000514

Miller County
Lake of the Ozarks State Park
Highway 134 Historic District
Brumley 2/26/85   85000533

Monroe County
Mark Twain State Park Picnic Shelter
at Buzzard's Roost
Santa Fe 3/04/85   85000515

St. Louis County
Dr. Edmund A. Babler Memorial
State Park Historic District
Grover 2/27/85   85000539

Arrow Rock State Historic Site
Bridge
Arrow Rock 3/04/85   85000516

Arrow Rock State Historic Site Grave
Shelter
Arrow Rock 2/27/85   85000534

Arrow Rock State Historic Site
Lookout Shelter
Arrow Rock 2/27/85   85000535

Arrow Rock State Historic Site Open
Shelter
Arrow Rock 2/28/85   85000536

Van Meter State Park Combination
Building
Van Meter State Park
Marshall 2/27/85   85000537

Van Meter State Park Shelter
Building
Van Meter State Park
Marshall 2/28/85   85000538

Washington State Park CCC Historic
District
Potosi 3/04/85   85000517

Wayne County
Sam A. Baker State Park Historic
District
Patterson 2/27/85   85000540

New Hampshire

Merrimack County
Bear Brook State Park CCC Camp
Historic District
Allenstown 6/11/92   92000632

New Jersey

Bergen County
Palisades Interstate Park
Fort Lee and vicinity 10/15/66
66000890

Passaic County
Skylands
Ringwood State Park
Ringwood 9/28/90   90001438

New York

Orange County
Palisades Interstate Park
Fort Lee and vicinity 10/15/66
66000890

North Carolina

Wake County
Crabtree Creek Recreational
Demonstration Area
Raleigh 06/30/95   95000783

Oregon

Lane County
Honeyman, Jessie M., Memorial
State Park Historic District
Florence 11/28/84   84000473

Marion County
Silver Falls State Park Concession
Building Area
Sublimity 6/30/83   83002164

Pennsylvania

Emergency Conservation Work (ECW)
Architecture in Pennsylvania State
Parks: 1933–42, TR
Berks County
French Creek State Park Six Penny
Day Use District
Morgantown 2/11/87   87000054

Centre County
Black Moshannon State Park
Maintenance District
Philipsburg 2/12/87   87000097

Black Moshannon State Park Day
Use District
Philipsburg 2/12/87   87000101

Black Moshannon State Park Family
Cabin District
Philipsburg 2/12/87   87000102

Clearfield County
Elliott, S. B., State Park Day Use
District
Clearfield 2/11/87   87000023

Elliott, S. B., State Park Family Cabin
District
Clearfield 2/11/87   87000024

Parker Dam State Park Family Cabin
District
Penfield 2/11/87   87000043

Parker Dam State Park — Parker Dam
District
Penfield 2/11/87   87000049

Clinton County
Ravensburg State Park
Loganton 5/18/87   87000741

Forest County
Cook Forest State Park Indian Cabin
District
Cooksburg 2/12/87   87000019

Cook Forest State Park River Cabin
District
Cooksburg 2/12/87   87000053

Fulton County
Cowans Gap State Park Family Cabin
District
Chambersburg 2/11/87   87000051

Huntington County
Whipple Dam State Park Day Use
District
Huntingdon 2/12/87   87000109

Jefferson County
Clear Creek State Park Day Use
District
Sigel 2/11/87   87000018

Clear Creek State Park Family Cabin
District
Sigel 2/12/87   87000106

Pike County
Promised Land State Park Whittaker
Lodge District
Canadensis 2/11/87   87000047

Promised Land State Park — Bear
Wallow Cabins
Canadensis 2/11/87   87000048

Somerset County
Kooser State Park Family Cabin
District
Jefferson 2/12/87   87000111

Laurel Hill RDA
Somerset 5/18/87   87000738

Sullivan County
Worlds End State Park Family Cabin
District
Forksville 5/18/87   87000742

Tioga County
Colton Point State Park
Ansonia 2/12/87   87000112

Westmoreland County
Linn Run State Park Family Cabin
District
Rector 2/12/87   87000107

Tennessee

*State Parks in Tennessee Built by the
CCC and the WPA, 1934—42, TR*
Overton County
Standing Stone Rustic Park Historic
District
Livingston 7/08/86   86002794

Pickett County
Pickett State Rustic Park Historic
District
Jamestown 7/08/86   86002795

Texas

Coryell County
Mother Neff State Park and F. A. S.
21-B(1) Historic District
Moody 10/02/92   92001303

Travis County
Barton Springs Archeological and
Historical District
Austin 11/27/85   85003213

Virginia

Alleghany County
Douthat State Park Historic District
Millboro 9/20/86   86002183

Washington

Clark County
Lewisville Park
Battle Ground 5/28/86   86001202

Other Associated Listings

California

Los Angeles County
Blacker, Robert R., House
Pasadena 2/06/86   86000147

Gamble House
Pasadena 9/03/71   71000155

Oaklawn Bridge and Waiting Station
Pasadena 7/16/73   73000406

Pitzer House
Claremont 9/04/78   78000689

Tulare County
Tenalu
Porterville, vicinity 9/04/86
86002194

Massachusetts

Bristol County
North Easton Historic District
Easton 11/03/72   72000119

New York

*Great Camps of the Adirondacks
Thematic Resources*
Essex County
Camp Santanoni
Newcomb 4/3/87   86002955

Franklin County
Camp Wild Air
Regis 11/07/86   86002930

Moss Ledge
Saranac Inn 11/07/86   86002942

Eagle Island Camp
Saranac Inn 4/03/87   86002941

Prospect Point Camp
Saranac Inn 11/07/86   86002947

Camp Topridge
Keese Hill 11/07/86   86002952

Hamilton County
Camp Pine Knot
Raquette Lake 11/7/86   86002934

Camp Uncas
Raquette Lake 4/3/87   86002937

Echo Camp
Raquette Lake 11/7/86   86002939

Sagamore Lodge (Boundary
Increase)
Raquette Lake 11/7/86   86002940

Oregon

Multnomah County
Columbia River Highway Historic
District
Troutdale 12/12/83   83004168

Notes

ABBREVIATIONS

ACA	American Civic Association
AR	*Annual Reports of the Department of the Interior*
ASLA	American Society of Landscape Architects
CCC	Civilian Conservation Corps
ECW	Emergency Conservation Work
EODC	Eastern Office of Design and Construction
FERA	Federal Emergency Relief Administration
LEM	Local experienced men
NRHP	National Register of Historic Places
PWA	Public Works Administration
RDA	Recreational demonstration area
WODC	Western Office of Design and Construction
WPA	Works Progress Administration

INTRODUCTION

1. National Park Service Act, 16 U.S.C. 1 et seq. (1988), August 25, 1916, ch. 408, 39 Stat. 535.

2. Landscape architects played a substantial role in the effort to create a national park service, which began in the early 1900s and was promoted by conservation groups such as the Sierra Club; scientists such as Joseph Grinnell of the University of California, Berkeley; and several members of Congress and other political leaders. The secretary of the interior urged the formation of the service in his 1910 annual report and enlisted the help of J. Horace McFarland and Frederick Law Olmsted Jr. in preparing a bill. McFarland encouraged President Taft to speak at the American Civic Association's annual convention in 1911. With McFarland's encouragement, Franklin Lane, who became secretary of the interior in 1913, hired an assistant in charge of parks. John Ise, *Our National Park Policy: A Critical History* (Baltimore: Johns Hopkins Press, 1961), 186–90.

3. Richard B. Watrous, "Our National Parks: A Conference," *Landscape Architecture* 6, no. 3 (1916): 100–105.

4. James Sturgis Pray with Robert B. Marshall, "The American Society of Landscape Architecture and Our National Parks," *Landscape Architecture* 6, no. 3 (1916): 119–20.

5. Henry Vincent Hubbard and Theodora Kimball, *An Introduction to the Study of Landscape Design* (1917; reprint, New York: Macmillan Co., 1924), 74.

6. Frank Albert Waugh, *The Natural Style in Landscape Gardening* (Boston: Richard G. Badger, 1917), 144–45.

7. Frederick Law Olmsted Jr., "The Distinction between National Parks and National Forests," *Landscape Architecture* 6, no. 3 (1916): 115–16.

8. Frederick Law Olmsted Jr., "Vacation in the National Parks and Forests," *Landscape Architecture* 12, no. 2 (1922): 107–11, from a paper read at the annual meeting of the American Civic Association on November 15, 1921.

9. Henry V. Hubbard, "The Designer in National Parks," *Landscape Architecture* 38, no. 2 (1948): 60; originally published in National Park Service, *1941 Yearbook: Park and Recreation Progress* (Washington, D.C.: GPO, 1941), 39.

10. Henry V. Hubbard, "Landscape Development Based on Conservation, As Practiced in the National Park Service," *Landscape Architecture* 29, no. 3 (1939): 105–21.

CHAPTER 1.   FROM PLEASURE GROUNDS TO PUBLIC PARKS

1. Andrew Jackson Downing, "A Visit to Montgomery Place," in *Rural Essays* (New York: Hagemann Publishing Co., 1894), 192–202. This essay was originally published in the *Horticulturalist* 2, no. 4 (1847): 153–60.

2. Andrew Jackson Downing, *A Treatise on the Theory and Practice of Landscape Gardening*, 9th ed. (New York: Orange Judd, 1875; reprint, Little Compton, R.I.: Theophrastus Publishers, 1977), 392, 396.

3. Henry G. Tyrrell, *Artistic Bridge Design: A Systematic Treatise on the Design of Modern Bridges According to Aesthetic Principles* (Chicago: Myron Clarke, 1912), fig. 161.

4. Downing, *Theory and Practice,* 401.

5. Andrew Jackson Downing, "On the Employment of Ornamental Trees and Shrubs in America," in *Rural Essays,* 375.

6. Ibid., 376; Andrew Jackson Downing, "A Word in Favor of Evergreens," in *Rural Essays,* 328–29. Note that Latin names are given throughout the text only in cases where they have been documented by historical records or where the identity of genus and species has been determined from literature, actual plantings, or other evidence.

7. Andrew Jackson Downing, "Neglected American Plants," in *Rural Essays,* 339–42.

8. Downing, *Theory and Practice,* 278–79.

9. Act of March 1, 1872.

10. Hubbard and Kimball, *Introduction,* 90.

11. National Park Service, *Frederick Law Olmsted: Six Principles of Landscape Design* (Brookline, Mass.: Frederick Law Olmsted National Historic Site, National Park Service, n.d., printed pamphlet).

12. Norman T. Newton, *Design on the Land: The Development of Landscape Architecture* (Cambridge: Harvard University Press, 1971), 233–41; quote is from Prince H. L. H. von Pückler-Muskau, *Hints on Landscape Gardening,* trans. Bernhardt Sickert, ed. Samuel Parsons (Boston: Houghton Mifflin, 1917), 65, and is given in Newton, *Design on the Land,* 239.

13. Newton, *Design on the Land,* 241–45.

14. Frederick Law Olmsted Sr., *Forty Years of Landscape Architecture: Central Park,* ed. Frederick Law Olmsted Jr. and Theodora Kimball (New York: G. P. Putnam's Sons, 1928; reprint, Cambridge: MIT Press, 1973), 256.

15. Ibid., 474, from Eighth Annual Report, Central Park Commission, 26.

16. Ibid., 258; Samuel Parsons Jr., *The Art of Landscape Architecture: Its Development and Its Application to Modern Landscape Gardening* (New York: G. P. Putnam's Sons, 1915), figs. opp. pp. 180 and 294.

17. Olmsted, *Forty Years,* 475.

18. Charles W. Eliot II, "The Influence of the Automobile on the Design of Park Roads," *Landscape Architecture* 13, no. 1 (1922): 28; Olmsted's quote appears on the same page.

19. Historic photographs, Franklin Park Files, Olmsted National Historic Site, Brookline, Mass.

20. Cynthia Zaitzevsky, *Frederick Law Olmsted and the Boston Park System* (Cambridge: Harvard University Press, 1982), 160–69.

21. Ibid., 176.

22. Ibid., 176–80.

23. William Robinson, *The Wild Garden or the Naturalization and Natural Grouping of Hardy Exotic Plants with a Chapter on the Garden of British Wild Flowers* (London: John Murray, 1870; reprint, London: Century Hutchinson with the National Trust, 1986).

24. Olmsted, *Forty Years,* 353–54.

25. Roger B. Martin, "Metropolitan Open Spaces," in *American Landscape Architecture: Designers and Places,* ed. William Tishler (Washington, D.C.: Preservation Press, 1989), 166.

26. E. Lynn Miller, "Charles Eliot," in Tishler, *American Landscape Architecture,* 53–54; Newton, *Design on the Land,* 318–36.

27. Charles W. Eliot, *Charles Eliot, Landscape Architect* (Boston: Houghton Mifflin, 1902), 709.

28. Ibid., 663–64; 652, October 25, 1894, Eliot to Commissioners of Boston Metropolitan Park System.

29. Ibid., 710, January 8, 1896, Eliot to Commissioners of Boston Metropolitan Park System.

30. Ibid., 665, January 27, 1897, Eliot to the editor of *Garden and Forest.*

31. Laura Wood Roper in an introductory note to Frederick Law Olmsted Sr., "The Yosemite Valley and the Mariposa Big Trees," *Landscape Architecture* 43, no. 1 (1953): 12–13.

32. Ise, *Our National Park Policy,* 18.

33. Statistics taken from Beatrice Ward Nelson, *State Recreation: Parks, Forests, and Game Preserves* (Washington, D.C: National Conference on State Parks, 1928); Newton, *Design on the Land,* 560–69.

34. National Park Service, *Proceedings of the National Parks Conference, Washington, D.C., January 2–6, 1917* (Washington, D.C.: GPO, 1917), 153–61.

35. Nelson, *State Recreation,* 4–5.

36. Ibid., 86; Newton, *Design on the Land,* 555–64.

37. *Annual Reports of the Department of the Interior, 1921* (Washington, D.C.: GPO, 1921), 56 (hereafter notes indicate references to annual reports by year and "AR"); P. H. Elwood Jr., ed., *American Landscape Architecture* (New York: Architectural Book Publishing Co., 1924), 168–70.

38. "Editorial: Outdoor Recreation," *Landscape Architecture* 14, no. 4 (1925): 287–88.

39. Nelson, *State Recreation,* 6; Raymond H. Torrey, *State Parks and Recreational Uses of State Forests in the United States* (Washington, D.C.: National Conference on State Parks, 1926); Herbert Evison, ed., *A State Park Anthology* (Washington, D.C.: National Conference on State Parks, 1930).

40. Laurie D. Cox, "Some Basic Principles of State Park Selection and Design," *Landscape Architecture* 22, no. 1 (1932): 11–13.

CHAPTER 2. AN AMERICAN STYLE OF NATURAL GARDENING

1. Waugh, *Natural Style*, 49–50.
2. Wilhelm Miller, *What England Can Teach Us about Gardening* (Garden City, N.Y.: Doubleday, Page, and Co., 1911), x, viii, 62.
3. Wilhelm Miller, *Prairie Spirit in Landscape Gardening*, Circular #184 (Urbana: Illinois Agricultural Experiment Station, 1915), 2, 5.
4. Jens Jensen, quoted in Miller, *Prairie Spirit*, 1–2.
5. Miller, *Prairie Spirit*, 11.
6. Bulletin on stratified rockwork was Circular 170 (Urbana: Illinois Agricultural Experiment Station).
7. Robert E. Grese, *Jens Jensen: Maker of Natural Parks and Gardens* (Baltimore: Johns Hopkins University Press, 1992), 106–10.
8. Ibid., 45–47; Catherine M. Howett, "Frank Lloyd Wright and American Residential Landscaping," *Landscape Journal* 26, no. 1 (1982): 33–40; Myron Hunt is probably best known for his design of the Rose Bowl (1932) in Pasadena.
9. Eugene O. Murmann, *California Gardens* (Los Angeles: Eugene Murmann, 1914), 7.
10. Gustav Stickley, "The Natural Garden: Some Things That Can Be Done When Nature Is Followed instead of Thwarted," in *Craftsman Homes*, ed. Gustav Stickley (New York: Craftsman Publishing House, 1909; reprint, New York: Dover Publications, 1979), 112–18.
11. "What May Be Done with Water and Rocks in a Little Garden." *Craftsman Homes*, 119–24.
12. Stickley, "Natural Garden," 118.
13. Tyrrell, *Artistic Bridge Design*, fig. 160.
14. Hubbard and Kimball, *Introduction*, ix–x. Hubbard classified the following styles: the Moorish style of Spain, the mogul style in India, the styles of the Italian Renaissance and baroque villas, the style of Le Notre (as apparent at Versailles and Vaux le Compte), the romantic landscape style, the English formal style of the Tudors (Dutch influence), the English cottage tyle, the New England colonial style, the modern German formal style, the Japanese styles, and finally, the modern American landscape style; the Newport garden is illustrated in plate 27.
15. Grese, *Jens Jensen*, 58; correspondence, Dorothy Waugh to Linda McClelland, 8 May 1989.
16. Waugh, *Natural Style*, 20, 24–25.
17. Parsons, *Art of Landscape Architecture*, 178.
18. Ossian Cole Simonds, *Landscape-Gardening*, Rural Science Series (New York: Macmillan Co., 1920; reprint, New York: Macmillan Co., 1931), 165.
19. Daniel Worster, *Nature's Economy: A History of Ecological Ideas*, 2d ed. (New York: Cambridge University Press, 1994), 205–20; Frederic E. Clements, *Dynamics of Vegetation: Selections from the Writings of Frederic E. Clements*, ed. B. W. Allred and Edith Clements (New York: H. W. Wilson Co., 1949), 272–73, originally published as "Ecology in the Public Service," *Ecology* 16, no. 3 (1935).

CHAPTER 3. SOURCES OF RUSTIC ARCHITECTURAL DESIGN

1. Information on the Shingle style features comes from Vincent J. Scully Jr., *The Shingle Style and the Stick Style* (New Haven: Yale University Press, 1977), 71–112.
2. James W. Steely, "Rustic Style in Depression Texas: Federal Architecture in the State Parks, 1933–1941" (M.S. thesis, University of Texas, Austin, 1985), 35–44; Zaitzevsky,

Frederick Law Olmsted, 166; Historic photographs, Franklin Park Files, Frederick Law Olmsted National Historic Site, Brookline, Mass.

3. Harvey H. Kaiser, *Great Camps of the Adirondacks* (Boston: David R. Godine, 1986), 12–13, 66.

4. Ibid., 65.

5. Ibid., 189–91; elevations are reproduced inside the back cover.

6. Augustus D. Shepard, *Camps in the Woods* (New York: Architectural Book Publishing Co., 1931), 1.

7. Hermann Valentin von Holst, *Modern American Homes* (Chicago: American Technical Society, 1913; reprinted as *Country and Suburban Homes of the Prairie School Period* (New York: Dover Publications, 1982), i.

8. Information on Japanese influences comes from Clay Lancaster, *The American Bungalow, 1880–1930* (New York: Abbeville Press, 1985), 122; Randell L. Makinson, *Greene and Greene: Architecture as a Fine Art* (Salt Lake City: Peregrine Smith Books, 1977), 32.

9. Lancaster, *American Bungalow,* 116; Makinson, *Greene and Greene,* 31.

10. Makinson, *Greene and Greene,* 70–73.

11. Ibid., 90–91; article was reprinted in *Craftsman Bungalows: 59 Homes from "The Craftsman,"* ed. Gustav Stickley (New York: Dover Publications, 1988), 40–43.

12. Stickley, *Craftsman Bungalows,* 40.

13. The Oaklawn Park designs by Greene and Greene are illustrated in Makinson, *Greene and Greene,* 113–15.

14. Monk's Hill shelter is illustrated in ibid., 187.

15. The Rudd and Pratt buildings are illustrated in Lancaster, *American Bungalow,* 132.

16. Makinson, *Greene and Greene,* 222.

17. Elmer Grey, "Some Country House Architecture in the Far West," *Architectural Record* 52, no. 289 (1922), quoted in Makinson, *Greene and Greene,* 226.

18. Makinson, *Greene and Greene,* 246–47.

19. For further explanation of the English influence on the work of Maybeck and other Bay Area architects, see Richard Longstreth, *On the Edge of the World: Four Architects in San Francisco at the Turn of the Century* (Cambridge: MIT Press, 1983).

20. Kenneth H. Cardwell, *Bernard Maybeck: Artisan, Architect, Artist* (Salt Lake City: Peregrine Smith Books, 1977), 153–55.

21. Laura Soullière Harrison, *Architecture in the Parks National Historic Landmark Theme Study* (Washington, D.C.: National Park Service, 1986), 77–80.

22. Ibid., 177; Cardwell, *Bernard Maybeck,* 185–86.

23. Harrison, *Architecture in the Parks,* 10, 62–69.

24. Virginia Grattan, *Mary Colter: Builder upon the Red Earth* (Flagstaff, Ariz.: Northland Press, 1980), 2, 26, 73.

25. Stickley, *Craftsman Homes,* 102–12.

26. Gustav Stickley, ed., *More Craftsman Homes* (New York: Craftsman Publishing House, 1912; reprint, New York: Dover Publications, 1982), 146–63.

27. William Phillips Comstock and Clarence Eaton Schermerhorn, *Bungalows, Camps, and Mountain Houses* (New York: W. T. Comstock Co., 1915; reprint, Washington, D.C.: American Institute of Architects Press, 1990), 26–27.

28. Ibid., 28, 30–31; Robert Winter, *The California Bungalow* (Los Angeles: Hennessey and Ingalls, 1980), 41.

CHAPTER 4. SCENERY PRESERVATION AND LANDSCAPE ENGINEERING

1. The National Park Service Act of August 25, 1916 (39 Stat. 535), established the National Park Service. The following year Stephen T. Mather was appointed the first director of the National Park Service, and Horace M. Albright was appointed assistant director.

2. National Park Service, *Proceedings of the National Parks Conference, Berkeley, California, March 11–13, 1915* (Washington, D.C.: GPO, 1915), 20 (hereafter cited as "*Proceedings, 1915*).

3. Stephen T. Mather, *Progress in the Development of the National Parks* (Washington, D.C.: GPO, 1916), 9, 19.

4. *Proceedings, 1915*, 17–19.

5. National Park Service, *Proceedings of the National Parks Conference*, 1.

6. 1917 *AR*, 26, 81.

7. 1918 *AR*, 815, 1076.

8. 1919 *AR*, 939; Punchard visited Yellowstone, Yosemite, Grand Canyon, Rocky Mountain, Mount Rainier, Crater Lake, Sequoia and General Grant, and Hawaii and inspected several national monuments.

9. Charles P. Punchard Jr., "Landscape Design in the National Park Service," *Landscape Architecture* 10, no. 3 (1920): 144–45.

10. 1919 *AR*, 1175.	11. 1922 *AR*, 34.
12. 1919 *AR*, 941.	13. 1920 *AR*, 339.
14. 1919 *AR*, 1081.	15. 1920 *AR*, 339.
16. 1919 *AR*, 1176.	17. 1921 *AR*, 275; 1920 *AR*, 256, 337.
18. 1920 *AR*, 93.	19. 1919 *AR*, 1081.
20. 1920 *AR*, 332.	21. 1919 *AR*, 1180.
22. Ibid., 987, 1177–78; 1920 *AR*, 336.	23. 1920 *AR*, 95.
24. 1920 *AR*, 94, 333; 1921 *AR*, 274.	25. 1920 *AR*, 95, 995.
26. 1919 *AR*, 1178.	27. 1920 *AR*, 332.
28. 1919 *AR*, 940.	29. Ibid., 966; 1920 *AR*, 211.
30. 1920 *AR*, 94.	31. 1919 *AR*, 1181; 1920 *AR*, 332.
32. 1920 *AR*, 336, 338.	

33. Official correspondence, Mather to Punchard, January 31, 1920, Record Group 79, National Archives, Washington, D.C.

34. Official correspondence, Punchard to Mather, February 6, 1920, Record Group 79, National Archives, Washington, D.C.

35. 1920 *AR*, 336.	36. 1919 *AR*, 1179.
37. 1920 *AR*, 333.	38. 1919 *AR*, 941.

CHAPTER 5. ACCOMMODATING THE PUBLIC

1. Daniel Ray Hull was born in 1890 in Lincoln, Kansas, and died in Alahambra, California, in 1964. After graduating from Harvard, Hull went to work for the landscape engineering firm of Daniels, Osmont, and Wilhelm in San Francisco. During World War I, he worked as a camp and hospital planner, and he was working in Milwaukee, Wisconsin, in 1920 when he became Punchard's assistant. Hull remained in California after leaving the National Park Service in 1927; he worked for Olmsted Jr. on the California State Parks Survey and was a designer for the California park system for many years. Biographical information has been gathered from telephone interviews, October 2, 1993, with Robert Chapel, University of Illinois, Urbana-Champaign, and James McCarthy, Harvard Archives, Harvard University; *Harvard Alumni Bulletin,*

November 18, 1914; and *Quinquennial Catalogue of the Officers and Graduates, Harvard University, 1636–1930* (Cambridge: Harvard University, 1930).

2. Paul Peter Kiessig received a B.S. in agriculture with a specialty in drafting from the University of Illinois, Urbana-Champaign, in 1916. In the same year he went to work as a draftsman for an airplane experiment station in Dayton, Ohio. He worked for the National Park Service from 1921 to 1923. He was born in San Diego in 1887 and died in Vista, California, in 1967. It appears that Kiessig and Gilbert Stanley Underwood worked together in California, where they became close friends. They both entered the University of Illinois in 1912, where Underwood and possibly Kiessig met Hull. Biographical information was gathered from a telephone interview, October 2, 1992, with Robert Chapel, University of Illinois, Urbana-Champaign, and Joyce Zaitlin, *Gilbert Stanley Underwood* (Malibu, Calif.: Pangloss Press, 1989), 8–14.

3. 1920 *AR*, 93; *Quinquennial Catalog*.

4. Paul Kiessig, "Landscape Engineering in the National Parks," December 2, 1922, Record Group 79, National Archives, San Bruno, Calif.

5. 1921 *AR*, 278. 6. Kiessig, "Landscape Engineering."

7. 1922 *AR*, 34. 8. 1921 *AR*, 57.

9. Kiessig, "Landscape Engineering." 10. 1923 *AR*, 40.

11. William Tweed, Laura E. Soullière, and Henry G. Law, "National Park Service Rustic Architecture: 1916–1942" (National Park Service, Western Regional Office, San Francisco, 1977), 30; 1920 *AR*, 96. The inspiration of this building has been attributed to Colter's work at Phantom Ranch, which was at the mouth of Bright Angel Creek.

12. 1923 *AR*, 39–40.

13. 1926 *AR*, 155.

14. 1921 *AR*, 169.

15. Herbert Maier, "The Purpose of the Museum in the National Parks," *Yosemite Nature Notes* 5, no. 5 (1926): 37–40; quote is from p. 38 and also appears in Tweed, Soullière, and Law, "Rustic Architecture," 39–41.

16. Harrison, *Architecture in the Parks*, 212–19.

17. 1926 *AR*, 157.

18. Tweed, Soullière, and Law, "Rustic Architecture," 30–31.

19. Zaitlin, *Gilbert Stanley Underwood*, 11, 14, 42–48; Tweed, Soullière, and Law, "Rustic Architecture," 41–44.

20. Zaitlin, *Gilbert Stanley Underwood*, 35–42; 1925 *AR*, 132.

21. 1925 *AR*, 135.

22. Ise, *Our National Park Policy*, 30, 127; Mary Shivers Culpin, *The History of the Construction of the Road System in Yellowstone National Park, 1872–1966*, Historic Resource Study, vol. 1 (Denver: Rocky Mountain Region, National Park Service, 1994), 43–68.

23. Culpin, *Road System in Yellowstone*, 50.

24. Dwight A. Smith, Columbia River Highway Historic District, NRHP Inventory-Nomination Form (National Park Service, National Register of Historic Places, Washington, D.C.), October 3, 1983.

25. Requirement for grade comes from Vint to Mather, official correspondence, August 14, 1928, Record Group 79, National Archives, Washington, D.C.

26. 1921 *AR*, 57.

27. Hubbard and Kimball, *Introduction*, 220; U.S. Forest Service, *Specifications for Forest Road Construction* (Washington D.C.: GPO, 1927); Harwood Frost, *The Art of Roadmaking: Treating of the Various Problems and Operations in the Construction*

and Maintenance of Roads, Streets, and Pavements (New York: McGraw-Hill, 1910); Arthur H. Blanchard and Henry B. Drowne, *Text-book on Highway Engineering: A Comprehensive Text-book for Students and a Reference Work for Engineers* (New York: John Wiley and Sons, 1913).

28. Hubbard and Kimball, *Introduction,* 310–11.

29. 1921 *AR,* 57; 1923 *AR,* 279. Despite its scenic grandeur, this road would prove vulnerable to flooding and thus was difficult and costly to maintain. Floods in 1924 necessitated emergency appropriations to construct log-crib revetments and diversion cribs as an effort to "save" the road. As a result of glacial flow, winter avalanches, and the like, the road never became the popular tourist route envisioned by Mather as early as 1916.

30. Hubbard and Kimball, *Introduction,* 222.

31. Waugh, *Natural Style,* 120–21.

32. Index of Waugh's Manuscripts, University of Massachusetts Archives, Amherst; Frederick Steiner, "Frank Waugh," in Tishler, *American Landscape Architecture,* 101–3.

33. Waugh, *Natural Style,* 82–83, 90–91.

34. Hubbard and Kimball, *Introduction,* 219–20.

35. 1925 *AR,* 136.

36. 1926 *AR,* 17; 1925 *AR,* 79.

37. 43 Stat. 90; Official correspondence, Demaray to John J. Blaine, U.S. Senate, October 10, 1927, Record Group 79, National Archives, Washington, D.C.

38. Ise, *Our National Park Policy,* 3237; 1931 *AR,* 111.

39. 1925 *AR,* 78–79.

40. 1926 *AR,* 155; "Memorandum of Agreement between the National Park Service and the Bureau of Public Roads Relating to the Survey, Construction, and Improvement of Roads and Trails in the National Parks and Monuments," January 18, 1926, no. 100072, Record Group 79, National Archives, Washington, D.C.

41. "Memorandum of Agreement."

42. Ibid.

43. Ibid.

44. Although revision to the interbureau agreement was considered to incorporate the chief engineer as a principal in preliminary planning and in the execution of road projects, having authority over the landscape engineer for the general approval of basic provisions, the director instead reorganized the San Francisco office, assigning to both Vint and Kittredge specific roles in the roads program. Official correspondence, Demaray to Albright, February 9, 1928, and Albright to Demaray, no date, ca. January 1928, Record Group 79, National Archives, Washington, D.C.

45. Mather in 1926 *AR,* 15–16. "Landscape protection" mentioned in earlier reports is now called "preservation of park scenery."

CHAPTER 6. PRINCIPLES AND PRACTICES FOR NATURALISTIC
ROADS AND TRAILS

1. Office Order, undated, Record Group 79, National Archives, Washington, D.C.

2. Ibid.

3. William G. Carnes, "Profiles of NPS 'Greats': Tom Vint," *Courier* 3, no. 9 (1980): 23.

4. "Personnel Information Sheet" for Thomas Chalmers Vint, U.S. Civil Service Commission, July 1940, Form 3464, Files of Charles E. Peterson, NRHP, Historic Landscape files, Washington, D.C.

5. Ibid.

6. Ibid.

7. Tweed, Soullière, and Law, "Rustic Architecture," 47.

8. Job Description for Assistant and Junior Landscape Architects, n.d., ca. June 1928, 1–2. Record Group 79, National Archives, Washington, D.C.; Tweed, Soullière, and Law, "Rustic Architecture," credits Sager with assisting Vint on the civil service standards.

9. Job Description, 1–2.

10. Job Analysis, Assistant Landscape Architect, n.d., ca. June 1928, Record Group 79, National Archives, Washington, D.C.

11. Official correspondence, Vint to Director, June 9, 1928, Record Group 79, National Archives, Washington, D.C.

12. 1929 *AR*, 163.

13. Ibid., 165; official correspondence, Vint to Albright, June 1929, Record Group 79, National Archives, Washington, D.C.

14. 1930 *AR*, 186.

15. Memorandum, Elliot to engineers in charge of park work, October 17, 1928, Record Group 79, National Archives, Washington, D.C.

16. General Provisions, Albright to Vint, June 16, 1929, Record Group 79, National Archives, Washington, D.C.

17. 1929 *AR*, 165; official correspondence, Mather to MacDonald, August 16, 1928, Record Group 79, National Archives, Washington, D.C.

18. Memorandum, Kittredge to Vint, October 27, 1928, Record Group 79, National Archives, Washington, D.C.

19. General Provisions of June 1929, Albright to Vint, June 16, 1929, Record Group 79, National Archives, Washington, D.C.

20. Memorandum, Vint to staff, June 8, 1929, Record Group 79, National Archives, Washington, D.C.

21. Correspondence, Albright to Vint, June 16, 1929, Record Group 79, National Archives, Washington, D.C.

22. John C. Olmsted, "The Treatment of Slopes and Banks," *Garden and Forest,* September 5, 1888, 326–27.

23. Hubbard and Kimball, *Introduction,* 149–50.

24. Official correspondence, Carpenter to Hewes, February 10, 1931, Record Group 79, National Archives, Washington, D.C.; official correspondence, Vint to Director, March 20, 1931, Record Group 79, National Archives, Washington, D.C.

25. 1932 *AR,* 28; 1932 *AR,* 28, 182; Plan 2015, February 23, 1938; Plan 2010, August 19, 1937, National Park Service, Denver Service Center, Technical Information Center.

26. Hubbard and Kimball, *Introduction,* 149–50.

27. Frank Albert Waugh, "Ecology of the Roadside," *Landscape Architecture* 21, no. 2 (1931): 81–92.

28. Landscape architect's reports, Davidson to Vint, 1927, Record Group 79, National Archives, San Bruno, Calif.

29. "1930 Fieldwork on Naturalization Data Requested," Record Group 79, National Archives, Washington, D.C.

30. 1931 *AR,* 131.

31. Report to Thomas Vint on Emergency Conservation Work in Mount Rainier National Park—1934 Season, Third Enrollment Period, Record Group 79, National Archives, Washington, D.C.

32. Hubbard and Kimball, *Introduction,* 198–99.

33. Ibid., 221 and illustration 28.

34. General Provisions of June 1929, Albright to Vint, June 16, 1929, Record Group 79, National Archives, Washington, D.C.

35. Hubbard and Kimball, *Introduction,* 199.

36. PG AP-3-2 sheets, December 16, 1929, National Park Service, Denver Service Center, Technical Information Center.

37. Quote is from Hubbard and Kimball, *Introduction,* 200.

38. PG 2042 and PG 2043, 1942, National Park Service, Denver Service Center, Technical Information Center.

39. NP-Yos-50, July 18, 1921, National Park Service, Denver Service Center, Technical Information Center; this design was similar to the Swan Bridge in Central Park.

40. 1928 *AR,* 165.

41. White River Bridge, Mount Rainier, June 14, 1928, Drawing R-814, National Park Service, Denver Service Center, Technical Information Center; *AR* 1928, 165.

42. White River Bridge, Drawing R-814.

43. Official correspondence, Carpenter to Albright, July 31, 1931, Record Group 79, National Archives, Washington, D.C.; Portfolio of Representative Park Structures, ca. 1932, National Park Service Historic Photography Collection, Harpers Ferry, W.Va.

44. Standard Architectural Details—Headwalls for Culverts, August 24, 1928, AP-81, National Park Service, Denver Service Center, Technical Information Center.

45. Ibid.

46. Draft report, Meeting of the Committee of Expert Advisers, Yosemite National Park, April 24–25, 1930, 1–2, F. L. Olmsted Jr. Job 8099, National Park Service, Frederick Law Olmsted National Historic Site.

47. Official correspondence, Albright to Vint, October 16, 1930, Record Group 79, National Archives, Washington, D.C.

48. The Mount Vernon Parkway was added to the National Park System by executive order in 1933.

49. 1929 *AR,* 30; 1931 *AR,* 111.

50. 1929 *AR,* 19.

51. 1930 *AR,* 187–88.

52. Dr. L. I. Hewes, in National Park Service, "Minutes of the Twelfth Conference of National Park Executives, Hot Springs National Park, Arkansas, April 3 to 8, 1932," document 65378 (National Park Service, Washington, D.C., mimeo.), 113.; the same year in *Civil Engineering,* Hewes credited the Landscape Division with "guiding the design of Bureau of Public Roads" and with influencing the state highways of western states; L. I. Hewes, "America's Park Highways," *Civil Engineering* 2 (1932), quoted in Culpin, *Road System in Yellowstone,* n. 25.

53. Hubbard, "Landscape Development," 108.

54. Report of the National Interregional Highway Committee, 1944, quoted in Christopher Tunnard and Boris Pushkarev, *Man-made America: Chaos or Control?* (New Haven: Yale University Press, 1963), 222.

55. Ibid., 222.

56. Informal notes, Harold Caparn to Superintendent Albright, 1926, Record Group 79, National Archives, Washington, D.C.

57. Informal correspondence, Davidson to Wosky, July 8, 1927, Record Group 79, National Archives, Washington, D.C.

58. Sanford Hill, "Final Narrative Report to the Chief Architect," Yellowstone National Park, Summer 1936, Record Group 79, National Archives, Washington, D.C.

59. William Tweed, National Register of Historic Places Inventory-Nomination Form for Moro Rock Stairway, May 29, 1977.

60. Ibid.

61. Ptarmigan Wall Tunnel, Drawing S4934, Glacier National Park, National Park Service, Denver Service Center, Technical Information Center.

62. Official memorandum, Kenneth McCarter to Superintendent Toll, August 30, 1929, Record Group 79, National Archives, Washington, D.C.

63. Horace M. Albright, "Picturesque America Seen from Trails in National Parks," *U.S. Daily* (Washington, D.C.), November 18, 1929.

64. Engineering Division, "Standards for Trail Construction," San Francisco, Calif., PG 5088, October 1934, National Park Service, Denver Service Center, Technical Information Center.

65. Ibid.

66. Ibid.

CHAPTER 7.   PARK ARCHITECTURE, LANDSCAPE NATURALIZATION, AND CAMPGROUND DEVELOPMENT

1. 1930 *AR,* 186; official correspondence, Vint to All Superintendents, September 5, 1930, Record Group 79, National Archives, Washington, D.C.; official correspondence, A. E. Demaray to P. J. Jennings, September 1931, Record Group 79, National Archives, Washington, D.C.; sheets were numbered A 912-A, B, and C, National Park Service, Denver Service Center, Technical Information Center.

2. 1931 *AR,* 130.

3. Albert H. Good, *Park Structures and Facilities* (Washington, D.C.: National Park Service, 1935); National Park Service, *Portfolio of Housekeeping Cabins,* PG-3032 (Washington, D.C.: Branch of Plans and Designs, n.d. [ca. 1934]).

4. Press Release, U.S. Department of the Interior, December 12, 1930, Record Group 79, National Archives, Washington, D.C.

5. "Portfolio of Representative Structures Designed by the Landscape Division, National Park Service" (Landscape Division, National Park Service, San Francisco, n.d., ca. 1932).

6. Good, *Park Structures and Facilities,* 176; Mary Shivers Culpin, NRHP Inventory-Nomination Form for Obsidian Cliff Kiosk, Historic Resources of Yellowstone National Park, November 30, 1981.

7. 1920 *AR,* 337.

8. Frank Albert Waugh, *Outdoor Theaters: The Design, Construction, and Use of Open-Air Auditoriums* (Boston: Richard G. Badger, 1917); this illustrated several well-known outdoor theaters, including those at the University of California, Berkeley, and Pomona State College.

9. 1932 *AR,* 109.

10. The Forestry Division was also concerned with insect control and measures to bring white pine blister rust and other forest infestations under control.

11. 1925 *AR,* 136.

12. Official correspondence, Vint to F. E. Kannermeyer, May 3, 1927, Record Group 79, National Archives, Washington, D.C.

13. Report to Landscape Division, September 5-15, 1927, Record Group 79, National Archives, San Bruno, Calif.; Report to Landscape Division, October 5-22, 1927, Record

Group 79, National Archives, San Bruno, Calif.; the list of plants has been compiled from Jerry F. Franklin and C. T. Dyrness, *Natural Vegetation of Oregon and Washington,* General Technical Report PNW-8 (Portland, Oreg.: Pacific Northwest Forest and Range Experiment Station, U.S. Department of Agriculture, 1973), and Jerry F. Franklin et al., *The Forest Communities of Mount Rainier National Park,* Scientific Monograph Series no. 19 (Washington, D.C.: National Park Service, 1988).

14. Landscape Architect's Report, Davidson to Vint, Spring 1928, Record Group 79, National Archives, San Bruno, Calif.

15. Correspondence, Tomlinson to All Residents of Mount Rainier Park, August 25, 1928, Record Group 79, National Archives, Washington, D.C.

16. Landscape Report, September 1928, Record Group 79, National Archives, San Bruno, Calif.

17. Correspondence, Davidson to Vint, October 11, 1928, Record Group 79, National Archives, San Bruno, Calif.; Information about the Douglas fir on the front lawn is drawn from a comparison of photographs from 1928 to 1932.

18. Landscape Report, October 10 to November 15, 1929, Record Group 79, National Archives, San Bruno, Calif.; Landscape Report, June 1–8, 1929, Record Group 79, National Archives, San Bruno, Calif.

19. The figures are taken from Davidson's "Landscape Transplanting Costs," which was included in the 1930 Naturalization Data Request, August 14, 1929, Record Group 79, National Archives, Washington, D.C. The names of plants are taken from Davidson's landscape reports; the plant lists for Longmire compiled by Lora J. Schiltgen, "Managing a Rustic Legacy: A Historic Landscape Study and Management Plan for Longmire Springs Historic District, Mount Rainier National Park" (M.L.A. thesis, University of Oregon, Eugene, June 1986), 118–22: and the recent plant ecology for the Longmire area as reported in Franklin et al., *Forest Communities of Mount Rainier.*

20. 1930 *AR,* 134.

21. Hubbard and Kimball, *Introduction,* 186.

22. Ibid., 182; Shepard, *Camps in the Woods,* 26–28, 78–79.

23. Hubbard and Kimball, *Introduction,* 187.

24. Official correspondence, Albright to Vint, May 21, 1929, Record Group 79, National Archives, Washington, D.C. Although the complete report seems to have been lost, sheets of mounted and labeled photographs on this work exist in the collection at the Mount Rainier National Park Library.

25. Vint to Resident Landscape Architects, "1930 Fieldwork on Naturalization Data Requested," Record Group 79, National Archives, Washington, D.C.

26. Ibid.

27. Ibid.

28. 1930 *AR,* 31.

29. Cathy Gilbert and Gretchen Luxenberg, *The Rustic Landscape of Rim Village, 1927–1941* (Seattle: Pacific Northwest Region, National Park Service, 1991), 67–79.

30. Merel S. Sager, "Report on Naturalization in the Rim Area, Crater Lake National Park," November 18, 1932, reproduced in Gilbert and Luxenberg, *Rustic Landscape,* 181–83.

31. Memorandum, Albright to All Superintendents and Concessionaires, November 11, 1930, National Archives, Record Group 79, Washington, D.C.

32. Joseph Grinnell and Tracy L. Storer, "Animal Life as an Asset of National Parks," *Science* 44, no. 1133 (1916): 375–80; Charles C. Adams, of the New York State College of Forestry, "The Relation of Wild Life to the Public in National and State Parks," in

National Park Service, *Proceedings of the Second National Conference on State Parks, 1922* (Washington, D.C.: National Park Service, 1922), 129–47.

33. Memorandum, Bryant to Albright, November 11, 1930, Record Group 79, National Archives, Washington, D.C.

34. Correspondence, Tomlinson to Albright, May 7, 1930, Record Group 79, National Archives, Washington, D.C.

35. Correspondence, Vint to Bryant, November 4, 1930, Record Group 79, National Archives, Washington, D.C.

36. 1932 *AR*, 8; CCC Handbook, Washington, D.C., undated, U.S. Department of the Interior, Natural Resources Library, Washington, D.C.; a memorandum issued to the CCC in 1935 reemphasizing the prohibition of introduced species made an exception for historic units of the National Park Service, many of which were added to the park system in 1933 and afterward.

37. Memorandum on the Ahwahnee Development, November 29, 1927, Job 8099, Yosemite National Park, National Park Service, Frederick Law Olmsted National Historic Site.

38. Ibid., 8–9.; P. R. Jones, Report of Visit, The Ahwahnee, Yosemite National Park, November 4–7, 1927, National Park Service, Frederick Law Olmsted National Historic Site.

39. 1929 *AR*, 18; when Davidson visited Yosemite in 1929, he was impressed by the splendid display of azaleas.

40. 1929 *AR*, 18; quote is from Master Plan, Mount Rainier, sheet 13, ca. 1937, National Archives, College Park, Maryland.

41. 1931 *AR*, 135.

42. Maier, "Purpose of the Museum in the National Parks"; Mabel E. Hibbard, "The Yosemite Museum Flower Show," *Yosemite Nature Notes* 6, no. 9 (1927), 65–67.

43. C. Edward Graves, "Dry or 'Moraine' Rock Garden at Yosemite Museum," *Yosemite Nature Notes* 9, no. 10 (1930), 89–91; Enid Michael, "Nature Garden a New Feature of Yosemite Museum," *Yosemite Nature Notes* 11, no. 10 (1932), 4–5.

44. Enid Michael, "Roadside Planting of the New Wawona Highway," *Yosemite Nature Notes* 13, no. 12 (1933), 113–14.

45. 1931 *AR*, 72.

46. 1930 *AR*, 31.

47. Memorandum, Cammerer to All Superintendents, August 30. 1930, Record Group 79, National Archives, Washington, D.C.

48. Lester Rowntree, *Flowering Shrubs of California and Their Value to the Gardener* (Stanford: Stanford University Press, 1939), vi–vii.

49. Emilio P. Meinecke, "Memorandum on the Effects of Tourist Traffic on Plant Life, Particularly Big Trees, Sequoia National Park, California," report in Sequoia–Kings Canyon Archives (May 1926), cited in Lary M. Dilsaver and William C. Tweed, *The Challenge of the Big Trees: A Resource History of Sequoia and Kings Canyon National Parks* (Three Rivers, Calif.: Sequoia Natural History Association, 1990), 144–45, 148–49.

50. E. P. Meinecke, *A Camp Ground Policy* (Ogden, Utah: U.S. Forest Service, U.S. Department of Agriculture, 1932), 1, cited E. P. Meinecke, "A Report upon the Excessive Tourist Travel on the California Redwood Parks" (California Department of Natural Resources, Division of Parks, Sacramento, 1928).

51. Official correspondence, Kittredge to Meinecke, January 30, 1935, Record Group 79, National Archives, Washington, D.C.

52. E. P. Meinecke, *Camp Planning and Camp Reconstruction* (n.p.: U.S. Forest Service, U.S. Department of Agriculture, n.d. [ca. 1934]), 8.

53. Meeting of the Committee of Expert Advisers, Yosemite National Park, draft of report, April 24–25, 1930, 13–14, by F. L. Olmsted Jr., Job 8099, National Park Service, Frederick Law Olmsted National Historic Site.

54. 1931 *AR*, 80.

55. 1932 *AR*, 7–9.

56. 1932 *AR*, 34.

CHAPTER 8.   A PROCESS FOR PARK PLANNING

1. National Park Service, "Minutes of the Twelfth Conference," 92; 1926 *AR*, 155.

2. Crater Lake Five Year Development Program, 1927, Record Group 79, National Archives, Washington, D.C.

3. "General Planning," Tentative Outline, February 1929, Record Group 79, National Archives, Washington, D.C.

4. 1929 *AR*, 163.

5. "General Planning," 1.

6. "Outline for Park Development," Mount Rainier National Park, enclosed in correspondence Vint to Tomlinson, August 19, 1927, Record Group 79, National Archives, Washington, D.C.

7. 1932 *AR*, 27.

8. Superintendent's Monthly Report, July 3, 1930, Record Group 79, National Archives, Washington, D.C.; 1930 *AR*, 30; General Development Plan, Mammoth Hot Springs, June 11, 1932, Record Group 79, National Archives, College Park, Maryland; A plan in 1940 shows that the plan did not evolve as Clarke envisioned it. The green that dominated the entrance to the village took an irregular form with curved edges and beveled corners. The concessioner developed a series of separate buildings, lodge, dining hall, and cabin courts to the rear in place of a large radiating hotel complex. The pair of U-shaped dormitories planned to house the park's many rangers were modified into an I-shaped building that would be repeated alongside to form a pair as demand arose and money permitted. The power house was built to the southwest and the campground developed in two distinctive sections according to designs worked out by the Branch of Plans and Design for tent camping and trailer camping. The museum was placed in the administration building in row with the superintendent's building. A new administration building was planned to face the planted boulevard alongside the post office. PWA funds were used in the construction of the rangers' dormitories and utility building. The CCC in the mid-1930s carried out an extensive program of planting around the new buildings and throughout the village.

9. National Park Service, "Minutes of the Twelfth Conference," 94.

10. Thomas C. Vint, "National Park Service: Master Plans," *Planning and Civic Comment* (April/June 1946); reprint (hereafter cited as "Vint, 'Master Plans'").

11. Ibid.

12. Park Development Outline, 1929, 9, Record Group 79, National Archives, Washington, D.C.; the sentiment for the wilderness movement which finally culminated in the 1964 Wilderness Act began in the Progressive Era: Frederick Law Olmsted Jr. called for such areas to be set aside in parks and forests following his tour of the West in the early 1920s.

13. 1929 *AR*, 19.

14. Mather, official correspondence, July 1928, Record Group 79, National Archives, Washington, D.C.; memorandum, Cammerer to Washington and Field Offices, April 3, 1936; Bryant in National Park Service, "Minutes of the Twelfth Conference," 97; S. Charles Kendeigh, "Research Areas in the National Parks, January 1942," *Ecology* 23, no. 2 (April 1942).

15. Memorandum, Vint to Albright, September 9, 1927, Record Group 79, National Archives, Washington, D.C.; quote is from Master Plan, Yellowstone National Park, n.d., ca. 1935, D.O 3146-G-2, Record Group 79, National Archives, Washington, D.C.

16. Memorandum, Superintendent Thomson, Yosemite National Park, to the Director, October 3, 1930, National Park Service, Frederick Law Olmsted National Historic Site; quote is from the Master Plan, Yosemite National Park, sheet 35, Record Group 79, National Archives, College Park, Maryland.

17. Master Plan, Mount Rainier, 1933, Record Group 79, National Archives, College Park, Maryland.

18. Ibid.

19. Ibid.

20. Master Plan, Mount Rainier, 1938, Record Group 79, National Archives, College Park, Maryland.

21. H. T. Thompson and L. E. Garrison, "Master Planning in National Parks," essay, n.d., ca. 1942, Record Group 79, National Archives, Washington, D.C.

22. National Park Service, *Master Plans: A Manual of Standard Practice for Use in the National Park Service* (Washington, D.C.: National Park Service, 1939).

23. Hubbard, "Landscape Development," 108.

24. Vint, "Master Plans."

25. Material for this section has been drawn from E. A. Davidson, "Landscape Work in Connection with the Development of the Yakima Park Area, Including the Approach Highway within Mt. Rainier National Park," A Report to Thomas C. Vint, Chief Landscape Architect, National Park Service, n.d., ca 1932, National Park Service, Columbia Cascades System Office, Seattle, Wash.; 1928–32 *AR;* Landscape architects' and superintendents' annual reports from 1928 to 1932, Record Group 79, National Archives, Washington, D.C., and San Bruno, Calif.

26. Davidson, "Landscape Work."

27. Quote is from ibid.

28. Davidson, "Landscape Work." Quotations in subsequent paragraphs are from this work, unless otherwise indicated.

29. Quote is from ibid.

30. Official correspondence, Vint to Tomlinson, October 20, 1929, Record Group 79, National Archives, Washington, D.C.

31. Davidson, "Landscape Work."

32. Ibid.

33. Ibid.

34. 1931 General Development Plan for Mount Rainier, Record Group 79, National Archives, Washington, D.C.; 1930 *AR*, 129.

35. Davidson, "Landscape Work."

CHAPTER 9. A DECADE OF NATIONAL PARK DEVELOPMENT

1. National Archives, *Records of the Public Works Administration,* Preliminary Inventory no. 125 (Washington, D.C.: National Archives and Records Service), 3. Ickes held this

position in tandem with his position at the Department of the Interior until 1939, when the agency was replaced by the Federal Works Agency and restructured under the Reorganization Act of 1939.

2. 1933 *AR*, 181.

3. Russ Olson, *Administrative History: Organizational Structures of the National Park Service, 1917 to 1985* (Washington, D.C.: National Park Service, 1985), chart 10; National Park Service, "Report on the Building Program from Allotments of the Public Works Administration, 1933–1937, Western Division" (San Francisco: National Park Service, 1938), 8. The report was compiled by Edward Nickel, architect, Branch of Plans and Design.

4. National Park Service, "Building Program from Allotments of the Public Works Administration," 10.

5. John C. Paige, *The Civilian Conservation Corps and the National Park Service, 1933–1942: An Administrative History* (Washington, D.C.: National Park Service, 1985), 15–17, 39; 1933 *AR*, 157.

6. Official correspondence, Owen Tomlinson to All Camp Superintendents, June 10, 1933, Record Group 79, National Archives, Washington, D.C.

7. Paige, *Civilian Conservation Corps,* 9–11.

8. Ibid., 18; quote is from 1933 *AR*, 157.

9. Paige, *Civilian Conservation Corps,* 19, 21–23; Paige says that the 1936 personnel reduction was partly an economy measure but also partly an effort by President Roosevelt to create a smaller agency that might be made permanent.

10. Official correspondence, Tomlinson to All Camp Superintendents, Mount Rainier National Park, June 10, 1933, Record Group 79, National Archives, Washington, D.C. Tomlinson's letter clearly echoed the 1918 and 1932 statements of policy.

11. Ibid.

12. Narrative Report, period ending September 30, 1934, Camp NP-2, Grand Teton National Park, Record Group 79, National Archives, Washington, D.C.

13. C. G. Thomson, "Summary of Work to Be Accomplished by Civilian Conservation Corps, Yosemite National Park," n.d., Record Group 79, National Archives, Washington, D.C.

14. "Emergency Conservation Work Programmed for Mount Rainier Park," July 3, 1933, Record Group 79, National Archives, Washington, D.C.; "Roosevelt's Tree Soldiers," *Tacoma Daily Ledger,* November 29, 1933; "Emergency Conservation Work, Mount Rainier National Park, Pictorial Record for Final Report, 1933," Record Group 79, National Archives, Washington, D.C. (hereafter cited as "Mount Rainier National Park, Pictorial Record, 1933")

15. Mount Rainier National Park, Pictorial Record, 1933.

16. Halsey M. Davidson, Report on ECW work at Mount Rainier National Park, Third Period Work, 1934, Record Group 79, National Archives, Washington, D.C.

17. ECW Narrative Report, White River Camp, NP-5, Mount Rainier National Park, 1935, Record Group 79, National Archives, Washington, D.C.; plan of amphitheater, R-3056, by Halsey Davidson, October 10, 1933, National Park Service, Denver Service Center, Technical Information Center.

18. Ibid.

19. Ibid.

20. Ibid.

21. "Statement of Operating Conditions for Associate Director A. E. Demaray," July 18, 1935, Record Group 79, National Archives, Washington, D.C.

22. Owen A. Tomlinson, Report on ECW activities, Mount Rainier National Park, August 1934, Record Group 79, National Archives, Washington, D.C.; Russell L. McKown, ECW Narrative Report, Mount Rainier National Park, 1934 season, Record Group 79, National Archives, Washington, D.C.

23. Ibid.

24. ECW Narrative Report, May and June 1934, Camp NP-1, Mount Rainier National Park, 11, Record Group 79, National Archives, Washington, D.C.

25. Final Report, Comfort Station, PWA Project FP-68, Ranger Station, PWA Project FP-71, February 1934, Denver Service Center, Technical Information Center.

26. ECW Quarterly Report, Wawona Camp, NP-1, Yosemite National Park, July 1934, Record Group 79, National Archives, Washington, D.C. Because this report gave only vague common names, the attributions of genus and species have been drawn from Willis Linn Jepson, *A Manual of the Flowering Plants of California* (1925; Berkeley: University of California Press, 1970), and "Landscape Plants for Yosemite Park," Files of the Planning Office, Yosemite National Park, Mimeo.

27. ECW Quarterly Report, Wawona Camp, NP-1, Yosemite National Park, October 1934, Record Group 79, National Archives, Washington, D.C.

28. ECW Quarterly Report, Cascades Camp, NP-6, Yosemite National Park, April 1934, Record Group 79, National Archives, Washington, D.C.

29. ECW Quarterly Report, Wawona Camp, NP-1, Yosemite National Park, October 1935, Record Group 79, National Archives, Washington, D.C.; R. L. McKown, Final Narrative Report, Yosemite National Park, Seventh Period ECW, April 1, 1936, through September 30, 1936, Record Group 79, National Archives, Washington, D.C. (hereafter cited as "McKown, Final Narrative Report, Yosemite").

30. Rowntree, *Flowering Shrubs of California,* 152.

31. Harold Fowler, "Report to Chief Architect, Sequoia National Park, October 1, 1934, to April 1, 1935," Record Group 79, National Archives, Washington, D.C.

32. Ibid.

33. ECW Quarterly Report, Camp NP-2, Yosemite National Park, October 1934, Record Group 79, National Archives, Washington, D.C.

34. ECW Quarterly Report, Cascades Camp, NP-6, Yosemite National Park, April 1935, Record Group 79, National Archives, Washington, D.C. (hereafter cited as "ECW Quarterly, Cascades, April 1935").

35. McKown, Final Narrative Report, Yosemite.

36. Frederic E. Clements, "Experimental Ecology in the Public Service," *Ecology* 16, no. 3 (1935): 360; also published in Clements, *Dynamics of Vegetation,* 272–73.

37. Fowler, "Report to Chief Architect."

38. ECW Quarterly Report, Cascades Camp, NP-6, Yosemite National Park, July 1934, Record Group 79, National Archives, Washington, D.C. (hereafter cited as "ECW Quarterly, Cascades, July 1934").

39. Sanford Hill, "Final Narrative Report to the Chief Architect, Seventh Period ECW, Yellowstone National Park, Summer 1936," Record Group 79, National Archives, Washington, D.C.

40. Lloyd Fletcher, "Report to the Chief Architect, ECW and PWA Projects, Fourth Enrollment Period, October 1, 1934, to April 1, 1935," Record Group 79, National Archives, Washington, D.C.

41. Fowler, "Report to Chief Architect."

42. ECW Semiannual Report, Camp NP-1, Sequoia National Park, April 1, 1935, to September 30, 1935, Record Group 79, National Archives, Washington, D.C.

43. ECW Quarterly, Cascades, July 1934. The report provided only common names for plants; Latin names are drawn from Jepson, *Flowering Plants of California.*

44. ECW Quarterly Report, Cascades Camp, NP-6, Yosemite National Park, January 1935, Record Group 79, National Archives, Washington, D.C. (hereafter cited as "ECW Quarterly, Cascades, January 1935").

45. ECW Semiannual Report, Cascades Camp, NP-6, Yosemite National Park, October 1935, Record Group 79, National Archives, Washington, D.C. (hereafter cited as "ECW Semiannual, Cascades, October 1935").

46. ECW Quarterly, Cascades, April 1935.

47. ECW Semiannual, Cascades, October 1935.

48. ECW Quarterly Report, Cascades Camp, NP-6, Yosemite National Park, October 1935, Record Group 79, National Archives, Washington, D.C. (hereafter cited as "ECW Quarterly, Cascades, October 1935").

49. ECW Quarterly, Cascades, April 1935.

50. ECW Semiannual, Cascades, October 1935.

51. ECW Quarterly, Cascades, October 1935.

52. ECW Quarterly Report, Cascades Camp, NP-6, Yosemite National Park, October 1934. The report provided common names of plants; Latin names have been taken from Jepson, *Flowering Plants of California;* further information on the ferns and grasses planted is not available.

53. McKown, Final Narrative Report, Yosemite.

54. Ibid.

55. Ibid.

56. ECW Quarterly Report, Walcott Camp, NP-3, Grand Canyon National Park, Second Enrollment Period; ECW Quarterly Report, Walcott Camp, NP-3, Grand Canyon National Park, Fourth Enrollment Period; ECW Semiannual Narrative Report, Walcott Camp, NP-3, Grand Canyon National Park, Second Enrollment Period; ECW Semiannual Narrative Report, Walcott Camp, NP-3, Grand Canyon National Park, Fourth Enrollment Period, Record Group 79, National Archives, Washington, D.C.

57. Ibid.

58. Hubbard, "Landscape Development," 120.

59. Ibid., 121; National Park Service, *Parkways: A Manual of the Revised Requirements, Instructions, and Information Relating to National Parkways for Use in the National Park Service,* (Washington, D.C.: National Park Service, 1938).

Chapter 10. A New Deal for State Parks

1. Conrad Wirth, *Parks, Politics, and the People* (Norman: University of Oklahoma Press, 1980), 76–77, 130.

2. Paige, *Civilian Conservation Corps,* 48–52.

3. National Park Service, *The CCC and Its Contributions to a Nation-Wide State Park Recreational Program* (Washington, D.C.: National Park Service, 1937), 12.

4. "A Year of Progress," in National Park Service, *1937 Yearbook: Park and Recreation Progress* (Washington, D.C.: GPO, 1938), 1.

5. Melvin B. Borgeson, "State Park Conservation Work: 2. District One," *Landscape Architecture* 24, no. 1 (1933): 27.

6. Norman T. Newton, "State Park Conservation Work: 3. New Jersey and Eastern New York," *Landscape Architecture* 24, no. 1 (1933): 28.

7. Harrison, *Architecture in the Parks,* 319; Inspector's Photographic Handbook, Region

Seven, Emergency Conservation Work, Record Group 79, National Archives, Washington, D.C.

8. Iowa State had instituted a landscape architecture degree program that included a specialty in "landscape engineering" designed for work in national forests and parks; information on Nason comes from Steely, "Rustic Style in Depression Texas," 20.

9. Manuscripts and Illustrations for Publications Concerning Emergency Conservation Work, 1933–36, Record Group 79, National Archives, College Park, Maryland.

10. Herbert Maier, "Proceedings of National Park Service Conference of State Park Authorities, Washington, D.C., February 25, 1935" (National Park Service, Washington, D.C., 1935, mimeo.), 84.

11. Ibid., 85–86; no documentary evidence has been uncovered to indicate whether the survey was ever conducted.

12. Ibid., 92–93.

13. Good, *Park Structures and Facilities*, 6–8.

14. Inspector's Photographic Handbook, Region Seven, National Park Service, Record Group 79, National Archives, Washington, D.C., plate 2.

15. 1934 *AR*, 172–73.

16. 1936 *AR*, 104.

17. "Administration Manual for Recreational Demonstration Areas" (National Park Service, Washington, D.C., 1941, mimeo.), 1–5.

18. Wirth, *Parks*, 178, 184–86; "Administration Manual," 2–5.

19. National Park Service, *Recreational Demonstration Areas, as Illustrated by Chopawamsic, Virginia* (Washington, D.C.: National Park Service, 1936); 1938 *AR*, 33; "Administration Manual," 1; Wirth, *Parks*, 188–89; Newton, *Design on the Land*, 588–94.

20. "The National Park Service in the Field of Organized Camping," in National Park Service, *1937 Yearbook: Park and Recreation Progress* (Washington, D.C.: GPO, 1938), 39.

21. Ibid., 38–40; Wirth, *Parks*, 176–77; Newton, *Design on the Land*, 594.

22. 1936 *AR*, 104; 1938 *AR*, 33–34.

23. 1936 *AR*, 104–5.

24. 1934 *AR*, 175; 1935 *AR*, 183–84; 1936 *AR*, 104–5.

25. 1935 *AR*, 179–80; 1938 *AR*, 35.

26. Wirth, *Parks*, 166–74; Newton, *Design on the Land*, 587; National Park Service, *A Study of the Park and Recreation Problem in the United States* (Washington, D.C.: GPO, 1941); 49 Stat. 1894, approved June 23, 1936.

27. National Park Service, *CCC and Its Contributions*, 13–17.

28. Conrad L. Wirth, "The National Aspect of Recreation," in National Park Service, *1937 Yearbook: Park and Recreation Progress*, v.

CHAPTER 11. PORTFOLIOS FOR NATURALISTIC PARK DESIGN

1. Correspondence, Dorothy Waugh to Linda McClelland, May 8, 1989; taped interview, Dorothy Waugh to James Steely, May 25, 1985.

2. Conrad L. Wirth, foreword to National Park Service, *Portfolio of Park Structures* (Washington, D.C.: National Park Service, 1934).

3. Manuscripts and Illustrations for Publications Concerning Emergency Conservation Work, 1933–36.

4. In May 1935, Waugh sent Wirth all the drawings and work that had been in progress at the time the portfolios were discontinued. These were absorbed into Good's files

and are now on record at the Cartographic Branch of the National Archives, Record Group 76, College Park, Maryland. Preliminary Inventory 144, entry 43. Unfortunately she saved very little of the correspondence accompanying plans and drawings.

5. Good, *Park Structures and Facilities,* 2.

6. Frank Albert Waugh, *Landscape Conservation: Planning for the Restoration, Conservation, and Utilization of Wild Lands for Park and Forest Recreation* (Washington, D.C.: National Park Service, 1935), 1–2.

7. Civilian Conservation Corps, *Construction of Trails,* Project Training Series no. 7 (Washington, D.C.: Civilian Conservation Corps, 1937).

8. Civilian Conservation Corps, *Signs and Markers,* Project Training Series no. 9 (Washington, D.C.: Civilian Conservation Corps, 1938).

9. Paige, *Civilian Conservation Corps,* 26–28, 33.

CHAPTER 12.   NATIONAL PARK DESIGN SINCE 1940

1. Paul V. McNutt, "Conservation for Recreation: The Landscape Architect as Land-Use Planner in Public Works," *Landscape Architecture* 30, no. 4 (1940): 174.

2. George Nason, "Architecture and Its Relationship to the Design of Parks," in National Park Service, *1940 Yearbook: Park and Recreation Progress* (Washington, D.C.: GPO, 1940), 56–57.

3. "ASLA Policies on Matters of Moment: Views on Public Questions Related to the Profession," *Landscape Architecture* 30, no. 4 (1940): 1–22.

4. Richard Lieber, "Nature's Balances in Parks and Elsewhere," in National Park Service, *1940 Yearbook: Park and Recreation Progress,* 82–85. Several master plans of the late 1930s, including those for Shenandoah National Park and White Sands National Monument, indicated a trend for locating park headquarters outside or on the edge of park boundaries. This trend seems to have been motivated more by practical issues of climate, topography, and administrative access than concerns for park preservation.

5. Quotation is taken from an address delivered July 11, 1940, at College Park, Maryland, and July 12, 1940, in George Washington National Forest, published as James J. McEntee, "The CCC and National Defense," *Regional Review* 5, no. 1 (1940): 28.

6. Civilian Conservation Corps, *Civilian Conservation Corps: Contributing to the Defense of the Nation* (Washington, D.C.: GPO, 1941), 1, 4, 8, 9.

7. Conrad Wirth, *Civilian Conservation Corps Program of the United States Department of the Interior, March 1933 to June 30, 1943* (Chicago: U.S. Department of the Interior, 1945), 1, 11, 13, 27–29.

8. "Landscape Architects at War: The ASLA in the Armed and Civilian Service as Revealed by Questionnaire," *Landscape Architecture* 33, no. 1 (1943): 8–13; "American Society of Landscape Architects: List of Officers and Trustees, Members, and Associates (as of December, 1942)," *Landscape Architecture* 33, no. 2 (1943): 63–74.

9. Henry L. Hornbeck, "Camouflage—Here and Now," *Landscape Architecture* 33, no. 1 (1942): 1–7. Armistead Fitzhugh, "Camouflage: Adaptation of Basic Principles of Landscape Architecture," *Landscape Architecture* 33, no. 4 (1943): 119–24.

10. "Landscape Architects at War"; "American Society of Landscape Architects."

11. "Cuts and Fills," *Landscape Architecture* 33, no. 1 (1943): 26–27; "Selected 1942 ASLA Committee Reports," *Landscape Architecture* 33, no. 2 (1943): 47–48.

12. Joseph L. Sax, *Mountains without Handrails: Reflections on the National Parks* (Ann Arbor: University of Michigan Press, 1980), 64–66; 1944 *AR,* 207–8.

13. 1944 *AR*, 218–19.

14. Paul V. Brown, "Planning Comments and Use Estimates, Big Bend National Park" [1942], enclosure 2888370, National Archives and Records Center, Fort Worth, Texas.

15. Hillory Tolson to Regional Director Tillotson, May 30, 1944, Memorandum Calling for a Preliminary Master Plan, National Archives and Records Center, Fort Worth, Texas.

16. Harvey H. Cornell to Director, Memorandum, February 8, 1946, National Archives and Records Center, Fort Worth, Texas.

17. National Park Service, "Mission 66 for the National Park System" (National Park Service, Washington, D.C., 1956, mimeo.), 5–14; Charles Stevenson, "Shocking Truth about Our National Parks: A Report on the Use of Park Areas and Supporting Funds," *Landscape Architecture* 45, no. 2 (1955): 57–60.

18. National Park Service, *Mission 66 in Action: Report on the First Year of Mission 66* (Washington, D.C.: National Park Service, 1957), 3.

19. National Park Service, "Mission 66 for the National Park System," 2a, 5a, 10.

20. Ibid., 12; Wirth, in National Park Service, *Mission 66 in Action*, 2.

21. Conrad Wirth, "The Basic Purpose of the National Park System," in National Park Service, "Mission 66 for the National Park System," iii–iv.

22. Conrad Wirth, "The Landscape Architect in National Park Work: His Projects, Opportunities, Problems, and Obligations," *Landscape Architecture* 46, no. 1 (1956): 15.

23. National Park Service, "Mission 66 for the National Park System," 26–27.

24. Ibid., 26, 93–94; also Ralph H. Lewis, *Museum Curatorship in the National Park Service, 1904–1982* (Washington, D.C.: National Park Service, 1993), 146.

25. National Park Service, "Mission 66 for the National Park System," 102–3.

26. National Park Service, *Mission 66 in Action*, 4–5, 8–11.

27. Conrad L. Wirth, "Mission 66 in the Headlines," *National Parks Magazine* 32, no. 132 (1958): 8.

28. Master Plan, Yellowstone National Park, n.d. (ca. 1935), National Archives, College Park, Maryland; Wirth, "Mission 66 in the Headlines," 8, 36; Richard A. Bartlett, *Yellowstone: A Wilderness Besieged* (Tucson: University of Arizona Press, 1985), 370. The idea for Canyon Village originated in the mid-1930s when the Yellowstone Master Plan identified the canyon rim as a sacred area and called for the removal of the existing hotel, cabins, and campground. Overnight accommodations, a campground, and visitor services were to be moved to a new location a short distance from the rim.

29. The following articles raised concern over Mission 66 park road construction: Ansel Adams, "Yosemite: 1958 Compromise in Action," *National Parks Magazine* 32, no. 135 (1958): 166–75; "Yosemite's Tioga Highway," *National Parks Magazine* 32, no. 134 (1958): 123–24; Anthony Wayne Smith, "The Tioga Road: Your NPA in Action," *National Parks Magazine* 33, no. 136 (1959): 10–13; Harold Bradley, "Roads in Our National Parks," *National Parks Magazine* 33, no. 137 (1959): 3–7; Marion Clawson, "Our National Parks in the Year 2000," *National Parks Magazine* 33, no. 142 (1959): 2–11; Weldon F. Heald, "Urbanization of the National Parks," *National Parks Magazine* 35, no. 160 (1961): 7–9; Paul M. Tilden and Nancy L. Machler, "The Development of Mount McKinley National Park," *National Parks Magazine* 37, no. 188 (1963): 10–15.

30. "A 'Sky-Post' for the Smokies," *National Parks Magazine* 33, no. 137 (1959): inside front cover; Hubert Bebb, "The Architect's Rebuttal," *National Parks Magazine* 33, no. 139 (1959): 16.

31. "Clingman's Dome," *National Parks Magazine* 33, no. 137 (1959): inside back cover.

32. Aldo Leopold, "Wilderness Values," in National Park Service, *1941 Yearbook: Park and Recreation Progress* , 28.

33. Thomas C. Vint, "Wilderness Areas: Development of National Parks for Conservation," in James Harlean, ed., *American Planning and Civic Annual* (Washington, D.C.: American Planning and Civic Association, 1938), 71; Jesse L. Nusbaum, "Wilderness Aspects of National Parks," in Harlean, *American Planning and Civic Annual,* 77.

34. National Park Service, *The National Park Wilderness* (Washington, D.C.: National Park Service, 1958).

35. F. Fraser Darling and Noel D. Eichhorn, *Man and Nature in the National Parks: Reflections on Policy,* 2d ed. (Washington, D.C.: Conservation Foundation, 1969), 73; legislation is quoted on 74.

36. George B. Hartzog Jr., "The Wilderness Act and the National Parks and Monuments," in *Wilderness and the Quality of Life,* ed. Maxine E. McCloskey and James P. Gilligan (San Francisco: Sierra Club, 1969), 19–20; National Parks and Conservation Association, *Preserving Wilderness in Our National Parks: A Program for Preventing Overuse of the National Parks through Regional Recreational Planning Outside the Parks* (Washington, D.C.: National Parks and Conservation Association, 1971), xvi.

37. National Park Service, *Administrative Policies for Natural Areas of the National Park System,* rev. ed. (Washington, D.C.: GPO, 1970), 56–57; criteria appear in McCloskey and Gilligan, *Wilderness and the Quality of Life,* 245–47.

38. National Parks and Conservation Association, *Preserving Wilderness,* xv-xviii.

39. Advisory Board on Wildlife Management, "Wildlife Management in the National Parks," March 4, 1963, in National Park Service, *Administrative Policies,* 99–112.

40. Darling and Eichhorn, *Man and Nature,* 3, 34, 38, 40, 44–45, 77.

41. National Park Service, *Administrative Policies,* 59.

42. "Park Roads Standards: A Report to the Director of the National Park Service," in National Park Service, *Administrative Policies,* 132.

43. National Park Service, *Administrative Policies,* 65.

44. "Park Roads Standards," 129–36.

45. National Park Service, *Administrative Policies,* 65; "Park Roads Standards," 135.

46. "Park Roads Standards," 135.

47. National Park Service, *Park Road Standards* (Washington, D.C.: National Park Service, 1984), i-ii.

48. Jean M. Muller and James M. Barker, "Design and Construction of Linn Cove Viaduct," *Journal of the Prestressed Concrete Institute* 30, no. 5 (1985): 2–17.

49. National Park Service, *Master Plan—Yellowstone National Park* (Denver: National Park Service 1973), 1.

50. National Park Service, *National Parks for the Twenty-first Century: The Vail Agenda* (Washington, D.C.: National Park Service, 1992), 84–86. This document summarizes the findings of the Seventy-fifth Anniversary Symposium, "Our National Parks: Challenges and Strategies for the Twenty-first Century," held in Vail, Colorado, October 1991.

Bibliography

BOOKS AND MANUSCRIPTS

Ahlgren, Carol Ann. "A Human and Landscape Architectural Legacy: The Influence of the Civilian Conservation Corps on Wisconsin State Park Development." M.A. thesis, University of Wisconsin, Madison, 1987.

Albright, Horace M. *The Birth of the National Park Service.* Salt Lake City: Howes Brothers, 1985.

Bartlett, Richard A. *Yellowstone: A Wilderness Besieged.* Tucson: University of Arizona Press, 1985.

Boeger, Palmer H. *Oklahoma Oasis: From Platt National Park to Chickasaw National Recreation Area.* Muskogee: Oklahoma Western Heritage Books, 1987.

Bramwell, Anna. *Ecology in the Twentieth Century: A History.* New Haven: Yale University Press, 1989.

Butler, George D. *Municipal and County Parks in the United States, 1935.* Washington, D.C.: National Park Service, 1937.

Butler, Ovid, ed. *American Conservation: In Picture and in Story.* Washington, D.C.: American Forestry Association, 1935.

Byrne, John P. "The Civilian Conservation Corps in Virginia, 1933–1942." M.S. thesis, University of Montana, 1982.

Cardwell, Kenneth H. *Bernard Maybeck: Artisan, Architect, Artist.* Salt Lake City: Peregrine Smith Books, 1977.

Chicago Historical Society. *Prairie in the City: Naturalism in Chicago's Parks, 1870–1940.* Chicago: Chicago Historical Society, 1991.

Civilian Conservation Corps. *Civilian Conservation Corps: Contributing to the Defense of the Nation.* Washington, D.C.: GPO, 1941.

———. *Construction of Trails.* Project Training Series no. 7. Washington, D.C.: Civilian Conservation Corps, 1937.

———. *Signs and Markers.* Project Training Series no. 9. Washington, D.C.: Civilian Conservation Corps, 1938.

———. *Woodsmanship for the Civilian Conservation Corps.* Washington, D.C.: Civilian Conservation Corps, 1938.

Clements, Frederic E. *Dynamics of Vegetation: Selections from the Writings of Frederic E. Clements.* Edited by B. W. Allred and Edith S. Clements. New York: H. W. Wilson Co., 1949.

Comstock, William Phillips, and Clarence Eaton Schermerhorn. *Bungalows, Camps, and Mountain Houses.* New York: W. T. Comstock Co., 1915. Reprint, Washington, D.C.: American Institute of Architects Press, 1990.

Conservation Foundation. *National Parks for a New Generation: Visions, Realities, Prospects.* Washington, D.C.: Conservation Foundation, 1985.

Cox, Thomas R. *The Park Builders: A History of State Parks in the Pacific Northwest.* Seattle: University of Washington Press, 1988.

Culpin, Mary Shivers. *The History of the Construction of the Road System in Yellowstone National Park, 1872–1966.* Historic Resource Study, vol. 1. Denver: Rocky Mountain Region, National Park Service, 1994.

Cultural Resources Information System Facility, Interagency Resources Division. "Historic Stonemasonry Road Features of the Great Smoky Mountains National Park." Open File Report no. 7. National Park Service, Washington, D.C., 1994.

Cutler, Phoebe. *Public Landscape of the New Deal.* New Haven: Yale University Press, 1985.

Dana, William S. B. *The Swiss Chalet Book.* New York: W. T. Comstock Co., 1913.

Darling, F. Fraser, and Noel D. Eichhorn. *Man and Nature in the National Parks: Reflections on Policy.* 2d ed. Washington, D.C.: Conservation Foundation, 1969.

Davidson, E. A. "Landscape Work in Connection with the Development of the Yakima Park Area, Including the Approach Highway within Mt. Rainier National Park." A Report to Thomas C. Vint, Chief Landscape Architect, National Park Service, Columbia Cascades System Office, Seattle, Wash., n.d. [ca. 1932].

Dilsaver, Lary M., and William C. Tweed. *The Challenge of the Big Trees: A Resource History of Sequoia and Kings Canyon National Parks.* Three Rivers, Calif.: Sequoia Natural History Association, 1990.

Downing, Andrew Jackson. *The Architecture of Country Houses.* New York: D. Appleton & Co., 1850. Reprint, New York: Dover Publications, 1969.

———. *Landscape Gardening.* Revised by Frank Albert Waugh. New York: John Wiley & Sons, 1921.

———. *Rural Essays.* Originally published in the *Horticulturalist.* New York: Hagemann Publishing Co., 1894.

———. *A Treatise on the Theory and Practice of Landscape Gardening.* 9th ed. New York: Orange Judd, 1875. Reprint, Little Compton, R.I.: Theophrastus Publishers, 1977.

Drury, Newton B. *National Park Service War Work, Dec. 7, 1941 to June 30, 1944.* Chicago: National Park Service, 1946.

Eaton, Leonard K. *Landscape Artist in America: The Life and Work of Jens Jensen.* Chicago: University of Chicago Press, 1964.

Eliot, Charles W. *Charles Eliot, Landscape Architect.* Boston: Houghton Mifflin, 1902.

Elwood, P. H., Jr., ed. *American Landscape Architecture.* New York: Architectural Book Publishing Co., 1924.

Engbeck, Joseph H., Jr. *State Parks of California from 1864 to the Present.* Portland, Oreg.: Graphic Arts Center Publishing Co., 1980.

Everhart, William C. *The National Park Service.* Boulder, Colo.: Westview Press, 1983.

Evison, Herbert, ed. *A State Park Anthology.* Washington, D.C.: National Conference on State Parks, 1930.

Firth, Ian. "Draft Historic Resource Study for the Blue Ridge Parkway." National Park Service, Southeast Region, Atlanta, 1992.

Foresta, Ronald A. *America's National Parks and Their Keepers.* Washington, D.C.: Resources for the Future, 1984.

Franklin, Jerry F., and C. T. Dyrness. *Natural Vegetation of Oregon and Washington.* General Technical Report PNW-8. Portland, Oreg.: Pacific Northwest Forest and Range Experiment Station, U.S. Department of Agriculture, 1973.

Franklin, Jerry F., William H. Moir, Miles A. Henstrom, Sarah E. Greene, and Bradley G.

Smith. *The Forest Communities of Mount Rainier National Park.* Scientific Monograph Series no. 19. Washington, D.C.: National Park Service, 1988.

Garland, Susan V. "The Civilian Conservation Corps in the Cuyahoga Valley." Files of the Cuyahoga Valley National Recreation Area, National Park Service, 1979.

Gilbert, Cathy, and Gretchen Luxenberg. *The Rustic Landscape of Rim Village, 1927–1941, Crater Lake National Park.* Seattle: Pacific Northwest Regional Office, National Park Service, 1990.

Good, Albert H., ed. *Park and Recreation Structures.* 3 vols. Washington, D.C.: National Park Service, 1938.

———. *Park Structures and Facilities.* Washington, D.C.: National Park Service, 1935.

Grattan, Virginia L. *Mary Colter: Builder upon the Red Earth.* Flagstaff, Ariz.: Northland Press, 1980.

Greene, Linda Wedel. *Yosemite: The Park and Its Resources.* Historic Resources Study. 3 vols. Washington, D.C.: National Park Service, 1987.

Grese, Robert E. *Jens Jensen: Maker of Natural Parks and Gardens.* Baltimore: Johns Hopkins University Press, 1992.

———. "Design with the Native Landscape, 1880–1940." University of Michigan, Ann Arbor, n.d. [ca. 1988], mimeo.

Haley, Jacquetta M., ed. *Pleasure Grounds: Andrew Jackson Downing and Montgomery Place.* Tarrytown, N.Y.: Sleepy Hollow Press, 1988.

Handlin, David P. *The American Home: Architecture and Society, 1815–1915.* Boston: Little, Brown and Co., 1979.

Harrison, Laura Soullière. *Architecture in the Parks National Historic Landmark Theme Study.* Washington, D.C.: National Park Service, 1986.

Hartzog, George B., Jr. *Battling for the National Parks.* Mt. Kisco, N.Y.: Moyer Bell, 1988.

Heatwole, Henry. *Guide to Skyline Drive and Shenandoah National Park.* Luray, Va.: Shenandoah Natural History Association, 1978.

Hewes, Laurence Ilsley. *American Highway Practice.* New York: John Wiley & Sons, 1942.

Hubbard, Henry Vincent, and Theodora Kimball. *An Introduction to the Study of Landscape Design.* 1917. Reprint, New York: Macmillan Co., 1924.

Huth, Hans. *Nature and the American: Three Centuries of Changing Attitudes.* Lincoln: University of Nebraska, 1957.

Ise, John. *Our National Park Policy: A Critical History.* Baltimore: Johns Hopkins University Press, 1961.

James, Harlean, ed. *American Planning and Civic Annual: A Record of Recent Civic Advance as Shown in the Proceedings of the Conference on National Parks, Held at Washington, D.C., January 20–21, 1938; the National Conference on State Parks, Held at Norris, Tennessee, May 11–14; and the National Conference on Planning, Held at Minneapolis, Minnesota, June 2–22, 1938.* Washington, D.C.: American Planning and Civic Association, 1938.

Jameson, John R. *Big Bend of the Rio Grande: Biography of a National Park.* New York: Peter Lang Publishing Co., 1987.

Jepson, Willis Linn. *A Manual of the Flowering Plants of California.* 1925. Berkeley: University of California Press, 1970.

Kaiser, Harvey H. *Great Camps of the Adirondacks.* Boston: David R. Godine, 1986.

Kieley, James. "A Brief History of the National Park Service." Paper written for the National Park Service, 1940. Mimeo.

———. "The Civilian Conservation Corps." Paper written for the National Park Service, 1939. Mimeo.

Krakow, Jere L. *Historic Resource Study: Rock Creek and Potomac Parkway, George Washington Memorial Parkway, Suitland Parkway, Baltimore-Washington Parkway.* Washington, D.C.: National Park Service, 1990.

Lancaster, Clay. *The American Bungalow, 1880–1930.* New York: Abbeville Press, 1985.

Lewis, Ralph H. *Museum Curatorship in the National Park Service, 1904–1982.* Washington, D.C.: National Park Service, 1993.

Lieber, Richard. *America's Natural Wealth: A Story of the Use and Abuse of Our Resources.* New York: Harper and Brothers, 1942.

Longstreth, Richard. *On the Edge of the World: Four Architects in San Francisco at the Turn of the Century.* Cambridge: MIT Press, 1983.

Makinson, Randell L. *Greene and Greene: Architecture as a Fine Art.* Salt Lake City: Peregrine Smith Books, 1977.

Massachusetts Horticultural Society. *Keeping Eden: A History of Gardening in America.* Edited by Walter T. Punch. Boston: Little, Brown and Co., 1992.

Mather, Stephen T. *Progress in the Development of the National Parks.* Washington, D.C.: GPO, 1916.

Maxwell, Ross A. *Big Bend Country: A History of Big Bend National Park.* Big Bend National Park: Big Bend Natural History Association, 1985.

———. *The Big Bend of the Rio Grande: A Guide to Rocks, Geologic History, and Settlers of the Area of Big Bend National Park.* Guidebook 7. 5th ed. Austin: University of Texas, Bureau of Economic Geology, 1987.

———. *Geologic and Historic Guide to the State Parks of Texas.* Guidebook 10. Austin: University of Texas, Bureau of Economic Geology, 1981.

McClelland, Linda Flint, J. Timothy Keller, Genevieve P. Keller, and Robert Z. Melnick. *Guidelines for Evaluating and Documenting Rural Historic Landscapes.* National Register Bulletin 30. Washington, D.C., 1990.

McCloskey, Maxine E., and James P. Guilligan. *Wilderness and the Quality of Life.* San Francisco: Sierra Club, 1969.

McCoy, Esther. *Five California Architects.* New York: Praeger Publishers, 1975.

McMinn, Howard E. *An Illustrated Manual of California Shrubs.* Berkeley: University of California Press, 1951.

Meinecke, E. P. *A Camp Ground Policy.* Ogden, Utah: U.S. Forest Service, U.S. Department of Agriculture, 1932.

———. *Camp Planning and Camp Reconstruction.* N.p.: U.S. Forest Service, U.S. Department of Agriculture, n.d. [ca. 1934].

Merrill, Perry H. *Roosevelt's Forest Army: A History of the Civilian Conservation Corps, 1933–1942.* Montpelier, Vt.: P. H. Merrill, 1981.

Meyer, Harold D., and Charles K. Brightbill. *State Recreation: Organization and Administration.* New York: A. S. Barnes and Co., 1950.

Meyer, Roy W. *Everyone's Country Estate: A History of Minnesota's State Parks.* St. Paul: Minnesota Historical Press, 1991.

Miller, Wilhelm. *The Prairie Spirit in Landscape Gardening.* Circular #184. Urbana: Illinois Agricultural Experiment Station, 1915.

———. *What England Can Teach Us about Gardening.* Garden City, N.Y.: Doubleday, Page, and Co., 1911.

Muir, John. *Our National Parks.* Boston: Houghton Mifflin, 1901. Reprint, Madison: University of Wisconsin Press, 1981.

Murmann, Eugene O. *California Gardening.* Los Angeles: Eugene O. Murmann, 1914.

Nash, Roderick. *Wilderness and the American Mind.* New Haven: Yale University Press, 1973.

National Conference on State Parks. *Proceedings of the Second National Conference on State Parks, Palisades Interstate Park, New York, May 22–25, 1922.* Washington, D.C.: National Conference on State Parks, 1923.

National Parks and Conservation Association. *Preserving Wilderness in Our National Parks: A Program for Preventing Overuse of the National Parks through Regional Recreational Planning Outside the Parks.* Washington, D.C.: National Parks and Conservation Association, 1971.

National Parks Centennial Commission. *Preserving a Heritage: Final Report to the President and the Congress of the National Parks Centennial Commission.* Washington, D.C.: National Parks Centennial Commission, 1973.

National Park Service. "Administration Manual for Recreational Demonstration Areas." U.S. Department of the Interior, Washington, D.C., 1941. Mimeo.

———. *Administrative Policies for Natural Areas of the National Park System.* Rev. ed. Washington, D.C.: GPO, 1970.

———. *Big Bend National Park Handbook.* Handbook no. 119. Washington, D.C.: U.S. Department of the Interior, 1983.

———. *Big Bend National Park Project, Texas.* Washington, D.C.: National Park Service, n.d. [ca. 1938].

———. *The CCC and Its Contributions to a Nation-Wide State Park Recreational Program.* Washington, D.C.: GPO, 1937.

———. *Emergency Conservation Work Handbook.* No. 182. Washington, D.C.: U.S. Department of the Interior, n.d. Mimeo.

———. "Inspector's Photographic Handbook." Regional Office, Region Seven, Oklahoma City. N.d. [ca. 1935].

———. *Master Plan Handbook.* Washington, D.C.: National Park Service, 1964.

———. *Master Plan — Yellowstone National Park.* Denver: National Park Service, 1973.

———. *Master Plans: A Manual of Standard Practice for Use in the National Park Service.* Washington, D.C.: National Park Service, 1939.

———. "Minutes of the Twelfth Conference of National Park Executives, Hot Springs National Park, Arkansas, April 3 to 8, 1932." National Park Service, Washington, D.C., 1932. Mimeo.

———. *Mission 66: Progress Report.* Washington, D.C.: National Park Service, 1966.

———. "Mission 66 for the National Park System." National Park Service, Washington, D.C., 1956. Mimeo.

———. *Mission 66 in Action: Report on the First Year of Mission 66.* Washington, D.C.: National Park Service, 1957.

———. *National Parks for the Twenty-first Century: The Vail Agenda.* Washington, D.C.: National Park Service, 1992.

———. *The National Park Wilderness.* Washington, D.C.: National Park Service, 1958.

———. *Park Road Standards.* Washington, D.C.: National Park Service, 1984.

———. *Parkways: A Manual of the Revised Requirements, Instructions, and Information Relating to National Parkways for Use in the National Park Service.* Washington, D.C.: National Park Service, 1938.

———. *Portfolio of Comfort Stations and Privies.* Washington, D.C.: National Park Service, 1934.

———. *Portfolio of Housekeeping Cabins.* PG-3032. Washington, D.C.: Branch of Plans and Design. n.d. [ca. 1934].

———. *Portfolio of Park Structures.* Washington, D.C: National Park Service, 1934.

———. "Portfolio of Representative Structures Designed by the Landscape Division, National Park Service." Landscape Division, National Park Service, San Francisco, n.d. [ca. 1932].

———. "Proceedings: National Park Service Conference of State Park Authorities, Washington, D.C., February 25, 1935." National Park Service, Washington, D.C., 1935. Mimeo.

———. *Proceedings of the National Parks Conference, Berkeley, California, March 11–13, 1915.* Washington, D.C.: GPO, 1915.

———. *Proceedings of the National Parks Conference, Washington, D.C., January 2–6, 1917.* Washington, D.C.: GPO, 1917.

———. *Proceedings of the Second National Conference on State Parks, 1922.* Washington, D.C.: National Park Service, 1922.

———. *Recreational Demonstration Areas, as Illustrated by Chopawamsic, Virginia.* Washington, D.C.: National Park Service, 1936.

———. "Report on the Building Program from Allotments of the Public Works Administration, 1933–1937, Eastern Division." National Park Service, Washington, D.C., 1938. Mimeo.

———. "Report on the Building Program from Allotments of the Public Works Administration, 1933–1937, Western Division." National Park Service, San Francisco, 1938. Mimeo.

———. *Sequoia and Kings Canyon National Parks: Architectural Character Guidelines.* Denver: National Park Service, 1989.

———. *Sequoia and Kings Canyon National Parks: Inventory of Significant Structures.* Denver: National Park Service, 1989.

———. *Sequoia and Kings Canyon National Parks: Road Character Guidelines.* Denver: National Park Service, 1990.

———. *A Study of the Park and Recreation Problem in the United States.* Washington, D.C.: GPO, 1941.

———. *Yearbook: Park and Recreation Progress, 1937–42.* Washington, D.C.: GPO, 1938–43.

———. *Yosemite Valley Cultural Landscape Report.* 2 vols. Denver: Denver Service Center, 1994.

National Research Council. *Science and the National Parks.* Washington, D.C.: National Academy Press, 1992.

Nelson, Beatrice Ward. *State Recreation: Parks, Forests, and Game Preserves.* Washington, D.C.: National Conference on State Parks, 1928.

Newton, Norman T. *Design on the Land: The Development of Landscape Architecture* Cambridge: Harvard University Press, 1971.

Olmsted, Frederick Law, Jr. *Report of State Park Survey of California.* Sacramento: California State Printing Office, 1929.

Olmsted, Frederick Law, Sr. *Forty Years of Landscape Architecture: Central Park.* Edited by Frederick Law Olmsted Jr. and Theodora Kimball. New York: G. P. Putnam's Sons, 1928. Reprint, Cambridge: MIT Press, 1973.

Olson, Gordon Cooper. "A History of Natural Resources Management within the National Park Service." M.S. thesis, Slippery Rock University, Pennsylvania, 1986.

Olson, Russ. *Administrative History: Organizational Structures of the National Park Service, 1917 to 1985.* Washington, D.C.: National Park Service, 1985.

Oregon State Parks Commission and Oregon State Planning Board. "A Study of Parks, Parkways, and Recreational Areas of Oregon." Vol. 1. Oregon State Planning Board, Portland, 1938. Mimeo.

Otis, Alison T., William D. Honey, Thomas C. Hogg, and Kimberly K. Lakin. *The Forest Service and the Civilian Conservation Corps: 1933–1942.* N.p.: U.S. Department of Agriculture, Forest Service, 1986.

Outdoor Recreation Resources Review Commission. *Outdoor Recreation for America: A Report to the President and to the Congress.* Washington, D.C.: GPO, 1962.

Paige, John C. *The Civilian Conservation Corps and the National Park Service, 1933–1942: An Administrative History.* Washington, D.C.: National Park Service, 1985.

Parsons, Samuel, Jr. *The Art of Landscape Architecture: Its Development and Its Application to Modern Landscape Gardening.* New York: G. P. Putnam's Sons, 1915.

———. *Landscape Gardening.* New York: G. P. Putnam's Sons, 1891.

Pearson, G. A. *Reforestation in the Southwest by CCC Camps.* Washington, D.C.: GPO, 1940.

———. *Timber Stand Improvement in the Southwest.* Washington, D.C.: GPO, 1940.

Pückler-Muskau, Prince H. L. H. von. *Hints on Landscape Gardening.* Translated by Bernhardt Sickert, edited by Samuel Parsons. Boston: Houghton Mifflin, 1917.

Quinquennial Catalogue of the Officers and Graduates, Harvard University, 1636–1930. Cambridge: Harvard University, 1930.

Rainier National Park Advisory Board. "Road and Trail Program for the Mount Rainier National Park." Report, July 5, 1934, U.S. Department of the Interior, Natural Resources Library.

Ranney, Victoria Post, ed. *The California Frontier.* The Papers of Frederick Law Olmsted, vol. 5. Baltimore: Johns Hopkins University Press, 1990.

Repton, Humphry. *The Art of Landscape Gardening Including His Sketches and Hints on Landscape Gardening.* Edited by John Nolen. Boston: Houghton Mifflin, 1907.

Rieley, William D., and Roxanne S. Brouse. "Historic Resource Study for the Carriage Road System, Acadia National Park, Mount Desert Island, Maine." 2 vols. National Park Service, North Atlantic Regional Office, Boston, 1989.

Roberts, Edith A., and Elsa Rehmann. *American Plants for American Gardens, Plant Ecology: The Study of Plants in Relation to Their Environment.* New York: Macmillan Co., 1929.

Robinson, William. *The Wild Garden or the Naturalization and Natural Grouping of Hardy Exotic Plants with a Chapter on the Garden of British Wild Flowers.* London: John Murray, 1870. Reprint, London: Century Hutchinson with the National Trust, 1986.

Roper, Laura Wood. *FLO: A Biography of Frederick Law Olmsted.* Baltimore: Johns Hopkins University Press, 1973.

Rowntree, Lester. *Flowering Shrubs of California and Their Value to the Gardener.* Stanford: Stanford University Press, 1939.

Runte, Alfred. *National Parks: The American Experience.* Lincoln: University of Nebraska Press, 1979.

Salmond, John A. *Civilian Conservation Corps, 1933–1942: A New Deal Case Study.* Durham, N.C.: Duke University Press, 1967.

Sanders, Barry. *A Complex Fate: Gustav Stickley and the Craftsman Movement.* New York: John Wiley & Sons, 1996.

Sax, Joseph L. *Mountains without Handrails: Reflections on the National Parks.* Ann Arbor: University of Michigan, 1980.

Schiltgen, Lora J. "Managing a Rustic Legacy: A Historic Landscape Study and Management Plan for Longmire Springs Historic District, Mount Rainier National Park." M.L.A. thesis, University of Oregon, Eugene, 1986.

Schmitt, Peter J. *Back to Nature: The Acadian Myth in Urban America.* Baltimore: Johns Hopkins University Press, 1990.

Scully, Vincent J., Jr. *The Shingle Style and The Stick Style: Architectural Theory and Design from Downing to the Origins of Wright.* New Haven: Yale University Press, 1977.

Shankland, Robert. *Steve Mather of the National Parks.* New York: Alfred A. Knopf, 1954.

Shepard, Augustus D. *Camps in the Woods.* New York: New York Architectural Book Publishing Co., 1931.

Simonds, Ossian Cole. *Landscape-Gardening.* Rural Science Series. New York: Macmillan Co., 1920. Reprint, New York: Macmillan Co., 1931.

Soullière, Laura E. *Special History Study: Historic Roads in the National Park System* Denver: National Park Service, 1995.

Steely, James Wright. *The Civilian Conservation Corps in Texas State Parks.* Austin: Texas Parks and Wildlife Department, 1986.

———. *Parks for Texas: The New Deal Fulfillment of a State Park System from Caddo Lake to Possum Kingdom, 1933–1945.* Austin: University of Texas Press, 1997.

———. "Rustic Style in Depression Texas: Federal Architecture in the State Parks, 1933–1941." M.S. thesis, University of Texas, Austin, 1985.

Steiner, Jesse Frederick. *Americans at Play: Recent Trends in Recreation and Leisure Time Activities.* New York: McGraw-Hill Book Co., 1933. Reprint, New York: Arno Press and the New York Times, 1970.

Stickley, Gustav, ed. *Craftsman Bungalows: Fifty-nine Homes from "The Craftsman."* New York: Dover Publications, 1988.

———. *Craftsman Homes: Architecture and Furnishings of the American Arts and Crafts Movement.* New York: Craftsman Publishing House, 1909. Reprint, New York: Dover Publications, 1979.

———. *More Craftsman Homes.* New York: Craftsman Publishing House, 1912. Reprint, New York: Dover Publications, 1982.

Story, Isabelle F. *The National Parks and Emergency Conservation Work.* Washington, D.C.: GPO, 1936.

Swain, Donald C. *Wilderness Defender: Horace M. Albright and Conservation.* Chicago: University of Chicago Press, 1970.

Tilden, Freeman. *The National Parks.* New York: Alfred A. Knopf, 1982.

———. *The State Parks: Their Meaning in American Life.* New York: Alfred A. Knopf, 1962.

Tishler, William, ed. *American Landscape Architecture: Designers and Places.* Washington, D.C.: Preservation Press, 1989.

Torrey, Raymond H. *State Parks and Recreational Uses of State Forests in the United States.* Washington, D.C.: National Conference on State Parks, 1926.

Tunnard, Christopher, and Boris Pushkarev. *Man-made America: Chaos or Control?* New Haven: Yale University Press, 1963.

Tweed, William. *Recreation Site Planning and Improvement in National Forests, 1891-1942.* Washington, D.C.: U.S. Department of Agriculture, 1980.

Tweed, William, Laura E. Soullière, and Henry G. Law. "National Park Service Rustic Architecture: 1916–1942." National Park Service, Western Regional Office, San Francisco, 1977. Mimeo.

Tweed, William, and Laura Soullière Harrison. *Rustic Architecture and the National Parks: The History of a Design Ethic.* Forthcoming.

Tyrrell, Henry G. *Artistic Bridge Design: A Systematic Treatise on the Design of Modern Bridges According to Aesthetic Principles.* Chicago: Myron Clarke, 1912.

Unrau, Harlan D. "Historical Overview and Preliminary Assessment of Rock Work, Bridges, and Roadway-Related Appurtenances along State Highways 410 and 123 in Mount Rainier National Park." Denver Service Center, National Park Service, 1988.

U.S. Department of the Interior. *Annual Report of the Department of the Interior.* 1914–42. Washington, D.C.: GPO, 1915–43.

————. *Glimpses of Our National Parks.* Washington, D.C.: GPO, 1916.

U.S. Forest Service. *Specifications for Forest Road Construction.* Washington, D.C.: GPO, 1927.

Vaux, Calvert. *Villas and Cottages: A Series of Designs Prepared for Execution in the United States.* New York: Harper and Brothers, 1864. Reprint, New York: Dover Publications, 1970.

von Holst, Hermann Valentin. *Country and Suburban Homes of the Prairie School Period.* Originally published as *Modern American Homes.* Chicago: American Technical Society, 1913. Reprint, New York: Dover Publications, 1982.

Washington State Planning Council. *A Study of Parks, Parkways, and Recreational Areas.* Olympia: Washington State Planning Council, 1941.

Waugh, Frank Albert. *Landscape Conservation: Planning for the Restoration, Conservation, and Utilization of Wild Lands for Park and Forest Recreation.* Washington, D.C.: National Park Service, 1935.

————. *Landscape Gardening: Andrew Jackson Downing.* Revision of *Treatise on the Theory and Practice of Landscape Gardening.* New York: John Wiley & Sons, 1921.

————. *The Natural Style in Landscape Gardening.* Boston: Richard G. Badger, 1917.

————. *Outdoor Theaters: The Design, Construction, and Use of Open-Air Auditoriums.* Boston: Richard G. Badger, 1917.

————. *Recreation Uses on the National Forests.* Washington, D.C.: GPO, 1918.

Wicks, William S. *Log Cabins: How to Build and Furnish Them.* New York: Forest and Stream Publishing Co., 1889.

Winter, Robert. *The California Bungalow.* Los Angeles: Hennessey & Ingalls, 1980.

Wirth, Conrad L. *Civilian Conservation Corps Program of the United States Department of the Interior, March 1933 to June 30, 1943.* Chicago: U.S. Department of the Interior, 1945.

————. *Parks, Politics, and the People.* Norton: University of Oklahoma Press, 1980.

Worster, Donald. *Nature's Economy: A History of Ecological Ideas.* 2d ed. New York: Cambridge University Press, 1994.

Wright, George M., Joseph S. Dixon, and Ben H. Thompson. *Fauna of the National Parks of the United States.* Fauna Series, no. 1. Washington, D.C.: GPO, 1933.

————. *Fauna of the National Parks of the United States.* Fauna Series, no. 2. Washington, D.C.: GPO, 1935.

Wright, R. Gerald. *Wildlife Research and Management in the National Parks.* Urbana: University of Illinois Press, 1992.

Yard, Robert Sterling. *The Book of National Parks.* New York: Charles Scribner's Sons, 1919.

————. *New Zion National Park: Rainbow of the Desert.* Washington, D.C.: National Parks Association, 1919.

————. *Our Federal Lands: A Romance of American Development.* New York: Charles Scribner's Sons, 1928.

Zaitlin, Joyce. *Gilbert Stanley Underwood: His Rustic, Art Deco, and Federal Architecture.* Malibu, Calif.: Pangloss Press, 1989.

Zaitzevsky, Cynthia. *Frederick Law Olmsted and the Boston Park System.* Cambridge: Harvard University Press, 1982.

ARTICLES

Abbott, Stanley W. "The Blue Ridge Parkway." *Regional Review* 3, no. 1 (1939): 3–6.

Adams, Ansel. "Yosemite: 1958 Compromise in Action." *National Parks Magazine* 32, no. 135 (1958): 166–75.

"An Adirondack Lodge." *House and Garden* 12 (December 1907): 203–7.

"An Adirondack Lodge for William A. Read." *American Architecture and Building News,* July 14, 1906, 90.

Albright, Horace. "Picturesque America Seen from Trails in National Parks." *U.S. Daily* (Washington, D.C.), November 18, 1929.

"American Society of Landscape Architects: List of Officers and Trustees, Members, and Associates (as of December, 1942)." *Landscape Architecture* 33, no. 2 (1943): 63–74.

"ASLA Policies on Matters of Moment: Views on Public Questions Related to the Profession." *Landscape Architecture* 30, no. 4 (1940): 2–22.

Beatty, M. E., C. A. Hartwell, and J. E. Cole, Jr. "101 Wildflowers of Yosemite." *Yosemite Nature Notes* 17, no. 6 (1938): 75–112.

Bebb, Hubert. "The Architect's Rebuttal." *National Parks Magazine* 33, no. 139 (1959): 16.

Benson, Harvey P. "The Skyline Drive: A Brief History of a Mountaintop Motorway." *Regional Review* 4, no. 2 (1940): 3–10.

Boerner, Alfred L. "Notes on Construction of a Footbridge." *Landscape Architecture* 21, no. 4 (1931): 329–34.

Borgeson, Melvin B. "State Park Conservation Work: 2. District One." *Landscape Architecture* 24, no. 1 (1933): 27–28.

Bradley, Harold. "Roads in Our National Parks." *National Parks Magazine* 33, no. 137 (1959): 3–7.

Caparn, Harold A. "Some Reasons for a General System of State Parks." *Landscape Architecture* 7, no. 1 (1917): 65–72.

Carnes, William G. "Landscape Architecture in the National Park Service." *Landscape Architecture* 41, no. 4 (1951): 145–50.

———. "Profiles of NPS 'Greats': Tom Vint." *Courier* 3, no. 9 (1980): 23.

Carr, Ethan. "Landmarks of Landscape Architecture: The Historical Context for National Park Service Landscape Architecture." In *Landscape Universe: Historic Designed Landscapes in Context,* edited by Charles A. Birnbaum. New York: Catalog of Landscape Records in the United States with the National Park Service, 1994.

———. "Landscape Architecture in National Parks, 1916–1942." *CRM* 16, no. 4 (1993): 7–9

Clarke, Gilmore D. "Landscape Construction Notes, XXXV: Notes on Texture in Stone Masonry." *Landscape Architecture* 21, no. 3 (1931): 197–201.

———. "Westchester Parkways." *Landscape Architecture* 28, no. 1 (1938): 40–42.

Clawson, Marion. "Our National Parks in the Year 2000." *National Parks Magazine* 33, no. 142 (1959): 2–11.

"Clingman's Dome." *National Parks Magazine* 33, no. 137 (1959): back cover.

Cox, Laurie D. "Some Basic Principles of State Park Selection and Design." *Landscape Architecture* 22, no. 1 (1931): 7–15.

Culley, Frank H. "Emergency Conservation Work in the National Parks: 2. Yellowstone National Park." *Landscape Architecture* 24, no. 1 (1933): 34–35.

"Cuts and Fills." *Landscape Architecture* 33, no. 1 (1943): 26–27.

Davidson, Ernest A. "Landscape Architecture: Its Future in the West." *Landscape Architecture* 30, no. 2 (1940): 66–67.

Dill, Malcom H. "Planting in Streets, Parkways, Highways, and Byways." *Landscape Architecture* 22, no. 2 (1932): 118–31.

"Editorial: Outdoor Recreation." *Landscape Architecture* 14, no. 4 (1925): 287–88.

Eliot, Charles W., II. "The Influence of the Automobile on the Design of Park Roads." *Landscape Architecture* 13, no. 1 (1922): 27–37.

Elwood, P. H., Jr. "Planning Highway Landscapes." *Landscape Architecture* 21, no. 3 (1931): 180–84.

———. "State Parks and Highways." *Landscape Architecture* 22, no. 1 (1932): 25–32.

Fitzhugh, Armistead. "Camouflage: Adaptation of Basic Principles of Landscape Architecture." *Landscape Architecture* 33, no. 4 (1943): 119–24.

Graves, C. Edward. "Dry or 'Moraine' Rock Garden at Yosemite Museum." *Yosemite Nature Notes* 9, no. 10 (1930): 89–91.

Grinnell, Joseph, and Tracy L. Storer. "Animal Life as an Asset of National Parks." *Science* 44, no. 1133 (1916): 375–80.

Hamblin, Stephen F. "Increased Interest in Plant Materials." *Landscape Architecture* 20, no. 4 (1930): 335–58.

———. "Increasing Native Perennial Flowers." *Landscape Architecture* 13, no. 1 (1922): 1–18.

———. "In Praise of Vines." *Landscape Architecture* 12, no. 3 (1922): 148.

———. "The Mental Planning of Planting." *Landscape Architecture* 14, no. 1 (1924): 92–94.

Hare, S. Herbert. "Are Your Parks Planned, or Do They 'Jus' Grow?" *Landscape Architecture* 22, no. 1 (1931): 16–24.

———. "The National Parks As Seen in the West: Some Random Impressions Gained through Recent Visits." *Landscape Architecture* 30, no. 2 (1940): 55–57.

Hartzog, George B., Jr. "The Wilderness Act and the National Parks and Monuments." In McCloskey and Gilligan, *Wilderness and the Quality of Life.*

Heald, Weldon F. "Urbanization of the National Parks." *National Parks Magazine* 35, no. 160 (1961): 7–9.

Hewes, L. I. "America's Park Highways." *Civil Engineering* 2 (September 1932): 537–40.

Hibbard, Mabel E. "The Yosemite Museum Flower Show." *Yosemite Nature Notes* 6, no. 9 (1927): 65–67.

Hornbeck, Henry L. "Camouflage—Here and Now." *Landscape Architecture* 33, no. 1 (1942): 1–7.

Howett, Catherine M. "Frank Lloyd Wright and American Residential Landscaping." *Landscape Journal* 26, no. 1 (1982): 33–40.

Hubbard, Henry V. "The Designer in National Parks." *Landscape Architecture* 38, no. 2 (1958): 60. Originally published in National Park Service, *1941 Yearbook: Park and Recreation Progress,* 1941, pp. 38–39.

———. "Landscape Development Based on Conservation, As Practiced in the National Park Service." *Landscape Architecture* 29, no. 3 (1939): 105–21.

Kendeigh, S. Charles. "Research Areas in the National Parks, January 1942." *Ecology* 23, no. 2 (April 1942): 236–38.

Kimball, Theodora. "Survey of City and Regional Planning in the United States, 1923." *Landscape Architecture* 14, no. 1 (1924): 95–107.

Kittredge, Frank A. "Preserving a Valuable Heritage." *Civil Engineering* 2, no. 9 (1932): 533–37.

Koehler, Hans J. "Planting a Naturalistic Garden in a Limestone Region." *Landscape Architecture* 14, no. 3 (1924): 153–55.

"The Landscape Architect in Public Works." *Landscape Architecture* 24, no. 1 (1934): 24–40.

"Landscape Architects at War: The ASLA in the Armed and Civilian Service as Revealed by Questionnaire." *Landscape Architecture* 33, no. 1 (1943): 8–13.

"Landscape Architecture in Public Park Design." *Landscape Architecture* 29, no. 3 (1939): 103–5.

Lawson, William J., and Will Mann Richardson. "The Texas State Park System: A History, Study of Development, and Plans for the Future of the Texas State Parks." *Texas Geographic Magazine* 2 (December 1938): 1–18.

Leopold, Aldo. "Wilderness Values." In National Park Service, *1941 Yearbook: Park and Recreation Progress*, 1941, pp. 27–29.

Lieber, Richard. "Nature's Balances in Parks and Elsewhere." In National Park Service, *1940 Yearbook: Park and Recreation Progress*, 1940, pp. 82–85.

Maier, Herbert. "The Purpose of the Museum in the National Parks." *Yosemite Nature Notes* 5, no. 5 (1926): 37–40.

Manning, Warren. "Travelways of Beauty." *Landscape Architecture* 20, no. 4 (1930): 323–26.

McClelland, Linda Flint. "Charles Pierpont Punchard." In *Pioneers of American Landscape Design: An Annotated Bibliography*, edited by Charles A. Birnbaum. Washington, D.C.: National Park Service, 1995.

———. "Gateway to the Past: Establishing a Landscape's Context for the National Register." In *The Landscape Universe: Historic Designed Landscapes in Context*, edited by Charles A. Birnbaum. New York: Catalog of Landscape Records in the United States with the National Park Service, 1994.

———. "The Historic Landscape Architecture of National Parks." In *Natural Areas and Yosemite: Prospects for the Future.* Yosemite Centennial Symposium Proceedings, October 13–20, 1990. Denver: Denver Service Center and the Yosemite Fund, 1991.

———. "Thomas Chalmers Vint." In *Pioneers of American Landscape Design: An Annotated Bibliography*, edited by Charles A. Birnbaum. Washington, D.C.: National Park Service, 1995.

McEntee, James J. "The CCC and National Defense." *Regional Review* 5, no. 1 (1940): 28.

McFarland, J. Horace. "Twenty Years of Scenery-Saving in America." *Landscape Architecture* 20, no. 4 (1940): 301–7.

McNutt, Paul V. "Conservation for Recreation: The Landscape Architect as Land-Use Planner in Public Works." *Landscape Architecture* 30, no. 4 (1940): 173–76.

Michael, Enid. "Nature Garden a New Feature of Yosemite Museum." *Yosemite Nature Notes* 11, no. 10 (1932): 4–5.

———. "Roadside Planting of the New Wawona Highway." *Yosemite Nature Notes* 13, no. 12 (1933): 113–14.

Morrison, Darrell. "Native Vegetation Restoration: Another Route to the Past." In *Yearbook of Landscape Architecture: Historic Preservation*, edited by Richard Austin, Suzanne Turner, Robert Z. Melnick, and Thomas J. Kane. New York: Van Nostrand Reinhold Company, 1983.

Muller, Jean M., and James M. Barker. "Design and Construction of Linn Cove Viaduct." *Journal of the Prestressed Concrete Institute* 30, no. 5 (1985): 2–17.

Nason, George L. "Architecture and Its Relationship to the Design of Parks." In National Park Service, *1940 Yearbook: Park and Recreation Progress,* 1940, pp. 56–58.

Newton, Norman T. "State Park Conservation Work: 3. New Jersey and Eastern New York." *Landscape Architecture* 24, no. 1 (1933): 28–29.

Nichols, Arthur R. "Landscape Design in Highway Development: A Coordinating Factor in the Layout of Traffic Ways." *Landscape Architecture* 30, no. 3 (1940): 113–20.

Nusbaum, Jesse L. "Wilderness Aspects of National Parks." In Harlean, *American Planning and Civic Annual,* 72–77.

Olin, Laurie. "Wide Spaces and Widening Chaos." *Landscape Architecture* 80, no. 5 (1990): 77–97.

Olmsted, Frederick Law, Jr. "The Distinction between National Parks and National Forests." *Landscape Architecture* 6, no. 3 (1916): 115–16.

———. "Vacation in the National Parks and Forests." *Landscape Architecture* 12, no. 2 (1922): 107–11, from a paper read at the annual meeting of the American Civic Association in 1921.

Olmsted, Frederick Law, Sr. "The Yosemite Valley and the Mariposa Big Trees." *Landscape Architecture* 43, no. 1 (1953): 12–25, with an introductory note by Laura Wood Roper, who discovered the report in the 1950s.

Olmsted, John C. "The Treatment of Slopes and Banks." *Garden and Forest,* September 5, 1888, 326–27.

Pillsbury, J. P. "Highway Planting." *Landscape Architecture* 20, no. 3 (1930): 201–6.

Pray, James Sturgis. "Danger of Over-Exploitation of Our National Parks." *Landscape Architecture* 6, no. 3 (1916): 113.

Pray, James Sturgis, with Robert B. Marshall. "The American Society of Landscape Architecture and Our National Parks." *Landscape Architecture* 6, no. 3 (1916): 119–25.

Punchard, Charles P., Jr. "Landscape Design in the National Park Service." *Landscape Architecture* 10, no. 3 (1920): 144–45.

"Resolutions of the American Society of Landscape Architects." *Landscape Architecture* 6, no. 3 (1916): 11–112.

Rogers, Roland W. "Emergency Conservation Work in the National Parks: 1. Shenandoah National Park." *Landscape Architecture* 24, no. 1 (1933): 32–34.

Roland, Carol. "Daniel Ray Hull." In *Pioneers of American Landscape Design: An Annotated Bibliography.* Edited by Charles A. Birnbaum. Washington, D.C.: National Park Service, 1995.

Roper, Laura Wood. "The Yosemite Valley and the Mariposa Big Trees." *Landscape Architecture* 43, no. 1 (1953): 12–13.

Runte, Alfred. "Joseph Grinnell and Yosemite: Rediscovering the Legacy of a California Conservationist." *California History* (Summer 1990): 170–81.

Scarfo, Robert A. "Stewardship and the Profession of Landscape Architecture." *Landscape Journal* 7, no. 1 (1988): 60–68.

Schoffelmayer, Victor H. "Big Bend Area of Texas: A Geographic Wonderland." *Texas Geographic Magazine* 1 (May 1937): 1–2.

"Selected 1942 ASLA Committee Reports." *Landscape Architecture* 33, no. 2 (1943): 47–48.

Sellars, Richard West. "Manipulating Nature's Paradise: National Park Management under Stephen T. Mather, 1916–1929." *Montana: The Magazine of Western History* 43, no. 2 (1993): 2–13.

———. "The Rise and Decline of Ecological Attitudes in National Park Management, 1929–1940," pt. 1. *George Wright Forum* 10, no. 1 (1993): 55–78.

Simonds, O. C. "Nature as the Great Teacher in Landscape Gardening." *Landscape Architecture* 22, no. 2 (1932): 100–108; from an address given before the students in the Department of Landscape Architecture of the University of Illinois on January 12, 1922.

"A 'Sky-Post' for the Smokies." *National Parks Magazine* 33, no. 137 (1959): inside front cover.

Smith, Anthony Wayne. "The Tioga Road: Your NPA in Action." *National Parks Magazine* 33, no. 136 (1959): 10–13.

Steely, James W. "Texas Treasures." *Texas Highways* 36 (October 1989): 22–29.

Stevenson, Charles. "Shocking Truth about Our National Parks: A Report on the Use of Park Areas and Supporting Funds." *Landscape Architecture* 45, no. 2 (1925): 57–60.

Stickley, Gustav. "The Natural Garden: Some Things That Can Be Done When Nature Is Followed instead of Thwarted." In idem, *Craftsman Homes.*

———. "What May Be Done with Water and Rocks in a Little Garden," in idem, *Craftsman Homes.*

Swain, Donald C. "The National Park Service and the New Deal, 1933–1940. *Pacific Historical Review* 41 (August 1972): 312–32.

———. "Passage of the National Park Service Act of 1916." *Wisconsin Magazine of History* 50 (Autumn 1966): 4–17.

Taylor, Albert D. "Notes on Garden Theaters." *Landscape Architecture* 21, no. 3 (1931): 209–27.

———. "Notes on the Construction of Ha-Ha Walls." *Landscape Architecture* 20, no. 3 (1930): 221–24.

———. "Notes with Reference to the Construction of Flagstone Walks." *Landscape Architecture* 12, no. 2 (1922): 117–19.

———. "Notes with Reference to the Construction of Walks, Trails, and Terraces." *Landscape Architecture* 13, no. 4 (1923): 253–57.

Tilden, Paul M., and Nancy L. Machler. "The Development of Mount McKinley National Park." *National Parks Magazine* 37, no. 188 (1963): 10–15.

Vint, Thomas C. "National Park Service: Master Plans." *Planning and Civic Comment* (April–June 1946). Reprint.

———. "Wilderness Areas: Development of National Parks for Conservation." In Harlean, *American Planning and Civic Annual,* 69–71.

Wagner, H. S. "What May Be Considered Adequate State Park Standards?" *Landscape Architecture* 22, no. 1 (1931): 1–6.

Watrous, Richard B. "Our National Parks: A Conference." *Landscape Architecture* 6, no. 3 (1916): 100–105.

Waugh, Frank Albert "Ecology of the Roadside." *Landscape Architecture* 21, no. 2 (1931): 81–92.

———. "Natural Plant Groups." *Landscape Architecture* 21, no. 3 (1931): 169–79.

———. "Notes on Outdoor Theaters." *Landscape Architecture* 18, no. 4 (1928): 261–66.

———. "The Physiography of Lakes and Ponds." *Landscape Architecture* 22, no. 2 (1932): 89–92.

———. "A Simple Outdoor Theater." *Landscape Architecture* 14, no. 4 (1924): 253–56.

Wheaton, Rodd L. "Park Roads and Highway Standards: Going-to-the-Sun Road." *CRM* 15, no. 6 (1992): 33–35.

Whiting, Edward C., and William L. Phillips. "Frederick Law Olmsted, 1870–1957: An

Appreciation of the Man and His Achievements." *Landscape Architecture* 47, no. 3 (1958): 145–57.

Wirth, Conrad L. "The Landscape Architect in National Park Work: His Projects, Opportunities, Problems, and Obligations." *Landscape Architecture* 46, no. 1 (1956): 13–18.

———. "Mission 66 in the Headlines." *National Parks Magazine* 32, no. 132 (1958): 8–9.

———. "State Park Conservation Work: 1. Office of National Parks, Buildings, and Reservations." *Landscape Architecture* 24, no. 1 (1933): 26.

"Yosemite's Tioga Highway." *National Parks Magazine* 32, no. 134 (1958): 123–24.

NATIONAL REGISTER OF HISTORIC PLACES DOCUMENTATION

Anderson, Rolf. "Minnesota State Park CCC/WPA Rustic Style Multiple Property Submission." National Register of Historic Places Multiple Property Documentation Form. Minnesota Historical Society, St. Paul, September 3, 1988.

Culpin, Mary Shivers. "Obsidian Cliff Kiosk." National Register of Historic Places Inventory-Nomination Form. Rocky Mountain Regional Office, Denver, November 30, 1981.

Denny, James M., and Bonita Marie Wright. "Emergency Conservation Work (E.C.W.) Architecture in Missouri State Parks, 1933–1942, Thematic Resources." National Register of Historic Places Inventory-Nomination Form. Department of Natural Resources, Historic Preservation Program, Jefferson City, Missouri, November 7, 1984.

McClelland, Linda Flint. "Historic Park Landscapes in National and State Parks." National Register of Historic Places Multiple Property Documentation Form. National Park Service, Washington, D.C., October 4, 1995.

McKay, Joyce. "CCC Properties in Iowa State Parks Multiple Property Submission." National Register of Historic Places Multiple Property Documentation Form. State Historical Society of Iowa, Des Moines, August 17, 1989.

Smith, Dwight A. "Columbia River Highway Historic District." National Register of Historic Places Inventory-Nomination Form. Oregon State Highway Division, Salem, October 3, 1983

Stager, Claudette. "State Parks in Tennessee Built by the CCC and WPA between 1934 and 1942." National Register of Historic Places Multiple Property Documentation Form. Tennessee Historical Commission, Nashville, February 1986.

Story, Kenneth. "Facilities Constructed by the CCC in Arkansas, 1933–1942." National Register of Historic Places Multiple Property Documentation Form. Arkansas Historic Preservation Program, Little Rock, December 1991.

Toothman, Stephanie. "Mount Rainier National Park Multiple Property Submission." National Register of Historic Places Multiple Property Documentation Form. Pacific Northwest Regional Office, National Park Service, Seattle, September 1983.

Tweed, William. "Moro Rock Stairway." National Register of Historic Places Inventory-Nomination Form. Sequoia and Kings Canyon National Park, Ash Mountain, California, 20 May 1977.

Index

Page numbers in italics refer to illustrations.

in Bryce Canyon, 171, *173*, 245; at Itasca
State Park (Minn.), 429, *441*

California Forest and Range Station,
Berkeley, 276

California Gardening (Murmann), 3, 66–
68

California state parks, 12, 54–55, 277, 382

Camden State Park, Minn., 70

Cammerer, Arno B., *13*, 394, 432

camouflage in World War II, 459–60

Camp, Edgar W., House, Sierra Madre,
Calif., 105–6, 114

Campfire Girls, 417

campground design, 7, 144, 411; CCC
work, 285, 350, 372–73; *Campground
Policy* (Meinecke), 7, 278–82; *Camp
Planning and Camp Reconstruction*
(Meinecke), 7, 282–85; Meinecke system, 7, 276–84, *281*, 466; Mission 66,
466–68, *467*; Punchard's work, 139, 143–
45; trailer-camping, 373, *374*, 442. *See
also* E. P. Meinecke

campgrounds, 7–8, 34, 164, 368, 466, 468;
Aspenglen (Rocky Mountain), 263, 411;
campgrounds in Mount Rainier, 131,
152, 278, *281*, 322, 350; Canyon campground, 152, 163, 308, 470; Flamingo
(Everglades), 464, *465;* Giant Forest
(Sequoia), 132, 144–45; in Yellowstone,
131, 139, 144–45, 152, 163, 308, 470

Camps in the Woods (Shepard), 100, 432,
442

Caparn, Harold A., 14, 58, 234

Carhart, Arthur, 160

Carlander, Guy, 108, 392

Carlsbad Cavern National Park, N.Mex.,
140, 272, 334; King's Palace Trail, *331*

Carnes, William G., 330, 464

Casa Grande National Monument, Ariz.,
272, 329

CCC (Civilian Conservation Corps), 7, 14,
85, 147, 328, 340–42, 450–52, 458; authorization and organization, 336, 382–83;
district inspectors and technicians,
400–404; ECW in national parks, 336–
45; ECW in state parks, 381–406, 423; in
national defense, 457–58; portfolios and
manuals, 7, 85, 425–43, *427, 428*, 441–

50; Project Training Series, 85, 450–51;
role of state park designers, 432; work
in RDAs, 414, 417

Central Park, N.Y.(city), 3, 36–40, 45–46,
52, 85–86, 89; Boulder Bridge, 39–40,
72; *Forty Years: Central Park* (Olmsted
and Kimball), 89

Chamberlin, Noel, 56

Chicago parks, 63–65

Chittenden, Hiram M., 126, 175

Chopawamsic RDA, Va., 416

Civilian Conservation Corps. *See* CCC

Civil Works Administration (CWA), 352,
404

Clarke, Gilmore D., 14, 57, 180–81, 224,
263, 376; exchange with Landscape
Division, 228–30, 376; general development plan for Mammoth Hot Springs
(Yellowstone), 214, 300, *301*

cleanup, 6, 139, 160, 342, 386, *387;* Jackson
Lake (Grand Teton), 342–43, *343;* Mirror Lake and Lake Eleanor (Yosemite),
140, 142, 342. *See also* roadside cleanup

Clements, Frederic E., 88, 208, 275, 356–58,
357

Cleveland, H.W.S., 47

Clifty Falls State Park, Ind., 54

Cobb, Albert Winslow, 117

Coffman, John, 255, 336, 338–39

Colonial Parkway, Va., 224, 230, 334, 378

Colorado River Storage Project, 475

Colter, Mary E. J., 108; collaboration with
NPS landscape engineers, 153, 164–65;
influence on national and state park
design, 113–14, 171, 246, 392; interest
in Mesa Verde, 112, 114, 246; work at
Grand Canyon, 112–13, *113*, 164, 245, 249

Columbian Exposition, 72, 104, 117

Columbia River Highway, Ore., 131, 176–
77, 225

comfort stations and privies, 244, 248,
352, 406, 425; *Portfolio* (D. Waugh),
425, *428;* Union Point Comfort Station
(Yosemite), 248, 425, *431*

Commission of Fine Arts (United States),
13–14, 157, 163, 173–74, 217, 300

community buildings, 70, 152, 163

Comstock, William, 100, 117–18

design, 81, 85, 143, 190, 192, 264, 372;
on national park plans, 312; on park
roads and parkways, 210, 232, 379; on
stewardship for national parks, 9–11, 73,
81. See also *Introduction* (Hubbard and
Kimball)
Huber, Walter, 110
Hull, Daniel R., 11, *13*, 14, 159–63, *161,*
171, 485; collaboration with concessionaires' architects, 171–74; design
of park roads, 182–92; design of park
structures, 165–66; education and experience, 81, 159–60; planning for park
villages, 163–65
Hunt, Myron, 13, 66, 119, 164–65, 167

Ickes, Harold L., 329, 382, 460
Illinois, Univ. of, 11, 159–60, 171, 199;
experiment station, 63–64, 207
Indiana state parks, 54, 58, 382, 385, 426
indigenous architecture, 5, 18, 104, 112, 114,
116, 118, 170–71, 394, 407, 438
"Inspector's Photographic Handbook,"
390, 406–13
interpretive shelters and exhibits, 34, 406–
9; Glacier Point Lookout (Yosemite),
107, 169–70, *169,* 408; Obsidian Cliff
Nature Shrine (Yellowstone), 249, 250–
51, *252,* 409
*Introduction to the Study of Landscape De-
sign* (Hubbard and Kimball), 3–4, 9, 39,
45, 71–81, 137; on Franklin Park, 39, 45,
74, 94; Modern American Landscape
style, 3, 61, 70–74; on naturalistic roads,
181, 183–85, 206–7, 215, 218; on planting
park structures, 259–60; on rockwork,
76–78; on scenic overlooks and vistas,
75–76, 84, 212; on shelters, 78–80, 94
Iowa State College, 11, 160, 199, 391
Iowa state parks, *27,* 54–55, 78, *79,* 382, *405,*
426, 430
Irving, Washington, 20
Itasca State Park, Minn., 53, 429, *441*

James, Dr. D. L., House, Carmel, Calif.,
107–8, 112
Japanese gardening style, 4, 67, 69–70, 91,
104, 115, 119, 376

Japanese Tea Garden (San Francisco), 70,
104
Jekyll, Gertrude, 45
Jennings, Allyn R., 230, 300
Jensen, Jens, 14, 63–65, 81, 104, 157, 164,
207, 376, 382
Jepson, Willis Linn, 88

Kent, William (landscape designer), 18
Kent, William (U.S. Cong.), 8
Kiessig, Paul, 160–62
Kimball, Theodora, 3, 5, 8, 71, 73, 89, 137
Kittredge, Frank A., 190, 204, 242, 334
Knight, Emerson, 58
Kragsyde, Manchester-by-the-Sea, Mass.,
92, 108
Kreinkamp, Herbert, 332

Lafayette National Park. *See* Acadia
National Park
Lake Guernsey State Park, Wyo., 416, *423,*
436
Lake Junction. *See* Fishing Bridge/Lake
Junction
Lake Murray Park, Okla., 420, 430
lakes and ponds, artificial, 7, 70, 87, 418,
448–50, *449*
Lamb, Hugo, 92
Lancaster, Samuel, 176
Land and Water Conservation Fund Act
(1964), 423, 476
Landscape Architecture (ASLA), 12, 58, 89,
137, 156, 207, 254, 444, 446, 455
Landscape Conservation (F. Waugh), 7, 85,
184, 418, 441–50
Landscape Division (NPS), 4, 11, 160, 255;
civil service standards, 198–99; collaboration with Educational Division,
220–35, 248–55; design of guardrail,
bridges, and culverts, 216–25; design
of tunnels, 225–28; development of
scenic overlooks, 211–14, 226, 233–36,
281; exchange with Westchester County,
180–81, 228–30, 376, 378, 425–26; expansion of building program, 243–48; job
responsibilities and qualifications, 196–
99; loop structures, grade separations,
and intersections, 214–15; naturalistic
trails, 233–42; organization, 199–200;

McEntee, James J., 457

McFarland, J. Horace, 8

McKim, Charles F., 92

McKim, Mead, and White, 93

McKown, Russell L., 358, 373, 459

McNutt, Paul V., 455

Mahoney, Marion, 66

Maier, Herbert, 5, 98, 99, 103, 166, 390, 429–30; as CCC district officer, 383, 389–402; education and influences, 68, 107, 114, 118–19; Library of Original Sources, 390, 432; NPS spokesperson, 392–400, 404; Yavapai Point Observation Building (Grand Canyon), 248, *273*, 392, 407–8, 430; Yellowstone amphitheaters, observation terraces, and nature shrines, 250–54, *250, 252, 253,* 408–9; Yellowstone museums, 70, 116, 166, 248–49, *251,* 407–8, 430; Yosemite Museum, 116, 166–69, *168,* 208, 394, 408. *See also* Inspector's Photographic Handbook; principles of NPS landscape design

maintenance facilities and industrial groups, 146, 148, 153

Mammoth Caves National Park, Ky., 140, 289–90

Mammoth Hot Springs, Yellowstone National Park, 14, 144, 300; campground, 144, 148; clean-up, 139; 1931 general development plan, 300, *301;* PWA construction, 332

Man and Nature (Darling and Eichhorn), 477, 485

Manning, Warren H., 47, 58

Manual of the Flowering Plants of California (Jepson), 88

Marshall, Robert B., 56, 124, 130, 474

Marston, Sylvanus, 118

Massachusetts Agricultural College, 81, 85, 160, 382

mass-planting, 61, 83–85, 446–47

master plans, 7, 300–306, 312–13, 453, 465, 478, 481; for Mount Rainier, 295–99, *296, 298,* 309–10, 313–23; for RDAs and state parks, 383, 419; tool for preservation, 306–10; for Yellowstone, 236, 300–301, 307–8, 481–82; for Yosemite, 308–9. *See also* park plans

Mather, Stephen T., 55, 124–38, 157, 195, 382; as NPS director, 8, 11, 110, 131, 134–36, 138, 152–53, 173–74, 196, 232, 310, *313; Progress in the Development of National Parks,* 124; on value of landscape engineers, 142, 162–63; visit to Yakima Park, *313, 315*

Maybeck, Bernard, 80, 109–11

Mayberry and Jones, 197

Mead, William R., 92

Meinecke, E. P., 7, 275, *279,* 285, 350. *See also* campground design

Merkel, Hermann, 180

Merriam, Lawrence C., 383

Mesa Verde National Park, Colo., 53, 112, 114, 126, 170, 246

Michael, Enid, 274

Miller, Wilhelm, 3, 62–66, 159; *Prairie Spirit in Landscape Gardening,* 63–65; *What England Can Teach Us,* 3, 62

Mills, Enos, 130

Minneapolis metropolitan parks, 47–48

Minnesota state parks, 53, 70, 382, *388,* 429, *447*

Minnewawa, Blue Mountain Lake, N.Y., 117

Mission Revival style of architecture, 107, 112, 118

Mission 66, 452, 462–73, 475, 480; Clingman's Dome Tower (Great Smoky Mountains), 464, 471–72, *471, 473;* Flamingo (Everglades), 464, *465,* 468; park roads, 470–71, 473; visitor centers, 464, 466, *467;* in Yellowstone, 468–70, *469*

Modern American Homes (von Holst), 104

Montezuma Castle National Monument, Ariz., 332

Moore, Barrington, 57

Moore, Charles, 13, 157, 163

More Craftsman Homes (Stickley), 114, 116

Morris, William, 45

Mount Hood National Forest, Ore., 85, 184, 444

Mount McKinley National Park (later Denali), Alaska, 332, 336, 471

Mount Nebo State Park, Ark., *77*

Mount Rainier National Park, Wash., 33, 53, 131, 215, 474; Carbon River Ranger Station, Wash., 340; Carbon River Road, 124, 140, 183; Christine Falls

Swiss style of architecture, 4, 98, 100, 110–12

Taylor, Albert D., 85, 89
Taylor, Oliver G., 429
Tennessee Valley Authority (TVA), 418, 455
Texas state parks, 55, 70, 160, *384, 389*, 430
Text-book on Highway Engineering (Blanchard and Drowne), 180
Thiene, Paul G., 197
Thompson, H. T., 306
Thomson, C. G., 268
Thoreau, Henry David, 20
Toll, Roger, 300
Tomlinson, Owen, 196, 257, 259, 313, *315,* 337
topographical maps, 128, 147, 303
trails and trail construction (foot and bridle), 4–5, 21, 28–29, 34, 84, 129–30, 233–42, *241,* 254–55, 334, *351,* 445–46, 450; Anhinga Trail (Everglades), 468; Appalachian Trail, 182; in Big Bend, *401,* 461; Bright Angel Trail (Grand Canyon), 70, *337;* Cadillac Mountain Summit Trail (Acadia), *240;* Cascade Crest Trail (later Pacific Crest), 182, 215, 348; *Construction of Trails* (CCC), 450; East Rim Trail (Zion), 241; formation trails in Yellowstone, 238, *239,* 364; Four-Mile Trail (Yosemite), 233, 242; Grand Canyon of the Yellowstone, 212, 234–36, 364; Half Dome Trail (Yosemite), 141, *363, 364;* High Sierra Trail (Sequoia), 241; Kaibab Trail (Grand Canyon), 226, 228, 240–41, 376, 430; King's Palace Trail (Carlsbad Cavern), *331;* Lost Lake Trail (Ludington State Park, Mich.), 70, *71;* Moro Rock Trail (Sequoia), 132–34, *133,* 236, 472; New River Trail (Grand Canyon), 233, 376; Ptarmigan Wall Trail (Glacier), 212, 226, 233, *234,* 238; Rim Village Promenade (Crater Lake), 154, 155, 212, 237; South Rim Trail (Grand Canyon), 212; West Rim Trail (Zion), 241; Wonderland Trail (Mount Rainier), 297
Treatise on the Theory and Practice of Landscape Gardening (Downing), 18, 21–35, 88

treatment of road banks. *See* roadside naturalization; slope stabilization
Tressider, Donald, 269
Tripp, B. Ashburton, 459
truck trails, 181–82, 359, 362, *362*
Trustees of Public Reservations, 48
Tugwell, Rex, 414
Tumacacori Mission National Monument, Ariz., 329–30
Tunnard, Christopher, 232
tunnels, 140, 182, 225–26; Mary's Rock Tunnel (Shenandoah), *227;* Mitchell Point Tunnel (Columbia River Highway), 176, *177;* Ptarmigan Wall Tunnel (Glacier), 212, *234;* Wawona Tunnel (Yosemite), 212, 226–28, *359;* Zion-Mt. Carmel Tunnel, 226
Turkey Run State Park, Ind., 54, 56, *385*
Turner, Albert M., 58
Turner Falls State Park, Okla., 412, *413*
Tyrrell, Henry G., 24, 70

Underwood, Gilbert Stanley, 99, 110, 159, 171–74, 197, 245
Union Pacific Railroad, 171
University of California, Berkeley, 11, 68, 88, 119, 126, 160, 196, 199, 252, 267
U.S. Department of the Interior Headquarters, Washington, D.C., 329
U.S. Forest Service, 7, 85, 143, 176, 180, 184, 187, 426, 444, 450, 474
Utah Parks Co., 99, 171, 245
Utz, W. T., 317

Vail Agenda (1991), 484–85
Vaux, Calvert, 35, 95
Vegetation and Forest Scenery for the Reservations (Eliot), 49
viaducts: Golden Gate Viaduct (Yellowstone), *203;* Linn Cove Viaduct (Blue Ridge Parkway), 480–81, *481*
Villas and Cottages (Vaux), 95
Vint, Thomas C., 5, 6, 11, 166, 196, 330, 429, 474; education and experience, 119–20; influences, 68, 103, 107, 118–19, 246–47; "Portfolio of Representative Structures," 247–48, 425, 430. *See also* Branch of Plans and Design; Landscape Division

About the Author

Linda Flint McClelland was born in Dedham, Massachusetts, and raised in nearby Boston, where she experienced firsthand the parks and parkways of Frederick Law Olmsted's Emerald Necklace and Charles Eliot's scenic reservations. She attended the University of Massachusetts, Amherst, and holds a bachelor's degree in education and a master's degree in art history. Most of her twenty-year career as a public historian for the United States government has been with the National Register of Historic Places in the National Park Service. She has published essays in the *Public Historian, CRM: Cultural Resources Management, Pioneers of American Landscape Design II: An Annotated Bibliography, Natural Areas and Yosemite: Prospects for the Future,* and other publications. She is the author/coauthor of several government publications including an earlier edition of this book (*Presenting Nature,* 1993) and *National Register Bulletin 30: Guidelines for Evaluating and Documenting Rural Historic Landscapes* (1990). She has taught landscape preservation at George Washington University, and, since 1984, she has lectured on landscape preservation and national park history at numerous landscape symposia, preservation conferences and workshops, and professional meetings including those sponsored by the Alliance for Historic Landscape Preservation, American Society of Landscape Architects, National Conference of State Historic Preservation Officers, National Council on Public History, National Park Service, and National Trust for Historic Preservation.

Library of Congress Cataloging-in-Publication Data

McClelland, Linda Flint.

Building the national parks : historic landscape design and construction / Linda Flint McClelland.

p. cm.

Originally published: Washington, D.C. : U.S. Dept. of the Interior, National Park Service, Cultural Resources, Interagency Resources Division, National Register of Historic Places, 1993.

Includes bibliographical references (p.   ) and index.

ISBN 0-8018-5582-9 (alk. paper). — ISBN 0-8018-5583-7 (pbk.)

1. United States. National Park Service — History.   2. Park facilities — United States — Design and construction — History.   3. National parks and reserves — United States — Design — History.   4. Parks — United States — Design and construction — History. 5. Landscape design — United States — History.   I. Title.

SB482.A4M3   1998

353.7′8 — DC21

97-12664

CIP